Fundamentals of
Management accounting

*The Willard J. Graham Series
in Accounting*

Consulting Editor
ROBERT N. ANTHONY   *Harvard University*

Fundamentals of
Management accounting

ROBERT N. ANTHONY
Graduate School of Business Administration
Harvard University

and

GLENN A. WELSCH
College of Business Administration
The University of Texas at Austin

 Revised edition   1977

RICHARD D. IRWIN, INC.   Homewood, Illinois   60430
Irwin-Dorsey Limited   Georgetown, Ontario   L7G 4B3

Revised Edition

First Printing, March 1977

Case material of the Harvard Graduate School of
Business Administration is made possible by the
cooperation of business firms who may wish to remain
anonymous by having names, quantities, and other
identifying details disguised while basic relationships
are maintained. Cases are prepared as the basis for
class discussion rather than to illustrate either effective
or ineffective handling of administrative situations.

ISBN 0-256-01896-0
Library of Congress Catalog Card No. 76–49312

Printed in the United States of America

LEARNING SYSTEMS COMPANY —
a division of Richard D. Irwin, Inc. — has developed a
PROGRAMMED LEARNING AID
to accompany texts in this subject area.
Copies can be purchased through your bookstore
or by writing PLAIDS,
1818 Ridge Road, Homewood, Illinois   60430.

To our wives,
Katherine and Irma

Preface

Many accounting instructors believe that it is sound pedagogy to divide the first course in accounting into two parts, the first semester or quarter focusing on financial accounting and the second on management accounting. Most texts, however, are not arranged so that such an approach is feasible with a single text. Consequently, instructors tend to select one text for financial accounting and a different text for management accounting, which causes a certain amount of confusion because of differences in terminology, point of view, and coverage. Moreover, the second text usually contains considerable review material on financial accounting because its author could not assume that students would have a common body of knowledge.

This volume and its companion, *Fundamentals of Financial Accounting,* are designed to overcome these problems. They provide material for a fully coordinated first course. Each volume can be used either for a one-semester or a one-quarter course. Both are designed to provide maximum flexibility for the instructor in the selection and order of materials for the classroom. They emphasize those aspects of accounting we believe essential for interpretation and use of accounting information. Mechanical and procedural details are minimized, while the conceptual, measurement, and communication aspects are emphasized.

Partly because the treatment of management accounting as a separate subject is relatively new, a satisfactory pedagogical framework for it — one that provides a way of organizing and unifying the several separate topics — has been difficult to devise. In financial accounting, the accounting equation, Assets = Liabilities + Owners' Equity, provides a unifying theme.

No such unified structure exists for management accounting. On the contrary, instructors spend much time emphasizing the point that "different figures are used for different purposes." This is a fundamental point, and it is valid, but it does tend to create confusion on the part of the student. In one chapter of the usual text students are told that in figuring cost they are supposed to include an allocated share of overhead costs; in another chapter they are told that the allocated costs are irrelevant and should be disregarded. In still another chapter they are told that costs must be related to personal responsibility, whereas in most other places no mention is made of personal responsibility.

The vagueness of the notion that there are *several* purposes adds to the student's problem of comprehending what the course is all about. How many purposes are there? Does each type of alternative choice problem (for example, make-or-buy, dropping a product, equipment replacement, buy-or-lease) constitute a separate purpose, with its own peculiar requirements for accounting information? Do the purposes mentioned in the book constitute *all* the purposes, or are there others? Are there topics not mentioned in the elementary course that students must learn about in advanced courses?

After a good many years of wrestling with the problem, the authors have concluded that it is possible to devise a framework for management accounting that overcomes these pedagogical difficulties. This volume is constructed around such a framework. We arrived at the framework by shifting the focus from the notion of "purpose" to the notion of "types of accounting information." It seems to us that there are three, and only three, different ways of constructing accounting information for use by management. One is conventional cost accounting, with its emphasis on full cost and its close ties to generally accepted financial accounting principles and to the financial accounting system. A second is the notion variously labelled as the "differential," "marginal," or "incremental" approach. The third is what has come to be called "responsibility accounting"; it focuses on the costs, revenues, and assets of responsibility centers.

It is not possible to relate each of these constructions to a single purpose. Planning, for example, uses all three types. For some pricing problems, full costs are relevant; whereas for others, differential costs are relevant. Nevertheless, if the three topics are arranged in the order given above, it is possible to describe, under the first topic, uses that require the use of full cost data; under the second topic, uses that require differential costs and revenue; and under the third topic, uses that require responsibility accounting data.

Another advantage of this approach is that it encourages the student to make a clear distinction among these three different types of information. Failure to appreciate this distinction is a basic cause of the difficulty that some students have in understanding what management accounting is all about.

We chose labels that are descriptive of the type of cost that is appropriate for each of the three purposes. These are: (1) full cost accounting, (2) differential accounting, and (3) responsibility accounting. Each of the three main parts of the book focuses on one of these topics. Together, they constitute the field of management accounting. The following brief descriptions will suggest their general nature:

Full cost accounting measures the total amount of resources used for a cost objective. These resources are the direct costs plus a fair share of the indirect costs associated with the cost objective.

Differential accounting focuses on the costs and revenues that are expected to be different if one alternative course of action, rather than another alternative, is adopted.

Responsibility accounting focuses on costs, revenues, and assets that are associated with the work of a responsibility center. It measures the inputs and outputs of responsibility centers.

In stressing the differences among the three types of management accounting information, we run the risk that the student will not appreciate that the three categories use many common elements, that they overlap, and that they constitute a single management accounting system, rather than three separate systems. We have taken steps to minimize these risks.

It can of course be argued that there are more than three types of management accounting information. Our three categories do not suggest such distinctions as long run versus short run, historical versus future, opportunity versus incurred, regulatory versus nonregulatory, direct versus indirect, or strategic planning versus management control. It would be possible to construct frameworks based on any or all of these distinctions. Instead of doing this, we have chosen to discuss these topics at the appropriate place in each of our main categories. We have found it feasible, without straining, to fit all these concepts under our three main topics, and this fact increases our confidence in the conclusion that the three categories are inclusive. If the student comes away from the course with the clear recognition that three types of management accounting information exist, and if he understands how to use them for appropriate purposes, he will be ahead of a great many people (including Congressmen and others in public life, and even some businessmen who imply in their speeches and actions that there is such a thing as "the" cost of something).

Plan of the book

Within each of the three categories, our objective is to discuss both the characteristics of the accounting information that is useful in that category, and also the way in which such information should be used.

The discussion of full cost accounting comes first because this topic is closely related to the subject matter of this text's companion volume, *Fundamentals of Financial Accounting*. Full costs are used to measure inventory amounts in financial accounting, and their construction is essentially governed by generally accepted financial accounting principles. Thus, this topic provides a good way of making the transition from financial accounting to management accounting. In discussing the uses of full cost information, more attention is given to its use as a basis for pricing than is the case with many accounting books. Whatever the theoretical merits of marginal-cost pricing may be, the fact is that in the real world the great majority of selling prices are based on full costs, and the student should therefore learn how costs are constructed and used for this purpose. (Marginal cost pricing is discussed in Part Two.)

Part Two deals with differential costs, differential revenues, and differential investments. These constructions are used in alternative choice decisions of various types, and the use of accounting information for these purposes is discussed in Chapters 7, 8, and 9. As background for this discussion, Chapter 6 contains a description of the behavior of costs, particularly the relationship among costs, volume, and profit.

Part Three focuses on responsibility accounting, that is, on costs, revenues, and investments that are associated with the activities of responsibility centers. As background, Chapters 10 and 11 discuss the management control structure and process respectively. Chapters 12, 14, and 15 discuss the use of accounting information in budgeting, in the analysis of variances, and in reports on performance. Part Three also contains a chapter on standard costs. Logically, this chapter could just as well have been located in Part One since standard costs are a part of many cost accounting systems. Students find standard costs quite difficult and complicated, however, and this is the reason for deferring this topic until a later chapter. (The chapter can be assigned following Chapter 4 if an instructor wants to treat standard costs along with other cost accounting topics.)

Chapter 16, on information processing, is more isolated from the main framework of the book than is ideal. We treat it separately because the subject is relevant for all three categories of accounting information, and therefore it is not appropriately included in any single one of them, to the exclusion of the other two.

Most books on management accounting do not contain a summary chapter. This one does, in Chapter 17. The essential rationale for a summary is that the emphasis on the three types of cost construction in the body of the book may have created the impression that management accounting consists of three separate, and largely unrelated, systems. The summary attempts to correct any such misconceptions by showing the interrelationships that in fact exist.

The revised edition

Although the basic structure described above has been retained, in this Revised Edition we have made major rearrangements of material within that structure. In Part One, the uses of cost accounting information precede the description of cost accounting so that uses can be emphasized from the beginning. In Part Three, several chapters have been rearranged for a similar reason.

Several specialized topics have been moved to chapter Appendixes so that instructors can assign them or not, as they wish. New material on income taxes, linear programming, and other quantitative techniques have been added as Appendixes.

Every chapter has been rewritten to update, simplify, improve clarity, and smooth the flow of topics. Many diagrams and examples have been added. There are a great many more questions, problems, and short cases than in the First Edition, and they are tied carefully to the text material.

Acknowledgments

We are grateful for comments received from many users of the First Edition. In addition, we much appreciate suggestions from the following, who read the entire manuscript of the Revised Edition: Keith Bryant, Jr., University of Alabama in Birmingham; Corine T. Norgaard, University of Connecticut; James Reece, University of Michigan; and James D. Suver, University of Colorado at Colorado Springs; and reviewers F. W. Schaeberle, Western Michigan University; and Patrick R. Delaney, Northern Illinois University. Christopher E. Nugent, Harvard Business School, did much of the revision of Chapter 16. Keith Bryant, Jr., assisted by Glenna Barstad, revised former problems and wrote many new problems. Gerald Holtz, Arthur Andersen & Company, made useful suggestions on the Appendix to Chapter 9. Joseph R. Curran, Northeastern University, revised and improved the Appendix to Chapter 12. Nancy Anthony did library research.

We are also grateful for the untiring, accurate work of manuscript preparation which was the responsibility first of Ann Carter, and then of Sandra Bardwell.

Cases are copyrighted by the President and Fellows of Harvard College. Permission to use these cases is appreciated.

Problems from the Uniform CPA Examinations, copyright by the American Institute of Public Accountants, and from the Certificate of Management Accounting Examinations, copyright by the Institute of Management Accounting, are used by permission.

February 1977   ROBERT N. ANTHONY
                                   GLENN A. WELSCH

Contents

The nature of
management accounting

The companion volume of this book, *Fundamentals of Financial Accounting,** focuses on financial accounting, where the principal objective is to furnish information that is useful to investors and other persons who are *outside* the organization. In this volume, the focus is on management accounting, where the principal objective is to furnish information that is useful to managers, that is, to persons who are *inside* the organization.

This chapter gives a general description of the work that managers do and the information that they use in doing this work. Accounting information is one type of information that managers use. The nature of management accounting and the similarities and differences between management accounting and financial accounting are discussed. The three types of management accounting information and the purposes for which they are used are introduced.

In *Fundamentals of Financial Accounting* we described the concepts, principles, and practices that are used in preparing the three financial statements that a company is required to furnish to outside parties: (1) the balance sheet, (2) the income statement, and (3) the statement of changes

---

* Glenn A. Welsch and Robert N. Anthony, *Fundamentals of Financial Accounting,* rev. ed. (Homewood, Ill.: Richard D. Irwin, Inc., 1977).

in financial position. As a reminder, examples of these financial statements (somewhat condensed) are shown in Exhibit 1–1.

The *balance sheet* reports the financial position of a business at a particular point in time. In Exhibit 1–1 the points in time for the two balance sheets are December 31, 1976, and December 31, 1975. The balance sheet is constructed according to the model:

$$\text{Assets} = \text{Liabilities} + \text{Owners' Equity}$$

The *income statement* reports the results of operations for a specified period of time. In Exhibit 1–1 the periods are the year ended De-

EXHIBIT 1–1
Financial statements, Morgan Ford Company

MORGAN FORD COMPANY
Balance Sheets

	At December 31			
Assets	1976		1975	
Current Assets:				
Cash		$ 19,180		$ 45,262
Accounts receivable		26,438		20,835
Inventory		316,602		262,433
Other current assets		14,863		12,888
Total Current Assets		377,083		341,418
Fixed Assets:				
Land		22,500		22,500
Building and equipment	$53,400		$53,400	
Less: Accumulated depreciation	14,451	38,949	10,820	42,580
Total Fixed Assets		61,449		65,080
Other assets		12,107		18,637
Total Assets		$450,639		$425,135
Liabilities				
Current Liabilities:				
Accounts and notes payable		$188,512		$163,178
Accrued liabilities		5,621		8,267
Total Current Liabilities		194,133		171,445
Mortgage loan payable		50,426		55,375
Total Liabilities		244,559		226,820
Shareholders' Equity				
Capital stock		60,000		60,000
Retained earnings		146,080		138,315
Total Shareholders' Equity		206,080		198,315
Total Liabilities and Shareholders' Equity		$450,639		$425,135

EXHIBIT 1–1 (*continued*)

MORGAN FORD COMPANY
Income Statements

	For the year ended December 31	
	1976	*1975*
Sales..	$1,352,840	$942,795
Cost of goods sold	1,097,468	755,236
Gross margin on sales..	255,372	187,559
Expenses:		
Selling expenses...	84,258	67,342
Administrative expenses...	106,452	98,681
Interest expense..	23,902	18,360
Total Expenses	214,612	184,383
Operating income...	40,760	3,176
Income tax expense..	7,503	720
Net Income...	$ 33,257	$ 2,456
Earnings per share	$5.54	$0.41

MORGAN FORD COMPANY
Statement of Changes in Financial Position
For the Year Ended December 31, 1976

Sources of Working Capital (inflows):

From operations:

Net income	$33,257	
Depreciation expense...	3,631	
Total Working Capital Generated by Operations.................		$36,888
From other sources:		
Sale of securities held as investment		6,530
Total Working Capital Generated....................................		43,418
Uses of Working Capital (outflows):		
Payment of cash dividend...	25,492	
Reduction in mortgage loan	4,949	
Total Working Capital Used		30,441
Net increase in working capital..		$12,977

cember 31, 1976, and the year ended December 31, 1975. An income statement shows, for the period,

$$\text{Revenues} - \text{Expenses} = \text{Net Income}$$

The income statement is related to the balance sheet. Net income is that portion of the increase in owners' equity which resulted from business operations during the period that it covers.

The *statement of changes in financial position* reports the inflows and outflows of financial resources during a period of time. It is constructed according to the model:

Fund Inflows − Fund Outflows = Change in Funds

These amounts are derived by rearranging information that originally appeared on the balance sheet and the income statement, using certain supporting detail behind these statements. In Exhibit 1–1 the statement reports inflows and outflows of working capital. An alternative form, not illustrated here, reports inflows and outflows of cash.

These three statements, and the notes accompanying them, are the principal source of information available to outside parties about the financial status and performance of a business. Not only do users study the information as it is stated, but they also calculate ratios which show the relationship of various categories to one another. For example, the user will note that in 1976 sales revenue and net income increased substantially over 1975, that inventory at the end of 1976 also increased substantially, that cash was much less at the end of 1976 than at the beginning of the year, and so on. Using ratios, the user can calculate that the return on shareholders' year-end equity in 1976 was 16 percent (= \$33,257 ÷ \$206,080), that the current (i.e., working capital) ratio at the end of 1976 was 1.9 to 1 (= \$377,083 ÷ \$194,133), and so on. Such information tells much about the performance of the company and about its financial condition.

Although prepared primarily for the use of outside parties, these financial statements are also useful to the management of the company. In addition, management needs information that is more detailed, for shorter time periods, and more directly related to specific management problems. This special information is the subject matter of **management accounting.** We shall describe the nature and uses of such information in an introductory way in this chapter.

In order to introduce the subject, one needs an understanding of what an organization is, who its managers are, and the nature of the job of managing an organization. The next section discusses these topics.

CHARACTERISTICS OF AN ORGANIZATION

An organization is a group of people who work together for some purpose. Let us look at a specific organization, the Morgan Ford Company. This company sells and services Ford automobiles in the city of Morgan. Such an organization is customarily called a "dealership."

Goals

The purposes for which the organization exists are called its goals. Morgan Ford Company is a corporation. Its owners, that is, its shareholders, have voluntarily invested money in the corporation. They did so with the expectation of earning a return, or profit, on that investment. A primary goal of Morgan Ford Company, therefore, is to earn profits. The shareholders have employed Martin Carroll as president and hold him responsible for managing the activities of the company in such a way that a satisfactory profit is earned. Earning a satisfactory profit is an important goal of most private businesses. For this reason such businesses are called **profit-oriented** companies to distinguish them from government organizations, hospitals, colleges, and other organizations. These **nonprofit organizations** have quite different goals.

Although earning profits is one goal, it is not the only goal of Morgan Ford Company. Its owners want to be well regarded in the community, they want to create jobs, they want to encourage the growth of the city of Morgan. The profit goal is tempered by the existence of these other goals.

Strategies

There are many alternative ways in which an automobile dealership can seek its goal of earning a satisfactory profit. The management of Morgan Ford Company has selected from the various possible alternatives certain courses of action that seem best for it. These are its **strategies.**

Martin Carroll, with the assent of the board of directors, has decided that the best strategies for Morgan Ford Company are to sell new Ford automobiles, to sell used cars of any make, and to service automobiles. He and the board have considered, but decided against, several other possible strategies. For example, they have decided not to sell trucks, not to operate a gasoline service station, not to lease automobiles, and not to operate a taxi service, because of doubts that the income that might be earned from these activities would provide an adequate return on the investment that the company would have to make in them. Other automobile dealers do engage in some or all of these activities; that is, they follow different strategies.

Carroll also has to choose from among a number of other types of strategies. Some automobile dealers are "volume" dealers; that is, they sell at low unit prices[1] and/or they spend much money on advertising, in the expectation that the lower profit per unit will be more than made up by the relatively large number of units sold. Others are "quality"

---

[1] Automobile dealers customarily quote the manufacturers' suggested retail price (the "sticker price") which is the same for everyone, but they vary the actual selling price by making allowances and discounts from the sticker price. Buyers therefore do not necessarily pay the suggested retail price.

dealers; that is, they charge a relatively high selling price but attract customers by providing excellent service and by creating an aura of trustworthiness. Again, the selection of one of these or similar strategies is a matter of management judgment. Some dealers make a profit one way, some another. (And, unfortunately, some dealers incur losses because the strategies they select do not work out satisfactorily.)

Every business has a set of strategies, although often they are not written down. Essentially they state (1) the goods the business has decided to manufacture, and/or the services it has decided to offer; and (2) which of the available alternatives for manufacturing and marketing these goods and services the management has decided on.

Incidentally, the fact that investors make their own decisions as to where to invest their money and the fact that individual companies can select their own strategies are two of the great strengths of the free enterprise system. They result in a constant search for new opportunities, and this helps to keep the economy dynamic. Governments in Soviet countries have discovered that the socialist system, as originally conceived, did not permit adequate flexibility in channeling investment funds or in selecting strategies, and they are now experimenting with various capitalistic devices that will provide more flexibility.

Organization structure

Martin Carroll does not execute the strategies by himself; Morgan Ford Company has 39 employees. Since he cannot personally supervise the work of so many people, Carroll has organized Morgan Ford employees into groups, called departments. Each department has an assigned job to do, and each is headed by a manager. Morgan Ford Company has four line departments and one staff department.

Line departments are responsible for activities that are directly associated with the production and marketing activities of the organization. They are (1) a new car sales department, which is responsible for selling new automobiles; (2) a used car sales department, which is responsible for selling used automobiles; (3) a service department, which services and repairs automobiles for customers and also reconditions used cars taken in trade; and (4) a parts and accessories department, which maintains an inventory of parts and accessories, furnishes these to the service department, and also sells them to customers. The managers of the new car and used car sales departments report to a vice president in charge of car sales.

Staff departments provide services to other departments. The controller department, which is the one staff department of Morgan Ford Company, collects, reports, and analyzes accounting information and other information, and prepares reports for both internal and external use. The controller department provides this service—that is, information—to the other departments and to top management. In this book we are particu-

EXHIBIT 1–2
Morgan Ford Company organization chart

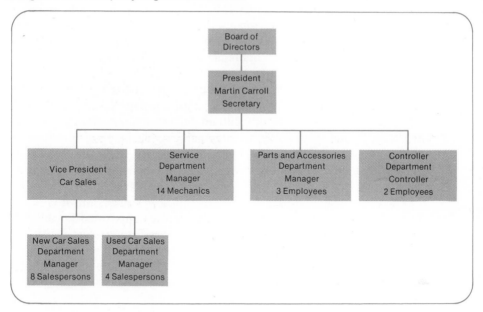

larly interested in the work of the controller department[2] and in the use of the information it prepares.

Exhibit 1–2 is an **organization chart** depicting this arrangement of people. The boxes represent the various organization units, and the lines connecting the boxes represent the relationships of the units to one another. The chart shows that the manager of the new car sales department and the manager of the used car sales department are responsible to the vice president for car sales. All other managers are directly responsible to the president, Martin Carroll. The president, in turn, is responsible to the board of directors, who are elected by the shareholders. **An organization chart shows the responsibility relationships among managers in an organization.**

The lines connecting the boxes on the organization chart show the *formal* responsibility relationships. The chart does not depict *informal* relationships. These exist and are important in any organization. For example, even though there is no line that connects the used car sales department with the service department, the managers of these departments must work closely together for the overall success of Morgan Ford Company.

---

[2] Although the word *controller* is widely used, the title *financial vice president* is used in many companies, and *chief accountant* is used in others (though less commonly). The word *comptroller* is an obsolete spelling of *controller* but continues to be used in some organizations; *comptroller* is *pronounced* the same as *controller*.

In its essentials, this organization chart is similar to that in many medium-size companies. In many companies there would be several staff departments that do not exist in Morgan Ford Company, including any or all of the following: finance, purchasing, research and development, personnel, labor relations, advertising, public relations, and legal.

In larger companies, the organization is naturally more complicated. There may be a number of layers in the organization, that is, subdepartments reporting to departments, subsubdepartments reporting to subdepartments, and so on. The complete organization chart for the Ford Motor Company, which has over 400,000 employees, requires many hundreds of $8\frac{1}{2}$-by-11-inch pages. It is so large and complicated that it is doubtful that any one person is familiar with all its details; each manager knows the part that affects his or her responsibility relationships within the company.

There is no standard designation of the names of organization units. The terms *divisions, departments, units,* and *sections* stand for different things in different companies. In this book, the word *division* is used for a relatively large and relatively self-contained organization, such as the Chicago dealership of a company that operates a number of separate automobile dealerships, and the word *department* is used for a unit that performs a single line or staff function. In other words, as used here, departments are parts of divisions, not vice versa.

Responsibility centers

Each box on Exhibit 1–2 represents a group of people (or, as in the case of "Vice President, Car Sales," a single person). The group has a job to do; that is, it has a defined responsibility. Each person in the group reports to someone, whom we shall designate the *manager*. We shall use the term **responsibility center** for any such group, that is, for **an organization unit with a defined responsibility and headed by a manager.** Moreover, we shall use the term responsibility center to include aggregations of individual boxes on the organization chart. Thus, each department is a responsibility center, and the company as a whole is also a responsibility center consisting of the aggregate of the lower level responsibility centers, with the president as its manager. If there were divisions, each of them would be a responsibility center. The responsibility center is a key concept in our discussion of management accounting.

The functions of management

The principal responsibility of a manager is to see to it that the work of the responsibility center gets done by the persons who report to him;[3]

---

[3] Throughout this text, when the male pronoun is used, it is for convenience only. All statements apply equally to both men and women.

managers are *not* responsible for doing the work personally. The principal responsibility of the service manager is to see to it that mechanics do a good job of repairing cars; it is *not* personally to repair cars. The manager of the new car sales department does not personally deal with each customer; there simply is not time for the manager to meet the dozens of customers who visit Morgan Ford Company on a typical day. Rather, the manager's primary responsibility is to see to it that the eight salespersons in the new car sales department do an effective sales job with these customers. The manager may, of course, spend some time dealing with customers, and he often participates in the closing of deals, but this is not his *primary* responsibility, and when he does these things he is *not* acting as a manager.

This is not the place for a detailed discussion of the functions that a manager performs in carrying out his responsibilities; textbooks on management discuss these at length.[4] Various authors classify these functions in different ways, but there is general agreement that they include at least the following:

1. Planning and coordinating.
2. Directing.
3. Controlling.

Each manager performs these functions for his own responsibility center, and he participates in the corresponding processes for the company as a whole.

In **planning, the manager decides what actions should be taken to help the organization achieve its goals.** Customers who walk into Morgan Ford Company see employees who are engaged in a variety of activities; they see service machinery and equipment, and they see bins full of parts. If they stop to think about this, they realize that much thought and action has been involved in creating the organization and the physical resources that are ready to serve them. This is planning. An important planning activity, especially at higher levels in the organization, is that of **coordination,** which means **melding the plans of individual responsibility centers into an integrated, balanced plan for the whole company.**

In **directing, the manager oversees the conduct of day-to-day operations.** The service manager assigns mechanics to jobs, he helps a mechanic who can't locate the source of trouble in an automobile, he settles disputes that arise between mechanics, he goes to bat for his mechanics in disputes that they have with the parts and accessories department. These are the activities that the customers observe, and outsiders may there-

---

[4] See Harold Koontz and Cyril J. O'Donnell, *Management,* 6th ed. (New York: McGraw-Hill Book Co., 1976); William H. Newman and E. Kirby Warren, *Process of Management,* 4th ed. (Englewood Cliffs, N.J.: Prentice-Hall, Inc., 1977); and Jerry B. Poe, *An Introduction to the American Business Enterprise,* 3d ed. (Homewood, Ill.: Richard D. Irwin, Inc., 1976).

fore believe that these activities are the only function of the manager; this is by no means the case. Directing is the process involved with the here and now.

In **controlling, the manager takes steps to insure that his responsibility center is operating in the best possible way.** In order to do this, he studies reports on past operations, and from these he tries to find ways of making operations better in the future. In other words, he uses the lessons learned from past experience to make better plans for the future. The process of using past experience to modify future plans is also called **feedback.** The manager's evaluations of the past are made in two general areas. First, there is an **appraisal of activities or functions** which may lead to improvements in ways of doing things or even to a change in strategy. Second, there is an **appraisal of the performance of individuals** which leads to praise, promotion, criticism, constructive suggestions, or other actions with respect to these individuals. As we shall see, the information that is needed for one of these types of appraisals is significantly different from that needed for the other type.

Decision making. In performing the planning, directing, and controlling functions, managers make decisions. In planning, the manager *decides* to buy a new machine or hire another mechanic. In directing, the manager *decides* which mechanics should work on various jobs. In controlling, the manager *decides* what if any corrective action should be taken. Thus, in a broad sense, the three functions can be regarded as being various types of decisions. For our purposes, however, it is more useful to discuss the three functions separately because each type of decision requires somewhat different management accounting information.

Similarities among organizations

Although each of the millions of organizations in the United States is in some sense unique, all of them except the smallest have the general characteristics described above; that is, they have one or more goals, they have strategies for achieving these goals, their personnel are grouped into responsibility centers, each responsibility center has a manager, and these managers plan, direct, and control the activities of the organization.

In this book we shall describe the nature and uses of management accounting in all types of organizations. Because of the basic similarities among organizations, many statements can be made that apply to organizations generally. Because of the differences among organizations of various types, however, some statements will apply only to certain types of organizations. For example, there are important differences between a profit-oriented organization, such as Morgan Ford Company, and a nonprofit organization, such as a government entity, a hospital, a college, or a church. A nonprofit organization, by definition, does not have profit as one of its goals. It does have goals, however; and the management accounting information in these organizations is intended to help management attain these goals, whatever they may be.

INFORMATION

The purpose of this section is to distinguish management accounting information from other types of information. First, let us define **information as a fact, datum, observation, perception, or any other thing that adds to knowledge.** The number 1,000 taken by itself is not information; it doesn't tell anyone anything. The statement that 1,000 students are enrolled in a certain school *is* information. Management accounting is one type of information. Its place in the whole picture is shown in Exhibit 1–3.

Information can be either quantitative or nonquantitative. Impressions from the senses (hearing, vision, etc.), conversations, television programs, and newspaper stories are examples of nonquantitative information. Management accounting is primarily concerned with quantitative information.

EXHIBIT 1–3
Types of information

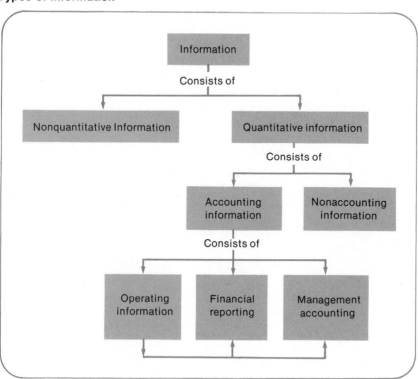

There are many types of quantitative information. Accounting information is distinguished from the other types in that it usually is expressed in monetary terms. Data on the age, experience level, and other characteristics of an employee are quantitative, but they are not usually designated as accounting information. The line here is not sharply drawn, however; nonmonetary information is often included in accounting reports when it assists the reader in understanding what the report is intended to convey. For example, reports on sales for Morgan Ford Company would show, in addition to the monetary amount of sales revenue, the number of automobiles sold, which is quantitative, nonmonetary information. There is no point in debating the question of whether this is or is not accounting. The important point is that the focus of accounting information is monetary, but that nonmonetary information is reported when it is useful to managers.

Operating information

The bottom section of Exhibit 1–3 indicates the general nature of accounting information. By far the largest quantity of such information consists of **operating information**. Operating information is detailed data generated in the course of operations. It is summarized to provide both financial accounting and management accounting information.

There are records showing the detail on orders received from customers, instructions for manufacturing the goods to meet these orders, and instructions for manufacturing goods that are to be held in inventory.

There are records having to do with material and services ordered, with their receipt, with keeping track of material while it is in inventory, and with its issue to the production departments.

There are records which show how much each employee has earned, the nature of the work done, and how much each has been paid.

There are records of the cost, location, and condition of each significant item of building, equipment, or other noncurrent asset used by the company, together with the related depreciation data.

For every cash sale, there is a cash register record of some sort. For every credit sale there is an invoice giving detail of what was sold and to whom. For every credit customer there is a record of the amounts of credit extended, the amount paid, and the unpaid balance.

There are the checkbook and bank deposit records; and records required to keep track of investments, the incurrence and payment of liabilities, and dividends and other transactions with stockholders.

Financial reporting

The financial statements are derived principally by classifying and summarizing this operating information, and the set of accounts in a company is designed so as to make it easy to prepare such summaries. The amount of sales revenue reported on the income statement is a summary total of the individual cash sales and credit sales transactions that have occurred in the accounting period. The amount of accounts receivable reported on the balance sheet is the total of the individual customer balances as of the balance sheet date, as shown in the detailed accounting records.

Management accounting

The detailed operating information also provides the source of most management accounting information. As is the case with financial reporting, management accounting information consists primarily of summaries drawn from underlying details. In the normal course of events, a manager does not care about the amount of money that an individual customer owes, or the amount that an individual employee earned last week, or the amount that was deposited in the bank yesterday, or the placement of an individual purchase order for the replenishment of parts. Records of these facts are used by operating personnel rather than by managers. The manager is interested in summaries drawn from these records rather than the details.

TYPES OF MANAGEMENT ACCOUNTING INFORMATION

Managers need information to carry out their responsibilities of planning, directing, and controlling. The nature of this information differs from that required for financial accounting in several important respects. The most important difference, and the most difficult one to grasp, is that in management accounting, information is summarized in different ways for different purposes, whereas in financial accounting there is an essential underlying unity.

Financial accounting is essentially a single process, governed by a single set of generally accepted accounting principles, and unified by the basic equation, Assets = Liabilities + Owners' Equity. All financial accounting transactions can be related to this basic equation, and the relationship is emphasized by the corresponding equation, Debits = Credits. By contrast, in management accounting *three* sets of principles govern the information that is used by managers. Information prepared according to each set of principles is used for certain purposes, but is not useful for other purposes.

In order to emphasize this distinction among principles, each of the three parts of this book focuses on the nature and use of one of these three types of management accounting information. In this introductory chapter we shall categorize them in terms of different cost constructions. They can also be categorized in terms of different revenue constructions or of different asset constructions, and we shall discuss these categories later on.

Cost is a monetary measure of the amount of resources used for some purpose. The three types of cost constructions that comprise management accounting are:

1. Full cost accounting.
2. Differential accounting.
3. Responsibility accounting.

We shall first describe each of these briefly and then indicate how they relate to the management functions of planning, directing, and controlling.

Full cost accounting

The *full cost* of an item is the sum of the costs that are incurred directly for that item plus a fair share of the indirect costs associated with the item. The full cost of a used car in the inventory of Morgan Ford Company consists of the purchase cost of the car, plus the cost of the labor and materials that were used in the service department to put the car into salable condition, plus a fair share of the general operating costs of the service department.

> *EXAMPLE:* If the company purchased a used car for $1,000, spent $50 of mechanics' time and used $70 worth of parts in fixing it up, and if a fair share of the service department's costs general applicable to this car were $30, the full cost of the used car is $1,150.

Full cost accounting is closely related to, and often is a part of, financial accounting because the inventory amount on the balance sheet is the full cost of the items in inventory, and the cost of goods sold item on the income statement is the full cost of the items sold.

Full cost is also used in many companies as a basis for arriving at selling prices. The customer who has an automobile serviced in the service department of Morgan Ford Company normally would be charged the full cost of the work done, plus a profit margin. In arriving at the selling prices for a line of manufactured products, which is part of the planning process, the full cost of these products is an important consideration.

Differential accounting

In making plans for the allocation of resources, managers often must make a choice between two or more alternatives. Resources are materials, services of employees, machines, electrical power, and so on. Each of these resources can be measured in terms of money, and this measurement is the cost of the resource. In any company, resources are limited. They should be used in the way most likely to accomplish the company's goals. Managers make many decisions involving the use of resources in one way rather than another, and these are called **alternative choice decisions.** A few examples from the long list of alternative choice problems that arise in the Morgan Ford Company are: the used car sales manager decides whether or not to place newspaper advertisements; the service manager decides whether or not to buy a new machine that will help the mechanics do a better job of servicing cars; or the parts and accessories manager decides whether or not to add a new item to the inventory, and if so, what quantity should be ordered.

The accounting information that is used in making alternative choice decisions is differential accounting. A *differential* cost is a cost that would be different if one alternative were selected than it would be if another alternative were selected. Costs that are not differential are irrelevant for alternative choice decisions and may be disregarded.

> EXAMPLE: Morgan Ford has purchased for $600 a used car with a badly dented body. The service manager has the alternative choice problem of sending the car to an outside body shop that specializes in such work or of repairing it in the company's service department. The following information is collected:

Alternative A. Price charged by outside body shop..........		$325
Alternative B. Differential costs of repairs in Morgan service department:		
Labor...	$180	
Parts...	90	−270
Difference, favoring Alternative B.......................		$ 55

The analysis indicates that the differential costs of making the repairs in the Morgan service department are $55 less than the cost that would be incurred if the work were sent outside; so, unless there were other considerations, the service manager would decide to do the work in the Morgan service department.

Note that in this analysis, no mention was made of the $600 cost of the used car itself. This cost is unaffected by the decision; it is not a differential cost.

Responsibility accounting

In making plans for the business as a whole and for the individual responsibility centers within the business, an important technique is called *budgeting.* A budget is a plan, usually annual, that is stated in financial terms. In controlling performance, an important part of the process is to measure how actual performance compares with planned, or budgeted, performance. Plans must be carried out by the managers of responsibility centers, and control can be exercised only through these managers. Therefore, it is essential that the information used for these purposes be arranged so that it corresponds to responsibility centers. Information arranged in this way is called **responsibility accounting** information.

> *EXAMPLE:* Exhibit 1–4 is a control report for the service department of Morgan Ford Company for September 1976. The first column shows the planned, or budgeted, expenses and revenues for September. The second column shows the actual expenses and revenues, and the third column shows the difference. The report shows that revenues were $2,766 less than planned, that wages and other expenses were higher than planned, and that these increases were partly offset by lower expenses for parts used and supplies used; but on balance the service department earned a profit that was $1,663 less than was planned.

A control report is essentially an *attention-directing* report. It alerts management to the possible existence of an unfavorable situation that needs correcting—in the case of Exhibit 1–4, low revenues, high wages, and high other expenses—but it does not, of course, automatically solve the problem if there is one. Martin Carroll, the president, uses such a report as the basis for discussion with the service department manager; and on the basis of this discussion he decides whether corrective action is needed.

Relation of accounting types to management functions

It should be emphasized that **there is not a one-to-one correspondence between the three types of management accounting information and the three management functions.** The task of understanding management accounting would be much simpler if such a correspondence existed, but it

EXHIBIT 1–4

MORGAN FORD COMPANY
Service Department Report
September 1976

	Planned	Actual	Difference*
Number of jobs completed................	200	183	(17)
Number of employee days.................	370	368	2
Revenues..	$34,000	$31,234	$(2,766)
Expenses:			
Employees wages	15,000	15,386	(386)
Parts used......................................	8,000	6,287	1,713
Supplies used..................................	2,500	2,412	88
Other expenses...............................	3,000	3,312	(312)
Total Expenses	28,500	27,397	1,103
Operating Income	$ 5,500	$ 3,837	$(1,663)

* ( ) = unfavorable.

does not. In making plans, managers often use responsibility accounting information, but certain types of plans require the use of full cost accounting information and others require differential accounting information. In making certain operating decisions, managers use full cost information; while for others, they use differential cost information. In controlling, managers use primarily responsibility accounting.

Thus, the central scheme of this book is to discuss each of the three types of management accounting separately, explaining what it is and discussing its use for various management purposes.

Place of management accounting

Since our interest is focused on management accounting, we may have a tendency to overemphasize its importance. In order to counteract this tendency, three points are emphasized here. They will be repeated in other contexts later on.

Financial accounting information. The financial statements shown in Exhibit 1–1 obviously are useful to the management of Morgan Ford Company. They help both in making plans and in controlling the operations of the company as a whole. In this sense, therefore, the companion volume, *Fundamentals of Financial Accounting,* is also concerned with management accounting. There is, however, no point in repeating the material we discuss in the companion volume; therefore, in this volume we shall discuss the *additional* accounting information that is useful to managers, beyond that contained in the financial statements.

Nonaccounting information. Accounting information is only part of the information that a manager uses. A manager uses whatever information is available, whether it be accounting or nonaccounting, quantitative or nonquantitative. A telephoned message, or even a rumor, that some customers are so dissatisfied with the Morgan Ford Company's service that they are about to take their business elsewhere, is not accounting and not even quantitative, but it is certainly an important piece of information.

Necessity for judgment. Accounting information, and indeed any information, rarely provides the complete answer to a management problem. The most that accounting information can do is to help the manager. The actual decision requires, in all except the most trivial situations, that judgment be exercised. Accounting information can help the manager make sound decisions. It assists the manager's judgment, but it is not a substitute for judgment.

MANAGEMENT ACCOUNTING AND FINANCIAL ACCOUNTING

We have mentioned one difference between management accounting and financial accounting. In order to facilitate the transition from the study of financial accounting to the study of management accounting in this volume, it seems desirable to restate this difference, add other differences to it, and also point out similarities.

Differences

In contrast with financial accounting, management accounting—

1. Has no single unified structure.
2. Is not necessarily governed by generally accepted principles.
3. Is optional rather than mandatory.
4. Includes more nonmonetary information.
5. Has more emphasis on the future.
6. Focuses on parts as well as on the whole of a business.
7. Has less emphasis on precision.
8. Is a means to an end, rather than an end in itself.

1. Lack of a single structure. As already noted, financial accounting is built around the fundamental equation, Assets = Liabilities + Owners' Equity; whereas in management accounting there are three types of accounting, each with its own set of principles.

2. Not governed by generally accepted principles. Financial accounting information must be reported in accordance with generally accepted accounting principles. Outsiders, who usually have no choice but to accept information just as the company provides it, need assurance that the financial statements are prepared in accordance with a mutually understood set of ground rules. Otherwise, they could not understand what the figures mean. Generally accepted accounting principles provide these common ground rules. The management of a company, by contrast, can make and enforce whatever rules it finds most useful for its own purposes, without worrying about whether these conform to some outside standard. Thus, in management accounting there may well be information on sales orders received (i.e., the order "backlog"), even though these are not financial accounting transactions. Also, in management accounting fixed assets may be stated at appraisal values, overhead costs may be omitted from inventories, or revenue may be recorded before it is realized, even though each of these concepts is inconsistent with generally accepted accounting principles. The basic question in management accounting is the pragmatic one: "Is the information useful?" rather than, "Does it conform to generally accepted principles?"

3. Optional. Financial accounting *must* be done. Enough effort must be expended to collect data in acceptable form and with an acceptable degree of accuracy to meet the requirements of outside parties, whether or not the accountant regards this information as useful. For most sizable corporations, these requirements are specified by the Securities and Exchange Commission (SEC), a government agency. Even those companies that are not covered by SEC regulations have their financial statements examined by professional outside accountants, in most cases; and these accountants insist that certain minimum requirements be met. Also, all companies must keep records for income tax purposes, according to regulations of the taxing authorities. Management accounting, by contrast, is entirely optional. No outside agencies specify what must be done, or indeed that anything need be done. Being optional, there is no point in collecting a piece of information for management purposes unless its value, as an aid to management, is believed to exceed the cost of collecting it.

4. Nonmonetary information. The financial statements, which are the end product of financial accounting, include primarily monetary information. Management accounting deals with nonmonetary as well as monetary information. Although the accounts themselves contain primarily money amounts, much of the information on management accounting reports is nonmonetary. They contain quantities of material, as well as the monetary cost of material; number of employees, as well as labor costs; units of products sold, as well as dollar amounts of sales revenue; and so on.

5. Future information. Financial accounting records and reports the financial history of an enterprise. Entries are made in the accounts only after transactions have occurred. Although financial accounting information is used as a basis for making future plans, the information itself is historical. Management accounting includes, in its formal structure, numbers that represent estimates and plans for the future, as well as information about the past. (Some financial accounting entries, such as those for depreciation, require that estimates of future conditions be made; but the basic thrust of financial accounting is nevertheless historical.)

6. Focus on parts. The financial statements relate to the business as a whole. Although some companies do subdivide revenues and expenses according to the main lines of business in which they engage, the main focus is on the entire business entity. In management accounting, by contrast, the main focus is on parts of the business, that is, on products, on individual activities, or on divisions, departments, and other responsibility centers. As we shall see, the necessity for dividing the total costs of the business among these individual parts creates important problems in management accounting that do not exist in financial accounting.

7. Less emphasis on precision. Management needs information rapidly, and is often willing to sacrifice some precision in order to gain speed in reporting. Thus, in management accounting, approximations are often as useful as, or even more useful than, numbers that are worked out to the last penny. Financial accounting cannot be absolutely precise either, so the difference is one of degree. The approximations used in management accounting are greater than those in financial accounting.

8. A means rather than an end. The purpose of financial accounting is to produce financial statements for external users. When the statements have been produced, the purpose has been accomplished. (The accountant can, to be sure, play an important role in helping users to analyze and understand the statements, but this activity takes place after the completion of the financial accounting process.) Management accounting information is only a means to an end, the end being the planning, directing, and controlling activities described above. Management accountants assist managers in using accounting data, but they should not adopt the attitude that the accounting numbers are an end in themselves.

Similarities

Although differences do exist, most elements of financial accounting are also found in management accounting. There are two reasons for this.

First, the same considerations that make generally accepted accounting principles sensible for the purposes of financial accounting are likely to be relevant for purposes of management accounting. For example, management cannot base its reporting system on unverifiable, subjective estimates of profits submitted by lower echelons which is the same reason that the cost and revenue concepts in financial accounting are based on the idea of objectivity.

Second, operating information is used both in preparing the financial statements and in management accounting. There is a presumption, therefore, that the basic data will be collected in accordance with generally accepted financial accounting principles, for to do otherwise would require duplication of data collecting activities.

ILLUSTRATIVE CASE

(Try to resolve this case before studying the suggested solution that follows.)

The Marker Pen Company manufactures and sells felt-tip pens of several styles, quality grades, and colors. The factory is managed by the production vice president. It is organized into four departments each headed by a supervisor: the barrel department, in which the barrels for the pens are molded from plastic; the wick department, which manufactures the wick and impregnates it with the writing fluid; the assembly department, which assembles the completed pen and packs it for shipment; and the factory service department, which provides general services to the other departments. The company also has a sales department, headed by a sales vice president; a personnel department; and a controller department. The production vice president, the sales vice president, the personnel department manager, and the controller report to the president.

Required:
1. Prepare an organization chart for this company.
2. Suggest the types of management accounting information that would

EXHIBIT 1–5
Marker Pen Company organization chart

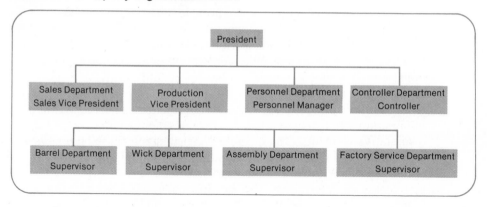

be useful to the managers in planning, directing, and controlling the activities of this company.

Suggested solution:

1. The organization chart is shown in Exhibit 1–5.
2. Following is a list of some of the uses of management accounting information:
   a. Full cost accounting information would be useful in valuing the pens for inventory purposes and in deciding on the prices to be charged for pens of various styles and qualities (but not different colors, unless cost varies with the color of the fluid, which is unlikely).
   b. Differential accounting information would be useful in deciding on whether to purchase new molding machines or retain existing machines; whether to buy some of the parts from an outside vendor, rather than making them; whether or not to adopt a new method of manufacture; or whether to increase advertising or other selling efforts (and a long list of other possible alternative choice decisions).
   c. Responsibility accounting information would be useful in preparing a budget for the company as a whole and for the individual responsibility centers, and for controlling the performance of the managers of each responsibility center by comparing budgeted performance with actual performance.

SUMMARY

Every organization has goals. In a profit-oriented business, an important goal is to earn a satisfactory profit. A company selects a set of strategies for attaining its goals, and the people in the company are organized in a way that is thought to be the best for carrying out these strategies. The various units in this organization are called responsibility centers. Each responsibility center is headed by a manager. The objective of management accounting is to provide useful information to these managers. Among other functions, managers perform the following for which accounting information is useful: (1) planning and coordinating the future activities of responsibility centers; (2) directing day-to-day operations; and (3) control, which involves evaluating results and taking appropriate action.

Accounting provides one type of information. The total amount of information needed by a manager includes nonquantitative as well as quantitative elements. The quantitative elements include both monetary and nonmonetary amounts. Accounting information is primarily monetary, but includes related nonmonetary data.

Accounting information can be divided into three categories. The largest, in terms of quantity, is operating information. Operating information is the source of both financial accounting and management accounting information; that is, accounting reports are essentially summaries of operating information, constructed in various ways to meet the needs (1) of investors and other outside parties, and (2) of managers inside the business.

There is no single, unified management accounting system. Rather, there are three different types of information, each used for different purposes. These are categorized as: (1) full cost accounting, (2) differential accounting, and (3) responsibility accounting. Each of the three main parts of this book is devoted to one of these types.

As contrasted with financial accounting, management accounting has several sets of principles rather than one; is not necessarily governed by generally accepted principles; includes more nonmonetary information; has more emphasis on the future; is optional rather than mandatory; focuses on segments of a business rather than on the whole; has less emphasis on precision; and is a means to an end rather than an end in itself. Nevertheless, the two types of accounting have much in common.

IMPORTANT TERMS

At the end of each chapter, a list of important terms introduced in the chapter is given. You should understand the meaning of these terms. The list for Chapter 1, arranged in the order in which they appear in the text, is:

Organization	Manager
Goals	Planning
Strategies	Directing
Controller	Controlling
Organization chart	Information
Responsibility center	Operating information

Financial reporting   Differential accounting
Management accounting   Responsibility accounting
Full cost accounting

1. A football team is an organization. Can you describe this organization in the terms used in the text: that is, its goals, its strategies, its organization structure, and the functions of its managers?

2. Describe some of the strategies that are available to a company in the retail grocery business.

3. A college or university is a nonprofit organization. Discuss the similarities and differences, in terms of the characteristics given in the text, between a college or university and the Morgan Ford Company.

4. Why is a business divided into departments?

5. What is the difference between a line department and a staff department? Which departments of the Marker Pen Company (Exhibit 1–5) are line departments and which are staff departments?

6. The controller department is generally responsible for all recordkeeping. Why don't the managers of line departments keep their own records?

7. The controller department is a staff or service organization. If the department consists of several sections such as accounts receivable, payroll, cost accounting, and so on, does the controller have line responsibility for these sections?

8. An important planning activity is *coordination*. Give examples of the coordination that must take place in the Morgan Ford Company.

9. Is the material in this book information? Is it management information?

10. Does a newspaper contain information? Is it management information?

11. How does information needed for planning differ from information needed for control?

12. Items on the income statement in Exhibit 1–1 are summaries of underlying detail. Some of this information (including detail not shown) is important to each manager in the Morgan Ford Company. Which items would each manager shown on the organization chart be especially interested in?

13. Refer to Exhibit 1–4. Does it contain both financial accounting and management accounting information? Describe the ways in which this management accounting report is similar to, and the ways in which it is different from, the financial accounting income statement in Exhibit 1–1.

14. For what uses is full cost accounting especially valuable? Differential accounting? Responsibility accounting?

15. The Marker Pen Company (see Illustrative Case) conceivably could change its strategy by closing down its factory and buying the pens from another manufacturer, ready for sale? What cost construction would be useful in deciding whether to do this?

16. What are the differences between management accounting and financial accounting?

17. "The goal of Morgan Ford Company is to make a profit. Management accounting information helps managers achieve this goal. But since a government agency (or other nonprofit organization) does not have profit as a goal, management accounting is of no use in such an organization." Do you agree?

18. Why is precision less important in management accounting than in financial accounting?

19. Why do generally accepted accounting principles affect management accounting even though there is no requirement that management accounting adhere to such principles?

20. "Accounting evidence is only partial evidence." Explain why this is so.

PROBLEMS

1–1. Suburbia Department Store sells four different lines:

a. Men's and boys' wear.
b. Ladies' wear.
c. Home furnishings.
d. Notions.

Each of these departments is headed by a manager (called the "buyer") who directs the activities of sales, inventory control, and clerical personnel in his or her department. There is a merchandising division manager who is directly responsible to the president. The buyers are responsible to the division manager. The store has three others also responsible to the president—an advertising manager, the controller of the accounting division, and the store personnel manager.

Required:

A. Prepare an organization chart for this company.
B. Classify each function depicted on your chart as either line or staff.
C. Suggest the types of management accounting information that would be useful to the managers in planning, directing, and controlling the activities of this company.

1–2. As controller of American Steel, you have been asked to provide information to management that would be helpful in answering a variety of questions.

Required:

A. For each of the questions below, classify the needed information as being an example of either full cost accounting, differential accounting, or responsibility accounting.
   1. Should the company own and operate its own iron ore mines or buy the ore from another firm?
   2. As a result of a new labor contract with the United Steel Workers Union, what will be the profit margin on a ton of steel at current prices?

3. Is the supervisor of the maintenance shop doing a good job?
4. How much money does the company have invested in finished goods inventory?
5. Should the company consider replacing its old open-hearth furnaces with new ones?
6. Which district sales manager is doing the best job?

B. In addition to management accounting information, what other types of information might be useful in attempting to answer each of the questions above?

1-3. Below is a list of management positions in the Morgan Ford Company and a list of various ledger accounts.

Management position	Accounts
Vice president—car sales	Wages—Mechanics
Manager—new car sales	Salary—Payroll Clerk
Manager—used car sales	Salary—New Car Sales Manager
Manager—parts and accessories department	Inventory—Parts
	Accounts Receivable
Manager—service department	Cash
Controller	Advertising—Used Cars
	Reconditioning Cost—Used Cars
	Maintenance—Repair Equipment
	Inventory—New Cars

Required:

Indicate which management position is most likely to be responsible for each account.

1-4. Following is a monthly report for a new branch office which the City National Bank recently opened in a rapidly developing section of the city.

CITY NATIONAL BANK
Eastside Branch Office Report
June 1977

	Planned	Actual	Difference*
Number of new accounts opened.....	100	80	(20)
Number of prospect calls made	50	37	(13)
Increase in deposit volume............	$50,000	$40,000	$(10,000)
Increase in loan volume	40,000	45,000	5,000
Expenses:			
Wages and salaries........................	$ 3,000	$ 2,400	$ 600
Utilities..	300	294	6
Rent on building	450	450	0
Supplies.......................................	150	153	(3)
Advertising	200	150	50
Other expenses............................	50	51	(1)
Total Expenses....................	4,150	3,498	652
Revenue from interest and service charges.....................................	4,000	3,800	(200)
Profit or (loss).............................	$ (150)	$ 302	$ 452

*( ) = unfavorable.

The branch manager is pleased that the report shows a $302 profit instead of the expected loss of $150.

Required:

What questions can be raised about the performance of the Eastside Branch and its manager based on information in the report?

1–5. State University is headed by a president who reports directly to a state board of regents. Four vice presidents are responsible to the president. The educational programs are administered by two of the four. A vice president for health affairs is responsible for separate schools of medicine, dentistry, and nursing. A vice president for general studies is responsible for separate schools of arts and sciences, business administration, education, and engineering. Each separate school is headed by a dean who reports directly to the appropriate vice president. The other two vice presidents are responsible for fiscal affairs and for administrative services.

Required:

A. Prepare an organization chart for State University.
B. Classify each function depicted on your chart as either line or staff.
C. Suggest the types of management accounting information that would be useful to the managers in planning, directing, and controlling the activities of this organization.

1–6. As controller of the city of Maple Heights, you have been asked to provide information to the mayor and city council which would be helpful in answering a variety of questions.

Required:

A. For each of the questions below, classify the needed information as an example of either full cost accounting, differential accounting, or responsibility accounting.
   1. As a result of a recent wage increase for airport workers, what does it now cost to operate the municipal airport?
   2. Should the city continue to own and operate its own garbage trucks or contract with a private firm?
   3. What does it cost to prepare and mail annual tax notices to property owners?
   4. Is the new police chief doing a better job than the former one?
   5. Should the city close its jail and contract with the county for detention of prisoners?
   6. Which department head is doing the best job of staying within his or her budget?
B. In addition to management accounting information, what other types of information might be useful in attempting to answer each of the questions above?

1–7. Below is a list of management positions at State University and a list of various ledger accounts.

Management positions	Accounts
Vice president—health affairs	Cash
Dean, School of Medicine	Salaries—Marketing Department
Dean, School of Dentistry	Travel—Dental Faculty
Dean, School of Business	Accounts Receivable—Tuition
Vice president—fiscal affairs	Salary—School of Medicine Dean
Vice president—administrative services	Cafeteria Expenses
	Secretary—Department of Surgery
	Maintenance—University Automobiles
	Endowment Fund Investments
	Supplies—Dental Clinic

Required:

Indicate which management position is most likely to be responsible for each account.

1–8. Following is a monthly report for the maintenance department of the Atlas Manufacturing Company.

ATLAS MANUFACTURING COMPANY
Maintenance Department Report
June 1977

	Planned	Actual	Difference*
Number of jobs completed:			
Scheduled maintenance	75	60	(15)
Breakdowns	25	40	15
Total Jobs	100	100	0
Labor hours worked:			
Scheduled maintenance	525	300	225
Breakdowns	325	576	(251)
Total Hours	850	876	(26)
Expenses:			
Wages and salaries	$ 7,650	$ 7,884	$ (234)
Parts and supplies	6,250	7,100	(850)
Depreciation—tools and equipment.................................	2,000	2,000	0
Other expenses.............................	1,100	1,326	(226)
Total Expenses	$17,000	$18,310	$(1,310)

*( ) = unfavorable.

Required:

A. What questions can be raised about the performance of the maintenance department and its manager based on information in this report?

B. What other questions might be raised about the company as a whole from an analysis of the report?

1-9. What questions can be raised about the performance of the Morgan Ford Company service department from the information given in the report in Exhibit 1-4?

1-10. As a review of financial accounting, calculate such ratios as you can from the data in Exhibit 1-1. (Refer to Chapter 16 of *Fundamentals of Financial Accounting* for a list of these ratios and how to calculate them.) What important information can you learn about the performance of the company in 1976 and its financial position as of December 31, 1975?

(For ease in making the computations, round all numbers to the nearest thousand dollars.)

CASE: CHARLES MAVIOLI

1-11. In the fall of 1974, Charles Mavioli, a general carpenter, decided to invest a part of his savings in woodworking machinery and in a building which had been used previously as a small garage. His plan for some time had been to prepare himself for contracting work of a modest sort, including small-home construction. He had always wanted to build low-priced dwellings "all on his own." So far in his career, Mavioli had been extraordinarily successful as a general carpenter, working at a wide variety of jobs. At times he had been hired as "boss carpenter" on large and important construction projects. For this kind of work he had received a good salary, a large part of which he and his wife had been able to save against the time when he could have a business of his own.

In October 1974, Mavioli had his shop completely fitted and had hired two mill hands and a shop mechanic to help him in his new undertaking. As a "fill-in" between jobs, it was his expectation to be able to provide fairly uniform employment for these people by manufacturing window and door frames, kitchen cabinets, and similar construction parts, both for stock and on order.

In the same month, in connection with a substantial order for kitchen cabinets requiring six to eight weeks of shop activity, Mavioli talked with the credit officer of his bank about his need for some temporary financial assistance in the purchase of necessary materials and supplies. This assistance the bank was glad to extend to him. In granting the loan, however, the credit officer stressed the fact that Mavioli would have to furnish regular financial statements to the bank so that the bank would be aware of his financial situation.

Mavioli had a friend who was an accountant for a local retail store. He asked the friend whether he would be interested in maintaining the necessary records on a part-time basis, and the friend readily agreed. The friend said, "I am well aware of what needs to be done in order to prepare the balance sheets and income statements that the bank requires, but I have had no experience with a business such as yours. In managing your business, you will need more information than is contained on the financial statements."

Required:

Make a list of information, in addition to financial accounting information, that Mavioli probably needs to manage his business successfully. Suggest what use Mavioli might make of each such item of information.

part one
Full cost accounting

In Chapter 1, we described briefly three different types of management accounting information. These are:

1. Full cost accounting.
2. Differential accounting.
3. Responsibility accounting.

Part One focuses on the first of these, that is, on full cost accounting. This type of accounting is discussed first because financial accounting, the subject of the companion volume of this book, uses full cost information. Full cost accounting therefore provides, in a sense, a bridge between this volume and its companion. Moreover, the earliest management accounting systems were systems for collecting full costs. We shall describe these systems and the uses of the information that they produce in Chapters 2 through 5.

There are two somewhat different reasons for studying systems for collecting full cost information. First, these systems provide data that are used in financial accounting, and an understanding of them is essential to a thorough understanding of the meaning of certain items on the balance sheet and income statement. Second, and quite apart from their financial accounting uses, full cost information is useful to managers.

By far the most important of these uses is to help set selling prices. The selling prices of many goods and services are related to the full cost of these goods and services. Also, many contracts provide that the buyer pay the seller an amount that equals the sum of full cost plus a specified profit. We hasten to add that in many other situations selling prices are based on differential costs rather than on full costs; these situations are discussed in Part Two.

Full cost information
and its uses

In the present chapter we give an introductory explanation of full costs; it will be considerably amplified in the next three chapters. We also describe some of the uses that management makes of full cost information. These uses are the following: (1) in financial accounting; (2) in answering the question: "What did it cost?"; (3) in arriving at prices in regulated industries; (4) in the analysis of profitability; and (5) in arriving at normal selling prices. Of these, we shall give special emphasis to normal pricing and shall describe a variety of pricing practices in which full cost information is used.

THE CONCEPT OF COST

"Cost" is one of the most slippery words used in accounting. It is used for a number of quite different notions. If someone says, without elaboration, "The cost of a widget is $1.80," it is practically impossible to understand exactly what is meant. The word "cost" becomes more meaningful when it is preceded by a modifier, making phrases such as "direct cost," "full cost," "opportunity cost," and so on; but even these phrases do not convey a clear meaning unless the context in which they are used is clearly understood. We shall be discussing the various contexts throughout this book.

General definition

In the broad sense,

Cost is a measurement, in monetary terms, of the amount of resources used for some purpose.

Three important ideas are included in the definition:

1. Most basic is the notion that cost measures the use of resources. The elements that constitute the cost of making something are physical quantities of material, hours of labor service, and quantities of other services. Cost measures how many of these resources were used.
2. Cost measurements are expressed in monetary terms. Money provides a common denominator that permits the amounts of individual resources, each measured according to its own scale, to be combined so that the total amount of all resources used can be determined.
3. Cost measurement always relates to a purpose. Much confusion can arise if the purpose is not clearly spelled out.

> *EXAMPLE:* Consider the building of a house. The resources used in building the house are lumber; hardware of various types; roofing material; hours of effort by carpenters, plumbers, electricians, and other tradespeople; hours of effort by supervisors; permit fees; trucks, power saws, and other items of equipment; and so on.
>
> For some purposes, the amount of resources used need not be expressed in monetary terms. In ordering the lumber, the construction supervisor can say: "Deliver 1,000 board feet of 2 by 4's." In assigning tradespeople, the construction supervisor can say: "X, you are to work all next week on the house."
>
> For other purposes, however, it is necessary to find the sum of all the resources used to build the house. In order to do this, the separate resources must be expressed in terms of some common denominator so that they can be added together. Since cost is expressed as a monetary amount, it provides such a common denominator. We cannot add together 1,000 board feet of lumber and 1,000 hours of labor; but if the price of the lumber is 50 cents a board foot and if the price of labor is $8 per hour, we can express the lumber as $500, the labor as $8,000, and add these to the monetary measures of other resources to obtain a useful measurement of the total amount of resources used for the house. Each of these amounts is an element of cost, and the total is the cost of building the house.
>
> Note that the purpose stated in this example was the "building of a house." If the purpose were something else, such as "building and *selling* a house", the cost would be different; it would include the selling cost as well as the construction cost.

Cost objective

Cost objective is the technical name for the purpose for which costs are measured.

A cost objective can be a product, such as a house; a part of a product, such as the construction of the foundation of a house; a whole company; a responsibility center within a company; an activity, such as the operation of a milling machine; or indeed anything for which one wants to measure the resources used. It is therefore a very broad term.

In each instance, the cost objective must be carefully stated and clearly understood. In a certain shoe factory, for example, the manufacture of one case (usually 12 pair) of Style 607 shoes may be one cost objective, the manufacture of one case of Style 608 shoes may be another cost objective, and the manufacture *and sale* of a case of Style 607 shoes may be still another cost objective.

A cost objective can be defined as broadly or as narrowly as one wishes. At one extreme, all the shoes manufactured in a shoe factory could be considered as a single cost objective, but if such a broad definition were used, differences in the resources used for the various styles of shoes would not be measured. At the other extreme, each pair of shoes manufactured could be considered as a single cost objective; but if such a narrow definition were used, the amount of recordkeeping involved in measuring costs would be tremendous. As it happens, many shoe factories use a "case" of shoes, which consists usually of 12 pair of a single style and color of shoes, as the unit of costing. The shoes in a single case may consist of several sizes, and each size requires slightly different amounts of leather, but these differences are not considered important enough to warrant the effort of measuring the cost of each size.

Full cost

The type of cost that we shall be discussing in these four chapters is called **full cost.** It means total cost, that is, **all the resources used for a cost objective.** In some circumstances, full cost is easily measured. If Ms. X pays $20 for a pair of shoes at a shoe store, the full cost of the pair of shoes to Ms. X is $20; that is, she used $20 of her resources – in this case, money – to acquire the pair of shoes.

But suppose we ask: What was the full cost of *manufacturing* the pair of shoes? This is a much more difficult question. A shoe factory may make thousands of pairs of shoes a month. Some are plain while others have intricate patterns, some are made of leather while others are made of synthetic material, and some are large while some are small. Clearly, different amounts of resources are used for these different styles of shoes; that is, they have different costs. One task of cost accounting systems is to assign amounts in such a way that significant differences in the amount of resources used are measured.

Direct and indirect costs.   In measuring the full cost of a cost objective, the various items of cost are divided into two categories, one called direct costs and the other, indirect costs.

A direct cost is an item of cost that is specifically traceable to or directly caused by a cost objective. The cost of the leather used in manufacturing a case of shoes is a direct cost, and so are the wages earned by the employees who worked directly in making that case of shoes.

An indirect cost is an item of cost that is associated with or caused by two or more cost objectives jointly but is not directly traceable to each objective individually. Indirect costs are also called **joint costs** or **common costs.** THe nature of an indirect cost element is such that it is not possible or feasible to measure directly how much of the cost is attributable to a single cost objective. Some part of the factory superintendent's salary and some part of the cost of heat and light used in the factory are elements of the cost of making each case of shoes, but there is no direct, observable way of measuring how much of these cost elements belongs to each case of shoes.

Governing principle.   **A governing principle of cost accounting is that the full cost of a cost objective is the sum of (1) its direct costs, plus (2) a fair share of its indirect costs.** This principle requires an explanation, for although it is intuitively obvious that the cost elements *directly traceable* to a cost objective are a part of the cost of that cost objective, it is by no means obvious that some fraction of the elements of indirect cost are part of the cost. One can actually see the leather in a pair of shoes, and it is obvious that certain labor services were involved in fashioning this leather into shoes, so there is no doubt of the appropriateness of counting such material and labor as part of the cost of the shoes. But what is the connection between the salary of the factory superintendent to the cost of a particular case of shoes made in the factory? The superintendent did not work on the shoes; for most of the time the superintendent probably was not even in the room where the shoes were being manufactured.

The basic rationale is that the indirect costs in the factory are incurred for the several cost objectives in the factory; to argue otherwise would be to assert that indirect costs are sheer waste. Therefore, some fraction of the indirect costs must be part of the full cost of each cost objective. The fact that indirect costs cannot be traced directly to *individual* cost objectives does not alter this conclusion.

> *EXAMPLE:* A certain factory manufactures wooden desks. Each desk is considered to be a separate cost objective. The records show that for desk No. 4,221, wood and hardware with a cost of $20.17 were used and that the earnings of persons who worked directly on that desk were $27.15. Desk No. 4,221 was one of 100 desks manufactured in the month of September. The total indirect costs of the factory in September

were \$3,218. The company assigned indirect costs equally to each desk; thus, the indirect cost of desk No. 4,221 was \$32.18 (\$3,218 ÷ 100). The full cost of manufacturing desk No. 4,221 was:

Direct material	\$20.17
Direct labor.........................	27.15
Indirect costs	32.18
Full cost	\$79.50

Techniques for measuring the full cost of a cost objective will be described in the next three chapters. In the remainder of this chapter the principal uses that are made of full cost information will be presented.

FINANCIAL ACCOUNTING

Financial statement items

In the companion volume, *Fundamentals of Financial Accounting,* brief references were made to financial statement items for which the measurement of full costs is needed. The principal items involved are inventory, as reported on the balance sheet, and cost of goods sold, as reported on the income statement. In a merchandising company, the inventory of goods on hand as of the balance sheet date is reported at the purchase cost of these goods, basically as shown on the vendor's invoice. When the goods are sold, this same cost is reported as an expense, cost of goods sold.[1]

In a manufacturing company, by contrast, the cost of a product includes not only the purchase cost of the material used in making the item but also all the other direct and indirect costs involved in manufacturing the item. In other words, in a manufacturing company, the costs used for inventory and cost of goods sold are the full manufacturing costs of the goods involved.

At the end of an accounting period, some goods may have been completed but are still on hand awaiting shipment to customers. These goods are called **finished goods inventory,** and they are measured at their full manufacturing cost.

> *EXAMPLE:* If Desk No. 4,221 (see preceding example) was completed and still on hand at the end of September, it would be included in finished goods inventory on the September 30 balance sheet at its cost of \$79.50.

Other goods may be partially completed and still in the factory at the end of the accounting period. These goods are called **goods in process**

---

[1] It will be recalled (Chapter 8 of *Fundamentals of Financial Accounting*) that these costs may be identified with specific items or they may be measured according to a Fifo, Lifo, or some other flow assumption. Here, we are concerned with measuring the *amount* of cost for a given item, and not with the flow assumption used in reporting the item in cost of goods sold or inventory on the financial statements.

inventory, and they are measured at the costs that have been incurred (that is, the resources used) up to that time.

> *EXAMPLE:* If another desk, No. 4,240, was partially finished at the end of September and costs of $62.15 had been incurred on it up to that time, it would be reported in goods in process inventory as of September 30 at $62.15.

When goods are sold, their costs are included in cost of goods sold at the full manufacturing cost.

> *EXAMPLE:* If Desk No. 4,221 were sold in October, its cost of $79.50 would be included as part of cost of goods sold on the October income statement.

The measurement of full cost is also needed for other financial accounting purposes. For example, if a company builds a building or makes a machine for its own use, the cost at which these fixed assets are reported on the balance sheet is the full cost of building or making them.

Segment reporting

Some companies, called **diversified companies** or conglomerates, do business in several different industries. These companies report separately the revenue, expense, and income for each of the principal industries in which they participate. Each such subdivision of the company is called a **segment** by the Financial Accounting Standards Board; and each is called a **line of business** by the Securities and Exchange Commission and by the Federal Trade Commission, which require similar reports.

The Financial Accounting Standards Board has not specified in detail what criteria are to be used in identifying segments. In general, a segment can be thought of as a separate industry, such as steel manufacturing as contrasted with electronics or with food. It is intended that the term be defined broadly enough so that no company is required to divide its total activities into more than about a dozen segments.

Revenues for a segment are usually easy to measure; they are the goods and services sold by that segment during the accounting period. In reporting the expenses of a segment, the principles of full cost measurement apply. The cost objective is the segment. Its full cost consists of the direct costs of the segment plus a fair share of the indirect costs, which are the general company costs that apply to two or more segments.

WHAT DID IT COST?

The problem of measuring the cost of something arises in a great many contexts: What was the cost of the campaign conducted by Candidate A? What did the last presidential election cost? What was the cost of police protection in City X? What was the cost to the U.S. Postal Service of sending a letter from Chicago to San Francisco? What was the cost of operating a school cafeteria? How does the cost of operating the supersonic Concorde aircraft between Washington and London compare with the cost of operating a Boeing 747? In arriving at answers to questions such as these, the appropriate cost construction usually is full cost.

The question also arises when two or more companies engage in a **joint venture.**[2] Several petroleum companies may agree to undertake a joint exploration program, or they may agree to develop a newly discovered oil field jointly, with each company paying for a specified fraction of the full cost. Company A may agree to do research that is also of interest to Company B, with Company B paying a stipulated percentage of the full cost.

In measuring the cost in such situations, there is a likelihood of misunderstanding and friction unless there is a clear and complete statement of exactly how "cost" is to be defined. There can be disagreement as to what the cost objective is; there can be disagreement as to what items of cost are to be assigned directly to the cost objective; and there can be disagreement as to how a "fair share" of indirect costs are to be determined. The first two of these possible sources of disagreement are discussed below; the third is deferred to later chapters.

Definition of cost objective

A televised public service message, whose purpose was to encourage gifts to higher education, contained the following statement: "Tuition covers only 25 percent of the cost of education in private colleges and universities." This percentage was arrived at by dividing tuition revenue by the *total* cost of operating these institutions. Such a calculation is incorrect because private colleges and universities engage in research, in community service programs, in providing board and room, and in many other noneducational activities. If the cost objective is taken as being the education of students, then all these noneducational costs should be excluded. The correct percentage of tuition to total *education* cost of all private colleges and universities is probably closer to 75 percent than to 25 percent.

Even if the cost objective is properly defined as education, there is room for disagreement as to exactly what constitutes educational activities. How does one distinguish between that part of the library which

---

[2] In a joint venture two or more companies organize a partnership or corporation, which they jointly own, for the purpose of carrying out a project of mutual interest.

exists for faculty research and that part which exists for student education? Are athletic facilities a part of education? Questions like these need to be thought about carefully in order to arrive at an unambiguous answer. In many cases, the description of the objective for which costs are collected is taken as being more obvious than it really is.

> *EXAMPLE:* A salesperson's boss says: "Please take Jones (a customer) out to dinner tonight; the company will pay what it costs." By "it," the boss may have in mind the bill for the two dinners; but the salesperson may have in mind that "it" means the cost of the dinners plus the cost of drinks before dinner, the cost of the automobile trip to pick up Jones, the cost of parking the car, and perhaps even the cost of having clothes cleaned so that the salesperson will look especially presentable.

After a few instances of misunderstanding which arose because of vagueness in the definition of "entertainment" in situations like that in the above example, a company undoubtedly would work out rules that clarified what the cost objective is to include. It must work out similar rules in a great many other situations. Does the product that is being costed include shipping costs to the customer? Is the company expected to furnish assistance in installation? If the product is unsatisfactory, will the company incur additional costs in remedying it? The list can be extended indefinitely.

Definition of cost

As we shall see there is much room for differences of opinion as to how full cost is to be measured. In particular, one cannot rely on the statement: "Measure costs according to generally accepted accounting principles," for accounting principles are not specific enough to resolve many of the detailed questions that arise. In some situations, one does not even know whether a cost is intended to represent full cost or some other type of cost.

> *EXAMPLE:* A and B are going on a trip, using A's automobile. They agree that they will "share the transportation costs." Unless they have a mutual understanding of exactly what is meant by *cost,* there can be bad feelings when it comes time to settle up. B may have in mind that *cost* means the gasoline only; whereas A may be thinking that *cost* includes repairs, a share of the cost of the tires, or even a share of the depreciation, insurance, and other costs involved in owning and operating the automobile.

In order to reduce confusion as to what is to be included in cost, it is often necessary to specify in some detail how direct costs are to be defined, what elements of indirect costs are to be included, how these elements are to be measured, and how the "fair share" of these costs assigned to the cost objective is to be determined.

Cost-type contracts

Agreement on the details of how cost is to be measured is especially important in situations in which one party has agreed to buy goods or services from another party at a price that is based on cost. There are tens of billions of dollars of such contracts annually. Under the Medicare and Medicaid programs, the federal government reimburses hospitals and other providers of health care for the cost of providing service to eligible patients. Blue Cross, Blue Shield, and insurance companies do the same thing for their subscribers and policyholders. The federal government pays for 90 percent of the cost of certain highway construction, and either 100 percent or some lesser percentage of the cost of urban renewal programs, welfare programs, programs for assistance to small business, disaster relief programs, and a variety of others. The prices of many construction projects, ranging in size from a private home to a skyscraper, are stated as cost plus an allowance for profit. When the cost of a product cannot be estimated accurately in advance, as is the case with new weapons systems and other newly developed products, the price is necessarily based on cost plus an allowance for profit.

In all these situations, the word *cost* means full cost. Again, because of differences in methods of measuring cost, it is necessary that the method to be used in the particular contract be spelled out in some detail so as to avoid misunderstanding.

SETTING REGULATED PRICES

Although Americans live in what is generally regarded as being a market economy, many of the prices that they pay are not set by the forces of the marketplace; rather, these prices are regulated. Regulated prices include prices for electricity, gas, and water; passenger and/or freight transportation by train, airplane, truck, bus, barge, and pipeline; telephone and telegraph; insurance premiums; and a long list of others. In each of these cases, prices are set by a regulatory agency (Federal Communications Commission, Interstate Commerce Commission, state public utility and insurance commissions, etc.). The regulatory agency allows a price that is equal to full cost plus an allowance for profit. In most cases, the regulatory agency provides a manual, which may contain several hundred pages, spelling out in great detail how costs are to be measured. These manuals are based generally on full cost principles, but the details differ greatly depending partly on the nature of the goods or services whose prices are regulated and partly on the personal preferences of the regulatory body.

In World War II, in the Korean War, and in the early 1970s, substantially all prices in the United States were made subject to regulation by a government agency. The general principle of these regulations was that prices could be increased only to the extent that full costs had increased.

ANALYSIS OF PROFITABILITY

In *Fundamentals of Financial Accounting* we discuss ratios and other techniques that are useful in analyzing the profitability of an entire business. Cost accounting makes it possible to make similar analyses of individual parts of a business. Such a part might be an individual product, a segment, a product line (which is a family of related products), a plant, a division, a sales territory, or any other subdivision of the whole business that is of interest. Using the principles of cost accounting, the direct costs and an appropriate share of the indirect costs of the part being reviewed can be determined. If the part of the business that is being analyzed does not earn a reasonable profit, that is, if the revenue generated by this part does not exceed its costs by an adequate amount, there is an indication that something is wrong.

In the short run, a product, a division, or other part of a business generally can be tolerated if its revenues at least exceed its out-of-pocket costs, but any part of the business which does not earn a satisfactory profit is not healthy, and consideration should be given to shifting the investment to a more attractive use. Techniques for pinpointing the cause of the unsatisfactory situation are discussed in Chapter 14.

NORMAL PRICING

Rationale for pricing

A principal goal of a profit-oriented business is to earn a satisfactory return on its investment, that is, on the assets that it uses. If the return on assets employed is too low, investors will refuse to put additional capital into the business. If the return on assets employed is too high, investors will observe the lucrative profit opportunities and pour funds into competing businesses; the additional capacity that results from this will lead to a reduction in selling prices and hence in the return on assets employed. Furthermore, a business with an extraordinarily high return on assets employed will be exposed to charges that it is gouging the public, which can lead to pressure — legal, political, and public — for price reduction. Thus, powerful forces work to keep return on assets employed within a range which can be designated as "satisfactory."

In order to earn a satisfactory return, revenues from the sale of goods and services must be large enough both to (1) recover full cost and (2) earn a profit that provides a satisfactory return on assets employed. One can therefore think of the selling price as consisting of two components: (1) an amount to recover full cost and (2) profit.

If a business makes a single product, the measurement of these two components is simple. Thus, if a contractor agrees to build a house for a customer at "cost plus 10 percent," a recordkeeping system can easily be set up that will measure the full cost of building the house, and the selling price of the house is found simply by adding 10 percent to that cost.

If, however, a business handles a number of products, either manufacturing them or selling them, or both, the problem is much more complicated. It essentially is this: The business will prosper if *for all the products combined,* total sales revenues exceed total costs by an amount sufficient to provide a satisfactory return. But selling prices must be set separately *for each product.* How can this be done for *each* product so that a satisfactory profit is earned for *all* products?

The general answer to this question is that each product should bear a *fair share* of the total costs of the business. We can expand this statement to say that **in general the selling price of a product should be high enough (1) to recover its direct costs, (2) to recover a fair share of all applicable indirect costs, and (3) to yield a satisfactory profit.** Such a price is a *normal price* (or, for reasons to be explained, a **target price**).

It must be understood that the foregoing is a statement of general tendency rather than a rule for setting the selling price of each product. For a number of reasons to be discussed later, the selling price of a given product is not set simply by ascertaining each of the components listed above and then adding them up. Nevertheless, measurement of the direct and indirect costs of a product provides a starting point in an analysis of what the actual selling price should be.

Adjustment of historical cost

If the purpose is to set selling prices for products that will be manufactured at some future time, the relevant costs are the costs that *will be* incurred at that time, not the costs that *were* incurred at some earlier time. Thus, in estimating costs for the purpose of arriving at selling prices, historical costs should be adjusted if it is believed that the costs that will be incurred to fill the future orders will be significantly different from the costs that have been incurred in the past. There are four principal reasons why future costs may not be the same as historical costs: (1) inflation, (2) volume, (3) productivity, and (4) product specifications. Each is discussed below.

Inflation. Since the United States, along with most countries of the world, seems to be in a more-or-less permanent condition of inflation, an adjustment for this factor often needs to be made. In many situations, this can be done by increasing total historical full cost by an appropriate percentage. If different elements of cost are expected to increase at different rates of inflation, however, more detailed calculations may be necessary.

EXAMPLE: For a certain product, direct material costs are expected to increase 7 percent, direct labor costs 5 percent, and other costs 6 percent. The revised estimate of unit costs is calculated as follows:

	Current Unit Cost	×	Adjustment for Inflation	=	Adjusted Unit Cost
Direct material............................	$10.00		107%		$10.70
Direct labor................................	15.00		105		15.75
Other costs	20.00		106		21.20
Total Cost.........................	$45.00				$47.65

Volume. Certain items of cost tend to vary, in total amount, with the number of units produced. If the leather in one pair of shoes costs $2, the leather in two pairs of the same style of shoes is likely to cost $4. Costs of this type are called **variable costs.** Other items of cost do not change in total amount with changes in the number of units produced in a given period, that is, with changes in volume. If the depreciation, supervisory salaries, heat, and light in a factory total $12,000 in a month in which 6,000 pairs of shoes are made, they are also likely to total $12,000 in a month in which only 5,000 pairs are made, and also $12,000 in another month in which 7,000 pairs are made. Costs of this type are called **fixed costs.**

We shall examine the behavior of variable and fixed costs in much more detail later on. For our present purpose, we need to point out that although fixed costs *in total* are unaffected by the level of volume, fixed costs *per unit* are different depending on the level of volume. Thus, in estimating future unit costs, the anticipated volume level needs to be taken into account.

EXAMPLE: In the current year, for a certain product, fixed costs are $120,000 in total, and 10,000 units are manufactured. The unit fixed cost is therefore $12. It is estimated that in the next year the dollar amount of fixed costs will be unchanged, but that 12,000 units will be manufactured. The fixed cost per unit is therefore estimated to be $10 (= $120,000 ÷ 12,000 units), a decrease of $2.

Productivity. More efficient methods of production are continually being developed, and these reduce costs. Output per man-hour increases, on the average, roughly 3 percent a year for all American industry, but there are wide variations among individual products and companies. In order to estimate the effect of productivity changes, the *quantity* of resources used for the product must be recalculated and then converted to monetary terms at the estimated prices.

EXAMPLE: If it is estimated that productivity gains will reduce labor required per unit of product from 3.0 hours to 2.7 hours, then there is a productivity gain of 10 percent. In estimating labor cost, the 2.7 hours must be costed at the estimated future labor rate, which usually is higher than the current labor rate because of inflation.

Product specification changes. The specifications of the product may be changed, and this causes corresponding change in its cost. The esti-

EXHIBIT 2-1
Alternative pricing methods

	Estimated unit costs	Pricing method	Cost base used	Calculation*
Direct manufacturing cost..............................	$4	Direct cost	Direct cost	$4 + (150% × $4) = $10
Indirect manufacturing cost.............................	2			
Total Manufacturing Cost....................	6	Gross margin	Manufacturing cost	$6 + (66.7% × $6) = $10
Selling and administrative cost.........	3			
Full cost	$9	Profit margin	Full cost	$9 + (11.1% × $9) = $10
Assets employed..............	$8	Return on assets	Full cost	$9 + (12.5% × $8) = $10
Desired return 12.5%				

* Calculations are explained in the text.
Note: Percentages shown are rounded.

mated cost must be calculated on the basis of the revised specifications. The specification for a 1977 Ford Granada automobile differ from those of a 1976 model in dozens of ways; each of these must be taken into account in estimating the 1977 cost.

Alternative approaches to pricing

In arriving at a normal selling price, one starts with cost, or some component of cost, and adds a margin to it. Exhibit 2–1 shows four of the common method of doing this, each of which will be explained in the following sections. In this example, the numbers have been constructed so that each of the methods produces the same selling price, $10, for the product. As we shall see, in certain situations, these methods can produce wide variations in selling prices for products with different cost characteristics; and it is this fact that makes the choice of a pricing method an important management decision.

Return-on-asset pricing

Since a principal goal of a business is to earn a satisfactory return on the assets that it employs, **the soundest way of arriving at the normal price is to compute a profit that is related to the assets employed on the product, and add this to the estimated full cost of the product.** In Exhibit 2–1, it is assumed that a satisfactory return is 12.5 percent of assets employed. If the assets employed are $8 per unit of product, then the profit must be 12.5 percent of $8, or $1, in order to yield a satisfactory return. Since the full cost of the product is $9 per unit, the selling price must be $1 more than this, or $10, to yield the desired return.

EXHIBIT 2–2

Effect of return-on-asset pricing

Income Statement
(assuming 100,000 units sold)

Revenue		$1,000,000
Direct manufacturing cost	$400,000	
Indirect manufacturing cost	200,000	
Cost of goods sold		600,000
Gross margin		400,000
Selling and administrative expense		300,000
Operating Income		$ 100,000

Assets employed, $800,000.
Return = $100,000 ÷ $800,000 = 12.5 percent.

Exhibit 2–2 demonstrates that this price does in fact yield the desired return. It shows what happens if the company sells its product for $10 per unit, assuming 100,000 units are sold in a year and that the assets employed during the year total $800,000. The income statement is derived simply by multiplying each of the numbers in Exhibit 2–1 by 100,000. Revenues are $1,000,000, expenses are $900,000, so the profit is $100,000. (Income taxes are omitted in the interest of simplicity.) Since assets employed are given as $800,000, the $100,000 profit is a return of 12.5 percent, which is the desired amount.

The return-on-asset method of pricing is the soundest method because it is based on a profit that is directly related to the company's goal of earning a return on assets employed. Nevertheless, it is not as widely used as some of the other methods. The basic reason is that this method requires that the amount of assets employed for each product be calculated, and in many companies it is not possible to do this. Furthermore, in certain situations, approximately the same results can be obtained by using one of the simpler methods.

Profit margin pricing

In profit margin pricing the full cost of making and selling the product is estimated and a profit margin is added. This profit margin is expressed as a percentage of the full cost.

The profit margin is calculated so as to produce, on the average, the desired return on assets employed for *all* products. No attempt is made to compute the assets employed on an individual product. For example, assume that company sells several different products and that its income statement is otherwise as shown in Exhibit 2–2. The company knows that in order to produce the desired return of 12.5 percent on the $800,000 of assets employed, it must earn a profit on *all* products of $100,000. Its costs are $900,000, so it computes the percentage of cost that will produce $100,000 profit. This is:

$$\$100,000 \div \$900,000 = 11.1 \text{ Percent}$$

It therefore calculates its normal price for each product by adding a profit margin of 11.1 percent (or perhaps, rounded, 11 percent) to its full cost.

Note that although assets employed were taken into account in arriving at the desired overall return, the calculation of the price for each product does not involve assets used for that product; rather, the profit margin is expressed as a percentage of cost.

Although setting the profit as a percentage of costs works satisfactorily if the assets employed for each product are proportionate to the full cost of each product, it breaks down if this condition does not exist. Products with a relatively low asset turnover require a relatively high profit as a percentage of costs in order to earn a satisfactory return on assets employed. (**Asset turnover** means revenues divided by assets employed. For example, if total sales revenue is $2,000,000 and total assets employed is $1,000,000, then asset turnover is two times. Each dollar of assets employed is said to "generate" two dollars of sales revenue.)

> *EXAMPLE:* A company manufactures two products, A and B, and the full cost of each product is $6 per unit. The company has $4,000,000 of assets, and it regards 15 percent as a satisfactory return. It therefore needs to price so as to earn $600,000 (= $4,000,000 × 0.15). If it expects to sell 200,000 units, its costs will be $1,200,000 (= $6 × 200,000 units). In order to earn a profit of $600,000, it will set a selling price of 50 percent above its cost (= $600,000 ÷ $1,200,000) if it uses the profit margin method. Its selling price will therefore be $9 per unit [= $6 + (0.5 × $6)] on each unit. As shown in Exhibit 2–3, Part A, at a $9 selling price and assuming 100,000 units of each product are sold, Product A will earn only 10 percent on the assets employed for it, while Product B will earn 30 percent.
>
> If, however, the company uses return-on-asset pricing, the profit margin would be $4.50 for Product A (= $30 × 15 percent) and $1.50 for Product B (=$10 × 15 percent). Thus, the selling prices would be $10.50 (= $6 + $4.50)

EXHIBIT 2–3
Difficulty with profit-margin pricing

	Product A Per unit	Product A Total	Product B Per unit	Product B Total	Total company
A. Profit margin pricing					
Assumed volume (units)..........		100,000		100,000	200,000
Revenue...............................	$ 9.00	$ 900,000	$ 9.00	$ 900,000	$1,800,000
Full cost..............................	6.00	600,000	6.00	600,000	1,200,000
Profit..................................	$ 3.00	$ 300,000	$ 3.00	$ 300,000	$ 600,000
Assets employed	$30.00	$3,000,000	$10.00	$1,000,000	$4,000,000
Return on assets employed		10%		30%	15%
B. Return on asset pricing					
Assumed volume (units)..........		100,000		100,000	
Revenue...............................	$10.50	$1,050,000	$ 7.50	$ 750,000	$1,800,000
Full cost..............................	6.00	600,000	6.00	600,000	1,200,000
Profit..................................	$ 4.50	$ 450,000	$ 1.50	$ 150,000	$ 600,000
Assets employed	$30.00	$3,000,000	$10.00	$1,000,000	$4,000,000
Return on assets employed		15%		15%	15%

for Product A and $7.50 (= $6 + $1.50) for Product B. At these selling prices, the total profit will also be $600,000, as shown in Part B of Exhibit 2–3. The $10.50 and $7.50 prices are more equitable than the $9 price, however, since they reflect the fact that more assets are required to make a unit of Product A than a unit of Product B.

Gross margin pricing

Some companies calculate selling prices by adding a percentage to the total cost of manufacturing their products. Since the difference between revenue and manufacturing cost is the gross margin, this method is called **gross margin pricing.** Again, using the data in Exhibit 2–2 as an example, the company knows that if it is to earn the desired return, the gross margin must be large enough to cover the selling and administrative expense of $300,000 plus the profit of $100,000, a total of $400,000. Since $400,000 is 66.7 percent of the total manufacturing cost of $600,000, the percentage used in arriving at the normal selling price would be 66.7 percent (or, rounded, 67 percent). This percentage is called the **mark-on percentage.**

For retailers, wholesalers, and other companies that sell but do not manufacture products, the gross margin is the difference between the selling price and the invoice cost of the goods sold. Many such companies use gross margin pricing.

The mark-on percentage should be high enough to cover the expenses of operating the business (other than the cost of the goods) and to provide a satisfactory return on assets employed. Operating costs and the amount of assets employed vary greatly in different types of companies, and there is a corresponding variation in their mark-on percentages. The higher the asset turnover and the lower the operating cost per dollar of sales, the smaller the mark-on percentage needs to be in order to produce a satisfactory return on assets employed.

> *EXAMPLE:* A food retailer that (1) provides a delivery service and personalized service to customers, (2) carries a relatively large inventory in relation to sales, and (3) has charge accounts outstanding for a month or two, requires a relatively high mark-on percentage. By contrast, a supermarket that (1) has no delivery service and hence a low operating cost per sales dollar, (2) has a relatively small inventory in relation to sales, and (3) has no assets tied up in accounts receivable, requires a relatively low mark-on percentage.

Products with high risks also tend to have high mark-on percentages. For example, the margins on women's fashion apparel are relatively high because of the risk that if the merchandise cannot be sold during a given season, it will become obsolete.

Direct cost pricing

Some manufacturing businesses set selling prices at **a certain percentage above the direct costs incurred in manufacturing their products;** this is called **direct cost pricing.** Referring again to Exhibit 2–2, direct manufacturing costs are $400,000. In order to cover the indirect manufacturing costs of $200,000, selling and administrative expenses of $300,-000, and earn a profit of $100,000, the price must exceed the direct manufacturing cost by $600,000. The percentage of direct cost that will result in such a price is $600,000 ÷ $400,000 = 150 percent.

The direct cost pricing method is sensible when the amount of other costs that equitably should be borne by each product is substantially the same percentage of direct costs, and when the assets employed in each product are also substantially similar in amount. When these conditions do not exist, the practice of setting selling prices as a certain percentage above direct cost can have unsatisfactory results. One reason why this practice is followed is that the allocation of indirect costs to products involves judgment, and some managers believe that the results are not sufficiently valid to be useful in making decisions on selling prices. They prefer to base pricing decisions on direct costs because these costs can be measured with a high degree of accuracy.

It can be argued that direct cost pricing gives satisfactory results, even when the cost characteristics of the products are different, because the differences in margin will offset one another and the company overall will make a satisfactory profit—"what we lose on the bananas, we make up on the oranges." There are two weaknesses in this argument. First, the differences will balance out only if the sales quantities of each product are in the same proportion as was originally contemplated when the prices were set. If a higher proportion of the high-cost products and a lower proportion of the low-cost products are sold, the company overall will earn less total profit than it estimated. Second, the differences may produce peculiar results in the marketplace. Some products will be sold for a price that is lower than reasonably can be justified, and profits on these products will be inadequate; other products will have a price that is higher than is justified by their cost, so business will be lost to competitors who price so as to earn only a satisfactory return on such products.

Time and material pricing

In the preceding discussion, it was assumed that the selling price was arrived at by first calculating costs and then adding an allowance for profit. An alternative approach is called **time and material pricing. In this method one pricing rate is established for direct labor and a separate pricing rate for direct material. Each of these rates is constructed so that it includes allowances for indirect costs and for profit.** This method of pricing is used in automobile repair shops, in job printing shops, in television repair shops, and in similar types of service establishments. It is also used by many professional persons and professional organizations, including physicians, lawyers, engineers, consultants of various types, and public accounting firms.

In time and material pricing the **time** component is expressed as a labor rate per hour, which is calculated as the sum of (1) direct salary and fringe benefit costs of the employee; (2) an equitable share of all indirect costs, except those related to material; and (3) an allowance for profit. The material component is found by adding a **material loading** to the invoice cost of parts and other material used on the job. This loading consists of an allowance for material handling costs and storage costs plus an allowance for profit. The material loading might well be approximately 20 percent to 40 percent of the invoice cost of the materials.

> *EXAMPLE:* A television repair shop has servicepeople who earn an
> average of $5 per hour. The manager estimates that other costs associated
> with repair work amount to $6 per hour and that a reasonable profit margin
> is $1 per hour. Customers are therefore charged $12 per hour of repair
> service. It is estimated that the cost of ordering parts and holding them in
> inventory until they are needed is 30 percent of the cost of the parts, and

that a reasonable profit margin on these parts is 10 percent of the cost of parts. Customers are therefore charged a material charge which is the cost of the parts used plus 40 percent of the cost. A job requiring three hours of labor and parts costing $20 would be priced as follows:

Labor, 3 hours @ $12.............. $36
Parts, $20 + 40% ($20).............. 28
Total Price of the Job...... $64

The time component of the time and material charge may be calculated on a machine-hour basis rather than on a labor-hour basis. A machine-hour basis is generally used in printing shops, for example, because there is a substantial difference in the costs of using the various types of presses and other printing equipment. An hourly rate is calculated for each type of equipment, in a manner similar to that described above for labor, and each job that used the equipment is charged at this hourly rate.

Adjusting costs to prices

Pricing, quite naturally, is usually thought of as the process of arriving at selling prices. There are some situations in which the process works in reverse; that is, the selling price that must be charged in order to meet competition is taken as a starting point. The problem then is to determine the maximum amount of cost the company can afford to incur if it is to earn a satisfactory profit at the given price.

In the apparel business, for example, it is customary to use discrete **price points** – $19.98, $24.75, $34.75, and so on. The manufacturer designs individual garments to "fit" one of these price points. The selling price is taken as a given, and the manufacturer calculates how much it can afford to spend on cloth, on labor, and on other elements of cost and still have a satisfactory profit margin. If an acceptable garment cannot be manufactured so as to be sold at the given price, then either the proposed item is dropped from the line or the calculations are redone, using the next higher price point. Similarly, when a manufacturer is thinking about making a product which competitors have already introduced and which has become well established in the market, it starts with the market price of the competitive product as a given. It calculates whether its costs are such that it can make a satisfactory profit at that price. If the results of such a calculation are disappointing, the manufacturer either attempts to redesign the product so that its costs are lower or, usually, the project is dropped. Occasionally, the manufacturer may decide to market the product at a price that is higher than that charged by competitors, but this is a risky course of action because consumers must be persuaded that the quality of the product justifies the higher price.

The approach of taking the selling price as a given is used for many products with a mass market, such as television and radio sets, most types of household appliances, clothing, branded foods, household furnishings, office supplies, office equipment, and general-purpose factory equipment.

Choice of a pricing method

A company selects the pricing method that strikes the best balance between, on the one hand, the advantages of simplicity and feasibility and, on the other hand, the desire to earn a satisfactory return on each product. At one extreme, the direct cost method is the simplest because it does not require that any indirect costs be assigned to products; and as we shall see, such assignment can be a complicated job. The direct cost method does not allow for any of a number of factors that may make the cost of one product different from that of another, however. At the other extreme, the return-on-asset method takes full account of all the costs and also the assets associated with each product. Many companies do not find it feasible to measure the amount of assets associated with each product, however.

The gross margin method is widely used when all products have approximately the same proportion of selling and administrative costs and of assets employed. Alternatively, as a variation on this method, a department store, for example, may calculate a satisfactory overall profit margin for each department, taking account of the selling expenses and assets employed in that department, and use a gross margin percentage on all products within the department. The gross margin percentage is set so that it produces the desired overall return on assets. Similarly, many companies use a profit margin percentage on all the products in a given product line or in a given division that takes account of the assets employed for that product line or in that division.

Price regulations

The Robinson-Patman Amendment to the Clayton Antitrust Act prohibits differentials in the prices charged competing customers unless these differentials "make due allowance for differences in the cost of manufacture, sale, or delivery resulting from the differing methods or quantities" of sales to such customers. The courts have interpreted these "due allowances" as related to full costs (i.e., the sum of direct costs and a fair share of indirect costs) rather than to only direct costs alone. This is another reason why it is advisable to calculate both the direct and the indirect costs attributable to products and to base prices on such calculations. Similarly, some states prohibit the sale of certain products or services below cost, with "cost" either specified as, or interpreted as meaning, full cost.

Pricing tactics

The foregoing discussion has emphasized the importance of measuring product costs in arriving at selling prices. It would be unfortunate if the reader were left with the impression that all prices are arrived at by adding up the product costs and tacking on a profit margin. Actually, many companies have no pricing problem. A market price exists, customers will not pay more than this price, and there is no reason why the product should be sold at a lower price. Wheat and other products traded on commodity markets are the classic examples, but the situation also exists for companies in many other industries, such as small companies in industries, such as small companies in industries where a few large companies exercise **price leadership.** Under such circumstances, a company may make no pricing calculations; it simply charges the market price.

If a company does have the problem of determining its selling prices, **cost information at best provides a first approximation to the selling price.** The price arrived at by the methods described above is often described as a **target price.** It is important information, but by no means is it the only information used in the final pricing decision.

The selling price is one of the tactics used in marketing a product. Marketing tactics can be compared with those used in a football game. Each team wants to win, and each has a set of offensive and defensive plays designed to achieve this objective; these are its tactics. Each uses these plays at various times according to its perception of the strengths and weaknesses of the opposing team. The situation in the competitive marketplace is roughly similar, but is is much more complicated because there are more than two teams, there are more variables in the environment, and the "plays" occur in much larger time and space dimensions than the 60 minutes and 100 yards of a football game. In the struggle to attain its profit objective, each company competes with a number of other companies. It attempts both to take business away from competitors and to expand the total amount of business in the industry. It has a number of tactics for use in this struggle—advertising, other promotional activities, salespersons, the product itself, its packaging, and the selling price.[3]

The selling price, therefore, is one tactical device in the competitive game. It can be varied in either direction—lowered in an effort to take business away from competitors, or raised in the hope that additional profits will be generated without undue loss of sales volume. Marketing managers use all the tactical devices, not just one. The selling price is, of course, an important one; and the manager needs information about the cost components of each product as a basis for making the pricing decision.

---

[3] For a more complete discussion, see Joe S. Bain, *Price Theory* (New York: Holt, Rhinehart and Winston, Inc., 1963).

Adjustments to the target price.   What does the marketing expert do with the first approximation of selling price that is given by the cost calculations? For one thing, the target price is regarded as *applying on the average;* prices of individual products often deviate from the average. A product line consists of a group of related products. For various reasons, it may be possible to obtain a relatively high profit margin on certain individual products in the line, whereas other products can be sold only at prices that yield a low profit margin. Still other products can be sold at a price that yields an average profit margin. Marketing experts know that if the profit margins on the some products are high enough to offset the low margins on other products, a satisfactory return on assets can be made on the product line as a whole. They therefore may compute the average profit margin required for the line as a whole, and vary the prices on individual products above or below this average, according to how they judge the market situation. The total profit on the whole product line will be satisfactory if the line consists of enough high-margin products and not too many low-margin products.

Moreover, marketing experts do not think solely about the selling price. It is the *difference* between selling price and cost that is important. In many circumstances, instead of raising selling prices, this difference can best be widened by redesigning the product so as to reduce its cost.

In making decisions about whether or not to discontinue an existing product, similar considerations normally govern. A new product is normally added to the line only if it is expected to produce a satisfactory return on the assets employed in making it. If an existing product has a low profit margin, and if the situation cannot be corrected by increasing prices or by reducing costs, then the product normally is replaced with a more profitable one. Again, marketing considerations may dictate departures from the normal procedure. Many low-margin products are retained so that the company may offer its customers a full line; for example, razors may be sold at a low margin in order to induce the sale of high-margin razor blades,[4] or a replacement product with an adequate margin may not be available, and so on.

Contribution pricing

A company does not always make pricing decisions with information on full costs as a first approximation. In some situations individual products may be sold at a loss, that is, at a price that is below full cost. These are special situations, and they require special cost constructions. This approach to pricing is called *contribution pricing,* and it is described in Chapter 7.

---

[4] A company cannot *compel* its customers to buy its own accessories and supplies. Such "tie-in" agreements are illegal.

ILLUSTRATIVE CASE

This case is designed to show the effect of various pricing methods when applied to products that have differing cost characteristics. Try to make the calculations and arrive at the correct conclusions before you look at the solution that follows.

EXHIBIT 2–4

MEADER COMPANY
Unit Costs for Certain Products

	Average for all Products	Product			
		A	B	C	D
Direct manufacturing cost	$ 5	$10	$ 5	$ 5	$ 5
Indirect manufacturing cost	5	10	10	5	5
Total Manufacturing Cost	10	20	15	10	10
Selling and administrative cost	5	10	5	2	5
Full cost	$15	$30	$20	$12	$15
Assets employed	$20	$40	$30	$20	$10

Exhibit 2–4 shows unit costs for certain products made and sold by Meader Company. The first column shows the average unit costs for all products, and the other columns show the unit costs for four of the dozens of individual products that are included in the average. The company considers a 10 percent return on assets employed as satisfactory.

Required:
1. Using the average unit costs for all products, calculate the percentages that the company would apply to costs or assets employed under each of the following pricing methods: (*a*) return on-asset pricing, (*b*) profit margin pricing, (*c*) gross margin pricing, and (*d*) direct cost pricing.
2. The unit costs for Product A are in proportion to the average for all products, but each element of cost is double the average. Compute the selling price using each of the four percentages you computed in No. 1. Would each method result in a price that gives a satisfactory profit for Product A?
3. Product B is a product that requires expensive manufacturing equipment. Consequently, its indirect manufacturing costs and the assets employed for it are higher than average. What selling price would you recommend for Product B? If the company used direct cost pricing, and based the price on the margin developed for the average of all products, what price would it arrive at for Product B? Why would this price not be satisfactory?

4. For Product C, selling costs are relatively low. What selling price would you recommend for Product C? If the company used gross margin pricing, what would be its selling price for Product C? Why would this price not be satisfactory?

5. For Product D, asset turnover is relatively high; it has only half the amount of assets employed per unit as the average product has. What selling price would you recommend for Product D? If the company used profit margin pricing, what price would it arrive at for Product D? Why would this price not be satisfactory?

Solution

1. A satisfactory price for the average product is one that provides a 10 percent return on assets employed, which is 10 percent of $20, or $2. The percentages that will arrive at selling prices that produce this profit are:

    a. Return-on-asset pricing, 10 percent of assets employed. Check: $15 full cost plus $2 ($20 × 10 percent) return on assets = $17.

    b. Profit margin pricing, 13.3 percent. To yield a $2 profit margin, the margin applied to full costs must be $2 ÷ $15, or 13.3 percent. Check: $15 + $15 (13.3 percent) = $17.

    c. Gross margin pricing, 70 percent. To cover the $5 of selling and administrative costs and the $2 profit, the margin applied to total manufacturing cost must be $7 ÷ $10 = 70 percent. Check: $10 + $10 (70 percent) = $17.

    d. Direct cost pricing, 240 percent. To cover the $5 of indirect manufacturing cost, the $5 of selling and administrative cost, and the $2 profit (a total of $12), the margin applied to direct manufacturing cost must be $12 ÷ $5 = 240 percent. Check: $5 + $5 (240 percent) = $17.

2. The selling prices for Item A would be:

Pricing method	Cost	Percentage (from above)	Price
Return on asset	$30	10% of $40	$34
Profit margin	30	13.3%	34
Gross margin	20	70%	34
Direct cost	10	240%	34

Since we know that the price should be $34 in order to earn the 10 percent return on assets employed, and since all the methods result in a price of $34, we can conclude that the methods can be used even if the absolute unit costs for a product are different from the average, so long as they have the same proportions as the average.

3. The selling price for Item B should be its full cost of $20 plus 10 percent of the $30 of assets employed equals $23. If the company

used direct cost pricing, it would apply the margin of 240 percent to the direct manufacturing cost of $5, arriving at a price of $17. At this price the company would not cover its full cost of $20, so it would lose money on the product. This shows that direct cost pricing is not appropriate when products have indirect costs that are relatively different from those of the average product.

4. The selling price for Product C should be its full cost of $12 plus 10 percent of the $20 assets employed equals $14. If the company used gross margin pricing, it would apply the margin of 70 percent to the total manufacturing cost of $10, arriving at a price of $17. This price is $3 higher than is needed to earn a satisfactory profit on the product. This shows that gross margin pricing is not appropriate when a product has selling and administrative costs that are relatively different from the average.

5. The selling price for Product D should be the full cost of $15 plus 10 percent of $10 assets employed equals $16. If the company used profit margin pricing, it would apply the margin of 13.3 percent to the full cost of $15, arriving at a price of $17. This price is $1 higher than needed to produce a satisfactory profit. This shows that gross margin pricing is not appropriate when a product has an asset turnover that is different from the average for all products.

SUMMARY

Cost is a measurement, in monetary terms, of the amount of resources used for some purpose, which is called a cost objective. The full cost of a cost objective is the sum of its direct costs plus a fair share of its indirect costs. Information about the full cost of products and services is used —

1. In financial accounting, to derive certain balance sheet and income statement amounts and to derive income by segments.
2. To answer the question, "What did X cost?" This question is asked in many contexts. Of particular interest is the fact that many contracts require that the buyer pay the seller either full cost or full cost plus a stipulated profit.
3. As a basis for setting regulated prices.
4. To measure the profitability of products, divisions, plants, or other parts of a business, so as to facilitate an analysis of the operation of these parts.
5. As a first approximation in deciding on selling prices under normal circumstances.

Of these uses, our attention was focused primarily on pricing decisions. The usual practice is to calculate a target price by adding a margin to cost. The margin preferably is calculated as a return on assets employed if this is feasible, but it is often calculated as a percentage of full costs, or of manufacturing costs, or even of direct costs. This target price is modified to take into account the strength of competition, the necessity of fitting the price into customary price lines (such as $19.98 dresses), and many other marketing considerations. Consequently actual prices, and hence actual profit margins on specific products, may differ widely from the cost-based first approximation. The intent is, however, that the desired profit will be obtained, on the average, with extra profits on high-margin products offsetting thin profits on low-margin products.

Adjustments to this first approximation may take the form of changing costs as well as changing profit margins. If it is thought that the target price is too high, then the product may be redesigned to reduce its cost so that a satisfactory profit can be earned at the attainable price.

IMPORTANT TERMS

Cost	**Profit margin pricing**
Cost objective	**Asset turnover**
Full cost	**Mark-on percentage**
Direct cost	**Direct cost pricing**
Indirect cost	**Time and material pricing**
Segment (line of business)	**Material loading**
Normal price	**Target price**
Return-on-asset pricing	

QUESTIONS FOR DISCUSSION

1. Explain why cost cannot be measured except in relation to something.

2. "The cost of a widget is $1.80." Why is this statement not meaningful, even to someone who knows what a widget is?

3. If you were asked to calculate the full cost of undergraduate education in a certain college or university, what items of cost would you include?

4. A buyer agrees to pay a builder the cost of building a house, plus 10 percent. Which of the following items should be included in the cost? Explain why or why not.

   a. Depreciation expense on the builder's trucks that haul material to the house.

   b. Lumber originally delivered to the site but later removed and used on another house.

   c. Scrap lumber, which was hauled off to the dump.

   d. Cost of the architect's plans which were used to build this and five other identical houses.

   e. Fees paid by the builder to the municipality because of the inspections required to see that the house conformed to building codes.

   f. Advertising expenses incurred to sell the house.

5. For what principal purposes is full cost information used?

6. The text uses "return on assets employed" and "return on investment"

interchangeably. Explain why these terms have the same meaning. (Hint: Recall the discussion in *Fundamentals of Financial Accounting* about the relationship between the left-hand and right-hand sides of the balance sheet.)

7. Consider a passenger automobile, such as a Ford Granada. In deciding on next year's selling prices, what types of adjustment to last year's costs should management take into account?

8. The principal determinants of the total profit of a business are (*a*) selling price per unit, (*b*) cost per unit, and (*c*) one other factor. What is that other factor? Why is it important?

9. In Exhibit 2–1, each of the four methods arrives at the same selling price ($10). Why, then, should a company be concerned about selecting the best method?

10. Some companies use the direct cost method of pricing and price all products at approximately the same percentage above direct costs. Under what circumstances will this policy lead to satisfactory prices, and under what circumstances will it lead to unsatisfactory prices?

11. Similarly, describe the circumstances in which gross margin pricing leads to satisfactory or to unsatisfactory results.

12. Similarly, describe the circumstances in which profit margin pricing leads to satisfactory or to unsatisfactory results.

13. "The higher the asset turnover and the lower the operating cost per dollar of sales, the smaller the mark-on percentage needs to be." Why is this so?

14. Profit margin pricing is often called full cost pricing. Why is this so?

15. Long-distance telephone rates are higher for operator-assisted calls than for direct-dial calls because of the higher labor and other costs involved in operator-assisted calls. But since a call dialed by the customer is handled completely automatically, why are the rates for direct-dial calls higher for long distances (such as New York to Seattle) than for short distances (such as New York to Philadelphia)?

16. Is the normal profit margin percentage that a retailer uses for setting the selling price of fine watches higher than that used by a supermarket in setting the selling price for cornflakes? List the factors that explain the difference.

17. Both retail food stores and wholesale food companies customarily use the gross margin method of pricing, that is, they add a mark-on percentage to cost. The mark-on percentage is typically higher for retailers than for wholesalers. Why is this so?

18. Some supermarkets vary their profit margin percentage according to the number of square feet of shelf space that a given item occupies. What is the rationale for this approach? Do you agree with this rationale?

19. In time and material pricing, a profit is included both in the time component and also in the material component. Does this mean that profits are double counted? Explain.

20. A shoe manufacturer is designing a new style of shoes to sell at $17 a pair. Estimates show that costs of the contemplated design will not produce a

satisfactory profit at this price. What types of action should the manufacturer consider?

PROBLEMS

2-1. The Brown Cabinet Shop makes a popular 30-inch wide bathroom vanity cabinet. Cost data are as follows:

Depreciation	$400 per month
Rent on building	300 per month
Cabinetmaker wages.................	20 per cabinet
Office expenses........................	600 per month
Utilities....................................	200 per month
Cabinet materials	25 per cabinet
Insurance	100 per month
Shop supervisor.......................	800 per month

Normal production volume is 200 cabinets per month. Brown assigns indirect costs equally to each cabinet.

Required:

A. Classify Brown's costs as either direct or indirect assuming that he uses the individual cabinet as his cost objective.
B. What is the full cost of a cabinet?
C. Brown's next door neighbor, Green had considered making a 30-inch cabinet for his bathroom and had priced the necessary materials. Green asked if Brown would sell him a finished cabinet at cost, and Brown agreed. Would you expect there to be any difference of opinion between the two men about the amount that Green should pay? Why?

2-2. The Taylor Company manufactures a number of products. In 1976 the selling price of Product A, whose sales are normally 10,000 units per year, was calculated as follows:

	Unit costs
Direct material	$ 2.00
Direct labor	4.00
Indirect manufacturing cost	3.00
Selling and administrative cost..	2.00
Full cost...	$11.00
Profit (10% of full cost)..	1.10
Selling price	$12.10

In 1977 the company estimates that direct material cost and direct labor cost will increase by 5 percent. It also estimates that indirect manufacturing cost will increase by a total of $5,000 and that selling and administrative cost and sales volume will remain unchanged.

Required:

What is the normal selling price for Product A in 1977?

2-3. The Crawford Company has prepared the following data pertaining to one of its products:

> Direct manufacturing cost—$8 per unit
> Indirect manufacturing cost—$4 per unit
> Selling and administrative cost—$4 per unit
> Assets employed—$40 per unit
> Desired rate of return on assets—10%

Required:

A. The company desires a normal selling price which yields the desired return on assets. Prepare calculations which show the determination of price using the following approaches:
  1. Return on assets.
  2. Profit margin.
  3. Gross margin.
  4. Direct cost.
B. Prepare an income statement for a year in which 80,000 units were sold.

2-4. The Jones Company uses the return-on-asset approach to pricing its single product. The price for the current year was calculated as follows:

	Per unit
Direct manufacturing cost	$100
Indirect manufacturing cost	50
Selling and administrative cost	30
Full cost	180
Profit margin	20*
Selling price	$200

> * Profit margin of $20 per unit was based on a desired rate of return on 12.5 percent, assets employed of $1,600,000, and expected sales volume of 10,000 units.

Required:

A. Calculate the asset turnover and return on sales for the current year.
B. A 25 percent increase in sales volume is expected next year, and unit costs and total assets employed are expected to remain constant. Recalculate the selling price, asset turnover, and return on sales.
C. Assume that sales volume remained constant next year at 10,000 units and that all unit costs increased 10 percent. Recalculate the selling price, asset turnover, and return on sales.
D. Comment on the effects of volume and cost changes on selling prices, asset turnover, and return on sales for a company using return on asset pricing.

2-5. Ellen Lacy, owner of Lacy Shoe Store, uses gross margin pricing. In a typical year the store normally sells shoes costing $300,000. Total operating costs of the store, including her salary, are $70,000 per year. Inventory, accounts receivable, and other assets are $200,000. Lacy desires a 15 percent return on her assets.

Required:

A. What mark-on percentage should Lacy use?
B. What is the normal selling price of a pair of shoes that has an invoice cost of $20?
C. The average shoe store in the community earns a profit that is 5 percent of sales. How do Lacy's profits compare with this?

2–6. Hallow Manufacturing Company makes a line of brooms and brushes. The following data relate to the production and sale of floor brush No. 826:

Sales per year—500,000 units @ $0.55 each
Direct costs per brush—$0.30
Other costs, per year—$100,000
Total assets employed—$100,000

Required:

A. How much operating income does the sale of brush No. 826 generate for the company?
B. How many brushes must be sold to earn a 10 percent return on assets employed?

2–7. The Foster Company manufactures two products, A and B. Estimated costs are presented below for a year in which 10,000 units of each product are expected to be sold:

	Total	Product A	Product B
Direct manufacturing cost................	$500,000	$300,000	$200,000
Indirect manufacturing cost	200,000	120,000	80,000
Selling and administrative cost.........	100,000	60,000	40,000

An annual profit of $80,000 is considered satisfactory. The company uses profit margin pricing with the same profit margin percentage for all products.

Required:

A. Calculate normal selling prices for Products A and B.
B. Using the prices calculated above, how much profit would result if the sales were 5,000 units of A and 15,000 units of B instead of 10,000 units of each?
C. Comment on the effect of changes in the product mix on total profit when profit margin pricing is used.

2–8. The owner of the Morgan Television Repair Company wants to begin using the time and material approach to pricing television services. The owner compiled the following data for a typical month:

Cost of repair parts—$1,500
Cost of handling and storing parts—$300
Salary and fringe benefits of repair personnel—$3,000
Other indirect costs (all related to repair
    personnel—$1,200
Total monthly costs—$6,000
Hours of labor available for repair work—500

Based on the assets employed in the business, a monthly profit of $1,500 is considered satisfactory.

Required:

A. Assuming that the company uses the same mark-on percentage for both labor and parts costs, what should be charged for a job that requires four hours of labor and parts costing $25?

B. If only 420 hours of labor time were available each month instead of 500 and costs were as above, what should be the charge to the customer for an hour of labor?

2–9. Tidwell Company and Marshall Company make similar snowblowers, and each sells 100,000 per year. Their unit costs are as follows:

	Unit costs	
	Tidwell	Marshall
Direct material..	$20	$56
Direct labor...	34	14
Indirect manufacturing cost..................................	26	10
Total costs...	$80	$80

These costs reflect the fact that Tidwell manufactures most of the components of the snowblowers while Marshall purchases components from other manufacturers and merely assembles them.

Required:

A. If the pricing policy of each company were to charge direct cost plus 80 percent, what would be the target selling price of each snowblower?

B. If the pricing policy of each company were to charge full cost plus 20 percent, what would be the target selling price of each snowblower?

C. Discuss briefly the relative merits of each pricing policy.

2–10. The Summers Company produces a wide variety of different products. Presented below are average unit cost data for all products and for four individual products:

	Average all products	Product W	Product X	Product Y	Product Z
Direct manufacturing cost	$ 8	$ 8	$ 6	$ 8	$ 8
Indirect manufacturing cost.....	8	8	6	16	8
Total Manufacturing Cost	16	16	12	24	16
Selling and administrative cost	8	8	6	8	4
Full cost	$24	$24	$18	$32	$20
Assets employed.....................	$40	$20	$30	$60	$40

The company considers a return on assets of 10 percent to be satisfactory.

Required:

A. Using the average unit costs for all products, calculate the profit percentages that the company would use under each of the following methods:
   1. Return-on-asset pricing.
   2. Profit margin pricing.
   3. Gross margin pricing.
   4. Direct cost pricing.
B. Calculate four possible selling prices for each of the four individual products using the profit percentages from Requirement A.
C. Which selling price seems most appropriate for each product? Explain your answer.
D. Suggest some reasons for the differing cost patterns and assets employed among the four products.

2–11. L. Frank is a student at State University. Recently she purchased a used car for $3,500 cash. Being concerned over the costs of owning and operating a car, she prepared the following estimates:

> License fees and taxes–$150 per year
> Maintenance and repairs–$200 per year
> Insurance–$400 per year
> Tires–$225 per set of four
> Useful life of tires–15,000 miles
> Cost of gasoline–$0.05 per mile
> Annual mileage to be driven–10,000

Also, Frank expects to keep the car for three years and then sell it for $500. She bought a set of new tires for the car during the first week of ownership and does not intend to replace tires at the time of final sale.

Required:

A. Classify the costs of Frank's car as either direct or indirect assuming that she selects the "car mile" as her cost objective and that she uses straight-line depreciation.
B. What is the full cost of a car mile for Frank's automobile? (Carry calculations to three decimal places.)
C. Frank and a classmate, J. Charles, plan a weekend at a beach resort and agree to share transportation costs equitably for the 500-mile trip. Actual expenditures were:

> Gasoline–$25
> Speeding ticket while Charles was driving–$50
> Replacement of broken fan belt–$15

If you were Frank, how much would you expect Charles to pay? Do you think Charles would agree? Why?

2–12. The James Company manufactures a number of products. In 1976 the selling price of Product M, whose sales are normally 12,500 units per year, was calculated as follows:

Unit costs

Direct material	$ 5
Direct labor	8
Indirect manufacturing cost	4
Selling and administrative cost	3
Full cost	20
Profit (10% of full cost)	2
Selling price	$22

In 1977 the company estimates that direct material cost and direct labor cost will increase by 10 percent. It also estimates that indirect manufacturing cost will increase by a total of $7,500 and that selling and administrative cost and sales volume will remain unchanged.

Required:

What is the normal selling price for Product M in 1977?

2–13. The Johnson Company has prepared the following data pertaining to one of its products:

> Direct manufacturing cost – $6 per unit
> Indirect manufacturing cost – $3 per unit
> Selling and administrative cost – $3 per unit
> Assets employed – $30 per unit
> Desired rate of return on assets – 10%

Required:

A. The company desires a normal selling price which yields the desired return on assets. Prepare calculations which show the determination of price using the following approaches:
  1. Return on assets.
  2. Profit margin.
  3. Gross margin.
  4. Direct cost.
B. Prepare an income statement for a year in which 75,000 units were sold.

2–14. The Stewart Company uses the return-on-asset approach to pricing its single product. The price for the current year was calculated as follows:

Direct manufacturing cost	$ 90
Indirect manufacturing cost	45
Selling and administrative cost	40
Full cost	175
Profit	15*
Selling price	$190

* Profit margin of $15 per unit was based on a desired rate of return of 15 percent, assets employed of $1,000,000, and expected sales volume of 10,000 units.

Required:

A. Calculate the asset turnover and return on sales for the current year.
B. A 25 percent decrease in sales volume is expected next year, and unit costs are expected to remain constant. Recalculate the selling price, asset turnover, and return on sales.
C. Assume that sales volume remained constant next year and that full unit cost increased $10. Recalculate the selling price, asset turnover, and return on sales.
D. Comment on the effects of volume and cost changes on selling prices, asset turnover, and return on sales for a company using return-on-asset pricing.

2–15. Marvin Dress Shop desires a 15 percent return on assets. It anticipates an asset turnover of one (i.e., annual sales equal assets employed). Cost of goods sold is estimated at $600,000 per year, and other operating expenses at $250,000 per year. The gross margin basis of pricing is used.

Required:

A. What should be the mark-on percentage?
B. What is the normal selling price of a dress that has an invoice cost of $60?

2–16. Bright, Inc., manufactures furniture polishes and cleaners. The following data relate to the production and sale of Shine, a large seller:

> Sales per year—250,000 cans @ $1.10 each
> Direct costs—$0.60 per unit
> Other costs—$105,000
> Total assets employed—$125,000

Required:

A. Compute the operating income which Shine generates for the company.
B. How many cans of Shine must be sold to earn a 10 percent return on assets employed?

2–17. The Gentry Company manufactures two products, X and Y. Estimated costs are presented below for a year in which 12,500 units of each product are expected to be sold:

	Total	Product X	Product Y
Direct manufacturing cost	$450,000	$300,000	$150,000
Indirect manufacturing cost	180,000	120,000	60,000
Selling and administrative cost	120,000	80,000	40,000

An annual profit of $75,000 is considered satisfactory. The company uses profit margin pricing with the same profit margin percentage for all products.

Required:

A. Calculate selling prices for Products X and Y.
B. Using the prices calculated above, how much profit would result if

sales were 15,000 units of X and 10,000 units of Y instead of 12,500 units of each?

C. Comment on the effect of changes in the product mix on total profit when profit margin pricing is used.

2-18. The owner of the Davis Auto Repair Shop wants to use the time and material approach to pricing services. The following data have been compiled for a typical month:

> Cost of repair parts — $3,000
> Cost of handling and storing parts — $500
> Wages and fringe benefits of mechanics — $5,000
> Other indirect costs (not related
>   to parts) — $1,500
> Total monthly costs — $10,000
> Hours of labor available for repair work — 780

Based on the assets employed in the business, a monthly profit of $2,000 is considered satisfactory.

Required:
A. Assuming that the company uses the same mark-on percentage for both labor and parts costs, what should be charged for a job that requires two hours of labor and parts costing $15?
B. If only 650 hours of labor time were available each month instead of 780 and costs were as above, what should be the charge to the customer for an hour of labor?

2-19. Thomas Company and Moore Company make similar lawnmowers, and each sells 100,000 per year. Their unit costs are as follows:

	Unit costs	
	Thomas	Moore
Direct material	$19	$53
Direct labor	32	13
Indirect cost	24	9
Total Costs	$75	$75

These costs reflect the fact that Thomas manufactures most of the components of the lawnmower, while Moore purchases components from other manufacturers and merely assembles them.

Required:
A. If the pricing policy of each company were to charge direct cost plus 80 percent, what would be the target selling price of each lawnmower?
B. If the pricing policy of each company were to charge full cost plus 20 percent, what would be the target selling price of each lawnmower?
C. Discuss briefly the relative merits of each pricing policy.

2-20. The Winter Company produces a wide variety of different products. Presented below are average unit cost data for all products and for four individual products:

	Average all products	Product A	Product B	Product C	Product D
Direct manufacturing cost	$ 9	$ 9	$ 6	$ 9	$ 9
Indirect manufacturing cost..............	9	9	6	18	9
Total Manufacturing Cost........	18	18	12	27	18
Selling and administrative cost	9	9	6	9	6
Full cost	$27	$27	$18	$36	$24
Assets employed.............................	$30	$15	$20	$45	$30

The company considers a return on assets of 10 percent to be satisfactory.

Required:

A. Using the average unit costs for all products, calculate the profit percentages that the company would use under each of the following methods:
 1. Return-on-asset pricing.
 2. Profit margin pricing.
 3. Gross margin pricing.
 4. Direct cost pricing.
B. Calculate four possible selling prices for each of the four individual products using the profit percentages from Requirement A.
C. Which selling price seems most appropriate for each product? Explain your answer.
D. Suggest some reasons for the differing cost patterns and assets employed among the four products.

2-21. Mary Martin is considering investing in a business and has narrowed the choice to two possibilities, A and B, with the following characteristics for first year's operations:

	Business A	Business B
Investment required..................	$ 50,000	$ 25,000
Sales revenue	150,000	100,000
Operating income.....................	4,000	2,500

Required:

A. Compute the asset turnover, percentage return on sales, and return on investment for each business.
B. Disregarding other considerations, which of these businesses is the better investment?

CASE: DEAN, EARLY, AND FINE

2-22. Dean, Early, and Fine formed a partnership. Dean contributed land with a fair-market value of $60,000, Early contributed $50,000 cash, and Fine contributed $50,000 cash. The partnership spent $100,000 in installing streets, sewers, and utilities. The land was divided into ten lots. Lots 1–5 had a selling price of $18,000 each; and lots 6–10, because of their more favorable location, had a selling price of $22,000 each.

It was agreed that Fine would sell the lots, receiving a commission of 5 percent, and that the remaining proceeds would be divided one third to each partner. It was further agreed that Early would acquire Lot No. 10 for personal use, and that in calculating the distribution of proceeds Lot No. 10 would be valued at cost. The nine lots were sold at the listed price, but when it came time to dissolve the partnership, there was a dispute about the distribution of the proceeds.

Required:

A. How much cash should each partner receive?
B. How should the agreement have been worded so as to avoid this dispute?

CASE: CONRAD TAXI

2–23.   Conrad owns a taxicab which he recently purchased for $6,000 cash. He operates it himself for 60 hours a week and rents it to Werner who also operates it 60 hours a week. Conrad pays all the bills. During the first year Conrad drove the taxicab 30,000 miles, of which 20,000 miles were "revenue miles" (i.e., miles for which fares were collected) and Werner drove 20,000 miles of which 10,000 miles were revenue miles.

Costs for the year were:

Registration and insurance	$1,500
Depreciation of the taxicab	1,200
Gasoline and oil	2,500
Tires (changed every 25,000 miles)	1,000
Routine maintenance (every month)	1,200

The taxicab was garaged in a space leased by Conrad at $900 per year. Conrad would pay this amount whether or not the taxicab was used by Werner.

During the year Werner paid $50 for his operator's license and a $10 fine for a parking violation. Conrad paid $50 for his operator's license, and a $20 fine for a second parking violation. (Parking fines were $10 for the first offense in a given year, $20 for the second offense, $30 for the third offense, and so on.)

Werner paid Conrad $50 per week ($2,600 per year), on account, and they agreed to settle up at the end of the year on an equitable basis. They could not agree on what this basis was, and they ask your help as an impartial outsider.

Required:

How much more should Werner pay Conrad?

CASE: GOVERNMENT CONTRACTS

2–24.   Many government contracts cannot be at a fixed price because the costs cannot be estimated closely in advance. Until 1976 the typical practice was to reimburse the contractor for its full cost plus a profit which was a certain percentage of cost (cost-based pricing). Beginning in 1976, some contractors were reimbursed at full cost plus a profit which was a certain percentage of assets employed (asset-based pricing).

For the purposes of discussion, assume that when the profit is based on cost, the rate is 7 percent and that when profit is based on assets employed, the rate is 14 percent. Assume three contracts, each with a cost of $1,000,000. Contractor A has assets of $1,000,000, Contractor B has assets of $500,000, and Contractor C has assets of $250,000. In other words, their asset turnovers (based on cost rather than revenue) are 1, 2, and 4, respectively.

Required:

A. Calculate the profit which each contractor would earn under (1) cost-based pricing and (2) asset-based pricing.
B. Assume that Contractor A owns assets costing $500,000 and that depreciation on these assets is a contract cost of $100,000 per year. Suppose, instead, Contractor A had leased these assets from another company, paying that company $110,000 per year. What would have Contractor A's profit have been under (1) cost-based pricing and (2) asset-based pricing? Which pricing policy encourages contractors to lease assets?
C. Assume that under cost-based pricing (with a 7 percent rate) the aggregate profit of government contractors is satisfactory. What should be the average industry turnover (based on cost) to warrant a profit of 14 percent of assets employed?
D. As a taxpayer, do you favor cost-based pricing or asset-based pricing?

SUGGESTIONS FOR FURTHER STUDY

(These books relate to the material in Chapters 2–5.)

Fremgen, James M. *Accounting for Managerial Analysis,* 3d ed. Homewood, Ill.: Richard D. Irwin, Inc., 1976.

Horngren, Charles T. *Cost Accounting: A Managerial Emphasis,* 3d ed. Englewood Cliffs, N.J.: Prentice-Hall, Inc., 1972.

Matz, Adolph, and Curry, Othel J. *Cost Accounting Planning and Control,* 6th ed. Cincinnati: Southwestern Publishing Co., 1976.

Neuner, John J. W., and Deakin, Edward B. *Cost Accounting: Principles and Practice,* 9th ed. Homewood, Ill.: Richard D. Irwin, Inc., 1977.

Shillinglaw, Gordon. *Cost Accounting: Analysis and Control,* 4th ed. Homewood, Ill.: Richard D. Irwin, Inc., 1977.

3

Cost accounting systems

This is the first of three chapters that describe the concepts and practices of cost accounting. As pointed out in Chapter 1, there are three distinct types of cost. Nevertheless, the term "cost accounting" usually refers only to the first type, full costs; that is, cost accounting systems are systems for collecting full costs.

In this chapter we describe the elements of cost that make up the full cost of a product. We also give an overview of the systems that are used for collecting product costs in a manufacturing company; trace the flow of costs from one account to another; and describe the characteristics of the two main types of systems, namely, job order costing and process costing.

SOURCES OF COST PRINCIPLES

In a merchandising company, goods are carried in inventory and are reported as cost of goods sold on the income statement at essentially the amount that the company paid suppliers for these goods. In a manufacturing company, by contrast, inventory and cost of goods sold amounts include the various elements of cost that were incurred in manufacturing these goods. A cost accounting system measures these costs.

Such a cost accounting system is an integral part of the financial accounting system of a manufacturing company. It is governed by the same "generally accepted accounting principles" that were described in *Funda-*

71

mentals of Financial Accounting. As it happens, however, the Financial Accounting Standards Board has not published many standards that specifically relate to cost accounting. In 1971 the Congress created the Cost Accounting Standards Board (CASB). Although the CASB's authority officially is limited to the measurement of costs on government contracts, its standards have a considerable influence on cost accounting in companies generally because in most respects the measurement of the costs for a government contract is similar to the measurement of the costs of products manufactured for commercial purposes. The standards published by the CASB are therefore incorporated in the description that follows.[1]

ELEMENTS OF COST

In Chapter 2 we said that the full cost of a cost objective is the sum of (1) its direct costs and (2) a fair share of indirect costs. Although a cost objective can be anything for which cost information is desired, in this chapter and the next chapter we shall limit the discussion to the measurement of the cost of a product, and even more specifically to the cost of *manufacturing* a product.

The elements of product cost are shown in Exhibit 3–1. The direct cost elements are direct labor cost and direct material cost. Together, these are called the **prime cost.** The indirect manufacturing cost is called **manufacturing overhead. The sum of direct material, direct labor, and manufacturing overhead is the total manufacturing cost.**

Direct labor and manufacturing overhead costs collectively are called **conversion costs** because these are the costs incurred in converting the raw materials into finished products.

The full cost of manufacturing and distributing the product includes, in addition to the manufacturing cost, its distribution cost and its general and administrative cost. These elements of cost will be discussed in Chapter 5.

Direct costs in general

A direct cost is a cost that can be traced to a single cost objective. (A direct cost is therefore often called a **traceable** cost.) In deciding whether or not a cost item is direct with respect to a specified cost objective, one should consider whether (1) that cost objective was the only cost objective to **benefit** from the item of cost and/or (2) that cost objec-

---

[1] These standards are initially published in the *Federal Register.* Every year or so the Cost Accounting Standards Board publishes a booklet containing the standards promulgated up to that time.

EXHIBIT 3-1
Elements of product cost

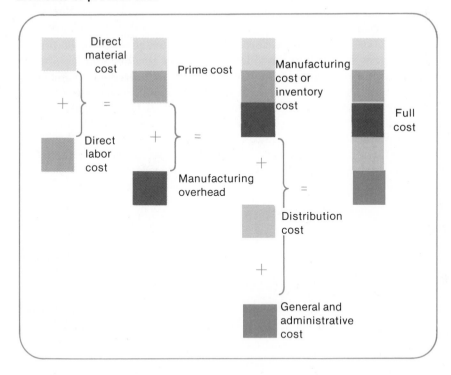

tive was the only cost objective that **caused** the item of cost. If either or both of these criteria apply, the item is direct.[2]

> *EXAMPLE:* Assume the cost objective is the manufacture of a specified case of shoes. The cost of the leather is a direct cost because that case of shoes both caused and benefited from the leather cost. The cost of inspecting the shoes is a direct cost because those shoes caused the cost, even though there was no measurable benefit to the shoes.

If the benefit or the causal relationship for a single item of cost applies to two or more cost objectives, the item is indirect with respect to any one of these cost objectives.

> *EXAMPLE:* The departmental supervisor's activities benefit all the shoes manufactured in the department, even though no specific case of shoes caused the supervisor's salary. The supervisor's salary is therefore an indirect cost of a specified case of shoes.

---

[2] Cost Accounting Standards Board, *Statement of Operating Policies, Procedures, and Objectives,* March 1973, p. 17.

In this chapter, the cost objectives we are interested in are manufactured goods, such as shoes. For such cost objectives, direct costs are those that directly benefit or are caused by the manufacture of the products. For other types of cost objectives, the word "direct" could refer to quite different items of cost. Thus, in a department manufacturing several products, the salary of a department supervisor is a direct cost of the department, but it is an indirect cost of the various products made in that department because no beneficial or causal relationship exists between any single product and the supervisor's salary. If the department made only a single product, however, the supervisor's salary could be classified as a direct cost of that product. Even in this situation, many companies classify the supervisor's salary as an indirect cost; they limit direct labor costs to the cost of employees who work physically on the product.

> EXAMPLE: In a factory that manufactures shirts, employees who operate the machines which are used to cut the cloth, sew the pieces together, make buttonholes, sew on buttons, attach the label, and press the completed shirt, and the employees who inspect the completed shirts are classified as direct labor. Employees who carry the material from one work station to another and those who do production planning, timekeeping, and supervision are classified as indirect labor.

We shall now discuss in more detail the two principal types of direct product costs: direct labor cost and direct material cost.

Direct material cost

A **direct material** (sometimes called "stores" or "raw materials") **is material which actually enters into and becomes part of the specified finished product.** It is to be distinguished from **supplies,** which are materials used in the operation of the business but not directly in the product itself, such as lubricating oil used in machinery.

There are two problems in the measurement of direct material cost: (1) measuring the **quantity** of material used for each product, and (2) measuring the **price** per unit of quantity.

In measuring the quantity, the cost accounting system has a procedure for recording the amount of raw material that is withdrawn from the raw materials inventory for use in the manufacturing process. Usually, the amount withdrawn is recorded on a document called a **requisition** which shows the quantity of each type of material and the product on which it is to be used.

The price per unit of quantity is often the purchase price of the material, as shown on the invoice. Purchase discounts may be deducted from the invoice price of goods purchased. The cost may be the cost of the specific item withdrawn from inventory, it may be determined by the Lifo, Fifo, or average cost method (as discussed in Chapter 8 of *Funda-*

mentals of Financial Accounting), or it may be a standard cost, which will be described in Chapter 13.

To the invoice cost, some companies add an allowance for **material-related costs.** These include inward freight cost, the cost of inspecting the material, costs of the purchasing department, costs of moving material within the factory, and costs of storing the material. Since these material-related items are really a part of the cost of the material as it enters the manufacturing process, it is theoretically desirable that they be included as direct material cost. Considerable recordkeeping is required to measure these material-related costs, however, and many companies believe that this recordkeeping is not worth the effort. They therefore price raw material at its purchase cost, disregarding material-related costs.

Direct labor cost

Direct labor is labor used to convert raw material into the finished product. **The direct labor costs of a product are those labor costs which can be specifically traced to or identified with the product or which vary so closely with the number of units produced that a direct relationship can be presumed to be present.** The wages and related costs of employees who assemble parts into a finished product, or who operate machines in the process of production, or who work on the product with tools, are direct labor costs of the product.

There are essentially two problems in the measurement of direct labor costs of a product: (1) measuring the *quantity* of labor time expended on the product, and (2) ascertaining the *price* per unit of labor time.

Measuring the **quantity** of labor time is relatively easy. A daily time-card, or comparable record, is usually kept for each direct labor employee; and the time spent on each cost objective is recorded on it. Or, if direct labor employees are paid a piece rate, the number of pieces completed is recorded. These labor records are used both to collect direct labor costs and also as a basis for payroll computations. Problems do arise concerning the treatment of such items as idle time, personal time, and overtime; but these problems are beyond the scope of this introductory treatment.

Deciding on the best way to **price** these labor times is conceptually more difficult than measuring the quantity of time. Many companies have a simple solution to this problem; they price direct labor at the amounts actually earned by the employees concerned (so much an hour if employees are paid on a day rate or an hourly rate; so much a piece if they are paid on a piece rate). They may use either a separate labor rate for each employee or an average labor rate for all the direct labor employees in a department.

> *EXAMPLE:* Assume that a certain job is worked on in four departments and that the time worked in each department (as shown by the timecards)

and the average direct labor rates are as indicated below. The direct labor cost of this job would be computed as follows:

Department	Direct labor hours on job	Departmental hourly rate	Total amount
A	20	$5.00	$100.00
B	3	4.50	13.50
C	6	3.80	22.80
D	40	3.00	120.00
Total Direct Labor Cost of Job			$256.30

Many companies add **labor-related costs** to the basic wage rate. They reason that each hour of labor effort costs the company not only the wages paid to the employee but also the social security taxes, pension contributions, and other fringe benefits paid by the employer.[3] The company must pay for these labor-related benefits; they are caused by the fact that the employee works, and they are therefore part of the real cost of using the employee's service. Other companies even include a share of the costs of the personnel department or of employee welfare programs as a part of direct labor cost. Using such a higher labor cost gives a more accurate measure of direct labor costs. It also requires additional record-keeping, however; and many companies do not believe the additional accuracy is worth the added recordkeeping.

Manufacturing overhead cost

The indirect cost of manufacturing a product is called manufacturing overhead cost (also called *factory overhead,* and occasionally *burden*). Thus, **manufacturing overhead includes all manufacturing costs other than direct material and direct labor.**

One element of manufacturing overhead cost is indirect labor, which represents wages and salaries earned by employees who do not work directly on a product but whose services are related to the overall process of production. Examples are janitors, forklift operators, toolroom personnel, inspectors, timekeepers, and supervisors. Another element of manufacturing overhead cost is indirect material cost, which is the cost of material used in the factory but not traced directly to specific products or other cost objectives. Examples are lubricants for machines, supplies, and raw materials which, although a part of the final products, are too insignificant to be included in direct material cost. Manufacturing overhead cost also includes such items of cost as heat, light, power, mainte-

---

[3] But not the employee's social security contribution. This is a deduction from the employee's earnings; it is therefore not a cost to the company.

nance, depreciation, taxes, and insurance on assets used in the manufacturing process.

Distinction between direct and indirect costs

It is conceptually desirable that a given item of cost be classified as a direct cost rather than as an indirect cost. This is because an item of direct cost is assigned directly to a single cost objective; whereas, as will be discussed in a later section, the assignment of indirect costs to cost objectives is a more roundabout and usually less accurate process. Nevertheless, the category of indirect costs does, and must, exist.

Certain costs are not traced directly to a specific product, and hence are indirect costs, for one of three reasons: (1) It is *impossible* to do so, as in the case of the supervisor's salary already mentioned. (2) It is *not feasible* to do so; that is, the recordkeeping required for such a direct tracing would cost too much. For example, the nails, the sewing thread, the eyelets, and the glue that are used in manufacturing a case of shoes cost only a few pennies, and it is not worthwhile to trace their cost to each case of shoes; these costs are therefore classified as indirect material. (3) Management *chooses* not to do so; that is, some companies classify certain items of costs as indirect simply because it is customary in the industry to do so.

Problems of drawing distinctions. Problems arise in attempting to draw a precise line between items of cost that are caused by or benefit a product and other costs. For example, a cost may not be caused by a product even though it is incurred at the same time as the product is being manufactured.

> *EXAMPLE:* In a certain factory, Products A, B, and C were manufactured during regular working hours, and Product D was manufactured after regular hours. Overtime wages were paid to the employees who worked on Product D. These overtime wages might, or might not, be a direct cost of Product D. If the factory worked overtime because the general volume of orders was high, then the overtime is attributable to all the products worked on, and is an indirect cost. If, on the other hand, the overtime work on Product D was occasioned by a special request of the customer for Product D, then the overtime is a direct cost of Product D. It could also happen that the overtime was caused by a special need to make Product C quickly, and in order to meet this need Product D was rescheduled from the regular work period to the overtime period; in this case, the overtime is truly a direct cost of Product C, even though overtime was not in fact paid during the hours in which Product C was being manufactured.

Moreover, there are differences of opinion as to how close the causal or beneficial relationship between a cost item and the cost objective must be in order to classify the item as direct. In many production operations, such as assembly lines, refineries, and similar continuous process operations, a basic work force is required no matter what products are manufactured. Some people argue that the labor cost of this work force constitutes a cost that is required to operate the plant as a whole, much like depreciation on the machinery, and that therefore it is an indirect cost. Nevertheless, most companies classify the costs of the basic work force as direct labor.

Manufacturing cost

As noted above, the manufacturing cost of a product is the sum of its direct material cost, direct labor cost, and manufacturing overhead cost. Under generally accepted accounting principles (i.e., the cost principle), this is the cost at which completed manufactured goods are carried as inventory, and the amount that is shown as cost of goods sold when the goods are sold.[4]

It should be emphasized that the cost at which goods are carried in inventory does not include distribution costs, or those general and administrative costs that are unrelated to manufacturing operations. It includes only the costs that are incurred "up to the factory exit door."

SYSTEMS FOR COST ACCUMULATION

A cost accounting system is a particular method of collecting costs and assigning them to cost objectives. We now describe the essentials of the system that is used to measure manufacturing costs of products. The measurement of the manufacturing cost of a product is essentially a two-step process: (1) the measurement of the costs that are applicable to operations during a given accounting period, and (2) the assignment of these costs to products.

The collection of costs applicable to the period is a problem in financial accounting. The underlying accounting concept is the accrual concept, which, as explained in *Fundamentals of Financial Accounting,* is to be distinguished from the cash basis of measurement. According to the accrual concept, labor costs for an accounting period represent the labor services *performed* in the period rather than the wages actually *paid* in cash in the period; material costs represent the amount of material *consumed* in the period rather than the amount of materials *purchased* or paid for in the period; and fixed asset costs are represented by depreciation for the period rather than by *outlays* for fixed assets. The accrual concept is consistent with the basic idea that cost measures the use of resources. Since these distinctions are discussed at length in *Fundamentals of Financial Accounting,* they will not be repeated here. Thus, in describing a cost accounting system, we shall take it for granted that

---

[4] As explained in *Fundamentals of Financial Accounting,* Chapter 8, inventory is carried at cost unless its market value is lower than its cost.

the costs applicable to the accounting *period* have been correctly measured in accordance with the accrual concept. The special problem of cost accounting is to assign these costs to products *worked on* during the period.

Inventory accounts

As of any moment in time, such as the date of a balance sheet, the current assets of a manufacturing company include three types of inventory accounts: raw materials, goods in process, and finished goods.[5] **Raw Materials Inventory** shows the acquisition cost of the raw materials on hand. These materials will be used subsequently in the manufacturing process and will be classified then either as direct material or as indirect material. **Goods in Process (or Work in Process) Inventory** shows the cost accumulated to date for those products on which production has been started but not yet completed. This cost includes the direct material, direct labor, and manufacturing overhead costs assigned to such products. **Finished Goods Inventory** shows the total manufacturing cost of products that have been manufactured but not yet sold. Finished Goods Inventory is comparable to the Merchandise Inventory account in a merchandising company, such as a retail store or a wholesaler. (A merchandising company has no raw materials or goods in process inventory.)

In brief, the process is as follows:

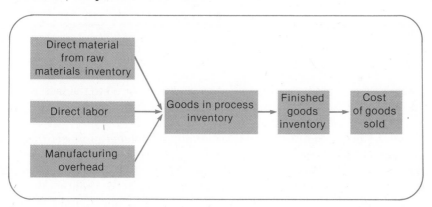

Exhibit 3–2 shows the flow of costs through these three inventory accounts. This exhibit provides an overview of the system for collecting costs, which can be read as follows:

At the beginning of the period, $90,000 of raw materials were on hand in the raw material storage area. During the period, raw material costing $52,000 was purchased and added to inventory, and raw material costing

---

[5] There may also be inventory accounts for supplies and other indirect materials.

EXHIBIT 3–2

Flow of costs through inventories ($000 omitted)

From vendors

Raw Materials Inventory

Balance, Jan. 1	90	Issued for use	49
→Purchases	52	To balance	93
	142		142
Balance, Feb. 1	93		

To factory

Goods in Process Inventory

Balance, Jan. 1	85	Goods manufactured	110
Direct material	49		
Direct labor	20	To balance	71
Manufacturing overhead	27		
	181		181
Balance, Feb. 1	71		

To finished goods warehouse

Finished Goods Inventory

Balance, Jan. 1	65	Cost of goods sold	115
Goods manufactured	110	To balance	60
	175		175
Balance, Feb. 1	60		

To customers

Cost of Goods Sold

115

$49,000 was withdrawn from inventory and transferred to the factory for use in manufacturing products. The Raw Materials Inventory on hand at the end of the period therefore cost $93,000.

At the beginning of the period, partially completed products then in the factory had a cost of $85,000. During the period, manufacturing costs incurred were the $49,000 of direct material cost, $20,000 of direct labor cost, and $27,000 of manufacturing overhead cost. Also, during the period, goods costing $110,000 were completed and transferred from the factory to the finished goods warehouse. Goods in Process Inventory at the end of the period therefore cost $71,000.

At the beginning of the period, the amount of finished goods on hand in the finished goods warehouse cost $65,000. During the period, goods that cost $110,000 were added to finished goods, as mentioned above, and goods that cost $115,000 were shipped to customers. Finished Goods Inventory at the end of the period therefore cost $60,000.

The $115,000 of goods shipped was the cost of goods sold during the period. The $115,000 appears on the income statement matched with the sales revenue from these goods.

The account flowchart

The accounting entries involved in the process sketched above are described in the next section. As an aid in visualizing the process, a flowchart is used. **A flowchart depicts the accounts used in a system, in T-account form, with arrows indicating the flow of amounts from one account to another.**

Most of the accounts on a cost accounting flowchart are either asset accounts or expense accounts. A characteristic of both asset and expense accounts is that increases are shown on the debit side and decreases are shown on the credit side. An arrow on a flowchart indicates a transfer from one account to another account, signifying that the first account is being decreased and the second account is being increased. The typical arrow on a cost accounting flowchart therefore leads from the credit side of one account to the debit side of another. These flows represent events that happen during the manufacturing process. In addition to the arrows designating "flow," other lines indicate entries for certain external transactions that are associated with the manufacturing process; an example is the entry for the purchase of raw material from an outside vendor, which is a debit to Raw Materials Inventory and a credit to Accounts Payable or Cash.

Flow of costs

Exhibit 3–3 illustrates the flowchart concept and shows the essential cost flows in a manufacturing company. The flowchart is an expansion of the situation depicted in Exhibit 3–2. Marker Pen Company, the entity involved, manufactures felt-tip pens (felt-tip pens are writing instruments similar to ball-point pens, but operating on a different principle).

The flowchart is divided into three sections: (1) *acquisition,* containing the accounts related to the acquisition of resources, which are asset and liability accounts; (2) *manufacture,* containing the accounts related to the manufacturing process; and (3) *sale,* the accounts related to the sale of products.

Events for a particular month depicted on the flowchart may be explained as follows:

1. During the month, $52,000 of raw materials were purchased on open account, $20,000 of various other assets were purchased for cash, and $60,000 of accounts payable were paid. The journal entries recording these transactions are as follows:

   a. Raw materials inventory 52,000
        Accounts payable   52,000

   b. (Various asset accounts) 20,000
        Cash   20,000

   c. Accounts payable 60,000
        Cash   60,000

EXHIBIT 3–3
Account flowchart of Marker Pen Company ($000 omitted)

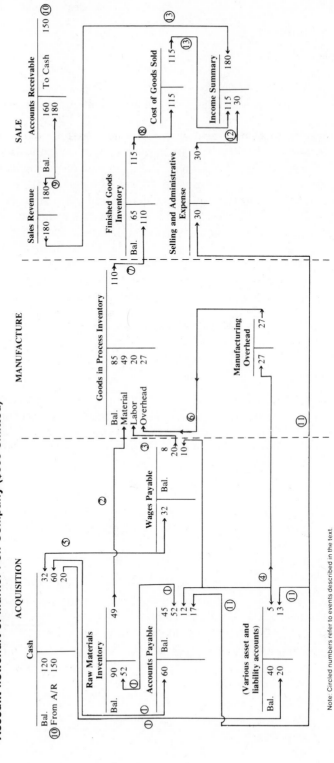

Note: Circled numbers refer to events described in the text.

2. During the month, raw materials costing $49,000 (principally felt tips, plastic compound, ink, and wicks) were withdrawn from inventory and sent to the factory to be worked on. This decrease in Raw Materials Inventory and increase in Goods in Process Inventory is recorded in the following journal entry:

Goods in process inventory	49,000	
Raw materials inventory		49,000

3. During the month, employees worked on this material and fashioned it into pens. The amount which they earned, $20,000, is the direct labor cost. It is added to Goods in Process Inventory, and the resulting liability increases Wages Payable, as recorded in the following journal entry:

Goods in process inventory	20,000	
Wages payable		20,000

4. Manufacturing overhead costs were incurred during the month amounting to $27,000. Of the total, $12,000 was ascertained from current invoices for such things as electricity and telephone bills, so the offsetting credits were to Accounts Payable. Indirect labor costs were $10,000, with the offsetting credit to Wages Payable. The remaining $5,000 represented depreciation, the charge-off of prepaid expenses, and other credits to asset accounts. All of these items are here collected in the general account, Manufacturing Overhead; but in practice they are usually recorded in separate overhead cost accounts, one for each type of cost. The journal entry follows:

Manufacturing overhead	27,000	
Accounts payable		12,000
Wages payable		10,000
(Various asset and liability accounts)		5,000

5. Employees were paid $32,000 cash. This decreased the liability account, Wages Payable, and also decreased Cash. (The payment of wages also involves social security taxes, withholding taxes, and certain other complications; for simplicity these have been omitted.) The journal entry follows:

Wages payable	32,000	
Cash		32,000

6. Since the manufacturing overhead is a part of the cost of the pens that were worked on during the month, the total cost incurred is transferred to Goods in Process Inventory, as in the following journal entry:

Goods in process inventory	27,000	
Manufacturing overhead		27,000

7. Pens that cost $110,000 were completed during the month and were transferred to Finished Goods Inventory. This resulted in a decrease in Goods in Process Inventory, as recorded in the following journal entry:

Finished goods inventory 110,000
    Goods in process inventory   110,000

8. Pens that cost $115,000 were sold during the month. Physically, these pens were removed from inventory and shipped to customers. On the accounting records, this is reflected by a credit to Finished Goods Inventory and a debit to Cost of Goods Sold, as in the following journal entry:

Cost of goods sold 115,000
    Finished goods inventory   115,000

9. For the same pens, sales revenue of $180,000 was earned; and this is recorded in the accounts as a credit to Sales and a debit to Accounts Receivable. Note that the Sales Revenue credit described here and the Cost of Goods Sold debit described in Entry No. 8 related to the same physical products, the same pens. The journal entry for the sales transaction is as follows:

Accounts receivable 180,000
    Sales revenue   180,000

10. Accounts receivable collected during the month amounted to $150,-000. Some of these collections were for sales made in the current month, but most were for sales made in previous months. The journal entry follows:

Cash 150,000
    Accounts receivable   150,000

11. During the month $30,000 of selling and administrative expenses were incurred, $17,000 of which represented credits to Accounts Payable and $13,000 credits to various asset and liability accounts. These are recorded in the following journal entry:

Selling and administrative expense 30,000
    Accounts payable   17,000
    (Various asset and liability accounts)   13,000

12. Since these expenses were applicable to the current period, the Selling and Administrative Expense account is closed to the Income Summary account, as in the following journal entry:

Income summary 30,000
    Selling and administrative expense   30,000

13. The balances in the Sales and Cost of Goods Sold accounts are also closed to Income Summary. The balance in Income Summary

then reflects the pretax income for the period. (To simplify the example, income taxes and certain nonoperating and financial items normally appearing on income statements have been excluded.) These closing journal entries follow:

```
Sales revenue.................................................... 180,000
        Income summary...........................................         180,000

Income summary................................................. 115,000
        Cost of goods sold..........................................         115,000
```

Strictly speaking, the cost accounting system as such ends with Entry No. 8. The other entries are given in order to show the complete set of transactions in the accounting cycle.

A condensed income statement for the Marker Pen Company is shown in Exhibit 3–4.

EXHIBIT 3–4

MARKER PEN COMPANY
Income Statement
For the Month of January

Sales revenue		$180,000
Cost of goods sold:		
Finished goods inventory, January 1	$ 65,000	
Cost of goods manufactured	110,000	
Goods available for sale..	175,000	
Finished goods inventory, February 1	60,000	
Cost of goods sold		115,000
Gross margin..		65,000
Selling and administrative expenses.............................		30,000
Operating Income..		$ 35,000

The form used is similar to the income statements illustrated in *Fundamentals of Financial Accounting.* However, many manufacturing companies do not show the detailed computation of cost of goods sold, as is done on Exhibit 3–4; rather, they simply report the amount of cost of goods sold as a single item, thus:

Sales revenue	$180,000
Cost of goods sold..	115,000
Gross margin...	$ 65,000

Manufacturing statement

Some companies prepare a **manufacturing statement,** which shows how the amount for cost of goods manufactured in a period was determined. Such a statement is shown in Exhibit 3–5. In order to find the cost of

EXHIBIT 3–5

MARKER PEN COMPANY
Manufacturing Statement
For the Month of January

Raw material:

Raw materials inventory, January 1	$ 90,000	
Add: Raw material purchased	52,000	
Raw material available for use	142,000	
Less: Raw materials inventory, February 1	93,000	
Raw material used		$ 49,000
Direct labor		20,000
Manufacturing overhead*		27,000
Total Manufacturing Costs		96,000
Add: Goods in process inventory, January 1		85,000
Total Goods in Process		181,000
Deduct: Goods in process inventory, February 1		71,000
Cost of goods manufactured		$110,000

* Usually, individual items of manufacturing overhead (indirect labor, electricity, repairs and maintenance, etc.) would be listed separately.

goods manufactured, we first must find the cost of raw material used. To do this, we start with the beginning inventory and add the amounts purchased to derive the total amount of raw material available for use. The amount of ending inventory is subtracted, and the difference is the cost of raw material used. Using goods in process inventory amounts, a similar approach is used to find cost of goods manufactured. Note that the final item, "Cost of goods manufactured," appears on the income statement in Exhibit 3–4. The manufacturing statement can therefore be viewed as an explanation of that item.

As a review of the cost accounting process, we suggest that you trace each item on this statement. It is derived from, and is exactly consistent with, the entries that were first shown in summary form on Exhibit 3–2 and then in more detail in Exhibit 3–3. You should be able to trace each number on the manufacturing statement to these earlier exhibits, and thereby reinforce your understanding of the meaning of the transactions.

A possible source of confusion is that the format of the manufacturing statement suggests that the cost of raw material used and the cost of goods manufactured are found by the process of deduction. The statement seems to say, for example: from the total raw material available for use of $142,000 there was deducted the ending inventory of $93,000 in order to find the raw material used of $49,000. As we have seen from the above description, this is not the way a cost accounting system actually works in practice. The amount of raw material used is found directly by adding up the individual material requisitions for withdrawals from inventory during the period. The conventional format matches the procedure used in the periodic inventory method, which was common some years ago, whereas modern cost accounting practice uses the perpetual inventory method.

JOB COSTING AND PROCESS COSTING

Consider the entries that transfer the cost of completed pens from Goods in Process Inventory to Finished Goods Inventory, and from Finished Goods Inventory to Cost of Goods Sold. (These were Entries No. 7 and No. 8 on Exhibit 3–3, in the amount of $110,000 and $115,000, respectively.) The number and types of physical units (i.e., pens) involved in these transfers can be ascertained readily by counting them; but in order to assign dollar amounts that correspond to these physical units, a *cost per unit* must be established.

If the company manufactured only one style of pen during a certain period and had no partially completed pens at the end or beginning of the period, it would be possible to divide the total amount of debits to Goods in Process Inventory by the total number of units worked on during the period to obtain the cost per unit. This unit cost could then be used to calculate the amount that is recorded for the transfer of completed pens from Goods in Process Inventory to Finished Goods Inventory; and when pens of this type were sold, the same unit cost could be used to calculate the amount that is debited to Cost of Goods Sold and credited to Finished Goods Inventory. If the factory made more than one kind of product, however, such a simple calculation would not give results that fitted the facts, since one product probably required more direct material, more direct labor, or more manufacturing overhead — that is, it cost more — than another. If the entries that transfer completed goods from Goods in Process Inventory to Finished Goods Inventory and subsequently to Cost of Goods Sold are to reflect the facts in such a situation, there must be some means of taking these differences into account.

> *EXAMPLE:* Assume the pen factory made two grades of pen, Style A with a manufacturing cost of $4 per dozen and Style B with a manufacturing cost of $6 per dozen. The transfers from Goods in Process Inventory to Finished Goods Inventory and from Finished Goods Inventory to Cost of Goods Sold should recognize these differences in cost. Assume that the company manufactures 15,000 dozen of each style a month but does not keep track of the costs of each style separately. Total manufacturing costs are $150,000 a month, and unit manufacturing costs are $5 (= $150,000 ÷ 30,000). If 30,000 dozen pens were sold in a month, cost of goods sold would be reported as $150,000 (= 30,000 × $5), regardless of the proportion of Style A and Style B. In any month in which the sales of Style A were higher or lower than those of Style B, the reported cost of goods sold would be incorrect. For example,

	Cost per unit	September		October	
		Units sold	Cost	Units sold	Cost
Style A	$4	10,000	$ 40,000	20,000	$ 80,000
Style B	6	20,000	120,000	10,000	60,000
Total		30,000	$160,000	30,000	$140,000

The total number of pens sold was 30,000 dozen in each month, but because the proportion of higher cost pens was greater in September than in October, the cost of goods sold actually was $160,000 in September and $140,000 in October. If the pens were costed at the *average* cost of $5 per dozen, cost of goods sold would be reported as $150,000 in each month, which is incorrect.

There are two principal systems for finding the costs of individual products. They are called, respectively, job order costing and process costing. These cost accounting systems correspond to the two principal types of manufacturing operations. In one type of manufacturing, which is often called the **job shop** type, the factory works on a series of discrete jobs, each one of which has different specifications. The different styles of shoes in a shoe factory have already been mentioned. Other examples are the various types of furniture made in a furniture factory and the products made in a machine tool factory. In the other type of manufacturing, often called the **process** type, a single product, or an unvarying mix of products, is produced continuously. Petroleum refineries and many other chemical processing plants are of this type.

Essentially, a job order cost system collects cost for each physically identifiable job or batch of work as it moves through the factory, regardless of the accounting period in which the work is done; while a process cost system collects costs for all the products worked on during an accounting period, and determines unit costs by dividing the total costs for the period by the total number of units worked on in the period.

Job order costing

The "job" in a job order cost system may consist of a single unit (e.g., a turbine or a computer), or it may consist of all units of identical or similar products covered by a single job or production order (e.g., 1,000 printed books or two dozen Style 652 blouses). Usually each job is given an identification number, and its costs are collected on a separate record that is set up for that number. Anyone who has had an automobile repaired at a garage has seen such a record, except that the amounts that the customer sees have been converted from costs to retail prices. Exhibit 3–6 shows such a **job cost record.** It contains spaces to record the individual elements of cost that are charged to that job. These costs are

EXHIBIT 3–6
Job cost record

Product: Item 607					Job No.: 2270
Date started: 3/28 Date completed: 4/12					
Units started: 100 Units completed: 100					

			Costs		
Week Ending	Dept. No.	Direct Material	Direct Labor	Manufacturing Overhead	Cumulative
March 31	12	$642.00	$108.00	$108.00	$ 858.00
April 7	12		222.00	222.00	1,302.00
7	16		200.00	160.00	1,662.00
14	16		250.00	200.00	2,112.00
Total		$642.00	$780.00	$690.00	$2,112.00
Unit cost		$ 6.42	$ 7.80	$ 6.90	$ 21.12

recorded as the job moves through the various departments in the factory. When the job is completed, these cost elements are totaled to find the total cost of that job. The sum of all the costs charged to all the jobs worked on in the factory during an accounting period is the basis for the entries debiting Goods in Process Inventory and crediting Raw Materials Inventory, Wages Payable, and Manufacturing Overhead accounts. When each job is completed, the total cost recorded on the job cost record is the basis for the entry transferring the product from Goods in Process Inventory to Finished Goods Inventory, and this same cost is the basis for the entry transferring the product from Finished Goods Inventory to Cost of Goods Sold when the product is sold. The total cost recorded on all job cost records for products that are still in the factory as of the end of an accounting period equals the total of the Goods in Process Inventory account at that time.

EXAMPLE: Using the data in Exhibit 3–6:

• Goods in Process Inventory on March 31 would include $858 as the cost of Job 2270; this is the cost incurred to that date.
• In April the transfer from Goods in Process Inventory to Finished Goods Inventory would include $2,112 for Job 2270.
• When units of Item 607 are sold, Finished Goods Inventory would be credited and Cost of Goods Sold would be debited at $21.12 per unit times the number of units sold.

In summary, in a job order cost system:

1. A separate job cost record is established for each job.
2. Costs chargeable to the job are entered on this record and are also debited to Goods in Process Inventory.

3. When the job is completed and transferred out of the factory, the total cost accumulated on the job cost record is the amount used to debit Finished Goods Inventory and to credit Goods in Process Inventory.
4. The balance in Goods in Process Inventory at the end of the accounting period is therefore the sum of the costs accumulated on all jobs remaining in the factory as reflected on the job cost records for uncompleted jobs.

Process costing

In a **process cost system,** all manufacturing costs for an accounting period, such as a month, are collected in Goods in Process Inventory. These costs are *not* identified with specific units of product. A record of the number of units worked on is also maintained. By dividing total costs by total units, one derives a cost per unit; and this cost per unit is used as the basis for calculating the dollar amount of the entries which record the transfer from Goods in Process Inventory to Finished Goods Inventory, and the subsequent transfer from Finished Goods Inventory to Cost of Goods Sold.

> *EXAMPLE:* In a factory using a process cost system, the total manufacturing cost in March was $200,000 and the number of units was 100,000. The cost per unit was therefore $2, and this unit cost is used to make the transfer from Goods in Process Inventory to Finished Goods Inventory. Assuming the 100,000 units were completed, the entry would be:
>
> Finished goods inventory 200,000
>   Goods in process inventory   200,000
>
> If in April 50,000 units were sold, the unit cost of $2 would be used in arriving at the amount of the entry:
>
> Cost of goods sold 100,000
>   Finished goods inventory   100,000

Equivalent production. One special problem that arises in a process cost system is that of taking into account the products that are only partially completed at the end of an accounting period. The units that were *worked on* in September include the following: (1) units that were both started and completed during September; plus (2) units that were worked on but not completed by the end of September; plus (3) units that were started in August (or earlier) and completed in September.

Since 100 percent of the costs of the first type were incurred in September but only a portion of the costs of the second and third types, production activity for September cannot be determined simply by adding up the number of units worked on during September. The three types of units must be converted to a common base, called **equivalent production,** that is, the equivalent of one completed unit. In order to convert the number of uncompleted products into their equivalence in terms of completed units, the assumption is often made that units still in process at the end of the period are half (i.e., 50 percent) complete, and similarly that units in process at the beginning of the period were half complete at that time. Using the 50 percent assumption, each unit started and completed during the period is given a weight of one, each unit in process at the end of the period is given a weight of one half, and each unit in process at the beginning of the period also is given a weight of one half. The sum of these amounts is the equivalent production of the period.[6]

> *EXAMPLE:* In a certain factory, costs incurred in September amounted to $22,000. During September, units were worked on as shown in Exhibit 3–7, that is, 100 units were completed that had been started in August; 2,000 units were started and completed in September; and another 300 units were started in September, but not completed. Thus, some work was done during September on a total of 2,400 units. The unit cost is *not* calculated by dividing $22,000 by the 2,400 units worked on, however; for to do so would be to neglect the costs incurred in the prior month for some units and the costs that will be incurred in the next month for still other units. Instead, it is assumed that in September one half of the work was done on the partially completed units, so that each of them is equivalent to one half a unit that was begun and completed within the month. The number of equivalent units was therefore $\frac{1}{2}(100) + 2,000 + \frac{1}{2}(300) = 2,200$ units. Since total manufacturing costs for September were $22,000, the unit cost was $10.
>
> The 2,100 units completed in September and transferred to Finished Goods Inventory would be costed at $10 per unit, a total of $21,000. The 300 partially completed units remaining in Goods in Process Inventory at the end of September would be costed at *one half* the unit cost, or $5 per unit, since it is assumed that they are only half completed.

The use of equivalent production units, described above, applies to direct labor cost and to manufacturing overhead cost. Direct material cost may or may not be treated differently, depending on when direct material enters the production process. If material is added evenly throughout the production process, it could reasonably be costed by use of the 50 percent assumption.

If, as is perhaps more common, all the raw material for a unit enters production at the beginning of the process, the direct material cost per unit would be obtained by dividing the total cost of material used during the month by the number of units *started* during the month.

In any event, some reasonable assumption has to be made. In a process cost system, there is no precise way of determining the amount of costs attributable to partially completed units.

---

[6] A more precise procedure would be to estimate the actual stage of completion, but this involves more effort. Another variation is to calculate the equivalent production for each department through which the product passes, rather than to the factory as a whole.

EXHIBIT 3–7

Calculation of equivalent production

	Period in which costs were incurred		
Type of units	*August*	*September*	*October*
100 started in prior month	$\frac{1}{2}$ of 100	$\frac{1}{2}$ of 100	
2,000 started and completed in current month..		2,000	
300 to be completed next month		$\frac{1}{2}$ of 300	$\frac{1}{2}$ of 300

Calculation of equivalent production for September

		Gross units	Equivalent production
A.	On hand at beginning	$100 \times \frac{1}{2}$	50
B.	Started and completed..............................	2,000	2,000
C.	On hand at end	$300 \times \frac{1}{2}$	150
	Total	2,400	2,200

Unit cost: $22,000 ÷ 2,200 units = $10.

Goods in Process Inventory

Balance, Sept. 1 (100 units @ $5)*	500	To finished goods inventory (2,100 units @ $10)	21,000
		Balance, Sept. 30	
Costs incurred	22,000	(300 units @ $5)	1,500
	22,500		22,500
Balance, Oct. 1	1,500		

* In this example, it is assumed that costs in August were also $10 per equivalent unit. If this was not in fact so, an error is introduced, but in a process cost situation, the beginning and ending inventories are usually so small that the error can be disregarded.

EXAMPLE: Assume that the $22,000 of cost in the above example excludes direct material cost. All the direct material is issued at the beginning of the production process. In September, the total cost of direct material put into production was $6,900. During the month, 2,300 units were started into production (see Exhibit 3–7). The unit raw material cost was therefore $3.

The inclusion of direct material costs would modify the amounts given in Exhibit 3–7. If we now take the $10 per unit cost computed there and add to it the $3 per unit direct material cost, the total unit cost becomes $13. The 2,100 units transferred to Finished Goods Inventory would be costed at $13 × 2,100 = $27,300. The 300 units in Goods in Process Inventory at the end of September would be costed at material cost of $3 per unit plus other costs of $\frac{1}{2}$($10) = $5 per unit, as before. The total unit cost for these items is therefore $8, and the total inventory amount for the 300 units is $2,400.

Summary. In summary, a process cost system works like this:

1. The costs of resources used in the manufacturing process during the accounting period are accumulated as debits to the Goods in Process Inventory account.
2. For cost elements, such as direct labor and manufacturing overhead, that are incurred *throughout* the manufacturing process:
    a. Production is measured in terms of the number of equivalent units of production.
    b. A cost per unit is found by dividing total cost by the number of equivalent units.
3. For cost elements, such as direct material, that are incurred at the *beginning* of the manufacturing process, the cost per unit is found by dividing total cost by the number of units that started the production process.
4. Finished Goods Inventory is debited, and Goods in Process Inventory is credited, by an amount that is equal to the number of units completed in the period multiplied by these costs per unit.
5. Assuming that all direct material is issued at the beginning of the production process, the balance in Goods in Process Inventory at the end of an accounting period is the direct material cost of the units still in the factory plus an appropriate share (say, 50 percent) of the total direct labor and manufacturing overhead cost of these units.

Choice of a system

In most situations, the nature of the manufacturing process indicates clearly which is more appropriate: a job order system or a process cost system. Nevertheless, since a process cost system requires less record-keeping than a job order system, there is a tendency to use it even though the products manufactured are not entirely alike. Thus, a manufacturer of children's shoes may use a process cost system, even though there are some differences in cost among the various sizes, styles, and colors of shoes manufactured. By contrast, manufacturers of men's or women's shoes usually use a job order system because the differences among the cost of the various styles are so significant that a process cost system would produce misleading results.

In a process cost system, the unit costs are averages derived from the total cost of the period. Differences in the costs of individual products are not revealed. Thus, if there are important reasons for keeping track of the differences between one product and another, or between one production lot of the same type product and another, then a job cost system is more appropriate. For example, a job cost system would invariably be used if the customer paid for the specific item or production order on the basis of its cost (as is often the case in machine shops, print shops, and other "job shop" companies). Also, use of a job cost system makes it possible to examine actual costs on specific jobs, and this may help one to locate trouble spots; in a process cost system, costs cannot be traced to specific jobs.

For our purposes, there is no need to study differences in the detailed records required for the two types of systems. Both systems are essentially devices for collecting manufacturing costs. Either furnishes the information required for the accounting entries illustrated in Exhibit 3–3. In practice, there are many cost accounting systems that use job costing in some departments and process costing in other departments.

VARIATIONS IN PRACTICE

An accounting system exactly like that outlined in Exhibit 3–3 will probably never be found in actual practice since it is a schematic representation of underlying structures. Companies build on the basic structure by adding accounts that collect the data in more detail so as to meet their particular needs for information. A company may, for example, set up several raw material inventory accounts, each one covering a different type of material, instead of a single account as shown in Exhibit 3–3. Alternatively, the Raw Materials Inventory account may be a controlling account, controlling thousands of individual subsidiary accounts. Another common variation is to have several goods in process accounts, one for each department in the factory. A system using several goods in process accounts is shown in Exhibit 3–8. It is assumed that the pen factory has three departments. Barrels are manufactured in the barrel department, wicks are manufactured in the wick department, and completed components are sent to the assembly department where they are assembled into pens. Completed pens are transferred to finished goods inventory. It will be noted that such a system is essentially like that shown in Exhibit 3–3 except that work is transferred from one department to another. The finished goods of one department become, in effect, the raw material of the next department.

DEMONSTRATION CASE

Part A. Flow of costs

Refer to Exhibit 3–8. You are asked to describe the meaning of each of the entries depicted on the flowchart diagram, and to calculate the ending balance in Goods in Process Inventory in each department. Although this requires careful attention to detail, it will aid your understanding of the flow of costs through a cost accounting system.

After you have traced the entries, you can check your understanding by referring to Exhibit 3–9. This exhibit shows how much of the three elements of cost—direct material, direct labor, and manufacturing over-

EXHIBIT 3–8

Cost system with departmental accounts ($000 omitted)

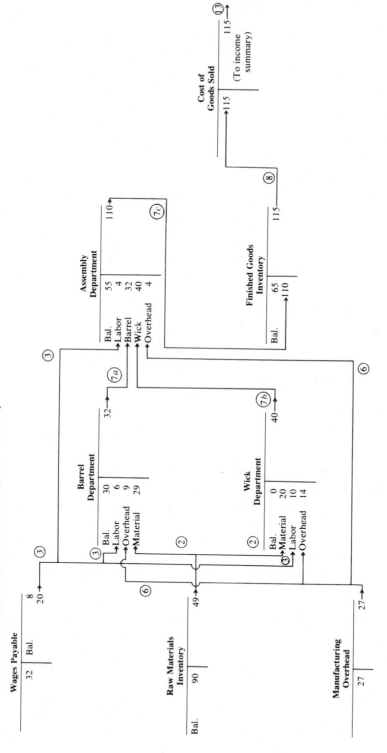

head—were debited to each of the three departments. For example, the balance in the Barrel Department goods in process account at the beginning of the period was $30,000. During the period, costs incurred in the department were $29,000 for direct material, $6,000 for direct labor, and $9,000 for manufacturing overhead. A total of $32,000 of finished barrels was transferred from the Barrel Department account to the Assembly Department account. The balance in the Barrel Department account at the end of the month was therefore $30,000 + $29,000 + $6,000 + $9,000 − $32,000 = $42,000.

EXHIBIT 3–9
Assignment of cost elements (000 omitted)

Entry	Total	Barrel	Wick	Assembly
Beginning balance............................	$85	$30	$ 0	$ 55
2. Direct material	49	29	20	0
3. Direct labor..	20	6	10	4
6. Manufacturing overhead	27	9	14	4
7a. From barrel..				32
7b. From wick				40
Total debits to department		74	44	135
Credits to department		32	40	110
Ending balance in goods in process..................	$71	$42	$ 4	$ 25

Above *Departments* spans the Barrel, Wick, and Assembly columns.

Observe that the sum of the three amounts for each cost item agrees with the amount debited to the Goods in Process Inventory account for that item shown on Exhibit 3–3. This correspondence arises because the Barrel Department, Wick Department, and Assembly Department accounts are in fact three goods in process inventory accounts.

Observe also the transfers between departments, that is, the $32,000 credited to Barrel Department and debited to Assembly Department, and the transfer of $40,000 from Wick Department to Assembly Department. The $32,000 represents the costs of the barrels completed during the month, and the $40,000 represents the cost of the wicks completed.

The other transactions on Exhibit 3–8 are the same as those on Exhibit 3–3. If you had difficulty in understanding any of them, refer back to the explanations given for that exhibit.

Part B.   Unit costs

To review your understanding of equivalent production units, assume that the pen factory used a process cost system, that raw material entered at the beginning of the process, and that the number of units in the Wick Department account was as follows:

Units (dozens)

On hand, beginning of month 0
Completed during the month 26,000
On hand, end of month 4,000

Using the data in Exhibit 3–9, you are asked to calculate the cost per dozen wicks for the month, and to explain how the ending balance of $4,000 in the Wick Department account and the transfer from Wick Department account to Assembly Department account of $40,000 were calculated.

After you have made this calculation, you can check your work, as follows:

For direct material, the total amount used was $20,000. Since material is used at the beginning of the process, this amount applies to all units started, which was 26,000 + 4,000 = 30,000. Direct material cost per unit was therefore $20,000 ÷ 30,000 units = $0.67.

For direct labor and manufacturing overhead costs, we must calculate the equivalent production. Since no wicks were on hand at the beginning of the month, equivalent production is the number of units completed plus one half the number of units on hand at the end of the month, that is, 26,000 + ½(4,000) = 28,000. Total direct labor and manufacturing overhead costs were $24,000. The cost per equivalent unit was therefore $24,000 ÷ 28,000 units = $0.86.

The unit cost applicable to the transfer to Assembly Department account was:

Material $0.67
Labor and overhead 0.86
Unit cost $1.53

The total cost of the wicks transferred to Assembly was therefore 26,000 × $1.53 = $39,780 (rounded to $40,000 in Exhibit 3–9).

The goods in process inventory of the Wick Department at the end of the month was $4,400, calculated as follows:

	Equivalent units	Unit cost	Cost
Direct material	4,000	$0.67	$2,680
Labor and overhead.......................................	2,000	0.86	1,720
Goods in process inventory			$4,400

This amount is rounded to $4,000 in Exhibit 3–9.

SUMMARY

Cost is a word of many meanings. In this chapter we have discussed cost in the sense of the full cost of a cost objective; cost in this sense measures all the resources used for a cost objective. Our cost objective was the manufacture of a product. The measurement of manufacturing costs is a two-step process: First, all the manufacturing costs applicable to an accounting period are collected; and, secondly, these costs are assigned to all the products that were worked on during that accounting period.

The second of these steps is the province of cost accounting. It is accomplished by assigning to cost objectives (1) their direct costs, that is, the costs that are directly traceable to each cost objective; and (2) a fair share of the indirect costs, that is, those costs incurred for several cost objectives.

A cost accounting system collects costs and assigns them to cost objectives. In a factory, costs are accumulated in a Goods in Process Inventory account as resources are used in the manufacturing process, and these costs are then transferred to a Finished Goods Inventory account when the products have been completed. In order to make the transfer from Goods in Process to Finished Goods, there must be some system for measuring the cost of individual completed units. There are two such systems: (1) job order costing, in which costs are accumulated separately for each individual item or for a lot of similar items; and (2) process costing, in which costs are accumulated for all units together, and then are divided between completed units and partially completed units according to some reasonable assumption as to the stage of completion at the end of the period.

IMPORTANT TERMS

Prime cost	Indirect cost
Manufacturing cost	Raw materials inventory
Conversion costs	Goods in process inventory
Direct cost	Finished goods inventory
Direct material cost	Job order cost system
Direct labor cost	Process cost system
Manufacturing overhead cost	Equivalent production

QUESTIONS FOR DISCUSSION

1. Why is it conceptually preferable to classify an item as a direct cost rather than an indirect cost?

2. Give three reasons, with an example for each, why not all items of cost are classified as direct costs.

3. Distinguish between direct labor cost and indirect labor cost, giving an example of each.

4. Distinguish between direct material cost and indirect material cost, giving an example of each.

5. Distinguish between material cost, supplies cost, and services cost.

6. What is the rationale for saying that indirect costs, which are not traced to an individual cost objective, are nevertheless part of the cost of that cost objective? (Refer to Chapter 2, page 36, if you are unsure of the answer to this question.)

7. The cost objectives in a certain motel are (a) room rentals and (b) meals. List some of the elements of cost you would expect to find in a motel, distinguishing between those that are direct costs of each of these cost objectives and those that are indirect costs.

8. Would you expect to find Raw Materials, Goods in Process, and Finished Goods Inventory accounts in the accounting system of a motel? Why?

9. A law firm may perform an engagement for a client that extends over a period of several months. It may bill the client when the engagement is completed. Would such a firm have a work in process inventory account? If so, how would the amount be arrived at? Give examples of costs that probably would be included.

10. Give as complete a list as you can of the items that constitute the direct cost, to your school, of the accounting course you are now taking. How should the amount of each item be arrived at?

11. Consider a division or subsidiary of a large corporation (such as the Chevrolet Division of General Motors Corporation) as a cost objective. Give examples of cost items that would be direct costs of that cost objective. Give examples that would be indirect costs.

12. A direct cost of a division of a company is the property taxes assessed on plant and equipment used by the division. It is unrealistic to say that these taxes "benefit" the division. What is the rationale for including such taxes as a direct cost?

13. Distinguish between the manufacturing cost of a month and the cost of goods manufactured in that month.

14. In an account flowchart for a cost accounting system, the flow is usually from the credit side of one account to the debit side of another account. Why is the flow in this direction rather than the reverse?

15. Marketing costs are not included in product costs reported in finished goods inventory. Why?

16. What is the essential difference between a job order cost system and a process cost system with respect to the way in which each arrives at unit costs?

17. Under what circumstances is job order costing rather than process costing appropriate?

18. What determines whether or not the equivalent production units method is used for direct material cost?

PROBLEMS

3–1. The following data pertain to the Bolton Company for July:

Raw materials inventory, July 1 .... $ 80,000
Goods in process inventory, July 1 100,000

Finished goods inventory, July 1	60,000
Raw material purchases	45,000
Raw material issued	65,000
Direct labor costs incurred	35,000
Manufacturing overhead costs incurred	42,000
Costs of goods completed and transferred	180,000
Costs of goods sold	175,000

Required:

A. Prepare T-accounts for the three inventory accounts and cost of goods sold.
B. Record the beginning balances and post the transactions for the month.
C. Draw arrows to show the transfers between accounts.
D. Calculate the inventory balances as of July 31.

3–2. Prepare journal entries for the transactions of the Bolton Company in Problem 3–1.

3–3. Sales revenue was $200,000 in July for the Bolton Company in Problem 3–1.

Required:

A. Prepare a manufacturing statement.
B. Prepare an income statement.

3–4. Costs incurred and other data pertinent to operations for the month of April for Simplex Manufacturing Corporation follow (000's omitted):

Raw material purchases	$230	Factory rent	$ 50
Freight–in on purchases	10	Rental of retail store	20
Factory supplies used	15	Office heat, light, power	8
Indirect labor	80	Raw material used in	
Direct labor	400	production	200
Depreciation of factory		Cost of goods completed	
machinery	75	during April	700
Factory heat, light, power	12	Finished goods ending	
Repairs to factory	10	inventory	150

Raw Materials Inventory

3/31	
Inventory 50	

Goods in Process Inventory

3/31	
Inventory 60	

Wages Payable

Finished Goods Inventory

3/31	
Inventory 200	

Manufacturing Overhead

Cost of Goods Sold

Required:

A. Complete the postings to a flowchart like the model above. Include arrows to show the flow of costs from raw material through the cost of goods sold.

B. Prepare journal entries for the flow of costs.

3–5. The Overhill Bicycle Company had the following account balances as of May 1:

Cash	$115,000 dr.
Accounts receivable..	150,000 dr.
Raw materials inventory	80,000 dr.
Goods in process inventory	75,000 dr.
Finished goods inventory	50,000 dr.
Accounts payable	42,000 cr.
Wages payable...	7,000 cr.
Various asset and liability accounts..............................	35,000 dr.

During the month of May, the following transactions occurred:

1. Raw materials of $50,000 were purchased on open account.
2. Various other assets in the amount of $19,000 were purchased for cash, and $57,000 of accounts payable were paid.
3. Raw materials costing $50,000 (mainly frames, wheels, tires, handlebars, seats, pedals, chains, gears, and brakes) were issued and sent to the factory for assembly into bicycles.
4. Direct labor costs of $18,000 were incurred.
5. The following items of manufacturing overhead costs were incurred but not paid:

Utilities	$10,000
Indirect labor............................	11,000
Depreciation.............................	4,000

6. Employees were paid $30,000 cash.
7. Manufacturing overhead costs for the month were charged to goods in process.
8. Bicycles costing $104,000 were completed and transferred to finished goods.
9. Bicycles costing $113,000 were sold for $175,000 on account.
10. Accounts receivable of $145,000 were collected.
11. Distribution and general and administrative expenses in the amount of $29,000 were incurred, $17,000 of which represented credits to accounts payable.

Required:

A. Prepare an account flowchart for May using the above information. Include arrows to indicate flows between accounts.

B. Prepare journal entries for the May transactions.

C. Prepare a manufacturing statement and an income statement for May.

3-6. The following data pertain to manufacturing activities of the Comfort Chain Company for April:

Raw materials inventory, April 1	$120,000
Raw material purchases	75,000
Raw material used	85,000
Goods in process inventory, April 1	70,000
Goods in process inventory, April 30	72,000
Finished goods inventory, April 1	42,000
Finished goods inventory, April 30	40,000
Direct labor costs incurred	55,000
Utilities	10,000
Indirect labor costs incurred	25,000
Depreciation of machinery	15,000
Repairs and maintenance	10,000

For April, sales revenue was $285,000, and distribution and general and administrative expenses were $35,000.

Required:

A. Prepare a manufacturing statement for April.
B. Prepare an income statement for April.

3-7. Job No. 1321 for the Staycool Company was the installation of air conditioning in a new 50-unit apartment building. Work began on March 7, and the job was completed on March 18. Costs were incurred as follows:

Mar. 8 Ductwork costing $2,500 was delivered to the job for installation.
      10 Wiring and other electrical items costing $750 were delivered to the job for installation.
      11 Direct labor on the job for the first week was 250 hours at $8 per hour.
      14 Fifty compressor and cooling coil units costing $400 each were delivered to the job for installation.
      18 Direct labor on the job for the second week was 240 hours at $8 per hour.

Overhead costs are assigned to jobs on the basis of 110 percent of direct labor.

Required:

A. Prepare a job cost record for Job No. 1321.
B. If the Staycool Company agreed to do Job No. 1321 at manufacturing cost plus 10 percent, what price would it bill to the customer?
C. What would be the Staycool Company's gross margin on this job?

3-8. The Handy Tool Company manufactures various tools and parts for small gasoline engines, some for special order and some for stock. At the end of April a summary of job cost sheets reflects the following data:

Job No.	Customer or stock No.	Total cost
1,002	Part No. 32	$4,500
1,100	Customer No. 45	7,800
1,205	Customer No. 69	7,200

During May two new jobs were started: 1,206 for stock Part No. 18, and 1,207 for Customer No. 70. Job Nos. 1,002, 1,100, and 1,206 were completed during May. Customer No. 45 paid $20,000 in full for his order. None of the stock parts were sold. Total costs incurred in May are shown below by job number:

Job No.	Amount
1,002	$4,900
1,100	8,000
1,205	600
1,206	5,000
1,207	3,100

Required:

A. Produce a summary job cost sheet to show the jobs still in process May 31.

B. Compute the cost of goods completed (manufactured) for May.

C. Compute the gross margin for May.

3-9. The Randall Company uses a process cost system. Total manufacturing costs for February were $100,000. Production data for the month were as follows:

	Units
Beginning goods in process	500
Started and completed..................................	9,000
Ending goods in process...............................	1,500

Required:

A. Assuming that the partially completed units were 50 percent complete, calculate equivalent production in units for February.

B. What is the unit cost and total cost of the units transferred to finished goods and the units remaining in goods in process inventory?

3-10. Purity Enterprises manufactures a single product, maple sundae topping. Syrup, flavoring, and preservatives are mixed, cooked for several hours in vats, cooled, and put into gallon cans to await shipment. On March 1, the vats were empty. During March, 20,000 gallons of topping were completed. On March 31, there were 5,000 gallons left in the vats, all completed as to raw materials and 50 percent complete as to direct labor and manufacturing overhead. Actual production costs for the month were $50,000 for direct materials, $9,000 for direct labor, and $13,500 for manufacturing overhead.

Required:

A. Compute the average cost of making a gallon of topping during March.

B. Prepare the journal entry to transfer the March production to finished goods.

3-11. The following data pertain to the Carter Company for September:

Raw materials inventory, September 1 .... $ 65,000
Goods in process inventory, September 1 80,000
Finished goods inventory, September 1 50,000
Raw material purchases 40,000
Raw material issued 75,000
Direct labor costs incurred 45,000
Manufacturing overhead costs incurred 60,000
Cost of goods completed and transferred 165,000
Cost of goods sold 190,000

Required:

A. Prepare T-accounts for the three inventory accounts and cost of goods sold.
B. Record the beginning balances and post the transactions for the month.
C. Draw arrows to show the transfers between accounts.
D. Calculate the inventory balances as of September 30.

3-12. Prepare journal entries for the transactions of the Carter Company in Problem 3-11.

3-13. Assume that sales revenue was $220,000 in September for the Carter Company in Problem 3-11.

Required:

A. Prepare a manufacturing statement.
B. Prepare an income statement.

3-14. Journalize the entries for the transactions reflected in the T-accounts below for the Connecticut Barrel Company for the month of December:

Cash		Accounts Receivable	
Bal. 11/30 10,000	60,000	Bal. 11/30 15,000	70,000
70,000		80,000	

Sales		Cost of Sales	
	80,000	50,000	
80,000			50,000

Raw Materials Inventory		Goods in Process Inventory	
Bal. 11/30 14,000	25,000	Bal. 11/30 12,000	65,000
27,000		23,000	
		25,000	
		18,000	

Finished Goods Inventory		Accounts Payable	
Bal. 11/30 25,000	50,000	60,000	Bal. 11/30 11,000
65,000			76,000

Wages Payable		Factory Indirect Costs	
23,000	23,000	18,000	18,000

Selling and Administrative Expense		Income Summary	
8,000	8,000	50,000	80,000
		8,000	

3–15. The Bright Lamp Company had the following account balances as of March 1, 1977:

Cash	$130,000 dr.
Accounts receivable	165,000 dr.
Raw materials inventory	95,000 dr.
Goods in process inventory	90,000 dr.
Finished goods inventory	75,000 dr.
Accounts payable	48,000 cr.
Wages payable	10,000 cr.
Various asset and liability accounts	45,000 dr.

During the month of March, the following transactions occurred:

1. Raw materials of $55,000 were purchased on open account.
2. Various other assets in the amount of $21,000 were purchased for cash, and $62,000 of accounts payable were paid.
3. Raw materials costing $53,000 (mainly bases, shades, and electrical parts) were issued and sent to the factory for assembly into lamps.
4. Direct labor costs of $24,000 were incurred.
5. The following items of manufacturing overhead costs were incurred but not paid:

Utilities	$15,000
Indirect labor	12,000
Depreciation	4,000

6. Employees were paid $33,000 cash.
7. Manufacturing overhead costs for the month were charged to goods in process.
8. Lamps costing $115,000 were completed and transferred to finished goods.
9. Lamps costing $120,000 were sold for $185,000 on account.
10. Accounts receivable of $165,000 were collected.
11. Distribution and general and administrative expenses of $32,000 were incurred, $20,000 of which represented credits to accounts payable.

Required:

A. Prepare an accounting flowchart for March using the above information. Include arrows to indicate flows between accounts.
B. Prepare journal entries for the March transactions.
C. Prepare a manufacturing statement and an income statement for March.

3–16. The following data pertain to manufacturing activities of the Folding Furniture Company for October:

Raw materials inventory, October 1	$125,000
Raw material purchases	78,000
Raw material used	100,000
Goods in process inventory, October 1	75,000
Goods in process inventory, October 31	85,000
Finished goods inventory, October 1	45,000
Finished goods inventory, October 31	50,000
Direct labor costs incurred	60,000
Utilities	12,000
Indirect labor costs incurred	27,000
Depreciation of machinery	16,000
Repairs and maintenance	10,000

Sales revenue was $300,000, and distribution and general and administrative expenses were $39,000 for October.

Required:

A. Prepare a manufacturing statement for October.
B. Prepare an income statement for October.

3–17. Establish a job order cost record to show the accumulation of costs for Job No. 786, for a special-order refrigeration unit. Data pertinent to the costs of the job are as follows:

Jan. 1 One hundred pounds of raw material C costing $10 per pound were requisitioned from the storeroom and used on the job.

7 Direct labor incurred on the job amounted to 100 hours at $7 per hour.

10 Raw material D was purchased at a cost of $1,500 for 150 pounds. This material will be used on Job No. 786 and on other future jobs requiring the same material.

11 Five pounds of raw material D were requisitioned from the storeroom and used on the job.

14 Direct labor cost incurred on the job amounted to 200 hours at $7 per hour and 10 hours at $10 per hour.

15 Factory indirect cost is assigned to the job on the basis of 150 percent of direct labor.

16 The job is completed.

Required:

A. Complete the job order cost record for Job No. 786.
B. If the company contracted to sell this refrigeration unit at manufacturing cost plus 10 percent, what price would it bill to the customer?
C. What would be the company's gross margin on this job?

3–18. The Able Assembly Company began business on January 1. Its employees are paid $7 per hour. It purchased and received $10,000 of raw material on January 2. Manufacturing overhead costs are charged to production based on 100 percent of direct labor costs. During January, there were three jobs with costs incurred as follows:

	Job No. 1	Job No. 2	Job No. 3
Direct materials..................	$1,600	$3,000	$2,000
Direct labor	100 hours	200 hours	50 hours
Status, January 31..............	Complete	Complete	Incomplete
	Sold for	Not sold	
	$4,000 cash		

Required:

A. What are the balances in each inventory account as of January 31?

B. Prepare an income statement for January.

3–19. The Steven Company uses a process cost system. Total manufacturing costs for May were $50,000. Production data for the month were as follows:

	Units
Beginning goods in process	1,000
Started and completed	8,500
Ending goods in process.................................	2,000

Required:

A. Assuming that the partially completed units were 50 percent complete, calculate equivalent production in units for May.

B. What is the unit cost and total cost of the units transferred to finished goods and the units remaining in goods in process inventory?

3–20. The Phideaux Company manufactures a single product, dry dog food. It began operations on June 1. During the month, 30,000 pounds of dog food were completed. On June 30, there were 5,000 pounds still in process, all completed as to ingredients and 50 percent complete as to direct labor and manufacturing overhead. Actual production costs for the month were $60,000 for ingredients, $13,000 for direct labor, and $16,250 for manufacturing overhead.

Required:

A. Compute the average cost of making a pound of Phideaux dog food during June.

B. Prepare the journal entry to transfer the June production to finished goods.

3–21. Diversified Products, Inc., manufactures a product in four processes. Below are data relating to the final process, Process 4, for the month of March:

Goods in Process 4 on March 1 were 600 units shown at a cost of $1,200. Of this amount, $600 was the cost as transferred from Process 3, and $600 was direct labor and overhead of Process 4. These units were assumed to be 50 percent complete as to labor and overhead.

During March, $6,000 of direct labor cost and $6,600 of overhead cost were incurred in Process 4.

During March, 4,400 units, at $1 each, were transferred from Process 3, and 4,000 units were completed and transferred to finished goods inventory.

Units in process at the end of March were assumed to be 50 percent complete as to direct labor and overhead. (No direct material was added in Process 4.)

Required:

A. What was the goods in process inventory in units on March 31?
B. What were the equivalent units of production in March?
C. What was the direct labor and overhead cost per equivalent unit in March?
D. What was the dollar amount transferred to finished goods inventory?
E. What was the balance in goods in process inventory as of April 1?

3–22. In Part B of the Demonstration Case, it assumed that raw material entered the wick department *at the beginning* of the process. Suppose, instead, that raw material entered the wick process *throughout* the process.

Required:

Calculate the total cost of the wicks transferred to the assembly department and the ending work in process inventory of the wick department.

3–23. Refer to the flowchart in Exhibit 3–3. Assume that each of the following events occurred, rather than the related events reflected in the exhibit and described in the text:

1. No raw materials were purchased during January.
2. Only $60,000 of pens were completed during January, rather than $110,000.
3. The factory shut down for the whole month of January. Manufacturing overhead costs of $15,000 were incurred and were charged as an expense on the January income statement. Pens costing $65,000 were sold for $100,000. No direct labor or direct material costs were incurred.

Required:

Consider each of these events separately:
A. What changes would be required in the journal entries for January?
B. What would be the effect on the income statement, Exhibit 3–4?

CASE: DAVIGO FOODS COMPANY

3–24. The Davigo Foods Company, located in a tomato-growing section, had for many years produced tomato specialties such as tomato juice cocktail, tomato paste, and ketchup. In 1973, it was able to extend its production season from four to nine months by the addition of various types of prepared spaghetti dinners and ravioli. In order to keep certain skilled personnel, the company had found a place for five employees in the shipping department during the three months when the remainder of the plant was closed.

These workers had been earning a wage of $3.90 an hour at their regular work, but they were willing to accept $2.91 an hour for the time they were in the shipping department. This meant that during the three months that they were in the shipping department the five workers had collectively received $2,580 less than they would have received at their regular rate of pay. However, the regular wage rate in the shipping department was $2.40 an hour, and the shipping department therefore had been charged with $1,320 more than it ordinarily would have paid for this type of work.

The head of the shipping department was indignant that his costs were increased by this amount and contended that he should be charged at a rate not higher than the regular $2.40 rate for his department and that a fairer rate would be the beginners' rate of $1.95, since these employees were not so efficient as his experienced work force.

Required:

How would you account for the $2.91 an hour paid the five workers when they worked in the shipping department?

4

Manufacturing overhead costs

In Chapter 3, we gave an overview of cost accounting. The essence of that description was that cost accounting measures the resources used for cost objectives and that the full cost of a cost objective is the sum of (1) its direct costs and (2) a fair share of its indirect costs. The measurement of direct costs is relatively straightforward. The measurement of indirect costs of manufacturing products, which is called manufacturing overhead, is somewhat more complicated, however. We shall describe each step in this measurement process in some detail in this chapter.

Knowledge of the cost accounting process is essential to an understanding of the meaning of the costs that are the end product of the process. The purpose of the chapter is to facilitate such an understanding.

MANUFACTURING ACTIVITIES

A factory (often called a *plant*) may be a single room in a building, it may be a whole complex of buildings spread out over many acres, or it may be anywhere in between. The procedures of accounting for manufacturing overhead costs are easier to visualize if one relates them to what is actually going on in the factory. For this purpose, we shall use Marker Pen Company, the relatively small company that manufactures felt-tip pens referred to in Chapter 3. A schematic of the parts of the pen is given in Exhibit 4–1.

110

EXHIBIT 4–1
Parts of a felt-tip pen

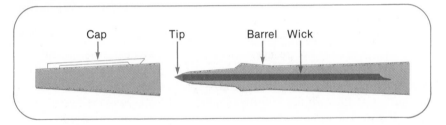

This company's factory consists of one building. In one room of this building, the barrel and the cap of the pens are manufactured. This room is called the barrel department. Employees who manufacture barrels and caps work in this room. The room contains the molding machines that are used to fabricate the barrels and caps. Employees who operate these machines are the direct workers of the department. The department is managed by a supervisor.

The factory has two other departments directly involved in the production of pens, the wick department and the assembly department. Each department has its own space, machinery, employees, and a supervisor. The factory also has a superintendent who is responsible for all manufacturing operations. The superintendent, together with production scheduling people, factory accountants, and clerical employees, work in the factory office.

The factory also contains storerooms for raw material and finished pens, and a maintenance department which keeps machinery and other assets in good condition. All employees other than those who work directly on products in the barrel, wick, and assembly departments are indirect employees, and their earnings are indirect labor costs.

Cost centers

In a cost accounting system, use is made of a device called a cost center. **A cost center is a cost objective for which costs of one or more related functions or activities are accumulated.** In the pen factory, the wick department is an example of a cost center; the costs incurred in that department are for the function or activity of manufacturing wicks for pens.

In a cost accounting system, items of cost are first accumulated in cost centers, and they are then assigned to products. For this reason a cost center is often called an **intermediate cost objective** to distinguish it from a product, which is a **final cost objective.**

Recall from Chapter 1 that a responsibility center is an organization unit headed by a manager. The wick department in the pen factory conforms to this definition, and it is therefore a responsibility center. The wick department is also a cost center. Indeed, most responsibility centers are also cost centers.

Not all cost centers are responsibility centers, however. The printing department in a company may operate a number of presses of different sizes and capabilities, some able to print several colors, and others, only black. In such a situation, each printing press may be a cost center, even though only the whole printing department is a responsibility center managed by one supervisor. Conversely, when the products flowing through the factory are essentially similar, an entire factory may be treated as a single cost center even though the factory consists of several responsibility centers each headed by a supervisor.

There are two types of cost centers: production cost centers and service cost centers.

A production cost center is a cost center that produces a product or a component of a product. The barrel, wick, and assembly departments in the pen factory are production cost centers. The individual printing presses mentioned above are also production cost centers.

All other cost centers are service cost centers. Service cost centers provide services to production cost centers and to other service cost centers, or they perform work for the benefit of the organization as a whole. A maintenance department that repairs machines and keeps the building in good condition is an example of a service cost center. The general factory office is a service cost center.

Not all service cost centers are identifiable organization units or other entities. For example, in many factories there is an "occupancy" cost center, in which all the costs associated with the physical premises are accumulated. These include the depreciation expense, property taxes, and insurance on the building and the costs of heating and lighting the premises.

Service cost centers are often called **indirect cost pools.** The term conveys the idea that they are devices in which indirect costs are accumulated; the costs subsequently flow out of these pools to other cost centers.

ALLOCATING OVERHEAD COSTS: GENERAL APPROACH

Suppose that in the month of September, the total overhead[1] cost in the pen factory was $27,000. This $27,000 was measured in accordance

---

[1] From here on, we shall use the word *overhead* in place of the more cumbersome term, *manufacturing overhead*. Our discussion focuses on the overhead costs in the manufacturing process, and all this overhead is manufacturing overhead.

with the accrual principle of financial accounting. A purpose of a cost accounting system is to assign this overhead cost to individual products.

Concept of overhead allocation

In Chapter 2, we stated the guiding principle that the cost of a cost objective includes, in addition to its direct costs, a *fair share* of the indirect costs that were incurred for several cost objectives, of which the cost objectives in question is one. Thus, if the cost objective is one production lot of pens, its cost includes a fair share of all the indirect, or overhead, costs in the pen factory. The idea of "fair share" sounds vague, and it is vague, but it is the best way of describing the basic approach to measuring the indirect costs of a cost objective.

What is a fair share? Perhaps the best way to think about this question is from the viewpoint of the customer. Under ordinary circumstances, customers should be willing to pay the cost of the products they buy plus a reasonable profit. Consider, for example, the customer of a job shop that offers printing services. A customer whose job requires the use of an expensive four-color printing press should expect to pay a fair share of the costs of operating that press, and should expect to pay more per hour of press time than the customer whose job requires only a small, inexpensive press. The customer whose job requires a long time should expect to pay a relatively larger share of the cost of plant facilities than the customer whose product requires the use of these facilities for only a short time. Collectively, moreover, all the customers should expect to pay all the costs.

Basic allocation principles

From the above line of reasoning, it follows that (1) all items of manufacturing cost should be assigned to product cost objectives, and (2) the amount assigned to an individual cost objective should be its proportional share of the total. More specifically, we can refer back to the criteria discussed in Chapter 3 and say that the amount of overhead assigned to a cost objective should be related to *benefits received* or a *causal incurrence*.

The process of assigning indirect costs to individual cost objectives is called allocation. The verb "to allocate" means "to assign indirect costs to individual cost objectives." Unfortunately, there is not general agreement on this terminology; some people use "allocate" to refer to direct costs as well as to indirect costs.

In this book we use *assign* as the general term applying to both direct and indirect costs. Whenever an item of cost is initially collected in a cost center, or moved from one cost center to another, or lodged in a final cost objective (such as a product), it is said to be **assigned.** Costs can be assigned to cost objectives in either of two ways: (1) they can be **assigned directly,** as is the case of direct material which is assigned directly to the product; or (2) they can be **allocated.**

Thus, an **allocated cost is a cost that is not assigned directly to a cost objective.** Overhead costs are allocated to products because they are, by definition, indirect costs of manufacturing products. However, in the process of collecting these costs in cost centers and moving them from one cost center to another, many of the transactions involve direct assignment. The supervisor's salary is *assigned directly* to the department supervised, but it is a part of the overhead cost of that department and is therefore *allocated* to the products passing through the department.

STEPS IN THE ALLOCATION PROCESS

Exhibit 4–2 is a diagram of the procedure involved in allocating overhead costs to products. The situation illustrated is that of the pen factory. The factory consists of three production cost centers and two service cost centers. The production cost centers are the barrel department, the wick department, and the assembly department. One of the service cose centers is the occupancy center, in which costs associated with the building are accumulated. The other is the general cost center, in which other overhead costs are accumulated. These include the costs of operating the storerooms, of the maintenance department, and of the factory office. (In many factories, there would be separate cost centers for each of these activities.)

Direct material and direct labor costs are assigned directly to product cost objectives by the techniques described in Chapter 3. The allocation of overhead cost to product cost objectives involves three steps:

1. **All overhead costs for an accounting period are assigned to some service or production cost center.** This flow is illustrated in Section A of Exhibit 4–2.
2. **The total cost accumulated in each service cost center is reassigned to production cost centers.** This flow is illustrated in Section B of Exhibit 4–2.
3. **The total of the overhead costs accumulated in each production cost center, including the reassigned service center costs, is allocated to products that pass through the production cost center.** This flow is illustrated in Section C of Exhibit 4–2.

We shall describe these three steps in more detail. First, as a pedagogical device for explaining the concept, we shall describe them in the order listed above. We shall then show that by changing this order we can arrive at the desired end result—the factory cost of products—by a

EXHIBIT 4–2
Allocating overhead costs to products

A. Initial assignment to cost centers

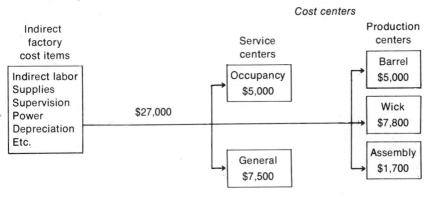

B. Reassignment to production centers   C. Allocation to products

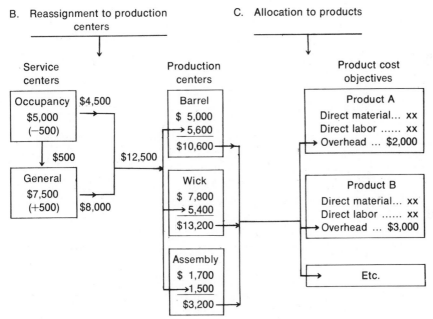

simpler technique and one that produces more useful information for management.

Initial assignment to cost centers

The first step in the allocation of overhead costs is to assign all items of manufacturing overhead costs for the month to some cost center.

EXHIBIT 4–3
Allocating overhead costs

		Service centers		Production centers		
Cost item	Total	Occupancy	General	Barrel	Wick	Assembly

		A. Initial assignment to cost centers				
Indirect labor	$10,000	$ 0	$ 5,000	$ 1,700	$ 3,300	$ 0
Supplies..................	5,000	600	1,500	500	1,500	900
Other	12,000	4,400	1,000	2,800	3,000	800
Subtotals..........	$27,000	5,000	7,500	5,000	7,800	1,700

		B. Reassignment of service center costs				
Occupancy..............		(5,000)	500	1,500	2,000	1,000
General..................			(8,000)	4,100	3,400	500
Indirect cost ...	$27,000	0	0	$10,600	$13,200	$3,200

		C. Calculation of overhead rates				
Direct labor hours	7,000			2,100	3,500	1,400
Overhead rate per direct labor hour ...				$5.05	$3.77	$2.29

( ) indicates subtraction.

Indirect labor costs are assigned to the cost centers in which the indirect employees work. The costs of supplies and other indirect materials are assigned to the cost centers in which the materials are used. Depreciation on machinery and power costs associated with the machines are assigned to cost centers in which the machines are located. In this step, each item of overhead cost is assigned to one, and only one, cost center, so that the sum of the costs for all the cost centers equals the total overhead costs for the whole factory.

Section A of Exhibit 4–3 shows how the $27,000 of overhead costs were assigned initially to cost centers. For example, of the $10,000 of indirect labor cost, zero was assigned to the occupancy cost center (because no personnel were charged to this cost center), $5,000 to the general cost center, $1,700 to the barrel department, $3,300 to the wick department, and zero to the assembly department (because its supervisor worked directly on products and it had no other indirect employees).

Reassignment of service center costs

The second step in the allocation of overhead costs is to reassign the total cost accumulated in each service cost center so that eventually all overhead costs are assigned to the production cost centers. Some service center costs are assigned directly to the cost centers that receive the service. Maintenance department costs may be assigned directly to production cost centers on the basis of the maintenance service actually performed, for example. The costs of a power-generating plant may be assigned according to the metered usage of electricity in each cost center, just as if the electricity had been purchased from an outside company.

Note, incidentally, the use of the word *directly* in the above paragraph. With respect to the final cost objective, that is, the product, all the items of cost that we are now discussing are indirect. With respect to individual cost centers, however, some of the items of cost are direct. We referred to this distinction earlier, and it is important that it not be overlooked.

Allocation bases. The costs of some service cost centers cannot be directly assigned to other cost centers. These costs must be allocated; that is, the costs must be assigned to other cost centers on some reasonable basis. The basis of allocation should correspond, as closely as is feasible, to one of the two basic criteria given in Chapter 3; that is, it should have some connection with either benefits received or a causal relationship. The dozens of alternative bases of allocations that are used in practice can be grouped into the following principal categories.

1. Payroll related. Social security taxes paid by the employer, accident insurance, fringe benefits, and other costs associated with amounts earned by employees may be allocated on the basis of the total labor costs. Alternatively, as mentioned in Chapter 3, some or all of these costs may enter into the calculation of direct labor costs; if so they will not appear as overhead costs at all. If certain overhead costs are ultimately charged to products by means of a direct labor rate (as will be described below), the ultimate effect of treating these costs as overhead is approximately the same as if they were charged as part of direct labor costs.

2. Personnel related. Personnel department costs, and other costs that are associated with the number of employees rather than with the amount that they are paid, may be allocated on the basis of number of employees. (The distinction between *payroll related* and *personnel related* is a subtle one. Many companies do not attempt to make such a distinction; instead they allocate both types of costs together, usually on the basis of direct labor costs.)

3. Material related. This category of cost may be allocated on the basis of either the quantity or the cost of direct material used in production cost centers, or, alternatively, it may be excluded from overhead costs and charged to products as part of direct material cost, as mentioned in Chapter 3. The latter practice is conceptually preferable, but it sometimes involves more recordkeeping than is believed to be worthwhile.

4. Space related. Some items of cost are associated with the space that the cost center occupies, and they are allocated to cost centers on the basis of the relative area or cubic content of the cost centers. Occupancy cost in Exhibit 4–3 is an example.

5. Activity related. Some costs are roughly related to the overall volume of activity in the cost center, or at least there is a presumption that the more work that a cost center does, the more costs are properly allocated to it. Electrical power costs and steam costs, if not directly assigned, fall into this category; and so do the costs of a variety of other service cost centers which, although not demonstrably a function of activity, are more realistically allocated in this way than in any other. The measure of activity may be an overall indication of the amount of work done by the cost center, such as its total labor cost, its total direct costs, or the total cost of its output. Alternatively, the measure of activity may be more closely related to the function of the service cost center whose costs are being allocated; for example, electric costs may be allocated on the basis of the total horsepower of motors installed in each cost center.

EXAMPLE: The middle section of Exhibit 4–3 shows the reassignment of service center costs to production cost centers.

Occupancy costs are space related, so the $5,000 of occupancy cost is allocated on the basis of the relative floor space in each cost center, as follows:

Cost center	Percent of floor space	Occupancy cost
General.............	10	$ 500
Barrel................	30	1,500
Wick..................	40	2,000
Assembly...........	20	1,000
	100	$5,000

The costs of the general cost center are allocated on the basis of the total direct costs (i.e., direct material + direct labor) charged to the three production cost centers. The total general cost is, after the addition of the allocated share of occupancy cost, $8,000. This amount is allocated as follows:

Cost center	Percent of direct costs*	General cost
Barrel................	51	$4,100
Wick	43	3,400
Assembly...........	6	500
Total	100	$8,000

* Calculated from Exhibit 3–9.

Step-down order. Note that in Exhibit 4–3, part of the cost of the occupancy service cost center is allocated to the general service cost center. It may well be that part of the cost of the general cost center should be allocated to the occupancy cost center, and this creates a problem. Whenever there are a number of service cost centers, the interrelationships among them could theoretically lead to a long series of distributions, redistributions, and re-redistributions. In practice, however, these redistributions are avoided by allocating the service center costs in a prescribed order, which is called the **step-down order.** In general, the cost of the service center with the greatest excess of services rendered to other cost centers over services received from other cost centers is allocated first, the service center with the second greatest excess is allocated next, and so on. In the illustration, the prescribed order is occupancy first, and general second. No additional cost is allocated to a service cost center after its costs have been allocated.

Allocation of overhead costs to products

Having collected all the overhead costs in production cost centers, the final step is to allocate these costs to the products worked on in these cost centers. In a process cost system, this is easy. The total equivalent units of production for the month is determined by the method described in Chapter 3, and the total overhead cost is divided by the number of equivalent units; this gives the unit overhead cost for each product.

In a job cost system, however, the procedure is more complicated. The various jobs worked on in the production center are of different sizes and complexities, and therefore they should bear different amounts of overhead cost. To the extent feasible, we want to allocate overhead costs to jobs such that each job bears its fair share of the total overhead cost of the cost center. In order to do this, an overhead rate is calculated.

Overhead rates. The function of the overhead rate is to allocate an equitable amount of manufacturing overhead cost to each product. In thinking about how this rate should be constructed, therefore, we need to address the question: Why, in all fairness, should one product have a higher overhead cost than another product? Depending on the circumstances, the following are among the plausible answers to this question:

1. Because more labor effort was expended on one product than on another, and overhead costs are presumed to vary primarily with the amount of labor effort.
2. Because one product used more machine time than another, and overhead costs are presumed to vary primarily with the amount of machine time.
3. Because one product had higher direct costs than another, and overhead costs are presumed to vary primarily with the amount of direct costs.

Each of these answers suggests a quantitative basis of activity that can be used to allocate overhead costs to products, viz:

1. If overhead costs tend to vary with the amount of labor effort, they can be allocated on the basis of the number of labor hours or labor dollars used for the product.
2. If overhead costs tend to vary with machine time, they can be allocated on the basis of the number of machine hours required for the product.

3. If overhead costs tend to vary with the amount of direct costs, they can be allocated on the basis of the total direct costs of the product.

The machine hours basis is common for production cost centers that consist primarily of one machine (such as a papermaking machine) or a group of related machines. The direct labor hours basis is frequently used in other situations. The decision as to the best measure of activity is judgmental. It is guided by the criteria of benefits received and causal relationships; but, by definition, there is no precisely accurate way of measuring how much overhead cost actually should attach to each product. If there were such a way, the item would be a direct cost.

Having selected what appears to be the most appropriate measure in a given production cost center, the overhead rate for that production cost center is calculated by dividing its total overhead cost by the total amount of activity for the period.

> EXAMPLE: Continuing with the example in Exhibit 4–3, let us assume that the number of direct labor hours is the appropriate activity measure for the allocation of overhead costs to products in all three production cost centers. In the barrel department, the direct labor hours for the month totaled 2,100. Dividing the 2,100 direct labor hours into the total overhead cost of $10,600, gives an overhead rate of $5.05 per direct labor hour.

Allocation to products. The overhead cost for each product that passes through the production cost center is calculated by multiplying the cost center overhead rate by the number of activity units accumulated for that product.

> EXAMPLE: Referring to the situation in Exhibit 4–3, if in this factory a certain lot of pens, Job No. 307, required 30 direct labor hours in barrel, 20 direct labor hours in wick, and 5 direct labor hours in assembly, its total overhead cost would be calculated as follows:

Production cost center	Direct labor hours	Overhead rate	Overhead cost
Barrel	30	$5.05	$151.50
Wick	20	3.77	75.40
Assembly	5	2.29	11.45
Total Overhead Cost of Job No. 307			$238.35

Predetermined overhead rates

The preceding description of the accumulation of overhead costs in cost centers and their eventual allocation to products followed the same chronological order as that used for the description of accounting for direct material and direct costs; that is, the amount of cost for the month was first ascertained, and subsequently this amount was allocated to products. This approach was used for pedagogical reasons; that is, it is the easiest way of relating the flow of overhead costs to the physical activities of the factory.

A better way of allocating overhead costs in most situations is to establish an overhead rate for each production cost center in advance, usually once a year, and then to use these predetermined overhead rates throughout the year. We shall limit the discussion of predetermined overhead rates to a job cost system, but similar considerations apply to a process cost system.

There are three reasons why the calculation of an annual overhead rate in advance is preferable to calculating a rate at the end of each month, based on the actual overhead costs incurred in that month.

1. If overhead rates were calculated monthly, they would be unduly affected by conditions peculiar to that month. Heating costs in the winter, for example, are higher than heating costs in the summer; but no useful purpose would be served by reporting that pens manufactured in the winter cost more than pens manufactured in the summer. As will be explained below, fluctuations in the volume of activity also can cause gyrations in the overhead rates; and misleading information on overhead costs would be presented if the overhead costs assigned to products were affected by month-to-month variations in the volume of activity.
2. The use of a predetermined overhead rate permits product costs to be calculated more promptly. Direct material and direct labor costs can be assigned to products as soon as the time records and material requisitions are available. If, however, overhead rates were calculated only at the end of each month, after all the information on overhead costs for the month had been assembled, overhead costs could not be assigned to products until after this calculation had been completed. With the use of a predetermined overhead rate, overhead costs can be allocated to products at the same time that direct costs are assigned to them.
3. Calculation of an overhead rate once a year requires less effort than going through the same calculation every month.

Procedure for establishing predetermined overhead rates

In order to establish overhead rates that will be used during a forthcoming year, a calculation is made that follows exactly the same steps described above, except that the numbers represent what the activity levels and costs are *estimated to be* during the coming year, rather than what they *actually were*.

The first step is to estimate what the level of activity, or volume, is going to be. For example, in the pen factory, it may be estimated that the volume will average 7,000 direct labor hours per month, the same as the actual volume in Exhibit 4–3.

The next step is to calculate the estimated overhead costs at the estimated volume in each cost center. Techniques for making these estimates are described in Chapters 12 and 13.

Having made estimates of the costs in each cost center, an overhead rate is developed by following the same procedure that has already been described: service center costs are reassigned to production cost centers, so that all overhead costs end up in some production cost center, the amount of activity (such as direct labor hours) in each production cost center is estimated, and total overhead costs are divided by the activity measure to arrive at an overhead rate.

The actual overhead rate described earlier was determined by

$$\frac{\text{Actual Overhead Costs}}{\text{Actual Volume}}$$

The predetermined overhead rate is calculated in the same way except that it is determined by

$$\frac{\text{Estimated Overhead Cost}}{\text{Estimated Volume}}$$

Because the calculation of predetermined overhead rates is otherwise exactly the same as the overhead rate calculation which has already been described and illustrated in Exhibit 4–3, the details are not repeated here.

Estimating volume. The most uncertain part of the process of establishing predetermined overhead rates is estimating what the volume of activity will be in the forthcoming year. This amount is called the **standard volume or the normal volume.**[2] This estimate of volume has a significant effect on overhead rates. In most companies, important items of overhead cost do not vary with changes in volume; they are called **fixed costs.** To take the extreme case, if *all* overhead costs are fixed, the overhead rate would vary inversely with the level of volume estimated for the forthcoming year. To the extent that not all costs are fixed, changes in overhead rates associated with changes in the estimate of volume are not as severe, but they are nevertheless significant in most situations. It is therefore important that careful attention be given to making the best possible estimate of volume as part of the procedure of calculating predetermined overhead rates.

> *EXAMPLE:* A papermaking machine is a large, expensive machine that either runs at capacity or does not run at all. Its depreciation, the costs associated with the building in which it is housed, and most other items of overhead cost are unaffected by how many hours a month the machine operates. Assume that these overhead costs are estimated to be $50,000 a month, and that they are entirely fixed, that is, they are estimated to be $50,000 regardless of how many hours the machine operates during the

---

[2] Alternative concepts of standard volume are described in the Appendix to this chapter.

month. If the measure of activity used in establishing the overhead rate is machine hours, overhead rates will vary as shown below for various estimates of machine hours to be operated during the month:

Number of machine hours	Overhead cost	Overhead rate (per machine hour)
500	$50,000	$100
400	50,000	125
250	50,000	200

The effect of the volume estimate on the amount of overhead cost assigned to products during the year is therefore great.

The important point to remember is that the predetermined overhead rate will be relatively low if the estimated volume of activity is relatively high because the same amount of fixed cost will be spread over a larger number of units. This point will be discussed in more depth in Chapter 6.

Underabsorbed and overabsorbed overhead

If a predetermined overhead rate is used, the amount of overhead costs allocated to products in a given month is likely to differ from the amount of overhead costs actually incurred in that month. This is because the actual overhead costs assigned to the cost center in the month, and/or the actual activity level for the month, are likely to be different from the estimates that were used when the predetermined overhead rate was calculated. If the amount of overhead cost allocated to products exceeds the amount of actual costs actually assigned to the cost center, overhead is said to be **overabsorbed;** and if the amount is less, overhead is **underabsorbed** (or **unabsorbed**). For management purposes, the amount of underabsorbed or overabsorbed overhead is useful information, as will be discussed in Chapter 14.

EXAMPLE: Assume in a certain production cost center, the predetermined overhead rate was calculated as follows:

Estimated direct labor hours (i.e., standard volume) 25,000
Estimated overhead costs at standard volume........................ $100,000
Overhead rate, per direct labor hour $4

Actual experience for January and February was as follows:

	January	February
1. Actual direct labor hours...............................	25,000	40,000
2. Actual overhead costs...................................	$110,000	$140,000
3. Overhead absorbed ($4 × line 1)	100,000	160,000
4. Underabsorbed overhead	$ 10,000	
Overabsorbed overhead		$ 20,000

For financial accounting purposes, the amount of underabsorbed or overabsorbed overhead in a given month should theoretically be divided among Goods in Process Inventory, Finished Goods Inventory, and Cost of Goods Sold in proportion to the relative size of these accounts. In practice, many companies hold the amount of suspense as a temporary item on the end-of-month balance sheet in the expectation that underabsorbed overhead in one month will be offset by overabsorbed overhead in another month; if a balance remains at the end of the year, it is ordinarily closed to Cost of Goods Sold. Many other companies close underabsorbed or overabsorbed overhead monthly to Cost of Goods Sold.

EXHIBIT 4–4
Overhead variance account (amounts in thousands)

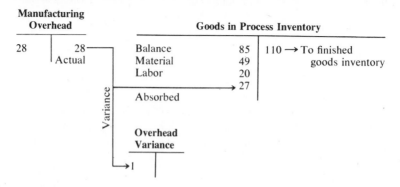

For simplicity, no account for overabsorbed or underabsorbed overhead was shown in the cost accounting flowchart given in Chapter 3, Exhibit 3–3. Such an account is often labeled an **Overhead Variance account.** The journal entry debits Goods in Process Inventory for the amount of costs absorbed, credits Manufacturing Overhead for the actual amount of overhead cost incurred, and debits or credits Overhead Variance for the difference.

Note that the variance account is needed solely because the company uses a predetermined overhead rate. The advantages of using such a rate, rather than waiting until the end of the period to allocate overhead, were explained above.

> *EXAMPLE:* Exhibit 3–3 (page 82) was constructed on the assumption that all overhead costs are allocated to products. If a predetermined overhead rate were used, and if its use gave rise to underabsorbed overhead, the accounts would be as depicted in Exhibit 4–4. The situation illustrated there is that in which actual overhead costs incurred exceeded the amount absorbed in a given month. The journal entry is:

Goods in process inventory 27,000
Overhead variance 1,000
    Manufacturing overhead..   28,000

JOINT PRODUCTS AND BY-PRODUCTS

Joint products are two or more dissimilar end products that are produced from a single batch of raw material or from a single production process. The classic example is the variety of end products that are made from a beef carcass. The end products include hides, many different cuts of meat, frozen meat dishes, pet food, fertilizers, and a variety of chemicals. Up to a certain point in the production process, the raw material is treated as a single unit. Beyond that point, which is called the **split-off point,** separate end products are identified, and costs are accumulated for each of these end products during subsequent stages of the manufacturing process. Up to the point at which cattle are slaughtered and dressed, for example, the purchase price of the cattle, feed, grazing, transportation, and other costs are accumulated for the animal as a whole; beyond that point, these costs must be divided among the many end products that are made from its carcass. The problem of joint costing is to find some reasonable basis for allocating to each of the joint products the costs that were incurred up to the split-off point.

This problem is essentially the same as that of allocating overhead costs. In both cases, the objective is to assign a fair share of the joint or common costs to the final cost objectives, and in neither case can the results be an entirely accurate measure of the actual costs.

One common basis of allocating joint costs is in proportion to the relative market value of the end products, minus the separate processing and marketing costs that are estimated to be incurred for each end product beyond the split-off point. If the selling price depends on cost, this method involves a certain amount of circular reasoning, but there may be no better alternative. If gasoline sells for twice the price of kerosene, per gallon, it is reasonable that gasoline should bear twice as much of the crude oil and joint refining costs.

Another basis of allocation is on a physical basis, such as *weight;* that is, the joint costs are divided in proportion to the weight of the joint material in the several end products. In the case of beef, this method implicitly assumes that the stew meat is as valuable as the tenderloin, which is unrealistic; but in other situations, the assumption that costs are related to weight might be reasonable. In any event, the amount of cost allocated to each end product must be recognized as resulting from a judgmental decision, and hence as not being entirely accurate.

EXAMPLE: A lumber company purchases logs and saws them into lumber. It allocates joint costs on a market value basis. A certain lot of logs is sawed into one million (1,000 thousand) board feet of lumber in three grades, as

EXHIBIT 4–5
Allocation of joint costs

A. Market value basis

Grade of lumber	Thousand board feet	Market value per 1,000 board feet	Market value each grade	Percent of market value	Allocation of cost
No. 1	200	$150	$30,000	36.6	$21,960
No. 2	500	80	40,000	48.8	29,280
No. 3	300	40	12,000	14.6	8,760
Total	1,000		$82,000	100.0	$60,000

B. Physical basis

Grade of lumber	Thousand board feet	Allocation of cost*
No. 1	200	200 × $60 = $12,000
No. 2	500	500 × 60 = 30,000
No. 3	300	300 × 60 = 18,000
Total	1,000	$60,000

* $60,000 total joint cost ÷ 1,000 thousand board feet = $60 per thousand board feet.

shown on Exhibit 4–5. The total market value of the 200 thousand board feet of Grade No. 1 is $30,000, which is 36.6 percent of the total market value of lumber cut from the logs. If the total joint cost, including the purchase price of the logs and the cost of transporting and sawing them, is $60,000, then 36.6 percent of this, or $21,960, would be assigned as the cost of Grade No. 1.

If the $60,000 cost were assigned on the basis of the number of board feet, or $60 per thousand board feet, then the cost of the No. 3 grade would be recorded as 300 × $60 = $18,000. This cost is more than the $12,000 market value of Grade No. 3, so it would appear that Grade No. 3 lumber was being sold at a loss. Such an impression is misleading because the company knows that three grades of lumber are necessarily produced from the logs.

If each grade is sold at the indicated market prices, a total gross margin of $22,000 (= $82,000 − $60,000) was earned on the whole transaction. It is reasonable to show that each grade of lumber contributed to this total.

Having allocated joint costs to products at the split-off point, the measurement of costs incurred *beyond* the split-off point is done in the usual manner. Each product is now a cost objective, and the additional direct labor and manufacturing overhead costs of completing the finished product are assigned to it.

By-products. By-products are a special kind of joint product. If management wishes to manufacture Products A and B in some predetermined proportion, or if it wishes to make as much of each end product as possible from a given quantity of raw material, then these products are ordinary joint products. On the other hand, **if management's objective is to make Product A, but in so doing some quantity of Product B inevitably emerges from the production process, then Product A is a main product and Product B is a by-product.** The intention is to make from a given amount of raw material as much of the main product and as little of the by-product as is possible. As management's intention changes, the classification changes. In the early part of the 20th century, kerosene was the main product made from crude oil; subsequently, with the growth in consumption of gasoline, kerosene became a by-product; currently, kerosene has become a main product again because it is an important component of jet engine fuel.

A number of alternative procedures are used in measuring the cost of by-products. At one extreme, a by-product may be assigned zero cost, with all the joint costs being assigned to the main products. In such a case, the profit on the by-product is equal to its sales revenue, less costs incurred beyond the split-off point. At the other extreme, the revenue from the by-product, less costs incurred beyond the split-off point, is deducted from the cost of the main product. The effect is to report no profit or loss for the by-product. Although these methods give quite different results, the overall effect is usually insignificant because by-products, by their nature, are usually unimportant. In some situations the results can be peculiar, however, as indicated in the example that follows.

EXAMPLE: A flour milling company arrives at the cost of flour by deducting the market value of the by-product, feed, from costs incurred up to the split-off point. In October, the market value of feed increased substantially over the value in September. The recorded cost of flour decreased correspondingly, as shown in the following data:

	Cost per bushel of wheat	
	September	October
Wheat cost and milling costs to split-off point..........................	$6.00	$6.00
Market value of feed from one bushel of wheat........................... $2.00		$3.00
Less processing and selling cost of this feed 1.00		1.00
Value of feed deducted	1.00	2.00
Cost of flour obtained from one bushel of wheat	$5.00	$4.00
Flour cost per pound (50 pounds per bushel of wheat)	$0.10	$0.08

Assuming that 50 pounds of flour is obtained from a bushel of wheat, the recorded cost of the flour was 10 cents per pound in September and 8 cents per pound in October, even though the cost of the wheat and processing costs remain unchanged. The change in the recorded cost of the flour resulted solely from the change in the market value of the by-product.

VALIDITY OF PRODUCT COSTS

From the above description, it should be apparent that the manufacturing cost of a product cannot be measured with complete accuracy if some items of cost are indirect, as is usually the case; and it should also be apparent that differences in cost accounting practice among companies result in different cost measures for the same physical item.

Accuracy of direct costs

Since companies differ in where they draw the line between direct and indirect costs, a comparison of the direct costs of two different companies may be misleading. If Company A classifies only the wages of direct workers as direct labor, but Company B includes labor-related costs as well as wages, then direct labor costs in Company A will be lower than those in Company B. Since labor-related costs (social security taxes, vacation pay, pensions, and the like) may amount to 20 percent or more of wages, this difference can be substantial. Corresponding differences usually do not exist within a single company, because all its responsibility centers presumably use similar definitions.

Accuracy of overhead costs

The overhead costs allocated to a product cannot measure the "actual" amount of resources used in making the product—that is, the "actual" cost incurred—in any literal sense of the word "actual." By means of the collection and allocation mechanism described in this chapter, we have indeed succeeded in adding a portion of building depreciation, for example, onto the cost of each unit of product. Nevertheless, judgments as to what is fair and reasonable were involved in each step of this process: (1) in deciding on the amount of costs applicable to the *accounting period* (what really is the depreciation expense of this period?), (2) in deciding how much of this item of cost is applicable to each *cost center*, and (3) in deciding how much of the cost center's cost is applicable to each product. Two equally capable accountants can arrive at different amounts of overhead cost for a given product: and there is no way of proving that one is right and the other wrong, that is, that one overhead figure is accurate and the other is inaccurate. Overhead costs are indirect costs, and there is no precisely accurate way of assigning indirect costs to cost objectives. By definition, indirect costs are incurred for two or more cost objectives.

Variations in cost centers

The amount of overhead cost allocated to a product can be significantly influenced by judgment as to how a cost center is defined. In some companies, each important machine is a cost center. At the other extreme, an entire plant may be a single cost center (giving rise to a **plantwide overhead rate**). There are a number of choices between these two extremes. In general, the more narrow the definition of a cost center, the more equitable is the resulting amount of overhead cost allocated to the product.

EXAMPLE: Assume a plant with two production cost centers, Departments A and B. In Department A, machining work is done with expensive machine tools requiring much floor space, power, and supplies; and in Department B bench work and assembly are done with inexpensive hand tools. Overhead rates are determined as follows:

Cost center	Estimated monthly direct labor hours	Estimated monthly overhead cost	Overhead rate per direct labor hour
A	2,000	$20,000	$10.00
B	4,000	10,000	2.50
Total Plant	6,000	$30,000	5.00

Assume a certain job required 20 direct labor hours in Department A and 100 direct labor hours in Department B. If each department were a cost center with its own overhead rate, the overhead cost allocated to this job would be:

Cost center	Overhead cost allocated
A	20 hours × $10.00 = $200
B	100 hours × 2.50 = 250
Total Overhead Cost	$450

By contrast, if the whole plant were a single cost center, with a plantwide overhead rate of $5 per direct labor hour, the overhead cost allocated to the same job would be:

$$120 \text{ Direct Labor Hours} \times \$5 = \$600$$

The amount of $600 is a less equitable allocation than the $450 derived from the use of separate departmental overhead rates because the plantwide rate charged $5 of overhead cost for each direct labor hour, despite the fact that almost all the direct labor hours on this job were incurred in Department B, where the overhead rate was only $2.50 per hour.

On the other hand, it is also true that the more narrow the definition of the cost centers, the more cost centers there will be; consequently, more clerical work will be required to compute and apply separate overhead rates. The choice of cost centers in a particular situation depends on the balance between the increase in the validity of the overhead rates as cost centers are more narrowly defined, on the one hand, and the increased clerical work involved on the other hand. If all products require approximately the same proportion of time in each department, the differences in overhead costs assigned by means of a series of rates for each department and the overhead costs assigned by a plantwide rate will be small. In such a situation, little increase in validity is gained by using a large number of overhead rates.

SOME IMPLICATIONS OF COST ACCOUNTING

At this point, let us summarize some of the important points in the description of cost accounting given in this and the preceding chapters.

First, observe that **cost accounting in a manufacturing company is not a separate accounting system.** It is an integral part of the financial accounting system, with accounts, journal entries, and the same rules for debit and credit that were described and illustrated in *Fundamentals of Financial Accounting.* Since there are books and manuals that have "cost accounting" in their title, some people may get the impression that cost accounting is a separate accounting system, off by itself; this is not so.

Second, note that the Goods in Process Inventory account can be visualized as an accounting representation of the factory itself. As labor, material, and services flow into the factory, the monetary representations of these resources flow to Goods in Process Inventory as debits. The physical movement of products out of the factory and into the finished goods warehouse is represented by a credit to Goods in Process Inventory and a debit to Finished Goods Inventory. The balance in the Goods in Process Inventory account represents the costs that have been accumulated on partially completed products that are still in the factory at the end of the period. This balance corresponds to physical quantities of products still in the factory.

Third, observe the difference in the timing of the impact of costs on net income between a merchandising company and a manufacturing company. If a clerk in a retail store earns $600 in September, that $600 is an expense in September, and income in September is reduced correspondingly. But if a factory employee in our pen factory earns $600 in September, that $600 becomes a part of the cost of the pens on which the employee works. In September, it appears in Goods in Process Inventory; then it moves to Finished Goods Inventory in the month in which the pens are completed, where it remains until the pens are sold. Thus, a factory employee's wages affect cost of goods sold, and hence income, only when the pens are sold, which may be in October or some later month. During the interval between the date of cost incurrence and the date of sale, the $600 of direct labor costs, together with the other costs of manufacturing the pens, is lodged in either Goods in Process or Finished Goods Inventory accounts; that is, these costs are part of the current assets.

In a merchandising company, costs of labor, supplies used, depreciation, and other elements affect income in the accounting period in which these costs are incurred; that is, wage expense for September, the supplies used in September, and depreciation expense for September, all have an impact on the income for September. In a **manufacturing company,** by contrast, those labor and other costs that are associated with the manufacturing process affect, initially, the value of inventory; **costs affect income only in the accounting period in which the products containing these costs are sold.** This may be a later accounting period than that in which the product was manufactured. The larger the inventory in relation to sales and the longer the production process, then the longer is the time interval that elapses between the incurrence of a manufacturing cost and its impact on income.

Finally, note the difference between "manufacturing cost" and "costs of goods manufactured." **Manufacturing cost** (or factory cost) **refers to all the resources put into the manufacturing process during the accounting period.** In other words, it is the sum of the debits to the Goods in Process Inventory account during the period. **Cost of goods manufactured refers to the cost of the products completed during the accounting period;** it is the credit to Goods in Process Inventory during the period. These two terms sound almost identical, but they stand for quite different concepts. Manufacturing cost would equal cost of goods manufactured in a given period only if the balance in the Goods in Process Inventory account were the same at the end of the period as at the beginning.

DEMONSTRATION CASE

As a means of solidifying your understanding of how overhead rates are established and used, you are asked to calculate overhead rates for 1977 for Marker Pen Company whose 1976 overhead costs are given in Exhibit 4–3. Assume that the company has prepared a budget which shows that estimates for the average month in 1977 will be changed from those shown in Exhibit 4–3 in the following respects:

1. Indirect labor costs are estimated to be 110 percent of the amounts shown.
2. Direct labor hours are estimated to be 120 percent of the amounts shown.

With these exceptions, the amounts of cost initially assigned to cost centers are the same as in Exhibit 4–3.

EXHIBIT 4–6
Solution for demonstration case

Question 1

		Service centers		Production centers		
Cost item	Total	Occupancy	General	Barrel	Wick	Assembly
		A.	Initial assignment to cost centers			
Indirect labor......	$11,000	$ 0	$ 5,500	$ 1,870	$ 3,360	$ 0
Supplies.............	5,000	600	1,500	500	1,500	900
Other.................	12,000	4,400	1,000	2,800	3,000	800
Subtotal....	28,000	5,000	8,000	5,170	8,130	1,700
		B.	Reassignment of service center costs			
Occupancy (%)....			10 %	30%	40%	20%
Occupancy ($).....		(5,000)	$ 500	$ 1,500	$ 2,000	$1,000
General (%).......				51%	43%	6%
General ($).........			$(8,500)	$ 4,335	$ 3,655	$ 510
Total........	$28,000			$11,005	$13,785	$3,210
		C.	Calculation of overhead rates			
Direct labor hours..............	8,400			2,520	4,200	1,680
Overhead rate per direct labor hour...............				$4.37	$3.28	$1.91

2. The overhead cost of Job 1020 is:

Department	Direct labor hours	Overhead rate	Overhead cost
Barrel	30	$4.37	$131.10
Wick..	20	3.28	65.60
Assembly	5	1.91	9.55
Total Overhead Cost...........			$206.25

3. *a.* The calculation of overhead variances is:

Department	Absorbed overhead			Actual overhead	Overabsorbed or (unabsorbed)
	Rate ×	Actual Hrs. =	Absorbed		
Barrel..............	$4.37	2,600	$11,362	$13,000	$(1,638)
Wick...............	3.28	4,000	13,120	14,120	(1,000)
Assembly	1.91	1,700	3,247	3,000	247
Total			$27,729	$30,120	$(2,391)

b. The journal entry is:

Goods in process inventory	27,729	
Overhead variance	2,391	
Manufacturing overhead......................................		30,120

( ) indicates subtraction.

Required:

1. Calculate 1977 predetermined overhead rates for each production cost center. Recall that service center costs are reassigned according to the following percentages:

To From	General	Barrel	Wick	Assembly
Occupancy	10	30	40	20
General		51	43	6

   (Calculate overhead rates to the nearest cent.)

2. Calculate the overhead cost that would be allocated to Job 1020. This job required 30 direct labor hours in barrel, 20 hours in wick, and 5 hours in assembly.

3. In January 1977, actual overhead costs and actual direct labor hours were as follows:

	Actuals for January	
	Overhead costs	Direct labor hours
Barrel.........................	$13,000	2,600
Wick	14,120	4,000
Assembly....................	3,000	1,700

   a. Calculate the overhead variance in each department.

   b. Make a journal entry crediting Manufacturing Overhead, debiting Goods in Process Inventory, and debiting or crediting Overhead Variance. (Do this for the factory in total; do not attempt to make separate entries for the three departments.)

   After you have made the calculations, check your answer with Exhibit 4–6.

SUMMARY

In addition to its direct costs, the manufacturing cost of a product includes a fair share of the indirect, or overhead, costs incurred in or for the factory. Items of cost are classified as indirect, rather than direct, because it is not possible to assign them directly, because it is not worthwhile to do so, or because the management chooses not to do so.

Manufacturing overhead costs are usually allocated to products by means of a predetermined overhead rate. This rate is calculated prior to the beginning of the year. The procedure is as follows:

1. A measure of activity for each production cost center is selected, and the level of activity, according to that measure, is estimated. This is the standard volume.

2. The amount of overhead costs for each cost center at the standard volume is estimated.
3. The estimated costs of service cost centers are assigned to production cost centers on some basis that reflects benefits received or a causal relationship. After this step has been completed, all overhead costs have been assigned to production cost centers.
4. For each production cost center, its standard volume is divided into its total overhead cost to arrive at its overhead rate.

The overhead rate is used to allocate overhead costs to the products that pass through the production cost center. The number of units of activity required for each product, multiplied by the overhead rate, gives the total amount of overhead cost allocated to that product.

Because allocations of overhead costs involve judgment about the definition of cost centers and the bases of allocation, the resulting amount of overhead cost allocated to a products is not precisely accurate.

When a manufacturing process involves joint products or by-products, allocation of costs incurred up to the split-off point is necessary. Any of several approaches may be used.

APPENDIX: CONCEPTS OF STANDARD VOLUME

The level of activity selected for use in calculating the overhead rate is called the *standard volume*. The text suggests that standard volume is the volume anticipated for the next year. Some companies are instead the *average volume* expected over a *number of years* in the future. The overhead rate is lower if the estimated volume is high because the same amount of fixed cost is spread over a larger number of units. Therefore, the overhead rates resulting from the use of one of these concepts of standard volume can differ substantially from those calculated on the other concept.

When the standard volume is taken as the volume expected next year, the resulting overhead rate is such that total overhead costs incurred in the year will be approximately absorbed onto products if the estimates are made with reasonable accuracy; that is, the amount of underabsorbed or overabsorbed overhead will be small. This method therefore meets the objective of financial accounting because it attaches all overhead costs to products. It may, however, cause difficulty if the costs are being used as a basis for pricing, for unit costs will tend to be high in a year of low volume and low in a year of high volume. If the low volume implies a business recession, the high unit cost may lead to an increase in selling prices at the very time when it is probably most unwise to attempt such an increase. Conversely, in a year of high volume, the low overhead rate may lead to a decrease in selling prices when such a decrease is unnecessary.

A standard volume based on an average of several years is used by automobile manufacturers and by a number of other leading companies. It avoids the pricing paradox mentioned above, but it does result in a large amount of overabsorbed overhead in a year of abnormally high

EXHIBIT 4–7
Effect of volume measure of costs

	High-volume year	Average year	Low-volume year
Units manufactured......................	50,000	40,000	30,000
Total direct cost (@ $5)................	$250,000	$200,000	$150,000
Total overhead cost......................	120,000	120,000	120,000
Total Cost...........................	$370,000	$320,000	$270,000

Unit costs:
A. Overhead rate based on annual volume:

	High-volume year	Average year	Low-volume year
Direct cost.......................	$ 5.00	$ 5.00	$ 5.00
Overhead cost...................	2.40	3.00	4.00
Total Cost per Unit.......................	$ 7.40	$ 8.00	$ 9.00

B. Overhead rate based on average volume:

	High-volume year	Average year	Low-volume year
Direct cost.......................	$ 5.00	$ 5.00	$ 5.00
Overhead cost...................	3.00	3.00	3.00
Total Cost per Unit.......................	$ 8.00	$ 8.00	$ 8.00

volume, and a large amount of underabsorbed overhead in a year of abnormally low volume.

> *EXAMPLE:* In a certain company, the number of units manufactured is as low as 30,000 in some years and as high as 50,000 in other years, but is 40,000 units in an average year. Overhead costs are entirely fixed; they are $120,000 a year, whatever the volume in that year may be. (The impact of inflation is ignored in the interest of simplicity.) Direct costs (material and labor) are $5 per unit. Exhibit 4–7 shows how the product costs would be calculated under the alternative ways of measuring volume.

If the overhead rate is based on the volume level in each year, then it will be $2.40 per unit (= $120,000 ÷ 50,000) in a year when volume is 50,000 units and $4 per unit (= $120,000 ÷ 30,000) in a year when volume is 30,000 units. The total cost per unit will be $7.40 in the year of high volume and $9 in the year of low volume. If selling prices are based on cost, there will be a tendency to charge low prices in a year in which volume is high, which is the very time when the heavy demand indicates that high prices can be obtained. Correspondingly, there will be a tendency to charge high prices in a year in which volume is low, which is the very time when customers are reluctant to buy the product.

If the overhead rate is based on the average volume of 40,000 units, the overhead rate will be $3 per unit (= $120,000 ÷ 30,000) regardless of what the volume is in a given year. Correspondingly, the total unit cost will not fluctuate with changes in volume.

IMPORTANT TERMS

Assign	Predetermined overhead rate
Allocate	Standard volume
Cost center	Overabsorbed overhead
Production cost center	Underabsorbed (or unabsorbed) overhead
Service cost center	Overhead Variance account
Indirect cost pool	Joint product
Step-down order	By-product
Overhead rate	Plantwide overhead rate

QUESTIONS FOR DISCUSSION

1. What are the differences and similarities between a cost center and a responsibility center?

2. Distinguish among *assign, assign directly,* and *allocate* as used in this text. Which term(s) applies to direct labor cost?

3. Below are listed certain service cost centers and five possible bases of allocation. Which basis of allocation is most appropriate for each cost center?

Service cost center	Basis for allocation
a. Medical department.	1. Labor hours.
b. Building maintenance.	2. Labor costs.
c. Personnel department.	3. Number of employees.
d. Employee pensions.	4. Square feet of floor space.
e. Employee cafeteria.	5. Total cost center cost.
f. Telephone department.	
g. Factory office.	
h. Heat and light.	

4. Exhibit 4–3 shows an amount of $10,000 for indirect labor cost. Describe in your own words each step in the procedure that results in some fraction

of this $10,000 becoming part of the cost of a lot of pens in finished goods inventory.

5.   Service center costs are first reassigned to production cost centers and then become part of the overhead rate which assigns them to products. Why not skip the step of assigning service center costs to production cost centers, and instead assign service center costs immediately to products?

6.   The overhead cost allocated to a certain job was $151.50 because the job required 30 direct labor hours and the overhead rate was $5.05 per direct labor hour. In what sense was $151.50 the actual overhead cost of the job, and in what sense was it not the actual overhead cost?

7.   Why are predetermined overhead rates better than overhead rates determined after the fact?

8.   In arriving at predetermined overhead rates, why is the estimate of volume an especially important consideration?

9.   Give several reasons why overhead costs might be underabsorbed in a given month.

10.   The text gives the journal entry for underabsorbed overhead. Give the corresponding entry for overabsorbed overhead, using any numbers that you wish.

11.   What is the theoretically correct way of disposing of a balance in the Overhead Variance account? What alternative is often used in practice? Why is the former way theoretically preferable to the latter?

12.   Suppose that before closing, the Overhead Variance account for a year has a credit balance. Does this fact indicate that the Finished Goods Inventory is overstated? Explain.

13.   Distinguish between joint products and by-products.

14.   The text illustrates how changes in the market value of the by-product, feed, can change the cost of the main product, flour, if feed is costed at its market value. Suppose wheat and milling costs were assigned to feed and flour in proportion to the weight of each. Would this eliminate the influence of changes in feed market value on flour costs? Would this alternative be preferable to treating feed as a by-product?

15.   "Since all manufacturing overhead costs are allocated to some product, they all wind up in inventory or in cost of goods sold. It therefore makes no difference how they are allocated." Comment.

16.   "The Delia Company sets selling prices on each job that are equal to cost plus 10 percent. Its total profit will therefore be 10 percent of cost, no matter how the costs are allocated to each job. It therefore makes no difference how the costs are allocated." Comment.

17.   "It is absolutely impossible to measure the true cost of any cost objective if indirect costs are present." Comment.

18.   Following is a diagram of the flow of costs into and out of inventory accounts in a certain period. Describe what amounts each of the letters represents.

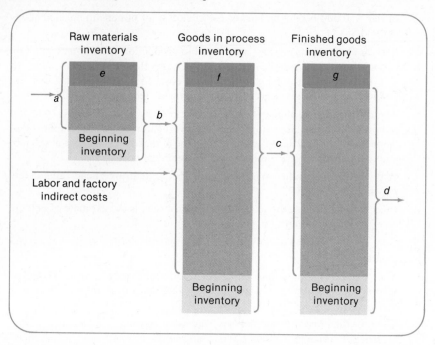

PROBLEMS

4–1. The Carter Company allocates overhead costs to jobs on the basis of direct labor hours. Its estimated average monthly costs for 1977 are as follows:

	Average monthly costs
Direct material...	$30,000
Direct labor (10,000 hours @ $8 per hour).........	80,000
Factory overhead..	50,000

Among the jobs worked on in November 1977 were two jobs, E and F, for which the following information was collected:

	Job E	Job F
Direct material cost........	$3,000	$3,000
Direct labor cost............	4,000	5,000

Required:

A. Compute the overhead rate and the total factory costs of Jobs E and F.

B. If the company charged customers 160 percent of manufacturing cost for its jobs, what would be the selling price of each job?

4-2. The Cable Company estimates that production costs for the operations of the coming year will be $400,000 for materials, $600,000 for labor, and $840,000 for factory overhead. Overhead is charged to cost objectives on the basis of percentage of direct labor cost.

Required:

A. Calculate the overhead rate for the estimated production for the coming year.
B. Compute the *debits* to goods in process for the month of January, assuming actual costs were $25,000 for direct materials, $35,000 for direct labor, and $75,000 for overhead.
C. Calculate the overabsorbed or underabsorbed overhead for January.
D. What disposition should be made of the overabsorbed or underabsorbed overhead for January? Why?

4-3. At the end of the accounting period a partial list of the accounts of Samson, Inc., shows the following balances:

	Debit	Credit
Raw materials ending inventory	$10,000	
Goods in process ending inventory	12,000	
Finished goods ending inventory	8,000	
Cost of goods sold	40,000	
Selling and administrative expenses	6,000	
Overhead variance		$ 3,000
Sales revenue		55,000

Required:

A. Show the allocation of the overabsorbed or underabsorbed overhead to the proper accounts.
B. Compute the net income for the period.

4-4. The Tempo Company has three production departments, A, B, and C, for which expected average monthly overhead cost and direct labor hours are as follows:

	Total	A	B	C
Overhead cost	$300,000	$210,000	$50,000	$40,000
Direct labor hours	60,000	30,000	10,000	20,000

Among the jobs worked on in January were the following, together with the direct labor hours of each:

		Direct labor hours		
Job	Total	A	B	C
150	600	200	100	300
151	600	300	100	200
152	600	100	100	400

The company considered the whole plant as one cost center (i.e., it used a plantwide overhead rate). The rate was based on direct labor hours.

Required:

A. Compute the overhead cost allocated to each job in January.

B. Suppose that instead of having a single cost center, each department was treated as a separate cost center. What would the factory overhead costs of the three departments have been?

C. Discuss whether the single cost center is preferable to having three cost centers.

4–5. Mid-City College is organized into three instruction centers and two service centers. The instruction centers are Arts and Sciences, Education, and Business Administration. The service centers are Buildings and Grounds and Central Administration. The president wants to know the cost per student in each of the three instruction centers. As a part of the task, you have been asked to assist with the reassignment of overhead costs from the service centers to the instruction centers. The following data represent estimates for the current school year:

	Total	Arts and Sciences	Educa- tion	Business Adminis- tration	Building and Grounds	Central Adminis- tration
Overhead costs (000)	$6,500	$2,000	$1,500	$1,500	$1,000	$500
Percent of space occupied	100	30	25	20	10	15
Number of employees	250	65	50	35	60	40
Number of students	8,000	4,000	2,500	1,500	–	–

Required:

A. Reassign the overhead costs from the service centers to the instruction centers, beginning with buildings and grounds.

B. Calculate the overhead cost for each instruction center on a number-of-students basis.

4–6. The Parker Manufacturing Company has two production departments (fabrication and assembly) and three service departments (general factory administration, factory maintenance, and factory cafeteria). A summary of costs and other data for each department prior to allocation of service department costs for the year ended June 30, 1977, appears below.

The costs of the general factory administration department, factory maintenance department, and factory cafeteria are allocated on the basis of direct labor hours, square footage occupied, and number of employees, respectively. There are no manufacturing overhead variances. Round all final calculations to the nearest dollar.

Assume that Parker elects to distribute service department costs to other service departments (starting with the service department with the greatest total costs) as well as the production departments.

	Fabrication	Assembly	General factory administration	Factory maintenance	Factory cafeteria
Direct labor costs................	$1,950,000	$2,050,000	$90,000	$82,100	$87,000
Direct material costs...............	$3,130,000	$ 950,000	–	$65,000	$91,000
Manufacturing overhead costs	$1,650,000	$1,850,000	$70,000	$56,100	$62,000
Direct labor hours...............	562,500	437,500	31,000	27,000	42,000
Number of employees........	280	200	12	8	20
Square footage occupied..........	88,000	72,000	1,750	2,000	4,800

Required:

A. Reassign the service department costs to the production departments.

B. Calculate predetermined overhead rates for the plant as a whole and for the two production departments using both a direct labor hour and a direct labor cost basis.

(AICPA adapted)

4–7. Yardley Corporation uses a joint process to produce products A, B, and C. Joint production costs for 1977 were $50,000. Relevant data follow:

Product	Units produced	Sales values	Additional processing costs
A...............	20,000	$60,000	$20,000
B	15,000	98,000	20,000
C	15,000	62,000	18,000

Required:

A. Calculate the amount of joint costs to be allocated to each product using the physical basis of allocation.

B. Calculate the amount of joint costs to be allocated to each product using the market value basis of allocation.

(AICPA adapted)

4–8. McLeod Manufacturing produces two joint products, C and D. Joint costs are $30,000 for a batch composed of 1,000 units of C and 1,000 units of D. Processing costs beyond the split-off point are $20,000 for C and $10,000 for D. Selling prices are $60 per units for C and $30 per unit for D.

Required:

A. Calculate the amount of joint cost per batch to be allocated to each product using the physical basis of allocation.

B. Calculate the amount of joint cost per batch to be allocated to each product using the market value basis of allocation.

C. Calculate the gross margin for each product which would result from the two different methods of allocating joint costs. Which method would you recommend? Why?

D. Repeat Requirements (B) and (C) assuming that McLeod lowers the price of C to $50 per unit.

4–9. Davis Company produces a product called Max. A by-product, called Min, also results from the manufacturing process. Min requires additional processing costs of $8,000 beyond the split-off point, and it can be sold for $0.80 a pound. Joint costs for the month were $170,000, and production consisted of 155,000 pounds of Max and 15,000 of Min. All production was sold.

Required:

A. Calculate the cost of Max for the month assuming that no joint costs are allocated to Min.

B. Calculate the cost of Max for the month assuming that by-product gross margin is treated as a reduction in the cost of the main product.

4–10. The production processes involved in making maple syrup can also produce maple sugar. Vermont Sugar Enterprises wishes to produce only syrup, but on occasion some sugaring takes place. Production for March produced the following results:

	Syrup	Sugar	Total
Units produced......................	10,000	500	10,500
Unit selling price	$ 7.50	$1.00	
Total process costs:			
After-split-off......................	$ 6,000	$ 155	$ 6,155
Joint costs			55,000

Required:

A. Calculate the cost of the syrup if the sugar is considered a by-product and the gross profit from its sale is considered to be a reduction of syrup cost.

B. Calculate product costs assuming this company decided to make and sell as much maple sugar as possible after filling all syrup orders.

4–11. The Middy Company uses a job order cost system. The following relate to the month of March:

Order	Raw materials	Direct labor	
No.	issued	Hours	Dollars
11	$ 2,000	1,000	$ 4,000
12	6,100	2,000	8,000
13	7,000	5,000	19,000
14	5,300	2,000	9,000
15	6,200	3,000	12,000
Total......................	$26,600	13,000	$52,000

Manufacturing overhead cost is applied to production on the basis of $4 per direct labor hour.

Manufacturing overhead cost for the month was $55,000.

Production orders 11, 13, 14, and 15 were completed during the month.

Production orders 11 and 14 were shipped and invoiced to customers during the month at a price double the total factory cost.

Required:

A. Prepare the following journal entries:
    1. Transferring raw material to goods in process.
    2. Transferring direct labor to goods in process.
    3. Transferring overhead cost to goods in process.
    4. Transferring from goods in process to finished goods inventory.
    5. Recording sales revenue and cost of goods sold.
B. Prepare a job cost record for Order No. 12.
C. What was the gross margin for the month?

4-12. The Wendell Canning Company has a busy season lasting six months from September through February and a slack season lasting from March through August. Typical data for these seasons are as follows:

	Busy season	Slack season
Average monthly direct labor hours.....................	12,000	4,000
Average monthly factory overhead costs..............	$24,000	$12,000

Manufacturing overhead cost is allocated to cases of canned goods on the basis of direct labor hours. The typical case requires one direct labor hour. The same type of products is packed in all months. On December 31, it has 20,000 cases in finished goods inventory.

Required:

A. If the company allocated each month's factory overhead costs to the products made in that month, what would be the factory overhead cost per case in the busy season and in the slack season, respectively? What would be the factory overhead cost component of finished goods inventory?
B. If, instead, the company used a predetermined annual overhead rate, what would be its cost per case? What would be the factory overhead cost component of finished goods inventory?
C. Discuss which method of overhead allocation is preferable.

4-13. Thrift-Shops, Inc., operates a chain of three food stores in a state that recently enacted legislation permitting municipalities within the state to levy an income tax on corporations operating within their respective municipalities. The legislation establishes a uniform tax rate that the municipalities may levy, and regulations that provide that the tax is to be computed on income derived within the taxing municipality, after a reasonable and consistent allocation of general overhead expenses. General overhead expenses have not been allocated to individual stores previously and include warehouse, general office, advertising, and delivery expenses.

Each of the municipalities in which Thrift-Shops, Inc., operates a store has levied the tax as provided by state legislation, and management is considering two plans for allocating general overhead expenses to the stores. The 1977 operating results before general overhead and taxes for each store were:

	Store			
	Ashville	Burns	Clinton	Total
Sales, net..	$416,000	$353,600	$270,000	$1,040,000
Less cost of sales	215,700	183,300	140,200	539,200
Gross margin	200,300	170,300	130,200	500,800
Less local operating expenses:				
Fixed...	60,800	48,750	50,200	159,750
Variable.....................................	54,700	64,220	27,448	146,368
Total.....................................	115,500	112,970	77,648	306,118
Income before general overhead and taxes...............................	$ 84,800	$ 57,330	$ 52,552	$ 194,682

General overhead expenses in 1977 were as follows:

Warehousing and delivery expenses:		
Warehouse depreciation	$20,000	
Warehouse operations.................................	30,000	
Delivery expenses	40,000	$ 90,000
Central office expenses:		
Advertising	18,000	
Central office salaries	37,000	
Other central office expenses.......................	28,000	83,000
Total General Overhead		$173,000

Additional information includes the following:

1. One fifth of the warehouse space is used to house the central office, and depreciation on this space is included in other central office expenses. Warehouse operating expenses vary with quantity of merchandise sold.
2. Delivery expenses vary with distance and number of deliveries. The distances from the warehouse to each store and the number of deliveries made in 1977 were as follows:

Store	Miles	Number of deliveries
Ashville	120	140
Burns...	200	64
Clinton.....................................	100	104

3. All advertising is prepared by the central office and is distributed in the areas in which stores are located.
4. As each store was opened, the fixed portion of central office salaries increased $7,000 and other central office expenses increased $2,500. Basic fixed central office salaries amount to $10,000, and basic fixed

other central office expenses amount to $12,000. The remainder of central office salaries and the remainder of other central office expenses vary with sales.

Required:

For each of the following plans for allocating general overhead expenses, compute the income of each store that would be subject to the municipal levy on corporation income:

Plan 1.   Allocate all general overhead expenses on the basis of sales volume.

Plan 2.   First, allocate central office salaries and other central office expenses evenly to warehouse operations and each store. Second, allocate the resulting warehouse operations expenses, warehouse depreciation and advertising to each store on the basis of sales volume. Third, allocate delivery expenses to each store on the basis of delivery miles times number of deliveries.

(AICPA adapted)

4–14.   Miller Manufacturing Company buys zeon for $0.80 a gallon. At the end of processing in Department 1, zeon splits off into products A, B, and C. Product A is sold at the split-off point, with no further processing. Products B and C require further processing before they can be sold; Product B is processed in Department 2, and Product C is processed in Department 3. Following is a summary of costs and other related data for the year ended June 30, 1977.

	Department		
	1	2	3
Cost of zeon	$96,000	–	–
Direct labor	14,000	$45,000	$ 65,000
Manufacturing overhead	10,000	21,000	49,000

	Products		
	A	B	C
Gallon sold	20,000	30,000	45,000
Gallons on hand at June 30, 1977	10,000	–	15,000
Sales in dollars	$30,000	$96,000	$141,750

There were no inventories on hand at July 1, 1977, and there was no zeon on hand at June 30, 1977. All gallons on hand at June 30, 1977, were complete as to processing. There were no manufacturing overhead variances. Miller uses the market value method of allocating joint costs.

Required:

A.   Calculate the amount of joint costs to be allocated to each product.
B.   Calculate the cost of goods sold for each product.
C.   Calculate the value of ending inventory for each product.

(AICPA adapted)

4–15. The Drake Company allocates overhead costs to jobs on the basis of direct labor hours. Its estimated average monthly factory costs for 1977 are as follows:

	Average monthly costs
Direct material	$ 50,000
Direct labor	160,000
Overhead costs	100,000

Its estimated average monthly direct labor hours is 20,000.

Among the jobs worked on in November 1977 were two jobs, G and H, for which the following information was collected:

	Job G	Job H
Direct material cost	$ 5,000	$ 5,000
Direct labor cost	16,000	20,000
Direct labor hours	2,000	2,500

Required:

A. Compute the overhead rate and the total factory costs of Jobs G and H.

B. At what amounts would customers be billed if the company's practice was to charge 180 percent of the manufacturing cost of each job?

4–16. The Smith Company estimated that costs of production for the following year would be:

Direct materials	$50,000
Direct labor	60,000
Factory overhead	90,000

Required:

A. Calculate the overhead rate for the next year, assuming that it is based on direct labor dollars.

B. Journalize the entry necessary to show the total cost of production for the month of April if the raw materials put into production totaled $4,000 and direct labor was $5,100.

C. If actual factory overhead costs incurred in April were $7,500, calculate the overabsorbed or underabsorbed overhead for the month.

D. What disposition should be made of the overabsorbed or underabsorbed overhead for April? Why?

4–17. At the end of the accounting period a partial list of the accounts of Seale, Inc., shows the following balances:

	Debit	Credit
Raw materials ending inventory	$12,000	
Goods in process ending inventory	14,400	
Finished goods ending inventory	9,600	
Cost of goods sold	48,000	
Selling and administrative expenses	7,200	
Overhead variance		$ 3,600
Sales revenue		66,000

Required:

A. Show the allocation of the overabsorbed or underabsorbed overhead to the proper accounts.

B. Compute the net income for the period.

4–18. The Northwest Company has been using an overhead rate based on direct labor dollars for each production center. A review of operations reveals the following facts:

1. Work starts in the stamping department where the use of costly stamping machinery is the prime reason for cost incurrence.
2. Stamped goods are then sent to the grinding department where the major cost is for the time spent grinding.
3. In assembly, a great deal of skill is required in some jobs, very little skill in others, causing varying hourly wages.

Required:

Use the following data to calculate the overhead rate for each production center, using the most appropriate allocation basis:

	Stamping	Grinding	Assembly
Expected overhead costs..............	$172,800	$152,000	$24,000
Total direct labor hours................	48,000	60,000	12,000
Total direct labor dollars	$180,000	$192,000	$48,000
Machine hours	9,600	240	120

4–19. The adjusted trial balance of Troy Corporation includes the following costs which are to be distributed before the books are closed to its three cost centers, A, B, and C.

	Total	Building	Furniture—fixtures	Machinery—equipment
Heat, light, power	$40,000			
Depreciation	23,800	$3,000	$800	$20,000
Insurance:				
Inventories...................	200			
Other.........................	2,210	1,300	60	850
Repairs.........................	5,900	4,000		1,900
Telephone expense..........	1,800			
	$73,910			

Data used for cost assignment follow:

	Cost center		
	A	B	C
Cubic feet...	700,000	200,000	100,000
Square feet of floor space	48,000	9,000	3,000
Number of telephone extensions....................	6	30	9

Three fourths of the furniture and fixtures are in Cost Center B, and one fourth are in Cost Center C. Half of the inventory is in Cost Center A, and half is in Cost Center B. Assume that all building costs except utilities are allocated on the basis of floor space. All machinery is in Cost Center A.

Required:

Calculate the amount of cost to be allocated to each cost center.

4-20.   The Northwest Company estimated the overhead costs for the coming year as shown below:

		Costs					
			Production centers			Service centers	
Expense	Basis for assignment	Stamping	Grinding	Assembly	Stores	Personnel	General Factory
Indirect wages	Payroll dollars	$ 50,000	$ 95,000	$10,000	$4,000	$29,000	$15,000
Rent	Square feet	1,200	1,200	600	1,200	240	360
Depreciation –							
Buildings..........	Square feet	2,400	2,400	1,200	2,400	480	720
Machinery	Value	89,750	8,650	1,785	10	15	820
Insurance...........	Value	300	280	150	15	15	60
Taxes – building ...	Square feet	600	600	300	600	120	180
Heat...................	Radiators	400	400	200	250	50	70
Power.................	Direct meter	450	450	175	25	80	40
Total.........		$145,100	$108,980	$14,410	$8,500	$30,000	$17,250

Additional data pertaining to the departments above:

Area in square feet.........................	10,000	10,000	5,000	10,000	2,000	3,000
Number of employees	10	15	2	1	5	2
Expected raw materials issued ($) ...	11,000	3,000	1,000			
Expected direct labor ($)	114,400	110,400	14,400			
Actual direct labor – January ($)	15,000	16,000	4,000			
Raw material – January ($)	40,000					
Actual indirect costs – January ($).....	23,000	19,000	6,000			

Required:

A.   Allocate the overhead costs of the service centers to the production centers utilizing the step-down procedure as follows:
Personnel – on basis of employees.
General factory – on basis of square feet of area.
Stores – on basis of requisitions.

B.   Compute the overhead rate per direct labor dollar for each production center.

C.   Calculate the overabsorbed or underabsorbed overhead for each production center for January.

4-21.   From a particular joint process, Watkins Company produces three products, X, Y, and Z. Joint production costs for the year were $60,000. Sales values and costs follow:

| | | Additional processing costs and sales values | |
| | | | |
Product	Units produced	Sales values	Added costs
X.......................... 6,000		$42,000	$9,000
Y.......................... 4,000		45,000	7,000
Z.......................... 2,000		32,000	8,000

Required:

A. Calculate the amount of joint costs to be allocated to each product using the physical basis of allocation.

B. Calculate the amount of joint costs to be allocated to each product using the market value basis of allocation.

(AICPA adapted)

4–22. Ellis Enterprises produces two joint products, L and M. Joint costs are $25,000 for a batch composed of 1,000 units of L and 500 units of M. Processing costs beyond the split-off point are $16,000 for L and $4,000 for M. Selling prices are $40 per unit for L and $20 per unit for M.

Required:

A. Calculate the amount of joint cost per batch to be allocated to each product using the physical basis of allocation.

B. Calculate the amount of joint cost per batch to be allocated to each product using the market value basis of allocation.

C. Calculate the gross margin for each product which would result from the two different methods of allocating joint costs. Which method would you recommend? Why?

D. Repeat Requirements B and C assuming that Ellis raises the price of L to $50 per unit.

4–23. Stewart Chemicals produces a product called Main-Pro. A by-product, called By-Pro, results from the manufacturing process. By-Pro requires additional processing costs of $10,000 beyond the split-off point, and it can be sold for $0.60 a pound. Joint costs for the month were $220,000, and production consisted of 200,000 pounds of Main-Pro and 20,000 pounds of By-Pro. All production was sold.

Required:

A. Calculate the cost of Main-Pro for the month assuming that no joint costs are allocated to By-Pro.

B. Calculate the cost of Main-Pro for the month assuming that by-product gross margin is treated as a reduction in the cost of the main product.

4–24. The Nutrient Company manufactures soybean oil and soybean meal. The company pays $64 per ton (2,000 pounds) for soybeans and incurs processing costs of $36 per ton. The average output from a ton of soybeans is 800 pounds of soybean oil and 1,200 pounds of soybean meal. Soybean oil is sold for $12 per cwt. (100 pounds), and soybean meal is sold for $3 per cwt.

Required:

A. Calculate the cost per cwt. of each product if—
   1. Costs are allocated on the basis of weight.
   2. Costs are allocated on the basis of market value.
   3. Soybean meal is treated as a by-product.
B. Which method of costing is preferable?
C. If output were 800 pounds of soybean oil, 1,100 pounds of soybean meal, and 100 pounds of chaff which had no market value, how, if at all, would your answer to Requirement A be different?

4–25. Department A uses a single raw material which costs $2 per pound. In October the department worked on four jobs, and the material used on each job was recorded as follows:

Job	Material used (*pounds*)
823	400
824	250
825	100
826	250

However, material was issued from raw materials inventory in an amount of $2,200.

Required:

A. How much material was wasted?
B. What do you think should be done about accounting for the waste?

CASE: STALCUP PAPER COMPANY

4–26. In March 1935 the president of the Stalcup Paper Company, while examining a group of charts regarding unit costs submitted to him by the cost department, noted that the unit costs of sorting rags had been rising for approximately two years. In order to determine the reason for this increase, he invited the foreman of the rag sorting department and the head of the cost department to his office to discuss the matter. The head of the cost department submitted three exhibits, as shown in Exhibits 4–8, 4–9, and 4–10, giving the details of the upward trend in costs shown in the charts. The foreman of the rag sorting department said

EXHIBIT 4–8
Output of rag sorting department in pounds

	1932	1934	Change
Old rags	3,220,000	2,460,000	− 23.6%
New rags	810,000	2,520,000	+211.1
	4,030,000	4,980,000	+ 23.6%
Percentage old rags	79.9%	49.4%	
Percentage new rags	20.1	50.6	

EXHIBIT 4–9
Expenses of rag sorting department

	1932		1934	
		Percent of direct labor		Percent of direct labor
Direct labor.................	$20,965		$17,185	
Rag sorting department burden:				
Indirect labor.............	$ 8,533		$ 9,540	
Repair labor..............	610		508	
Repair materials	123		271	
Supplies	156		160	
Power.......................	612		553	
Investment	15,549		15,204	
	25,853	122	26,236	153
General overhead	19,128	91	15,186	88
	$65,676		$58,607	

EXHIBIT 4–10
Rag sorting department, costs of sorting old and new rags (as shown in cost records)

	1932		1934	
	Dollars	Cents per pound	Dollars	Cents per pound
Old rags:				
Wages............................	$20,475	0.636	$15,645†	0.636
Department overhead.......	24,985*	0.776	23,885†	0.971
General overhead	18,681	0.580	13,825	0.562
	$64,141	1.992	$53,355	2.169
Increase				0.177·
New rags:				
Wages............................	$ 490	0.0605	$ 1,540	0.0611
Department overhead.......	598*	0.0738	2,351†	0.0933
General overhead	447	0.0552	1,361	0.0540
	$ 1,535	0.1895	$ 5,252	0.2084
Increase				0.0189

* 122 percent of wages.
† 153 percent of wages.

that his costs were lower rather than higher than they had been in past years, and that the basis of the cost department's estimates was unsound. He submitted Exhibit 4–11 in support of this contention.

The Stalcup Paper Company used old rags, new rags, and pulp in manufacturing its papers. The proportions in which these materials were

EXHIBIT 4–11

Rag sorting department, costs of sorting old and new rags (as estimated by foreman)

| | 1932 | | 1934 | |
	Dollars	Cents per pound	Dollars	Cents per pound
Old rags:				
Wages	$20,475	0.636	$15,645	0.636
Department overhead	20,441	0.635	12,960	0.527
General overhead	15,285	0.475	7,502	0.305
	$56,201	1.746	$36,107	1.468
Decrease				0.278
New rags:				
Wages	$ 490	0.060	$ 1,540	0.061
Department overhead	5,142	0.635	13,276	0.527
General overhead	3,843	0.475	7,684	0.305
	$ 9,475	1.170	$22,500	0.893
Decrease				0.277

mixed were varied in accordance with the requirements for different grades and types of paper. The new rags, which were purchased from textile converters, cost substantially more per pound than old rags, which were purchased through junk dealers. The old rags were usually received in the form of garments, from which it was necessary to remove carefully all foreign materials such as buttons, rubber, and metal. New rags were largely remnants containing only a small percentage of foreign matter requiring removal; consequently, they could be sorted much more rapidly than old rags.

The sorters sat at benches. Their task was to remove all foreign matter from the material placed before them and to distribute the usable cloth, according to quality, into containers placed beside them. The sorters inspected and graded, on the average, 55 pounds of old rags of 575 pounds of new rags per hour. They were paid on a day rate basis, the management having discovered by experience that payment on a piece rate basis resulted in picking over rags less carefully.

Between 1932 and 1934 the composition of rags purchased by the Stalcup Paper Company changed considerably, as shown in Exhibit 4–8. The percentage of old rags to the total dropped from approximately 80 percent to approximately 50 percent. During the same interval the total quantity of rags handled increased nearly 25 percent. In spite of the large increase in total volume, labor costs declined over the period because of the smaller amount of old rags handled.

Costs charged to the rag sorting department were of three types: first, those incurred for direct labor in the department; second, overhead charged directly to the department; and third, general factory overhead. The amount of general factory overhead charged to a department was obtained by multiplying the direct labor in the department by the ratio of total general overhead to total direct labor in the entire plant.

Both departmental burden and the department's share of general factory overhead were charged to products processed by the department as a percentage of the direct labor applied to these products. This percentage was obtained by dividing total overhead by total direct labor in the department.

The items included in rag sorting department burden were as shown in Exhibit 4–9. The most important of these were indirect labor, including the salary of the foreman and wages of employees engaged in taking material to and from the sorters, and investment, which included the charge against the department for taxes, depreciation, and insurance on the premises and equipment it used. General overhead included miscellaneous factory labor, building repair labor and materials, manufacturing executive salaries, and expenses of functional departments, such as planning, costing, and research.

The head of the cost department pointed out to the president that between 1932 and 1934 the rag sorting department burden charge had increased from 122 percent of direct labor to 153 percent and that the difference in the cost of rag sorting in the two years was, as shown in Exhibit 4–10, almost entirely attributable to this increase.

The foreman differed with the cost department's estimated unit costs and pointed out that it was hard to conceive of unit costs increasing while total costs were diminishing and while volume of output was rising. He stated that the cost department was not charging the proper proportion of overhead charges to the new rags and that therefore old rags were taking more than their share of total department burden. He said that, in his opinion, a much sounder method of allocating burden charges would be on a per-pound basis rather than on the percentage-of-direct-labor basis previously used; and he recommended that costs in the rag department in the future should be calculated on the basis shown in Exhibit 4–11.

In 1935 the Stalcup Paper Company was operating at about 55 percent of capacity.

Required:

A. How can you explain the difference between the costs shown in Exhibit 4–10 and those shown in Exhibit 4–11?

B. What really has happened to the costs in 1934 as compared to 1932? Is the foreman to be congratulated, or should he be criticized?

5

Other aspects of cost accounting

In Chapters 3 and 4 we focused on the measurement of costs for one type of cost objective; namely, the manufacture of goods. We now expend the description to include other types of costs: (1) costs incurred by manufacturing companies other than for manufacturing; (2) costs of merchandising companies; and (3) costs of service companies, including nonprofit organizations. We also point out some of the implications that can be derived from a discussion of cost accounting systems.

The general principles of cost measurement are the same for nonmanufacturing costs as for manufacturing costs, and the same for services as for goods. In this chapter, we are simply extending these principles to additional types of cost and to additional cost objectives.

NONMANUFACTURING COSTS

Until the last two or three decades, most cost accounting systems dealt solely with the measurement of the manufacturing costs of goods. This was probably because manufacturing costs are the only items of cost that need to be collected in order to prepare the external financial statements. The manufacturing costs of goods must be measured in order to obtain the amounts for the Goods in Process Inventory and Finished Goods Inventory accounts on the balance sheet and the amount for cost of goods sold on the income statement. Other costs are reported as expenses on the income statement in aggregate amounts, and hence there is no need to assign them to specific cost objectives for external reporting purposes.

In more recent years, cost accounting systems have been expanded to include other types of cost. A list of the types of nonmanufacturing costs, as they are found in many industrial companies, is given below.

1. Distribution costs.
    a. Marketing costs.
    b. Logistics costs.
2. Research and development costs.
3. General and administrative costs.
    a. Staff and service units.
    b. General corporate costs.
4. Capital costs.

These types of cost are part of the full cost of *manufacturing and selling* a product. Nevertheless, because of the traditional focus on manufacturing costs in cost accounting systems, some people use "full cost" to mean only the *manufacturing* cost of a product. Care must be taken to distinguish between these two quite different uses of the term "full cost." Although there is considerable diversity in the way companies classify nonmanufacturing activities, this list is sufficiently representative to serve as a basis for the discussion that follows.

For nonmanufacturing costs, the guiding principles of cost measurement are the same as those already discussed in connection with manufacturing costs; namely, (1) the full cost of a cost objective is the sum of its direct costs plus an equitable share of indirect costs, (2) as many items of cost as are feasible should be treated as direct costs, and (3) indirect costs should be allocated to individual cost objectives on the basis of intended benefits or a causal relationship.

Distribution costs

Distribution costs comprise the costs of performing two quite dissimilar activities: (1) marketing (or order getting) and (2) logistics (or order filling). Both activities are involved in getting the finished product from the factory to the customer. The basic distinction between them is that marketing costs are incurred *before* the receipt of a sales order, whereas logistics costs are incurred *after* the order has been received.

From a management standpoint, this distinction is of fundamental importance. Logistics costs are *caused by* the sales transaction in the sense that once a sales order has been accepted, a chain of events begins that culminates in the delivery of the product to the customer and the collection of cash from the customer. These events involve costs, and the costs are a more-or-less inevitable consequence of accepting the order. Marketing costs have an opposite cause-and-effect relationship.

They *cause* the sales order, rather than being *caused by* the sales order. They are in the nature of "bread cast upon the waters."

Marketing costs. **Marketing costs are costs that are incurred in efforts to make sales.** They include: advertising and other sales promotion costs; the costs of field salespersons and sales offices, including the salaries, travel, and entertainment expense, costs of training salespersons and holding sales meetings, commissions of salespersons, and the costs associated with operating sales offices; market research costs; and the costs of general marketing management activities.

Marketing costs are as necessary to the profitable operation of a business as are manufacturing costs. It is, however, much more difficult to measure the marketing cost of a single product than to measure its manufacturing cost. Marketing activities are often carried on in field sales offices which may be widely dispersed geographically, whereas manufacturing is usually carried on within the four walls of one plant. Usually, salespersons and others in the marketing organization handle several products; consequently, most of the marketing costs applicable to a single product are indirect costs. Manufacturing activities tend to be standardized and repetitive, whereas each call made by a salesperson must be tailored to fit the needs and whims of the particular customer. Most importantly, although many marketing activities cannot be traced to specific sales orders, the cost of the *entire* marketing effort is properly associated with the sales revenue that results from those orders that are obtained. For example, if a salesperson's cost averages $50 per call (i.e., a visit to a customer's office) and if one order is received, on the average, for every three calls that the salesperson makes, the cost per sales order is not the $50 cost of the call which resulted in the order; rather, it is the $150 cost of the three calls.

For these and other reasons, few companies attempt to measure the marketing cost of each product separately. Instead, they measure the cost of each marketing *function,* that is, advertising, direct selling, market research, and so on. These functions are cost centers in the same sense that the manufacturing functions discussed in Chapter 4 are cost centers, and the same principles of cost measurement apply to them. The total cost of each function includes some elements that are direct and other elements that are indirect. Expenses for newspaper and other advertising are direct costs of the advertising function, for example. Compensation of salespersons, their travel expenses, and costs of operating branch offices are direct costs of the selling function. (If the salesperson is paid on a commission basis, the compensation can even be traced directly to the products sold.) The marketing organization also has service cost centers, such as occupancy, information processing, and sales engineers, and these indirect costs are assigned to the functional cost centers in the same manner as service center costs are assigned in the factory.

Classification of costs.   In the factory, the final cost objectives are products; that is, all costs eventually get assigned to products. In the marketing organization, by contrast, cost information is used for a variety of purposes. Sales revenue and marketing costs may be classified in a number of ways, including:

1. Sales territories or sales offices.
2. Individual salespersons.
3. Customers, classified by —
   a. Industry.
   b. Size of order.
   c. Geographical territory.
   d. Frequency of salesperson's call.
4. Types of selling effort, such as media advertising, point-of-sale advertising, sales promotion, coupons, and so on.
5. Products and product lines.

Each of these categories is a cost objective. In order to assign costs to these cost objectives, the original classification of costs by functions must be quite detailed. After they are accumulated in the functional cost centers, costs are reclassified according to the categories indicated above, or such other categories as management finds useful. Although it might seem that much recordkeeping would be required to make such cross classifications, they are in fact easily accomplished with modern computer processing. Exhibit 5–1 shows reports that classify sales data in four different ways: (1) by item, (2) by classes of item, (3) by customers, and (4) by salesman.

Logistics costs. **Logistics costs are those costs incurred between the time goods enter finished goods inventory and the time they are delivered to the customer, together with the recordkeeping costs associated with processing the customer's order and account receivable.** These costs include: costs of warehousing, that is, holding the completed product in inventory until it is shipped to the customer; costs of packing and otherwise preparing the product for shipment; costs of shipping the product to the customer, including transportation costs if the customer does not pay for these separately; costs of installation and servicing the product if the customer does not pay for these separately; costs of preparing the invoice and the related costs of recording the transaction in the company's accounts; the costs of processing the payment when it is received from the customer, collection cost, and bad debt expense. In the terminology of economics, most logistics costs provide **place utility,** in contrast with manufacturing costs which provide **form utility.**

As is the case with marketing costs, logistics costs are part of the full costs of products in the sense that a product cannot be said to be profitable unless its sales revenue exceeds all its costs, including logistics costs. Thus, in estimating full costs as a basis for setting selling prices, both marketing costs and logistics costs must be taken into account.

EXHIBIT 5-1

Multiple classification of sales information

```
                          LAURENTIAN INDUSTRIES, INC.

                       COMPARATIVE ANALYSIS OF SALES BY ITEM


                          PERIOD ENDING 10/31/--                    PAGE


    ITEM                             CURR. PERIOD QUAN.   PCT    YTD QUANTITY     PCT
    NO.          DESCRIPTION         THIS YR   LAST YR    CHG   THIS YR  LAST YR  CHG
   624634   D20068 OVERHAUL GASKET     10        14       29-     90       98     8-
   624832   17D0011 BELT DYNAMIC FAN  190       150       27    1,820    1,905    4-
   624901   DMK6448 HUB ASSEMBLY J2     1-        5      120-     18       18     0
```

```
                          LAURENTIAN INDUSTRIES, INC.

                             SALES BY ITEM CLASS

                            MONTH ENDING 03/31/--


    ITEM                      SOLD THIS   GROSS    PROFIT   SOLD THIS    GROSS    PROFIT
    CLASS  CLASS DESCRIPTION    MONTH     PROFIT   PERCENT    YEAR       PROFIT   PERCENT

      1    ABRASIVES          2,720.19   271.36      10      9,900.17    907.60      9

      2    ACIDS AND CHEMICALS 1,216.27  170.27      14      3,139.68    408.07     13

      3    BRASS              6,220.83   435.45       7     16,341.47  1,143.87      7
```

```
                          LAURENTIAN INDUSTRIES, INC.

                         COMPARATIVE SALES ANALYSIS

                       BY ITEM CLASS FOR EACH CUSTOMER

                            MONTH ENDING 05/31/--                   PAGE


    CUST  ITEM    CUSTOMER/ITEM CLASS      MONTHLY SALES      PRCNT   YEAR TO DATE SALES   PRCNT
    NO   CLASS         NAME            THIS YEAR  LAST YEAR   CHG    THIS YEAR  LAST YEAR   CHG
    3310         TARDELL HARDWARE
            11   BUILDER HARDWARE         103.19    91.31     13     515.92     729.43     29-
            12   ELECTRICAL SUPPLIES       87.58    85.02      2     435.57     375.29     16
            13   GIFTS AND SUNDRIES        63.01      .00            315.09     490.36     35-
            14   HOUSEWARES               198.05   150.23     32     990.32   1,123.19     12-
```

```
                          LAURENTIAN INDUSTRIES, INC.

                       COMPARATIVE SALES ANALYSIS BY CUSTOMER

                             FOR EACH SALESMAN

                            PERIOD ENDING 07/31/--                  PAGE


    SLMN  CUST.   SALESMAN/CUSTOMER    THIS PERIOD   THIS PERIOD   YEAR-TO-DATE   YEAR-TO-DATE
    NO.   NO.          NAME            THIS YEAR     LAST YEAR     THIS YEAR      LAST YEAR
     10          A R WESTON
          1426   HYDRO CYCLES INC       3,210.26     4,312.06     10,010.28       9,000.92
          2632   RUPP AQUA CYCLES       7,800.02     2,301.98     20,322.60      11,020.16
          3217   SEA PORT WEST CO          90.00CR     421.06        900.00         593.10

                 SALESMAN TOTALS      10,920.28      7,035.10     31,732.88      20,614.18

     12          H T BRAVEMAN
          0301   BOLLINGER ASSOCIATES     100.96         0.00        100.96          0.00
```

Source: Courtesy of Data Processing, IBM Corporation.

Also, like marketing costs, logistics costs are classified in various ways in order to facilitate their use for management planning and control.

Research and development costs

Research and development costs are the costs associated with efforts to find new or improved products or processes. Although there is a technical distinction between *research* and *development,* it is unimportant for our purposes since both types of effort are usually carried on by the same organization unit.

Research and development is a gamble. Only a relatively few research projects—in many companies, fewer than 5 percent—produce successful results. Although the money spent on the unsuccessful projects is lost, it is an unavoidable loss since no one knows at the beginning of a research effort whether the effort will succeed. Thus, it may be realistic to view the whole research and development effort as an overall cost of the company. In this view, all the research and development costs would be allocated to all the products.

Modifications of this broad view are possible. Some product lines may inherently require more research and development effort than others because they are threatened by early obsolescence unless extensive research and development effort is undertaken to keep them up to date. Management may decide to allocate all, or greater than a proportional share of, research and development costs to these product lines. Also some research and development projects may be specifically identifiable with a particular product, such as research that is undertaken to correct a defect that has been discovered in that product; if so, the cost of such a project is a direct cost of that product.

Project costing. Within the research and development organization, the unit of costing—that is, the cost objective—is generally the individual research and development project. If management decides that the therapeutic possibilities of some new chemical formulation should be investigated, it sets up a **project** for this specific purpose and assigns one or more researchers to work on that project. The resources used for the project are measured in a way that is similar to the job order cost system in the factory. Each project is a job, to which is assigned its direct costs and an allocated portion of the indirect costs of the research and development organization. In order to allocate overhead costs to projects, a research and development overhead rate is calculated, using a procedure similar to that described in Chapter 4.

In addition to working on projects, researchers typically spend some of their time on nonproject investigations, trying out their own ideas. The costs of such work are collected in a miscellaneous project account that is set up for this purpose.

General and administrative costs

General and administrative is a catchall category. It **includes general costs and also the costs of various administrative activities applicable to the company as a whole.** The distinction between *general* and *administrative* is not important enough to warrant separate treatment of these two categories. Costs of these functions are sometimes referred to as *corporate* costs or as *home office* costs. For the purpose of measuring and analyzing costs, these functions can be classified as either (1) staff and service units or (2) general corporate costs.

Staff and service units. All companies except the smallest have central staff units that provide assistance to the line units and to top management. These include the *controller department,* headed by the controller, whose functions were described in Chapter 1; the *finance department* (or treasurer department), which is responsible for negotiating loans, arranging for issues of stock, and managing cash and short-term securities; the *manufacturing staff,* which sets manufacturing policies and does engineering work for manufacturing facilities; the *purchasing department,* which sets purchasing policy and which may do the actual purchasing of certain raw materials and services; the *personnel department,* which is responsible for hiring and training personnel, for establishing wage and salary scales and other personnel policies and for operating cafeterias and recreational facilities and providing medical services; the *industrial relations department,* which deals with employee complaints and union negotiations (often a part of the personnel department); the *corporate secretary department,* which is responsible for general corporate affairs and relationships with stockholders; the *public relations department,* which is responsible for maintaining a favorable public attitude toward the company; the *legal department,* which prepares or checks contracts and other legal documents and represents the company in litigation; and a number of others. In some companies there is a separate information processing department that operates computers; in other companies, this function is part of the controller department.

To the extent that these staff units provide services that can be traced directly to individual line departments, the cost of these services is a direct cost of the departments receiving them. If these line departments are production cost centers, the costs of the staff units become part of the costs of the products that these departments work on. For example, if employees of the manufacturing staff redesign the production work flow in a plant, the costs are a direct cost of that plant and become part of the overhead cost of products manufactured in the plant. Other staff and service costs are indirect and hence are allocated to cost objectives.

General corporate costs. Corporate costs include the costs of general management, that is, the chief executive, other top executives who have general management (as distinguished from functional management) responsibilities, and their personal staffs. Corporate costs also include donations to charitable organizations, dues and other costs associated with trade association membership, settlement of lawsuits and other litigation costs that are in addition to the costs of the legal staff, expenditures to meet the company's public responsibilities, and similar activities. Since the activities of general management are spread across the whole business and since these and other general corporate costs can rarely be traced directly to a specific cost center, almost all general corporate costs are indirect costs.

Relation to manufacturing costs.   Although general and administrative costs are not incurred physically inside the factory, some of them are incurred, at least in part, *for the benefit of* the manufacturing process. The personnel department, for example, may be responsible for hiring and training employees some of whom are factory employees; the controller maintains accounting records, some of which are factory records. Despite the conceptual justification for assigning a part of the general and administrative costs as factory costs, many companies do not do so. They have decided that the extra paperwork that would be required would not be worthwhile.

Assignment of general and administrative costs

For some purposes it is necessary to assign general and administrative costs to cost objectives. The Cost Accounting Standards Board (CASB) has prescribed bases for assigning such costs in some detail in two standards, Nos. 403 and 410. Although Standard No. 403 is specifically related to the problem of allocating "home office" (i.e., corporate headquarters) costs to segments (i.e., divisions, plants, or other major subdivisions of a company), the same general principles apply to the allocation of general and administrative costs to other types of cost objectives.

Exhibit 5–2 gives examples of allocation bases that are suggested by CASB for various general and administrative functions.

Residual expenses.   Those items of general and administrative costs that cannot realistically be related to activities on a causal or benefits received basis are called **residual expenses.** They include the general corporate costs and in some companies a portion of staff and service costs. The Cost Accounting Standards Board has a complicated formula for the allocation of residual expenses, but most companies allocate them according to the overall size of the various cost objectives. For example, residual expenses might be assigned to divisions in the same ratio as the total direct costs of each division bore to the total of the direct costs of all divisions. Consequently, each division would be allocated residual expenses in proportion to its size, which usually is a reasonable basis.

EXHIBIT 5-2

Bases for allocating general and administrative costs

Home office expense or function	Alternative allocation bases
Centralized service functions:	
1. Personnel administration...............	1. Number of personnel, labor hours, payroll, number of hires.
2. Data processing services...............	2. Machine time, number of reports.
3. Centralized purchasing and sub-contracting	3. Number of purchase orders, value of purchases, number of items.
4. Centralized warehousing...............	4. Square footage, value of material, volume.
5. Company aircraft service...............	5. Actual or standard rate per hour, mile, passenger mile, or similar unit.
6. Central telephone service..............	6. Usage costs, number of instruments.
Staff management of specific activities:	
1. Personnel management.................	1. Number of personnel, labor hours, payroll, number of hires.
2. Manufacturing policies (quality control, industrial engineering, production scheduling, tooling, inspection, and testing, etc.).	2. Manufacturing cost input, manufacturing direct labor.
3. Engineering policies	3. Total engineering costs, engineering direct labor, number of drawings.
4. Material/purchasing policies..........	4. Number of purchase orders, value of purchases.
5. Marketing policies	5. Sales, segment marketing costs.

Source: Cost Accounting Standards 403.60.

Converting allocated costs to direct costs. Some costs which are allocated could, with some effort, be assigned directly to cost objectives. For example, if the controller department operates a computer, a common practice is to allocate the costs of this computer to other costs centers on the basis of an overall measure of their size. Alternatively, a preferable procedure is to assign computer costs directly to users by calculating a rate per minute for the cost of computer usage and charging each user for computer time at this rate. It is worthwhile to go to some effort to develop procedures for assigning costs directly, for at least two reasons: (1) direct assignment is a more accurate way of assigning costs than allocating them; and (2) as will be discussed in Chapter 11, direct assignment of costs assists in the control of these costs.

Capital costs

Capital costs are the costs of using the capital that the company has invested in its assets. For debt capital (i.e., funds borrowed from creditors), this cost is called *interest*. For equity capital (i.e., funds supplied by shareholders), no explicit cost is recognized in financial accounting. (Dividends paid to shareholders are *not* a measure of the cost of equity capital; dividends are a distribution of earnings, rather than a cost.)

Many companies do not include capital costs in their cost accounting systems; that is, they do not attempt to assign capital costs to cost objectives. When they measure the profitability of a division, a product line, or some other segment of the business, they exclude capital costs. When capital costs are omitted, income is not the true profit in the economic sense since in economics the cost of using capital is a cost. Income so calculated is income from operations. Unless this operating income is large enough to cover the capital costs, the division or other cost objective is not really profitable.

Some companies do assign capital costs to cost objectives. When the expenses subtracted from revenue include an item for capital costs, the resulting income amount is a better measure of the real profitability of the cost objective. When capital costs are included, it is important to recognize that these costs are *not* solely the interest cost of using borrowed capital but also include the cost of using equity capital. In Chapter 8 we shall discuss how such a cost can be estimated.

Assets employed.   Even though the cost of using capital is not explicitly recognized in most systems, there are several types of analyses in which the measurement of this cost is important. For example, in Chapter 2 we emphasized the importance of setting selling prices for products in a way that recognized differences in the amount of capital employed. Also, in order to analyze the profitability of a division, it is necessary to relate the division's income to the capital it uses. The amount of capital that a business uses is listed on the right-hand side of its balance sheet, classified according to its source—mortgage loans, bonds, shareholders equity, and so on. The uses made of this capital are listed on the left-hand side of the balance sheet, classified according to the types of assets that have been acquired with the capital. Analyses of the type mentioned above use data on the left-hand side of the balance sheet rather than data on the right-hand side; that is, they measure assets employed.

There are two main categories of assets employed: fixed assets and current assets. We shall describe how each can be associated with a product cost objective. Similar techniques can be used for assigning assets to other cost objectives.

Fixed assets.   The fixed assets employed for a product can be either direct or indirect, with respect to that product. The machinery used to manufacture a product is directly traceable to that product. Some part of the factory building, warehouses, and even general corporate office space are indirectly attributable to that product. One cost of using the fixed assets is depreciation, and it is allocated to products as part of the overhead allocation procedure described in Chapter 4. The capital costs of the fixed assets employed for a product can be assigned to the product in essentially the same way that depreciation costs are assigned. In this context fixed assets are often called **facilities capital.**

EXAMPLE: In Cost Center No. 27, a production cost center, overhead costs are allocated to products by means of an overhead rate per unit of product. This overhead rate includes the depreciation cost of fixed assets. By means of this overhead rate, 10 percent of the depreciation cost in Cost Center No. 27 is allocated to Product A. Cost Center No. 27 has $1,000,000 of fixed assets; and 10 percent of this amount, or $100,000, is therefore calculated as the cost center fixed assets employed for Product A.

The costs of various service centers are also allocated to Cost Center No. 27. Included in these costs are depreciation costs which total 20 percent of the total depreciation of all service centers. The fixed assets in all service centers total $2,000,000. Cost Center No. 27 is therefore allocated 20 percent of this amount, or $400,000; and 10 percent of the $400,000, or $40,000 is in turn allocated to Product A.

The total fixed assets employed for Product A is therefore $100,000 + $40,000 = $140,000. The capital cost of Product A is found by multiplying $140,000 by the rate selected as the cost of capital.

Current assets. The current assets whose capital cost is allocated to products usually consist of inventory and accounts receivable. Cash, prepaid expenses, and other current assets are typically of such minor importance that the work involved in associating their capital cost with products is not worthwhile. In most cases, no attempt is made to trace inventory and accounts receivable directly to product cost objectives. Instead, overall relationships are established, and the amount of working capital applicable to a product is calculated from these relationships.

EXAMPLE: In a certain company, the balance in accounts receivable typically is 10 percent of annual sales revenue. The company therefore estimates that the amount of the accounts receivable asset employed for each product is 10 percent of the estimated sales revenue of that product. In the same company, the inventory amount averages 20 percent of the annual cost of goods sold. The company therefore estimates that the amount of the inventory asset employed for each product is 20 percent of the estimated manufacturing cost of that product. The capital cost of the current asset associated with Product A is found by multiplying these amounts by the rate selected for the cost of capital.

Contract costing. Effective in 1976, the Cost Accounting Standards Board, in its Standard No. 414, required that the cost of using facilities capital be included as an item of cost in government contracts. The CASB currently does not require that the cost of using current assets be so included.

IMPLICATIONS FOR USERS OF COST INFORMATION

We have now completed our description of the methods used by companies to measure full costs. Before turning to another topic, it is appropriate to think about the description in this and the two preceding chapters from the viewpoint of the user of cost information, for the user needs to understand the effect of cost accounting practices in order to understand the nature and significance of the cost information that is generated by these practices.

Effect of alternative practices on income measurement

Cost measures the use of resources. The total costs of a period can be classified into one of three categories depending on the purpose for which resources were used: (1) capital expenditures, (2) product costs, or (3) expenses.

Capital expenditures are the costs associated with the acquisition, construction, and installation of fixed assets. (Note that this term does not have the same meaning as *capital costs* discussed in the preceding section.) These costs are reported in the fixed assets section of the balance sheet. At the moment of acquisition, capital expenditures have no effect on income. They are amortized (i.e., depreciated) and become expenses in the future years during which the assets provide benefits to the company. In *Fundamentals of Financial Accounting* we discuss how the line between capital expenditures and other costs should be drawn.

Product costs (also called **inventoriable costs** or **factory costs**) consist of the direct costs plus a fair share of the factory indirect costs that are involved in manufacturing products. These costs "attach" to the product; that is, as the product physically moves through the factory, the accounting system accumulates its cost in each of the production cost centers through which it moves. Initially, these costs appear as Goods in Process Inventory, an asset. When the manufacturing process has been completed, the product physically moves to finished goods inventory, and its cost enters Finished Goods Inventory, another asset. When the product is sold, its cost is reported on the income statement as cost of goods sold. Thus, **product costs affect income only in the period in which the product is sold.**

Note that in financial accounting the product cost is the cost of *manufacturing* the product; it does not include costs incurred "beyond the factory door." Product costs are therefore less than the full cost of a product; full cost includes distribution and general and administrative costs as well as manufacturing cost.

Cost of goods sold is matched against revenue on the income statement. **Expenses are the other costs that are matched against revenue in a given accounting period.** They are also called **period costs.**

As discussed earlier, it is important to understand that although the terms *costs* and *expenses* are sometimes used interchangeably, they are in fact different concepts. **All expenses derive from cost, but not all costs are expenses.** The acquisition of a building involves a cost but not an expense in the period in which the building was acquired; the acquisition cost becomes an expense in future periods via the depreciation mechanism. The manufacture of a product involves a cost in the period of manufacture; the corresponding expense is reported in the period in which the product is sold.

Importance of the distinction. The decisions on how a given item of cost is classified can have an important effect on the amount of income reported for a given accounting period. The effect is shown in the diagram in Exhibit 5–3. Consider any resource, such as labor services, material,

EXHIBIT 5–3
Effect on income of alternative cost practices

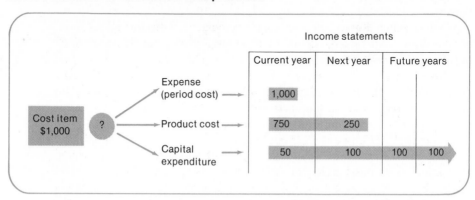

supplies, or whatever. The cost of this resource, assumed to be $1,000, can be recorded in one of three ways. If it is classified as an expense, the whole $1,000 affects income of the current year. If it is classified as a product cost and three fourths of the products containing this cost are sold in the current year, then $750 of the cost affects income in the current year. The remaining $250 winds up in inventory and affects income in the next year, the year in which these products are sold. Finally, if the $1,000 is a capital expenditure, it affects income in a succession of future years. In Exhibit 5–3, it is assumed that the asset is depreciated over a period of ten years, with one half a year's depreciation occurring in the first year. If the fixed asset is used in the manufacturing process, the impact is even more roundabout because depreciation first becomes a part of the product cost, and it affects income only when the product is sold.

Differences and similarities in practice

In addition to differences in the way in which companies distinguish between capital expenditures, product costs and expenses, other differences in practice have been described in this and the two preceding chapters. In order to understand the full meaning of an item of cost information, therefore, one must understand the system from which it comes. Does it or does it not include an allocation of distribution costs, or of some or all of general and administrative costs? If so, what basis of allocation is used? What items of cost are counted as direct costs? How are indirect manufacturing costs allocated? The way that a particular company answers these questions has an effect on the way it measures costs.

Despite these differences, there are forces which result in a basic similarity in the cost accounting systems of many companies. The set of generally accepted accounting principles is one such force. Moreover, in certain industries, companies have similar cost accounting systems because a trade association has fostered a common accounting system for use by the industry (as is the case with hospitals, most of which use a system developed by the American Hospital Association), or because companies in the industry have adopted the system of a leading company (as in the automobile manufacturing industry, in which all systems are similar to that developed by General Motors Corporation).

VARIABLE COSTING

Because of the importance of identifying direct and variable items of cost, some companies use what is called a **variable cost system** (often, but incorrectly, called a **direct cost systems**).[1] **In a variable cost system, the cost of a product includes only its variable manufacturing costs.** These consist of direct labor costs, direct material costs, and those items of manufacturing overhead costs that are variable with the level of activity. All fixed manufacturing costs are charged as expenses of the current period, rather than being included in inventory as part of product costs. This practice is *not* in accordance with generally accepted accounting principles, because these principles require that an appropriate share of *all* manufacturing costs be assigned to products. Nevertheless, some companies use it for internal purposes. The conventional cost accounting system, as described in Chapters 3 and 4, is called an **absorption cost system,** to indicate that fixed costs are absorbed as a part of product costs.

In a variable cost system, fixed manufacturing costs are viewed as costs that are associated with being in a state of readiness to produce, rather than costs associated with the actual production of specific units of product. Fixed costs are said to be *time* costs, whereas variable costs are said to be *activity* costs. Proponents of variable costing assert that

---

[1] Recall that in cost accounting systems direct product cost includes only direct material cost and direct labor cost. In variable cost systems, variable manufacturing overhead is included in the same category as direct material and direct labor.

management can be misled if these fixed costs are intermingled with variable costs in the measurement of inventory and costs of goods sold. This point is discussed in more detail in the Appendix. Variable costing is the extreme case of differences of opinion about which items of costs are *product costs* and which are expenses of the current period, that is, *period costs*.

Variable costs may be separately identified from fixed costs in an absorption cost system. The difference is that in an absorption cost system, fixed costs are allocated to products, whereas in a variable cost system no such allocations are made.

MERCHANDISING COMPANIES

In drugstores, department stores, supermarkets, and other merchandising companies, cost of goods sold is essentially the invoice cost of these goods. These companies therefore do not need a cost accounting system in order to find the cost of good sold. They do, however, use cost information for other purposes, a principal one being to measure the profitability of various selling departments within the company.

The selling departments in a store are usually set up according to categories of merchandise. They correspond to the production cost centers in a factory in the sense that the productive activities of the company take place in these departments. Merchandising companies also have units that are responsible for various general and administrative activities, and these correspond to the service cost centers in a factory. The cost of a selling department includes its direct costs plus a fair share of the indirect costs, that is, the costs of these service centers.

EXHIBIT 5–4

REGIS MEN'S STORE
Income Statement
March

	Total	Suits	Furnishings	Shoes
Sales revenues	$53,000	$26,000	$17,000	$10,000
Less: Returns	1,200	500	400	300
Net sales	51,800	25,500	16,600	9,700
Cost of goods sold	31,500	15,000	11,000	5,500
Gross margin	20,300	10,500	5,600	4,200
Sales salaries	4,000	1,500	2,000	500
Sales commissions	5,000	1,500	2,000	1,500
Occupancy expense	1,200	600	400	200
Advertising	800	800	0	0
Depreciation on fixtures	600	300	100	200
General and administrative	4,000	2,000	1,200	800
Total Expenses	15,600	6,700	5,700	3,200
Operating Income (loss)	$ 4,700	$ 3,800	$ (100)	$ 1,000

Exhibit 5–4 is an income statement for a men's clothing store in which there are three selling departments: suits, furnishing (e.g., underwear, shirts, ties), and shoes. The sales revenue and gross margin of each department are of great interest because one of the department manager's principal responsibilities is to sell an adequate volume of merchandise at an adequate margin.

In the expense section of this income statement, some of the expenses (such as sales salaries, sales commissions, and depreciation on fixtures) are incurred directly in the selling departments. Other expenses are assigned to selling departments in a way that is similar to the assignment of service center costs to production cost centers in a factory. To the extent feasible, the assignment is direct. Thus, in Exhibit 5–4 advertising expense for the month was entirely for newspaper advertising of suits, so the total advertising expense was assigned to the suit department.

Other expenses are allocated on the basis of the same general criteria that we have already discussed: causal relationship or benefits received. Occupancy cost (heat, light, building depreciation, property taxes, janitorial services) may be assigned on the basis of the square feet of space occupied by each department. General and administrative expenses that cannot be allocated according to the causal or benefits criteria are residual expenses that may be allocated on the basis of some overall measure of activity, such as sales revenue or gross margin. Many companies do not allocate such expenses to selling departments.

Although the details differ, the general approach to the assignment of costs to selling departments in a merchandising company follows the same principles as those already discussed for the assignment of costs to production cost centers in manufacturing companies.

SERVICE ORGANIZATIONS

Products, which are the outputs of any organization, consist of either goods or services. Goods are tangible; that is, they have physical substance and can be touched or seen. Services are intangible.[2] Our description of cost accounting systems has focused on measuring the cost of goods. The same general approach is applicable to measuring the cost of services.

In the United States many more persons are employed in service organizations than in organizations that manufacture goods; and as is characteristic of highly developed economies, the proportion of the total work force that is employed in service industries is steadily increasing. Exhibit 5–5 gives an indication of the magnitude of various types of non-organizations that are generally included.

---

[2] Some people use the word *products* to refer only to tangible goods; they therefore do not count services as products. The context usually makes the intended meaning clear.

EXHIBIT 5–5
Size of certain U.S. nonmanufacturing industries, 1974

	National income ($ billion)
Transportation	45.1
Communication	23.8
Electric, gas, sanitary services	20.0
Wholesale and retail trade	178.5
Finance, insurance, real estate	130.3
Hotels and lodging	7.2
Personal services (e.g., laundries, beauty shops)	8.2
Business services	21.4
Auto and other repair services	9.0
Motion picture and other recreation	6.7
Health care	46.8
Legal services	10.8
Educational services	10.1
Nonprofit membership organizations	10.1
Miscellaneous professional services	14.7

Source: "National Income and Product Accounts of the United States, 1929–1974," Statistical Table 6.3, *Supplement to the Survey of Current Business.*

Similarity to measurement of manufacturing costs

As in the case with manufacturing companies, some service organizations use job order cost systems and others use process cost systems. Garages that service and repair automobiles use a *job cost system,* that is, they accumulate on a job cost record the costs incurred for each automobile that they service. Hospitals and medical clinics set up a job cost record for each patient. Many other service organizations use a *process cost system;* that is, they assign costs to cost centers, they measure in some way the number of units of service furnished by the cost center, and they find the unit cost by dividing the total cost of the center by the number of units of services rendered.

Some of the terminology used in service organizations differs from that discussed earlier for manufacturing companies. For example, instead of the term "production cost center," the term **mission cost center** is used. A mission cost center works directly on the services that the organization provides, as contrasted with a **support cost center** that provides services to other cost centers in the organization. A support cost center corresponds to a service cost center in a manufacturing company, and the only reason for the difference in terminology is to avoid the confusion that might otherwise arise if the word "service" was used both for a type of cost center and for the output of the whole organization.

Because of the basic similarity in the methods of measuring cost in both service organizations and manufacturing organizations, there is no need to repeat the description of cost measurement methods that has already been given.

Pricing

Many service organizations, especially law, engineering, accounting and other firms that provide professional services, arrive at normal selling prices by a version of the time and material method described in Chapter 2. They establish a **billing rate** for each hour of professional time, and charge the customer at this rate plus the cost of supplies and other materials and services used on the job. The billing rate is established by adding together the annual salary cost of the professional, a fair share of overhead costs, and a profit margin, and dividing the total by the number of hours that the professional is expected to work on billable assignments during the year.

Defining cost objectives and outputs

The outputs of a manufacturing company are tangible; goods have physical properties that can be described and that can be readily counted or measured in most cases. The outputs of a service organization, by contrast, are intangible: in many situations the services cannot be clearly described, let alone counted or measured. The output of a university, for example, is education; but it is difficult to describe what education consists of and impossible to measure it. In the absence of a practical way of measuring the real outputs of the organization, a surrogate measure is used. A **surrogate** measure is one that approximates the real output, although it is not the same as the real output. For example, the number of students who attend the university or the number of students who graduate is used as a surrogate output measure, even though output does not actually consist of numbers alone.

The cost objectives of a service organization are related to these surrogates of output. In designing a cost accounting system, much thought needs to be given to defining cost objectives in the most useful way. Usually, two criteria are important in deciding on what the cost objectives should be: (1) they should be useful as a basis for setting selling prices, and (2) they should provide useful information for management planning and control.

> *EXAMPLE NO. 1:* A university may designate its entire educational program as a single cost objective. Alternatively, it may establish two cost objectives: one for undergraduate and the other for graduate education. Going into still more detail, it may decide to measure the cost of individual fields of instruction, or even of individual courses in each field. Depending on the cost objectives selected, the university can arrive at a cost per student, a cost per undergraduate (as distinguished from graduate) student, a cost

per student majoring in a given field, or a cost per course or per credit hour. The choice of cost objectives depends on how, if at all, the resulting cost information will be used for pricing (e.g., setting tuition charges in private universities or obtaining funds from the legislature in the case of public universities), and the usefulness of the cost detail in making management decisions.

EXAMPLE NO. 2: Long-distance trucking companies collect goods, move them from one city to another, and deliver them. Each city in which a company operates is called a terminal. Movement of goods between two cities is called a traffic lane. Three types of cost objectives are used in the trucking industry. Some companies assign all costs and revenues to *terminals,* including a share of the costs of hauling goods from one terminal to another. Other companies assign costs and revenue to *traffic lanes,* including a share of the costs of operating facilities in each terminal. Still other companies assign costs to *classes of commodities* transported. Some companies use two of these approaches in combination. Their choice depends on their judgment as to which type of cost objective provides the most useful information to management.

Systems prescribed by regulatory agencies

Many service organizations are regulated by government agencies. Among these are gas companies, electric companies, water companies, trucking companies, railroads, airlines, bus companies, pipeline companies, telephone companies, broadcasting companies, banks, investment trusts, and insurance companies. Most regulatory agencies require that each regulated company submit revenue and cost reports; and the agency prescribes, usually in considerable detail, how costs are to be measured.

The fact that the method of measuring costs is prescribed in detail has one important advantage, but in certain industries it has an equally important disadvantage. The advantage is that the data are comparable among companies so that valid comparisons of the costs of various cost objectives can be made. Indeed, the regulatory agency usually publishes averages and other compilations of the cost of various cost objectives in order to facilitate such comparisons. The disadvantage is that in some regulated industries, the cost objectives and the methods of assigning costs to cost objectives specified by the regulatory agency are of little use for management. Many systems were instituted prior to the development of modern cost accounting principles and have not been modified in the light of recent developments. In these industries, the regulated companies are in the unfortunate position of being required to maintain two "sets of books," one to meet the requirements of the regulatory agency, but useless for other purposes, and the other to meet the needs of management. Not only does this requirement cause additional record-keeping expense, but also it leads to misunderstanding when information from one set of books is confused with that from the other set of books.

EXAMPLE: The cost accounting system prescribed by the Civil Aeronautics Board for airline companies is an example of a system that provides information that is useful both to the regulatory agency and to the managements of airline companies. By contrast, the system prescribed by the Interstate Commerce Commission for railroads is an antiquated one which requires that costs be collected in a way that is not useful to management, and probably of little use to the needs of the ICC.

Estimates of volume

In Chapter 4 we emphasized the importance of making a good estimate of volume, that is, the level of activity, as a part of the process of arriving at overhead rates. We also emphasized the difficulty of making a reliable volume estimate in a manufacturing company because of the uncertainties about what the level of sales activity in the forthcoming year will be. Service organizations also must make volume estimates in order to arrive at overhead rates; but in some of them, the problem is much less difficult than that in the typical manufacturing company. A college or university knows, within reasonably close limits, what its level of activity will be for the whole academic year as soon as students have registered in the fall. The activity level of religious organizations and of many other membership organizations is determined by the amount that can be raised from dues or contributions, and this amount often can be estimated within close limits prior to the beginning of the year. Government organizations that depend on financial support from the legislature know, usually before the beginning of the year, how much money they are going to receive; and this determines the level of services that they can furnish. In these organizations, the problem of estimating the level of activity is much less serious than it is in a typical manufacturing company.

Nonprofit organizations

A nonprofit organization is an organization whose primary objective is something other than earning a profit; it is to be contrasted with a *profit-oriented* organization. Most nonprofit organizations provide services rather than manufacture tangible products, so they are included in the services category. Of the types listed in Exhibit 5–5, health care, educational and membership organizations are predominantly nonprofit organizations. Government organizations are nonprofit organizations. The cost accounting practices of nonprofit organizations are in many respects similar to those of profit-oriented organizations. Both nonprofit and profit-oriented organizations use resources; and in both cases, the problem of cost measurement is to identify the amount of resources that are used for each of the various cost objectives that the organization has.

Two important differences exist, however: (1) nonprofit organizations tend to make less use of the accrual concept and (2) some of them do not measure depreciation. Each is discussed below.

Less use of accrual accounting. Since cost measures the use of resources, valid information on costs cannot be collected unless the underlying accounting data are structured in such a way that monetary information on the use of resources is available. In a profit-oriented organization, adherence to the accrual and matching concepts assures that cost measures the *use* of resources. Some service organizations have accounting systems that adhere to these concepts. However, a great many government organizations — local, state, and federal — do not have accrual accounting systems; that is, their systems measure the cost of resources *acquired* in a given period but not the cost of resources *used* in that period.

The reason for this discrepancy is primarily historical. Accrual accounting started in manufacturing companies because of the need to measure the costs of goods in inventory. It developed further in manufacturing companies as those companies found ways in which management could make additional uses of accounting data. The trend toward accrual accounting in profit-oriented service organizations has been a fairly recent one. In the last few years banks, other financial institutions, and insurance companies have adopted accounting principles that permitted independent accountants to certify that their financial statements were "prepared in accordance with generally accepted accounting principles." Such a statement still cannot be made for many nonprofit organizations, particularly colleges and universities, religious organizations, and government organizations. In the absence of accrual accounting, monetary information on the amount of resources used for cost objectives cannot be obtained from the accounting records. Instead, approximations must be made on the basis of information obtained outside the accounting records. Without the control that debit and credit provides, such approximations are often unreliable.

> *EXAMPLE:* In many government organizations, an accounting record is made when material is *purchased* but no record is made when material is *used.* Material cost is deducted from revenue in the period in which the material was purchased, in clear violation of the matching principle. Thus, no accounting record shows the monetary amount of material *used* in a given period, either in individual cost centers or for the organization as a whole. Similarly, contracts (such as for painting a building) are recorded as costs in the period in which the contract was signed rather than in the period in which the work was done (e.g., the period in which the building was painted).

Less use of depreciation. Many nonprofit organizations do not record depreciation expense. In profit-oriented companies, depreciation accounting is essential; a company cannot be said to have made a profit unless its revenue exceeds all its costs, including the cost of the fixed assets that it uses. Many nonprofit organizations do not have the same need to match depreciation expense with revenue because they derive funds for fixed assets from gifts (as in the case of private colleges and religious organizations) or from special appropriations made for that purpose (as in the case of government organizations), rather than from operating revenues. However, nonprofit organizations whose operating revenues are supposed to cover all costs (e.g., government-owned electric, water, and transportation organizations) do use depreciation accounting.

DEMONSTRATION CASE

The following problem has two purposes: (1) to encourage you to review your understanding of methods of allocating nonmanufacturing costs to products, and (2) to permit you to see the impact of various allocation methods on the data that are furnished to management. Exhibit 5–6 shows revenue and cost information for the Allstol Company. This company makes two products. Product A is sold in large quantities to a relatively few buyers. Product B requires extensive advertising and sales promotion effort, and has relatively high logistics costs because the average size of each order is small. In Exhibit 5–6 costs have been allocated to products by first collecting elements of cost in a number of service centers and then allocating the total amount in each service center to the products according to benefits received or a causal relationship.

You are asked to calculate what the costs assigned to each product would have been if, instead of the basis actually used, the company had used either of the following methods of handling indirect costs:

1. Distribution and general and administrative costs are allocated on the basis of the relative direct labor cost of each product.

EXHIBIT 5–6
Revenue and cost data for Allstol Company (000 omitted)

	Total	Product A	Product B
Sales	$2,400	$1,600	$800
Manufacturing cost:			
Direct material	200	150	50
Direct labor	500	400	100
Manufacturing overhead	500	450	50
Total Manufacturing Cost	1,200	1,000	200
Distribution costs	600	280	320
General and administrative	400	220	180
Full costs	2,200	1,500	700
Operating Income	$ 200	$ 100	$100
Income as percent of sales revenue	8.3%	6.3%	12.5%

2. Distribution and general and administrative costs are allocated on the basis of the relative amount of total manufacturing costs.

Required:

Calculate the dollar amount of income and its percentage of revenue for each product under each of the above methods. Having made these calculations, evaluate the usefulness of the results of these various approaches to management.

Solution:

The calculations for the allocation of distribution and general and administrative costs on the basis of direct labor are made after determining that the direct labor of Product A is 400 ÷ 500 = 80 percent of total direct labor, and of Product B, 20 percent.

Allocated on basis of direct labor

	Product A	Product B
Sales	$1,600	$800
Total manufacturing cost	1,000	200
Distribution, general, and administrative cost	800	200
Full costs	1,800	400
Operating income (loss)	$ (200)	$400
Income as percent of sales	(12.5%)	50.0%

Calculations for the allocation of distribution and general and administrative costs on the basis of total factory costs are derived from the fact that the total factory costs of Product A are 1,000 ÷ 1,200 = 83 percent of total factory costs, and those of Product B are 17 percent. The calculations are:

Allocated on basis of total factory cost

	Product A	Product B
Sales	$1,600	$800
Total manufacturing cost	1,000	200
Distribution, general and administrative cost	830	170
Full costs	1,830	370
Operating Income (loss)	$ (230)	$430
Income as percent of sales	(14.4%)	53.8%

These three methods of calculation give quite different results. The carefully worked out allocations given in Exhibit 5–6 show that Product B has 12.5 percent profit per dollar of revenue compared with 6.3 percent for Product A; that is, each revenue dollar of Product B produces twice as much income as a revenue dollar of Product A.

By contrast, the message conveyed by either of the other two methods is that Product A is being sold at a loss and all the company's income is being generated by Product B. This message is misleading.

The conclusion is that unless care is exercised in selecting the method of indirect cost allocation, management may be misled by the resulting cost information. The most useful information is the careful allocation shown in Exhibit 5–6, because this is the closest approximation to the amount of resources actually used for each of the two products.

SUMMARY

This chapter concludes our description of cost accounting systems whose purpose is to measure the full costs of cost objectives. For a manufacturing company, costs incurred outside the factory are distribution costs, research and development costs and general and administrative costs. Distribution consists of two quite different activities, marketing (or order getting) and logistics (or order filling). The differences must be kept in mind in examining the costs related to each type. Distribution costs are usually recorded by functions, customers, and activities, rather than by products. Research and development costs are collected by projects using a procedure that is similar to the job order cost system in a factory. General and administrative costs are collected by functions and assigned to cost objectives, to the extent feasible, on a basis that reflects intended benefits or causal relationship. There is usually a class of residual expenses for which no rational basis for allocation exists, and an arbitrary formula must be used to allocate such costs. In some companies, the cost of using capital is measured.

There is no uniform way of measuring costs, so cost comparisons among companies must be made cautiously. Nevertheless, the measurement procedures for companies within a given industry tend to be similar.

In a retail store or other merchandising company, the cost objectives are usually selling departments. Costs assigned to a selling department include both its direct costs and a fair share of the costs of service departments, as is the case with production cost centers in a manufacturing company.

Service organizations include nonprofit as well as profit-oriented organizations. The cost accounting problems and practices of service organizations are similar to those of manufacturing organizations, except that: some nonprofit service organizations do not use accrual accounting and some do not account for depreciation; cost objectives are more difficult to define and measure in service organizations; regulated service organizations must adhere to practices prescribed by the regulatory agency; and volume is relatively easy to estimate in some service organizations.

IMPORTANT TERMS

Distribution costs

Marketing costs

Logistics costs

Research and development costs

General and administrative costs

Residual expenses

Capital cost

Product cost

Period cost (or expense)

Variable costing

Absorption costing

Products

Goods

Services

Surrogate

Nonprofit organizations

APPENDIX: EFFECT OF VARIABLE COSTING ON INCOME

When the number of units of product *sold* in a given period is different from the number of units *manufactured* in that period, a variable cost system gives a quite different income figure for the period than does an absorption cost system. The difference is demonstrated in Exhibit 5–7. The assumed situation is as follows:

Selling price.. $100 per unit

Costs:

    Variable manufacturing................................. 25 per unit

    Fixed manufacturing..................................... 175 per period

    Distribution and administration...................... 30 per period

Assuming that five units are manufactured each period, the product costs per unit will be as follows:

	Product costs per unit	
	Absorption costing	Variable costing
Variable costs..	$25	$25
Fixed manufacturing cost..............................	35*	0
Product cost per unit....................................	$60	$25

    * $175 ÷ 5 = $35.

In Period No. 1 five units are manufactured, but only three units are sold. The other two units are in finished goods inventory as of the end of the period. The income reported under absorption costing is higher than that reported under variable costing. This is because in absorption costing $70 of fixed manufacturing cost is part of the cost of the two units that are in finished goods inventory, and hence this $70 does not

EXHIBIT 5-7

Comparison of absorption costing and variable costing

Period 1. Production exceeds sales
Units manufactured = 5
Units sold   = 3

Income Statements

	Absorption costing	Variable costing		Difference*
Sales revenue (three units)	$300		$300	$ 0
Cost of goods sold	180		75	105
Gross margin	120		225	105
Fixed manufacturing costs		$175		
Distribution and administrative	30	30	205	(175)
Operating Income	$ 90		$ 20	$ (70)
Ending inventory (two units)	$120		$ 50	

Period 2. Sales exceeds production
Units manufactured = 5
Units sold   = 7

Income Statements

Sales revenue (seven units)	$700		$700	$ 0
Cost of goods sold	420		175	245
Gross margin	280		525	245
Fixed manufacturing costs		$175		
Distribution and administration	30	30	205	(175)
Operating Income	$250		$320	$ 70
Ending inventory	0		0	

* ( ) = unfavorable.

affect income for the period, whereas in variable costing the entire $175 of fixed manufacturing cost affects income for the period.

In Period 2, five units are manufactured but seven units are sold (i.e., the five units manufactured in Period 2 plus the two units that were in finished goods inventory). In Period 2, the income reported under absorption costing is lower than that reported under variable costing. This is because the cost of goods sold under absorption costing includes the $70 of fixed manufacturing cost that were assigned to the two units that were in finished goods inventory, whereas in variable costing this $70 was part of the expense of Period 1.

In summary, in periods when production volume is greater than sales volume, income as reported in an absorption costing system is higher than income as reported in a variable costing system. In periods when sales volume is greater than production volume, income as reported in an absorption costing system is lower than income as reported in a variable costing system.

Note that this difference is associated with a fluctuation in the size of finished goods inventory from one period to the next. At the end of Period 1, there were two units in inventory; whereas at the end of Period 2 there were zero units in inventory. If inventory remains relatively constant from period to period, the difference in net income as reported by the two systems is not great.

Note also that the *total* income for the two periods is $340 under either method. A costing method may affect the allocation of costs to a given accounting period, and hence the income reported for the period; but it does not affect the total amount of costs of income for periods for which combined production volume equals combined sales volume. In the two years combined, sales volume and production volume are ten units.

Although there is much debate over which system provides a better measure of income, the fact is that only an absorption costing system is permitted by generally accepted accounting principles.

QUESTIONS FOR DISCUSSION

1. A conventional income statement often contains an item labeled "Selling, general, and administrative expenses." Which of the types of cost discussed in this chapter would be included in such an item?

2. What is the principal difference, from an analytical standpoint, between marketing costs and logistics costs?

3. Why are marketing costs ordinarily not collected by products? Under what circumstances would it be appropriate to collect marketing costs by products?

4. "If each call a salesperson makes costs $80, and if the salesperson obtains an order, on the average, once in four calls, the salesperson cost per order is nevertheless $80 because the other three calls were nonproductive." Explain why you agree or disagree with this statement.

5. Why are production activities said to give *form utility* and logistics activities, *place utility?*

6. Describe the similarities between accounting for research and development costs and accounting for job order costs in a factory.

7. Referring to the staff units and their functions given in the text, give examples of functions whose costs are probably residual expenses.

8. How, if at all, do the costs of general and administrative activities become part of finished goods inventory?

9. Why is it preferable to charge users so much a minute for the computer time they use rather than to allocate computer costs along with other general and administrative costs?

10. What is the difference between capital costs and capital expenditures?

11. How does the item *interest expense* on an income statement differ from *capital cost* as used in this chapter?

12. Suppose that for management accounting purposes capital cost was included as an element of cost. How would income as reported in the management accounting system differ from income as reported for financial accounting purposes?

13. Distinguish between product costs and period costs.

14. As between capital expenditures, product costs, and expenses, which has the most immediate impact on income, and which has the least immediate impact? Why?

15. Referring to Exhibit 5-4, explain the similarities and the difference between the information reported for selling departments in Regis Men's Store and the information reported for production cost centers in a manufacturing company.

16. Distinguish among the words *products, goods,* and *services.*

17. Why, if at all, should the cost accounting system for a profit-oriented electric power company be different from that of a government-owned, nonprofit electric power company?

18. The U.S. Postal Service is a large nonprofit organization. Does it need a cost accounting system? Why?

19. What would be appropriate cost objectives for a large church or synagogue?

20. Many government organizations do not have an accrual accounting system. How would management benefit from such a system?

21. Exhibit 5-3 shows the effect on income of alternative cost practices. A government agency may record an item as a "cost" in the period in which the contract to perform the service is signed (as in the case of painting a building, mentioned in the text). Describe how such a practice affects the timing of the effects of cost on income.

PROBLEMS

5-1. The Whitney Company incurred the following costs in manufacturing and selling its products:

Salespersons' commissions	$20,000
Raw materials purchased	80,000
Cost of salespersons' salesbooks	350
Cost of invoices used to bill customers	500
Salary of finished goods warehouse janitor	5,000
Wages of credit department clerks	8,000
Salespersons' travel expense	3,700
Rent on materials warehouse	800
Rent on finished goods warehouse	1,200
Interest on finished goods warehouse loan	500

Required:

Compute separately the marketing and logistics costs included above.

5-2. Below is a breakdown, by product, of the 1977 sales and costs of producing and selling the four products in the line of East-West, Inc.

For the year ended December 31, 1977

	Product A	Product B	Product C	Product D
Sales..................................	$60,000	$40,000	$50,000	$30,000
Cost of goods sold	33,000	20,800	26,000	15,300
Distribution expenses	11,000	10,000	9,500	10,700
General expenses...............	9,000	6,000	9,500	3,000
Operating income..............	7,000	3,200	5,000	1,000

Required:

A. Calculate the change in gross margin which would result if logistics costs which were 10 percent of total distribution expenses were treated as a manufacturing cost instead of marketing cost.

B. Rate the products according to their profitability.

5–3. The central regional sales manager for the Toddler Toy Company is held responsible for the control of the following expenses incurred in June and July:

Expense	June	July
Supervision......................................	$ 5,000	$ 5,500
Salespersons' salaries......................	8,334	8,000
Commissions	4,500	4,666
Salespersons' travel.........................	7,000	6,600
Supplies–sales office	1,000	1,080
Salaries–sales office	2,500	2,834
Miscellaneous sales expense............	1,240	1,330
Rent..	2,500	3,000
Total	32,074	33,010
Net sales revenue	$151,600	$170,000

Required:

A. Compute the amount of expense per $100 of net sales for each expense category.

B. What was the total cost per dollar of the added July sales?

C. What can be said about the sales manager's control of salespersons' salaries?

D. What possible relationship might exist between travel expense and sales?

5–4. The controller of Taylor Sales, Inc., produced the following statement of income by product line for the month of October:

		Product		
	Total	L	M	N
Sales	$15,000	$3,000	$4,500	$7,500
Cost of goods sold............................	6,000	1,220	1,800	2,980
Gross margin....................................	9,000	1,780	2,700	4,520
Marketing...	7,000	900	2,300	3,800
Profit before general and administrative.................................	$ 2,000	$ 880	$ 400	$ 720

Marketing costs were allocated by charging each product with its fair share according to the number of customer calls, number of miles traveled by salespersons, number of telephone calls made, number of invoices sent, number of orders received, and similar bases.

The sales manager said that these allocations of marketing costs were so much "hocus-pocus," and that the commonsense way of allocating the $7,000 was either in proportion to sales revenue or in proportion to gross margin.

Required:
A. Calculate the profitability of the three products in accordance with each of the two methods suggested by the sales manager.
B. Which product is actually the most profitable? Explain your answer as if you were the controller discussing the matter with the sales manager.

5–5. The Day Company manufactures eyeglass frames which it sells to wholesalers, optometrists, and opticians. Data pertaining to its customers and distribution costs are as follows:

Customer class	Sales revenue	Cost of goods sold	No. of sales calls	No. of invoice lines	No. of orders
Wholesalers	$190,000	$154,000	230	2,200	110
Optometrists	230,000	158,000	360	4,500	580
Opticians	310,000	235,000	410	3,300	310
	$730,000	$547,000	1,000	10,000	1,000

Function	Costs	Allocation base
Salespersons' salaries	$68,000	Number of salespersons' calls
Packing and shipping	10,000	Customers' orders
Advertising	12,000	Dollar sales
Credit and collections	14,000	Invoice lines
General accounting	17,000	Customers' orders

Required:
Prepare an analysis of profitability by customer class.

5–6. The Flory Company recorded the following data pertaining to sales of its single product during 1977:

Cost of goods sold (40% of sales)	$120,000
Salespersons' commissions (2% of sales)	6,000
Sales salaries	25,000
Order processing and billing costs	5,000
Credit and collection costs	7,500

The orders filled during the year have been analyzed as follows:

Order size	No. of orders	Total sales value
$ 1–$10..............................	3,000	$ 24,000
11– 20..............................	6,000	108,000
21– 30..............................	3,600	84,000
31– 40..............................	1,800	57,000
41– 50..............................	600	27,000
	15,000	$300,000

Flory employs two salespersons—Rogers and Brown. Rogers has been with the firm longer and is paid a salary of $13,300 per year: Brown receives $11,700 per year. The salespersons spend equal amounts of time with each customer, and most orders are single-line invoices. Orders have been credited to the two salespersons as follows:

	Rogers		Brown	
Order size	No. of orders	Sales	No. of orders	Sales
$ 1–$10.....................	2,640	$ 21,600	360	$ 2,400
11– 20.....................	3,600	70,800	2,400	37,200
21– 30.....................	1,800	42,000	1,800	42,000
31– 40.....................	360	11,400	1,440	45,600
41– 50.....................	120	5,400	480	21,600
	8,520	$151,200	6,480	$148,800

Required:

A. Prepare a statement showing the relative profitability of each order size group.

B. Prepare a statement showing the relative profitability of the two salespersons.

C. Comment on the significance of the statement prepared in Requirement B.

5–7. You are the general manager of a brand-new hotel and are interested at this early date (during the period of preopening training, etc.) in obtaining some ideas as to the potential profitability of your location. The experts have provided you with summaries of data (based on their recent feasibility study and rounded to the nearest $10,000 on an annual basis).

Rooms: 200 rooms with an average room rate of $20.

Foods: 365 days a year with the following covers served and approximate average guest check receipts per meal period.

	Maximum daily covers	Average receipts
Breakfast......................	200	$2.00
Lunch..........................	300	2.75
Dinner.........................	200	5.00

Beverages: 304 days per year (52 weeks × 6 days, holidays subtracted) for eight hours per day (5 P.M. to 1 A.M.). The lounge will generate a maximum of $125 in sales per operating hour. In addition, during the dinner hours (5 P.M. to 9 P.M.), a maximum of $65 per hour can be derived from the sale of beverage to food customers in the dining room.

During the first three years the following levels of activity are expected:

Rooms........................... 65% of occupancy
Foods........................... 72% of maximum covers served
Beverages..................... 97% of maximum beverage sales

Further, a projected statement of maximum gross operating profit is provided for the first three years' operations. (All percentages are based on total firm revenues.)

	Rooms	Food and beverage	Total
Revenues...	55%	45%	100%
Cost of goods sold		14*	14
Direct department expense.....................	20	20*	40
Gross operating income.........................	35%	11%	46
Overhead (deductions from income, etc.)...			20
House profit..			26%

* It is assumed that food costs will approximate $33\frac{1}{3}$ percent of food revenues, and beverage costs 25 percent of beverages revenue, and direct operating expenses are divided evenly between food and beverages.

Required:

A. Compute rooms, food and beverage earnings capacity for:
   1. Maximum.
   2. Expected.
B. Compute gross operating income:
   1. Maximum.
   2. Expected.
C. Allocate overhead (total deduction from income) by departments and determine the resulting departmental house profit using the sales dollar basis and the gross operating income dollar basis.
   1. Maximum revenue.
   2. Expected revenue.

5-8. The following data pertain to activities of the Dow Company during 1977:

Sales revenue...	$1,600,000
Variable manufacturing costs...	700,000
Fixed manufacturing costs...	300,000
Variable selling and administrative costs.........................	100,000
Fixed selling and administrative costs.............................	200,000
Production (units)..	200
Beginning finished goods inventory.................................	0
Ending finished goods inventory (units)............................	40

Required:

A. Prepare an income statement using absorption costing.
B. Prepare an income statement using variable costing.
C. Explain why net income was different on the two statements.

5–9. The following data relate to a year's budgeted activity for Patsy Corporation, a single product company:

	Units
Beginning inventory	30,000
Production	120,000
Available	150,000
Sales	110,000
Ending inventory	40,000

	Per unit
Selling price	$5.00
Variable manufacturing costs	1.00
Variable selling costs	2.00
Fixed manufacturing costs (based on 100,000 units)	0.25
Fixed selling costs (based on 100,000 units)	0.65

Fixed costs remain constant within the range of 25,000 units to 160,000 units.

Required:

A. Prepare an income statement using absorption costing.
B. Prepare an income statement using variable costing.
C. Explain why net income was different on the two statements.

(AICPA adapted)

5–10. The president of the Newport Company has received a condensed profit report for 1977, and he is puzzled by a decline in net income which accompanied a significant increase in sales. Sales rose 50 percent, and profit fell $200,000. He phoned the controller and asked for an explanation. The following data pertain to the two years:

	1976	1977
Net income	$ 450,000	$ 250,000
Sales in units	200,000	300,000
Production in units	300,000	200,000
Standard activity in units	300,000	300,000
Sales price per unit	$15	$15
Variable cost per unit	$ 5	$ 5
Fixed manufacturing overhead	$1,800,000	$1,800,000
Fixed manufacturing overhead per unit	$ 6	$ 6
Fixed selling and administrative expense	$ 350,000	$ 350,000

Required:

A. Prepare income statements for 1976 and 1977 using both absorption costing and variable costing.
B. Write a letter of explanation for the controller to send to the president.

5–11. The administrator of Wright Hospital has presented you with a number of service projections for the year ending June 30, 1977. Estimated room requirements for inpatients by type of service are:

Type of patient	Total patients expected	Average number of days in hospital		Percent of regular patients selecting types of service		
		Regular	Medicare	Private	Semi-private	Ward
Medical............	2,100	7	17	10%	60%	30%
Surgical	2,400	10	15	15	75	10

Of the patients served by the hospital, 10 percent are expected to be Medicare patients, all of whom are expected to select semiprivate rooms. Both the number and proportion of Medicare patients have increased over the past five years. Daily rentals per patient are: $40 for a private room, $35 for a semiprivate room, and $25 for a ward.

Operating room charges are based on man-minutes (number of minutes the operating room is in use multiplied by number of personnel assisting in the operation). The per man-minute charges are $0.13 for inpatients and $0.22 for outpatients. Studies for the current year show that operations on inpatients are divided as follows:

Type of operation	Number of operations	Average number of minutes per operation	Average number of personnel required
A	800	30	4
B	700	45	5
C	300	90	6
D	200	120	8
	2,000		

The same proportion of inpatient operations is expected for the next fiscal year, and 180 outpatients are expected to use the operating room. Outpatient operations average 20 minutes and require the assistance of three persons.

The budget for the year ending June 30, 1977, by departments, is:

General services:
Maintenance of plant............................	$ 50,000
Operation of plant................................	27,500
Administration	97,500
All others	192,000

Revenue producing services:
Operating room	68,440
All others	700,000
	$1,135,440

The following information is provided for cost allocation purposes:

	Square feet	Salaries
General services:		
Maintenance of plant.....................................	12,000	$ 40,000
Operation of plant...	28,000	25,000
Administration	10,000	55,000
All others	36,250	102,500
Revenue producing services:		
Operating room	17,500	15,000
All others	86,250	302,500
	190,000	$540,000

Basis of allocations:
Maintenance of plant—salaries
Operation of plant—square feet
Administration—salaries
All others—8% to operating room

Required:

Prepare schedules showing the computation of—

A. The number of patient days (number of patients multiplied by average stay in hospital) expected by type of patients and service.

B. The total number of man-minutes expected for operating room services for inpatients and outpatients. For inpatients show the breakdown of total operating room man-minutes by type of operation.

C. Expected gross revenue from routine services.

D. Expected gross revenue from operating room services.

E. Cost per man-minute for operating room services assuming that the total man-minutes computed in Requirement B is 800,000 and that the step-down method of cost allocation is used (i.e., costs of the general services departments are allocated in sequence first to the general services departments that they serve and then finally to the revenue producing departments).

(AICPA adapted)

5-12. The New Mode Corporation incurred the following costs in the manufacturer and sale of its products:

Processing of salespersons' orders.............................	$ 2,200
Processing of raw material purchase orders	1,100
Insurance on raw material storage..............................	100
Insurance on finished goods storage...........................	250
Salaries of salespersons	18,000
Cost of customer billing..	3,000
Accounts receivable collection costs...........................	700
Transportation-in—materials	1,500
Transportation-out—sales...	2,000
Salary of raw material clerk.......................................	6,000
Salary of purchasing agent	10,000

Required:

Compute separately the marketing and logistics costs included above.

5–13. The results of operations for the year 1977 for the North-South Company are summarized below:

	For the year 1977			
	Product A	*Product B*	*Product C*	*Product D*
Sales.............................	$120,000	$80,000	$100,000	$60,000
Cost of goods sold...........	66,000	41,600	52,000	30,600
Distribution expenses.......	22,000	20,000	19,000	21,400
General expenses............	18,000	12,000	19,000	6,000
Net income.....................	14,000	6,400	10,000	2,000

Required:

A. Logistics costs total 10 percent of distribution expenses. Calculate the change in gross margin which would result if these were treated as factory costs.

B. Which product is the most profitable? The least profitable?

5–14. The following are items relating to the marketing expenses and sales of Callo Cosmetics for a week in January and February. The sales manager is held responsible for all expense items below:

Expense	*January*	*February*
Supervisory...	$ 1,250	$ 1,375
Salespersons' salaries.............................	2,083	2,000
Commissions...	1,125	1,167
Salespersons' travel................................	1,750	1,650
Supplies–sales office	250	270
Salaries–sales office	625	708
Miscellaneous sales expense	310	333
Rent...	625	750
Total...	8,018	8,253
Net sales revenue	$37,900	$42,500

Required:

A. Compute the amount of expenses per $100 of net sales for each expenditure.

B. What was the total cost per dollar of added February sales?

C. What can be said about the manager's control of salespersons' salaries?

D. What is a possible relationship between travel expense and sales?

5–15. The controller of Canton Sales, Inc., produced the following statement of income by product line for the month of May:

	Total	Product A	Product B	Product C
Sales..................................	$14,000	$2,800	$4,200	$7,000
Cost of goods sold	5,400	1,120	1,600	2,680
Gross margin	8,600	1,680	2,600	4,320
Marketing	6,600	800	2,200	3,600
Profit before general and administrative..................	$ 2,000	$ 880	$ 400	$ 720

Individual items of marketing costs were allocated to products according to the number of customer calls, number of miles traveled by salespersons, number of telephone calls made, number of invoices sent, number of orders received, and similar bases.

The sales manager challenged these allocations of marketing costs as unnecessarily complicated and said that the proper way of allocating the $6,600 was either in proportion to sales revenue or in proportion to gross margin.

Required:

A. Calculate the profitability of the three products in accordance with each of the two methods suggested by the sales manager.

B. Which product is actually the most profitable? Explain your answer as if you were the controller discussing this matter with the sales manager.

5-16. The Weems Company manufactures baby furniture which it sells to wholesalers, department stores, and specialty shops. Data pertaining to customers and distribution costs are as follows:

Customer class	Sales revenue	Cost of goods sold	No. of sales calls	No. of invoice lines	No. of orders
Wholesalers	$180,000	$144,000	240	2,100	120
Department stores	240,000	168,000	360	4,600	580
Specialty shops	300,000	225,000	400	3,300	300
	$720,000	$537,000	1,000	10,000	1,000

Function	Costs	Allocation base
Salespersons' salaries.........	$65,000	Number of salesperson's calls
Packing and shipping	12,000	Customers' orders
Advertising.........................	10,000	Dollar sales
Credit and collection...........	15,000	Invoice lines
General accounting	18,000	Customers' orders

Required:

Prepare an analysis of profitability by customer class.

5-17. The Myrick Company recorded the following data pertaining to sales of its single product during 1977:

Cost of goods sold (40% of sales)	$100,000
Salespersons' commissions (2% of sales)...................	5,000
Sales salaries..	24,000
Order processing and billing costs...........................	5,000
Credit and collection costs......................................	7,500

The orders filled during the year have been analyzed as follows:

Order size	No. of orders	Total sales value
$ 1-$10	2,500	$ 20,000
11- 20	5,000	90,000
21- 30	3,000	70,000
31- 40	1,500	47,500
41- 50	500	22,500
	12,500	$250,000

Myrick employs two salespersons – Hawkins and Hines. Hawkins has been with the firm longer and is paid a salary of $12,800 per year; Hines receives $11,200 per year. The salespersons spend equal amounts of time with each customer, and most orders are single-line invoices. Orders have been credited to the two salespersons as follows:

	Hawkins		Hines	
Order size	No. of orders	Sales	No. of orders	Sales
$ 1-$10	2,200	$ 18,000	300	$ 2,000
11- 20	3,000	59,000	2,000	31,000
21- 30	1,500	35,000	1,500	35,000
31- 40	300	9,500	1,200	38,000
41- 50	100	4,500	400	18,000
	7,100	$126,000	5,400	$124,000

Required:

A. Prepare a statement showing the relative profitability of each order size group.

B. Prepare a statement showing the relative profitability of the two salespersons.

C. Comment on the significance of the statement prepared in Requirement B.

5-18. The Airport Hotel is organized into three revenue-generating departments: rooms, food, and beverage. The results of its operations for 1977 were as follows:

Total revenue $2,000,000

Expenses:

Payroll..	720,000
Departmental expenses	180,000
Food...	160,000
Beverages...	60,000
Administration and general........................	100,000
Advertising and promotion.........................	60,000
Utilities...	80,000
Repair and maintenance............................	60,000
Rent, taxes, and insurance........................	280,000
Interest..	100,000
Depreciation..	120,000
Total Expenses............................	1,920,000
Net Income...	$ 80,000

The manager is interested in the relative profitability of the individual departments. The costs of food and beverages may be assigned directly. Payroll and departmental expenses are to be assigned as follows: rooms, $630,000; food, $180,000; and beverage, $90,000. The remaining expenses are to be allocated on the basis of sales dollars, which were rooms, $1,160,000; food, $580,000; and beverage, $260,000.

Required:

A. Prepare a statement showing the relative profitability of the rooms, food, and beverage departments.

B. Comment on the allocation bases used for those costs which were not assigned directly.

5-19. The following data pertain to activities of the Lewis Company during 1977:

Sales revenue...	$1,300,000
Variable manufacturing costs...	600,000
Fixed manufacturing costs...	300,000
Variable selling and administrative costs.........................	100,000
Fixed selling and administrative costs.............................	200,000
Production (units)..	200
Beginning finished goods inventory (units)......................	0
Ending finished goods inventory (units)...........................	40

Required:

A. Prepare an income statement using absorption costing.

B. Prepare an income statement using variable costing.

C. Explain why net income was different on the two statements.

5-20. The following information is available for Keller Corporation's new product line:

Selling price per unit	$	15
Variable manufacturing costs per unit of production		8
Total annual fixed manufacturing costs		25,000
Variable administrative costs per unit of production		3
Total annual fixed selling and administrative expenses		15,000

There was no inventory at the beginning of the year. During the year 12,500 units were produced and 10,000 units were sold.

Required:

A. Prepare an income statement using absorption costing.
B. Prepare an income statement using variable costing.
C. Explain why net income was different on the two statements.

(AICPA adapted)

5–21. A stockholder wrote the president of the Campbell Company asking how he managed to turn a 50 percent increase in sales into a $200,000 decline in profits from 1976 to 1977. The letter was sent to the controller who assembled the following data for the two years:

	1976	*1977*
Net income	$ 550,000	$ 350,000
Sales in units	200,000	300,000
Production in units	300,000	200,000
Standard activity in units	300,000	300,000
Sales price per unit	$15	$15
Variable cost per unit	$ 5	$ 5
Fixed manufacturing overhead	$1,800,000	$1,800,000
Fixed manufacturing overhead per unit	$ 6	$ 6
Fixed selling and administrative expenses	$ 250,000	$ 250,000

Required:

A. Prepare income statements for 1976 and 1977 using both absorption costing and variable costing.
B. Write a letter of explanation for the president to send to the puzzled stockholder.

5–22. Consider two hypothetical companies, A and B. Their operations are identical in all respects, and certain income statement data for 1977, *excluding the four items listed below,* are also identical, as follows:

Sales revenue	$1,100,000
Cost of goods sold	600,000
Marketing expense	130,000
General and administrative expense	200,000

One half of the manufacturing costs for the year remain in Finished Goods Inventory as of December 31, and the other half are in Cost of Goods Sold.

The companies' accounting treatment of certain items differs as follows:

1. Freight on shipments to customers is $50,000. Company A classifies this as a marketing expense. Company B deducts this from sales revenue in arriving at net sales.
2. Freight on shipments from one company warehouse to another is $40,000. Company A classifies this as a product cost. Company B classifies it as a marketing cost.
3. Certain staff costs, not included in the $200,000 listed above, amount to $20,000. Company A classifies these as a product cost. Company B classifies them as a period cost because they were incurred for the benefit of the manufacturing division.
4. Certain other administrative costs not included in the $200,000 listed above, and amounting to $30,000, are for the administration of the marketing function. Company A classifies these as marketing expenses, and Company B as general and administrative expenses.

Required:

A. Prepare an income statement for Company A and another for Company B.
B. Calculate the percentage of each item to net sales. Explain why these differ for the two companies.
C. Discuss which of the alternative treatments is preferable for each of the four items.

5-23. Kellogg Company has developed a new type of circulating fan. It manufactured a trial lot of 100 fans as a basis for working out production problems and to provide information that would assist in arriving at the selling price of the fans. Manufacturing costs of this lot were as follows:

	Total cost
Electric motor	$ 450
Sheet metal	600
Other fittings	100
Direct labor	400
Manufacturing overhead (100% of direct labor)	400
Total	$1,950

The production engineer concluded that in normal production sheet metal costs and direct labor costs would probably be reduced by 10 percent.

It was estimated that 10,000 fans would be sold annually, and that the distribution and administrative costs properly chargeable to the fans would amount to $100,000. Assets employed for the manufacture of the fans were estimated at $200,000. The company required a return of 10 percent on assets employed.

Required:

A. From the information given, what should be the target selling price of the fan?
B. Discuss the uncertainties that probably are present in the above calculation.

part two

Differential accounting

In Part One we focused on the collection and use of information on the full costs of products or other cost objectives. We now turn to a second type of management accounting information. Various names are given to this type; we shall use the term *differential* accounting. Differential accounting has three closely related facets: differential costs, differential revenues, and differential investment. Of these, we shall give most emphasis to differential costs because these involve the most difficult problems of understanding. Similar principles apply to differential revenues and differential investment, however.

Chapter 6 introduces the concept of differential costs and describes how costs of certain items change with the level of activity and with other factors. It provides a technical background for Chapters 7, 8, and 9, which discuss the use of differential accounting information in various types of business problems.

The student should note carefully the contrast between differential costs and the full costs which were the subject of Part One. The full cost accounting system does provide much of the raw data that is used to construct differential costs. In Part Two, however, we shall not use full costs as such, but rather we shall use only those items of cost that are relevant to a particular decision.

In Part Two, we shall also use some cost data that do *not* come from a cost accounting system. Cost accounting systems are generally governed by the principles of financial accounting. In Part Two, we are not constrained by these principles. For example, although in financial accounting assets are recorded at their historical cost, in Part II we shall use other bases for measuring cost.

The essential reason for the differences in the cost constructions that are relevant to Part Two and those that were relevant in Part One is *purpose*. A thorough understanding of the central idea that *different purposes require different cost constructions* will clear up the confusion that often arises because there *are* different cost constructions.

The differential concept:
Cost-volume-profit
relationships

In this chapter we introduce the concept of differential costs (and also differential revenues) and contrast this concept with that of full costs which was our focus in Part One. The chapter explains in an introductory way what the differential cost concept is and how differential costs aid the decision maker in analyzing business problems. As a background for discussing the analysis of business problems, we describe how costs behave in certain situations, and particularly the effect that a change in volume has on costs and on profits.

CONCEPT OF DIFFERENTIAL COSTS AND REVENUES

Some people have difficulty in accepting the idea that there is more than one type of cost construction. They say; "When I pay a company $180 for a desk, the desk surely cost me $180. How could the cost be anything else?" It is appropriate therefore that we establish the points (a) that "cost" does have more than one meaning, (b) that differences in cost constructions relate to the *purpose* for which the cost information is to be used, and (c) that unless these differences are understood, serious mistakes can be made.

Consider a furniture company that manufactures desks after orders for them have been received. According to its cost accounting records, maintained as described in Part One, the full cost of manufacturing a

197

certain desk is $200. Suppose that a customer offered to buy such a desk for $180. If the company considered that the only relevant cost for this desk was the $200 full cost, it would of course refuse the order because its revenue would be only $180 and its cost would be $200; therefore the management would conclude that the company would incur a loss of $20 on the order.

But it might well be that the additional *out-of-pocket costs* of making this one desk—the lumber, other material, and the wages paid to the cabinetmaker who worked on the desk—would be only $125. The other items making up the $200 of full cost were items of cost which would not be affected by this one order. The management might therefore decide to accept this order at $180. If it did, the company's costs would increase by $125, its revenue would increase by $180, and its operating income would increase by the difference, or $55. Thus, the company would be $55 better off by accepting this order than by refusing it. Evidently in this problem, the wrong decision might be made if the company relied on the full cost information.

In this example, we used both $200 and $125 as measures of the "cost" of the desk. These numbers represent two types of cost constructions, each of which is used for a different purpose. The $200 measures the full cost of the desk, which is the cost used for the purposes described in Chapter 2. The $125 is another type of cost construction; and it is used for other purposes, one of which is to decide, under certain circumstances, whether an order for the desk should be accepted. We shall label this latter type of cost construction *differential cost.*

Differential costs are costs that are different under one set of conditions than they would be under another set of conditions.[1] The term refers both to certain items of cost and to amounts of cost. Thus, in many situations direct labor is an *item* of differential cost; also, if the *amount* of cost that differs in a certain problem is $1,000, the $1,000 is said to be the amount of differential cost.

Differential costs always relate to a specific situation. In the example described above, the differential cost of the desk in question was $125. Under another set of circumstances—for example, if a similar problem arose several days later—the differential cost might well be something other than $125. From the viewpoint of the *buyer* of the desk, its differential cost was $180. The buyer paid $180 for the desk, which the buyer would not have been paid if the desk had not been purchased.

Contrasts with full costs

There are three important differences between full costs and differential costs.

---

[1] Differential costs are also called *relevant* costs.

1. Nature of the cost. The full cost of a product or other cost objective is the sum of its direct costs plus an equitable share of applicable indirect costs. Differential costs include only those elements of cost that are different under a certain set of conditions. This is the most important distinction between full costs and differential costs.

2. Source of data. Information on full costs is taken directly from a company's cost accounting system. The system is designed to measure full costs on a regular basis, and to report these costs routinely. There is no comparable system for collecting differential costs. The appropriate items that constitute differential costs are assembled to meet the requirements of a specific problem. Each problem is different. Some of the data used to construct differential costs may come from the cost accounting system, but other data come from other sources.

3. Time perspective. The full cost accounting system collects costs on a historical basis; that is, it measures what the costs *were*. For certain purposes, such as setting selling prices, these historical costs are adjusted to reflect the estimated impact of future conditions; but for other purposes, such as financial reporting, the historical costs are used without change. **Differential costs always relate to the future; they are intended to show what the costs would be if a certain course of action were adopted, rather than what the costs were.** Historical costs are often useful in estimating what the future costs are likely to be because the past is often the best available guide to the future.

RELATION OF COSTS TO VOLUME

In the example of the desk given above, the volume, or output, of the furniture manufacturer would be higher — by one desk — if the company accepted the order compared with what the volume would have been if the company did not accept the order. The proposal under consideration therefore had an effect on volume as well as on costs. This is the case with many problems involving differential costs, and we shall therefore discuss in some detail the relation of costs and volume. In order to do so, we discuss in more depth the concepts of variable costs and fixed costs which were introduced in earlier chapters.

Variable, semivariable, and fixed costs

There are three general types of cost patterns: variable, fixed, and semivariable.

Variable costs are items of cost that vary directly and proportionately with volume. If variable costs are $4,000 in a period when volume is 1,000 units of product, they should be $6,000 in a period when volume is 1,500 units. A 50 percent increase in volume causes a 50 percent increase in variable cost. Direct labor, direct material, lubricants, power costs, and supplies are typical examples of variable costs.

In general usage, the word *variable* means simply *changeable,* but in accounting, *variable* has a more restricted meaning. Variable refers not to changes in cost that take place over time, nor to changes associated with the seasons of the year, but only to changes associated with the *level of activity,* that is, with the volume of output. If an item of cost increases as volume increases, the item is a variable cost; otherwise, it is not.

Fixed costs do not vary at all with volume. If fixed costs are $4,000 in a period when volume is 1,000 units, they should also be $4,000 when volume is 1,500 units. Building depreciation, property taxes, supervisory salaries, and occupancy costs (heat and light) often behave in this fashion. These costs are incurred because of the passage of time, rather than because of the volume within a specified period of time.

Although the term *fixed cost* may imply that the amount of cost is fixed and hence cannot be changed, such an implication is incorrect. The term refers only to items of cost that do not change with changes in *volume.* Fixed costs can be changed for other reasons; for example, a deliberate management decision to change them. The term *nonvariable* is therefore more appropriate than *fixed;* but since *fixed cost* is in widespread business use, we use it here.

> *EXAMPLE:* Plant protection costs, such as the wages of security guards, are ordinarily fixed costs since these costs do not vary with changes in volume. Plant protection costs will increase, however, if management decides that the current level of plant protection is inadequate and hires additional guards, or if salary levels are increased. Alternatively, they will decrease if management decides that reductions in the current level of plant protection are prudent.

Semivariable costs vary in the same direction as, but less than proportionately with, changes in volume. If semivariable costs are $4,000 in a period when volume is 1,000 units, they should be higher than $4,000, but less than 50 percent higher, when volume is 1,500 units. Semivariable costs are also called *semifixed* or *partly variable* costs. Examples may be indirect labor, maintenance, and clerical costs.

Relation to unit costs. The foregoing description of the three types of cost was expressed in terms of *total costs* for a period. In terms of *unit costs,* the description of these types of cost is quite different. The variable cost per unit of volume is a *constant;* that is, it does not change as volume changes. Fixed cost per unit does change with changes in volume; as volume increases, fixed cost per unit decreases. Semivariable cost per unit also changes with changes in volume, but the amount of change is smaller than that for fixed cost. These relationships have already been described briefly in Part One, but an additional example is given for emphasis.

EXAMPLE: Costs at three levels of volume are given below:

Volume (units)	1,000	1,200	1,500
Total cost for the period:			
Variable cost	$4,000	$4,800	$6,000
Fixed cost	4,000	4,000	4,000
Semivariable cost....................................	4,000	4,400	5,000
Unit cost:			
Variable cost	$4.00	$4.00	$4.00
Fixed cost	4.00	3.33	2.67
Semivariable cost....................................	4.00	3.67	3.33

Observe that as volume increases by 50 percent (i.e., from 1,000 to 1,500 units)—

- Total variable cost increases by 50 percent.
- Total fixed cost remains unchanged.
- Total semivariable cost increases but by less than 50 percent.
- Variable cost per unit remains unchanged.
- Fixed cost per unit decreases.
- Semivariable cost per unit decreases, but not as rapidly as fixed cost per unit.

Variable costs versus direct costs. We need to distinguish carefully between variable cost and direct cost. A *direct cost* is an element of cost that can be traced to a single cost objective, as contrasted with an indirect cost, which applies to more than one cost objective.

The direct labor costs and the direct material costs in a production cost center are direct costs of that cost center. They are also *variable* costs because normally twice as much direct material and direct labor cost are required for two units of output as for one unit.

There are, however, many circumstances in which an item of direct cost is not a variable cost. The costs of supervision and depreciation on the machinery located in a cost center are direct costs of that cost center, but they are fixed costs, *not* variable costs. Also, in a cost accounting system, only direct material and direct labor costs are classified as direct manufacturing costs of products, but some items of manufacturing overhead are *variable* costs; that is, they vary with volume. Electrical power and lubricants are examples.

Cost-volume diagrams

The relationship between costs and volume can be displayed on a cost-volume diagram. Three such diagrams are shown in Exhibit 6–1. In a cost-volume diagram, cost is plotted on the vertical, or *y,* axis, and volume is plotted on the horizontal, or *x,* axis. This follows a conventional

EXHIBIT 6-1
Types of costs

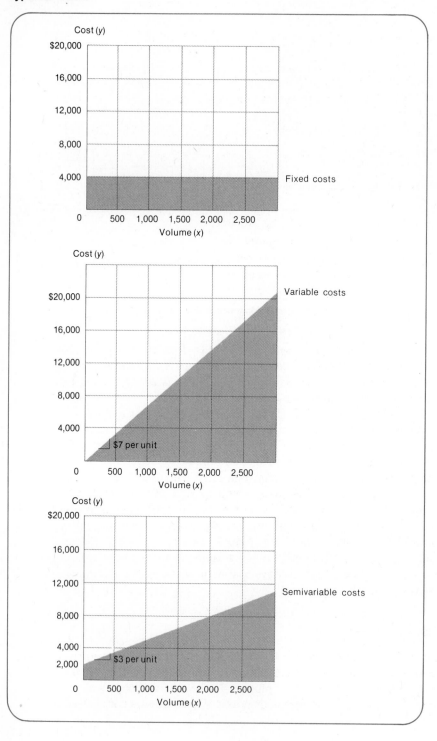

rule for graphs: the *dependent variable* is plotted on the *y* axis and the *independent variable* is plotted on the *x* axis. In a cost-volume diagram, therefore, cost is implicitly assumed to be the dependent variable and volume the independent variable; that is, the amount of the cost *depends on* the volume or level of activity, rather than *vice versa*.

In introducing the subject, we shall describe a company that makes and sells only one product. In such a company, volume is best measured by the number of units of product manufactured or sold in a given time period, such as a month. Later on, we shall describe techniques for measuring cost-volume relationships in companies that have several products.

Each of the diagrams in Exhibit 6–1 shows the behavior of one of the three types of cost described above. The fixed cost is $4,000 per period, regardless of the volume in that period. It is therefore represented by a horizontal line. The variable cost is $7 per unit of volume. The line therefore is zero at zero volume; and it goes up proportional with the volume, at a rate of $7 per unit. The semivariable cost line starts at $2,000 at zero volume and increased at a rate of $3 per unit of volume. Note that the semivariable cost can be decomposed into two elements, a fixed element of $2,000 per period of time and a variable element of $3 per unit of volume.

Behavior of total costs

If each separate cost element behaves according to one of the three patterns shown in Exhibit 6–1, then the total cost, which is the sum of these separate elements, must vary with volume in the manner shown in Exhibit 6–2, which was constructed simply by combining the three separate elements shown in Exhibit 6–1.

Since a semivariable cost can be split into fixed and variable components, the **behavior of total costs can be described in terms of only two components — a fixed component, which is a total amount per period, and a variable component, which is an amount per unit of volume.** In Exhibit 6–2, the fixed amount is $6,000 per period, which is the sum of the $4,000 fixed cost and the $2,000 fixed component of the semivariable cost. The variable cost is $10 per unit of volume, which is the sum of the $7 per unit variable cost and the $3 per unit variable component of the semivariable cost. The semivariable cost has disappeared as a separate entity, part of it being combined with the variable cost and the remainder being combined with the fixed cost. Such combining can be done for any semivariable cost item that is expressed as a fixed dollar amount per period plus a rate per unit of volume. There is therefore no need to consider semivariable costs as a separate category. Accordingly, from this point on, we shall consider only the fixed and variable components of cost. Subsequently, we shall describe techniques for separating a semivariable

EXHIBIT 6–2
Relation of total cost to volume

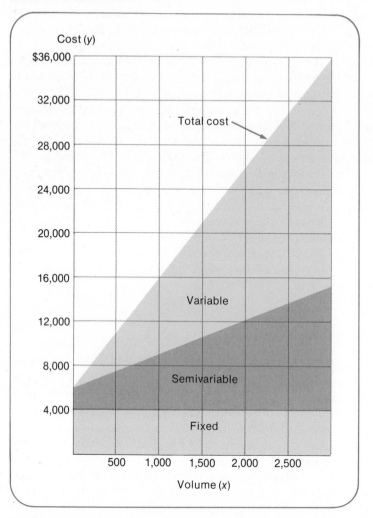

cost into a variable rate per unit of volume and a fixed amount per time period.

Meaning of the cost-volume diagram

The cost-volume diagram in Exhibit 6–2 shows the relationship between costs and volume. Its appearance implies certain things about this relationship, which are discussed below.

The linear assumption. The lines on Exhibit 6–2 are straight lines, not curves. Thus, the diagram implies that the relationship between costs and volume is *linear*. Actually, some items of costs may vary in steps, as in Exhibit 6–3. This happens when the cost occurs in discrete "chunks," as when one indirect worker is added for every 500 additional hours of direct labor per month. Other items of cost may vary along a curve rather than a straight line; and in rare circumstances still others, such as the maintenance cost of idle machines, may actually decrease as volume increases.

In most situations, however, the effect of these discontinuities and nonlinear cost functions on total costs is minor, and the assumption that

EXHIBIT 6–3
A cost element with a step function

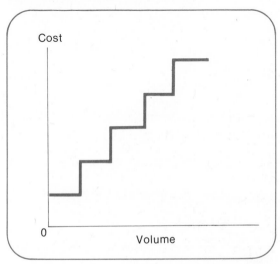

total costs vary in a linear relationship with volume is a satisfactory working approximation. This is a most fortunate fact. Many theoretical treatises discuss cost functions with various types of complicated curves. Such complicated curves are rarely used in practice, however, for it is usually found that the simple straight-line assumption, although perhaps not a perfect representation of cost-volume relationships, is close enough for practical purposes. In this book, therefore, we describe only linear relationships. If a real-life problem does involve nonlinear relationships, the general approach is similar to that described here; the only difference is that the arithmetic is more complicated.

Relevant range. Exhibit 6–2, as drawn, suggests that the indicated relationships apply over the whole range of volume, from zero to whatever number is at the far right of the diagram. This implication is incorrect. For example, at zero volume (i.e., when the factory is not operating at all), management decisions may cause costs to be considerably higher or considerably lower than the $6,000 shown in Exhibit 6–2. When production gets so high that a second shift is required, costs may behave quite differently from the way they behave under one-shift operations. Even within the limits of a single shift, it is to be expected that costs will behave differently when the factory is very busy, from the way they behave when the factory is operating at a significantly lower volume. In short, a straight line gives a good approximation of the behavior of costs *only* *within a certain range of volume.* This range is referred to as the **relevant** **range** because it is the range that is relevant for the situation being analyzed.

EXHIBIT 6–4
Designation of relevant range

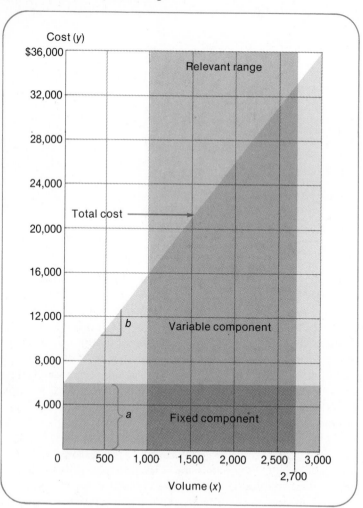

Exhibit 6–4 shows the same cost pattern as Exhibit 6–2, and the relevant range is indicated by the shaded area from 1,000 to 2,700 units. Although the cost line is extended to zero volume, it does not imply that costs actually will behave in this fashion at volumes lower than 1,000 units; rather, the line is drawn on the diagram solely as a means of identifying the fixed component of total costs. The fixed component (i.e., $6,000 per period) is the amount of cost indicated by the point where the cost line crosses the y axis, which is at zero volume.

In Exhibit 6–4, the relevant range is shown explicitly. It does clutter up the diagram somewhat; and for this reason it is omitted from most cost-volume diagrams, including those that we shall be using. Even though the relevant range is not explicitly shown, the reader should always remember that the cost-volume relationships depicted are valid only within a certain range; different relationships exist both above and below that range.

Single set of conditions.   The diagram shows the estimated relationship between costs and volume under a certain set of conditions: assumed wage rates, assumed material prices, assumed manufacturing methods, and so on. If any of these conditions should change—for example, if there is an increase in wage rates—the diagram is obsolete, and a new one must be drawn.

Volume the only causal variable.   A cost-volume diagram shows only the impact that *volume* has on costs. It tells nothing about other factors that affect costs in a given period. Some of these other factors are:

- *Rate of change.* Rapid changes in volume are more difficult for factory personnel to adjust to than moderate changes.
- *Direction of change.* When volume is increasing, costs tend to lag behind the straight-line curve because supervisors try to get by with the existing work force. When volume is decreasing, costs also lag because supervisors try to avoid laying off workers.
- *Duration of change.* A temporary change in volume tends to have a smaller effect on costs than a longer, more permanent change.
- *Efficiency.* For many reasons, costs may be better controlled in one period than in another.
- *Management discretion.* Management may decide that certain cost items should be changed.

For these and other reasons, it is not possible to predict the costs of operating a factory for a certain period merely by predicting the volume for that period and then reading off the costs at that volume from a cost-volume diagram. Nevertheless, the effect of volume on costs is so important that the cost-volume diagram is an extremely useful tool in analysis. In using it, the interpretation of the diagram should be tempered by the influence of other factors, to the extent that they can be estimated.

Equation for the cost line

On the cost-volume diagram, total costs are read on the y axis and volume is shown on the x axis. The total costs at any volume are the sum of the fixed component ($6,000 per period in Exhibit 6–4) and the variable component ($10 per unit times the number of units). For example, total cost at a volume of 2,000 units is: $6,000 + (2,000 units @ $10 per unit) = $26,000. The general equation for any straight line is $y = a + bx$. In a cost-volume diagram, these symbols mean the following:

$$y = \text{total cost}$$
$$x = \text{volume}$$
$$a = \text{the fixed cost per period}$$
$$b = \text{the variable cost per unit}$$

Thus, the equation can be used to find the total cost at any volume within the relevant range as follows:

Equation:	a	$+$	(b	$\bullet$ x)	$=$	y
Words:	Fixed per Period	+	(Variable per Unit	$\bullet$ Units)	=	Total Cost
Numbers:	$6,000	+	($10	$\bullet$ 2,000)	=	$26,000

Unit costs

It should be emphasized that the line we are studying represents *total* costs at various volumes. A line that represents *unit* costs is quite different. If total costs have a linear relationship with volume, and if some costs are fixed, then unit costs will always be a curve that slopes downward to the right. This curve shows that unit costs decrease as volume increases. Exhibit 6–5 is a unit cost curve derived from Exhibit 6–4. Since a unit cost is total cost divided by the number of units, Exhibit 6–5 was obtained simply by dividing total cost at various volume levels by the amount of volume at those levels, plotting the results of each such calculation, and joining the points.

Estimating the cost-volume relationship

In order to construct a cost-volume diagram, estimates must be made of what the amount of costs are expected to be. These estimates often are made as part of the *budgeting* process, which is described in Chapter 12. In this process, estimates are made of all significant items of revenue and cost; these show what revenues and costs are expected to be in some future period, usually the following year or the average month in the following year.

Any of the following methods can be used to derive the a and b terms for the cost-volume formula as a part of this process.

EXHIBIT 6–5
Behavior of unit costs

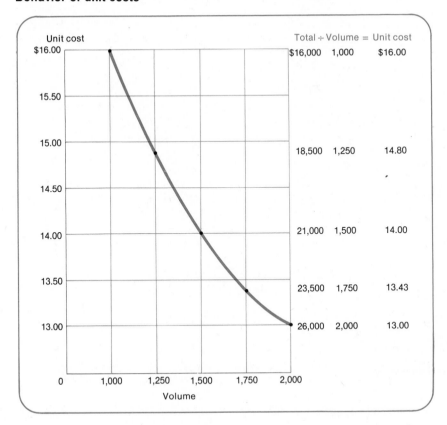

High-low method. Estimate total costs at each of two volume levels; this establishes two points on the line. This is called the high-low method because one of the volumes selected is likely to be quite high and the other is likely to be quite low; the upper and lower limits of the relevant range often are selected for this purpose. Then proceed as follows:

1. Subtract total cost at the lower volume from total cost at the higher volume, and subtract the number of units for the lower volume from the number of units for the higher volume.
2. Divide the difference in cost by the difference in volume, which gives *b*, the amount by which total cost changes with a change of one unit of volume (i.e., the variable unit cost).
3. Multiply either of the volumes by *b* and subtract the result from the total cost at that volume, thus removing the variable component and leaving the fixed component *a*.

This is simply an application of the general procedure for deriving the equation of a straight line, given two points on the line.

EXAMPLE: It is estimated that costs will be $33,000 when volume is 2,700 units and $21,000 when volume is 1,500 units. The calculation of the formula for the line is as follows:

	Estimates	
	Costs	Volume
High	$33,000	2,700
Low	21,000	1,500
Difference	$12,000	1,200

$b = \$12,000$ Difference in Cost $\div$ 1,200 Difference in Units
$= \$10$ per unit; this is the *variable* component.
$a = \$33,000 - (2,700$ units @ $\$10)$
$= \$6,000$; this is the *fixed* component.

or

$a = \$21,000 - (1,500$ units @ $\$10) = \$6,000$

Therefore, the formula for the line is:

$$y = \$6,000 + \$10x$$

Direct estimate.   Estimate total costs at one volume, and estimate how costs will change with a unit change in volume. The estimate of change is the variable component, b; and the fixed component, a, can be found by subtraction, as described above.

Built-up estimate.   Consider each item of cost separately. Decide which items are variable, which are fixed, and which are semivariable. Estimate the variable rate for each variable cost item and the fixed amount for each fixed cost item. Estimate the behavior of semivariable costs in terms of their variable and fixed components. Add up these separate estimates.

Scatter diagram.   Use a volume-cost diagram. On it plot actual costs recorded in past periods (on the y axis) against the volume levels in those periods (on the x axis). Data on costs and volumes for each of the preceding several months might be used for this purpose. Draw a line that best fits these observations. Such a diagram is shown in Exhibit 6–6. The line of best fit either can be drawn by visual inspection of the plotted points, or it can be fitted by a statistical technique called the **method of least squares** (see Appendix at the end of this chapter). In many cases a line drawn by visual inspection is just as good as, and in some cases is better than, a mathematically fitted line, because judgment can be used to adjust for unusual observations.

If the line is fitted visually, the a and b values can be determined by reading the values for any two points on the line and then using the high-

EXHIBIT 6–6
Scatter diagram

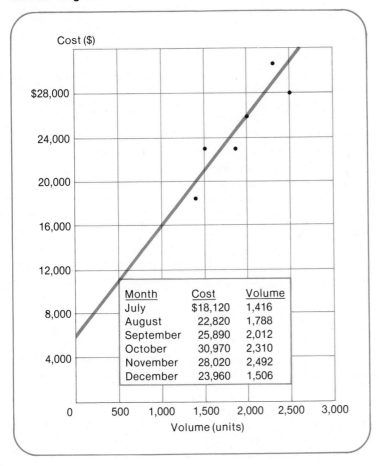

Month	Cost	Volume
July	$18,120	1,416
August	22,820	1,788
September	25,890	2,012
October	30,970	2,310
November	28,020	2,492
December	23,960	1,506

low method described above. If the line is fitted statistically, the procedure gives the a and b values directly.

Problems with scatter diagrams. Estimating cost-volume relationships by means of a scatter diagram is a common practice, but the results can be misleading. In the first place, this technique shows, at best, what the relationship between costs and volumes **was in the past,** whereas we are interested in what the relationship **will be in the future.** The past is not necessarily a mirror of the future. Also, the relationship we seek is that obtaining under a *single set of operating conditions,* whereas each point on a scatter diagram may represent changes in factors other than the two being studied, namely, cost and volume. Similar problems arise when historical data are used in connection with the other methods.

Measures of volume

So far we have been describing a single-product company in which volume can be measured by the number of units produced. In a company that makes several products, the number of units produced is unlikely to be a reliable measure of activity for the obvious reason that some products cost more per unit than others. To regard them as of equal importance would be like adding apples and oranges. In these companies, therefore, other measures of volume must be used. The problem of selecting the appropriate volume measure in these circumstances is similar to that of selecting the basis for the overhead rate in Chapter 4. An overhead rate can be expressed as an amount per unit of product, per direct labor hour, per direct labor dollar, or in other ways. Each of these bases of overhead allocation reflects different measures of volume. Presumably, a certain measure is selected because it most closely reflects the conditions that cause costs to change.

In selecting a volume measure, two basic questions must be answered: (1) should the measure be based on *inputs,* or should it be based on *outputs?;* and (2) should the measure be expressed in terms of *money amounts,* or should it be expressed in terms of *physical quantities?* Each of these questions is discussed below.

Input versus output measures. Input measures relate to the resources that are used in a cost center. Examples for a production cost center are the number of direct labor hours worked, dollars of direct labor cost, number of machine-hours operated, or pounds of raw material used. Output measures relate to the goods and services that flow out of the cost center.

For cost-volume diagrams that show the relationship between overhead costs and volume, an input measure, such as direct labor costs, may be a good measure of volume since many elements of overhead cost tend to vary more closely with other input factors than with output. For example, it is reasonable to expect that indirect cost items associated with direct labor, such as fringe benefits, social security taxes, and payroll accounting, varv with the amount of direct labor used. Some indirect costs, such as inspection costs, might vary more closely with the quantity of products produced.

If the diagram represents total costs for a cost center, and if volume is measured in terms of direct labor, which is itself one element of cost, it can be argued that the same numbers affect both costs and volume. This is true, but the diagram nevertheless reflects changes in costs other than direct labor and is therefore useful.

Monetary versus nonmonetary measures. A volume measure expressed in physical quantities, such as direct labor hours, is often better than one expressed in dollars, such as direct labor cost, because the former is unaffected by changes in prices. A wage increase would cause direct labor costs to increase, even if there were no actual increase in the volume of activity. If volume is measured in terms of direct labor dollars, such a measure could be misleading. On the other hand, if price changes are likely to affect both labor and overhead to the same degree, the use of a monetary measure of volume may be a means of allowing implicitly for the effect of these price changes.

Choice of a measure. The ease of obtaining the measure must be taken into account. Total direct labor costs are often available in the cost accounting system without extra calculation, whereas the computation of total direct labor hours, or machine-hours, may require considerable additional work. Also, since the measure of volume for analytical purposes is often (but not always) the same as that used in allocating overhead costs to products for the purpose of financial accounting, the appropriateness of the measure for the latter purpose must also be considered.

THE PROFITGRAPH AND CONTRIBUTION ANALYSIS

The cost-volume diagram in Exhibit 6–4 can be amplified into a useful device called the *profitgraph* (or *cost-volume-profit graph*, or *P/V graph*) simply by the addition of a revenue line to it, for a **profitgraph is a diagram showing the expected relationship between total cost and revenue at various volumes.**[2] A profitgraph can be constructed either for the business as a whole, or for some segment of the business such as a product, a product line, or a division.

In a single-product company, total revenue at any volume is the unit selling price times the number of units sold. Just as the cost-volume diagram shows the relationships under a single set of conditions, so does a revenue line show the relationship under a single condition, namely, a constant selling price per unit. We designate total revenue as y_r (the subscript r distinguishes this line from the cost line which henceforth we shall designate as y_c.) Designating the unit selling price as p, the equation for total revenue at any volume, x, is

$$y_r = px$$

For example, if the unit selling price is $15, revenue at a volume of 2,000 units is $30,000.

In Exhibit 6–7, we have added this revenue line to the cost-volume diagram shown in Exhibit 6–4, thereby turning it into a profitgraph. Although not shown explicitly on the diagram, it should be understood that the relationships are expected to hold only within the relevant volume range, as in Exhibit 6–4. Sometimes, several revenue lines are drawn on a profitgraph, each one showing what revenue would be at a specified unit

---

[2] This device is also called a *break-even chart*, but such a label has the unfortunate implication that the objective of a business is merely to break even.

EXHIBIT 6–7
Profitgraph

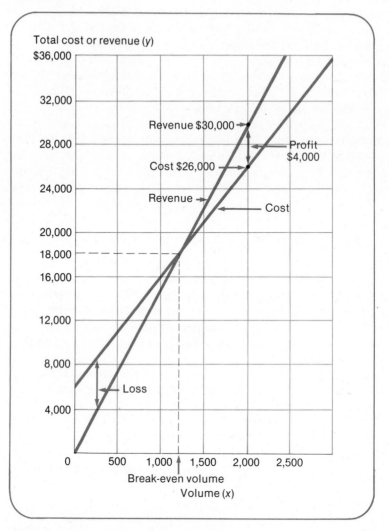

selling price. This procedure helps to show how a change in selling price affects the profit at any given volume.

Contribution income statement

Before describing the uses that can be made of the profitgraph and the equations underlying it, we introduce another device for showing the relationships among revenue, variable cost, and fixed cost. This is the contribution income statement. **A contribution income statement is an income statement arranged so as to emphasize the contribution margin.**

EXHIBIT 6-8

Contribution Income Statement
(assuming volume of 2,000 units)

Revenue (2,000 units @ $15)..................................... $30,000
Variable expenses* (2,000 units @ $10) 20,000
Contribution margin.. 10,000
Fixed expenses.. 6,000
Operating Income .... $ 4,000

* Since this is an income statement, the amounts deducted from revenue are called *expenses*. As pointed out in Chapter 4, expenses are one type of cost. Thus, although the description in this chapter uses the broader term, *costs*, it applies equally well to the type of cost that is deducted from the revenue of a period and which is labeled *expense*.

The contribution margin is the difference between revenue and variable expenses. An example is shown in Exhibit 6-8. It was constructed from the equations used in drawing Exhibit 6-7, at a volume of 2,000 units, which we will assume is the expected volume for the period.

The contribution income statement shows the relationships at one level of volume. It is therefore a vertical slice of the profitgraph. The statement in Exhibit 6-8 is in the simplest possible form. In practice, additional detail would be shown; that is, items of variable cost such as direct material, direct labor, variable manufacturing overhead, and variable marketing expenses would be listed separately; and items of fixed cost, such as fixed manufacturing overhead and administrative costs, would also be listed separately.

Uses of the profitgraph and contribution income statement

The profitgraph and the contribution income statement are useful devices for analyzing the overall profit characteristics of a business. We shall illustrate their uses with the data already developed, which are summarized below.

Assuming that the business expects to sell 2,000 units, the same volume as was used in Exhibit 6-8, we shall show the calculations for that volume.

Symbol	Meaning	Numbers
a	Fixed cost	$6,000 per period
b	Variable unit cost	$10 per unit
p	Selling price	$15 per unit
x	Volume	2,000 units
y_r	Total Revenue =	
	$px = \$15 \times 2,000$	$30,000
y_c	Total Cost =	
	$a + bx = \$6,000 + (\$10 \times 2,000)$	$26,000
i	Income =	
	$y_r - y_c = \$30,000 - \$26,000$	$4,000

Marginal income

In the conventional income statement, at a volume of 2,000 units, total cost would be calculated as $13 per unit (= $26,000 ÷ 2,000) and income as $2 per unit (= $4,000 ÷ 2,000). This unit cost and unit income are correct, but they are correct only at a volume of 2,000 units. At higher volumes, income will be more than $2 per unit. This is because at higher volumes the $6,000 of fixed cost is spread over more units, making the unit cost lower and the unit income higher. At lower volumes, the converse will happen.

The equations given above can be rearranged in a way that shows specifically how changes in volume affects income. The approach follows that of the contribution margin income statement in Exhibit 6–8. This statement says that

$$\text{Revenue} - \text{Variable Costs} - \text{Fixed Costs} = \text{Income}$$

Substituting letters:

$$p \cdot x \quad - \quad b \cdot x \quad - \quad a \quad = \quad i$$

Rearranging,

$$(p - b)x \quad - \quad a \quad = \quad i$$

In words, this says that income can be found by taking the difference between unit selling price and unit variable cost, multiplying by volume, and subtracting the fixed costs. In the example,

$$[(\$15 - \$10) \times 2{,}000 \text{ Units}] - \$6{,}000 = \$4{,}000$$

The difference between unit selling price and unit variable cost is the marginal income. It is also called the *unit contribution*. Marginal income is the amount that income changes with a change of one unit of volume. Note that marginal income, $5 in the above example, is the same at all volume levels within the relevant range. It therefore is much easier to understand than the income per unit ($2 at 2,000 units), which is different at each volume. Marginal income times the number of units at a given volume gives the contribution margin as shown on the contribution income statement. In Exhibit 6–8, the contribution margin is $5 × 2,000 units = $10,000.[3]

Contribution profitgraph

Using the marginal income, we can construct another form of profit-graph, as shown in Exhibit 6–9. The y axis on this profitgraph is income,

---

[3] In this book, we use *contribution margin* for the difference *in total* between revenue and variable costs, and we use *marginal income* for the difference *per unit*. The term *unit contribution margin* is often used instead of marginal income.

EXHIBIT 6-9
Contribution profitgraph

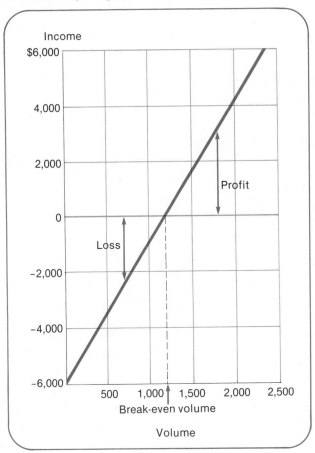

or loss. The line shows that at zero volume the loss would be $6,000 and that it would decrease by $5 per unit, becoming zero at 1,200 units, and then turning into income of $5 per unit (for example, $4,000 at a volume of 2,000 units). **A contribution profitgraph shows the income or loss at each volume level.**

Break-even volume

The relationships given above can also be used to find the **break-even volume, the volume at which total costs equal total revenue.** Since we know from the marginal income analysis that each unit of marginal income reduces the loss caused by the existence of the fixed costs, it follows that at the break-even volume the marginal income times the volume is equal to the fixed costs, or

$$(p - b) \cdot x = a$$

Solving for x, we have

$$\text{Break-Even Volume } x = \frac{a}{p - b} = \frac{\text{Fixed Costs}[4]}{\text{Marginal Income}}$$

This equation says that the break-even volume can be found by dividing the fixed cost (a) by the marginal income, which is the difference between selling price per unit (p) and variable cost per unit (b). Using the illustrative numbers,

$$\frac{\text{Fixed Costs}}{\text{Marginal Income}} = \frac{a}{p - b} = \frac{\$6,000}{\$15 - \$10} = 1,200 \text{ Units}[5]$$

If enough units are sold so that the contribution margin equals the fixed costs, the business will break even, that is, income will be zero. At higher volumes, income increases by the marginal income per unit. In the example, with fixed costs of $6,000, 1,200 units must be sold to break even. Above 1,200 units, income will be earned at the rate of the marginal income, which is $5 per unit. At volumes below the break-even point a loss is expected. The amount of loss or profit expected at any volume is the difference between points on the total cost and revenue lines at that volume.

That the break-even volume is indeed 1,200 units can be verified by calculating total revenue and total costs at 1,200 units:

Revenue, $15 × 1,200 units $18,000
Costs, $6,000 + ($10 × 1,200 units) 18,000
Income 0

---

[4] Since at the break-even volume total cost equals total revenue, the break-even volume (x) can also be found as follows:

$$\text{Total Cost} = \text{Total Revenue}$$
$$a = bx = px$$
$$a = px - bx$$
$$\frac{a}{p - b} = x$$

[5] Using totals, the break-even volume (x) can be found as follows:

$$\text{Total Cost} = \text{Total Revenue}$$
$$a + bx = px$$
$$\$6,000 + \$10x = \$15x$$
$$\$6,000 = \$5x$$
$$x = \$1,200$$

The break-even volume is not the same as the *standard* volume used as a basis for determining overhead rates. In a profitable business, standard volume is considerably higher than break-even volume.

Planned income

Another use made of the above relationships is to find the volume level that must be attained in order to earn a specified level of income. In order to do this, we simply add the desired income (i) to the fixed costs and divide the total by the marginal income, or

$$\frac{\text{Fixed Costs} + \text{Desired Income}}{\text{Marginal Income}} = \text{Needed Volume } x = \frac{a+i}{p-b}$$

If an income of $5,000 is desired, the volume must be

$$\frac{\$6,000 + \$5,000}{\$15 - \$10} = 2,200 \text{ Units}$$

Margin of safety

Another calculation made from a profitgraph is the **margin of safety. This is the amount or ratio by which the current volume exceeds the break-even volume.** Since current volume is 2,000 units, the margin of safety in our illustrative situation is 800 units ($= 2,000 - 1,200$) or 40 percent of current volume. Sales volume can decrease by 40 percent before a loss is incurred, other factors remaining equal.

Improving profit performance

These cost-volume-profit relationships suggest that a useful way of studying the basic profit characteristics of a business is to focus not on the profit per unit (which is different at every volume) but rather on the total fixed costs and the marginal income per unit. In these terms, there are four basic ways in which the profit of a business that makes a single product can be increased:

1. Increase the selling price per unit.
2. Decrease variable cost per unit.
3. Decrease fixed costs.
4. Increase volume.

The separate effects of each of these possibilities are shown in the following calculations and in Exhibit 6–10. Each starts from the current situation that is assumed to be: selling price, $15 per unit; variable cost, $10 per unit; fixed costs, $6,000 per period; and volume, 2,000 units. Income in this situation is $4,000. The effect of a 10 percent improvement in each factor would be:

Factor	Effect on—		New income	Percent income increase*
	Revenue	Cost		
Increase selling price by 10%..........	$+3,000	$ 0	$7,000	75
Decrease variable cost by 10%........	0	−2,000	6,000	50
Decrease fixed cost by 10%............	0	− 600	4,600	15
Increase volume 10%	+3,000	+2,000	5,000	25

* Increase over present income of $4,000.

EXHIBIT 6–10
Improving profit performance

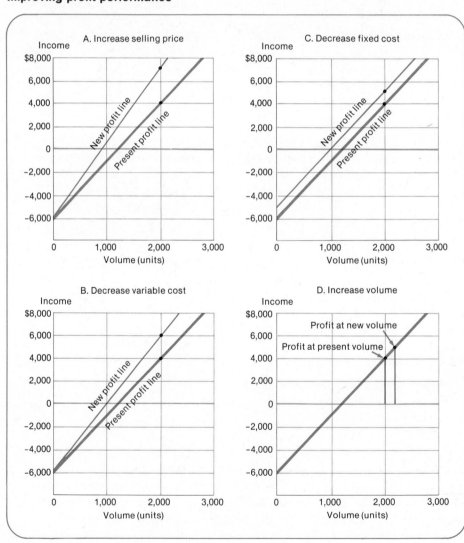

Instead of varying each factor separately, we can look at some of the interrelationships among them. We can calculate, for example, that a 20 percent (i.e., $1,200) increase in fixed costs could be offset either by a 4 percent increase in selling price, or a 12 percent increase in volume, or a 6 percent decrease in variable costs.

The foregoing calculations assume that each factor is independent of the others, a situation that is rarely the case in the real world. An increase in selling price often is accompanied by a decrease in volume, for example. Changes in the factors therefore must usually be analyzed simultaneously, rather than separately as was done above.

Several products

The cost-volume-profit relationships described above apply in a company that makes only a single product. If the company makes several products, a slightly different approach must be used because the unit costs of the products will differ and the number of units of products cannot be used as a valid measure of volume.

We can get around this problem by using sales revenue as the measure of volume and by expressing the variable unit costs as a *percentage* of sales revenue rather than as a *dollar* amount per unit. Thus, if for all products, revenue is estimated to be $30,000 and variable costs are estimated to be $20,000, then variable costs are $66\frac{2}{3}$ percent of revenue. Simply by changing the volume label on Exhibit 6–7, we turn it into a profitgraph for this situation. The variable costs can be thought of as $66\frac{2}{3}$ cents for each revenue dollar, and the marginal income is similarly $33\frac{1}{3}$ cents for each revenue dollar.

These relationships can be easily fitted into the equations given above:

$$\text{Break-Even Point} = \frac{\text{Fixed Costs}}{\text{Marginal Income}} = \frac{a}{p-b}$$

$$= \frac{\$6,000}{0.33\frac{1}{3}}$$

$$= \$18,000 \text{ of Revenue}$$

The revenue needed to attain an income of $5,000 equals

$$\frac{\text{Fixed Costs} + \text{Desired Income}}{\text{Marginal Income}} = \frac{a+i}{p-b}$$

$$= \frac{\$6,000 + \$5,000}{0.33\frac{1}{3}}$$

$$= \$33,000 \text{ of revenue}$$

These relationships are valid if each dollar of revenue produces approximately the same marginal income. This is the case in many companies; that is, they set selling prices so as to earn a profit that is constant percentage above the variable costs. The relationships are also valid, even if marginal incomes on the various products differ, if **product mix** (i.e. the proportion of products with different marginal incomes) is relatively constant. If the product mix changes, the profitgraph does not give valid results. For example, even if total sales revenue does not change from one period to the next, the income in the second period will be higher than the income in the first period if a relatively high proportion of products that have a high marginal income is sold in the second period.

EXHIBIT 6–11
Fallacious profitgraph

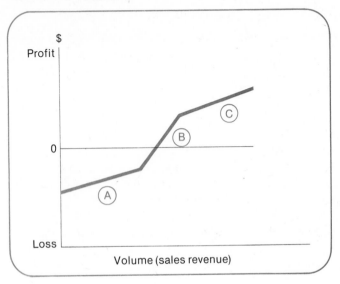

Thus, it is important to understand that the profitgraph shows the *average* marginal income for all products.

If products have different marginal incomes, and if the mix of products is likely to change, the preferable approach is to construct a separate profitgraph for each product. Such a profitgraph shows the marginal income for that product and an appropriate share of the total fixed costs of the company.

Another, but fallacious, approach to this problem is shown in Exhibit 6–11. In this profitgraph, the first line shows the income for Product A, the second that for Product B, and the third that for Product C. The fallacy is that this construction assumes a sequence of events that does not exist in the real world; namely, that Product A is sold *first*, that no units of Product B are sold until after the last unit of Product A, and no units of Product C until after the last unit of Product B. Actually, all products are being sold at the same time.

Problems with scatter diagrams

Scatter diagrams (see page 210) are often a useful way of finding the average relationship between costs and revenues in a multiproduct company. Revenues are plotted on the volume or x axis and costs on the y axis. The marginal income is found by the methods described earlier in this chapter. A problem with such an approach, however, is that the

EXHIBIT 6–12
Scatter diagram illustrating drift

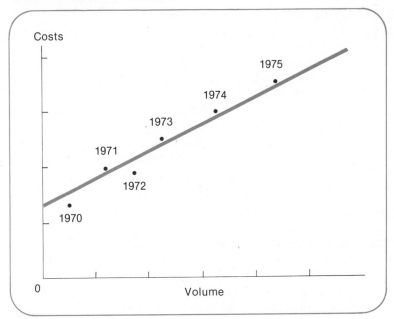

plotted points may not represent the relationships between costs and revenue under a given set of circumstances. The reason is indicated in Exhibit 6–12. In this scatter diagram, each point is located by plotting the costs for one year on the y axis and the sales revenue for that year on the x axis. The points lie along a well-defined path, which is indicated by the straight line; but this line may *not* indicate a relationship between costs and volume.

In fact, the line may indicate nothing more than the tendency for both revenues and costs to increase over the past six years because of inflationary factors. If this is the case, then the line shows the trend, or **drift,** of costs **through time,** not the relationship between cost and volume **at a given time.** Any scatter diagram covering a period of years in which sales were generally increasing each year, or generally decreasing each year, is likely to have this characteristic; and the longer the period covered, the more unreliable the diagram becomes. When the points are strongly influenced by drift, a scatter diagram cannot be used to find cost-volume-profit relationships.

DEMONSTRATION CASE

This case has two purposes. First, it gives practice in making the calculations described in this chapter. Second, and basically much more important, it shows how the relative proportion of fixed costs and variable costs influences management's decisions. You should answer the questions before looking at the suggested solution.

Harvey Cannon is thinking of operating his own ice cream stand at a nearby beach during the 12 weeks of the summer season. In discussions with the ice cream manufacturer who would supply the stand, the following estimates emerged. It was estimated that revenue for the season would be $40,000, but this depended, of course, on the weather and on Cannon's ability to attract customers. The ice cream manufacturer would sell ice cream and other supplies at a cost of 60 percent of revenue. Cannon would pay $300 for a license and for other incidental costs. Three possible arrangements were discussed.

A. The ice cream manufacturer would lease the stand, including all necessary equipment, to Cannon for 20 percent of sales revenue. Cannon would hire part-time help as needed, on an hourly basis, at an estimated cost of 17 percent of sales revenue.

B. The manufacturer would lease the stand and equipment to Cannon for 20 percent of sales revenue, as in A. Harvey would hire helpers for the season at a salary of $5,000.

C. The manufacturer would lease the stand and equipment at $7,000 for the season. Cannon would hire helpers at a salary of $5,000 for the season.

Required:

1. For each of the three alternatives, calculate (*a*) the marginal income per sales dollar, (*b*) the break-even volume in sales dollars, and (*c*) the operating income if sales revenue is $40,000.
2. Which alternative would you recommend that Harvey Cannon should accept?

Suggested solution:

1. The calculations are given in Exhibit 6–13. For Alternative A, for example, variable costs per sales dollar are $0.60 for the merchandise, $0.20 for the lease, and $0.17 for the helpers, a total of $0.97. Marginal income is therefore $0.03 per sales dollar. Fixed costs are $300 for the license, and so forth. The break-even volume is $300 ÷ $0.03 = $10,000 of revenue. At sales revenue of $40,000,

EXHIBIT 6–13
Calculations for Harvey Cannon

	Alternative		
	A	B	C
Variable cost (per sales $):			
Merchandise.................................	$ 0.60	$ 0.60	$ 0.60
Lease...	0.20	0.20	0
Helpers......................................	0.17	0	0
Total	$ 0.97	$ 0.80	$ 0.60
Marginal income (per sales $).........	0.03	0.20	0.40
Fixed cost per season:			
License, etc.	$ 300	$ 300	$ 300
Lease...	0	0	7,000
Helpers......................................	0	5,000	5,000
Total Fixed Cost.....................	300	5,300	12,300
Break-even volume.......................	$10,000	$26,500	$30,750
Income statement:			
Revenue.....................................	$40,000	$40,000	$40,000
Variable cost.............................	38,800	32,000	24,000
Fixed cost	300	5,300	12,300
Total Cost..............................	39,100	37,300	36,300
Operating Income........................	$ 900	$ 2,700	$ 3,700

variable costs would be 97 percent of revenue, or $38,800, and fixed costs would be $300, making total costs $39,100. Operating income would therefore be $900. Similar calculations are made for the other two alternatives.

2. There is no "right answer" to the second question. The choice depends basically on how much risk Cannon is willing to assume. If he keeps fixed costs low, as in Alternative A, the business will break even at a volume of $10,000, which is only 25 percent of the estimated volume, so he is relatively certain of not losing money if he chooses this alternative. On the other hand, he is unlikely to make much profit if he decided on Alternative A: $900 for the estimated volume, and only $0.03 for every dollar of revenue above that, which is not much for a summer's work.

At the other extreme, with the high fixed costs in Alternative C, the break-even volume increases to $30,750, which is 77 percent of the estimated volume. If he selects this alternative, Cannon runs the risk of not making any profit if sales are less than expected, and he could lose money if the weather was really bad. On the other hand, if sales volume works out as estimated, he will earn $3,700 for the summer, much more than either of the other alternatives, and he will earn $0.40 profit on every sales dollar above $40,000.

The choice that Cannon faces is common in business. If a company is willing to assume the risk of heavy fixed costs, it can earn large profits if volume turns out to be as good as estimated. If it is unwilling to assume this risk, it usually must expect to earn lower profits. The decision turns on management's willingness or reluctance to assume risks.

SUMMARY

Differential costs are costs that are different under one set of conditions than they would be under another set of conditions. The costs that are differential depend on the specific situation that is being analyzed.

In many situations costs differ because of differences in volume or activity, and it is therefore important to understand the relationship between costs and volume. Within a relevant range, variable costs vary proportionately with volume. Fixed costs remain constant. A third category of cost, semivariable cost, need not be considered separately since it can be decomposed into variable and fixed components.

In most situations, the cost-volume relationship is linear, and can be expressed by the equation for a straight line, $y = a + bx$. This line is often drawn on a cost-volume diagram. When a revenue line is added to such a diagram, the diagram is called a profitgraph.

From the relationships shown on the profitgraph, important information about the business can be discerned. The marginal income is the difference between revenue per unit and variable cost per unit. The break-even volume is the volume at which total revenue equals total cost. These relationships can be used to estimate the volume that is necessary to earn a desired amount of income, and also to estimate the effect of various ways of improving profit performance.

APPENDIX: THE LEAST-SQUARES METHOD

The least-squares method is the commonly used mathematical method for determining the values in the equation for the line showing the relationship between volume and costs. It can be used only when a straight-line relationship exists; but as noted in the text, most cost-volume relationships are approximately straight lines.

The general equation for a straight line is

$$y = a + bx$$

in which y stands for total cost, a for fixed cost, b for variable cost per unit, and x for volume. A series of observations of costs and volume gives pairs of x, y values, and these are used to find the values of a and b. The least-squares technique determines a and b values such that the resulting line has this characteristic: **the sum of the squares of the distances of each observation from the line is at a minimum.** For any other line, the sum of the squares of the distances would be greater. Hence, the name *least squares.* The distances from the individual observations to the line are measured *vertically,* that is, they are parallel to the y axis.

Exhibit 6–14 is a scatter diagram on which cost-volume observations for five months have been plotted. Each x, y dot represents the volume

EXHIBIT 6–14
Scatter diagram

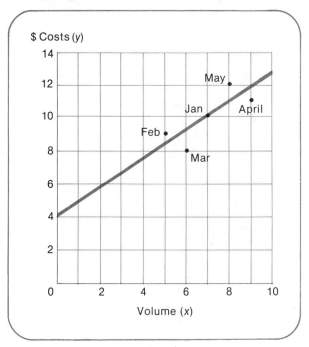

and the costs for one of these months. The numerical amounts for each month are shown in the table below. A straight line has been drawn to represent the relationship between costs and volume that can be deduced from these five observations. The least-squares method obtains the a and b values for this line by solving two simultaneous equations:

$$Na + (\Sigma x)b = \Sigma y$$
$$(\Sigma x)a + (\Sigma x^2)b = \Sigma xy$$

In this equation, N is the number of observations; in our example, 5. To use these equations, the values for Σx, Σy, Σx^2, and Σxy are first calculated, as in the following table:

Month	Volume x	Cost y	x^2	xy
January	7	$10	49	70
February....................	5	9	25	45
March	6	8	36	48
April...........................	9	11	81	99
May............................	8	12	64	96
$N = 5$	$\Sigma x = 35$	$\Sigma y = 50$	$\Sigma x^2 = 255$	$\Sigma xy = 358$

These values are then substituted in the two simultaneous equations as follows:

$$5a + 35b = 50$$
$$35a + 255b = 358$$

The procedure for solving two simultaneous equations is first to multiply one or both of the equations by a constant so that the resulting value for one of the terms is the same amount in both equations. In this case, the easiest way to do this is to multiply the first equation by 7, so that the a term becomes 35, the same as a in the second equation:

$$7 \cdot (5a + 35b) = 7 \cdot 50$$
$$35a + 245b = 350$$

Next, one equation is subtracted from the other. The a term drops out, leaving a simple linear equation which can be solved for b:

$$35a + 255b = 358$$
$$\underline{35a + 245b = 350}$$
$$0 \qquad 10b = 8$$
$$b = 0.80$$

We now know that b, which is the variable cost per unit, is $0.80. Substituting this amount in either one of the equations makes it possible to solve for a:

$$5a + 35b = 50$$
$$5a + (35 \cdot 0.8) = 50$$
$$5a + 28 = 50$$
$$5a = 22$$
$$a = 4.40$$

Thus, the fixed cost is $4.40.

The complete equation for the straight line is therefore:

$$y = 4.4 + 0.8x$$

Most computers and some hand-held calculators are programmed so that the values for a least-squares straight line can be obtained automatically after the observed x, y pairs are entered.

IMPORTANT TERMS

Differential cost	Output measure
Variable cost	Profitgraph
Fixed cost	Contribution income statement
Semivariable cost	Marginal income
Relevant range	Contribution profitgraph
High-low method	Break-even volume
Scatter diagram	Margin of safety
Input measure	Drift

QUESTIONS FOR DISCUSSION

1. The accounts contain an item, "Wages earned, $1,000." Describe, so as to distinguish between them, situations in which this $1,000 would be (a) a product cost, (b) a direct cost, (c) a variable cost, (d) a differential cost, (e) an indirect cost, and (f) a fixed cost.

2. Explain in your own words the differences between full costs and differential costs.

3. "Any item of cost can change, but only certain items are variable." Explain and illustrate each half of this sentence.

4. "My records show that gasoline costs me 5 cents a mile, regardless of how many miles I drive my car, whereas my insurance cost per mile obviously varies with the number of miles I drive. Therefore, gasoline is a fixed cost and insurance is a variable cost?" Explain why this statement is wrong.

5. If costs do not behave the same way at zero volume as they do within the relevant range, why are the lines on a cost-volume diagram extended to zero volume?

6. In all the examples given in the text, unit cost decreases as volume increases. Can you think of circumstances in which unit cost would *increase* with an increase in volume?

7. The cost-volume diagram, Exhibit 6–4, does not identify semivariable costs. Why?

8. "The cost-volume diagram shows the relationship between costs and volume under the conditions prevailing at a certain time." How would Exhibit 6–4 be affected if (a) there was an increase in wage and salary rates? (b) if the company added a safety engineer? (c) if direct material costs per unit decreased? and (d) if the company purchased an automatic machine to perform certain operations that currently are done manually?

9. How would the unit cost diagram in Exhibit 6–5 be affected by each of the changes listed in Question 8?

10. In Exhibit 6–4, the top of the relevant range is a volume of 2,700 units. What conditions could cause a difference in cost behavior at a volume higher than 2,700 units?

11. Similarly, suggest conditions that could cause a difference in cost behavior at a volume lower than the bottom of the relevant range.

12. Describe methods for estimating the fixed cost per period and the variable cost per unit of volume.

13. Identify the numbered components on the profitgraph in Exhibit 6–15.

EXHIBIT 6–15

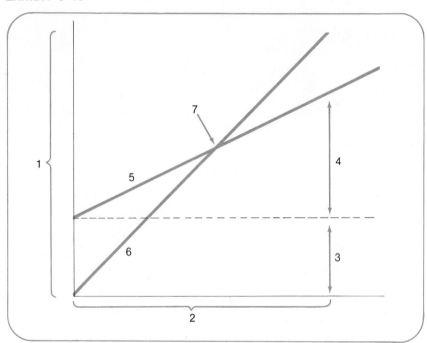

14. Under what circumstances could machine-hours appropriately be used as a measure of volume on a profitgraph?

15. Under what circumstances can a profitgraph such as that shown in Exhibit 6–7 be used if a company makes several products? Why is it invalid under other circumstances?

16. Why are differential costs not labeled as such in an accounting system?

17. Distinguish between the meaning of the terms *contribution margin* and *marginal income*.

PROBLEMS

6–1. The graphs below relate to the behavior of certain costs involved with the operation of a summer basketball camp for boys:

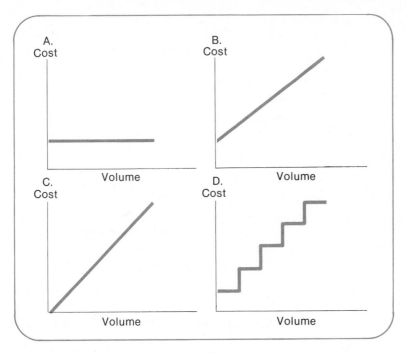

Required:

A. Title each graph to show the type of cost it described (fixed, variable, semivariable, etc.)

B. From the list of costs described below select those which each graph described.

Costs

1. Cost of food served campers.
2. Counsellors' salaries. A counsellor is hired for every 20 campers.
3. Repairs and maintenance. The maintenance supervisor is on salary. Other repairs and labor depend on funds available as campers increase.
4. Depreciation of camp buildings and equipment.

6–2. Listed below are the expected costs of several items at the upper and lower levels of the Baxter Company's relevant range of activity.

	Lower level	Upper level
Production (units)	10,000	20,000
Raw materials	$50,000	$100,000
Direct labor	75,000	150,000
Depreciation of machinery	25,000	25,000
Indirect labor	40,000	70,000
Supervisory salaries	36,000	36,000
Maintenance	25,000	45,000

Required:

A. For each item, calculate the cost per unit at both levels of activity.
B. For each item, does the behavior of cost per unit over the relevant range of activity indicate the general type of cost (fixed, variable, or semivariable)? Explain your answer.

6-3. The Lance Company has developed the following equation for manufacturing overhead cost:

Total Cost = $15,000 per Year + $5 per Direct Labor Hour

Required:

Prepare an estimate of the manufacturing overhead cost for a month in which 4,000 direct labor hours are expected.

6-4. An examination of past records of maintenance costs of the Roman Company disclosed the following cost and volume measures:

	October	July
Cost per month	$96,500	$68,500
Machine-hours	25,000	17,000

Required:

A. Using the high-low method, prepare the equation for monthly maintenance cost.
B. Use the equation from Requirement A to estimate the maintenance cost for a month having 18,500 machine hours.

6-5. Production costs in Department A for the preceding six months were as follows:

	Month					
	Jan.	Feb.	Mar.	Apr.	May	June
Units of production	220	200	240	260	300	280
Total cost	$9,500	$9,000	$9,650	$10,100	$11,000	$10,750

Required:

A. Estimate fixed and variable costs by the high-low method.
B. Estimate fixed and variable costs by drawing a scatter diagram.
C. If production in a certain month is estimated to be 250 units, what is your estimate of total cost?

6-6. Using the equation $y = a + bx$ for the cost at any volume and the equation $px = a + bx$ for the break-even volume, answer the questions below, using the following data:

Fixed costs per period	$45,500
Variable costs per unit	$ 25
Standard sales volume per period (units)	30,000
Selling price per unit	$ 60

Required:

A. Calculate the total cost at standard volume.
B. Calculate the break-even point in units.

C. Calculate the profit or loss at standard volume.

D. What is the marginal income?

E. Compute the income which would result at the standard volume if both the variable cost per unit and the selling price per unit increased by 20 percent.

6-7. The 1977 budget for Collegiate Gift Shoppe contains the following data:

Total assets............................	$180,000
Revenues..............................	200,000
Total expenses	160,000
Fixed expenses....................	40,000

Required:

A. What is the equation for estimating the operating income at various volumes under these circumstances?

B. What is the expected break-even point for 1977?

C. If the maximum capacity of this firm is $300,000 sales without further investment, what is the maximum potential rate of return on assets?

D. If $10,000 of fixed expenses could be transferred to variable costs of sales, what is the dollar effect on —
  1. Operating income, and
  2. Break-even point?

6-8. Blaine, manager of the Radio Hut, a retail store specializing in radio, stereo, and tape equipment, is trying to decide whether there is a predictable relationship between store wages and sales volume. Employees of the store include general office help and two full-time clerks, whose costs were the same each week. In periods of peak activity part-time clerks are hired. Average weekly amounts for selected accounts for the last year are as follows:

Sales......................	$12,500
Wages....................	1,155 (total)
Wages....................	625 (part-time clerks)

Required:

A. Use the equation $y = a + bx$ to predict the future amount of wages for a week when estimated sales will be $15,000.

B. If sales increased enough to warrant the addition of another full-time clerk adding $150 a week to wages, predict (1) the wages expected to be paid part-time clerks in a week when sales were $20,000, and (2) the total wages which will be paid.

C. What sales volume would warrant the expenditure of $800 a week for part-time help, assuming fixed wages remained the same as in Requirement A above?

D. Does there seem to be a predictable relationship between wages and sales volume that can aid Blaine in future planning? Explain.

6-9. Bolter Company sells two products, A and B. In 1977 it sold 2,000 units of A at $100 per unit. It had purchased these 2,000 units at a cost of $60 per unit and had repackaged them at an additional cost of $10 per unit. It sold 2,000 units of Product B at $50 per unit. The purchase cost of these units was $35 per unit, and there were no repackaging costs. All other costs of Bolter Company were fixed. In 1977 they amounted to $60,000 and were allocated to Products A and B in proportion to sales revenue.

Required:

A. Prepare an income statement for 1977 in which all costs are assigned to each product.

B. Prepare an income statement for 1977 that shows the contribution of each product and for the company as a whole. Discuss the differences between this income statement and the income statement prepared in Requirement A.

C. In 1978 it is expected that the sales price of Product B must be decreased to $40 per unit in order to meet competition, other conditions remaining as in 1977. Prepare an estimated income statement for 1978.

D. Under the circumstances given in Requirement C, should Product B be discontinued?

6–10. Refer to Exhibit 6–10.

Required:

A. Describe in words and numbers why the position of the "new profit" line changes in each of the four situations that are diagrammed.

B. What has happened to the break-even volume in each situation and why?

6–11. On page 221 it is said that an increase of 20 percent in fixed costs can be offset by a 4 percent increase in selling price, a 12 percent increase in volume, or a 6 percent decrease in variable cost.

Required:

Explain, using illustrative numbers, how each of the latter three percentages were arrived at.

6–12. Bradford Company produces two products, A and B. Expected data for the first year of operations are:

	A	B
Expected sales (units)	10,000	15,000
Selling price per unit	$50	$60
Variable costs per unit	38	40

Total fixed costs are expected to be $400,000 for the year.

Required:

A. If sales, prices, and costs are as expected, what will be the operating income and the break-even volume in sales revenue?

B. Assume that costs and prices were as expected but Bradford sold 15,000 units of A and 10,000 units of B. Recalculate the operating income and the break-even volume in sales revenue.

C. Draw a contribution profitgraph with a solid expected profit line and a dotted actual profit line.
D. Comment on the impact of a change in the product mix on break-even points and profits.

6-13. Rosalind, Inc., manufactures and sells a single product with a price of $50 per unit. The following estimated annual cost data have been prepared for the upper and lower levels of the firm's relevant range of activity:

	Lower level	Upper level
Production (units)...	5,000	7,500
Manufacturing costs:		
Direct materials...	$ 50,000	$ 75,000
Direct labor..	40,000	60,000
Overhead:		
Indirect labor	21,000	28,500
Supplies	20,000	30,000
Depreciation	12,000	12,000
Distribution expenses:		
Salespersons	45,000	62,500
Travel...	8,000	8,000
Advertising	5,000	5,000
Other	29,000	41,500
General and administrative expenses.................	30,000	37,500
Total	$260,000	$360,000

Required:
A. Classify each individual element of cost according to its behavior pattern (fixed, variable, or semivariable), and explain why you made each classification.
B. Prepare a diagram like the one for Exhibit 6-4 which shows the relationship between total costs and volume and also shows the relevant range.
C. What is the equation for the total cost line in Requirement B?
D. Calculate the break-even point both in units and sales revenue.
E. Add a revenue line to your diagram for Requirement B. At what volume does the revenue line cross the total cost line? Is it the break-even point?
F. Prepare a contribution income statement assuming sales of 7,000 units. What is the margin of safety at this volume, if any?
G. Prepare a contribution profitgraph. Does it indicate the same break-even point as determined above?
H. Recalculate the break-even point assuming that all of the following happen simultaneously:
   1. Price increases to $55 per unit.
   2. All variable costs increase 10 percent.
   3. Total fixed costs are reduced $1,700.

6–14. Following are the partially completed results of a least-squares calculation:

$$N = 10$$
$$\Sigma x = 1,000$$
$$\Sigma y = 20,000$$
$$\Sigma x^2 = 2,000,000$$
$$\Sigma xy = 4,000,000$$

Required:

Find the *a* and *b* values.

6–15. Following are simplified data for costs and volume in four months:

Month	Volume (units)	Cost
September	4	$6
October	3	5
November	5	7
December	2	4

Required:

Compute fixed cost and variable cost per unit by the method of least squares.

6–16. The graphs below relate to the behavior of certain costs involved in the operation of a mechanical arts course offered by a local corporation in a program of adult education:

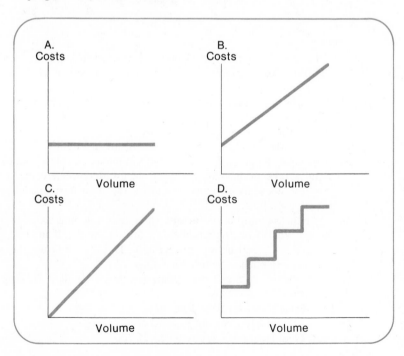

Required:

A. Title each graph to show the type of cost it described (fixed, variable, semivariable, etc.).
B. From the list of costs described below select those which each graph describes:

Costs

1. Cost of materials used by students.
2. Depreciation of machinery and equipment used.
3. Cost of blueprints and manuals. Copies must be acquired for every six students who enroll.
4. Utilities and maintenance. Utilities remain constant each month, but maintenance tends to vary with the usage of machinery and equipment.

6-17. Listed below are the expected costs of several items at the upper and lower levels of the Bailey Company's relevant range of activity.

	Lower level	Upper level
Production (units)	12,000	18,000
Supplies	$ 24,000	$ 36,000
Direct labor	120,000	180,000
Property taxes	18,000	18,000
Indirect labor	66,000	96,000
Clerical costs	15,600	21,600
Occupancy costs	24,000	24,000

Required:

A. For each item, calculate the cost per unit at both levels of activity.
B. For each item, does the behavior of cost per unit over the relevant range of activity indicate the general type of cost (fixed, variable, or semivariable)? Explain your answer.

6-18. The Grant Company has developed the following equation for manufacturing overhead cost:

$$\text{Total Cost} = \$9,600 \text{ per Year} + \$1 \text{ per Machine-Hour}$$

Required:

Prepare an estimate of the manufacturing overhead cost for a month in which 15,000 hours of machine time are expected.

6-19. An examination of past records of maintenance costs of the Beeland Company disclosed the following cost and volume measures:

	March	July
Cost per month	$53,000	$38,000
Machine-hours	18,000	12,000

Required:

A. Using the high-low method, prepare the equation for monthly maintenance cost.

B. Use the equation in Requirement A to estimate the maintenance cost for a month having 16,000 machine-hours.

6-20. Production costs in Department B for the preceding six months were as follows:

	Month					
	July	Aug.	Sept.	Oct.	Nov.	Dec.
Units of production ...	700	900	1,100	1,000	800	600
Total cost...............	$10,000	$12,500	$13,000	$12,000	$8,500	$8,000

Required:

A. Estimate fixed and variable costs by the high-low method.
B. Estimate fixed and variable costs by drawing a scatter diagram.
C. If production in a certain month is estimated to be 850 units, what is your estimate of total cost?

6-21. Following are data on the behavior of costs in four departments:

Department	Fixed cost	Variable cost per unit	Volume units	Total cost
A...............	$30,000	$ 3	1,000	$?
B...............	?	6	200	3,000
C...............	5,000	10	?	7,000
D...............	80,000	?	2,000	110,000

Required:

Calculate the missing term in each equation.

6-22. The 1977 budget for the College Soda Shop contains the following data:

Liabilities.................................	$ 40,000
Capital stock............................	42,500
Retained earnings	7,500
Sales.......................................	100,000
Fixed expenses	20,000
Variable expenses	60,000

Required:

A. What is the equation for estimating the income at various volumes under these circumstances?
B. What is the break-even volume in 1977?
C. If the maximum capacity of this firm is $150,000 of sales utilizing the current level of assets, what is the maximum potential rate of return on these assets?
D. If the cost of goods sold can be reduced by $5,000 by changing suppliers, what is the dollar effect on —
    1. Operating income, and
    2. Break-even point?

6-23. The manager of Motor-Magic Shop, a repair business specializing in the maintenance and repair of small engines and motors, is studying costs in relation to service revenue and is currently concerned with the relationship of wages paid mechanics to sales revenue. The shop employs two full-time mechanics who are paid $200 each per week, and uses part-time help who are students from a local vocational training program when volume is more than these two mechanics can handle. The part-time help is paid on an hourly basis. Last year, part-time wages averaged $100 per week and sales averaged $1,000 per week.

Required:

A. Use the equation $y = a + bx$ to predict the future amount of wages for a week in which sales are expected to be $900.
B. What weekly revenue would warrant wages of $180 per week for part-time workers?
C. A bookkeeper was hired at the wage rate of $120 per week. Predict the total wages which would be paid in a week which had total sales of $950.
D. Does there seem to be a predictable relationship between wages and sales volume? Explain.

6–24. Austin Company sells two products, A and B. In 1977 it sold 3,000 units of Product A and 1,000 units of Product B. For Product A, the unit selling price was $100 and the unit purchase cost was $60. For Product B, the unit selling price was $100 and the unit purchase cost was $70. A sales commission of 10 percent of the selling price was paid for each product. All other costs were fixed. They totaled $80,000, and $40,000 was allocated to each product.

Required:

A. Prepare an income statement for 1977 in which all costs are assigned to each product.
B. Prepare an income statement for 1977 that shows the contribution of each product and for the company as a whole. Discuss the differences between this income statement and the income statement prepared in Requirement A.
C. Should Product B be discontinued?
D. In 1978 it is expected that the sales volume of each product will be 2,000 units, other conditions remaining as in 1977. Prepare an estimated income statement for 1978.
E. What accounts for the difference in operating income of 1978 as compared with that of 1977?

6–25. The Taylor Company produces two products, A and B. Expected data for the first year of operations are:

	A	B
Expected sales (units)	8,000	12,000
Selling price	$45	$55
Variable costs	30	35

Total fixed costs are expected to be $360,000 for the year.

Required:

A. If sales, prices, and costs are as expected, what will be the operating income and the break-even volume in sales revenue?

B. Assume that prices and costs were as expected but Taylor sold 12,000 units of A and 8,000 units of B. Recalculate the operating income and the break-even volume in sales revenue.

C. Draw a contribution profitgraph with a solid expected profit line and a dotted actual profit line.

D. Comment on the impact of a change in the product mix on break-even points and profits.

6–26. Schaffer, Inc., manufactures and sells a single product with a price of $60 per unit. The following estimated annual cost data have been prepared for the upper and lower levels of the firm's relevant range of activity.

	Lower level	Upper level
Production (units)..	4,000	6,000
Manufacturing costs:		
Direct materials...	$ 32,000	$ 48,000
Direct labor..	40,000	60,000
Overhead:		
Indirect labor	25,000	33,000
Supplies...	12,000	18,000
Depreciation	18,000	18,000
Distribution expenses:		
Salespersons	39,000	51,000
Travel...	12,000	12,000
Advertising	7,000	7,000
Other	22,000	30,000
General and administrative expenses.................	43,000	53,000
Total	$250,000	$330,000

Required:

A. Classify each individual element of cost according to its behavior pattern (fixed, variable, or semivariable), and explain why you made each classification.

B. Prepare a diagram like the one for Exhibit 6–4 which shows the relationship between total costs and volume and also shows the relevant range.

C. What is the equation for the total cost line in Requirement B?

D. Calculate the break-even point both in units and sales revenue.

E. Add a revenue line to your diagram for Requirement B. At what volume does the revenue line cross the total cost line? Is it the break-even point?

F. Prepare a contribution income statement assuming sales of 5,000 units. What is the margin of safety at this volume, if any?

G. Prepare a contribution profit graph. Does it indicate the same break-even point as determined above?

H. Recalculate the break-even point assuming that all of the following happen simultaneously:
1. Price decreases to $55 per unit.
2. All variable costs decrease 5 percent.
3. Total fixed costs decrease $5,000.

6–27. In a recent period Zero Company had the following experience:

Sales (10,000 units @ $200) $2,000,000

	Fixed	Variable	
Costs:			
Direct material..................... $	–	$ 200,000	
Direct labor.........................	–	400,000	
Factory overhead.................	160,000	600,000	
Administrative expenses	180,000	80,000	
Other expenses....................	200,000	120,000	
Total Costs.................... $ 540,000		$1,400,000	1,940,000
Operating Income			$ 60,000

Required:

A. Calculate the break-even point for Zero in terms of units and sales dollars.

B. What sales volume would be required to generate an operating income of $96,000?

C. What is the break-even point if management makes a decision which increases fixed costs by $18,000?

(AICPA adapted)

6–28. The following data relate to a year's estimated activity for Patsy Corporation, a single product company:

	Units
Beginning inventory...	30,000
Production..	120,000
Available...	150,000
Sales...	110,000
Ending inventory	40,000

	Per unit
Selling price	$5.00
Variable manufacturing costs	1.00
Variable selling costs..	2.00
Fixed manufacturing costs (based on 100,000 units)	0.25
Fixed selling costs (based on 100,000 units).........................	0.65

Total fixed costs remain unchanged within the relevant range of 25,000 units to total capacity of 160,000 units.

Required:

A. What is the expected annual break-even point in both units and sales revenue?

B. What is the estimated operating income for the year using direct costing?

C. Assume that selling price increases by 20 percent; variable manufacturing costs increase by 10 percent; variable selling costs remain the same; and total fixed costs increase to $104,400. How many units must now be sold to generate a profit equal to 10 percent of the contribution margin?

(AICPA adapted)

6–29. All-Day Candy Company is a wholesale distributor of candy. The company services grocery, convenience, and drugstores in a large metropolitan area.

Small but steady growth in sales has been achieved by the All-Day Candy Company over the past few years while candy prices have been increasing. The company is formulating its plans for the coming fiscal year. Presented below are estimated data for the current year.

Average selling price	$4.00 per box
Average variable costs:	
Cost of candy	$2.00 per box
Selling expenses	0.40 per box
Total	$2.40 per box
Annual fixed costs:	
Selling	$160,000
Administrative	280,000
Total	$440,000

Expected annual sales volume (390,000 boxes), $1,560,000

Manufacturers of candy have announced that they will increase prices of their products an average of 15 percent in the coming year due to increases in raw material (sugar, cocoa, peanuts, etc.) and labor costs. All-Day Candy Company expects that all other costs will remain at the same rates or levels as the current year.

Required:

A. What is All-Day Candy Company's break-even point in boxes of candy for the current year?

B. What selling price per box must All-Day Candy Company charge to cover the 15 percent increase in the cost of candy and still maintain the current contribution margin ratio?

C. What volume of sales in dollars must the All-Day Candy Company achieve in the coming year to maintain the same operating income as projected for the current year if the selling price of candy remains at $4 per box and the cost of candy increases 15 percent?

(IMA adapted)

6–30. R. A. Ro & Company, maker of quality handmade pipes, has experienced a steady growth in sales for the past five years. However, increased competition has led Ro, the president, to believe that an aggressive advertising campaign will be necessary next year to maintain the company's present growth.

To prepare for next year's advertising compaign, the company's accountant has prepared and presented Ro with the following data for the current year, 1977:

Cost schedule

Variable costs:

Direct labor	$ 8.00/pipe
Direct materials	3.25/pipe
Variable overhead	2.50/pipe
Total Variable Costs	$13.75/pipe

Fixed costs:

Manufacturing	$ 25,000
Selling	40,000
Administrative	70,000
Total Fixed Costs	$135,000

Selling price, per pipe	$25.00
Expected sales, 1977 (20,000 units)	$500,000

Ro has set the sales target for 1978 at a level of $550,000 (or 22,000 pipes).

Required:

A. What is the projected operating income for 1977?
B. What is the break-even point in units for 1977?
C. Ro believes an additional selling expense of $11,250 for advertising in 1978, with all other costs remaining constant, will be necessary to attain the sales target. What will be the operating income for 1978 if the additional $11,250 is spent?
D. What will be the break-even point in dollar sales for 1978 if the additional $11,250 is spent for advertising?
E. If the additional $11,250 is spent for advertising in 1978, what is the required sales level in dollar sales to equal 1977's operating income?
F. At a sales level of 22,000 units, what is the maximum amount which can be spent on advertising if an operating income of $60,000 is desired?

(IMA adapted)

6-31. Gondol Company is a wholesaler of a line of soft drinks. In 1977 its income statement was as follows:

Revenue (200,00 cases)..........................		$240,000
Cost of goods sold	$180,000	
Variable operating expenses...................	10,000	
Fixed operating expenses......................	30,000	220,000
Operating Income.................................		$ 20,000

Required:

A. What was Gondol Company's contribution margin and its marginal income in 1977?

B. Assuming 1977 is typical, what is Gondol Company's break-even point?

C. The company believed that if it added another delivery truck at an annual fixed cost of $15,000, it could increase sales by 40 percent. Assuming such a sales increase, should the truck be added?

D. What is the minimum sales increase necessary to justify adding the additional delivery truck?

E. As another alternative, the company was considering raising its selling price to $1.30 per case. It estimated that it would lose 50,000 cases of volume if it did so. Should it raise the price? (Assume it did *not* buy the additional truck.)

F. What is the minimum amount of sales volume, in cases, that must be sold in order to make the $1.30 price a sound decision?

G. Assume that the company added the delivery truck and also raised its selling price to $1.30 per case. How many cases must it sell to be as well off as it was in 1977?

CASE: HARCORD WHOLESALE GROCERS, INC.

6-32. Prior to 1972, Harcord Wholesale Grocers, Inc., had kept no departmental income statements. In order to control operations more effectively, the management decided at the beginning of that year to install departmental cost accounts. At the end of 1972, the new accounts showed that although the business as a whole had a gross margin of 13.1 percent and a net profit of 1.1 percent on net sales of $4,816,000, the fresh fruit and produce department had shown a substantial loss, with a gross margin of only 9.8 percent of its $832,032 net sales, against an expense rate of 14.2 percent. The income statement for this department is shown in Exhibit 6–16.

This loss led one executive to argue that the department should be discontinued. The executives agreed that so far as the factor of customer satisfaction with the completeness of the company's line was concerned, it was not essential to continue selling fresh fruits and produce. Elimination of this department, in other words, was not expected to result in loss of sales by other departments.

EXHIBIT 6–16

HARCORD WHOLESALE GROCERS, INC.
Income Statement
Fresh Fruit and Produce Department

		Percent
Net sales	$832,032	100.0
Cost of sales	750,492	90.2
Gross margin	81,540	9.8

Expenses:

Payroll, direct labor, and supervision in the department	41,280	
Salespersons' commissions (fruits sold by general salespersons selling for all departments on straight, uniform, commission basis)	12,792	
Rent (charged to department on basis of yearly rental per square foot occupied; the company rented and occupied an entire building)	32,880	
Taxes (assessed by state on average value of inventory)	1,200	
Insurance (for protection of inventory)	960	
Depreciation (basis: 5 percent on departmental equipment)	3,120	
Administration and general office (allocated on basis of departmental sales)	25,648	
Interest on inventory (an accounting charge; actually there was no outside borrowing for working capital)	470	
Total Expenses	118,350	14.2
Net loss	$(36,810)	(4.4)

After several protracted discussions of the proposal, one of the executives sought to end the controversy by saying that the company should discontinue either the department or the new accounting system.

Required:

What action should be taken?

7

Alternative choice decisions

In Chapter 6 we introduced the concept of differential costs and differential revenues. The purpose of Chapter 7 is to describe in more detail how differential costs and revenues are measured and how they are used in analyzing a wide variety of problems. These are called *alternative choice* problems, because in each case the manager seeks to choose the best one of several alternative courses of action.

NATURE OF ALTERNATIVE CHOICE PROBLEMS

In an alternative choice problem, two or more alternative courses of action are specified, and the manager decides which one to adopt.[1]

In many alternative choice problems, the decision is made on a strictly judgmental basis; that is, there is no systematic attempt to define, measure, and assess the advantages and disadvantages of each alternative. Managers who make judgmental decisions may do so simply because they are not aware of any other way of making up their mind, or they may do so, with good reason, because the problem is one in which a systematic attempt to assess alternatives is too difficult, too expensive, or simply not possible. No mathematical formula will help solve a problem in which the attitudes or emotions of the individuals involved are dominant factors,

---

[1] In a broad sense, *all* business problems involve a choice among alternative courses of action. The problems discussed here are those in which the alternatives are clearly specified.

246

nor is there any point in trying to make calculations if the available information is so sketchy or so inaccurate that the results would be completely unreliable.

In many situations, however, it is useful to make quantitative estimates of at least some of the consequences of each alternative and to analyze these consequences in a systematic manner. In this and the next two chapters, we discuss techniques for making such an analysis.

Business goals

In an alternative choice problem, the manager seeks the *best* alternative. "Best" refers to that alternative which is most likely to accomplish the goals of the organization. An important goal of most business organizations is to earn profits. Presumably, the more profits that are earned on the funds that have been invested in the business, the greater the satisfaction of the investors. This idea leads to the economists' statement that the goal of a business is to *maximize the return on its investment.*

The maximization idea, however, is too difficult to apply in most practical situations. The manager does not know, out of all the very large number of alternative courses of action available, which one will produce the maximum return on investment. Furthermore, many actions which could increase return on investment are ethically unacceptable. Setting selling prices that charge all the traffic will bear is one example. For these reasons, the idea that an important goal of a business is to earn a *satisfactory* return on its investment is more realistic and more ethically sound than the idea that the sole goal is to maximize return on investment.

Although return on investment is an important goal, it is by no means the only goal of a business. In many practical problems, personal satisfaction, friendship, patriotism, reputation in the community, self-esteem, or other considerations may be much more important than return on investment. The company may have other measurable goals, such as maintenance of its market position, stabilization of employment, or avoidance of undue risk. When these considerations are important or dominant, the solution to an alternative choice problem cannot be reached by the techniques discussed here. The most these techniques can do is show the effect on return on investment of seeking some other goal. The problem then becomes one of deciding whether the attainment of the other goal is worth the cost.

STEPS IN ANALYSIS

The analysis of most alternative choice problems involves the following steps:

1. Define the problem.
2. Select the most likely alternative solutions.

3. Measure and weigh those consequences of each selected alternative that can be expressed in quantitative terms.
4. Evaluate those consequences that cannot be expressed in quantitative terms and weigh them against each other and against the measured consequences.
5. Reach a decision.

In this book, we focus primarily on information that can be expressed in quantitative terms. Thus, we are here interested primarily in Step 3 of the above list. Brief mention will be made of the other steps.

Steps 1 and 2.   Definition of the problem and of alternative solutions

Unless the problem is clearly and precisely defined, quantitative amounts that are relevant to its solution cannot be determined. In many situations, the definition of the problem, or even the recognition that a problem exists, may be the most difficult part of the whole process. Moreover, even after a problem has been identified, the possible alternative solutions to it often are by no means clear at the outset.

> *EXAMPLE:* A factory manager is considering a machinery salesperson's proposal that a certain machine should be used to manufacture a part that is now being made by manual methods. At first glance, there may appear to be two alternatives: (1) continue to make the part by manual methods, or (2) buy the new machine. Actually, however, several additional alternatives should perhaps be considered, such as these: (3) buy a machine other than the one recommended by the salesperson, (4) improve the present method of making the part, or even (5) eliminate the manufacturing operation altogether and buy the part from an outside source. Some thought should be given to these other alternatives before attention is focused too closely on the original proposal.

On the other hand, the more alternatives that are considered, the more complex the analysis becomes. For this reason, having identified all the possible alternatives, the analyst should eliminate on a judgmental basis those that are clearly unattractive, leaving only a few for detailed analysis.

In most problems, one of the alternatives is to continue what is now being done, that is, to reject a proposed change. **This alternative is referred to as the base case. It is used as a benchmark against which other alternatives are compared.**[2]

Note that there must always be at least two alternatives. If only one course of action is possible, the manager literally has "no choice" and

---

[2] For convenience, the base case may be identified as Case 1, and the other alternatives as Case 2, Case 3, and so on.

therefore has no need to make an analysis. If a government safety inspector orders a safety device to be installed on a certain machine, the manager often has no need to weigh alternatives; there may be no choice except to have the device installed.

Step 3. Weighing and measuring the quantitative factors

Usually, a number of advantages and a number of disadvantages are associated with each of the alternatives. The task of the decision maker is to evaluate each of the relevant factors and to decide, on balance, which alternative has the largest net advantage. If the factors, or variables, are expressed solely in words, such an evaluation is an exceedingly difficult task.

> *EXAMPLE:* Consider the statement: "A proposed manufacturing process will save labor, but it will result in increased power consumption and require additional insurance coverage." Such a statement provides no way of weighing the relative importance of the saving in labor against the increased power and insurance costs. If, by contrast, the statement is "The proposed process will save $1,000 in labor, but power costs will increase by $200 and insurance costs will increase by $100," the net effect of these three factors can easily be determined; that is, $1,000 - ($200 + $100) indicates a net advantage of $700 for the proposed process.

As is demonstrated by the above illustration, the reason why we try to express as many factors as possible in quantitative terms, is that once this has been done the net effect of these factors can easily be found by the simple arithmetic operations of addition and subtraction.

Step 4. Evaluating the unmeasured factors

For most problems, there are important factors that are not measurable; yet the final decision must take into account all differences between the alternatives being considered, both those that are measured and those not measured. The process of weighing the relative importance of these unmeasured factors, both as compared with one another and as compared with the net advantage or disadvantage of the measured factors, is a judgmental process.

It is easy to underestimate the importance of these unmeasured factors. The numerical calculations for the measured factors often require hard work, and they result in a figure that has the appearance of being definite and precise. Nevertheless, all the measured factors may be collectively less important than a single factor that cannot be measured. For example, many persons could meet their transportation needs less expensively by using public conveyances rather than by operating an automobile, but they nevertheless own an automobile for reasons of prestige, convenience, or other factors that cannot be measured quantitatively.

To the extent that calculations can be made, these make it possible to express as a single number the net effect of many factors that bear on the decision. They therefore reduce the number of factors that must be considered separately in the final judgment process that leads to the decision; that is, they narrow the area within which judgment must be exercised. Rarely, if ever, do they eliminate the necessity for this crucial judgment process.

Step 5.   Reaching a decision

After the first attempt to identify, evaluate, and weigh the factors, the manager has two choices: (1) additional information can be sought or (2) the manager can make a decision and act on it. Many analyses could be improved by obtaining additional information, and it is usually possible to obtain such information. However, obtaining the additional information always involves effort (which means cost); and what is more important, it requires that the decision be postponed. There comes a point, therefore, when the manager concludes that it is better to act than to defer a decision until more data have been collected.

DIFFERENTIAL COSTS

In Chapter 6 we introduced the type of cost construction called differential costs. Since differential costs are normally used in analyzing alternative choice problems, we now discuss them in more depth.

If some alternative to the base case (i.e., the present method of operation or "status quo") is proposed, differential costs are those that will be different under the proposed alternative than they are in the base case. Items of cost that will not be affected by the proposal are not differential.

There is no general category of costs that can be labeled "differential." The costs that are differential depend on the particular problem being analyzed. To illustrate this point, we shall use the data in Exhibit 7–1 which shows an estimated monthly income statement for Ajax Cleaners. This company has two activities, laundry and dry cleaning. This income statement is constructed on the contribution margin basis introduced in Chapter 6. (Recall from Chapter 6 that the contribution margin for the business as a whole, or for any part of it, is the difference between its revenue and its variable costs, and that variable costs are those that vary proportionately with volume.)

The income statement indicates that the business is expected to operate at a loss. In an effort to correct this situation, management is considering three proposals. We shall identify the differential costs and revenues associated with each proposal.

Proposal A.   The manager of an apartment house has offered to solicit dry cleaning business from her tenants. She asks a commission of 15

EXHIBIT 7–1

AJAX CLEANERS
Estimated Monthly Income Statement
Contribution Basis

	Dry cleaning		Laundry	
Revenues		$5,400		$3,200
Variable Expenses:				
Salaries...	$1,300		$1,400	
Supplies..	1,500		700	
Other	250		200	
Total Variable	(56%)	3,050	(72%)	2,300
Contribution margin	(44%)	2,350	(28%)	900
Direct fixed expenses		600		300
Contribution to indirect expenses..................		1,750		600
Total Contribution............................			2,350	
Indirect Fixed Expenses:				
Salaries...		1,300		
Heat and Light..		200		
Advertising		300		
Rent		700		
Other...		300		
Total Indirect Expense.........................			2,800	
Net loss...			$ (450)	

percent of revenues. Should this offer be accepted or rejected? In this case, there is differential dry cleaning revenue. The variable dry cleaning costs are also differential. For each dollar of additional revenue, there will be $0.56 of additional variable cost. The difference between these is $0.44; this, as explained in Chapter 6, is the marginal income. Thus, for each dollar of additional revenue, Ajax will earn the marginal income of $0.44 less the commission of $0.15, so it will be better off by the difference of $0.29 if it accepts the offer. For every additional $100 of monthly sales, the relevant amounts are:

Differential revenues..............................		$100
Variable dry cleaning costs..................	$56	
Commissions	15	71
Differential income		$ 29

Other costs are not differential and can be disregarded.

Proposal B. Noting that the contribution margin of the laundry business is relatively small, it is suggested that Ajax should get out of the laundry business. Would this be a sound decision? Since the laundry business makes a contribution of $600, this would not be a sound decision.

In more detail, the effect would be that the revenues and the direct costs of the laundry business would be eliminated, as follows:

Lost revenues....................................		$3,200
Costs saved:		
Variable laundry costs......................	$2,300	
Other direct laundry costs.................	300	2,600
Loss in contribution...........................		$ 600

In the analysis of this proposal, both the variable costs and the other direct costs are differential since both will be saved if the laundry business is discontinued. The indirect costs are unaffected and can be disregarded.

Proposal C. Since the income statement shows that the business is expected to operate at a loss, it is suggested that the whole company be closed. Unless other actions (such as Proposal A) are sufficient to offset the loss, this would be a sound decision. In this proposal, the total revenues and the total expenses are differential since all of them would be eliminated by closing the business. The owners would be better off by $450 a month to do this.

The above brief examples are intended solely to illustrate the point that the amounts of differential revenues and differential costs depend on the nature of the alternative being considered. For a thorough study of each proposal, the analyst should examine the cost items more carefully so to determine whether the differential costs are actually as indicated on the estimated income statement. Such an analysis might show, for example, that if Ajax got out of the laundry business, some part of the indirect costs could be reduced; if so, these amounts would properly be part of the calculation.

Variable costs

As the above example illustrates, **differential costs are not necessarily the same as variable costs.** Variable costs are those that vary directly with the volume of output. If in a specific problem, the alternatives being considered involve a change in volume (as in Proposal A above), then variable costs, by definition, are differential costs; differential costs may include fixed costs as well as variable costs (as in Proposal B). A proposal to increase the number of plant guards, which are a component of fixed costs, involves no element of variable cost.

Economists use the terms **marginal costs** and **incremental costs** with approximately the same meaning as what accountants call variable costs. The marginal or incremental cost of a product is the cost of producing one additional unit of that product. Thus, marginal or incremental costs are differential costs in problems that involve changing the volume of output, but not otherwise.

MECHANICS OF THE CALCULATION

There is no prescribed format for making a comparison between the differential costs of each alternative. The arrangement should be whatever is most convenient and which most clearly sets forth the facts to the decision maker. One common practice is to list amounts of differential cost for the base case alternative (i.e., the status quo) in one column, the amounts for Case 2 (i.e., the proposal) in a second column, and then find the difference between the amounts for each item of cost.

EXAMPLE: A company is considering a proposal to buy Part No. 101 from an outside supplier instead of manufacturing the part as it is now doing. The base case is to continue manufacturing Part No. 101, and the alternative (or Case 2) is to purchase Part No. 101 from the outside supplier. All revenue items, all selling and administrative expenses, and all production costs other than those directly associated with the manufacture of Part No. 101 will probably be unaffected by the decision. If so, there is no need to consider them. Items of differential cost could be listed as follows:

	Annual costs			
	If Part No. 101 is manufactured (base case)	*If Part No. 101 is purchased (Case 2)*	*Difference*	
			−	+
Direct material...............	$ 570	0	$ 570	
Purchased parts	0	$1,700		$1,700
Direct labor....................	600	0	600	
Power...........................	70	0	70	
Other costs	150	0	150	
Total	$1,390	$1,700	1,390	1,700
				−1,390
Net differential cost.........				$ 310

Since costs would be increased by $310 if Part No. 101 were purchased, the indication is that the proposal to purchase Part No. 101 should be rejected.

In an alternative format, the total differential costs of each alternative are listed, and one total is subtracted from the other to give the net advantage or disadvantage of the alternative.

EXAMPLE: Using the same data as in the above example:

Differential costs of purchasing (Case 2)...........................	$1,700
Differential costs of manufacturing (base case).................	1,390
Difference (disadvantage of purchasing)	$ 310

Exactly the same results can be obtained by calculating the net difference between the alternatives.

EXAMPLE: Again using the same data as above, the calculation could be made as follows:

		Costs if Part No. 101 is purchased
Purchase price of Part No. 101...............		$1,700
Costs saved by not manufacturing Part No. 101:		
Direct material...................................	$570	
Direct labor......................................	600	
Power..	70	
Other costs	150	
Total Costs Saved..........................		−1,390
Net disadvantage in purchasing		$ 310

Costs that are unaffected. Although items of cost that are unaffected by the decision are not differential and may be disregarded, a listing of some or all of these unaffected costs nevertheless may be useful so as to insure that all cost items have been considered. If this is done, it is essential that the unaffected costs be treated in exactly the same way under each of the alternatives. The net difference between the costs of the two alternatives, which is the result we seek, is not changed by adding equal amounts to the cost of each alternative.

EXAMPLE: Part No. 101 is one component of Product A. It may be convenient to list each of the items of cost, and perhaps even the revenue, for each of the alternatives, as in Exhibit 7–2. The difference in profit is the same $310 that was arrived at in the earlier examples. This is because the proposal to purchase Part No. 101 had no effect on the revenue of Product A, nor on the costs of Product A, other than those already listed.

The calculation in Exhibit 7–2 requires somewhat more effort than those in the preceding examples, but it may be easier to understand, and the practice of listing each item of cost and revenue helps to insure that no differential items are overlooked.

Danger of using full cost

The full costs that are measured in a cost accounting system may be misleading in alternative choice problems. In particular, when estimating differential costs, items of cost that are allocated to products should be viewed with skepticism. Full costs usually do not reflect, and are not intended to reflect, the differential costs for most alternative choice problems. A company may allocate overhead costs to products as 100 percent of direct labor costs; but this does not mean that if direct labor costs are decreased by $600 by purchasing Part No. 101, there will be a corresponding decrease of $600 in overhead costs. Overhead costs may not decrease at all, they may decrease, but by an amount less than $600; or

EXHIBIT 7–2
Calculation of differential profit

	Annual profit on Product A	
	Base case	Purchase of Part No. 101
Revenue..............................	$10,000	$10,000
Costs:		
Direct material.......................	$1,570	$1,000
Purchased parts	0	1,700
Direct labor..........................	3,000	2,400
Power.................................	200	130
Other costs..........................	450	300
Occupancy costs...................	800	800
General and administrative	3,000	3,000
Total Costs	9,020	9,330
Profit..................................	980	$ 670
	− 670 ←	
Differential profit	$ 310	

they may even increase, as a result of an increased procurement and inspection work load resulting from the purchase of Part No. 101. In order to estimate what will actually happen to overhead costs, we must go behind the overhead rate and analyze what will happen to the various elements of overhead.

> *EXAMPLE:* The full costs of Product A, as shown on Exhibit 7–2, included an item of $800 for occupancy costs and an item of $3,000 for general and administrative costs. Occupancy cost is the cost of the building in which Product A is manufactured, and the $800 represents the share of total occupancy cost that is allocated to Product A. If Part No. 101, one part in Product A, is purchased, the floor space in which Part No. 101 is now manufactured no longer would be required. It does not necessarily follow, however, that occupancy costs would thereby be reduced. The costs of rent, heat, light, and other items comprising occupancy costs might not be changed at all by the decision to purchase Part No. 101. Unless the actual amount of occupancy cost were changed, this item of cost is not differential.
>
> Similarly, general and administrative costs of the whole company probably would be unaffected by a decision to purchase Part No. 101. Unless these costs would be affected, they are not differential.

Fringe benefits

Labor cost is one of the important items of cost in many business decisions. The real cost of labor is significantly higher than the dollar amount of pay earned by employees. In addition to the pay for the work performed on a given job, labor costs include such items as the employers' taxes for old-age and unemployment compensation; insurance, medical, and pension plans; vacation and holiday pay; and other fringe benefits. For business in general, these benefits average about 25 percent of wages earned, although there is a wide variation among different companies. In estimating differential labor costs, fringe benefits usually should be taken into account.

Opportunity costs

Opportunity cost measures the opportunity which is lost or sacrificed when the choice of one course of action requires that an alternative course of action be given up. Opportunity costs are not measured in accounting records, and they are not relevant in many alternative choice problems, but they are significant in certain situations.

EXAMPLE: Able now earns $25,000 a year in a job that he feels is secure for the forseeable future. He is thinking about giving up his job and buying and operating a retail store. In analyzing the profitability of this proposal, Able's salary of $25,000 is an opportunity cost of operating the retail store, because if he no longer works at his present job, he gives up the opportunity to continue to earn the $25,000 salary.

In general, if accepting an alternative requires that facilities or other resources must be devoted to that alternative that otherwise could be used for some other purpose, there is an opportunity cost, and it is measured by the profit that would have been earned had the resources been devoted to the other purpose.

EXAMPLE: If the floor space required to make Part No. 101 can be used for some other revenue-producing purpose, then the sacrifice involved in using it for Part No. 101 is an opportunity cost of making that part. This cost is measured by the income that would be sacrificed if the floor space is used for Part No. 101; this is not necessarily the same as the allocated occupancy cost per square foot of floor space as developed in the cost accounting system.

If the floor space used for Part No. 101 could be used to manufacture another item that could be sold for a profit of $400, the $400 then becomes a differential cost of continuing to manufacture Part No. 101. The inclusion of this item would change the numbers as calculated in previous examples as follows:

	If Part No. 101 is manufactured (base case)	If Part No 101 is purchased	Difference
Differential costs, as above	$1,390	$1,700	+$310
Opportunity cost of floor space	400	0	− 400
Net differential cost (in favor of purchasing)			$ 90

The inclusion of this item of opportunity cost therefore changes the results of the calculation; the alternative of purchasing Part No. 101 now has a lower cost.

Opportunity costs are by their very nature "iffy." In most situations, it is extremely difficult to estimate what, if any, additional profit could be earned if the resources in question were devoted to some other use.

Out-of-pocket costs

The term out-of-pocket cost refers to cost items that will cause the company to pay money out of its "pocket" if the alternative under consideration is adopted, that it would not pay if the alternative is not adopted. Out-of-pocket costs therefore are the same thing as differential costs in many situations. Opportunity costs, however, often are not out-of-pocket costs, so the out-of-pocket idea is not always relevant.

Estimates of future costs

Differential costs are estimates of what costs will be in the future. Nevertheless, in many instances our best information about future costs is derived from an analysis of historical costs. One can easily lose sight of the fact that historical costs, per se, are irrelevant. Historical costs may be a useful guide as to what costs are likely to be in the future, but using them as a guide is basically different from using them as if they were factual statements of what the future costs are going to be.

Except where future costs are determined by long-term contractual arrangements, differential costs are necessarily estimates, and they usually cannot be close estimates. An estimated labor saving of $1,000 a year for five years, for example, implies assumptions as to future wage rates, future fringe benefits, future labor efficiency, future production volume, and other factors that cannot be known with certainty at the time the estimate is prepared. Consequently, there is ordinarily no point in carrying computations of cost estimates to several decimal places. In fact, there is a considerable danger of being misled by the illusion of precision that such meticulous calculations give.

Sunk costs

A sunk cost is a cost that already has been incurred. Depreciation is ordinarily a sunk cost because depreciation is a write-off of the cost of a fixed asset, and the cost of the asset was incurred when the asset was acquired. Similarly, the book value of a fixed asset is a sunk cost; it represents that portion of the acquisition cost that has not yet been written off as depreciation expense. A sunk cost exists because of actions taken in the past; therefore, **a sunk cost is not a differential cost.** No decision made today can change what has already happened. The past is history; decisions made now can affect only what *will* happen in the future.

This point is often a troublesome one to grasp because we know that in financial accounting, depreciation is unquestionably an element of expense. It is sometimes suggested that when a proposed alternative results in the disposition of an existing machine, the depreciation on that machine will no longer be a cost, and that the saving in depreciation expense should therefore be taken into account as an advantage of the proposed alternative. This is not so. This argument overlooks the fact that the book value of the machine will, sooner or later, be recorded as a cost, regardless of whether the proposed alternative is adopted. If the alternative is not adopted (i.e., the base case), depreciation on the machine will continue; whereas if the alternative *is* adopted, the remaining book value will be written off when the machine is disposed of. In either case, the total amount of cost is the same, so the book value is not a differential cost.

> *EXAMPLE:* Assume the same situation as in Exhibit 7–2, and assume further that Part No. 101 is manufactured on a machine that was purchased six years previously for $1,000, that it is being depreciated over ten years at $100 per year, that $600 of depreciation has been accumulated, and that the book value of the machine is therefore $400. If Part No. 101 is purchased, however, the machine cannot be used for any other purpose, so it will be scrapped; it has no resale value.
>
> It is sometimes argued that if Part No. 101 is purchased, $100 of depreciation expense for each of the next four years will be saved, and this makes depreciation a differential cost. This is a fallacious argument. It overlooks the fact that the $400 book value will be written off the books, whether or not the fixed asset continues to be used. If the asset continues in use, the write-off comes by way of the annual depreciation expense. If the asset is scrapped, there will be a write-off of the remaining book value at that time. In either case the total amount involved is $400, so the cost is not differential.
>
> This point can be illustrated by comparing income over the four-year period involved, as is done in Exhibit 7–3. Revenues and costs other than the item related to the fixed asset are the same as those in Exhibit 7–2 except that they have been multiplied by 4 because we are examining a four-year period. As the exhibit shows, if Part No. 101 continues to be manufactured, depreciation expense over the four-year period will be $400; whereas if Part No. 101 is purchased, there will be a write-off of the $400 book value when the machine is scrapped. The fixed asset cost therefore does not affect the difference between the two alternatives; it is the same $310 per year as was shown in Exhibit 7–2.

The cost of an asset is supposed to be depreciated over its service life. In the above example, if the machine is scrapped at the end of six years,

EXHIBIT 7–3
Irrelevance of sunk costs

	Base case	Purchase of Part No. 101	Difference	Average annual basis (difference ÷ 4)
	Income statement for four years			
Revenue............................	$40,000	$40,000	$ 0	
Costs (from Exhibit 7–2)	−36,080	−37,320	1,240	$310
Profit, before depreciation......	3,920	2,680	1,240	310
Depreciation........................	400		−400	−100
Loss on disposal		400	400	100
Profit	$ 3,520	$ 2,280	$1,240	$310

we know by hindsight that its service life was actually six years. The original estimate of a ten-year service life therefore turns out to be an error; however, it was an error made at the time the depreciation schedule was set up six years previously, and no current decision can change it.

If the machine had a market value, its market value *would* be a relevant consideration, since its disposal would then bring in additional cash. If the income tax effect of writing off the loss on disposal were different from the tax effect of writing off depreciation over the four-year period, the effect of taxes is relevant. (The method of allowing for this tax effect will be discussed in Chapter 9.) **The book value of the machine itself is not relevant.** Ultimately, the book value is going to be charged against income, but whether this is done through the annual depreciation charge or through a lump-sum write-off makes no ultimate difference.

Importance of the time span

The question of what costs are relevant depends to a considerable extent on the time span of the problem. If the proposal is to make only one unit of Part No. 101, only the direct material costs may be relevant; the work could conceivably be done without any differential labor costs if employees were paid on a daily basis and had some idle time. At the other extreme, if the proposal involves a commitment to manufacture Part No. 101 over the foreseeable future, practically all items of manufacturing costs would be differential.

In general, the longer the time span of the proposal, the more items of cost are differential. In the very long run, all costs are differential. Thus, in very long-run problems, differential costs include the same elements as full costs, for in the long run one must consider even the replacement of buildings and equipment, which are sunk costs in the short run. (Although the items are the same, the amounts are different, since alternative choice problems involve future costs, not historical costs.) In many short-run problems, relatively few cost items are subject to change by a management decision.

TYPES OF ALTERNATIVE CHOICE PROBLEMS

In the remainder of this chapter and in Chapters 8 and 9, we describe general approaches to the main types of alternative choice problems. In the Appendix to this chapter we describe some techniques that are useful for certain specific analyses.

As noted earlier, a dominant objective of a business is to earn a satisfactory return on investment. The return on investment percentage is income divided by investment. Income is the difference between revenue and costs. Thus, three basic elements are involved in a company's return on investment: (1) costs, (2) revenue, and (3) investment, or

$$\text{Return on Investment} = \frac{\text{Revenue} - \text{Costs}}{\text{Investment}}$$

Although the general approach to all alternative choice problems is similar, it is useful to discuss three subcategories separately. First, there are problems that involve only the cost element. In these problems, since revenue and investment elements are unaffected, the best alternative is normally the one with the lowest cost. Problems of this type are discussed in the next section. Second, there are problems in which both the revenue and costs elements are involved. Problems of this type are discussed in the latter part of this chapter. Third, there are problems that involve investment as well as revenue and costs. These are discussed in Chapters 8 and 9.

PROBLEMS INVOLVING COSTS

Alternative choice problems involving only costs have these general characteristics: The base case is the status quo, and an alternative to the base case is proposed. If the alternative is estimated to have lower differential costs than the base case, it is accepted (assuming nonquantitative factors do not offset this). If there are several alternatives, the one with the lowest differential cost is accepted. Problems of this type are often called **trade-off problems** because the set of costs associated with the proposal is traded off for the set associated with the base case. Thus, the basic question is: Are the differential costs of the proposed alternative lower than those of the base case? Examples are given in this section.

Methods change

In a problem involving a methods change, the base case is to maintain the status quo, and the alternative being proposed is the adoption of some new method. The method may be associated with manufacturing products or with any other activity that is part of the operation of the business. The cost analysis for many problems in this class is quite simple. The costs of continuing the present method are estimated and compared with the estimated costs under the proposed method. If the differential costs of the proposed method are significantly lower, the method should be adopted (unless nonquantitative considerations are significant). Thus, if a new method of routing the product through the several machines in a department is found to save two hours of labor per unit of product, and the labor cost is $8 per hour, the differential savings is $16 per unit; the analysis therefore indicates that the proposed method should be adopted.

A practical difficulty in such problems is in deciding whether certain items of costs are in fact differential. If, for example, the computed labor time in the base case is 20 hours, and under the proposed method, labor time is estimated to be 18 hours, the calculated saving is two hours. This calculated savings may not be a real saving, however. If the number of employees is indeed reduced by 10 percent, or if the employees use the additional two hours to do other productive work, then the amount of the savings is genuine. If no change in the size of the work force or in its use occurs, then the labor cost is not differential, and the proposed method will not in fact add to profits.

Overtime versus second shift

In many factories, the work is planned to be done in a single shift (or "turn") of eight hours per day, or 40 hours per five-day week. If the number of sales orders received is so large that the products cannot be manufactured in this time period, the problem arises of how the additional orders should best be filled. Normally, there are two alternatives: (1) work the current work force more hours, or (2) add a second shift. The decision as to which alternative is preferable involves a comparison of the differential costs of each.

If overtime is used, each overtime hour must normally be paid for at 150 percent of the usual, or *straight-time,* rate. If a second shift is added, employees are paid at the straight-time rate, plus a relatively small shift premium for the inconvenience of working at night. If a second shift is organized, however, employees usually would expect to work at least four hours, and possibly longer, and to be paid even though they work fewer than four hours. Thus, if the increased demand can be satisfied by only a few hours beyond the normal workday, and especially if the increase is temporary, use of present employees on an overtime basis is usually preferable. In other cases, organization of a second shift is the better solution. The calculation of differential costs under each alternative helps to resolve this problem.

Operation versus shutdown

The opposite problem to that described above arises when demand is low. The question then is whether to operate the facility at a low volume or to shut down until enough orders have accumulated to justify normal operations. Again, the differential costs of each alternative can be calculated. The differential costs of continued operations are normally approximately the same as the variable costs. Determining the costs of shutdown, however, usually requires a special calculation. This is because the variable costs only are valid within a relevant range, as described in Chapter 6. If the plant is closed, certain fixed costs, such as supervision, may be eliminated; but certain other costs, such as security costs, must be increased. Thus, the differential costs of a shutdown never can be arrived at by reading a cost-volume diagram; they must be estimated according to the facts in the particular situation.

Make or buy

Make-or-buy problems are among the most common type of alternative choice problems. At any given time, a business performs certain activities with its own employees, and it pays outside firms to perform certain other activities. It constantly seeks to improve the balance between these two types of activities by asking: Should we contract with some outside party to perform some function that we are now performing ourselves? Or, conversely, should we ourselves do something that we now pay someone else to do? The possibilities are practically endless. They include such questions as whether to manufacture or to buy a given part (which was illustrated in a preceding section), contracting for computer services, contracting for all or part of maintenance work, or hiring an outside legal firm rather than having lawyers on the company payroll. Make-or-buy problems even include such fundamental alternatives as whether to turn the entire selling function over to brokers or commission agents, or whether to discontinue manufacturing operations and become solely a marketing organization.

As the example given above for Part No. 101 shows, the cost of the outside service (the "buy" alternative) usually is easy to estimate; the difficult problem is to find the differential costs of the "make" alternative. Perhaps the greatest difficulty in analyzing such problems is in deciding on the appropriate time span to be covered by the analysis. The Part No. 101 example pinpoints this problem. The analysis given above indicated that the cost of purchasing Part No. 101 was $1,700 a year, and the estimated differential cost of manufacturing was $1,390, so there was an estimated saving from "making" of $310. But this saving might be earned only in the very short run. As noted above, in the longer run, overhead costs might become differential. Thus, for an item that is currently being made, as a general rule, the "make" alternative is often attractive in short-run situations, especially when idle facilities exist, but the "buy" alternative may be attractive when a longer time span is considered.

Another problem in evaluating make-or-buy alternatives is that of controlling quality. There are many services which an outside specialist may perform more satisfactorily than company personnel, especially if the amount of services required is a relatively insignificant part of the company's activities. Most companies buy letterheads and forms from an outside printer, for example. On the other hand, if the company performs the service itself, it may have better control over its quality than if it relies on an outside source. These are highly judgmental matters.

PROBLEMS INVOLVING BOTH REVENUES AND COSTS

In the second class of alternative choice problems, both costs and revenues are affected by the proposal being studied. Insofar as the quantitative factors are concerned, the best alternative is the one with the largest difference between differential revenue and differential cost, that is, the alternative with the most **differential income.**

The following types of problems will be discussed:

1. Contribution pricing.
2. Price/volume/profit analysis.
3. Changes in selling prices.
4. Discontinuing a product.
5. Sale versus further processing.
6. Other marketing tactics.
7. Benefit/cost analysis.

Contribution pricing

In Chapter 2, techniques for using cost to arrive at the "normal" or "target" price for a product were described. Briefly, the approach is to add up the full costs of the product, add a profit margin that produces a satisfactory return on investment, and use the result as a first approximation to the price. The target price is then adjusted to take account of competitive conditions. This is the approach that is used for the great majority of pricing decisions in American business.

Although full cost is the normal basis for pricing, and although a company must recover its full cost or eventually go out of business, there are some pricing situations where differential costs and revenues are appropriately used. In normal times, a company may refuse to take orders at prices that will not yield a satisfactory profit; but if times are bad, such orders may be accepted if the differential revenue obtained from them exceeds the differential costs involved. Differential costs are the costs that will be incurred if the order is accepted and that will not be incurred if it is not accepted. Differential revenue is the revenue that will be earned if the order is accepted and that will not be earned if it is not accepted. **The company is better off to receive some revenue above its differential costs than to receive nothing at all.** Such orders make some contribution to profit; and such a selling price is therefore called a **contribution price,** to distinguish it from a normal price.

Dumping, which is the practice of selling surplus quantities of a product in a selected marketing area at a price that is below full costs, is another version of the contribution idea. However, dumping may violate the Robinson-Patman Amendment in domestic markets, and is in general prohibited by trade agreements in foreign markets.

It is difficult to generalize on the circumstances that determine whether full costs or differential costs are appropriate. Even in normal times, a company may accept an opportunity to make some contribution to profit by using temporarily idle facilities. Conversely, even when current sales volume is low, the contribution concept may be rejected on the grounds that the low price may "spoil the market," or that orders can in fact be obtained at normal margins if the sales organization works hard enough.

> *EXAMPLE:* The estimated unit costs of Product X, in the relevant range of volume, are:

	Cost per unit
Direct material cost	$ 1.20
Direct labor cost	5.60
Variable manufacturing overhead cost	1.40
Variable distribution cost	3.00
Total Variable Costs	11.20
Fixed costs (at normal volume)	6.00
Full cost	$17.20

In this case, the variable costs are the differential costs because if an additional unit is sold, the additional costs will be only the costs that vary with volume. Thus, if a unit can be sold for any price above $11.20, differential income will result. For example, if the item can be sold for $14 per unit, the differential income, or marginal income, is $2.80 per unit (= $14.00 − $11.20). The company would be $2.80 better off to sell a unit at $14 than not to sell it at all. Note that the fixed costs of $6 do not enter into the calculation. Of course, the company would be even better off if it could sell the item at a price that is higher than its full cost of $17.20; it would use contribution pricing only when it was unable to obtain adequate volume at the higher price.

In the example above, it was implicitly assumed that the sale of a unit at $14 was a separate transaction and did not affect other transactions. If the company's normal price was $20, and customers who were paying $20 learned about the special deal at $14, they would quite likely insist on a corresponding reduction in the price they paid. The consequent reduction in profit on other sales could far offset the $2.80 marginal income on the sale made at the contribution price. For this reason, contribution pricing must be used with great care. Companies use different brand names, or sell to different categories of customers, in order to distinguish sales made at contribution prices from sales made at normal prices. These distinctions must be made with due regard for the requirements of the Robinson-Patman Act which prohibits differences in selling prices to competing customers not justified by differences in costs.

Price/volume/profit analysis

As a general rule, the lower the selling price of a product, the greater the quantity that will be sold. This is the economists' law of demand. If

EXHIBIT 7–4
Analysis of cost/volume/price relationships

(1) Unit selling price	(2) Unit variable cost	(3) = (1) − (2) Marginal income	(4) Estimated quantity sold	(5) = (3) × (4) Contribution margin
$300	$150	$150	1,000	$150,000
270	150	120	1,500	180,000
250	150	100	2,000	200,000
220	150	70	2,500	175,000
200	150	50	3,000	150,000

a business can estimate how many units will be sold at various prices, it can use the techniques of marginal income and contribution margin described in Chapter 6 to arrive at the optimum selling price, that is, the selling price that will yield the highest profit. It does this by calculating the contribution margin at various selling prices, and selecting the selling price that gives the highest contribution margin.[3]

An example of the calculation is given in Exhibit 7–4. In this case the company estimates that if its selling price is $300 per unit, it will sell 1,000 units monthly. If the selling price is $270, it will sell 1,500 units, and so on. The variable cost is assumed to be $150 per unit, so the marginal income is the difference between the unit selling price and $150. The contribution margin is calculated for each selling price, and it turns

---

[3] Recall that marginal income is the difference between the selling price and the variable cost per unit; a $1 change in selling price therefore results in a $1 change in marginal income. The contribution margin is the marginal income times the quantity sold.

out that the contribution margin is highest at a selling price of $250.

Note that fixed costs do not enter into this calculation. They are the same in total, within the relevant range, regardless of the selling price, so they are not differential costs and can be disregarded. Alternatively, fixed costs could be included in the calculation, in order to arrive at the profit at each selling price, but this would not change the conclusion. For example, if fixed costs were $100,000 per month, the subtraction of $100,000 from each of the contribution margins would not change the conclusion that the $250 selling price is best. (The student can easily verify this fact.)

The relationship between unit selling prices and the quantity sold is called the **demand curve** for a product. In the real world, there are relatively few products for which even a rough approximation of the demand curve can be arrived at. Who knows how many more Chevrolets would be sold if the price of a Chevrolet were reduced by 10 percent? If a demand curve cannot be estimated, then the technique described above cannot be used.

Changes in selling prices

The cost/volume/profit relationships described in Chapter 6 can also be used in a similar, but simpler, problem; namely, when a change in an established selling price is being considered. If the company is considering an increase in its price, the question is: Will the increase in marginal income be large enough to offset the loss in contribution margin resulting from the lower quantity sold? Conversely, if the company is thinking of reducing its price in order to increase sales volume, the question is: Will the added volume produce enough contribution margin to offset the lower marginal income? An approach to these questions is to calculate the maximum amount by which the quantity sold can decrease without reducing the contribution margin at a higher price, or, conversely, the minimum amount that the quantity sold must increase in order to warrant a lower price. The relationships described in Chapter 6 suggest how these calculations should be made.

EXAMPLE: At its $15 unit selling price, a company expects to sell 2,000 units. Its variable costs are $10 per unit, so its marginal income is $5. The company is considering reducing its selling price to $14. It can calculate the minimum increase in quantity sold that will warrant such a reduction, as follows:

- Contribution margin at $15 = $5 marginal income × 2,000 units = $10,000.
- At a $14 selling price, the marginal income will decrease by $1, that is, to $4.

- In order to maintain a contribution margin of at least $10,000, the quantity must increase to $10,000 ÷ $4 = 2,500 units, an increase of 500 units.
- If the company believes that the quantity will increase by *at least* 500 units, the price reduction is warranted.

Conversely, the company may be thinking of increasing its price to $16.

- Its marginal income will then be $6.
- In order to have a contribution margin of at least $10,000, the quantity cannot decrease to less than 1,667 units (= $10,000 ÷ $6).
- If the company believes that the quantity will not decrease to less than 1,667 units, the price increase is warranted.

Discontinuing a product

If the selling price of a product is less than its full cost, then conventional accounting reports will indicate that the product is being sold at a loss; and this fact may lead some people to recommend that the product be discontinued. Actually, such an action may make the company worse off rather than better off. The company is better off to have a product that makes some contribution to overhead and profit than not to have the product at all. An analysis of differential revenues and differential costs is the proper approach to problems of this type.

EXAMPLE: Hanson Manufacturing Company makes three products, A, B, and C. Exhibit 7–5 shows the profit or loss on each product as reported on the full cost basis. Note that Product B has sales revenue of $2,594,000, full costs of $2,426,000, and hence a loss of $332,000. Should Product B be discontinued because it is being sold at a loss?

The costs that are relevant for this analysis are differential costs; the full costs shown on Exhibit 7–5 are not appropriate. If we ask what costs are differential if Product B is discontinued, then it is clear that the costs related to the building, to equipment, and to general administration, are not likely to be affected. These costs would continue (except in the unlikely event that part of the building could be sold); therefore, they are not differential costs. The differential costs are principally the direct labor and direct material costs, and certain other items that are labeled as direct.

If Product B were dropped, the revenue earned from it would of course be lost. Exhibit 7–6 shows the differential costs and revenues in this situation. It shows that if Product B had not been sold in 1977, costs would have been reduced by $1,290,000 but revenues would have been reduced by $2,594,000, so the company would have been worse off by $1,304,000. Under these circumstances, Product B should not be dropped.[4]

---

[4] This conclusion is based on the analysis of the available data. In a practical situation, further study would be warranted to determine if other items of cost are differential.

EXHIBIT 7–5

HANSEN MANUFACTURING COMPANY
Product Costs, 1977
(in thousands)

Costs	Product A	Product B	Product C	Total	Direct	Allocated	Basis of allocation
Rent	$ 587	$ 457	$ 388	$ 1,432		X	Square feet
Property taxes	62	50	40	152		X	Square feet
Property insurance	52	40	53	145		X	Val. of equip.
Direct labor	1,445	995	768	3,208	X		
Indirect labor	398	273	212	883		X	Direct labor
Power	22	25	30	77		X	Machine-hours
Light and heat	15	13	10	38		X	Square feet
Building service	10	8	7	25		X	Square feet
Materials	909	232	251	1,392	X		
Supplies	52	48	35	135	X		
Repairs	18	15	10	43	X		
Total	3,570	2,156	1,804	7,530			
Selling expense	935	445	458	1,838		X	Sales
General and administrative	332	158	163	653		X	Sales
Depreciation	165	127	165	457		X	Val. of equip.
Interest	52	40	53	145		X	Val. of equip.
Total Cost	5,054	2,926	2,643	10,623			
Sales revenue	5,457	2,594	2,672	10,723			
Profit or (loss)	$ 403	$ (332)	$ 29	$ 100			

EXHIBIT 7-6

Effect of discontinuing Product B
Differential revenues and costs (in thousands)

Decrease in revenue		$2,594
Decrease in costs:		
Direct labor	$995	
Materials	232	
Supplies	48	
Repairs	15	1,290
Decrease in profits if Product B discontinued		$1,304

Before a final decision is reached, other alternatives need to be considered. For example, if a new product with a higher profit margin could be found to use the facilities now used to make Product B, then it indeed might be desirable to drop Product B and add the new product.

Sale versus further processing

Many companies, particularly those that manufacture a variety of finished products from basic raw materials, must address the problem of whether to sell a product that has reached a certain stage in the production process or whether to do additional work on it. Meat-packers, for example, can sell an entire carcass of beef, or they can continue to process the carcass into hamburger and various cuts, or they can go even further and make frozen dinners out of the hamburger. The decision requires an analysis of the differential revenue and differential costs.

Let us designate the alternative of selling the product at a certain stage as the base case and that of processing it further as Case 2. For the base case, the relevant numbers are the sales revenue less any differential costs that are required to market the product at that stage. For Case 2, the numbers are the (presumably higher) sales revenue for the processed product, less the differential costs of the additional processing. If the differential income (i.e., revenue minus costs) of further processing exceeds that of the base case, then Case 2 is preferred. The important point to note about this analysis is that all costs incurred prior to the point in the production process where this decision is made may be disregarded. These costs are incurred whether or not additional processing takes place, and they are therefore not differential.

EXAMPLE: A meat-packer is considering whether to sell unprocessed meat (base case) or to process it into frozen dinners (Case 2). Estimates of differential revenue and costs per pound are:

	Base case (sell unprocessed)	Case 2 (process)	Difference
Revenue...............................	$0.70	$1.30	$0.60
Differential marketing costs... $0.03		$0.20	
Differential material cost....... ...		0.10	
Other differential costs......... ...		0.18	
Total Differential Costs...	−0.03	−0.48	−0.45
Differential income	$0.67	$0.82	$0.15

Since the differential income for Case 2 is $0.15 higher than that for the base case, the alternative of making frozen dinners appears to be attractive. Neither the cost of the steer nor the cost of slaughtering and dressing it is relevant since these costs are incurred under both alternatives.

The preceding example provides a good opportunity to contrast the differential approach with the full cost approach that was discussed in Part One. The two approaches are diagrammed in Exhibit 7–7.

In the full cost approach, the central problem is to decide how to divide the joint costs among the joint products. These are the costs incurred up to the split-off point. In this case, assume that the company has decided to sell *both* meat and frozen dinners, and that joint costs are $25,000 for 100,000 pounds, or $0.25 per pound. Using the sales value basis of allocation (see Chapter 5), $0.23 per pound is allocated to meat and $0.27 per pound to frozen dinners. Beyond the split-off point, both variable costs and fixed costs are accumulated for each product, using the techniques described in Part One. (Detailed calculations are omitted.)

In the differential cost approach, the joint costs incurred up to the point where the decision to sell or process further is made are irrelevant; they do not enter into the calculations. The fixed costs are also disregarded. On the assumption that variable costs are the same as differential costs, the two approaches are similar only in their treatment of this component of cost.

Each approach has its purpose. The full cost approach is used for measuring the value of inventory and of cost of goods sold and as a basis of normal pricing. The differential approach is useful in making the decision on whether to sell meat or to process it into frozen dinners. It is important that each approach be used for the appropriate purpose, and not for the wrong purpose.

Other marketing tactics

The differential approach also can be used for a number of other marketing problems, such as deciding which customers are worth

EXHIBIT 7–7

Contrast between differential costs and full costs

Full cost approach

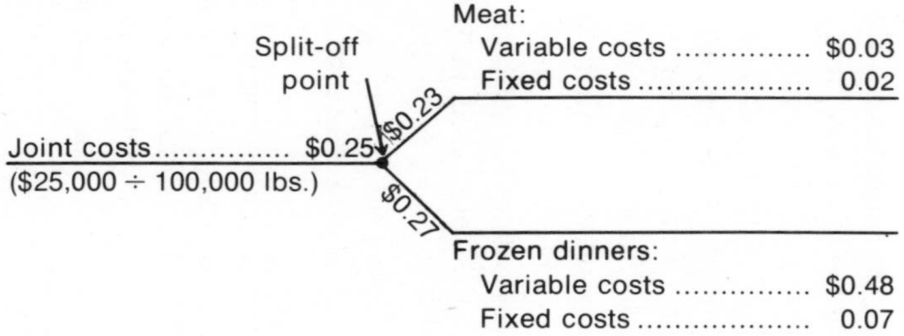

```
Split-off                    Meat:
point                          Variable costs ........... $0.03
                               Fixed costs .............    0.02
            $0.23
Joint costs ....... $0.25
($25,000 ÷ 100,000 lbs.)
            $0.27
                             Frozen dinners:
                               Variable costs ........... $0.48
                               Fixed costs .............    0.07
```

Differential cost approach

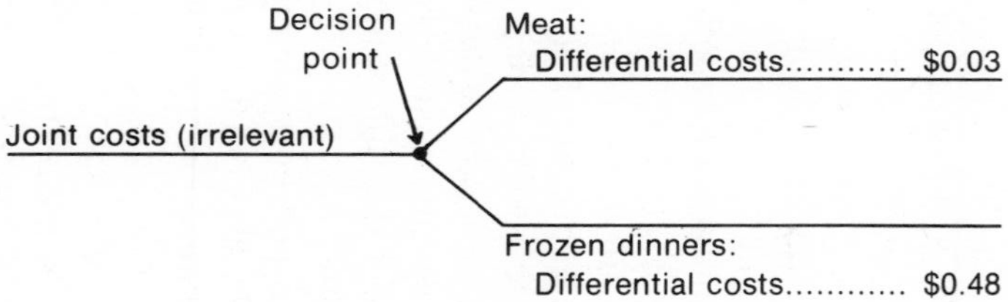

```
Decision                     Meat:
point                          Differential costs........... $0.03

Joint costs (irrelevant)

                             Frozen dinners:
                               Differential costs........... $0.48
```

Income statements
(per pound)

	Meat	Frozen dinners
Revenue...............	$0.70	$1.30
Expenses:		
Joint...............	0.23	0.27
Variable...............	0.03	0.48
Fixed...............	0.02	0.07
Total...............	0.28	0.82
Income...............	$0.42	$0.48

Analysis

	Meat	Frozen dinners
Revenue...............	$0.70	$1.30
Costs...............	0.03	0.48
Differential Income...............	$0.67	$0.82

soliciting by sales personnel and how often the salesperson should call on each customer; deciding whether to open additional warehouses or, conversely, whether to consolidate existing warehouses; deciding whether to improve the durability of a product in order to reduce the number of maintenance calls; and deciding on the minimum size of order that will be accepted.

Benefit/cost analysis

In the preceding examples the purpose of the analysis was to find the alternative that increased profits, that is, that widened the difference between revenue and cost. Revenue is the monetary measure of the value of goods and services sold. In a nonprofit organization, the objective is something other than increasing profits, and the value of goods and services furnished cannot usually be measured in monetary terms. For both these reasons, nonprofit organizations cannot use the technique of comparing differential costs and differential revenues. Nevertheless, it is sometimes possible to use a similar approach by **comparing differential costs with some measure of the benefits that are expected as a consequence of incurring the additional costs. This approach is called benefit/cost analysis.**

Benefit/cost analysis is widely used in nonprofit organizations. It is also used in profit-oriented companies for analyzing such proposals as spending more money to improve the company's reputation with the public, to provide better information to management, or for other proposals in which a measure of the differential revenue is not feasible.

In a benefit/cost analysis, the cost calculations are usually straightforward; the difficult part of the analysis is the estimate of the value of the benefits. In many situations, no reliable estimate of the quantitative amount of benefits can be made. In such situations, the anticipated benefits are carefully described in words, and then the decision maker must answer the question: Are the perceived benefits worth *at least* the estimated cost? For example, "If we add $25,000 to the costs of the market research department, will the increased output of the department be worth at least $25,000?" The answer to this question is necessarily judgmental, but the judgment can be aided by a careful estimate of the differential costs and a careful assessment of the probable benefits.

If a nonprofit organization is analyzing a problem that involves differential costs but does not require the measurement of benefits, then the techniques described in the first part of this chapter are fully applicable. Nonprofit organizations have proposals for methods improvements, and they have make-or-buy problems. The decision rule for these problems is the same as that already illustrated, namely, the preferred alternative is the alternative with the lowest differential costs.

Estimating sales

In problems in which both revenues and costs are differential, the most difficult part of the analysis usually is the estimate of the sales volumes for the alternatives being considered. No one knows *for sure* what will happen to sales volume if the product is priced on a contribution basis, or if a product is sold after further processing rather than being sold in a less finished state, or if additional sales personnel are hired, or if additional warehouses are operated. Nevertheless, the analysis requires that estimates of sales volume be made. Some companies employ sizable market research staffs which prepare such estimates. They may test a proposed marketing tactic in a few cities to find out what happens to sales volume before making the decision to extend the tactic nationwide. Notwithstanding these efforts, the fact remains that in a free market economy the customer is king. Customers' collective decisions determine how many sales are made, and it is most difficult to estimate in advance what these decisions will be.

DEMONSTRATION CASE

As a device for demonstrating your understanding of the fact that the cost elements that are relevant in an alternative choice problem vary with the nature of the problem, consider the costs that are relevant for various decisions that may be made about owning and operating an automobile. A study made by Runzheimer and Company and published by the American Automobile Association gives the national average cost in 1975 of operating a 1975 Chevelle eight-cylinder hardtop sedan (equipped with standard accessories — radio, automatic transmission, power steering, and power disc brakes) as follows:

	Average per mile
Variable costs:	
Gasoline and oil	4.82 cents
Maintenance	0.97
Tires	0.66
Total Variable Costs	6.45 cents

	Amount per year
Fixed costs:	
Fire and theft insurance	$ 53
Other insurance	330
License and registration	30
Depreciation	773
Total Fixed Costs	$1,186

Assume that these costs are valid estimates of future costs (which actually is not the case because of inflation).

Required:

1. You own an automobile like that described above and have it registered. You are thinking about making a trip of 1,000 miles. What is the differential cost?
2. You own an automobile but have not registered it. You are considering whether to register it for next year or to use alternative forms of transportation that you estimate will cost $1,200 for the 10,000 miles you expect to drive. Should you register it? (Disregard convenience and other nonquantitative factors.)
3. You do not own an automobile but are considering the purchase of the automobile described above. If your estimate is that you will drive 10,000 miles per year for five years and that alternative transportation will cost $1,200 per year, should you do so?

Suggested solution:

1. When a person owns an automobile, already has it registered, and is deciding whether it is worthwhile to make a proposed trip, the relevant costs are 6.45 cents a mile times the estimated mileage of the trip; a trip of 1,000 miles therefore has a differential cost of $64.50. The fixed costs are not relevant since they will continue whether or not the trip is made.
2. When a person owns an automobile and is deciding whether to (*a*) register it for a year or (*b*) leave it idle and use some other form of transportation, the relevant costs are the insurance and fees of $413 plus 6.45 cents a mile times the 10,000 miles of expected travel by automobile, a total of $1,058. The $413 has become a cost because it is affected by the decision as to registration. If alternative transportation costs $1,200 a year, the owner is well advised to register the automobile.
3. When a person is deciding whether to (*a*) buy an automobile or (*b*) use some other means of transportation, the relevant costs are $1,186 a year plus 6.45 cents a mile times the 10,000 miles of expected travel, or $1,186 + $645 = $1,831. If alternative transportation costs $1,200 a year, the person is well advised to use alternative transportation.

Each of the above answers is, of course, an oversimplification because it omits nonquantitative factors and relies on averages. In an actual problem, the person would have data that more closely approximated the costs of his or her own automobile.

SUMMARY

When an alternative choice problem involves changes in costs but not changes in revenue or investment, the best solution is the one with the lowest differential costs, insofar as cost information bears on the solution. Although historical costs may provide a useful guide to what costs will be in the future, we are always interested in future costs, and never in historical costs for their own sake. In particular, sunk costs are irrelevant. The longer the time span involved, the more costs are differential. Among the problems involving changes in cost are proposed changes in methods and make-or-buy problems.

When the problem involves both cost and revenue considerations, differential revenues, as well as differential costs, must be estimated. Among the problems in this area are: contribution pricing (i.e., selling below normal price temporarily in order to obtain some differential income), cost/volume/price analysis, discontinuing a product, sale versus further processing, and other marketing tactics. When revenue cannot be estimated, benefit/cost analysis is helpful in certain types of problems.

Differential cost and revenue rarely provide the answer to any business problem, but they facilitate comparisons and narrow the area within which judgment must be applied in order to reach a sound decision.

APPENDIX: QUANTITATIVE TECHNIQUES FOR CERTAIN PROBLEMS

In this Appendix we describe techniques that are helpful in the analysis of certain types of alternative choice problems. The general approach to all problems is that described in the text. The techniques described here are refinements which are applicable in certain types of problems.

Economic order quantity

One common problem is to decide what quantity of an item to order for the replenishment of inventory. If the demand for the item is predictable and is reasonably steady throughout a year, it is possible to calculate the **economic order quantity,** that is, the optimum amount to order at one time. If the item is manufactured by the company, the same technique can be used to determine the **economic lot size,** that is, the quantity that should be manufactured in one lot.

When an item is ordered, certain differential costs are incurred that are related to the order itself and are not substantially influenced by the quantity of an item that is included in the order. These include the cost of obtaining quotations and selecting the vendor, the paperwork associated with writing the purchase order, the cost of receiving and inspecting the goods when they arrive, and the paperwork of paying the invoice and making the accounting records. When an item is manufactured, costs are involved in production scheduling and in setting up machines that also are not related to the quantity of items manufactured. We shall describe the technique in terms of an order placed with an outside vendor, and hence will refer to *ordering costs,* but the same technique applies to manufactured items, where the corresponding term is *setup costs.*

Costs also are involved in carrying an item in inventory, and these costs essentially vary with the size of the inventory. They include the cost of the storage space and the cost of the capital that is tied up in inventory.

Exhibit 7–8 shows how alternative ordering policies affect these two types of cost. It is assumed that usage of a certain item is 1,200 units

EXHIBIT 7–8
Different practices regarding size of orders

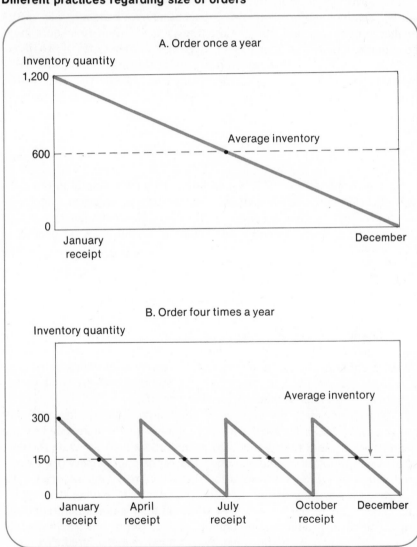

per year, and that usage is at a fairly even rate, approximately 100 units per month. Part A shows that if a single order were placed for the annual requirement of 1,200 units, the inventory carrying cost would be relatively high because the inventory would start at 1,200 units and would average 600 units during the year.[5] Since only one order is placed for the whole year, the ordering costs are relatively small.

By contrast, as shown in Part B, placing orders four times per year would involve four times as much ordering cost but a relatively low inventory carrying cost since there would be an average of only 150 units in inventory throughout the year.

It is apparent that there is some ordering quantity at which the sum of the annual ordering cost and the annual inventory carrying cost is at a minimum. By the use of calculus, it can be demonstrated that this quantity is **the quantity at which the annual ordering costs equals the annual inventory carrying cost.** This is the economic order quantity. This quantity can be found from the equation

$$Q = \sqrt{\frac{2OR}{C}}$$

In this equation,

Q = economic order quantity (number of units in one order)
O = ordering costs for one order
R = annual requirements in units
C = inventory carrying costs per unit, per year

EXAMPLE: Estimates for a certain item are:

O (ordering cost for one order) $300
R (annual requirements) .... 1,200 units
C (inventory carry cost)............................... $2 per unit

$$\text{Economic Order Quantity} = \sqrt{\frac{2 \times \$300 \times 1,200}{\$2}}$$
$$= \sqrt{360,000}$$
$$= 600 \text{ Units}$$

Since 1,200 units are required per year, there must be $1,200 \div 600 = 2$ orders placed; that is, one order every six months.

The costs used in this equation are differential costs. The differential ordering costs include the costs associated with placing an order and handling its receipt. The differential inventory carrying charge includes

---

[5] Inventory is 1,200 units immediately after the goods are received and declines to zero a year later. Assuming that the decline is at a roughly even rate throughout the year, the average inventory during the year is one half the sum of the beginning and ending inventories; or $\frac{1}{2}(1,200 + 0) = 600$ units.

an estimate of interest costs, and of the costs associated with the occupancy of warehouse space.

In the example given above, it was assumed that the inventory reached zero just before an additional order is received. For safety's sake, the company needs additional inventory in case demand is higher than anticipated or the receipts of the replenishment order is delayed. This additional inventory is called *safety stock,* and techniques for estimating the optimum amount of safety stocks are available. They do not affect the calculation of economic order quantity, which is a separate problem.

Probabilities and expected value

All the numbers used in alternative choice problems are estimates of what will happen in the future. In the foregoing examples, we used **single value** estimates; that is, each estimate was a single number representing someone's best estimate as to what differential costs or revenues would be. Some companies are experimenting with estimates made in the form of probability distributions rather than as single numbers. Instead of stating, "I think sales of Item X will be $100,000 if the proposed alternative is adopted," the estimator develops a number of possible sales volumes, together with his or her estimate of the probability that each will occur. Each possible outcome is weighted by the probability that it will occur. Probability is expressed as a decimal between zero and one. A probability of 0.1 means there is one chance in ten that the outcome will occur, and a probability of 0.5 means that the chances are even. The sum of the separate probabilities always equals one, which simply means that *some* value must occur.

The sum of these weighted amounts is called the **expected value** of the probability distribution. It is computed as in the following example:

(a) Possible sales volume	(b) Estimated probability		(a) × (b) Weighted amount
$ 60,000	0.1		$ 6,000
80,000	0.1		8,000
100,000	0.4		40,000
120,000	0.2		24,000
140,000	0.2		28,000
	1.0	Expected value	$106,000

The probability 0.1 opposite $60,000 means that there is one chance in ten that sales will be $60,000.

The expected value of $106,000 would be used as the best estimate of differential revenue. If a single value estimate rather than an expected value were used, it would be $100,000 because this is the number with the highest probability. The $106,000 expected value is a better estimate of sales because it incorporates the whole probability distribution.

Business executives do not find it easy to develop estimates in the form of probability distributions; but if they can do so, the validity of the estimates can be greatly increased.

Sensitivity analysis

In a calculation of differential costs or differential income, some items have a greater influence on the final result than others. In thinking about the validity of the result, it is useful to focus attention on the most significant part of the calculation. In some problems, the most significant item is obvious. For example, the estimate of sales volume is often a major factor in a problem in which the quantity sold varies among the alternatives. In other problems, it is useful to locate the items that have an important influence on the final results so that they can be subjected to special scrutiny. Techniques for doing this are called **sensitivity analysis.**

One such technique is to vary each of the estimates, in turn, by a given percentage, say 10 percent, and determine what effect the variation in that item has on the final results. If the effect is large, the result is *sensitive* to that item.

Another technique is to calculate a number of results, varying each of the elements according to an amount that is selected by chance from a probability distribution. A computer can calculate 1,000 such results in a few seconds. Because the numbers are selected by chance, as in a gambling situation, this approach has come to be called the *Monte Carlo method.* If all the results fall within a narrow range, it can safely be assumed that they are relatively insensitive to the estimates of individual items. If the range is wide, the indication is that the calculation is quite uncertain, and the numerical results must therefore be used cautiously.

Decision trees

A characteristic of the problems described in this chapter was that a *single* decision had to be made, and as a consequence of that decision estimated revenues would be earned and estimated costs would be incurred. There is another class of problems in which a *series* of decisions has to be made, at various time intervals, with each decision influenced by the information that is available at the time it is made. An analytical tool that is useful for such problems is the *decision tree.*

In its simplest form, a decision tree is a diagram that shows the several decisions or *acts* and the possible consequences of each act; these consequences are called *events.* In a more elaborate form, the probabilities and the revenues or costs of each event's outcomes are estimated, and these are combined to give an *expected value* for the event.

Since a decision tree is particularly useful in depicting a complicated series of decisions, any brief illustration is highly artificial. Nevertheless, the decision tree shown in Exhibit 7–9 will suffice to show how the technique works.

The assumed situation is this. A company is considering whether to develop and market a new product. Development costs are estimated to be $100,000 and there is a 0.7 probability that the development effort

EXHIBIT 7–9
Simple decision tree

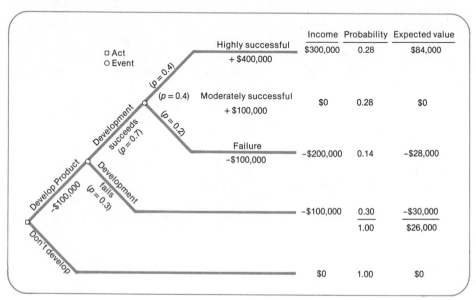

will be successful. If the development is successful, the product will be marketed, and it is estimated that –

a. If the product is highly successful, it will produce differential income of $400,000 (or a net of $300,000 after subtracting the development cost);
b. If the product is moderately successful, it will break even, that is, its income of $100,000 will just offset the development cost;
c. If the product is a failure, it will lose $100,000 (or a total loss of $200,000 after taking account of the development cost).

The estimated probability of high success is 0.4; of moderate success, 0.4; and of failure, 0.2.

The expected value of each outcome is the monetary income or loss times the probability of that outcome's occurrence. Thus,

1. If development fails, the expected value is the development cost times the probability of failure: $-\$100,000 \times 0.3 = -\$30,000$, that is, a \$30,000 loss.
2. If development succeeds, but the product is a failure, the loss is \$100,000 development cost plus \$100,000 marketing costs, a total loss of \$200,000. The total probability of development success *and* product failure is $0.7 \times 0.2 = 0.14$. The expected value of this outcome is $0.14 \times -\$20,000 = -\$28,000$.
3. If development succeeds and the product is moderately successful, the probability is 0.28 (0.7×0.4) and the differential net income is zero; hence the expected value is $0.28 \times \$0 = \$0$.
4. If development succeeds and the product is highly successful, the net income is $\$400,000 - \$100,000$ development costs, or \$300,000, and the probability is again 0.28; hence the expected value of this outcome is $0.28 \times \$300,000 = \$84,000$.

The *total* expected value of the act "Develop Product" is the algebraic sum of the expected values of all possible outcomes on the "Develop Product" branch of the tree, that is, \$26,000. This amount is then compared with the expected value of the other alternative act, "Don't Develop" (which is the base case). If the development is not undertaken there is a 100% chance (1.0 probability) that the incremental income will be \$0; hence the expected value of "Don't Develop" is zero. Because the act "Develop Product" has the larger expected value, the decision would be to proceed with the development effort. This does not mean, of course, that the ultimate outcome is "guaranteed" to be differential income of \$26,000; rather it means that based on the estimates that have been made in considering this decision, management should "gamble" and go ahead with the development, because the *expected* payoff from this gamble is positive, whereas if the gamble is not taken there will be zero payoff.

Linear programming

In the situations described in the text it was assumed implicitly that available resources are adequate to carry out whichever alternative is selected. However, in some situations this assumption is not valid. For example, a machine has only a certain amount of capacity, and if that capacity is used by one product it cannot be used for another. Similarly, a factory building has room for only so many machines. In these situations, there are *constraints* on the uses of resources. Linear programming is a model for solving problems with several constraints.

In linear programming, a series of mathematical statements is developed. The first, called the *objective function,* is the quantity to be optimized; this is usually a formula for differential costs which the model will minimize, or one for differential income, which is to be maximized. The other statements express mathematically the constraints of the situation.

> EXAMPLE: A company makes two products, each of which is worked on in two departments. Department 1 has a capacity of 500 labor hours per week; Department 2, 600 labor hours. The labor requirements of each product in each department are as follows:

	Labor hours per unit	
	Product A	Product B
Department 1	5	2.5
Department 2	3	5

As many units of B as can be made can also be sold, but a maximum of 90 units of A can be sold per week. The marginal income (i.e., unit price minus unit variable costs) is $2 for A and $2.50 for B. How many units of each should be made in order to maximize total contribution?

The problem can be expressed mathematically as follows:

Maximize $P = 2A + 2.5B$ (maximize profit, the objective function)
Subject to $5A + 2.5B \leq 500$ (Department 1 capacity constraint)
     $3A + 5B \leq 600$ (Department 2 capacity constraint)
     $A \leq 90$ (Product A sales constraint)
     $A \geq 0, B \geq 0$ (A negative number of units cannot be made.)

In words, the above says: find the number of units of A and B that should be made each week so as to maximize contribution margin when the marginal income is at $2 per unit for A and $2.50 per unit for B, subject to the constraint that a unit of A requires 5 hours in Department 1 and a unit of B requires 2.5 hours there, and only 500 hours per week are available in Department 1; and so forth.

This situation can be illustrated graphically as in Exhibit 7–10. One can see from the table above that Department 2 could make 200 units of A if it worked only on A, or 120 units of B if it worked only on B; in Exhibit 7–10 the line between these two extremes, labeled "Dept. 2 Capacity Constraint," shows all of the possible A–B product combination that would utilize all of Department 2's available capacity of 600 hours. The other lines are drawn in the same manner.

The shaded area in Exhibit 7–10 bounded by the axes and the three constraint lines, is called the *feasible set,* because any A–B combination in that area can be produced and sold, whereas combinations outside that area are infeasible. A moment's reflection will reveal that the optimum A–B combination must lie on the "northeast" boundary of the feasible set because any point inside that boundary does not use up all the available manufacturing capacity and/or A sales capacity, and hence does not maximize contribution since more units could be made and sold.

What is also true, but is not intuitively obvious, is the fact that the optimum A–B combination lies at a *vertex* of that boundary; that is, at either point *w*, *x*, *y*, or *z*.

What a linear programming computer program does, in effect, is calculate the profit, P, at each vertex of the feasible set boundary and identify

EXHIBIT 7–10

Linear programming graphical solution

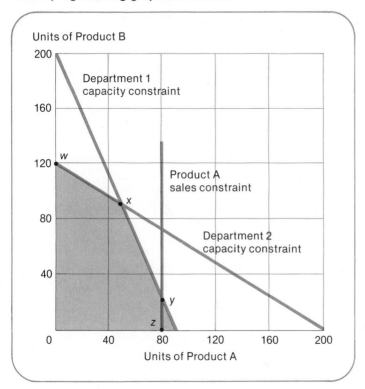

that point which gives the highest profit. Of course, for more realistic problems, such as determining the least costly delivery routes for a fleet of trucks or determining the most profitable mix of petroleum products to be refined from a quantity of crude oil, tens or even hundreds of mathematical statements are involved, and the problem cannot be solved manually. Computers can, and do, solve such problems rapidly.

Shadow prices.   As part of the solution to a linear programming problem, the computer program also calculates a *shadow price* for each constrained resource, that is, for each resource that is completely utilized in the optimum solution. For example, if the optimum solution involves using all of Department 2's capacity, the shadow price for this capacity would indicate the amount by which profit would increase if the capacity could be increased by one hour (to 601 hours); this shadow price would be the maximum amount the company should be willing to spend to add a unit of capacity (i.e., one labor hour) in Department 2.

IMPORTANT TERMS

Alternative choice problem	Sunk cost
Base case	Make or buy
Marginal cost	Differential income
Incremental cost	Contribution pricing
Opportunity cost	Benefit/cost analysis
Out-of-pocket cost	

QUESTIONS FOR DISCUSSION

1. A satisfactory return on investment is one goal of most businesses. Name some additional business goals.

2. A company has learned that a new machine has been developed that might be better than a machine it now uses for a certain production operation. List the steps it should go through in investigating this matter.

3. In connection with the new machine referred to in Question 2, give examples of quantitative and nonquantitative factors that should be considered, and distinguish between these two types of factors.

4. What is the advantage of using numbers to express the importance of factors in an alternative choice problem?

5. What is the difference between contribution margin and marginal income?

6. Referring to Exhibit 7–1 and the three proposals given in connection with it, give examples of variable costs that are differential costs, and of differential costs that are not variable costs. Can you think of a problem involving Ajax Cleaners in which variable costs would not be differential costs?

7. Explain in your own words the story told by Exhibit 7–2. In particular, how do you reconcile the direct material costs given there with the direct material cost of $570 for the same item given in earlier examples?

8. "Overhead costs are allocated to products at 200 percent of direct labor costs. This means that if direct labor costs increase, overhead costs also increase. Therefore, if direct labor costs are differential, so are overhead costs." Do you agree?

9. Historical costs are irrelevant in alternative choice problems, but the numbers used in many such problems are in fact historical costs. Explain this apparent paradox.

10. The book value of a machine on the balance sheet is genuinely an asset, but in alternative choice problems this asset amount is disregarded. Why?

11. In Exhibit 7-3, explain in your own words the meaning of "depreciation" and "loss on disposal," and why they are treated as they are.

12. Suppose the machine referred to in Exhibit 7-3 could be sold for $100. Should this $100 enter into the calculation? If so, what happens to the $300 difference between the market value of $100 and the book value of $400?

13. An accounting principle is "cost or market, whichever is lower." How can a machine be carried on the balance sheet as an asset at $400 if its market value is only $100?

14. The book value of a machine is a sunk cost. However, if the same machine is rented rather than owned, the rental payments are *not* a sunk cost. Explain this apparent paradox.

15. Opportunity costs, as such, are not recorded in accounting records. Why not?

16. "In the very long run, all costs are differential." Explain what this means.

17. In a certain company, return on investment is calculated as follows:

$$\frac{\text{Revenue } \$100 - \text{Costs } \$80}{\text{Investment } \$200} = 10 \text{ Percent}$$

Give *four* ways in which the return on investment could be increased to approximately 11 percent.

18. Under some circumstances, a reduction of two hours of labor time required to make a product reduces differential costs and in other circumstances it does not. Distinguish between these circumstances, with examples.

19. Holvelt Company manufactures and sells power lawnmowers. It owns its factory and a separate office building. List some of the make-or-buy alternatives that the company might consider.

20. If allocated costs can give misleading impressions, as on Exhibit 7-5, then why should cost allocations be made?

21. "A company must recover its full costs or eventually go out of business." Do you agree? Why?

22. An analyst estimated that a proposed new advertising campaign would increase sales of a certain product by 10 percent. Since sales currently were $1,487,462, the analyst estimated the differential revenue at $148,746.20. What wrong impression could this number give? What number should the analyst have used?

23. Airlines have special low rates for families who fly on certain days. Explain why they do this, using concepts described in this chapter. Under what circumstances should airlines have low rates for students?

24. A company is considering a proposal that involves using an item of raw material in inventory that cost $100. If the item is used for the proposal, it must be replaced at a cost of $150 because it is normally used in the manufacturing process. What is the differential cost of the item? Would your answer be different if the item were not going to be used in the manufacturing process and instead would be discarded as junk?

PROBLEMS

7–1.   Vapner Construction Company wants to establish a decision rule on when to rent a house trailer for an on-site construction office, and when to build an on-site office. Trailers of the kind which Vapner uses can be rented for $100 per month, with a minimum rental of eight months. Construction of an on-site office generally costs Vapner $900 for materials, 20 percent of which are salvagable upon dismantling, and $1,200 in labor. Other costs would be unaffected.

Required:

In terms of length of construction project, when should Vapner rent a trailer and when should it construct its own on-site office?

7–2.   The Woodward Company publishes two monthly magazines, *Feminine Fashions* and *Farmer's Monthly.* Estimated revenue and expenses for a typical month are as follows:

	Feminine Fashions	Farmers' Monthly
Revenues	$25,000	$20,000
Variable expenses:		
Salaries	6,000	5,000
Paper, printing, and postage	7,000	7,000
Other	3,000	2,000
Direct fixed expenses	1,000	1,000

	Woodward Company
Indirect fixed expenses:	
Salaries	$6,000
Utilities	4,000
Advertising	3,500
Rent	2,500
Other	2,000

Required:

A.   Prepare a contribution basis income statement by magazine similar to Exhibit 7–1.

B.   A company has offered to sell subscriptions to the magazines for a 20 percent commission. Should Woodward accept the offer? Why?

7–3.   Addy Company manufactures a toy with a retail price of $9.95 and a manufacturing cost of $3. It sells the toy through specialty stores, and it bills the stores at the retail price less 30 percent. Sales are about 20,000 units annually. An acquaintance suggested to W. Addy that the toy would be an attractive item in airport gift shops. Addy replied, "I've already looked into that. Our marketing costs would be about the same as sales to specialty stores, but airport gift shops require a discount of 50 percent from the retail price. We therefore would have to sell $1\frac{2}{3}$ as many units to an airport gift shop to make the same gross margin as we make in sales to specialty stores, and it is highly unlikely that we could do this. Therefore, I am not sure your idea is a good one."

Required:

Explain why you agree or disagree with Addy's reasoning.

7–4. Macklin Insurance Company is considering adding a coffee-and-snack bar to its employee lounge. The lounge is open 250 days per year. On the average, 200 employees visit it each day. The average item sold by the snack bar would cost 20 cents. Half of the employees visiting the lounge would make a purchase each day at the snack bar. The snack bar would be operated by a commercial caterer whose terms are that the company must pay her $50 per week (50 weeks per year) to operate the snack bar; she in turn will give the company 25 percent of her total snack sales.

Required:

Should the company accept these terms? If so, what will its profit probably be? If not, how much additional profit must it have in order to install a snack bar?

7–5. A manufacturer of motorcycles has been operating at 80 percent of plant capacity. In order to utilize more capacity the plant manager is considering making a headlight which had been previously purchased for $7.10 per unit. The plant has the equipment and labor force necessary to manufacture this light, which the design engineer estimates would cost $1.40 for direct materials and $3 for direct labor. The plant overhead rate is $1.50 per direct labor dollar of which $0.75 is variable cost.

Required:

A. On the basis of the information given, should the company make or buy the light? Show computations to support your answer.

B. Comment on unmeasured factors that should be considered also.

7–6. ABC Electronics was contemplating the manufacturing of a component part of an electronic testing device which the company sold. Parts were presently being purchased for $6.17 each. Terms of the arrangement were 2/10, net 30, f.o.b. seller's factory. Shipping charges amounted to $0.08 per unit.

Company cost accountants estimated that after an initial training period of one week, the five workers needed to assemble the parts would average 66 completed parts for a normal seven-hour workday. Net material costs per unit would amount to $4.30 if the part were to be produced. The plant manager estimated that one supervisor would have to devote about 25 percent of his or her time to supervision of the workers, and that demand for the component part would remain relatively constant at 16,500 units annually. Labor rates were as follows:

Assembly labor .... $2.80 per hour
Supervision .... 4.25 per hour

Required:

A. Should ABC Electronics make the component part or continue to buy it?

B. Will either increases or decreases in demand for the component part change your answer to (A) above?

C. Establish a make-or-buy decision rule for this component part to include rules for—

1. When to utilize overtime hours (assume overtime pay to be 150 percent of regular pay).

2. When to hire additional workers.

7-7. Seavy Equipment Company produces a line of wrought-iron lawn ornaments. Current sales average 70 percent of the 100,000 unit plant capacity, and a large contractor has offered the company an order for 10,000 ornaments at $7 each. The usual selling price is $10 per unit. Company cost accountants have computed the cost per ornament as follows:

Variable costs of materials and labor......................	$5
Fixed costs	3
	$8

Acceptance of the 10,000-unit order is not expected to change the total fixed costs.

A. On the basis of the information given, should Seavy accept the order for 10,000 units at $7 each? Support your answer with appropriate computations.

B. Comment on unmeasured factors that should be considered also.

7-8. Nubo Manufacturing, Inc., is presently operating at 50 percent of practical capacity producing about 50,000 units annually of a patented electronic component. Nubo recently received an offer from a company in Yokohama, Japan, to purchase 30,000 components at $6 per unit, f.o.b. Nubo's plant. Nubo has not previously sold components in Japan. Budgeted production costs for 50,000 and 80,000 units of output follow:

Units	50,000	80,000
Costs:		
Direct material	$ 75,000	$120,000
Direct labor...	75,000	120,000
Factory overhead...	200,000	260,000
Total Costs	$350,000	$500,000
Cost per unit...	$7.00	$6.25

The sales manager thinks the order should be accepted, even if it results in a loss of $1 per unit, because the sale may build up future markets. The production manager does not wish to have the order accepted primarily because the order would show a loss of $0.25 per unit when computed on the new average unit cost. The treasurer has made a quick computation indicating that accepting the order will actually increase gross margin.

Required:

A. On the basis of the information given, should the order be accepted or rejected? Show computations to support your answer.

B. In addition to revenue and costs, what additional factors should be considered before making a final decision?

(AICPA adapted)

7-9. Tracy Enterprises can produce 10,000 snowblowers a month at capacity operations. Average normal production and sales have been 8,000 per month, but an economic slump in the area has caused the sales manager to believe that only 4,000 units can be sold through usual outlets during the coming month. Tracy has received an offer from a large mail-order concern requesting a total of 5,000 units of production. Tracy would receive $150 per unit. The blowers normally sell through regular channels for $160 each, the amount which the company feels allows for a satisfactory return on investment. Monthly fixed costs are $400,000; and the variable costs of production, distribution, and administration are $60 per unit.

Required:

A. What is the maximum unit cost allowable on the mail-order contract if a profit of $45 per unit is desired? How many units must be sold to meet this requirement?

B. How much does it cost Tracy to produce and sell a snowblower at volume levels of 10,000, 9,000, and 8,000 units? What do you consider to be the most reasonable unit cost?

C. Should Tracy use regular channels or sell to the mail-order firm? Justify your recommendation.

7-10. E. Berg & Sons build custom-made pleasure boats which range in price from $10,000 to $250,000. For the past 30 years, Berg, Sr. has determined the selling price of each boat by estimating the costs of material, labor, a prorated portion of overhead, and adding 20 percent to these estimated costs.

For example, a recent price quotation was determined as follows:

Direct materials	$ 5,000
Direct labor	8,000
Overhead	2,000
	15,000
Plus 20%	3,000
Selling price	$18,000

The overhead figure was determined by estimating total overhead costs for the year and allocating them at 25 percent of direct labor.

If a customer rejected the price and business was slack, Berg, Sr. would often be willing to reduce his markup to as little as 5 percent over estimated costs. Thus, average markup for the year is estimated at 15 percent.

Ed Berg, Jr. has just completed a course on pricing and believes the firm could use some of the techniques discussed in the course. The course emphasized the contribution margin approach to pricing and Berg, Jr. feels such an approach would be helpful in determining the selling prices of their custom-made pleasure boats.

Total overhead which includes selling and administrative expenses for the year has been estimated at $150,000 of which $90,000 is fixed and the remainder is variable in direct proportion to direct labor.

Required:

Assume the customer in the example rejected the $18,000 quotation and also rejected a $15,750 quotation (5 percent markup) during a slack period. The customer countered with a $15,000 offer.

A. What is the difference in net income for the year between accepting or rejecting the customer's offer?
B. What is the minimum selling price Berg, Jr. could have quoted without reducing or increasing net income?
C. Comment on the advantages and disadvantages of the contribution margin approach to pricing in contrast to the approach used by Berg, Sr.

(IMA adapted)

7-11. City College sponsors rock concerts once a week for ten weeks during the summer. The concerts are held in the college gymnasium which has a seating capacity of 1,000. Portable stands for an additional 1,000 may be rented for $8,000 for the summer. Profit from the concerts goes into a student scholarship fund. Fixed costs for 1,000 persons are $15,000 for the summer and variable costs are $0.20 per person. Last summer cert. In an effort to increase attendance, consideration is being given to lowering the ticket price this summer. A group of marketing students prepared the following estimates of attendance per concert for a range of prices:

Price per ticket	Estimated attendance per concert
$3.50	800
3.00	1,200
2.50	1,600
2.00	2,000

Required:

A. Prepare an analysis showing which of the four ticket prices should be charged this summer.
B. Calculate the difference in operating income which would result if the price were changed to the amount calculated in (A) above.

7-12. Atlas Manufacturing Company is considering discontinuing its Western Sales Division. A 1977 income statement for the division follows:

Revenue	$500,000
Cost of goods sold	400,000
Gross margin	100,000
Selling and administrative expenses	150,000
Net loss	$ (50,000)

Factory overhead accounts for 25 percent of the cost of goods sold and is one-half fixed. One third of the selling and administrative expenses are fixed. These data are believed to reflect conditions in the immediate future.

Required:

Should Atlas discontinue sales in its Western Division? Show computations to support your answer.

7–13. Yardley Corporation uses a joint process to produce products A, B, and C. Each product may be sold at its split-off point or processed further. Additional processing costs are entirely variable and are traceable to the respective products produced. Joint production costs for 1977 were $50,000 and are allocated by Yardley using the relative-sales-value at split-off approach. Relevant data follow:

			Sales values and additional costs if processed further	
Product	Units produced	Sales value at split-off	Sales values	Additional costs
A	20,000	$ 45,000	$60,000	$20,000
B	15,000	75,000	98,000	20,000
C	15,000	30,000	62,000	18,000
		$150,000		

Required:

A. To maximize profits, which products should Yardley sell at the split-off point and which should be sold after further processing? Show your computations.

B. Are the joint production costs of $50,000 relevant in making the decision to sell or process further in Requirement A? Explain why.

(AICPA adapted)

7–14. The U.S. Army Corps of Engineers frequently uses benefit/cost analysis to evaluate proposed navigation projects. One such project involved making the Damp River navigable for barge traffic from Southtown, where it flowed into a navigable waterway, to Northtown, its origin. The project would require the construction and operation of locks at six dams along the river plus the dredging and maintenance of a channel at least 150 feet wide and nine feet deep. The entire distance is 220 miles; and a major city, Midtown, is located on the river 170 miles north of Southtown.

The benefits of the project would be the savings in freight charges expected to result from shipping by water, instead of by rail or truck, such bulky commodities as iron ore, iron and steel products, coal, and woodpulp. Data on benefits and costs are as follows:

Segment	Distance	Average annual savings	Average annual cost
Southtown to Midtown	170 miles	$24,000,000	$21,000,000
Midtown to Northtown...........	50	3,000,000	3,600,000
Total..........................	220 miles	$27,000,000	$24,600,000

Required:

A. Calculate the benefit/cost ratio for each of the two segments of the river and for the entire project.
B. What recommendation would you make in regard to funding the Damp River navigation project? Why?
C. Another federal agency is seeking funding for a program to reduce deaths resulting from head and neck cancer. This program estimates costs of $7.8 million and savings of $9.0 million based on the expected lifetime earnings of those whose deaths would be averted. Calculate the benefit/cost ratio and contrast the merits of the cancer program and the navigation project.
D. Comment on the strengths and weaknesses of benefit/cost analysis as an aid to decision making for programs such as the two above.

7–15. The Masters Company wants to determine the number of units of a particular component it should order each time an order is entered. Monthly usage is a constant 20 units. Ordering costs are $12 per order, and inventory carrying costs are $10 per unit per year.

Required:

A. Calculate the economic order quantity.
B. Calculate the number of orders needed per year.

7–16. Ralph Brown owns a collection of rare stamps which he purchased two years ago for $15,000. Today, he received a firm offer of $22,000 for his collection. There is to be a national meeting of stamp collectors and dealers in one week. Much buying and selling activity takes place at such a meeting. Based on his knowledge of the stamp market, Ralph developed the following estimates of prices he might be able to obtain if he waits for the meeting to sell his collection:

Possible prices	Estimated probabilities
$10,000	0.1
15,000	0.1
20,000	0.4
25,000	0.3
30,000	0.1
	1.0

Required:

Assume that Ralph wants to sell his stamp collection, should he accept the $22,000 offer now or should he wait for the meeting? Why?

7–17. Dairy Pure Stores, a small supermarket chain, is considering opening all its stores on Sundays. Salary expense for a Sunday would amount to $8,000, and other additional costs would be approximately $1,300. Gross margins on sales at Dairy Pure average 15 percent.

Required:

What volume of sales would be necessary to justify Sunday opening?

7–18. Randy's Place consists of a restaurant and a lounge. Estimated revenue and expenses for a typical month are as follows:

	Restaurant	*Lounge*
Revenues	$20,000	$10,000
Variable expenses:		
Salaries	5,000	2,000
Food and drink	7,000	4,000
Other	3,000	1,000
Direct fixed expenses	1,000	1,000

Randy's Place

Indirect fixed expenses:	
Salaries	$3,000
Utilities	2,500
Rent	2,000
Other	2,500

Required:

A. Prepare a contribution basis income statement by major activity similar to Exhibit 7–1.

B. A local diners' club wants to add Randy's to its list of clients who give a 20 percent discount to customers and who pay the club a 5 percent commission. Should the offer be accepted? Why?

C. What would be the effect of closing the lounge? Show computations to support your answer.

D. Should Randy's Place consider closing the entire operation? Why?

7–19. Two competing food vendors were located side by side at a state fair. Both occupied buildings of the same size, paid the same rent, $1,250, and charged similar prices for their food. Vendor A employed three times as many employees as B and had twice as much income as B even though B had more than half the sales of A. Other data:

	Vendor A	*Vendor B*
Sales	$8,000	$4,500
Cost of goods sold	50% sales	50% sales
Wages	$2,250	$750

Required:

A. Present the data given in the form of a marginal income analysis statement.

B. Explain why Vendor A is twice as profitable as Vendor B.

C. By how much would Vendor B's sales have to increase in order to justify the doubling of the number of employees at the same rate of pay if B's desired operating income is $350?

7–20. The Baxley Company operates a cafeteria for its employees. Fixed operating costs are $3,000 per month, and variable costs are $0.40 per dollar of sales. Sales for an average month are $8,000. Able Vending Company has offered to replace the cafeteria with a set of vending machines for which revenue is estimated to be $7,000 monthly. Baxley would receive 12 percent of total revenue as rental income, and would avoid all cafeteria fixed and variable costs.

Required:

Should Baxley accept Able's offer to replace the cafeteria with vending machines? Support your answer with computations.

7–21. A manufacturer of home laundry equipment has been operating at 75 percent of plant capacity, and management is considering ways of raising the rate of capacity utilization. Among the proposals under study is to make an electric motor which is currently being purchased for $50 each. Costs to manufacture this motor have been estimated as follows:

Direct materials...	$15
Direct labor (3 hours @ $7)..	21
Factory overhead ($5 per direct labor hour)...............	15
Total...	$51

Fixed factory overhead is budgeted at $500,000 per year, and the overhead rate is calculated using a capacity level of 250,000 direct labor hours per year.

Required:

A. On the basis of the information given, should the company make or buy the motor? Show computations to support your answer.

B. Comment on unmeasured factors that should be considered also.

7–22. The Vernon Corporation, which produces and sells to wholesalers a highly successful line of summer lotions and insect repellents, has decided to diversify in order to stabilize sales throughout the year. A natural area for the company to consider is the production of winter lotions and creams to prevent dry and chapped skin.

After considerable research, a winter products line has been developed. However, because of the conservative nature of the company management, Vernon's president has decided to introduce only one of the new products for this coming winter. If the product is a success, further expansion in future years will be initiated.

The product selected (called Chap-off) is a lip balm that will be sold in a lipstick type tube. The product will be sold to wholesalers in boxes of 24 tubes for $8 per box. Because of available capacity, no additional fixed charges will be incurred to produce the product. However, a $100,000 fixed charge will be absorbed by the product to allocate a fair share of the company's present fixed costs to the new product.

Using the estimated sales and production of 100,000 boxes of Chap-off as the standard volume, the accounting department has developed the following costs:

Direct labor... $2.00/box
Direct materials $3.00/box
Total overhead $1.50/box
      Total... $6.50/box

Vernon has approached a cosmetics manufacturer to discuss the possibility of purchasing the tubes for Chap-off. The purchase price of the empty tubes from the cosmetics manufacturer would be $0.90 per 24 tubes. If Vernon accepts the purchase proposal, it is estimated that direct labor and variable overhead costs (included with the fixed cost allocation in "total" overhead above) would be reduced by 10 percent and direct material costs would be reduced by 20 percent.

Required:
A. Should Vernon make or buy the tubes? Support your answer with computations.
B. What would be the maximum price that Vernon could pay for the tubes? Explain.
C. Revised sales estimates show sales of 125,000 boxes. At this higher level, additional equipment at an annual rental of $10,000 must be acquired to manufacture all tubes required. However, this would be the only additional fixed cost required even if sales increase as high as 300,000 boxes. Under this circumstance, should Vernon make or buy the tubes? Explain.

                                          (IMA adapted)

7-23. Hooker Rubber Company has been offered a contract to supply 500,000 automobile tires to a large car manufacturer at a price of $15 per tire. Hooker's full cost of producing the tire is $16. The normal sales price for the tire is $20 to both distributors and some selected retailers. Variable costs per tire amount to $14; however, in order to meet the needs of the auto manufacturer, Hooker will have to cut its sales to regular customers by 100,000 tires annually. The auto maker has clearly indicated that it will enter into the agreement only if Hooker will agree to supply all 500,000 of the tires requested.

Required:

A. Should Hooker accept the offer? Show computations to support your answer.

B. Comment on unmeasured factors that should be considered also.

7–24. Ace Fastener Company, a manufacturer of nails, has received a request from Sunshine Builders for Ace to supply Sunshine with ten 100-pound kegs of nails per week for a one-year period, at a price of $5.15 per keg. Ace is presently working at 100 percent capacity for one eight-hour shift and would have to incur overtime expense in order to meet Sunshine's request. Ace's normal sales price for nails is $5.65 per 100-pound keg.

The steel used for manufacture of nails is purchased by Ace at a cost of $80 per ton. Ace experiences a 5 percent material waste factor in production. Labor costs per 100 pounds of output are $0.50; however, overtime production would increase labor costs by 50 percent. Overhead, which is currently 18 percent variable and 82 percent fixed, is allocated on a 100 percent-of-direct-labor-dollars basis.

Required:

A. On the basis of the information given, should Ace Fastener Company accept Sunshine's order at the $5.15 per keg price? Show computations to support your answer.

B. In addition to costs and revenue, what additional factors should be considered before making a final decision?

7–25. Scoville Manufacturing Company has just received an order for 2,500 garden tillers for which the buyer, a large agricultural cooperative, would pay $108 each. Average tiller production and sales have been 4,000 per month, but an economic recession in the area has caused management to believe that only 2,000 tillers could be sold through usual channels. Scoville has the capacity to produce 5,000 units per month with a fixed monthly cost of $200,000 and variable production, distribution, and administrative costs of $30 per unit, which management feels has provided a satisfactory return on investment. The regular selling price is $115 per unit.

Required:

A. What is the maximum unit cost allowable on the cooperative order if a total profit of $87,000 was desired on the order? How many units must be sold to meet this requirement?

B. Calculate what you consider to be the full cost to Scoville of one tiller. Justify your answer.

C. What should Scoville do: take the cooperative offer or manufacture to sell through regular channels? Why?

7–26. George Jackson operates a small machine shop. He manufactures one standard product available from many other similar businesses and he also manufactures products to customer order. His accountant prepared the annual income statement shown below:

	Custom sales	Standard sales	Total
Sales	$50,000	$25,000	$75,000
Material	10,000	8,000	18,000
Labor	20,000	9,000	29,000
Depreciation	6,300	3,600	9,900
Power	700	400	1,100
Rent	6,000	1,000	7,000
Heat and light	600	100	700
Other	400	900	1,300
	44,000	23,000	67,000
	$ 6,000	$ 2,000	$ 8,000

The depreciation charges are for machines used in the respective product lines. The power charge is apportioned on the estimate of power consumed. The rent is for the building space which has been leased for ten years at $7,000 per year. The rent and heat and light are apportioned to the product lines based on amount of floor space occupied. All other costs are current expenses identified with the product line causing them.

A valued custom parts customer has asked Jackson if he would manufacture 5,000 special units for him. Jackson is working at capacity and would have to give up some other business in order to take this business. He can't renege on custom orders already agreed to but he could reduce the output of his standard product by about one-half for one year while producing the specially requested custom part. The customer is willing to pay $7 for each part. The material cost will be about $2 per unit, and the labor will be $3.60 per unit. Jackson will have to spend $2,000 for a special device which will be discarded when the job is done.

Required:

A. Recast the income statement using the contribution approach.
B. Calculate and present the following costs related to the 5,000-unit custom order:
   1. The incremental cost of the order.
   2. The full cost of the order.
   3. The opportunity cost of taking the order.
   4. The sunk costs related to the order.
C. Should Jackson take the order? Explain your answer.

(IMA adapted)

7-27. Johnson's Health Club sponsors boxing matches twice a week for 25 weeks during the fall and winter. The charge per ticket has been $3.50 with an average attendance of 900 spectators at each match. In an effort to increase attendance, the club manager is considering decreasing the ticket price. There are 1,000 seats available now, but for an added $15,000 per year, capacity can be doubled. Yearly fixed costs are now $90,000, and variable costs are $0.25 per spectator. Expected ticket sales and attendance follow:

Price per ticket	Estimated attendance
$3.50	900
3.00	1,250
2.50	1,750
2.00	2,000

Required:

A. Prepare an analysis showing which of the four ticket prices should be adopted.

B. Calculate the difference in operating income which would result if the price were changed to the amount calculated in A above.

7–28. Delta Venus Swimsuit Company is considering dropping its line of ladies' beach robes. A 1977 product statement for the robe line follows:

Revenue	$417,000
Cost of goods sold	378,000
Gross margin	39,000
Selling and administrative expenses	60,000
Net loss	$ (21,000)

Factory overhead accounts for 26 percent of the cost of the goods sold and is one-third fixed. Two thirds of the selling and administrative expenses are fixed. These data are believed to reflect conditions in the immediate future.

Required:

Should Delta Venus drop the beach robe line? Show computations to support your answer.

7–29. From a particular joint process, Watkins Company produces three products, X, Y, and Z. Each product may be sold at the point of split-off or processed further. Additional processing requires no special facilities, and production costs of further processing are entirely variable and traceable to the products involved. In 1977 all three products were processed beyond split-off. Joint production costs for the year were $60,000. Sales values and costs needed to evaluate Watkins' 1977 production policy follow:

Product	Units produced	Sales values at split-off	Additional costs and sales values if processed further	
			Sales values	Added costs
X	6,000	$25,000	$42,000	$9,000
Y	4,000	41,000	45,000	7,000
Z	2,000	24,000	32,000	8,000

Joint costs are allocated to the products in proportion to the relative physical volume of output.

Required:

A. To maximize profits, which products should Watkins have sold at the split-off point and which should have been sold after further processing? Show your computations.

B. Are the joint production costs of $60,000 relevant in making the decision to sell or process further in Requirement A? Explain why.

(AICPA adapted)

7–30. The Johnson Company wants to determine the number of units of Product 814 to manufacture during each production run. Annual production requirements are 1,000 units, and setup costs are $500. Inventory carrying costs are $10 per unit per year.

Required:

A. Calculate the economic lot size.

B. Calculate the number of production runs needed per year.

7–31. Dawson owns a rare painting which was purchased last year for $10,000. Today, Dawson received a firm offer of $14,000 for the painting. Early next month, Dawson plans to attend a national meeting of art collectors and dealers. Much buying and selling activity takes place at such a meeting. With the help of the director of the local art museum, Dawson developed the following estimates of prices that might be obtained for the painting if it is sold at the meeting:

Possible prices	Estimated probabilities
$ 5,000	0.1
10,000	0.2
15,000	0.3
20,000	0.3
25,000	0.1
	1.0

Required:

Assuming that Dawson wants to sell the painting, should the $14,000 offer be accepted now or should Dawson wait for the meeting? Why?

7–32. The Justa Corporation produces and sells three products. The three products, A, B, C, are sold in a local market and in a regional market. At the end of the first quarter of the current year, the following income statement has been prepared:

	Total	Local	Regional
Sales	$1,300,000	$1,000,000	$300,000
Cost of goods sold	1,010,000	775,000	235,000
Gross margin	290,000	225,000	65,000
Selling expenses	105,000	60,000	45,000
Administrative expenses	52,000	40,000	12,000
	157,000	100,000	57,000
Net Income	$ 133,000	$ 125,000	$ 8,000

Management has expressed special concern with the regional market because of the extremely poor return on sales. This market was entered a year ago because of excess capacity. It was originally believed that the return on sales would improve with time, but after a year no noticeable improvement can be seen from the results as reported in the above quarterly statement.

In attempting to decide whether to eliminate the regional market, the following information has been gathered:

	Products		
	A	B	C
Sales..	$500,000	$400,000	$400,000
Variable manufacturing expenses as a percentage of sales..............	60%	70%	60%
Variable selling expenses as a percentage of sales...................	3%	2%	2%

Sales by Markets

Product	Local	Regional
A.....................	$400,000	$100,000
B.....................	300,000	100,000
C.....................	300,000	100,000

All administrative expenses and fixed manufacturing expenses are common to the three products and the two markets and are fixed for the period. Remaining selling expenses are fixed for the period and separable by market. All fixed expenses are based upon a prorated yearly amount.

Required:

A. Prepare the quarterly income statement showing contribution margins by markets.

B. Assuming there are no alternative uses for the Justa Corporation's present capacity, would you recommend dropping the regional market? Why or why not?

C. Prepare the quarterly income statement showing contribution margins by products.

D. It is believed that a new product can be ready for sale next year if the Justa Corporation decides to go ahead with continued research. The new product can be produced by simply converting equipment presently used in producing Product C. This conversion will increase fixed costs by $10,000 per quarter. What must be the minimum contribution margin per quarter for the new product to make the changeover financially feasible?

(IMA adapted)

7–33. Anchor Company manufactures several different styles of jewelry cases. Management estimates that during the third quarter of 1976 the company will be operating at 80 percent of normal capacity. Because the company desires a higher utilization of plant capacity, the company will consider a special order.

Anchor has received special order inquiries from two companies. The first order is from JCP, Inc., which would like to market a jewelry case similar to one of Anchor's cases. The JCP jewelry case would be marketed under JCP's own label. JCP, Inc., has offered Anchor $5.75 per jewelry case for 20,000 cases to be shipped by October 1, 1976. The cost data for the Anchor jewelry case which would be similar to the specifications of the JCP special order are as follows:

Regular selling price per unit	$9.00
Costs per unit:	
Raw materials	$2.50
Direct labor 0.5 hours @ $6	3.00
Overhead 0.25 machine-hours @ $4	1.00
Total Costs	$6.50

According to the specifications provided by JCP, Inc., the special order case requires less expensive raw materials. Consequently, the raw materials will only cost $2.25 per case. Management has estimated that the remaining costs, labor time, and machine time will be the same as the Anchor jewelry case.

The second special order was submitted by the Krage Company for 7,500 jewelry cases at $7.50 per case. These jewelry cases, as with the JCP cases, would be marketed under the Krage label and have to be shipped by October 1, 1976. However, the Krage jewelry case is different from any jewelry case in the Anchor line. The estimated per unit costs of this case are as follows:

Raw materials	$3.25
Direct labor 0.5 hours @ $6	3.00
Overhead 0.5 machine-hours @ $4	2.00
Total Costs	$8.25

In addition, Anchor will incur $1,500 in additional setup costs and will have to purchase a $2,500 special device to manufacture these cases; this device will be discarded once the special order is completed.

The Anchor manufacturing capabilities are limited to the total machine-hours available. The plant capacity under normal operations is 90,000 machine-hours per year or 7,500 machine-hours per month. The budgeted fixed overhead for 1976 amounts to $216,000. All manufacturing overhead costs are applied to production on the basis of machine-hours at $4 per hour.

Anchor will have the entire third quarter to work on the special orders. Management does not expect any repeat sales to be generated from either special order. Company practice precludes Anchor from subcontracting any portion of an order when special orders are not expected to generate repeat sales.

Required:

Should Anchor Company accept either special order? Justify your answer and show your calculations.

(IMA adapted)

7–34. Marshall Manufacturing, Inc., has produced two products, Z and P, at its Richmond plant for several years. On March 31, 1973, P was dropped from the product line. Marshall manufactures and sells 50,000 units of Z annually, and this is not expected to change. Unit material and direct labor costs are $12 and $7, respectively.

The Richmond plant is in a leased building; the lease expires June 30, 1977. Annual rent is $75,000. The lease provides Marshall the right of sublet; all nonremovable leasehold improvements revert to the lessor. At the end of the lease, Marshall intends to close the plant and scrap all equipment.

P has been produced on two assembly lines which occupy 25 percent of the plant. The assembly lines will have a book value of $135,000 and a remaining useful life of seven years as of June 30, 1973. This is the only portion of the plant available for alternative uses.

Marshall uses one unit of D to produce one unit of Z. D is purchased under a contract requiring a minimum annual purchase of 5,000 units. The contract expires June 30, 1977. A list of D unit costs follows:

Annual purchases (units)	Unit cost
5,000– 7,499	$2.00
7,500– 19,999	1.95
20,000– 34,999	1.80
35,000– 99,999	1.65
100,000–250,000	1.35

Alternatives are available for using the space previously used to manufacture P. Some may be used in combination. All can be implemented by June 30, 1973. Should no action be taken, the plant is expected to operate profitably, and manufacturing overhead is not expected to differ materially from past years when P was manufactured. Following are the alternatives:

1. Sell the two P assembly lines for $70,000. The purchaser will buy only if the equipment can be acquired from both lines. The purchaser will pay all removal and transportation costs.
2. Sublet the floor space for an annual rental of $12,100. The lease will require that the equipment be removed (cost nominal) and leasehold improvements costing $38,000 be installed. Indirect costs are expected to increase $3,500 annually as a result of the sublease.
3. Convert one or both P assembly lines to produce D at a cost of $45,500 for each line. The converted lines will have a remaining useful life of ten years. Each modified line can produce any number of units of D up to a maximum of 37,000 units at a unit direct material and direct labor cost of $0.10 and $0.25, respectively. Annual manu-

facturing overhead is expected to increase from $550,000 to $562,000 if one line is converted and to $566,000 if both lines are converted.

Required:

Prepare a schedule to analyze the best utilization of the following alternatives for the four years ended June 30, 1977. Ignore income taxes and the time value of money.

1. Continue to purchase D; sell equipment; rent space.
2. Continue to purchase D; sell equipment.
3. Produce D on two assembly lines; purchase D as needed.
4. Produce D on one assembly line; purchase D as needed.

(AICPA adapted)

7-35. French Company operates a retail store with 5,000 square feet of selling floor space. It is divided into three departments. Annual revenues and expenses for each department are currently as follows:

	Frozen food	Dry groceries	Sundries	Total
Revenue.........................	$300,000	$1,000,000	$200,000	$1,500,000
Direct costs (including Cost of goods sold)......	250,000	900,000	150,000	1,300,000
Indirect costs..................	9,600	52,800	17,600	80,000
Total Departmental Cost	259,600	952,800	167,600	1,380,000
Departmental profit.........	$ 40,400	$ 47,200	$ 32,400	120,000
Administrative costs........				60,000
Operating Income				$ 60,000

Indirect costs are allocated to departments in proportion to the square feet of floor space that each occupies since there is a close relationship between the sales volume of each department and its floor space.

Management is considering adding a line of paperbook books and magazines. This line can be deployed in space now used for either groceries or sundries with only minor alterations in shelving arrangements. It cannot be taken from the frozen food department. It is estimated that this line would produce $100,000 in revenue and incur $82,500 of cost of goods sold and other direct costs. It would require 500 square feet of floor space.

It is expected that revenues of other departments would decrease in proportion to the floor space that they gave up. Costs, including indirect costs, would also decrease proportionally. (Indirect costs would decrease proportionally because the allocations are based on floor space.)

Required:

A. If groceries and sundries each give up 250 square feet of floor space for the new department, should the decision be made to add the book and magazine department?

B. Would it be preferable to take the space entirely from one of the existing departments, and if so, from which one?

C. Assume that additional floor space could be rented at annual fixed cost of $20,000. Would this be preferable to either of the other alternatives?

D. If the company should change its basis of allocating fixed costs so that fixed costs were allocated as a proportion of the revenue of each department, how, if at all, would your conclusions be changed?

7–36. DBA Chemical Company is considering changing the material content of chemical compound 12XC2, which it produces in batches, on order, for one customer in the plastics industry. DBA salespersons have been informed by the customer that if the order lead time for 12XC2 could be reduced to 10 days from the present 17 days, orders for the compound would double. 12XC2 cannot be carried in inventory due to rapid deterioration after completion.

12XC2 is produced in batches of 10,000 pounds, using special equipment. The compound is made up of various petroleum by-products and other chemicals. The company's chief chemist has informed sales management that substitution of Chemical B for Chemical A in the mix would not change the quality of the product and would cut the processing time in half. Processing time is presently 14 days.

The sales department, in conjunction with company cost accountants, prepared a summary of the cost data for 12XC2 under the present processing method and has also summarized the changes which would result if Chemical B were substituted for Chemical A, as follows:

Costs for compound 12 × C2

	Per pound
Materials (except for Chemical A)	$0.20
Chemical A	0.05
Labor (3 workers @ $3/hour × 24 hours × 14 days ÷ 10,000 pounds)	0.3024
Overhead (@ 65% of direct material dollars, 85% fixed)	0.1625
Full cost	$0.7149

Summary of changes as a result of substituting Chemical B for Chemical A

1. Labor time and costs per pound cut in half.
2. $0.18 material cost component per pound of 12XC2 for Chemical B.
3. Sales volume will double from 180,000 pounds annually to 360,000 pounds annually.

Required:

If DBA can sell 12XC2 at $0.62 per pound, would you recommend acceptance of the proposed change in the manufacturing method?

7–37. In mid-1970, in reaction to the sharply declining demand for can openers which resulted from the introduction of the "tab top" can, A. Keen, manager of the Kitchen Implements Division (K.I.D.) of Household Products, Inc., has gathered cost data on the division's "Party Time" can opener, in the hope that some action can be taken to reverse the upward spiral of cost per unit.

The data accumulated by Keen shows, among other things, that it may be more profitable to purchase the plastic handles which are attached to the "Party Time" can opener then to continue to produce them. K.I.D. has frequently been approached by J. E. Plastics Company salespersons who have offered (1) to produce the handles for K.I.D. and sell them to K.I.D. for 4 cents each, and (2) to purchase K.I.D.'s plastic-handle producing machinery for $27,000 if a sufficiently large contract for handles can be agreed upon.

The data shows that in 1967, handles could be produced for $0.0291125 each with volume at 1.2 million handles annually, as follows:

	1967	
	Annual	Per unit
Factory overhead:		
Depreciation............................ $2,500		
Supervision............................. 7,000		
Supplies 1,000		
Utilities................................... 2,000		
Maintenance 500	$13,000	1.08333¢
Labor	13,200	1.10000
Materials.................................	8,735	0.72792
	$34,935	2.91125¢

Demand for handles has dropped to a level of 300,000 units annually, and Keen, recognizing the fixed nature of most of the overhead items, knows that per-unit cost at this reduced level of volume may well exceed the 4 cents per-unit cost of purchase.

Additional data:

1. Variable costs per unit have remained unchanged between 1967 and 1970.
2. Estimated annual factory overhead for 1970 is as follows:

Depreciation.........................	$ 2,500
Supervision	5,000
Supplies...............................	800
Utilities	1,500
Maintenance.........................	550
	$10,350

3. The net book value of the plastic-handle producing machinery was $32,500 at January 1, 1970.

Required:

Should Keen accept the offer of J. E. Plastics Company?

7-38. Fine Foods, Inc., a regional supermarket chain, orders 400,000 cans of frozen orange juice per year from a California distributor. A 24-can case of frozen juice delivered to the Fine Foods central warehouse costs $4.80, including freight charges. Fine Foods borrows funds at a 10 percent interest rate to finance its inventories.

The Fine Foods purchasing agent has calculated that it costs $200 to place an order for frozen juice, and that the annual storage expenses for one can of juice (electricity, insurance, handling) amounts to $0.05 per can.

Required:

A. How many cans of frozen juice should Fine Foods request in each order?

B. If the California distributor offers Fine Foods a 10 percent discount off the delivery price for minimum orders of 80,000 cans, what should Fine Foods do?

CASE: ATHERTON COMPANY

7-39. Early in January 1975 the sales manager and the controller of the Atherton Company met for the purpose of preparing a joint pricing recommendation for Item 345. After the president approved their recommendation, the price would be announced in letters to retail customers. In accordance with company and industry practice, announced prices were adhered to for the year unless radical changes in market conditions occurred.

The Atherton Company was the largest company in its segment of the textile industry; its 1974 sales had exceeded $12 million. Company salespersons were on a straight-salary basis, and each salesperson sold the full line. Most of Atherton's competitors were small. Usually they waited for the Atherton Company to announce prices before mailing out their own price lists.

Item 345, an expensive yet competitive fabric, was the sole product of a department whose facilities could not be utilized on other items in the product line. In January 1973 the Atherton Company had raised its price from $3 to $4 a yard. This had been done to bring the profit per yard on Item 345 up to that of other products in the line. Although the company was in a strong position financially, it would require considerable capital in the next few years to finance a recently approved long-term modernization and expansion program. The 1973 pricing decision had been one of several changes advocated by the directors in an attempt to strengthen the company's working capital position so as to insure that adequate funds would be available for this program.

Competitors of the Atherton Company had held their prices on products similar to Item 345 at $3 during 1973 and 1974. The industry and Atherton Company volume for Item 345 for the years 1969–74, as estimated by the sales manager, is shown in Exhibit 7–11. As shown by this exhibit, the Atherton Company had lost a significant portion of its former market position. In the sales manager's opinion, a reasonable forecast of industry volume for 1975 was 700,000 yards. The sales manager was certain that the company could sell 25 percent of the 1975 industry total if it adopted the $3 price and feared a further volume decline if it did not

EXHIBIT 7–11

Item 345, prices and production, 1969–1974

| | Volume of production (yards) | | Price | |
| | | | | |
Year	Industry total	Atherton	Charged by most competitors	Atherton Company
1969............	610,000	213,000	$4	$4
1970............	575,000	200,000	4	4
1971............	430,000	150,000	3	3
1972............	475,000	165,000	3	3
1973............	500,000	150,000	3	4
1974............	625,000	125,000	3	4

meet the competitive price. As many consumers were convinced of the superiority of the Atherton product, the sales manager reasoned that sales of Item 345 would probably not fall below 75,000 yards, even at a $4 price.

During the pricing discussions, the controller and sales manager had considered two other aspects of the problem. The controller was concerned about the possibility that competitors would reduce their prices below $3 if the Atherton Company announced a $3 price for Item 345. The sales manager was confident that competitors would not go below $3 because they all had higher costs and several of them were in tight financial straits. The sales manager believed that action taken on Item 345 would not have any substantial repercussions on other items in the line.

The controller prepared estimated costs of Item 345 at various volumes of production (Exhibit 7–12). These estimated costs reflected

EXHIBIT 7–12

Estimated cost per yard of Item 345 at various volumes of production

	75,000	100,000	125,000	150,000	175,000	200,000
Direct labor.........................	$0.800	$0.780	$0.760	$0.740	$0.760	$0.800
Material..............................	0.400	0.400	0.400	0.400	0.400	0.400
Material spoilage.................	0.040	0.040	0.038	0.038	0.038	0.040
Department expense:						
Direct*.............................	0.120	0.112	0.100	0.100	0.100	0.100
Indirect†..........................	0.800	0.600	0.480	0.400	0.343	0.300
General overhead‡	0.240	0.234	0.228	0.222	0.228	0.240
Factory cost........................	$2.400	$2.166	$2.006	$1.900	$1.869	$1.880
Selling and administrative						
expense§......................	1.560	1.408	1.304	1.236	1.215	1.222
Total Cost..................	$3.960	$3.574	$3.310	$3.136	$3.084	$3.102

* Indirect labor, supplies, repairs, power, and so on.
† Depreciation, supervision, and so on.
‡ 30 percent of direct labor.
§ 65 percent of factory cost.

current labor and material costs. They were based on past experience except for the estimates of 75,000 and 100,000 yards. The company had produced more than 100,000 yards in each of the last ten years, and earlier experience was not applicable because of equipment changes and increases in labor productivity.

Required:

A. How, if at all, did the company's financial condition relate to the pricing decision?

B. Should $3 or $4 have been recommended? (Assume no intermediate prices are being considered.)

C. What information not in the case would you like to have in making this pricing decision? (Do not let the lack of information prevent your answering Requirement B!)

CASE: HELVIN BLANKET COMPANY

7–40.   The Helvin Blanket Company was a large producer of cotton blankets. Since the company performed all the operations from the baled cotton to the finished blankets, and since a market existed for cotton in various stages of manufacture, an ever-present problem before its management was, at what point in the manufacture of a blanket the alternative of selling the uncompleted product was more profitable than continuing with the manufacturing process toward a later market. During a period of undercapacity operations, an incident occurred that raised the question of the validity of using the familiar total average cost accumulations and prorations of the accounting department as a basis for deciding at which point to terminate manufacturing and to sell the product in process.

At a meeting of the principal executives, the sales manager proposed that the carding and spinning capacity of the mill be used to produce warp yarn which, she said, the company could sell currently at a profit. The production manager, on the other hand, contended that the loom capacity of the plant rendered it desirable to continue all yarn operations through to the stage of blankets. The sales manager defended her position with the following figures, which the cost office had prepared for her on the basis of current standard costs:

	Cost per pound, warp yarn	Cost per blanket
Labor	$0.1316	$ 0.2937
Overhead	0.1053	0.2327
Processing materials	0.0083	0.0521
Raw materials	0.3812	1.1436
Cost at standard	0.6265	1.7221
Current selling price	0.6450	1.7000
Profit or (loss)	$0.0185 per lb.	$(0.0221) per blanket

Each blanket contained one pound of warp yarn and two pounds of filling yarn. The figures for cost per blanket were cumulative. Thus, the $0.2937 labor item under cost per blanket included the $0.1316 labor cost of making one pound of warp yarn, plus the labor cost of making two pounds of filling yarn and the labor cost of weaving the blanket.

The production manager challenged the validity of any figures that indicated that the optimum move for the management was to shut down the greater part of the mill in the face of a reasonably favorable market demand for blankets. He argued that the plant was set up to manufacture blankets, not yarn, and to sell yarn was, in effect, to get out of the blanket business, in which the company had made its name. Moreover, he wasn't sure but that the company, despite the generally weak market, might do better financially by keeping the blanket room open.

The head of the cost office stated that the figures presented by the sales manager had been based on painstaking studies of labor and material costs and of methods of distributing overhead to products. He admitted that certain allocations were rough and that different kinds of costs were reported together. On being questioned, he said that for both yarn and blankets about 15 percent of the labor cost was fixed and that about 60 percent of overhead was fixed.

The executives had to reach a decision on the issue. The sales manager was opposed to selling blankets at a loss when she could be selling yarn at a profit. The production manager certainly did not want to close his blanket mill.

Required:

A. What different courses of action might be taken, and what arguments can be made to support them?

B. What information or forecasts might be useful to round out the story?

C. On balance, and in the light of the probable state of affairs, what would you decide?

D. If the current selling price of warp yarn was $0.725 a pound, instead of $0.645, as given in the case, would your decision be changed?

SUGGESTIONS FOR FURTHER READING

Bierman, H.; Bonini, C. P.; and Hausman, W. H. *Quantitative Analysis for Business Decisions,* 5th ed. Homewood, Ill.: Richard D. Irwin, Inc., 1977.

Christenson, C. J.; Vancil, R. F.; and Marshall, P. W. *Managerial Economics: Text and Cases,* Rev. ed. Homewood, Ill.: Richard D. Irwin, Inc., 1973.

National Association of Accountants. *Criteria for Make-or-Buy Decisions,* New York: NAA, 1973.

Raiffa, Howard. *Decision Analysis.* Reading, Mass.: Addison-Wesley Publishing Co., Inc. 1968.

8

Capital investment decisions

In Chapter 7 we discussed those types of alternative choice problems which involved the use of differential *costs* and differential *revenues*. In Chapters 8 and 9 we extend the discussion to problems that involve differential *investments*. These are problems in which the proposal is to invest funds, that is, capital, at the present time in the expectation of earning a return on these funds over some future period. Such problems are called *capital investment problems*. They are also called *capital budgeting problems* because a company's capital budget is a list of the investment projects which it has decided to carry out. In these problems, the only new element is the consideration of the differential investment; differential costs and differential revenues are treated in the same manner as already discussed in Chapter 7.

The analysis of capital investment problems is complicated. It is important that these problems be solved correctly because they often involve large sums of money and because they may commit or "lock in" the business to a certain course of action over a considerable period in the future. The basic approach is described in Chapter 8, and some variations on this approach and some additional considerations are discussed in Chapter 9.

THE CONCEPT OF PRESENT VALUE

The analysis in this chapter is built around a concept called *present value*. Many people have great difficulty in understanding this concept,

310

and we shall therefore discuss it carefully.[1] The reason for this difficulty may stem from a failure to appreciate that there is a fundamental difference between the operation of a business and the conduct of one's personal affairs.

Difference between personal and business attitude

Children are taught that it is a good thing to put money into a piggybank. Their parents congratulate them when the bank is finally opened and the accumulated coins are counted out. But a manager's heart is not gladdened when only the same amount can be taken out of the company's "piggybank" as was put into it. The manager expects that the company's money will earn more money.

By their emphasis on piggybanks and similar devices to teach the importance of thrift, parents encourage children to believe that it is better to have money in the future than to spend it today. Stated more formally, parents teach that the value of money today is *less than* its value at some future time.

Managers think differently. They expect that money invested today will increase in amount as time passes because they expect to earn a profit on that investment. It follows that an amount of money that is available for investment today is more valuable to the manager than an equal amount of money that will not be available until some time in the future. This is because the money available today can be invested to earn still more money, whereas money that has not yet been received obviously cannot be invested today. If a manager is asked, "Would you prefer to have a dollar today or a promise of receiving a dollar a year from now?" The manager would answer, "Of course, I prefer a dollar today because I can put that dollar to work and end up a year from now with more than a dollar." To the manager, therefore, the value of money that is available today is *more than* the value of the same amount that will be received at some future time.

Present value

The value of money today is called its *present value.* The present value of $1 that is available today is, obviously, $1. The present value of $1 that is not available today, but that will be available at some future time, is less than $1. How much less, is a matter to be discussed in a following section.

---

[1] This concept is introduced in *Fundamentals of Financial Accounting,* Chapter 11, in relation to certain financial accounting matters. If you have difficulty with the discussion that follows, we suggest that you reread that chapter.

To make this idea more concrete, consider Able Company. Its management expects that the company can earn a return of 10 percent per year on funds that are invested in the company's assets. (Incidentally, the rate of return is invariably expressed on a *per annum* basis; that is, the statement "return of 10 percent" is invariably taken to mean "10 percent per year.") If Able Company invested $100 today for one year, at an anticipated return of 10 percent, it would expect to have $110 at the end of the year. Thus $100 invested today is expected to have a *future value* of $110 one year from today. Conversely, it can be said that the expectation of having $110 one year from today has a *present value*—a value today—of $100 if funds are expected to earn 10 percent; that is, the value of $110 to be received one year from today is equal to the value of $100 today.

Suppose Able Company expects to receive $100 one year from now. What is the present value of that amount? In a following section the technique for answering this question is described; but for now, the answer simply is stated: the present value of $100 to be received a year from now is $90.91 if the business expects to earn 10 percent on its investments. That this *is* the correct answer can easily be demonstrated. If $90.91 is invested today for one year at 10 percent, it will earn 10 percent of $90.91, or $9.09, which added to the $90.91 makes $100. This exercise leads to a definition of present value.

> The present value of an amount that is expected to be received at a specified time in the future is the amount which if invested today at a designated rate of return would cumulate to the future amount.

Finding present values

It is easy to demonstrate, as was done above, that the present value of $100 to be received one year from now at a rate of return of 10 percent is $90.91. For periods that are longer than a year, the arithmetic is more complicated because of the force of compound interest. Thus, we can demonstrate that at a 10 percent rate of return, $100 expected to be received two years from today has a present value of $82.64 because in the first year 10 percent of this amount, or $8.26, will be earned, bringing the total to $90.90, and in the second year 10 percent of $90.90, or $9.09, will be earned, bringing the total to $100. (The amount does not come exactly to $100 because the calculations were not carried to enough decimal places.)

In Chapter 11 of *Fundamentals of Financial Accounting* the formula is given for calculating the present value of a payment of $1 to be received n years hence at an interest rate i. It is:

$$\frac{1}{(1 + i)^n}$$

The same formula is applicable to the investment problems discussed here. The term *i*, which stood for "interest rate" in *Fundamentals of Financial Accounting,* refers to "rate of return," as used above. Indeed, economists refer to the rate used in investment problems as an interest rate, but business executives customarily use "earnings rate" or "rate of return" for the same notion. We shall not use the formula directly, however, because it is more convenient to use a table of present values computed from it.[2] Such a table, for the present value of $1, is Table S, which appears on page 723. The present value amounts used in the above examples were taken from Table S. The number opposite Year 1 in the 10 percent column is $0.909. Since this is the present value of $1, to be received one year from now, the present value of $100 is 100 times this, or $90.90.

Inspection of Table S will reveal two fundamental points about present value:

1. **Present value decreases as the number of years in the future in which the payment is to be received increases.**

> *EXAMPLE:* For a rate of return of 10 percent, some present values of $1 are:

Time	Present value
1 year hence	$0.909
5 years hence	0.621
10 years hence	0.386
20 years hence	0.149

2. **Present value decreases as the rate of return increases.**

> *EXAMPLE:* For an amount to be received five years hence, some present values of $1 are:

At a rate of return of—	Present value
6%	$0.747
10	0.621
15	0.497
20	0.402

Application to investment decisions

When a company purchases a machine, it makes an **investment;** that is, it commits funds today in the expectation of earning a return on those funds over some future period. Such an investment is similar to that

---

[2] Also, computer programs and minicalculators are available that handle the calculations automatically.

made by a bank when it loans money. The essential characteristic of both types of transactions is that funds are committed today in the expectation of earning a return in the future. In the case of the bank loan, the future return is in the form of interest plus repayment of the principal. In the case of the machine, the future return is in the form of earnings generated by profitable operation of the machine. We shall designate such earnings as the **cash inflow.**

When a company is considering whether or not to purchase a new machine, the essential question that it seeks to answer is **whether the future cash inflow is likely to be large enough to warrant making the investment.** The problems discussed in this chapter all have this general structure: It is proposed that a certain amount be invested at the present time in the expectation of earning a return on this investment in future years. The question is whether the anticipated cash inflows will be large enough to justify investing this amount in the proposal. Illustrative of these problems are the following:

1. *Replacement.* Shall we replace existing equipment with more efficient equipment? The future cash inflows from the investment in the new equipment are the cost savings resulting from lower operating costs, or the cash profits from additional volume produced by the new equipment, or both.
2. *Expansion.* Shall we build a new plant? The future cash inflows from this investment are the cash profits from the products produced in the new plant.
3. *Cost reduction.* Shall we buy equipment to perform an operation now done manually; that is, shall we spend money in order to save money? The future cash inflows on this investment are the savings resulting from lower operating costs.
4. *Choice of equipment.* Which of several proposed items of equipment shall we purchase for a given purpose? The choice often turns on which item is expected to give the largest return on the investment made in it.
5. *Buy or lease.* Having decided that we need a building or a piece of equipment, should we lease it or should we buy it? The choice turns on whether or not the investment required to purchase the asset will earn an adequate return because of the cash inflows that will result from avoiding the lease payments. (Avoiding a cash outflow is equivalent to receiving a cash inflow.)
6. *New product.* Should a new product be added to the line? The choice turns on whether the expected cash inflows from the sale of the new product are large enough to warrant the investment in equipment, working capital, and the costs required to make and introduce the product.

General approach

Note that all these problems involve two quite dissimilar kinds of amounts. First, there is the investment, which is usually made in a lump sum at the beginning of the project. Although not literally made "today," it is made at a specific point in time which for analytical purposes is called "today," or **Time Zero.** Second, there is a stream of future cash inflows, which it is anticipated will result from this investment, usually over a period of years.

These two types of amounts cannot be compared directly with one another because they occur at different points in time. As we have seen, the present value of $1 today is $1, but the present value of $1 that is to be received at some time in the future is less than $1. Thus, in order to make a valid comparison, we must bring the amounts involved to equivalent values at the same point in time. This could be done in any of a number of ways. We could, for example, convert all the amounts to future values, that is, their equivalent values at the termination of the project. It is more convenient, however, to convert them to *present values,* that is, to the values at Time Zero. In order to do this, we need not adjust the amount of the investment since it is already stated at its Time Zero or present value. We need only to convert the stream of future cash inflows to their present value equivalents, and we can then compare them directly with the amount of the investment. To do this, we multiply the cash inflow for each year by the present value of $1 for that year at the appropriate rate of return. This process is called **discounting** the cash inflows. The rate at which the cash inflows are discounted is called the **required rate of return.**

The difference between the present value of the cash inflows and the amount of investment is called the net present value. If the net present value is zero or a positive number, the proposal is acceptable.

EXAMPLE: A proposed investment of $1,000 is expected to produce a cash inflow of $600 per year for each of the next two years. The required rate of return is 10 percent. The present value of the cash inflows can be compared with the present value of the investment as follows:

	Year	Amount	Present value of $1 @ 10%	Total present value
Cash inflow	1	$600	$0.909	$ 545
Cash inflow	2	600	0.826	496
Present values of cash inflows.....				1,041
Less: Investment....................				1,000
Net present value......................				$ 41

The proposed investment is acceptable.

After the amount of cash inflows has been made comparable with the amount of investment by discounting each cash flow, the basic decision rule is:

A proposed investment is acceptable if the present value of its future expected net cash inflows equals or exceeds the amount of investment.

This is a general rule and some qualifications to it will be discussed in a later section. To apply it, the approach is as follows:

1. Estimate the amount of investment.
2. Estimate the amount of cash inflow in each future year.
3. Find the present value of these cash inflows. This is done by discounting each cash inflow amount at the required rate of return.
4. Subtract the amount of investment from the total present value of the cash inflows.

We shall recapitulate by listing and defining the terms used in the above process:

Investment means the amount of funds committed to a project at Time Zero.

Cash inflow means the amounts expected to flow into the company as a consequence of making the investment. Usually cash inflows are expected for several years in the future.

Discounting means finding the present value of future cash inflows.

Required rate of return means the rate at which future cash inflows are discounted in order to find their present value. It is also called the **required earnings rate** or the **discount rate.**

Net present value means the amount by which the total present value of cash inflows exceeds the investment.

Meaning of return on investment

So far, we have shown how the present value of amounts to be received in the future can be calculated if cash inflows and the rate of return are given. It is useful to look at the situation from another viewpoint: How can the rate of return be calculated when the investment and the cash inflows are given?

Consider the familiar situation of a bank loan. When a bank lends $1,000 and receives interest payments of $80 at the end of each year for five years, with the $1,000 principal being repaid at the end of the fifth year, the bank correctly is said to have earned a return of 8 percent on its investment of $1,000. Note that the return percentage is always expressed on an annual basis and that it is found by dividing the annual return by the amount of the investment outstanding during the year. In this case, the amount of loan outstanding each year was $1,000 and the return was $80 in each year, so the rate of return was $80 ÷ $1,000, or 8 percent.

If, however, a bank lends $1,000 and is repaid $250 at the end of each year for five years, the problem of finding the return becomes more complicated. In this situation, only part of the $250 annual cash inflow represents the return, and the remainder is a repayment of part of the principal. It turns out that this loan also has a return of 8 percent, in the same sense as the loan described in the preceding paragraph: namely, the $250 annual payments will repay the loan itself and in addition will provide a

EXHIBIT 8–1
Demonstration of meaning of return on investment

Year	(a) Cash inflow	(b) Return at 8% of investment outstanding	(c) = (a) – (b) Balance, to apply against investment	(d) Investment outstanding end of year
0	$ ...	$...	$ ...	$1,000
1	250	80	170	830
2	250	66	184	646
3	250	52	198	448
4	250	36	214	234
5	250	19	231	3*

* Arises from rounding.

return of 8 percent of the *amount of principal still outstanding each year.* The fact that the return is 8 percent is demonstrated in Exhibit 8–1. Of the $250 repaid in the first year, $80, or 8 percent of the $1,000 then outstanding, is the return, and the remainder, or $170, reduces the investment, or principal, making it $830. In the second year, $66 is a return of 8 percent on the $830 of investment then outstanding, and the remainder, $184, reduces the investment to $646. And so on. (The residual of $3, rather than $0, at the end of the fifth year arises strictly from rounding; the true return is not exactly 8.000 percent.)

It can be seen from the above examples that when an investment involves annual interest payments with the full amount of the investment being repaid at its termination date, the computation of the return is simple and direct; but when the annual payments combine both principal and interest, the computation is more complicated. Some business problems are of the simple type. For example, if a business buys land for $1,000, rents it for $80 a year for five years, and then sells it for $1,000 at the end of five years, the return is 8 percent. Many business investment decisions, on the other hand, relate to depreciable assets, whose characteristic is that they have no, or very little, residual value at the end of their useful life. The cash inflow from these investments must therefore be large enough for the investor both to recoup the investment itself during its life and also to permit him or her to earn a satisfactory return on the amount not yet recouped, just as in the situation shown in Exhibit 8–1.

The concept of present value and the concept of return on investment are intimately related. To demonstrate this point, the following example applies the present value calculation to the one-year investment that was described above, for which we already know the rate of return.

EXAMPLE: Should a proposed investment of $1,000 with expected cash inflow of $1,080 one year from now be accepted if the required rate of return is 8 percent? In Table S, we find that the present value of $1 to be received one year hence at 8 percent is $0.926. The present value of $1,080 is therefore $1,080 × $0.926 = $1,000. Using the format given above:

Present value of cash inflow	$1,000
Investment	1,000
Net present value	0

The proposal is acceptable.[3]

Stream of cash inflows

The cash inflows on most business investments are not a single amount, as in the preceding example, but rather a series of amounts received over several future years as in Exhibit 8–1. The present value of the stream of cash inflows can be found by discounting each year's cash inflow by the appropriate factor from Table S.

EXAMPLE: Is a proposed investment of $1,000 with expected cash inflow of $250 a year for five years acceptable if the required rate of return is 8 percent? The present value of the cash inflows can be computed as follows:

Year	(a) Cash inflow	(b) Present value of $1 at 8% (from Table S)	(a) × (b) Present value
First	$250	$0.926	$232
Second	250	0.857	214
Third	250	0.794	198
Fourth	250	0.735	184
Fifth	250	0.681	170
Total Present Value			$998

[3] In order to illustrate certain points, the numbers in this and some other examples have been structured so that the amount of investment is the same, or almost the same, as the present value of cash inflows. Since the numbers are estimates, with an inevitable margin of error, the decisions in a real-world problem would not be as clear-cut as the examples indicate.

The total present value of the cash inflows is slightly less than $1,000, which means that the rate of return on the proposed investment would be slightly less than 8 percent; therefore, the proposal is not acceptable.

The above computation using Table S was laborious. Table A (page 724) has, for many problems, a more convenient set of present value amounts than those in Table S. It shows the present value of $1 to be received annually for *each* of the next *n* years in the future. Each number on Table A was obtained simply by cumulating, that is, adding together, the amounts for the corresponding year and all preceding years in the same column on Table S.[4] The relationship is shown in Exhibit 8–2.

EXHIBIT 8–2
Relation of Tables S and A
(present values at 10%)

Year	$1 (Table S)		$1 per year (Table A)
1	$0.909	=	$0.909
	+		
2	0.826	=	1.736
	+		
3	0.751	=	2.487
	+		
4	0.683	=	3.170
	+		
5	0.621	=	3.791

Table A can be used directly to find the present value of a stream of *equal* cash inflows received annually for any given number of years; therefore it reduces considerably the arithmetic required in problems of the type illustrated in the preceding example. Note that in order to use Table A, the amount of cash inflows must be the same for each year.

> *EXAMPLE:* Assume the same facts and question as in preceding example. Table A shows that the present value of $1 *to be received each year* for five years at 8 percent is $3.993; therefore, the present value of $250 a year for five years is $250 × $3.993 = $998, which is the same result as that computed in the preceding example.

Although the values in Table A are cumulative from Year 1, they can be used also to find the present value of a stream of cash inflows between any two points in time. The procedure is to subtract the value for the year *preceding* the first year of the cash inflow from the value for the last year of the cash inflow.

---

[4] Table A is technically known as a table of "Annuity, present value of $1."

EXAMPLE: What is the present value of $1,000 a year to be received in Years 6 through 10 if the required rate of return is 8 percent?

Solution:

Time period	Present value of $1 per year at 8%
For 10 years..	$6.710
For Years 1–5	3.993
Difference (Years 6–10)..	$2.717
For $1,000 a year: 1,000 × $2.717 =	$2,717

Other present value tables

Tables S and A are constructed on the assumption that cash inflows are received once a year and on the last day of the year. For many problems this is not a realistic assumption because cash in the form of increased revenues or lower costs is likely to flow in throughout the year. Nevertheless, annual tables are customarily used in business investment problems, on the grounds that they are easier to understand than tables constructed on other assumptions, such as monthly or continuous discounting, and that they are good enough considering the inevitable margin of error in the basic estimates.

The calculations in this book will therefore use annual tables: Table S for the present value for a single amount to be received *n* years from now; and Table A for the present value of a stream of equal amounts to be received for each of the next *n* years. The two tables are often used in combination, as illustrated in the next example, which also relates the computation discussed here to the concept of return on investment discussed at the beginning of this section.

EXAMPLE: Is a proposed investment of $1,000 with annual cash inflows of $80 a year for the next five years with the $1,000 to be repaid at the end of five years acceptable if the required rate of return is 8 percent?

Solution:

As shown by the following calculation, the cash inflows have a present value of $1,000, so the proposal is acceptable:

Year	Payment	8% discount factor	Present value
1–5..	$80/year	$3.993 (Table A)	$319
End of 5	$1,000	0.681 (Table S)	681
Total Present Value			$1,000

Notations

In the preceding examples, we have used words to describe the discount rates used to find present values. Space can be saved by using the following symbols:

For the present value of a *single* payment of $1, to be made n years in the future at a discount rate (i.e., interest rate) of i percent, use

$$S_{\overline{n}|i}$$

These amounts are found in Table S.

A stream of payments is called an *annuity*. Thus, for the present value of an annuity of $1 a year for n years at i percent, use

$$A_{\overline{n}|i}$$

These amounts are found in Table A.

EXAMPLES:

1. Label the present value of $1 to be received five years hence at a discount rate of 8 percent (from Table S):

$$S_{\overline{5}|8\%} = \$0.681$$

2. Label the present value of $1 a year to be received in the next five years at a discount rate of 8 percent (from Table A):

$$A_{\overline{5}|8\%} = \$3.993$$

Incidentally, numbers in these calculations should never be carried to cents. The present value of $100 a year for five years at 8 percent should be stated as $399, not $399.30. In most practical problems the numbers are rounded even further. To show cents gives a false impression of accuracy.

ESTIMATING THE VARIABLES

This completes the description of the concept and mechanics of calculations involving a proposed investment. In general, the analysis can be presented in the following format (in this case for a proposed $1,000 investment, with earnings of $400 a year for five years, and a required rate of return of 10 percent):

Present value of cash inflows $400 × $3.791 ($A_{\overline{5}|10\%}$)............................	$1,516
Investment...	1,000
Net present value..	$ 516

We now turn to a discussion of how to estimate each of the four elements involved in such calculations. These are:

1. The required rate of return.
2. The amount of cash inflows.
3. The economic life, which is the number of years for which cash inflows are anticipated.
4. The amount of investment.

Required rate of return

When a bank loans money at an interest rate of 8 percent, it does so with the knowledge that repayment of the loan plus interest is *highly likely*. But when a company makes an investment in machinery, plant, or similar income-producing assets, the return is much less certain. The return depends on the cash inflows that actually will be generated by the investment; and, as will be explained in the next section, these cash inflows usually cannot be estimated accurately in advance. Because of this greater uncertainty, the business executive ordinarily requires a greater return on investments in tangible assets than a banker requires on a loan. The selection of an appropriate required rate of return is a crucial top management decision.

Two alternative ways of arriving at the required rate of return will be described: (1) trial and error and (2) cost of capital.

Trial and error. Recall that the higher the required rate of return, the lower the present value of the cash inflows. It follows that the higher the required rate of return, the fewer investment proposals will have cash inflows whose present value exceeds the amount of the investment. Thus, if a given rate results in the rejection of many proposed investments that management intuitively feels are acceptable, there is an indication that this rate is too high, and a lower rate is selected. Conversely, if a given rate results in the acceptance of a flood of projects, there is an indication that it is too low. As a starting point in this trial-and-error process, companies often select a rate of return that other companies in the same industry use.

Cost of capital. In economic theory, the required rate of return should be equal to the company's **cost of capital,** which is the cost of debt capital plus the cost of equity capital, weighted by the relative amount of each in the company's capital structure.

> EXAMPLE: Assume a company in which the cost of debt capital (e.g., bonds) is 4 percent and the cost of equity capital (e.g., common stock) is 15 percent, and in which 40 percent of the total capital is debt and 60 percent is equity.[5] The cost of capital is calculated as follows:

Type	Capital cost	Weight	Weighted
Debt (bonds)	4%	0.4	1.6%
Equity (stock)	15	0.6	9.0
Total		1.0	10.6%

Thus, the cost of capital is 10.6 percent or, rounded, 11 percent. In the above example, the 4 percent used as the cost of debt capital may appear

---

[5] For a more complete description of debt capital and equity capital, see *Fundamentals of Financial Accounting,* Chapters 12 and 13.

to be low. It is low because it has been adjusted for the income tax effect of debt financing. The reason for making such an adjustment is discussed in Chapter 9.

The difficulty with the cost-of-capital approach is that although the cost of debt capital is usually known within narrow limits, the cost of equity capital is difficult to estimate realistically.[6] Presumably, the rate of return that investors expect, which is the cost of equity capital, is reflected in the market price of the company's stock, but the market price is also influenced by such other factors as general conditions of the economy, investors' estimate of the company's future earnings, and dividend policy. Techniques for isolating the cost of equity capital from these other factors are complicated; moreover, they do not usually give reliable results. For this reason, the cost-of-capital approach is not widely used in practice.

Selection of a rate.   Most companies use a judgmental approach in establishing the required rate of return. Either they experiment with various rates, by the trial-and-error method described above, or they judgmentally settle upon a rate of 10 percent, 15 percent, or 20 percent because they feel that elaborate calculations are likely to be fruitless. In the examples in this book, a required rate of return of 10 percent is usually used. This seems to be a widely used rate in industrial companies, and it is the rate prescribed by the federal government for use in the analysis of proposed government investments. Few industrial companies would use a lower rate than 10 percent. Higher rates are used in certain industries in which profit opportunities are unusually good.

The required rate of return is higher than the going rate of interest on bonds or other types of debt capital. Because bondholders have a prior claim on both their interest and on their principal in the event of liquidation, an investment in bonds is less risky to the investor than an investment in the common stock of the same company. The return demanded for an investment varies with its risk; therefore, an investor in stock requires a higher return than an investor in bonds. Since the overall rate of return is an average of the return for bonds and the return for stocks, it is bound to be higher than the return for bonds alone.

Allowance for risk.   The required rate of return that is selected by the techniques described above applies to investment proposals of *average* risk. For essentially the same reason that the required rate of return for capital investment projects in general is higher than interest rates on debt, the return expected on an individual investment project of greater-than-average risk and uncertainty should be higher than the average rate of return on all projects. Conceptually, it would be possible to use a higher-

---

[6] For methods of deriving such estimates, see Hunt, Williams, and Donaldson, *Basic Business Finance: Text and Cases,* 4th ed. (Homewood, Ill.: Richard D. Irwin, Inc., 1971).

than-average required rate of return in the calculation of the net present value of projects of higher-than-average risk and uncertainty, but in practice most companies do not do this. Instead, they either introduce an element of conservatism into the calculations by deliberately shortening the estimate of economic life or lowering the estimate of cash inflows, or they take the risk characteristics into account as a judgmental matter when the final decision on the project is made. A few companies use mathematical techniques that are designed to incorporate an allowance for uncertainty; these techniques are described in advanced texts.

Cash inflows

The cash inflows that result from an investment consist of two elements. The first, and by far the more important, is the stream of annual inflows that results from operations that the investment makes possible. The second is the inflow that may result at the end of the project's economic life; it arises from the residual value of the assets. Since this latter inflow is usually unimportant, and often nonexistent, the term *cash inflows* can be taken to mean inflows from operations unless specific mention is made of residual values.

Operating cash inflows.   The operating cash inflows are often called the *earnings* from the investment. They are essentially the additional *cash* that the company estimates will flow in as a consequence of making the company's cash inflow would be if it did not make the investment. The *differential* concept emphasized in Chapters 6 and 7 is therefore equally applicable here, and the discussion in Chapters 6 and 7 should carefully be kept in mind in estimating cash inflows for the type of problem now being considered. In particular, recall that the focus is on cash inflows; accounting numbers derived from the accrual concept or from the allocation of overhead costs are not necessarily relevant.

Consider, for example, a proposal to replace an existing machine with a better machine. What are the cash inflows associated with this proposed investment? We note first that the existing machine must still be usable, for if it can no longer perform its function, there is no alternative and hence no analytical problem; it *must* be replaced. The comparison, therefore, is between (1) continuing to use the existing machine (the base case, or Case 1) and (2) operating the proposed machine (Case 2). The existing machine has certain labor, material, power, repair, maintenance, and other costs associated with its future operation. If the alternative machine is proposed as a means of reducing costs, there will be different, lower costs associated with its use. The difference between these two amounts of cost is the cash inflow anticipated if the new machine is acquired. These cash inflows usually are estimated on an annual basis.

Note that the cash inflows are arrived at by comparing the estimated costs associated with the proposed machine with the estimated costs associated with continuing to operate the existing machine. The relevant costs are therefore differential costs, the costs that are different in the proposed investment from those in the base case.

If the proposed machine increases the company's productive capacity, and if the increased output can be sold, the differential income on this increased volume is a cash inflow anticipated from the use of the proposed machine. This differential income is the difference between the added sales revenue and the incremental costs required to produce that sales revenue. These costs usually include direct material, direct labor, direct selling costs, and any other costs that would not be incurred if the increased volume were not manufactured and sold.

In short, the cash inflows from an investment are either a reduction in cash costs, an increase in cash receipts, or some combination. A reduction in costs has the same effect on the company's income as an equal increase in receipts.

Depreciation. **Depreciation on the proposed equipment is not an item of differential cost.** Depreciation is omitted from the calculation of net present value because the procedure itself allows for the recovery of the investment. When we say (as in a preceding example) that an investment of $1,000 which produces a cash inflow of $400 a year for five years has a net present value of $516 at a required earnings rate of 10 percent, we mean that the cash inflow is large enough to (1) recover the investment of $1,000, (2) earn 10 percent on the amount of investment outstanding, and (3) earn $516 in addition. The recovery of investment is equivalent to the sum of the annual depreciation charges that are made in the accounting records; therefore it would be incorrect to include a separate item for depreciation in calculating cash inflow.

One of the most common errors made in analyzing proposed investments in depreciable assets is to include depreciation as an element of cost. It is important to remember that the technique described here provides for recovery *of* the investment as well as earnings *on* the investment. To include depreciation would be double counting.

Depreciation on the existing equipment is likewise not relevant because the book value of existing equipment represents a sunk cost. For the reason explained in Chapter 7, sunk costs should be disregarded.

Make-or-buy proposals. In Chapter 7 we discussed the type of problem in which the company is considering buying from an outside vendor a part which it is now making. Ordinarily, such a proposal does not involve an investment. The converse of this problem, in which the company is considering making an item that it is now buying, *does* involve an investment and therefore belongs in this chapter. The investment is the cost of the additional equipment that will be purchased in order to manufacture the item. The cash inflow on such a proposal is the *difference* between the price paid to the outside vendor for the item and the cash costs that will be incurred if the item is made by the company.

EXAMPLE: Part No. 102 is currently purchased from an outside vendor at a price of $10 per unit. It is proposed that the part be manufactured. Equipment with a cost of $18,000 and an economic life of five years would be purchased. The required rate of return is 10 percent. The cash costs of making the part, including direct labor, direct material, and other direct costs, are estimated to be $6 per unit. Annual requirements are 1,000 units. The annual cash inflow is:

Purchase cost of Part No. 102 (1,000 × $10)	$10,000
Cost of making Part No. 102 (1,000 × $6)	−6,000
Annual cash inflow	$ 4,000

The calculation of the net present value is:

Present value of cash inflows:

$4,000 × $3.791 ($A_{5\rceil 10\%}$)	$15,164
Investment	18,000
Net present value..	$ (2,836)

Conclusion: The part should continue to be purchased.

Buy-or-lease proposals. The proposal under consideration may be whether to buy an asset or to lease it. (Usually, such a proposal is considered *after* the basic decision to acquire and use the asset has been made.) If the asset is bought, the purchase price represents an investment. If the asset is leased, no investment is required; instead a series of lease payments must be made. By buying the asset, the cash outflows for the lease payments are not required, and the avoidance of these outflows therefore constitutes the cash inflows on the investment. In other words, if the investment is made, there will be no cash outflows for lease payments. The avoidance of these cash outflows is equivalent to cash inflows resulting from the investment. If the lessor agrees to perform certain services, such as maintenance or insurance, then these should be subtracted from the lease payments because such services would also be required if the asset were purchased, and they therefore are not differential.

EXAMPLE: A company has decided to acquire a computer. It can be purchased for $100,000, or it can be leased for $22,000 a year. The lease payment includes maintenance service, which the company estimates is worth $2,000 a year. The estimated economic life of the computer is eight years. The required rate of return is 10 percent.

The calculation is as follows:

Cash inflow:

Saving in annual lease payments........................	$22,000
Less maintenance included in payments	2,000
Annual cash inflow	$20,000

Present value of cash inflows:

$20,000 \times \$5.335$ ($A_{\overline{8}\|10\%}$)	$106,700
Investment	100,000
Net present value..	$ 6,700

Conclusion: The machine should be purchased, rather than leased.

Uncertainties. Since investments in machinery and other operational assets are usually expected to produce cash inflows for a number of years, the earnings estimates may well extend a considerable distance into the future. The farther ahead one attempts to make estimates, the more uncertain they become. Estimates of the relatively distant future must be treated accordingly; that is, as rough approximations rather than as numbers that have a high degree of precision.

Inflation. A particularly troublesome aspect of estimating cash inflows is what assumption to make about future changes in price levels. If the analyst believes, as many people do, that labor rates and material prices will generally tend to move upward indefinitely, it may be desirable to incorporate in the estimate of cash inflows an explicit adjustment for the effect of inflation. For example, if there is an estimated annual savings of direct labor of 1,000 hours per year, and if the current direct labor cost is $5 per hour, the annual savings will be $5,000 currently; but it will be some higher amount if the hourly cost increases in the future. If annual wage increases of 5 percent are foreseen, then the saving will be $5,250 in the second year, $5,512 in the third year, and so on. Despite the likelihood of such increases, many companies do not make an adjustment for inflation. They reason that the rate of inflation is highly uncertain and that its effect on the total company's operations are so unpredictable that the effort to make the adjustment is not worthwhile, or that cost increases will be offset by equivalent increases in selling prices.

Income taxes. In most investment problems the effect of income taxes must be taken into account. Because the procedure for doing this is fairly complicated, this subject is deferred to Chapter 9.

Residual value. A machine may have a **residual value** (i.e., salvage or resale value) at the end of its economic life. In a great many cases, the estimated residual value is so small and occurs so far in the future that it has no significant effect on the decision. Moreover, any salvage or resale value that is realized may be approximately offset by removal and dismantling costs. In situations where the estimated residual value is significant, the net residual value (after removal costs) is viewed as a future cash inflow in the year of disposal. Other assets, such as repair parts or inventory, may also be liquidated at the end of the project; and these are treated in the same fashion.

EXAMPLE: The economic life of a proposed riverboat is estimated to be 20 years. It is estimated that the boat could be sold at the end of 20 years for $50,000. Costs associated with making the sale would be $5,000. The present value of the residual value is computed as follows:

Resale value at end of Year 20	$50,000
Cost of making the sale	−5,000
Net proceeds	$45,000
Present value of $45,000 in Year 20 = $45,000 × $0.149 ($S_{\overline{20}|10\%}$)	$ 6,700

(Note that the present value, which actually works out to $6,705, has been deliberately rounded in view of the uncertainty of the estimate. Even greater rounding, say to $7,000, would be acceptable.)

Economic life

The economic life of an investment is the number of years over which cash inflows are expected as a consequence of making the investment. Even though cash inflows may be expected for an indefinitely long period, the economic life is usually set at a specified maximum number of years, such as 10, 15, or 20. This maximum is often shorter than the life that is actually anticipated both because of the uncertainty of cash inflow estimates for distant years and because the present value of cash inflows for distant years is so low that the amount of these cash inflows has no significant effect on the calculation. For example, at a discount rate of 10 percent, a $1 cash inflow in Year 21 has a present value of only 15 cents, and the *total* present value of a $1 cash inflow in *each* of the 30 years from Year 21 through Year 50 is only $1.40.

The end of the period selected for the economic life of a proposed investment is called the investment horizon. The word "horizon" suggests that beyond this time cash inflows are not visible. Economic life can rarely be estimated exactly; nevertheless, it is important that the best possible estimate be made, for the economic life has a significant effect on the calculations.

When a proposed project involves the purchase of equipment, the economic life of the investment corresponds to the estimated useful life of the equipment to the user. There is a tendency, when thinking about the life of a machine, to consider primarily its **physical life,** that is, the number of years the machine will provide service before it wears out. The physical life of an automobile, for example, is more than 10 years; and that of a brick building more than 50 years. Although the physical life is an upper limit, in most cases the economic life of an asset is considerably shorter than its physical life.

There are several reasons for this. Technological progress makes machinery obsolete. Improvements will almost certainly be made sometime in all machines now in existence, but the question of *which* machines will be improved and *how soon* the improved machines will be on the market is a most difficult one to answer. Unless special information is available, the answer can be little more than an educated guess. Yet it is a guess that must be made, for the investment in a machine will cease to earn a return when it is replaced by an improved machine.

The economic life also ends when the company ceases to make profitable use of the machine. This can happen because the particular operation performed by the machine is made unnecessary by a change in style or a change in process, or because the market for the product itself has vanished, or because the company decides, for whatever reason, to discontinue the product. A machine for making buggy whips may last physically for 100 years; yet such a machine cannot continue to earn a return on its investment after the buggy whips produced on it are no longer in demand. The uncertainties associated with product demand vary widely with different industries. The equipment used to make a novelty item, such as a skateboard, may have an economic life of only a few years — perhaps only a single year — whereas a nuclear power reactor may reasonably be expected to provide cash inflows for several decades.

Finally, the economic life of a machine ends if the company goes out of business. Most managements quite properly operate on the premise that the company will be in business for a long time to come. There are instances, however, when management foresees an end to the business, or to a particular part of it, in the relatively near future. In such a case, the economic life of a machine is limited to the period during which management believes the business is going to operate.

The key question is: Over what period of time is the investment likely to generate cash inflows for this company? For whatever reason, when the investment no longer produces cash inflows, its economic life has ended. In view of the uncertainties associated with the operation of a business, most companies are conservative in estimating what the economic life of a proposed investment will be.

Investment

The investment is the amount of funds that a company risks if it accepts an investment proposal. The relevant investment costs are the differential costs. These are the outlays that will be made if the project is undertaken and that will not be made if it is not undertaken. For simplicity, they are regarded as being made at Time Zero, although some of these outlays may be made somewhat earlier than when the investment starts to generate cash inflows. The cost of the machine itself, its shipping costs, cost of installation, and the cost of training operators are examples of differential investment costs. These outlays are part of the investment, even though some of them may not be capitalized in the accounting records.

Existing equipment. If the purchase of new equipment results in the sale of existing equipment, the net proceeds from the sale reduces the amount of the differential investment. In other words, the differential investment is the total amount of *additional* funds that must be committed to the investment project. The net proceeds from existing equipment are its selling price less any costs incurred in making the sale and in dismantling and removing the equipment.

> EXAMPLE: Following is the calculation of the investment for the proposed purchase of a Beager shirt-pressing machine for a laundry:

Gross investment:		
Cost of new Beager Model 85...............................		$18,585
Freight from factory		525
Installation, including new wiring...........................		600
Training of operators..		300
Gross investment		20,010
Less proceeds from sale of old Beager Model 70:		
Sales price	$1,000	
Less: Packing and crating..................................	−100	
Net proceeds		900
Net investment...		$19,110

Sunk costs. In Chapter 7 we emphasized that sunk costs are irrelevant. If $100,000 already has been expended for research on a new product and if the new product will require an additional investment in new facilities of $50,000, the relevant investment figure is $50,000, not $150,000. The $100,000 is a sunk cost. Human nature is such that there is a temptation to try to work sunk costs such as these into the calculation, but this temptation must be resisted. In considering a proposed investment, the analyst must always look forward, never backward. Only future events and their associated costs and revenues are relevant to current decisions.

Investments in working capital. An investment is the commitment or locking up, of funds in any type of asset. Although up to this point depreciable assets have been used as examples, investments also include commitments of funds to additional inventory and to other current assets. In particular, if the proposal is to produce a new product, additional funds will probably be required for inventories, accounts receivable, and increased cash needs. Part of this increase in current assets may be supplied from increased accounts payable and accrued expenses; the remainder must come from permanent capital. This additional working capital is as much a part of the differential investment as the equipment itself.

Often it is reasonable to assume that the *residual value* of investments in working capital is approximately the same as the amount of the initial investment; that is, that at the end of the project, these items can be liquidated at their cost. Under these circumstances, the amount of working capital is treated as a cash inflow in the last year of the project, and its present value is found by discounting that amount at the required rate of return.

EXAMPLE: A proposed new product is estimated to require an investment of $300,000 in equipment and $100,000 in additional working capital (primarily for accounts receivable and inventory). The economic life of the proposal is estimated to be ten years. At the end of that time, the equipment is estimated to have a net residual value of zero, but working capital can probably be liquidated at the full amount of $100,000. The calculation of the investment is as follows:

Equipment..	$300,000
Working capital..	100,000
Total Investment	$400,000

At the end of Year 10 there will be a cash inflow from the release of the $100,000 working capital. Its present value is found by multiplying $100,000 by $0.386 ($S_{\overline{10}|10\%}$). This present value of $38,600 should be included as one of the cash inflows associated with the project.

NONMONETARY CONSIDERATIONS

We have described the quantitative analysis involved in a capital investment proposal. It should be emphasized that this analysis does not provide the complete solution to the problem because it encompasses only those elements that can be reduced to numbers. A full consideration of the problem involves nonmonetary factors. Many investments are undertaken without a calculation of net present value. They may be necessary for the safety of employees; they may be undertaken for the convenience or comfort of employees (such as a new cafeteria or a new recreation room); they may be undertaken to enhance community relations, or because they are required in order to meet pollution control or other legal requirements, or because they increase plant protection safeguards. For some proposals of this type, no economic analysis is necessary; if an unsafe condition is found, it must be corrected regardless of the cost. For other proposals, these nonmonetary factors must be considered along with the numbers that are included in the economic analysis. For all proposals, the decision maker must take into account the fact that all the numbers are estimates, and that personal judgment as to the validity of these estimates must be used in arriving at a decision.

Based on a survey of 177 industrial companies, Fremgen reports that only 27 percent believed that the economic analysis was the most critical part of the decision process and only 12 percent believed it was the most difficult.[7] The others said that the proper definition of the proposal, the estimation of cash inflows, and the implementation of a decision after it had been made were more important. Thus, the techniques described in this chapter are by no means the whole story. They are, however, the only part of the story that can be described as a definite procedure; the remainder must be learned through experience.

Overall analytical process

The technique described above is often called the **net present value method.** Following is a summary of the steps involved in using this method in analyzing a proposed investment:

1. Select a required rate of return. Presumably, once selected, this rate will be used in all calculations. It need not be reconsidered for each proposal.
2. Find the differential investment, which includes the additional outlays made at Time Zero, less the net proceeds from disposal of existing equipment.
3. Estimate the economic life of the proposed project.
4. Estimate the differential cash inflows for each year during the economic life.
5. Estimate the residual values at the end of the economic life, which consist of the disposal value of equipment and working capital that is to be released.
6. Find the present value of all the inflows identified in Steps 4 and 5 by discounting them at the required rate of return, using Table S for a single amount or Table A for a series of annual flows.
7. Find the net present value by subtracting the differential investment from the present value of the inflows. If the net present value is zero or positive, decide that the proposal is acceptable, insofar as the monetary factors are concerned.
8. Taking into account the nonmonetary factors, reach a final decision. (This part of the process is at least as important as all the other parts put together, but there is no way of generalizing about it.)

DEMONSTRATION CASE

As an aid to visualizing the relationships in a proposed investment, it is often useful to diagram the flows similar to that illustrated in Exhibit 8–3.

This flow diagram reflects the following investment proposal. A pro-

---

[7] James M. Fremgen, "Capital Budgeting Practices; a Survey," *Management Accounting,* May 1973, p. 19.

EXHIBIT 8–3
Cash-flow diagram

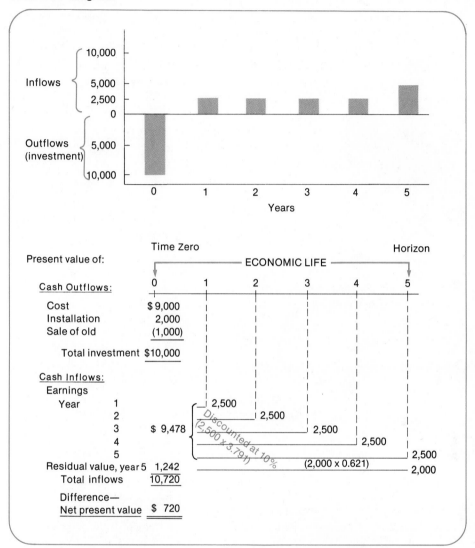

posed machine will cost $9,000, and $2,000 will be spent to install it. It will replace an existing machine which has a book value of $2,000, but which can be sold for $1,000. It is estimated that the machine will save $2,500 a year in labor costs, that its economic life is five years, and that it can be sold at the end of that time for $2,000, net of removal costs. The company requires a rate of return of 10 percent. Should the proposed machine be purchased?

Analysis:

(This analysis is arranged in order of the steps given above.)

1. The required rate of return is 10 percent. (The company derived this rate by one of the approaches described above.)
2. The estimated investment is the $9,000 purchase price, plus the $2,000 installation cost, less the $1,000 resale value of the existing equipment, or $10,000. The $2,000 book value of the existing equipment is a sunk cost and is irrelevant.
3. The estimated economic life is five years.
4. The estimated cash inflows are $2,500 a year for five years.
5. The estimated residual value is $2,000 at the end of Year 5.
6. The present values are computed as follows:

Cash inflows	Amount	Year	Table	Factor	Present value
From operations.....................	$2,500/year	1–5	A	$3.791	$ 9,478
Residual..............................	2,000	5	S	0.621	1,242
Total Present Value of Inflows......................					$10,720

7. The net present value is:

Inflows...	$10,720
Investment	10,000
Net present value.......................................	$ 720

8. Unless there are nonmonetary factors that weight the decision in the other direction, the proposal is acceptable.

SUMMARY

A capital investment problem is essentially one of determining whether the anticipated cash inflows from a proposed project are sufficiently attractive to warrant risking the investment of funds in the project. The investment is typically made at one moment of time, whereas cash inflows occur over a period of time in the future. The analytical technique must take this difference in timing into account. This is done by using the concept of present value, namely, that an amount of money to be received in the future has a lower value, today, than the same amount of money that is on hand today. Tables are available that show the present value of amounts that are to be received at any specified time in the future and also amounts that are to be received annually for a specified number of years.

The basic decision rule is that a proposal is acceptable if the present value of the cash inflows expected to be derived from it exceeds the amount of the investment. In order to use this rule, one must estimate: (1) the required rate of return, (2) the amount of cash inflow in each year, (3) the economic life, and (4) the amount of investment.

The required rate of return is the minimum rate that a company expects to earn on its investments. Although usually arrived at judgmentally, it is sometimes possible to arrive at it by computing the company's cost of capital. The cash inflows are discounted at the required rate of return.

Cash inflows are those that are anticipated as a consequence of the investment. They are differential inflows, in the same sense as those discussed in Chapter 7. Depreciation on the proposed assets is not a cash flow. If there is a residual value, its present value is also a cash inflow.

Economic life is the number of years that the investment is expected to generate cash inflows. It is never longer than the physical life of the assets acquired, and is usually shorter than the physical life, reflecting the likelihood that technological improvements, the discontinuance of the product line, or other factors will cause a cessation of earnings prior to the expiration of physical life.

The amount of investment is the differential amount of funds that will be committed to the project. It includes not only the invoice cost of the assets themselves but also all costs associated with making the assets ready to begin producing cash inflows. Also, it includes working capital required for the project. The gross amount of investment is reduced by the net proceeds from the sale of assets that are disposed of if the project is undertaken.

The foregoing are monetary considerations that can be incorporated in an economic analysis. Nonmonetary considerations are also important in making the actual decision; they are often as important as the monetary considerations and are in some cases so important that no economic analysis is worthwhile.

IMPORTANT TERMS

Present value   Net present value
Investment   Cost of capital
Cash inflow   Residual value
Time Zero   Economic life
Discounting   Investment horizon
Required rate of return

QUESTIONS FOR DISCUSSION

1. In a "Christmas Club" plan, a person deposits a specified amount weekly in a bank savings account and the total amount accumulated is paid back just before Christmas. No interest, or very little interest, is paid on these deposits. Is a Christmas Club member acting irrationally by depositing

money under these conditions? Would a business be acting irrationally if it joined a Christmas Club? Explain.

2. Would you prefer cash inflows of $600 a year for four years or cash inflows of $400 a year for six years, assuming your required rate of return is 10 percent? Explain. Is there any required rate of return that would change your answer?

3. In what one way do the problems discussed in this chapter differ from the alternative choice problems discussed in Chapter 7?

4. The true return in Exhibit 8–1 is not exactly 8.000 percent. Is it slightly higher than 8.000 percent, or is it slightly lower? Explain.

5. Table A is used to find the present value of a stream of equal annual cash inflows. Suppose that payments were $250 a year in each of Years 2, 3, 4, and 5, and $300 in Year 1. Without making calculations, explain how Table A could be used in such a situation.

6. If the required rate of return is 8 percent and the investment is $1,000, is the proposal described in Question 5 acceptable? Answer without making calculations. (Hint: Compare these facts with those in the example on page 318.)

7. "A proposal that has zero net present value should be rejected because the company will get no return on its capital." Comment.

8. "Our company can borrow money at not more than 9 percent interest. Therefore our cost of capital can't be higher than 9 percent." Comment.

9. Should the discount rate used on unusually risky proposals be higher or lower than the rate used on proposals of average risk? Explain your answer carefully.

10. "The higher a company's required rate of return, the more money the company will be willing to invest because the more it will earn." Comment.

11. Companies are said to expect higher profits on investments in underdeveloped countries than in Western European countries with stable economic conditions, and this is said to be an example of exploitation of underdeveloped countries. Is there another explanation for this?

12. Is a stream of relatively certain cash inflows preferable to a stream of cash inflows of the same annual amount that is relatively uncertain? Why?

13. Why is the cost-of-capital method not widely used in practice?

14. It is said that investors basically have a choice between eating well and sleeping well. Explain what is meant by this statement, using differences in required rates of return in your explanation.

15. Explain why depreciation on the proposed equipment is omitted from the calculation of net present value.

16. "Depreciation is most certainly an item of cost. Any decision model that ignores depreciation is wrong." Comment.

17. How does the economic life of a jet aircraft compare with the economic life of the airport runways that the aircraft uses? Why?

18. Why is the economic life of a machine usually shorter than its physical life? Is the economic life ever longer than the physical life?

19. For each of the following types of investment projects, state how estimates should be made of the investment, the economic life, and the cash inflows:
    a. Building a new plant.
    b. Replacing existing equipment with more efficient equipment.
    c. Buying a machine to perform an operation now done manually.
    d. Adding a new product.

20. A company has invested $100,000 to develop a new item of electronic equipment, but it doesn't operate properly. It then decides to invest $50,000 additional, but the equipment still doesn't work. Under what circumstances would the company be well advised to spend yet another $50,000?

21. The techniques discussed in this chapter are applicable to capital investment decisions in government and other nonprofit organizations. Suppose a proposal is made to introduce labor-saving equipment in a maintenance shop of a nonprofit organization. What one change needs to be made in the approach described in the text?

22. How would you go about finding the cost of capital for the federal government? For a university that has a large endowment fund?

PROBLEMS

Note: Disregard income taxes in these problems.

8–1. The following is taken from a "financial advice" column in a daily newspaper:

Question. A professor friend tells me that whenever he buys a new car he takes out a passbook loan and it only costs him 2 percent on a $5,000 loan.

His reasoning is that if the bank pays him 5 percent on his savings and puts a 7 percent charge on his loan, his total cost is 2 percent.

I think my friend is 100 percent wrong because no matter how he juggles these figures he's still paying 7 percent—therefore his cost is 7 percent. Right?

Answer. In theory, of course, your friend is right: if he could buy a car on a 7 percent loan and use his passbook as collateral (on which he is earning interest of 5 percent), then the total cost to him would be 2 percent.

Using your passbook as collateral is the cheapest way to borrow money from a bank (at a rate about 2 percentage points above your passbook rate), but why shouldn't it be? After all, the bank isn't doing a thing but lending you your own money, skimming off 2 percent, and blocking you from using your own money for any other purpose. Under those circumstances, I'd lend it to you myself.

Required:

Is the answer correct? Explain.

8–2. To be sure that you understand how to use Tables S and A, solve the following and show your computations:

A. What is the present value of $5,000 to be received at the end of five years if the required rate of return is 12 percent?

B. What is the present value of $1,000 per year for each of the next five years if the required rate of return is 12 percent?

C. What is the present value of $8,000 to be received at the end of four years if the required rate of return is 8 percent?

D. What is the present value of $1,700 per year for each of the next four years if the required rate of return is 8 percent?

E. What is the present value of an investment which is expected to produce cash inflows of $2,500 per year in Years 1 through 3 and $1,500 per year in Years 4 through 5 if the required rate of return is 10 percent?

F. What is the present value of an investment which is expected to produce cash inflows of $2,500 in Year 1, $2,000 in Year 2, and $1,500 in Year 3 if the required rate of return is 10 percent?

G. What is the present value of an investment which is expected to produce cash inflows of $2,000 per year for each of the next six years plus $1,200 at the end of Year 6 if the required rate of return is 12 percent?

H. What rate of return is earned on an investment which produces cash inflows of $1,000 per year for six years and has a present value of $3,889?

8-3. The Ellis Company estimates that it can save $3,100 per year in cash operating costs over the next ten years if it buys a new machine at a cost of $12,000. The machine will have no residual value, and the required rate of return is 12 percent.

Required:

A. Calculate the net present value of the proposed investment in the new machine.

B. Do you recommend that Ellis purchase the machine? Why?

C. Assuming that the new machine would save only $2,500 per year for five years, recalculate the net present value. Do you recommend purchase? Why?

8-4. The Bowmar Company is considering three proposed investments, A, B, and C. Each requires an investment of $4,900, and each has an economic life of three years and total cash inflow over that period of $6,000. The pattern of cash inflows for each proposal differs, however, as indicated below:

	Annual cash inflows		
Year	A	B	C
1	$1,000	$2,000	$3,000
2	2,000	2,000	2,000
3	3,000	2,000	1,000
	$6,000	$6,000	$6,000

Required:

A. Calculate the net present value of each proposal if the required rate of return is 10 percent.

B. Do you recommend that Bowman make any or all of the proposed investments? Why?

C. Explain why the net present values of the three proposed investments differ even though the total cash inflow is the same for all three.

8–5. The Burgess Company has a capital structure which is 30 percent debt and 70 percent equity. The cost of debt capital is 5 percent, and the cost of equity capital is 13 percent.

Required:

A. Calculate the cost of capital for Burgess.

B. Burgess needs to raise additional capital and is considering a new issue of bonds that would raise the debt portion of the capital structure to 40 percent and raise the cost of debt capital to 6 percent. Recalculate the cost of capital for Burgess assuming the new bonds are issued.

8–6. Last year Main Line Company installed a group of machines with the expectation of substantial labor cost savings. The expected results for the first year of operations follow:

Cost of machines, installed	$15,000
Useful life	5 years
Labor savings	$ 6,000
Increased power costs	450
Increased insurance and property taxes	550

The company actually paid $15,500 for the machines as installation costs were greater than expected. Actual labor savings were only $5,700. Maintenance costs had been expected to remain unchanged, but they increased $600. All other costs were as expected.

Required:

A. Assuming the company has a required earnings rate of 15 percent, should the proposal have been accepted, based on expected results? Show all computations.

B. If all other costs remain the same as the actual results of the first year of operations, do you feel this company made a sound investment decision? Comment.

8–7. The Jane Company has just developed a new product which is expected to have the following projected cash inflows over the economic life of the project.

Year	Cash flow
1	$25,000
2	30,000
3	35,000
4	40,000

Jane does not invest in productive assets unless they feel the investment will return at least 20 percent. The equipment necessary to produce the product can be bought or made by Jane.

Required:

A. Calculate the maximum amount of capital investment which can be budgeted for if the company undertakes the production of the new product under the conditions shown above.

B. Assume that the cash inflow is expected to be $32,500 each year for four years instead of the flows above. Recalculate the maximum amount of capital investment which can be budgeted.

C. Explain why your answers to Requirements A and B differ.

8–8. Parsons Company is considering the purchase of a new machine to replace an existing machine. The purchase price is $10,000 delivered and installed. The new machine is estimated to produce savings of $2,000 in direct labor and other direct costs annually, as compared with the present equipment. The new machine has an estimated economic life of ten years and zero residual value. The company requires a rate of return of 20 percent of an investment of this type.

Required (consider each part separately):

A. Assuming the present equipment has zero book value and zero salvage value, should the new machine be purchased?

B. Assuming the present equipment has a book value of $4,800 (cost $8,000, less accumulated depreciation of $3,200) and zero salvage value today, should the new machine be purchased?

C. Assuming the present equipment has a book value of $4,800 and a salvage value today of $3,000, should the new machine be purchased?

D. Assume that the new machine will save only $1,000 a year, but that its estimated economic life is 20 years. Other conditions are as described in Requirement A. Should the new machine be purchased?

E. Assume that estimated savings are $2,500 in each of the first five years and $1,500 in each of the next five years. Other conditions are as described in Requirement A. Should the new machine be purchased?

8–9. Parsons Company decided to buy the machine described in Problem 8–8 (hereafter called "Model A" machine). Two years later Model B machine comes on the market. Model B costs $20,000 delivered and installed, and it is estimated to result in annual savings of $5,000 as compared with the cost of operating the Model A machine, and to have an economic life of ten years. Because the Model B machine is such an improvement, the Model A machine has no resale value.

Required:

A. What action should the company take?

B. If the company purchases the Model B machine, a mistake has been made somewhere because the Model A machine, purchased only two years previously, is being scrapped. How did this mistake come about?

8–10. The City Bus Company has just installed a new machine for washing its buses. The machine cost $16,000, and its annual operating costs exclusive of depreciation are expected to be $12,000. It will have a four-year useful life and no salvage value.

After the first day of use, a machine salesperson tells the company about a better bus washing machine which costs $20,000 and will do the same job for an annual operating cost of $8,000 exclusive of depreciation. The new machine has a four-year useful life and no salvage value. The market for used bus washers is rather weak, and the original machine can be sold to net only $9,000.

Required:

A. Should City Bus buy the new bus washer or keep its day-old machine? Support your answer with computations.

B. Is the cost of the original washer relevant to the decision on the new washer? Explain your answer.

8–11. The County Board of Education has decided to acquire a computer. It can be purchased for $152,000 or leased for $31,000 a year. The lease payment includes maintenance which is estimated to be worth $2,500 a year. The estimated economic life of the computer is eight years, and it is expected to have a residual value of $10,000. Additional working capital of $2,000 will be required and can be recovered at the end of eight years. The County uses a 10 percent rate in the analysis of proposed investments.

Required:

Should the County Board of Education lease or purchase the computer? Show computations to support your answer.

8–12. Bill Coyne is considering opening a self-service laundromat which would require an investment of $54,000 for washers, dryers, and related equipment. Bill estimates that the equipment will have a seven-year life, and seeks a return of 25 percent without regard to tax considerations, which he recognizes will reduce his actual return.

Bill plans to charge $0.50 for the use of a washing machine and $0.25 for the use of a dryer for 25 minutes. He has estimated that he will gross $450 and $225 from the washers and dryers respectively each week. Variable costs would amount to $0.04 per wash for water and electricity and $0.03 per 25-minute dryer cycle for gas and electricity. Bill has estimated that his monthly fixed expenses will consist of rent of $450 and maintenance and cleanup labor of $200.

Required:

Can Bill Coyne obtain the return he desires, given the revenue and expense estimates? Show computations to support your answer.

8–13. C. Smith of the Smith-Link Company is considering the purchase of a new machine to replace older, less efficient machinery with a net book value of $35,000. The new machine carries a $220,000 price tag, which includes delivery and installation. Smith knows that she will incur a loss of $25,000 on the sale of the old machinery, which bothers her, since she is convinced that the present machinery will probably last as long as the proposed new machinery would. Smith has estimated the economic life of the new machine to be 30 years. On the other hand, Smith's cost accountants have told her that the new machinery would save the company $18,650 annually in reduced labor and material costs. The required rate of return is 12 percent.

Required:

What would the net present value of the new machinery be if it were to be purchased? Show your computations.

8-14. The Lance Company is considering the replacement of a machine with a newer more efficient model. The old machine currently has a book value of $8,000, present resale value of $6,000, and expected residual value of $2,000 after the remaining four years of its economic life. Data on the new machine and the estimated effect on annual operating costs are as follows:

Cost...	$55,000
Delivery and installation...............................	4,000
Residual value	5,000
Additional working capital required................	6,000
Reduction in labor costs..............................	10,000
Reduction in maintenance costs...................	3,000
Increase in utility costs...............................	1,000
Economic life	10 years

The reduction in maintenance costs applies only to the first five years, after which maintenance costs of new machines are expected to be the same as for old. Lance's required rate of return is 15 percent.

Required:

A. Diagram the cash flows and calculate the net present value of the proposed investment in the machine using the format in Exhibit 8-3.
B. Do you recommend purchase of the new machine? Why?
C. The cost analyst who prepared the data above just called to say she has discovered some errors in her computations. The cost of the new machine should be $60,000 instead of $55,000, but the savings in labor costs should be $11,000 per year instead of $10,000. Using the new data, recalculate the net present value and reassess your recommendation on possible purchase of the new machine.

8-15. A bank makes the following offer: If you will deposit $15,000 cash, the bank will immediately give you a brand-new automobile worth $3,800, and it will also return your $15,000 at the end of five years.

Required:

A. What earnings rate is implicit in this offer?
B. If you had $15,000 to invest, would you accept this proposition?

8–16. To be sure that you understand how to use Tables S and A, solve the
following and show your computations.

    A. What is the present value of $6,000 to be received at the end of
six years if the required rate of return is 8 percent?

    B. What is the present value of $1,000 per year for each of the next
six years if the required rate of return is 8 percent?

    C. What is the present value of $12,000 to be received at the end of
four years if the required rate of return is 10 percent?

    D. What is the present value of $2,500 per year for each of the next
four years if the required rate of return is 10 percent?

    E. What is the present value of an investment which is expected to
produce cash inflows of $3,000 per year in Years 1 through 4 and
$1,500 per year in Years 5 through 7 if the required rate of return is
12 percent?

    F. What is the present value of an investment which is expected to
produce cash inflows of $4,000 in Year 1, $3,000 in Year 2, and
$2,000 in Year 3 if the required rate of return is 12 percent?

    G. What is the present value of an investment which is expected to
produce cash inflows of $2,500 per year of each of the next seven
years plus $1,300 at the end of Year 7 if the required rate of return
is 10 percent?

    H. What rate of return is earned on an investment which produces
cash inflows of $1,000 per year for five years and has a present
value of $3,605?

8–17. The Carter Company estimates that it can save $2,900 per year in cash
operating costs over the next ten years if it buys a new machine at a cost
of $12,000. The machine will have no residual value, and the required
rate of return is 10 percent.

Required:

    A. Calculate the net present value of the proposed investment in the
new machine.

    B. Do you recommend that Carter purchase the machine? Why?

    C. Assuming that the new machine would save only $2,500 per year
for six years, recalculate the net present value. Do you recommend
purchase? Why?

8–18. The Barrett Company is considering three proposed investments, A,
B, and C. Each requires an investment of $6,100, and each has an eco-
nomic life of three years and total cash inflow over that period of $7,500.
The pattern of cash inflows for each proposal differs, however, as indicated below:

| | Annual cash inflows | | |
Year	A	B	C
1.....................	$3,500	$2,500	$1,500
2.....................	2,500	2,500	2,500
3.....................	1,500	2,500	3,500
	$7,500	$7,500	$7,500

Required:

A. Calculate the net present value of each proposal if the required rate of return is 10 percent.

B. Do you recommend that Barrett make any or all of the proposed investments? Why?

C. Explain why the net present values of the three proposed investments differ even though the total cash inflow is the same for all three.

8–19. The Hyde Company has a capital structure which is 45 percent debt and 55 percent equity. The cost of debt capital is 4 percent, and the cost of equity capital is 14 percent.

Required:

A. Calculate the cost of capital for Hyde.

B. Hyde needs to raise additional capital and is considering a new issue of bonds that would raise the debt portion of the capital structure to 55 percent and raise the cost of debt capital to 5 percent. Recalculate the cost of capital for Hyde assuming the new bonds are issued.

8–20. Shortly before the beginning of 1977 Delbert Company was considering the installation of a new piece of equipment which was designed to automate what had been an operation that required direct labor. Expected results for the first year of operations are as follows:

Cost of equipment	$28,200
Installation cost	1,800
Labor savings, 2,000 hours @ $6	12,000
Increased power costs	900
Increased insurance and taxes	500
Increased maintenance costs	1,000

The company did buy the equipment. It actually paid $3,500 for installation costs. In 1977, actual labor hours saved totaled 2,000, but labor rates increased to $7 per hour. Other costs were as expected. The expected useful life of the equipment was five years.

Required:

A. Assuming the company has a required earnings rate of 15 percent, should the proposal have been accepted, based on expected results? Show all computations.

B. If costs for the five years remain the same as the actual results of the operations of the first year, what can be said about the management's decision to invest in the equipment?

8–21. Wyman Company has just developed a new product which should have the following projected cash inflows over the economic life of the product:

Year	Cash flow
1	$35,000
2	30,000
3	25,000
4	20,000

Wyman does not invest in productive assets unless they feel the investment will return at least 20 percent. The equipment necessary to produce the product can be bought or made by Wyman.

Required:

A. Calculate the maximum amount of capital investment which can be budgeted for if the company undertakes the production of the new product under the conditions shown above.

B. Assume that the cash inflow is expected to be $27,500 each year for four years instead of the flows above. Recalculate the maximum amount of capital investment which can be budgeted.

C. Explain why your answers to Requirements A and B differ.

8-22. The University Computer Center has a Model 4 computer which it purchased for $600,000 one year ago. It had an expected useful life of five years and resale value after five years of $50,000. Annual operating costs are $100,000, exclusive of depreciation.

A new Model 5 computer is being offered to the school at a cost of $750,000. It also has an expected useful life of five years and resale value after five years of $50,000. Annual operating costs exclusive of depreciation are $60,000. The market for used Model 4 computers is rather weak, and the old computer can be sold to net only $150,000. The university uses a 10 percent discount rate.

Required:

A. Should the university buy the new Model 5 computer or keep its Model 4? Support your answer with computations.

B. Is the book value of the Model 4 relevant to the decision on buying the Model 5? Explain your answer.

8-23. The City of Brownville has decided to acquire a computer. It can be purchased for $148,000 or leased for $30,000 a year. The lease payment includes maintenance, which is estimated to be worth $2,500 a year. The estimated economic life of the computer is eight years, and it is expected to have a residual value of $10,000. Additional working capital of $2,000 will be required and can be recovered at the end of eight years. The City uses a 10 percent rate in the analysis of proposed investments.

Required:

Should Brownville lease or purchase the computer? Show computations to support your answer.

8-24. The Grant Company is considering the replacement of a machine with a newer more efficient model. The old machine currently has a book value of $10,000, present resale value of $7,000, and expected residual value of $2,000 after the remaining four years of its economic life. Data on the new machine and the estimated effect on annual operating costs are as follows:

Cost	$50,000
Delivery and installation	4,000
Residual value	5,000
Additional working capital required	6,000
Reduction in labor costs	8,000
Reduction in maintenance costs	3,000
Increase in utility costs	1,000
Economic life	10 years

The reduction in maintenance costs applies only to the first five years, after which maintenance costs of the new machine are expected to be the same as for the old. Grant's required rate of return is 14 percent.

Required:

A. Diagram the cash flows and calculate the net present value of the proposed investment in the machine using the format in Exhibit 8–3.

B. Do you recommend purchase of the new machine? Why?

C. The cost analyst who prepared the data above just called to say she had discovered a couple of errors in her computations. The cost of the new machine should be $60,000 instead of $50,000, but the savings in labor costs should be $9,000 per year instead of $8,000. Using the new data, recalculate the net present value and reassess your recommendation on possible purchase of the new machine.

8–25. In the 1960s, a federal agency used benefit/cost analysis to evaluate the proposal for a five-year program designed to prevent accidental deaths due to head injuries of motorcycle riders. The intent of the program was to persuade motorcyclists to wear protective helmets and eyeshields on the premise that such devices would be effective in reducing deaths.

The expected cost of the program was $1.6 million per year for a five-year period. Benefits were measured first in terms of the expected number of deaths averted and second in terms of the present value of the lifetime earnings of those whose lives were saved. The program was expected to save an average of 750 lives per year of persons whose lifetime earnings had a present value of $120,000, on the average. A discount rate of 4 percent was used to calculate the present value of the costs and the present value of the lifetime earnings of those whose deaths would be averted. The benefit/cost ratio was calculated by dividing the present value of the benefits by the present value of the costs.

Required:

A. Calculate the benefit/cost ratio for the program.

B. Calculate the program cost per death averted. Use the present value of the total five-year cost and the total number of deaths averted.

C. Another program was designed to reduce deaths through improved driver licensing. This program offered a reduction in deaths of 442, discounted program costs of $6.1 million, and discounted program benefits of $22.9 million. Calculate the benefit/cost ratio and the cost per death averted.

D. If you could recommend funding of only one of the two programs, which would you favor? Why?

E. Comment on the strengths and weaknesses of benefit/cost analysis as an aid to decision making for programs such as the two above.

SUGGESTIONS FOR FURTHER READING

Grant, Eugene L., and Ireson, William G. *Principles of Engineering Economy,* 5th ed. New York: The Ronald Press Co., 1970.

Hunt, Pearson; Williams, Charles M.; and Donaldson, Gordon. *Basic Business Finance: Text and Cases,* 4th ed. Homewood, Ill.: Richard D. Irwin, Inc., 1971.

Quirin, G. David. *The Capital Expenditure Decision.* Homewood, Ill.: Richard D. Irwin, Inc., 1967.

Solomon, Ezra, ed. *The Management of Corporate Capital.* Glencoe, Ill.: The Free Press, 1959.

Weston, J. Fred, and Brigham, Eugene F. *Managerial Finance,* 4th ed. New York: Holt, Rinehart and Winston, Inc., 1972.

9

Additional aspects
of investment decisions

This chapter completes the discussion of the analysis of capital investment decisions. First, we describe how the effect of income taxes is taken into account in such analyses. Next, we describe techniques for making analyses of investment problems that supplement, or are used in place of, the net present value technique described in Chapter 8. These techniques are the discounted cash-flow method, the payback method, and the unadjusted rate of return method. They are not as sound as the net present value technique, but they are often found in practice. Finally, the application of the present value concept to a class of problems called *preference problems* is discussed.

INCOME TAXES

Nature of income tax impact

In Chapters 7 and 8, we intentionally disregarded the impact of income taxes on the calculation of costs and earnings of proposed alternative courses of action. Obviously, income taxes do affect a company's profitability. If a proposed price increase is estimated to increase a company's pretax income by $100,000, and if the government takes 50 percent of the additional income in the form of additional income taxes, then the price increase will add only half of the $100,000, or $50,000, to net income. In general, a course of action that increases income also increases the amount of income tax that the company must pay.

With a few important differences (some of which are discussed in the Appendix to this chapter), the amount of income subject to the federal income tax (i.e., taxable income) is calculated in the same way that a company calculates net income for financial accounting purposes. Thus, as a general rule, if the income tax rate is 48 percent, the government takes 48 cents out of every dollar that the company adds to its income before income taxes.

The relevant tax rate

The current federal income tax rate on corporations is 20 percent of the first $25,000 of taxable income, 22 percent of the next $25,000, and 48 percent of taxable income over $50,000. Since the problems we are analyzing involve proposed increases in income, the 20 percent and the 22 percent rates are not relevant, except in companies that expect *total* taxable income to be lower than $50,000. Neither is the average tax rate relevant. The relevant rate for most companies is the rate that the corporation pays on *additional* profits, which for the federal tax is 48 percent.

EXAMPLE: Corporation X has taxable income of $100,000. It therefore pays income tax as follows:

	Taxable income	Tax rate	Tax
First increment	$ 25,000	20%	$ 5,000
Second increment	25,000	22	5,500
Remainder	50,000	48	24,000
Total	$100,000	34.5%	$34,500

The corporation's *average* tax rate is 34.5 percent ($34,500 ÷ $100,000). If, however, Corporation X made a decision that increased its taxable income by $10,000, its income taxes would be increased by 48 percent of the $10,000, or $4,800. Since the *differential* income is taxed at the 48 percent rate, both the 20 and 22 percent rates and the average rate should be disregarded; they are not relevant to the decision. As emphasized in Chapters 7 and 8, the income that is relevant in the analysis of alternative choice problems is the differential income.

In addition to the federal tax, most states impose income taxes of a few percent, and so do some cities. In the problems and examples in this chapter, we shall assume total income tax rate of 51 percent.[1] The

---

[1] Although the general principles for calculating income taxes are unlikely to change, rates and some other details change from year to year. This discussion is based on the situation that existed in 1976. The rule of thumb that federal, state, and municipal taxes together take 50 percent of taxable income is widely used in practice. Nevertheless, for illustrative purposes we prefer not to use a 50 percent rate. If such a rate were used, we would have difficulty in communicating which of the numbers in the calculations referred to the income tax and which referred to the net income after tax, since the two numbers would be identical.

term *net income,* without a qualifying term, is always supposed to refer to income after income taxes have been deducted. Nevertheless, in order to avoid any possibility of confusion, the term **aftertax income** is often used for net income, and the term **pretax income** is used for income before the deduction of income taxes. Similarly, we shall refer to the **pretax cash inflow,** which is the same as the cash inflow discussed in Chapter 8, and to the **aftertax cash inflow,** which is the cash inflow after income taxes have been taken into account.

Implications for depreciable assets

For many alternative choice problems, if the income tax is 51 percent, aftertax income is 49 percent of pretax income. Thus, if a proposed cost reduction method is estimated to save $10,000 a year pretax, it will save $4,900 a year aftertax:

Differential pretax cash inflow $10,000
Additional income tax.................................... 5,100
Differential aftertax cash inflow .... $ 4,900

Although $4,900 is obviously not as welcome to the shareholders as $10,000 would be, the proposed cost reduction method would increase income, and, disregarding nonmonetary considerations, the decision should be made to adopt it. This is the case with *all* the alternative choice problems discussed in Chapter 7. Income taxes reduce the differential pretax cash inflow by the amount of the tax bite; however, a proposal that shows additional profits on a pretax basis will also show additional profits on an aftertax basis. For this reason, calculations for problems of the type discussed in Chapter 7 (e.g., contribution pricing, new methods, make or buy) are often made on a pretax basis, in the interests of simplicity.

When depreciable assets are involved in a proposal, however, the situation is quite different. In proposals of this type, **there is no simple relationship between pretax cash inflow and aftertax cash inflow,** primarily because depreciation is disregarded in estimating the pretax cash inflow of such proposals, whereas depreciation is an expense that is taken into account in calculating taxable income. This is the case with the capital investment proposals in Chapter 8. We now describe how income taxes should be taken into account in analyzing such proposals.

Taxes in capital investment decisions

The basic rule for evaluating a proposed investment, given in Chapter 8, is that the investment is acceptable if the present value of the cash inflows equals or exceeds the amount of the investment.

EXAMPLE: A proposed machine that costs $1,000 is expected to produce cash inflows in the form of savings in labor and other costs amounting to $320 a year for five years. The required rate of return is 10 percent. The calculation of net present value is:

Present value of cash inflows:
$320 × 3.791 ($A_{5| 10\%}$) $1,213
Investment 1,000
Net present value .... $ 213

Since the proposal has a positive net present value, it is acceptable if taxes are disregarded.

Assuming a tax rate of 51 percent, one might jump to the conclusion that if the pretax cash inflows were $320 per year, the aftertax cash inflows would be 49 percent of $320, or $157 per year. If such were the case, the proposal described in the preceding example would not be acceptable:

Present value of aftertax cash inflows:
$157 × 3.791 ($A_{5| 10\%}$)... $ 595
Investment 1,000
Net present value... $ (405)

Note: In these examples, ( ) indicates a negative present value.

Actually, the calculation of aftertax cash inflow in this situation is more complicated than simply taking 49 percent of the pretax cash inflow. As explained in Chapter 8, depreciation is omitted from the calculation of net present value because the net present value is the amount in excess of the recovery of the investment, and to count depreciation as a cost would be double counting. In calculating taxable income, however, depreciation is an expense, which is subtracted from revenue, just as it is on the usual income statement.

Exhibit 9–1 shows how the $1,000 proposed investment used in the

EXHIBIT 9–1
Effect of income taxes on investment calculation

Annual Income Statements

	Without investment		With investment		
	(base case)		(Case 2)		Difference
Revenue		$1,002,000		$1,002,000	0
Depreciation	$ 50,000		$ 50,200		$+200
Other expenses	851,000		850,680		−320
Total Expense		901,000		900,880	−120
Pretax income................		101,000		101,120	+120
Income tax (51%)............		51,510		51,571	+ 61
Net Income		$ 49,490		$ 49,549	$+ 59

above example would affect the company's income statement and the calculation of its income tax. The relationships shown in that exhibit should be studied carefully. The first pair of columns shows how the company's income statement would appear if it did not purchase the proposed machine, and the next pair of columns shows how the income statement would look if the machine were purchased, other conditions remaining unchanged. Revenue is unaffected. Depreciation expense increases by $200, which is the annual charge for a $1,000 machine being depreciated over a period of five years on a straight-line basis. Other expenses decrease $320 a year because of the savings arising from use of the new machine. Pretax income therefore increases by $120, which is the difference between the additional depreciation and the lower amount of other expense. Since income tax is assumed to be 51 percent of taxable income, income tax increases by 51 percent of $120, or $61. Net income therefore increases by $59.

The important fact to note from Exhibit 9–1 is that the **additional income tax is much less than 51 percent of the pretax cash inflow.** The reason is that depreciation offsets part of what would otherwise be additional taxable income. Depreciation is therefore called a **tax shield** in investment calculations. It shields the pretax cash inflow from the full impact of income taxes. Taxable income will not correspond to pretax cash inflows in any problem where depreciation is a significant factor. The increase in taxable income will be *less than* the increase in pretax cash inflow by the amount of the depreciation expense on the assets acquired.

Procedure for incorporating depreciation.   In order to calculate the aftertax cash inflow, therefore, we must take account of the depreciation tax shield. At the same time, we must be careful not to permit the amount of depreciation itself to enter the calculation of *cash inflow* because this would lead to the double counting that must be avoided. We must find the amount of additional income tax, which is indeed a cash outflow, without counting the depreciation expense, which is not a cash outflow. The way to do this is to make a separate calculation of the additional income tax and subtract this from the pretax cash inflow. More specifically, the procedure is as follows:

1. Estimate the pretax cash inflows resulting from the investment, as in Chapter 8.
2. Estimate the additional income tax by, in effect, preparing a regular income statement as in Exhibit 9–1.
3. Subtract the additional income tax from the pretax cash inflows to find the aftertax cash inflows.
4. Discount the aftertax cash inflows at the required rate of return to find their present value.

5. Subtract the investment from the present value of the inflows to find the net present value of the proposal.

   EXAMPLE: Continue with the example of a proposed machine costing $1,000 with estimated pretax cash inflows of $320 a year for five years. The required rate of return is 10 percent.

   1. Pretax cash inflows are, as stated, $320 a year.
   2. Additional income tax is, as calculated in Exhibit 9–1, $61 a year.
   3. Therefore, annual aftertax cash inflows are $320 − $61 = $259.
   4. The cash inflows of $259 have a present value of $259 × 3.791 $(A_{\overline{5}|10\%})$ = $982. The net present value is therefore $982 − $1,000 = $−18. The net present value is still a negative amount, and the proposal is therefore not acceptable, but the negative amount of $18 is much less than the $405 derived above from the erroneous calculation that assumed that aftertax cash inflow was 49 percent of pretax cash inflow.

Exhibit 9–2 shows a convenient format for displaying the calculations. The proposal is the same as that used in the previous example. Additional taxable income is subtracted from the pretax cash inflow. The additional income tax is 51 percent of additional taxable income, or $61. This is subtracted from the pretax cash inflow to find the annual aftertax cash inflow. The present value of this stream of cash inflows for five years is then calculated by using the appropriate discount factor from Table A. **Note that the additional income tax is subtracted from the pretax cash inflow, not from the additional taxable income.**

Accelerated depreciation. In the preceding example we assumed, for simplicity, that depreciation was calculated by the straight-line method. In fact, most companies use one of the accelerated methods of depreciation in calculating their taxable income. They use an accelerated method because it increases the present value of the depreciation tax shield. The present value of the depreciation tax shield is relatively high in the early years and correspondingly lower in the later years of the investment. (Re-

EXHIBIT 9–2
Calculation of net present value with tax shield

	Taxable income calculation	Present value calculation
Annual pretax cash inflow...................................	$320	$ 320
Less: Additional depreciation	200	
Additional taxable income..................................	$120	
Additional income tax ($120 × 51%)		−61
Aftertax cash inflow...		259
Present value $259 × 3.791 $(A_{\overline{5}|10\%})$........................		982
Investment..		1,000
Net present value		$ (18)

call from Chapter 8 that the present value of an amount to be received in the near future is higher than the present value of the same amount to be received in the more distant future.)

Since with the accelerated methods the amount of depreciation varies from year to year, calculations of aftertax cash inflows must be made separately for each year, and each must be discounted using present values in Table S. Table A cannot be used to find the present value because in order to use Table A the cash inflows must be equal in each year.

> *EXAMPLE:* Assume the same situation as in the preceding example, namely a proposed machine costing $1,000 with estimated pretax cash inflows of $320 a year for five years. The required rate of return is 10 percent. Assume, however, that the company uses the sum-of-the-years'-digits method, which is one of the acceptable accelerated depreciation methods for calculating its taxable income.[2] Calculations are shown in Exhibit 9–3. For the first year, depreciation expense would be 5/15 of $1,000, or $333. This amount *exceeds* the amount of pretax cash inflow by $13, so the tax impact in the first year would be a *reduction* in taxes of 51 percent of $13 = $7. The aftertax cash inflow would be $320 − (−$7) = $327. In the second year, depreciation expense would be 4/15 of $1,000, which is $267. The additional inflow subject to tax would therefore be $320 − $267 = $53. The additional income tax would be $27, making the aftertax cash inflow $293. And so on, for the third, fourth, and fifth year.
>
> The present value of the aftertax cash inflow is found by discounting the aftertax cash inflow amounts for each year at the appropriate discount rate from Table S. The sum of these discounted amounts, $1,007, is the total present value of the inflows. Subtracting the investment, $1,000, gives the net present value of the proposal, which is $7.

In Exhibit 9–3, note how the use of accelerated depreciation increases the attractiveness of the investment. Its present value rises from $982 with straight-line depreciation to $1,007 with accelerated depreciation, and the proposal now meets the criterion that the present value of its net cash inflows exceeds the investment. This result occurs because a larger fraction of the depreciation tax shield occurs in the early years, where present values are relatively high.[3]

---

[2] Recall that in the sum-of-the-years'-digits method, the annual depreciation is the fraction in which the denominator is the sum-of-the-years'-digits, and the numerator is n for the first year, $n − 1$ for the second year, and so on. For an asset with a five-year life, the denominator is $5 + 4 + 3 + 2 + 1 = 15$, and the fraction is 5/15 for the first year, 4/15 for the second year, and so on. The Internal Revenue Code permits accelerated depreciation for most, but not all, depreciable assets.

[3] In practice, accelerated depreciation is usually used in calculating taxable income because of the higher present value of the depreciation tax shield. Nevertheless, we use straight-line depreciation in most of the problems and examples in this book, simply to reduce the amount of arithmetic.

EXHIBIT 9–3

Calculation of net present value, accelerated depreciation

Year	(a) Pretax cash inflow	(b) SYD depre- ciation	(c) = (a) − (b) Inflow subject to tax	(d) Tax at 51%	(e) = (a) − (d) Aftertax cash inflow	Discount rate (Table S)	Present value
1.............	$ 320	$ 333	$−13	$ −7	$ 327	0.909	$ 297
2.............	320	267	53	27	293	0.826	242
3.............	320	200	120	61	259	0.751	195
4.............	320	133	187	95	225	0.683	154
5.............	320	67	253	129	191	0.621	119
Total	$1,600	$1,000	$ 600	$305	$1,295		1,007
Investment							1,000
Net present value							$ 7

Investment tax credit

Income tax regulations permit a company under certain specified conditions to take an **investment credit** when it purchases new machinery, equipment, and certain other types of depreciable assets. The investment credit may be as high as 10 percent of the purchase price.[4] It is subtracted directly from the amount of the tax bill. Thus, if a company buys a new machine for $10,000, it may be able to subtract 10 percent of that amount, or $1,000, from its current tax obligation. This is a direct reduction of $1,000 in the investment. In other words, the cost of the machine to the corporation is actually only 90 percent of the invoice amount.

The effect of this reduction in the investment is to make investment proposals that much more attractive, and thus to stimulate businesses to buy additional capital assets. For example, if a proposal required an investment of $100,000 and its cash inflows had an estimated net present value of only $95,000, it would be unattractive. If, because of the investment credit, the investment became only $90,000, the proposal would have a $5,000 positive net present value and would meet the test of acceptability.

OTHER METHODS OF ANALYSIS

So far, we have limited the discussion of techniques for analyzing capital investment proposals to one method, the net present value method. We now describe three alternative ways of analyzing a proposed capital investment project: (1) the project rate-of-return method, (2) the payback method, and (3) the unadjusted return on investment method.

---

[4] The percentage tends to change from one year to another, and in some years Congress has eliminated the investment credit entirely. The credit cannot exceed 50 percent of the company's total tax liability.

Project rate-of-return method

When the net present value method is used, the required rate of return must be selected in advance of making the calculations, because this rate is used to discount the cash inflows in each year, so as to find their present value. As we noted in Chapter 8, there is no practical formula for arriving at the required rate of return that is exactly correct in a given company. Thus, calculations based on whatever rate is selected are open to challenge. An alternative approach avoids the necessity of deciding on a required rate of return in advance. This is the **project rate-of-return (PRR) method. It computes the rate of return that equates the present value of the cash inflows with the amount of the investment.** In other words, the PRR is the discount rate which makes the net present value of the project equal to zero. This rate is also called the **internal rate of return,** and the technique is also called the **discounted cash flow method** (although this term is confusing because the net present value method also discounts the cash flows), the **time-adjusted-return method,** and the **investor's method.**

If the management is satisfied that the PRR is high enough, then the project is acceptable; if the PRR is not high enough, then the project is unacceptable. In deciding what rate of return is "high enough," the same considerations as those involved in selecting a required rate of return apply (see Chapter 8).

Level inflows. If the cash inflows are level – that is, the same amount each year – the computation is simple. It will be illustrated by a proposed investment of $1,000 with estimated cash inflow of $250 a year for five years. The procedure is as follows:

1. Divide the investment, $1,000, by the annual inflow, $250. The result, 4.0, is called the **investment/inflow ratio.**

2. Look across the five-year row of Table A. The column in which the figure closest to 4.0 appears shows the project rate of return. Thus, some rates in the five-year row are:

	4%	6%	8%	10%
Present value	4.452	4.212	3.993	3.791

The closest figure to 4.0 is 3.993 in the 8 percent column, and the return is therefore approximately 8 percent. (If there is doubt about this, refer back to Exhibit 8–1 where it is demonstrated that the return is indeed approximately 8 percent.)

3. If management is satisfied with a return of approximately 8 percent, then it should accept this project (aside from nonquantitative considerations). If management requires a higher return, then it should reject the project.

The number 4.0 in the above example is simply the ratio of the investment to the annual cash inflows. Each number in Table A shows the ratio of the present value of a stream of cash inflows to an investment of $1 made today, for various combinations of rates of return and numbers of years. The number 4.0 opposite any combination of year and rate of return means that the present value of a stream of inflows of $1 a year for that number of years discounted at that rate is $4. The present value of a stream of inflows of $250 a year is in the same ratio; therefore the total present value is $250 times 4, or $1,000. If the number is less than 4.0, as is the case with 3.993 in the example above, then the return is correspondingly less than 8 percent.

In using Table A, in this method, it is usually necessary to interpolate, that is, to estimate the location of a number that lies between two numbers appearing in the table. There is no need to be precise about these interpolations because the final result can be no better than the basic data, and the basic data are ordinarily only rough estimates. A quick interpolation, made visually, is usually as good as the accuracy of the data warrants. Calculation of a fraction of a percent is rarely warranted.

As a device for understanding the investment/inflow ratio, the reader is encouraged to think about other relationships that are implicit in Table A. For example, a project with an investment of $20,000 and an annual cash inflow of $5,000 has an investment/inflow ratio of 5. Looking for numbers in Table A that are close to 5, this ratio can be used to determine how long the economic life of the project must be to give a specified rate of return. If the required return is 10 percent, Table A shows that the economic life must be more than seven years, because the number 5 is between the 4.868 for seven years and the 5.335 for eight years.

Uneven inflows. If cash inflows are not the same in each year, the project rate of return must be found by trial and error. The cash inflows for each year are listed, and various discount rates are applied to these amounts until a rate is found that makes their total present value equal to the amount of the investment. This rate is the project rate of return. This trial-and-error process can be quite tedious if the computations are made manually; however, computer programs are available that perform the calculations automatically.

Payback method

The number referred to above as the investment/inflow ratio is also called the **payback period** because **it is the number of years over which the investment outlay will be recovered or paid back from the cash inflow** *if* the estimates turn out to be correct; that is, the project will "pay for itself" in this number of years. If a machine costs $1,000 and generates cash inflow of $250 a year, it has a payback period of four years. Thus, the equation is:

$$\text{Payback Period} = \frac{\text{Investment}}{\text{Annual Cash Inflow}}$$

Payback is often used as a quick, but crude, method for appraising proposed investments. If the payback period is equal to or only slightly less than the economic life of the project, then the proposal is clearly unacceptable, because its PRR (project rate of return) is zero or very small. (If a project has a payback of five years and an economic life of five years, its PRR obviously is zero; it does not generate any profit. If it has an economic life of six years, Table A shows that its PRR is about 6 percent.) If the payback period is considerably less than the economic life, then the project is attractive.

If several investment proposals have the same general characteristics, then the payback period can be used as a valid way of screening out the acceptable proposals. For example, if a company finds that production equipment ordinarily has a life of ten years and if it requires a return of at least 15 percent, then the company may specify that new equipment will be considered for purchase only if it has a payback period of five years or less; for Table A shows that a payback period of five years is equivalent to a return of approximately 15 percent if the life is ten years. Stating the criterion in this fashion avoids the necessity of explaining the present value concept to supervisors in the operating organizations.

The danger of using payback as a criterion is that it gives no consideration to differences in the length of the estimated economic lives of various projects. There may be a tendency to conclude that the shorter the payback period, the better the project; whereas a project with a long payback may actually be better than a project with a short payback if it will produce cash inflows for a much longer period of time.[5]

EXAMPLE: Project A involves an investment of $20,000 and cash inflows of $4,000 a year for ten years. Project B involves an investment of $60,000 and cash inflows of $15,000 for only six years:

	Project A	Project B
Investment	$20,000	$60,000
Annual cash inflow	4,000	15,000
Payback, years	5	4
Economic life years	10	6
Project rate of return (Table A)	15%	13%

Project A is the preferable project, even though it has a longer payback period.

[5] The simple payback method takes no account of present value; that is, it does not recognize that cash inflows in early years have a higher present value than cash inflows in later years. In order to overcome this weakness, the *discounted payback* method has been developed. The simple payback period is the number of years required to make cash inflows equal the amount of investment. The discounted payback period, by contrast, is the number of years of cash inflows that are required to (*a*) recover the amount of the investment, *and also* (*b*) earn the required rate of return on the investment during that period. The computations can be quite complicated if done manually, but are a simple task for a computer.

Unadjusted return on investment method

The *unadjusted return* method computes the net income expected to be earned from the project each year, in accordance with the principles of financial accounting, including a provision for depreciation expense. **The unadjusted return on investment is found by dividing the annual net income by either the amount of the investment or by one half the amount of investment.** (The use of one half the investment is on the premise that over the whole life of the project, an average of one half the initial investment is outstanding because the investment is at its full amount in Time Zero and shrinks gradually to nothing, or substantially nothing, by its horizon year.) The equation is:

$$\text{Unadjusted Return} = \frac{\text{Annual Net Income}}{\text{Investment*}}$$

* Or investment ÷ 2.

Since normal depreciation accounting provides, in a sense, for the recovery of the cost of a depreciable asset, one might suppose that the return on an investment could be found by relating the investment to its income after depreciation, but such is *not* the case. In Exhibit 8–1 we demonstrated that the return on an investment of $1,000 with cash inflows of $250 a year for five years was truly 8 percent. Over the five-year period the company would recover its $1,000 and in addition would earn 8 percent a year on the amount of investment not recovered in that year.[6] No method of accounting can change that economic fact. In the unadjusted return method, however, the calculation would be as follows:

Gross annual earnings	$250
Less depreciation ($\frac{1}{5}$ of $1,000)	200
Annual Income	$ 50

Dividing net income by the investment ($50 ÷ $1,000) gives an indicated return of 5 percent. But we know that this result is incorrect; the true return is 8 percent. If we divide the $50 net income by one half the investment, that is, $500, the result is 10 percent, which is also incorrect.

This method is called the unadjusted return method because it makes no adjustment for the differences in present value of the inflows of the various years; that is, it treats each year's inflow as if it were as valuable as that of every other year, whereas actually the prospect of an inflow of $250 next year is more attractive than the prospect of an inflow of $250 two years from now, and that $250 is more attractive than the prospect of an inflow of $250 three years from now, and so on.

---

[6] For simplicity, income taxes are omitted from this example. This omission has no effect on the point being illustrated.

The unadjusted return method, based on the gross amount of the investment, will always *understate* the true return. The shorter the time period involved, the more serious is the understatement. For investments involving very long time periods, the understatement is insignificant. If the return is computed by using one half the investment, the result is always an *overstatement* of the true return. No method which does not consider the time value of money can produce an accurate result.

Until fairly recently, the unadjusted return method was widely used, and it is still used in companies whose managers are unaware of the importance of the present value concept. Despite its conceptual weakness, the unadjusted return method does have a place in capital investment analysis, for it shows the effect of a proposal on the company's income statement. This effect, which is not shown in present value computations, may be significant in certain situations because of the importance that investors attach to the amount of reported net income.

PREFERENCE PROBLEMS

There are two classes of investment problems, called, respectively, *screening* problems and *preference* problems. **In a screening problem the question is whether or not to accept a proposed investment.** The discussion so far has been limited to this class of problem. A great number of individual proposals come to management's attention, and by the techniques described above those that are worthwhile can be screened out from the others.

In **preference problems** (also called **ranking** or **rationing** problems), a more difficult question is asked: **Of a number of proposals, each of which has an adequate return, how do they rank in terms of preference?** If not all the proposals can be accepted, which ones do we prefer? How do we ration a limited amount of funds so that the funds go to the most desirable projects? The decision may merely involve a choice between two competing proposals, or it may require that a series of proposals be ranked in order of their attractiveness. Such a ranking of projects is necessary when there are more worthwhile proposals than there are funds available to finance them, which is often the case.

Criteria for preference problems

Both the project rate-of-return and the net present value methods are used for preference problems.

If the project rate-of-return method is used, the preference rule is as follows: the higher the PRR, the better the project. A project with a PRR of 20 percent is said to be preferable to a project with a PRR of 19 percent.

If the *net present value method* is used, the present value of the cash inflows of one project cannot be compared directly with the present value of the cash inflows of another project unless the investments are of the same size. Most people would agree that a $1,000 investment that produces cash inflows with a present value of $2,000 is better than a $1,000,-000 investment that produces cash inflows with a present value of $1,001,000, even though they each have a net present value of $1,000. In order to compare two proposals under the net present value method, therefore, we must relate the size of the discounted cash inflows to the amount of money that is risked. This is done simply by dividing the present value of the cash inflows by the amount of investment, to give a ratio that is generally called the *profitability index*. **The preference rule then is as follows: the higher the profitability index, the better the project.** Note that the present value of the cash inflows is used in the numerator of this ratio, *not* the net present value of the project. If the net present value of a project is zero, its profitability index is 1.0, which is the same as saying that the present value of its cash inflows equals its investment.

Comparison of preference rules

Conceptually, the profitability index is superior to the project rate of return as a device for deciding on preference. This is because the PRR method will not always give the correct preference as between two projects with different lives or with different patterns of earnings.

> *EXAMPLE:* Proposal A involves an investment of $1,000 and cash inflow of $1,200 received at the end of one year; its PRR is 20 percent. (The discount rate for one year at 20 percent is 0.833; $1,200 × 0.833 = $1,000.) Proposal B involves an investment of $1,000 and cash inflows of $300 a year for five years; its PRR is only 15 percent. (The discount rate for five years at 15 percent is 3.352; $300 × 3.352 = $1,000, approximately.) But Proposal A is *not* necessarily preferable to Proposal B. It is preferable only if the company can expect to earn a high return during the following four years on some other project in which the funds released at the end of the first year are reinvested. Otherwise, Proposal B, which earns 15 percent over the whole five-year period, is preferable.[7]

The incorrect signal illustrated in the above example is not present in the profitability index method. Assuming a required rate of return of 10 percent, the two proposals described above would be analyzed as follows:

(a) Proposal	(b) Cash inflow	(c) Discount factor	(d) = (b) × (c) Present value	(e) Investment	(f) = (d) ÷ (e) Profitability index
A	$1,200 — 1 yr.	0.909	$1,091	$1,000	1.09
B	300 — 5 yr.	3.791	1,137	1,000	1.14

---

[7] Note that this problem arises when a choice must be made between two competing proposals, only one of which can be adopted. If the proposals are noncompeting and the required rate of return is less than 15 percent, then both of them are acceptable.

The profitability index signals that Proposal B is better than Proposal A, which is in fact the case if the company can expect to reinvest the money released from Proposal A so as to earn only 10 percent on it.[8]

Although the profitability index method is conceptually superior to the PRR method, and although the former is also easier to calculate since there is no trial-and-error computation, the PRR method is widely used in practice. There seem to be two reasons for this. First, the profitability index method requires that the required rate of return be established before the calculations are made, whereas many analysts prefer to work from the other direction — that is, to calculate the project rate of return and then see how it compares with their idea of the rate of return that is appropriate in view of the risks involved. Second, the profitability index, like any index, is an abstract number that is difficult to explain; whereas the project rate of return is similar to interest rates and earnings rates with which every business executive is familiar.

COMPARISON OF METHODS

As a means of summarizing and comparing all the analytical methods described in Chapters 8 and 9, these methods are now applied to a simple fact situation, as follows: Two capital investment proposals are under consideration. Case 1 involves an investment of $1,000 with estimated pretax cash inflows of $400 a year for five years. Case 2 involves an investment of $10,000 and pretax cash inflows of $3,000 a year for ten years. The income tax rate is estimated to be 51 percent, straight-line depreciation is used for tax purposes, and the required rate of return is 10 percent. These facts, together with computations made under various methods, are summarized in Exhibit 9–4.

Calculations are given for Case 2. To review, the reader might well work out the same calculations for Case 1.

First, we calculate the annual aftertax cash inflow, which for Case 2 is as follows:

	Taxable income calculation	Present value calculation
Annual pretax cash inflow	$3,000	$3,000
Less: Additional depreciation	1,000	
Additional taxable income	$2,000	
Additional income tax (51 percent)		1,020
Aftertax cash inflow		$1,980

---

[8] Proof of this statement is complicated, and we do not give it here. In most problems, the PRR gives the same signal as the profitability index.

EXHIBIT 9–4
Methods of evaluating investment proposals

	Case 1	Case 2
Assumed estimates:		
Investment	$1,000	$10,000
Life, years	5	10
Annual pretax cash inflow	$ 400	$ 3,000
Annual aftertax cash inflow	$ 298	$ 1,980
Analytical results:		
Net present value	$ 130	$ 2,167
Profitability index	1.13	1.22
Project rate of return	15%	15%
Payback, years	3.4	5
Unadjusted return, initial investment	10%	10%
Unadjusted return, average investment	20%	20%

To find the *net present value,* the amount of investment is subtracted from the present value of the stream of aftertax cash inflows:

Present value of aftertax cash inflows:

$1,980 × 6.145 $(A_{\overline{10}|10\%})$	$12,167
Investment	10,000
Net present value	$ 2,167

To find the *profitability index,* the present value of the aftertax cash inflow is divided by the investment:

$$\$12,167 \div \$10,000 = 1.22$$

To find the *project rate of return,* the investment/inflow ratio is first calculated. It is $10,000 ÷ $1,980 = 5.05. Then the ten-year row of Table A is examined to find the number closest to this ratio. This is the $5.019 under 15 percent. The project rate of return is therefore approximately 15 percent.

The *payback period* is the same as the investment/inflow ratio, that is, about five years.

The *unadjusted return* is found by constructing an income statement:

Pretax cash inflows	$3,000
Less depreciation	1,000
Pretax income	2,000
Income tax (51%)	1,020
Net Income	$ 980

The net income, $980, divided by the amount of investment, $10,000, gives a return of about 10 percent. If the average investment of $5,000 ($10,000 ÷ 2) is used, the return is about 20 percent.

What can we conclude from all these numbers? First, the net present value of both proposals is positive, and the PRR of both projects exceeds the required rate of return of 10 percent. These are valid tests, and they show that both proposals are acceptable. (These two methods always give the same *screening* signal; that is, if one method says a proposal is acceptable, so will the other.)

From the payback test, we can conclude that the payback period for each proposal is shorter than its life, but we cannot say for sure that this fact, by itself, makes the proposal acceptable because we do not know if it is *enough* shorter to provide an acceptable rate of return.

The unadjusted return understates the true return if it is calculated on the basis of the initial investment, and it overstates the true return if it is calculated on the basis of the average investment. It is not a meaningful figure.

Turning to the more difficult *preference* question, we ask whether Proposal B is more desirable than Proposal A. The profitability index, which is the most valid test, does rank Proposal B higher. The project rate-of-return method ranks them as equally desirable, each having a PRR of 15 percent. The payback period does not provide a valid preference measure since there is no way of knowing whether a five-year project with a payback of three years is preferable to a ten-year project with a payback of five years, without using present values. The unadjusted return is not a valid measure of preference.

It should be emphasized that the calculation of a variety of measures, as in Exhibit 9–4, was for illustrative purposes only. In the real world, a company would select one principal measure and perhaps supplement it by other measures for special purposes. It would not calculate all these measures routinely.

CONCLUDING COMMENTS

Additional intricacies

The discussions in this book are introductory. Chapters 8 and 9, however, are even more introductory than most. The concepts and the general approach to solving practical problems are described, but a great many complexities that are encountered in real-life situations are necessarily omitted. For example, we have not described how to handle the situation in which an existing piece of equipment has a shorter useful life than the proposed equipment, or the situation in which some parts of the proposed investment are made prior to Time Zero, or the situation in which investments are made in increments during the life of the project. Such situations are dealt with in the references cited at the end of Chapter 8.

Nonquantitative factors

Neither have we discussed how to handle the considerations that cannot be reduced to quantitative terms. We repeat the admonition made in Chapter 8: these qualitative factors are usually at least as important as those that are encompassed in the calculations. We omit them simply because there is no way of describing what to do about them other than to say: use good judgment. Indeed, the use of good judgment is the essence of the whole approach. The techniques described in these chapters permit rational analysis of *some* of the important factors. This analysis should be done first. Management should accept the results of this analysis, weigh it together with the qualitative factors, and then make the decision.

Nonuse of discounting

Some companies do not use discounting techniques in analyzing investment proposals. In some of them the reason is that the manager is not familiar with the techniques. But there is a much better reason in many instances. Some managers, having studied the approach carefully, have concluded that it is like trying "to make a silk purse out of a sow's ear"; that is, in their opinion the underlying estimates of cash flows and economic life are so rough that the refinement of using discounting techniques is more work than it is worth. Therefore they prefer the simple payback method or the unadjusted return method.

Those managers who do use one of the discounting methods argue that the extra work involved is small, and that the results, although admittedly rough, are nevertheless better than the results of calculations that do not take into account the time value of money.

DEMONSTRATION CASE

Exhibit 9–5 shows an analysis of an investment proposal made in 1912, which was a long time prior to the use of present value techniques. The analysis compares the investment and operating costs of three one-horse vans with those of one motor van, which presumably could do the same job. It is an erroneous analysis. Before reading further, it is suggested that the student try his or her hand at making a valid analysis of this situation, using the data in Exhibit 9–5. The errors are discussed below.

In the first place, note that the calculation includes both the investment cost and the depreciation of this cost (for the van, $2,150 investment and $2,150 depreciation); thus the investment cost is in effect counted twice,

EXHIBIT 9–5

Illustration of incorrect investment analysis (from a 1912 advertisement)

DELIVERY VAN

Cost of Operating Three One-Horse Vans for Five Years		Cost of Operating One Schacht Delivery Van for Five Years	
3 Vans at $250 each	$ 750.00	One Van	$ 2,150.00
7 Horses at $200 each	1,400.00	Gasoline, averaging 60 miles per day,	
3 Sets Harness at $40 per set	120.00	300 days per year, 10 miles per gal.	1,440.00
Repairs to harness at $5 per set per year	75.00	Oil at 50¢ gal., 120 miles per gal.	375.00
Repairs to vans, including repainting	525.00	Grease, transmission and cup, averaging 15¢ per lb., running 100	
Insurance at $25 per policy	375.00	miles to the lb.	135.00
Wages of three drivers at $15 per week	11,700.00	Battery charging at 50¢ per month	30.00
Wages of stablemen and general help (one at $10)	2,600.00	Tire renewals, averaging 5,000 miles per tire	3,300.00
Feed, stabling, vet. service, shoeing, etc., at $25 per horse per month	4,500.00	Oil for lamps	100.00
Depreciation, 20 percent	1,870.00	Repairs	375.00
Interest on investment at 6 percent	480.00	Liability and fire insurance	750.00
	$24,395.00	Driver at $15 per week	3,900.00
		Incidentals at $25 per year	125.00
		Interest at 6 percent	645.00
		Depreciation at 20 percent	2,150.00
			$15,475.00

Cost of operating three one-horse vans for five years	$24,395.00
Cost of operating one Schacht Delivery Van for five years	15,475.00
Savings in operating van for five years	8,920.00
Net saving, per year, in favor of Schacht Delivery Van	$ 1,785.00

Ask for Diagnosis Blank, fill in and return, and we will analyze your problems for you, and advise you, without prejudice and without incurring any obligation of the feasibility of Motor Trucks or Vans for your delivery service. It will be worth your while.

which is wrong. Depreciation is the recovery of the investment; if should not be added to the investment itself.[9]

Next, note that an attempt was made to incorporate the notion of present value by including interest as a cost. There are two errors in the method used. First, the rate of interest of 6 percent is today, as it was then, too low as a measure of the risk of a business investment; it corresponds to a rate for borrowing money. Second, interest was calculated on the initial amount of the investment, which overlooks the fact that the funds committed to the investment are gradually released over time. In a rough way, these two errors tend to offset one another, but the extent to which one counterbalances the other is a matter of happenstance. A valid approach would be to discount the future cash flows as described in the text.

Exhibit 9–6 illustrates how the analysis of this investment proposal might be made today. The essential problem is to express the cost of the

---

[9] The depreciation of $1,870 on the horse-drawn vans excluded depreciation on two of the horses, for a reason that is not known. Perhaps it was an attempt to recognize the residual value of the horses.

investment and annual operating costs for each alternative so they can be aggregated correctly. This is done by computing the present value of the stream of future operating costs. We can omit income taxes since they were insignificant in 1912. For the three one-horse vans, the operating costs are given as $3,955 per year. In the absence of other information,

EXHIBIT 9–6
Modern analysis of delivery van proposal

Three one-horse vans:

Investment...		$ 2,270
Annual operating costs:		
Repairs	$ 120	
Insurance	75	
Wages..	2,860	
Feed, stabling, etc.	900	
Total Annual Operating Cost	3,955	
Present value, 5 years, 10%..		14,993
Total Present Value of Costs		$17,263

One Schacht delivery van:

Investment...		$ 2,150
Annual operating costs:		
Gasoline, oil, grease, battery	396	
Tire renewals...	660	
Repairs	75	
Insurance	150	
Wages..	780	
Lamp oil, incidentals	45	
Total Annual Operating Cost	2,106	
Present value, 5 years, 10%..		7,984
Total Present Value of Costs		10,134
Net advantage of Schacht van ($17,263 − $10,134)		$ 7,129

a discount rate of 10 percent is assumed. From Table A, we find that a stream of payments of $1 per year for five years, at 10 percent, has a present value of $3.791. Therefore, a stream of $3,955 per year has a present value of $3,955 × 3.791, or $14,993. This, added to the investment, makes the total present value of the costs equal to $17,263. The costs of the Schacht delivery van computed in a similar way, comes out to $10,134, so the Schacht delivery van has a net advantage of $7,129.

We might note that the revised calculation uses the same estimates as those used in the original advertisement. For a full-blown analysis, we should also question the assumption that a truck driver will receive the same wages as the driver of a van, that one truck will in fact do as much work as three horse-drawn vans, that gasoline costs 16 cents per gallon, and so on. But from the facts given we have no way of addressing such questions.

SUMMARY

The impact of income taxes must be taken into account in analyzing proposed capital investments. This cannot be done by applying the applicable income tax rate to the amount of pretax cash inflows, however, because depreciation shields part of the cash inflows from the effect of income taxes. A separate calculation is made to determine the additional income tax that will result from the proposed investment, and this amount is subtracted from the pretax cash inflows to arrive at the aftertax inflows. The use of accelerated depreciation has the effect of increasing the present value of the depreciation tax shield.

In addition to the net present value method of analyzing proposed capital investments discussed in Chapter 8, several other methods are in use. The project rate-of-return (PRR) method finds the rate of return that equates the present value of cash inflows to the amount of investment; it is a valid method. The simple payback method finds the number of years of cash inflows that are required to equal the amount of investment. The unadjusted return on investment computes net income according to the principles of financial accounting and expresses this as a percentage of either the initial investment or the average investment. The simple payback and unadjusted return methods have serious weaknesses.

Preference problems are those in which the task is to rank two or more investment proposals in order of their desirability. The profitability index, which is the ratio of the present value of cash inflows to the investment, is the most valid way of making such a ranking. The PRR method is also valid in most, but not all, preference problems. Other methods are generally not useful for ranking purposes.

APPENDIX: EFFECT OF INCOME TAXES ON BUSINESS DECISIONS

Some readers already have experienced the trauma of calculating their personal federal income tax. In this Appendix, the corporate income tax is contrasted with the individual tax and some of the ways in which the income tax affects business decisions are described. The description relates to 1976; details can be expected to be different in later years.

Individual income tax

The main items involved in the calculation of an individual's federal income tax are shown in Exhibit 9–7, and each is discussed below.

Gross income. Gross income includes all items of income that an individual receives, except for a few things that are specifically excluded. (Most individuals report on a cash basis, rather than an accrual basis, so income refers to cash receipts, not to revenue as is the case with a busi-

EXHIBIT 9–7
Elements of individual income tax

Gross income		$15,000
Less: Adjustments		1,000
Adjusted gross income		14,000
Less: Deductions	$2,000	
Exemptions	750	2,750
Taxable income		$11,250
Income tax (calculated)		$ 2,100
Less: Tax withheld	1,800	
Prepayment and other	200	2,000
Balance of tax due		$ 100

ness.) Included are salaries, wages, fees, commissions, bonuses, tips, and other compensation for personal services; most dividends and interest income; rent and royalty income; income from a proprietorship or partnership business (which is calculated generally according to the principles to be described below for corporations); income from trusts, estates, pensions, and annuities; and gains from the sales of securities and other property (although only one half of such *capital gains* are counted if the property has been owned for more than six months).

Cash receipts that are *excluded* from gross income are gifts, inheritances, certain types of scholarships, social security benefits, death benefits from most life insurance policies, proceeds from the sale of property equal to its cost (as distinguished from the gain on such a sale), the first $100 of dividend income ($200 if the return is for husband and wife), and interest on *tax-exempt* bonds, which are mostly bonds of states and municipalities.

Adjustments in gross income. Gross income is reduced for certain costs that are associated with earning the related income. As already noted, if the taxpayer operates a business, these are essentially the business expenses that would be recorded as such in accounting. Even if the taxpayer is an employee of someone else, he or she may deduct costs under certain highly restricted circumstances. For a salesperson, these include travel costs not reimbursed by an employer. When an employee moves permanently from one city to another, moving costs can be deducted.

Deductions. The taxpayer can deduct interest expense, including interest on a mortgage; state and local property taxes, income taxes, and sales taxes; contributions to charities (including the College Alumni Fund – Adv.); one half the cost of health insurance, but not over $150; large medical and hospital bills; contributions to a qualified retirement plan; alimony payments; costs of making investments and preparing tax returns; and casualty losses over $100. The taxpayer can either itemize each of these deductions, or can take a *standard deduction* for such items combined. The standard deduction is 16 percent of adjusted gross income up to a maximum of $2,300 for a single person or $2,600 for a couple who file a joint return. Instead of these deductions, the taxpayer can take a *low-income allowance* ($1,600 for a single taxpayer; $1,900 for a married couple). This allowance, together with the exemptions described below, has the effect of removing many low-income people from the tax rolls.

Exemptions. The taxpayer is allowed one personal exemption and one exemption for each dependent. Additional exemptions are allowed if the taxpayer and/or his spouse is over age 65 and/or blind. Each exemption is worth $750 and is subtracted from adjusted gross income.

Calculation of the tax. After the subtraction of deductions and exemptions, the remainder is *taxable income.* The income tax is calculated according to a table that shows the amount for each level of income. The table is structured so that the tax is *progressive;* that is, the higher the taxable income, the higher the tax as a percentage of that income. The minimum rate is 14 percent, which applies to the first $500 of taxable income for a single taxpayer and the first $1,000 for married taxpayers filing joint returns. The maximum rate is 70 percent, which applies to income of over $100,000 for a single taxpayer and to income of over $200,000 for a joint return. However, to the extent that the income is earned, the maximum rate is 50 percent. Earned income comes from compensation, business income, and the like, as distinguished from interest and dividend income.

From the amount of tax, the taxpayer deducts the amount that his or her employer has withheld, amounts prepaid to the Internal Revenue Service during the year, and certain other credits. The difference is remitted to the IRS (or, if withholding and payments exceed the tax, the IRS sends the taxpayer a check for the difference.)

Individual tax planning

The government does not want taxpayers to pay more income taxes than they are required to pay. The tax regulations and their implications are so complicated, however, that many taxpayers do pay more than they need to. The foregoing description is only a brief outline of the main provisions of the regulations, as anyone who has read the fine print of the instructions accompanying Form 1040 and the related tax forms will appreciate. Most wealthy taxpayers and many taxpayers of moderate income therefore consult tax experts to learn about ways of legitimately reducing their taxable income. Some of these are discussed below.

An obvious, but sometimes overlooked, rule is that taxpayers should take all the deductions and exemptions to which they are entitled. Many taxpayers do not know, for example, that certain costs incurred in seeking employment are allowable deductions in calculating taxable income.

Income postponement. A person normally has a lower income after retirement than during his working years. Since the tax rates are progressive, the lower income in the retirement years may be taxed at a lower rate than the higher income in the working years. Under some circumstances, therefore, a taxpayer is well advised to shift income to the retirement years. If, for example, a married taxpayer has taxable income of $30,000 during a certain year, he must pay a tax rate of 39 percent on the last $2,000 of that income (assuming a joint return is filed). If, however, $2,000 of income is postponed until the taxpayer retires, and his income then drops to $15,000, the $2,000 will be taxed at a rate of only 25 percent. Taxable income is postponed by various types of retirement plans, including pension plans paid for by the employer, and plans to which the taxpayer contributes some of his current income. Provided certain conditions are met, these retirement contributions are not counted as income until the year in which the retirement payments are received.

Tax-exempt securities. Since interest on most state and municipal bonds is tax exempt, wealthy investors may increase their aftertax income substantially by investing in such securities. A taxpayer in the top (70 percent) tax bracket keeps, after taxes, only $30 of every $100 of interest or dividends that is received from investing in corporate securities, but the taxpayer keeps $100 of every $100 received from tax-exempt securities. Put another way, for a top-bracket investor, an investment in a $1,000 tax-exempt security paying 5 percent interest provides $50 after taxes, which is the same as he would keep from $1,000 invested in a taxable bond at 16 2/3 percent interest [$1,000 × 16 2/3 percent = $167; $167 − ($167 × 0.7) = $50]. Because of the tax advantage of exempt securities, they are issued at lower interest rates than corporate bonds of comparable risk.

Capital gains. As noted above, only one half the capital gain arising from the sale of securities or other property held more than six months is counted as gross income, so the effective tax rate on these gains is only half the tax rate on income from ordinary sources. If a taxpayer has a choice between receiving $1,000 that is counted as ordinary income and $1,000 that is counted as a capital gain, he would much prefer the latter.

Of the several ways in which this general principle may be used to advantage, perhaps the most common relates to the payment of dividends by corporations. Dividends are ordinary income. If earnings are retained by the company, rather than being paid out as dividends, and if they can be put to work in the company to earn additional earnings, the market price of the stock should eventually reflect these additional earnings. The investor can then sell the stock at a higher price than would otherwise be the case, and the gain is a capital gain. Investors who are interested in capital gains seek companies that pay relatively small dividends, hoping that the relatively large retained earnings will result in an increase in the price of the stock. (There are several "ifs" in the above line of reasoning; the gain from such an investment policy is by no means a sure thing.)

Tax shelters. Consistent with generally accepted accounting principles, the Internal Revenue Code permits the cost of a fixed asset to be written off by means of periodic depreciation charges. Some assets, however, do not decline in market value with the passing of time, and others decline at a rate that is less than the depreciation charge. A well-constructed and well-located office building, for example, can sometimes be sold for more than the owner paid for it several years previously. The tax deductions, including depreciation expense, on such properties may even exceed the rental revenue in the early years, yet the property may nevertheless be an attractive investment because of its "depreciation tax shield" and its ultimate resale value. Such properties are called **tax-sheltered investments.**

An individual taxpayer, or a partnership, may acquire property for these reasons. In the early years, expenses may exceed revenue, thus resulting in a loss which is an offset to the income received from other sources. (See the calculation of accelerated depreciation in Exhibit 9–3, Year 1, for an example of such a loss.) After some years, the property is sold, hopefully for more than its book value. The gain is taxed as a capital gain.[10] Calculations of the present value of proposed tax-sheltered investments are made in the same fashion as for any investment. The anticipated resale value is treated as an estimated cash inflow in the year in which sale of the property is planned. Note that the total amount of income over the life of this investment is *not* what causes the tax advantage in a tax-sheltered investment. The tax advantage arises because (1) taxable income is low or negative in the early years when present value is high, and (2) the gain when the property is sold is taxed as a capital gain rather than as ordinary income.

Exploring for oil and gas, leasing equipment, farming, cattle raising, other agricultural activities, and timber growing have special tax provisions that, under certain circumstances, make them attractive as tax-sheltered investments. As is the case with any business investments, however, if the proposition turns out to be unsound, the investor loses.

Although capital gains, accelerated depreciations, and tax shelters reduce the income tax below what it otherwise would be, the Internal Revenue Code offsets part of the benefits by imposing a special tax of 10 percent of the amount of such *tax preference* items above a prescribed minimum.

---

[10] Special rules apply to the calculation of this gain.

Corporation income tax

The deductions and exemptions in the individual income tax calculations are designed partly to take account of the individual's ability to pay taxes (e.g., the rates are higher for wealthy taxpayers; the exemption of $750 per dependent reflects ability to pay), partly to provide an incentive for socially desirable activities (e.g., contributions to charities are tax deductible), and partly for political reasons (e.g., the federal government is reluctant to tax the income on state bonds because of state opposition to such a tax).

Somewhat different considerations govern the calculation of the corporation income tax. In general, the corporation tax calculation approximates the calculation of the net income of a business. Deviations from the generally accepted accounting principles that govern such calculations are made primarily for one of two reasons (1) because generally accepted accounting principles are believed to be too subjective, or (2) in order to encourage socially desirable actions. In addition, special interest groups sometimes succeed in persuading the Congress to give them special tax benefits.

As an example of a departure from generally accepted principles in income tax calculations a corporation cannot deduct its estimated future expense for warranty costs. This item is an expense that should be matched with current revenue, but the amount has to be estimated, and the estimate is a matter of subjective judgment. As an example of incentives for socially desirable actions, businesses are given special treatment for transactions involving the acquisition, disposition, and sale of capital assets, in order to encourage them to invest in modern equipment.

If the corporation has a taxable loss in a given year, the Internal Revenue Service will pay it an equivalent amount from taxes paid in the three preceding years (the "tax carryback"). If the loss is greater than this amount, it may be used to offset income taxes during the next five years (the "tax carryforward").

Another difference between the corporation tax and the personal tax is that the corporation tax is essentially not progressive. Instead of the schedule of personal tax rates that rise in 25 steps from 14 percent to 70 percent, in the corporation tax structure there are essentially only three steps. The first $25,000 of a corporation's income is taxed at 20 percent, the next $25,000 at 22 percent, and all income above $50,000 is taxed at 48 percent.

One might suppose that this rate structure would cause a large company to organize itself into many small subsidiary corporations, each with a taxable income of less than $50,000. In reality, this does not happen because the Internal Revenue Code looks through the form to the substance; it regards all the corporations in such an arrangement as a single consolidated corporation, and levies the income tax on the total income of the entity.

Capital gains and losses

In the text of Chapter 9, we discussed how depreciation is a tax deductible expense that shields the cash flows from the full effect of income taxes, and how accelerated depreciation and the investment credit increase the attractiveness of capital investment proposals in most circumstances. Other tax features are also important in such decisions. One of these is the treatment of capital gains and losses.

When an existing machine is replaced by a new machine, the net book value of the existing machine is removed from the accounting records. This transaction may give rise either to a gain or to a loss, depending on whether the amount realized from the sale of the existing machine is greater than or less than its net book value (see *Fundamentals of Financial Accounting,* Chapter 10). The income tax treatment of this gain or loss may well differ from the accounting treatment, however. Depending on the circumstances, (1) a gain or loss may be included in the calculation of taxable income and thus subject to the regular income tax rate; (2) a gain may be subject only to a 30 percent tax rate, which is applicable to capital gains; (3) if the new machine replaces one of "like kind," no gain or loss may be recognized, but, instead, the *book value* of the replaced machine is added to the cash paid for the new machine, and the total becomes the cost of the new machine for income tax purposes; or (4) if the machine is treated as a member of a group, the value of the replaced machine may be disregarded entirely. Expert tax advice is needed on problems involving gains and losses on the sale of depreciable assets, for it is difficult to know which of these alternatives is applicable in a given case. In any event, when existing assets are disposed of, the relevant amount by which the net investment is reduced is the proceeds of the sale, adjusted for taxes.

Forms of business organization

The income of a corporation is taxed twice. It is taxed by the corporation income tax in the year it is earned, and the same income is taxed a second time when it is distributed to investors in the form of dividends, because dividends are taxable income to the recipient. The income of a proprietorship or a partnership is taxed only once, at the time it is earned by the proprietor or partner; there is no separate income tax on an unincorporated business. Despite this double taxation, a large entity with widespread ownership has no choice but to organize itself as a corporation. The complications of operating as a gigantic partnership would be too great, and investors would ordinarily be unwilling to assume the unlimited liability that partners have.

The question arises, however, as to why a small, closely held business would choose to organize as a corporation and thereby suffer double taxation of its income. One reason is that a corporation with fewer than ten stockholders can elect to be taxed as if it were a partnership. (They are called *Subchapter S Corporations* because this is the applicable subchapter of the Internal Revenue Code.) The more fundamental reason for incorporating is the limited liability advantage that corporations have.

In any event, tax considerations are important in deciding on which form of organization is best in a given situation. Other considerations were discussed in Chapter 12 of *Fundamentals of Financial Accounting.*

Methods of financing

The interest paid to bondholders or other creditors is a tax deductible expense to the corporation, whereas no tax deduction is given for dividends paid to shareholders. The effect of this is that the true cost of debt financing is much less than the cost of equity financing, that is, obtaining funds from shareholders.

Exhibit 9–8 shows the effect of debt financing, compared with equity financing. Currently, the company has $40 million of permanent capital, all of which is equity capital (either furnished by shareholders or from retained earnings). Management estimates that with $10 million of additional capital, income before interest and income taxes will be $12 million annually. It is considering obtaining the additional capital either from debt financing (bonds) at an interest rate of 9 percent, or with equity financing (issuance of additional common stock).

As can be seen from Exhibit 9–8, if the $10 million is obtained from debt financing, there will be an additional interest cost of $900,000. This is a tax deductible expense, so it shields the pretax income from the full effect of the income tax. If the company uses equity financing, however, the full $12,000,000 of pretax income is subject to the income tax. Thus, if debt financing is used, income taxes will be $459,000 lower than if equity financing is used. This reduces the effective cost of the debt financing, making it 4.4 percent, rather than 9 percent. Indeed, as a general rule, it can be said that the effective interest cost of debt financing is about one half the actual interest rate, because of the impact of income taxes.

Note also that although net income is higher with equity financing ($5,880,000 compared with $5,439,000), equity capital is also higher, so the return on shareholders' equity is only 11.8 percent under equity financing compared with 13.6 percent with debt financing.

EXHIBIT 9–8

Effect of alternative financing methods (000 omitted)

Assumptions:
1. Current capital is $40,000, all equity.
2. Additional capital required is $10,000.
3. Income before interest and taxes will be $12,000.
4. Debt capital will cost 9 percent interest.

Return on equity capital

	Debt financing	Equity financing
Capital:		
Debt (bonds)	$10,000	$ 0
Equity (stock)	40,000	50,000
Total Capital	$50,000	$50,000
Income:		
Income before interest and taxes	$12,000	$12,000
Interest expense (9 percent)	900	0
Taxable income	11,100	12,000
Income tax (51 percent)	5,661	6,120
Net income	$ 5,439	$ 5,880
Return on equity capital	13.6%	11.8%

Effective interest cost

	Amount	Percent
Interest expense	$900	9.0
Less: Savings in income tax ($6,120 − $5,661)	459	4.6
Effective interest cost	$441	4.4

For these reasons, companies are strongly motivated to use debt financing rather than equity financing whenever it is feasible to do so. The tax advantages of debt financing must be weighed against its additional risk, however. The higher the proportion of debt financing the greater the risk of financial difficulty if business conditions should become unfavorable.

Treatment of interest in calculation. In analyzing capital investment proposals, it would be possible to take the interest deduction into account in the form of a tax shield, just as was described above for depreciation. This is done, however, only when the method of financing is an integral part of the proposed investment. In the more usual situation, as explained in Chapter 8, interest is included as one element in calculating the required rate of return. When such a calculation is made, it is the aftertax interest cost that is relevant.

EXAMPLE: In computing a company's cost of capital, what rate should be used for bonds that have a pretax interest rate of 8 percent if the company expects its income tax rate to be 51 percent?

Answer: If the income tax rate is 51 percent, the aftertax interest cost of the bonds is 1 minus 51 percent = 49 percent of the interest rate. The rate to be used for bonds is therefore 0.49 × 0.08 = 3.9 percent.

Preferred stock. From the point of view of common shareholders, preferred stock is much inferior to bonds as a source of financing. Preferred stock dividends must be paid ahead of dividends on the common, but they are not tax deductible to the corporation. Thus, although the effective cost of a 9 percent bond is about 4.5 percent, the effective cost of 9 percent preferred stock is the full 9 percent. Preferred stock is therefore used primarily in special situations, such as in connection with acquisitions or reorganizations.

Tax incentives

We have already described the tax incentives that exist to encourage a company to acquire additional capital assets. Income tax considerations must be taken into account whenever a proposal involves the acquisition of depreciable assets. In addition to this general case, there are a number of special situations in which income tax considerations have a significant effect on the analysis of alternative choice problems. These involve tax incentives that the government has provided to encourage what it believes to be socially desirable actions on the part of business. If the proposal involves the acquisition of, or the search for, certain mineral resources, special tax regulations relating to depletion need to be taken into account. The government also provides special income tax treatment for expenses associated with the hiring and training of members of disadvantaged minority groups, for expenditures made for pollution abatement, for building low-income housing, for childcare facilities, for business conducted in Puerto Rico, for products that are exported for sale abroad, and for a number of other special situations. A description of these special tax treatments is not appropriate for an introductory text. The point is that business executives must be familiar with their existence and must be prepared to call in tax experts whenever a proposal involving these matters is being analyzed so that cash-flow estimates will be based on correct tax facts.

Concluding comment

Income tax regulations and explanations of them are compiled by several publishing companies. A single set consists of several thousand pages of fine print and requires about three feet of shelf space. Obviously, the description above is only a brief summary of some of the important points. It should be adequate, however, to convey the following general ideas:

- Income taxes make a big difference in the analysis of many business problems; their impact should always be considered.
- Expert tax advice is needed on all except the most routine problems.
- Taxable income is in most respects calculated in the same way as income is calculated under generally accepted accounting principles, but there are enough differences so that a knowledge of accounting principles is not adequate to answer tax questions.

IMPORTANT TERMS

Aftertax income	Payback method
Pretax income	Unadjusted return on
Pretax cash inflow	investment method
Aftertax cash inflow	Screening problem
Tax shield	Preference problem
Project rate-of-return method	Profitability index
Investment/inflow ratio	

QUESTIONS FOR DISCUSSION

1. Income taxes were not considered in any of the calculations of alternative choice problems in Chapter 7. Does this mean that of these calculations lead to incorrect decisions?

2. Teddall Company expects to pay federal and state income taxes at the following rates:

	Amount	Rate	Income tax
Puerto Rican income	$ 75,000	0%	$ 0
First taxable increment	25,000	20	5,000
Second taxable increment	25,000	22	5,500
Other, federal only	100,000	48	48,000
Remainder, federal and state	775,000	51	395,250
	$1,000,000	45.4%	$453,750

What income tax rate is relevant in analyzing a typical investment proposal? Does the size of the proposed investment affect your answer?

3. Supposing the Congress made the following changes in income taxes, what effect would each probably have on the total amount of capital investments made in the United States? Why?
   a. Reduce the income tax rate from 48 percent to 40 percent.
   b. Permit only straight-line depreciation for tax purposes; forbid the use of accelerated depreciation.

c. Permit an investment to be fully depreciated over one half its economic life.

d. Eliminate the investment credit.

4. For an investment proposal that results in a cost saving, is "cash inflow" as used in the chapter the same as "differential cost" as used in Chapter 7? For an investment proposal that involves additional revenue, is "cash inflow" the same as "differential revenue"? Explain.

5. In analyzing an investment proposal, why is depreciation excluded from the calculation of pretax cash inflows but included in the calculation of the income tax effect?

6. In your own words, explain how the net difference of $59 in Exhibit 9–1 was derived.

7. Can there be an acceptable proposal to acquire a machine for the purpose of reducing direct labor costs in which the depreciation completely shielded the pretax cash inflow; that is, so that no additional income tax payments would be required? Explain.

8. The total amount of depreciation is the same whether accelerated depreciation or straight-line depreciation is used. Why, then do most companies use accelerated depreciation in calculating taxable income?

9. In Exhibit 9–3, the first amount in the "Tax" column is *minus* $7. Explain how there can be a minus income tax.

10. Explain the difference between the project rate-of-return method and the net present value method.

11. Does the net present value method and the project rate-of-return method lead to the same decision in screening problems? In preference problems? In case they lead to different decisions, which decision is correct?

12. Explain the weakness of the payback method as a decision rule.

13. What is the relationship between the two rates of return found by the unadjusted return on investment method and the rate of return found by the project rate-of-return method? Explain which rate is correct, and why.

14. In a preference problem, two or more proposals are ranked in order of their desirability. If each of the proposals is acceptable, why does anyone want to know how they rank; that is, why aren't they all accepted?

15. The chapter explains how the numbers for Case 2 in Exhibit 9–4 were derived. Make a similar explanation for Case 1.

16. What are some of the nonquantitative considerations that are important in a capital investment problem? Can you think of any practical, important problem that does not require the use of judgment?

17. Discuss issues involved in deciding between the following investment opportunities, only one of which can be undertaken. Assume a 10 percent required rate of return.

Case No. 1. provides a 17 percent return, with moderate risk, for a 13-year period.

Case No. 2. provides a 25 percent return, with moderate risk, for a five-year period.

PROBLEMS

Note: Unless otherwise specified, use a tax rate of 51 percent and assume straight-line depreciation for tax purposes.

9–1. The Williams Company is trying to decide whether to continue using an old machine with a remaining useful life of five years, or replace it with a new machine costing $6,000 which is expected to save $1,800 of labor costs each year of its five-year life. The old machine is fully depreciated and has no salvage value. The company requires a 10 percent rate of return after taxes.

Required:
A. Calculate the net present value of the proposed investment.
B. Should Williams purchase the new machine? Why?

9–2. Ecolab, Inc., has acquired new equipment costing $8,000 with an estimated useful life of four years and an estimated salvage value of $1,200. The company wishes to use the depreciation method which gives the better cash flow. Under consideration are the straight-line and the sum-of-the-years'-digits methods.

Required:
A. Prepare a schedule which will show the difference in aftertax cash flow of the two methods being considered.
B. Which depreciation method is preferable for tax purposes? Why?
C. Assume that pretax cash inflows associated with the new equipment are $3,000 per year and that Ecolab requires a 10 percent rate of return after taxes. Calculate the net present value of the investment using both depreciation methods. Why do the two methods yield different answers?

9–3. (Disregard income taxes in this problem.) Compute the following:
A. The rate of return for an investment expected to yield an annual cash inflow of $400 is 5 percent. How much is the investment if the investment/inflow ratio is 12.50?
B. An investment of $9,000 has an investment/inflow ratio of 8.6 and a useful life of 15 years. What is the annual cash inflow? What is the time-adjusted rate of return?
C. What is the maximum price a company can afford to pay for an asset expected to produce a cash inflow of $6,000 per year for five years if its required rate of return is 8 percent?
D. How much investment per dollar of expected annual operating savings can a company afford if the investment has an expected life of ten years and its required rate of return is 12 percent?

9–4. The Johnson Company is considering the purchase of a new machine which is expected to result in an aftertax cash inflow of $3,000 per year. The machine will cost $15,000 and have an economic life of ten years with zero residual value.

Required:

A. Calculate the project rate of return for the new machine.

B. If Johnson's required rate of return is 12 percent, do you recommend purchase of the new machine? Why?

C. Assume that the cost of the machine is $18,400 instead of $15,000. Recalculate the project rate of return.

D. Assume the situation as in Requirement A except that the economic life of the machine is eight years instead of ten. Recalculate the project rate of return.

E. Assume the situation as in Requirement A except that the aftertax cash inflow is $3,300 per year instead of $3,000. Recalculate the project rate of return.

F. Try to generalize about the effect on the project rate of return of changes in the cost of an asset, the economic life of the asset, and the aftertax cash inflows resulting from an asset.

9–5. The Ellis Company estimates that it can save $3,100 per year in pretax cash operating costs over the next ten years if it buys a new machine at a cost of $12,000. The machine will have no residual value. Ellis has a required rate of return of 12 percent after taxes.

Required:

A. Calculate the project rate of return for the new machine.

B. Do you recommend purchase? Why?

C. What would be the project rate of return if the economic life of the machine were five years instead of ten? Do you recommend purchase now? Why?

9–6. Refer to the Ellis Company (Problem 9–5).

Required:

A. Calculate the payback period.

B. Do you recommend purchase? Why?

9–7. Under certain circumstances, the reciprocal of the payback period (i.e., annual cash inflow divided by investment) is an approximation of the project rate of return. (Disregard income taxes in this problem.)

Required:

A. What is the project rate of return for three projects in which the investment is $1,000, annual cash inflows are $300, and the economic life is respectively five, eight, and ten years.

B. Compare your answers in Requirement A with the reciprocal of the payback period (i.e., 30 percent).

C. Using numbers from the lower portions of the 25, 30, 40, and 50 percent columns, determine the useful lives at which the reciprocals of the payback periods give the same result as the project rate-of-return method.

D. Using your answers to Requirements B and C, try to generalize about the accuracy of the payback reciprocal as an approximation of the project rate of return.

9–8.   Refer to the Ellis Company (Problem 9–5).

Required:

A.   Calculate the unadjusted return on investment using both the initial and the average investment.

B.   Explain why the unadjusted return on investment will normally differ from the project rate of return for the same project.

9–9.   Yale Corporation is considering these two alternative investment proposals, only one of which can be accepted.

	Case 1	Case 2
Added investment.............................	$20,000	$20,000
Useful life...	5 years	10 years
Expected aftertax inflow....................	$ 6,000	$ 3,000

Required:

A.   Assuming that Yale requires a 10 percent rate of return after taxes, calculate the net present value and profitability index for both cases.

B.   Calculate the project rate of return for both cases.

C.   Which proposal, if either, should be accepted? Explain your answer.

9–10.   Cornell Corporation estimates that it will be able to approve up to $30,000 in capital investment projects at a meeting next week. The following proposals will be considered, none of which has a residual value:

Project number	Additional investment	Expected aftertax cash inflow	Estimated life of project (years)
1.................	$ 5,000	1,200	5
2.................	10,000	3,000	4
3.................	15,000	2,700	11
4.................	10,000	3,000	7
5.................	5,000	2,000	3

Required:

A.   Calculate the project rate of return after taxes for each of the five projects.

B.   Calculate the profitability index for each of the five projects using a required rate of return of 10 percent after taxes.

C.   Rank the projects and recommend which should be accepted. Explain your answer.

9–11.   The Bradford Company has decided to buy new equipment which will cost $1,200,000 and is expected to produce pretax cash inflows of $500,000 per year. The equipment is expected to have an economic life of three years and have a residual value of $300,000. F. Bradford strongly believes that corporate income taxes will soon be increased from the present 51 percent and wonders about the depreciation method that should be used for the new equipment. The company requires a 10 percent return after taxes.

Required:

A. Prepare depreciation schedules using both straight-line and sum-of-the-years'-digits methods.

B. Assume that the tax rate is raised to 65 percent for Years 2 and 3. Calculate the net present value of the aftertax cash inflows for each of the two depreciation methods.

C. Which depreciation method do you recommend to Bradford? Why?

9-12. The Savory Corporation wants to acquire new equipment with which to make a new product. The equipment may be purchased at a cost of $51,000 or leased for an annual payment of $18,300 per year for three years. The increased cash inflow anticipated is $20,000 per year, before tax considerations and any applicable straight-line depreciation and lease payments. The equipment would have no residual value at the end of three years.

Required:

A. Calculate the aftertax cash flow for each of the three years if the equipment is purchased with $50,000 borrowed funds to be repaid with interest of $2,500, $1,700, and $875 for each of the three years. The loan principal will be repaid in three equal annual payments.

B. Calculate the aftertax cash flow for each year if the equipment is leased.

C. Which is more profitable, leasing or buying? Why? (In comparing profitability disregard the required rate of return and use the interest costs instead.)

D. Comment on the decision to acquire the equipment if the company has a required rate of return of 10 percent after taxes on all such projects. (In answering this question, consider carefully how interest should be treated.)

9-13. The Brewer Company is considering the purchase of a new machine which is expected to save $4,000 per year in cash operating costs for five years, pretax. The cost of the machine is $14,000, and it will have zero residual value. Brewer has a required rate of return of 12 percent after taxes. The machine qualifies for the 10 percent investment tax credit. (*Note:* Depreciation expense for tax purposes is based on the original cost of the asset before subtracting the investment credit.)

Required:

A. Calculate the project rate of return for the new machine.

B. What would the project rate of return have been without the investment credit?

C. What would the project rate of return have been if the investment credit were 15 percent instead of 10 percent?

D. Comment on the potential implications of the changes in the investment credit percentage as a means to encourage business to invest in fixed assets.

9-14. Refer to the data for the Lance Company (Problem 8-14). In addition, assume that the new machine qualifies for the 10 percent investment credit, and that any gain or loss on the disposal of the old machine is treated as ordinary revenue or expense for tax purposes.

Required:

A. Calculate the aftertax net present value.
B. Calculate the payback period.
C. Calculate the unadjusted return on investment using both initial and average investment.
D. Do you recommend purchase? Why?

9–15. The Nelson Corporation has an opportunity to replace an old machine with no book value or salvage value with a new machine costing $9,000 with a ten-year useful life. Expected annual labor savings are $2,000. The company requires a 10 percent return on investment after taxes.

Required:

A. Calculate the net present value of the proposed investment.
B. Should Nelson purchase the new machine? Why?

9–16. The Re-Cycle Company is just starting operations with new equipment costing $30,000 and a useful life of four years. At the end of four years the equipment probably can be sold for $6,000. The company is concerned with its cash flow and wants a comparison of straight-line and sum-of-the-years'-digits depreciation to help management decide which depreciation method to use.

Required:

A. Calculate the difference in aftertax income and cash inflow under each method.
B. Which depreciation method is preferable for tax purposes? Why?
C. Assume that pretax cash inflows associated with the new equipment are $10,000 per year and that Re-cycle requires a 10 percent rate of return after taxes. Calculate the net present value of the investment using both depreciation methods. Why do the two methods yield different answers?

9–17. (Disregard income taxes in this problem.) Compute the following:
A. An investment of $12,000 has an investment/inflow ratio of 6.2 and a useful life of 12 years. What is the annual cash inflow and the time-adjusted rate of return?
B. The time-adjusted rate of return for an investment expected to yield an annual cash inflow of $1,500 is 14 percent. How much is the investment if the investment/inflow ratio is 6.14?
C. What is the maximum investment a company would make in an asset expected to produce annual cash inflow of $5,000 a year for eight years if its required rate of return is 18 percent?
D. How much investment per dollar of expected annual operating savings can a company afford if the investment has an expected life of seven years and its required rate of return is 15 percent?

9–18. The Jackson Company is considering the purchase of a new machine which is expected to result in an aftertax cash inflow of $5,000 per year. The machine will cost $20,000 and have an economic life of eight years with zero residual value.

Required:

A. Calculate the project rate of return for the new machine.

B. If Jackson's required rate of return is 20 percent after taxes, do you recommend purchase of the new machine? Why?

C. Assume that the cost of the machine is $18,000 instead of $20,000. Recalculate the project rate of return.

D. Assume the situation as in Requirement A except that the economic life of the machine is seven years instead of eight. Recalculate the project rate of return.

E. Assume the situation as in Requirement A except that the aftertax cash inflow is $4,000 per year instead of $5,000. Recalculate the project rate of return.

F. Try to generalize about the effect on the project rate of return of changes in the cost of an asset, the economic life of an asset, and the aftertax cash inflows resulting from an asset.

9-19. The Carter Company estimates that it can save $2,900 per year in pretax cash operating costs over the next ten years if it buys a new machine at a cost of $12,000. The machine will have no residual value. Carter has a required rate of return after taxes of 10 percent.

Required:

A. Calculate the project rate of return for the new machine.

B. Do you recommend purchase? Why?

C. Assume that the machine would save only $2,500 per year for six years. Recalculate the project rate of return. Do you recommend purchase now? Why?

9-20. Refer to the Carter Company (Problem 9-19).

Required:

A. Calculate the payback period.

B. Do you recommend purchase? Why?

9-21. Refer to the Carter Company (Problem 9-19).

Required:

A. Calculate the unadjusted return on investment using both the initial and the average investment.

B. Explain why the unadjusted return on investment will normally differ from the project rate of return for the same project.

9-22. Jan Shoe Company is considering the following two investment proposals (disregard taxes):

	Case 1	Case 2
Initial cash outlay..............	$10,000	$10,000
Investment life..................	10 years	10 years
Cash inflows	$ 2,000 annually	$20,000 at the end of the 10th year

Required:

A. Assuming that Jan requires a 10 percent rate of return, calculate the net present value and profitability index for both cases.
B. Calculate the project rate of return for both cases.
C. Which proposal should be accepted, if any? Explain your answer.

9–23. Dartmouth Corporation estimates that it will have $50,000 available for capital investments during 1977. Half of this will be reserved for emergency projects and half will be invested in the most desirable projects from the following list. None of the investments has a residual value.

Project number	Added investment	Expected aftertax cash inflow	Estimated life of project
1.................	$ 5,000	$1,250	3 years
2.................	10,000	2,500	5
3.................	11,000	3,500	4
4.................	4,000	500	15
5.................	2,000	1,100	2

Required:

A. Calculate the aftertax project rate of return for each of the five projects.
B. Calculate the profitability index for each of the five projects using a required rate of return of 10 percent after taxes.
C. Rank the projects and recommend which should be accepted, if any. Explain your answer.

9–24. The King Company has decided to buy new equipment which will cost $1,400,000 and is expected to produce pretax cash inflows of $600,000 per year. The equipment is expected to have an economic life of three years and have a residual value of $200,000. C. King strongly believes that corporate income taxes will soon be increased from the present 51 percent and wonders about the depreciation method that should be used for new equipment. The company requires a 10 percent rate of return after taxes.

Required:

A. Prepare depreciation schedules using both straight-line and sum-of-the-year's-digits methods.
B. Assume that the tax rate is raised to 66 percent for Years 2 and 3. Calculate the net present value of the aftertax cash inflows for each of the two depreciation methods.
C. Which depreciation method do you recommend to King? Why?

9–25. The McGowan Soup Company needs more cold storage space. A building adequate for anticipated needs for the next three years may be leased for $51,000 per year, or the company can build its own storage house on company owned property at a cost of $150,000. At the end of three years the building would have no salvage value. Increased cash inflow is expected to be $60,000 per year before any applicable taxes, straight-line depreciation, or lease payments.

Required:

A. Calculate the aftertax cash flow for each of the three years if the building is purchased with funds borrowed with interest payable of $7,500, $5,100, and $2,600 for each of the three years, respectively. The loan principal will be repaid in three equal annual payments.

B. Calculate the aftertax cash flow for each year if the building is leased.

C. Which is more profitable, leasing or buying? Why? (In comparing profitability, disregard the required rate of return and use the interest costs instead.)

D. Comment on the decision to acquire the building if the company has a required rate of return of 10 percent after taxes on all such projects. (In answering this question, consider carefully how interest should be treated.)

9–26. The Wallace Company is considering the purchase of a new machine which is expected to save $5,000 per year in pretax cash operating costs for five years. The cost of the machine is $16,000, and it will have zero residual value. Wallace uses straight-line depreciation and has a required rate of return of 10 percent after taxes. The machine qualifies for the 10 percent investment tax credit. (*Note:* Depreciation expense is based on the original cost of the asset before subtracting the investment credit.)

Required:

A. Calculate the project rate of return for the new machine.

B. What would the project rate of return have been without the investment credit?

C. What would the project rate of return have been if the investment credit were 15 percent instead of 10 percent?

D. Comment on the potential implications of changes in the investment credit percentage as a means to encourage business to invest in fixed assets.

9–27. Refer to the data for the Grant Company (Problem 8–24). In addition, assume that the new machine qualifies for the 10 percent investment credit, and that any gain or loss is treated as ordinary revenue or expense for tax purposes.

Required:

A. Calculate the aftertax net present value.

B. Calculate the payback period.

C. Calculate the unadjusted return on investment using both initial and average investment.

D. Do you recommend purchase? Why?

9–28. The Baxter Company manufactures toys and other short-lived fad type items.

The research and development department came up with an item that would make a good promotional gift for office equipment dealers. Aggressive and effective effort by Baxter's sales personnel has resulted in almost firm commitments for this product for the next three years. It is expected that the product's value will be exhausted by that time.

In order to produce the quantity demanded Baxter will need to buy additional machinery and rent some additional space. It appears that about 25,000 square feet will be needed; 12,500 square feet of presently unused, but leased, space is available now. (Baxter's present lease with 10 years to run costs $3 a foot.) There is another 12,500 square feet adjoining the Baxter facility which Baxter will rent for three years at $4 per square foot per year if it decides to make this product.

The equipment will be purchased for about $900,000. It will require $30,000 in modifications, $60,000 for installation, and $90,000 for testing; all of these activities will be done by a firm of engineers hired by Baxter. All of the expenditures will be paid for on January 1, 1973.

The equipment should have a salvage value of about $180,000 at the end of the third year. No additional general overhead costs are expected to be incurred.

The following estimates of revenues and expenses for this product for the three years have been developed:

	1973	1974	1975
Sales..	$1,000,000	$1,600,000	$800,000
Material, labor, and incurred overhead	400,000	750,000	350,000
Assigned general overhead	40,000	75,000	35,000
Rent...	87,500	87,500	87,500
Depreciation	450,000	300,000	150,000
	977,500	1,212,500	622,500
Income before tax	22,500	387,500	177,500
Income tax (40%)	9,000	155,000	71,000
	$ 13,500	$ 232,500	$106,500

Required:

A. Prepare a schedule which shows the incremental, aftertax, and cash flows for this project.

B. If the company requires a two-year payback period for its investment, would it undertake this project? Show your supporting calculations clearly.

C. Calculate the aftertax unadjusted rate of return for the project.

D. A newly hired business school graduate recommends that the company consider the use of the net present value analysis to study this project. If the company sets a required rate of return of 20 percent after taxes will this project be accepted? Show your supporting calculations clearly. (Assume all operating revenues and expenses occur at the end of the year.)

(IMA adapted)

9-29. It is sometimes argued that companies would be better off if the Congress allowed depreciation based on the replacement cost of assets, rather than on the historical cost. Examine this argument by examining a machine that costs $1,000 and has a useful life of five years. Assume that under present laws a company would (a) take a 10 percent investment credit in Year 1, (b) depreciate the $1,000 over four years (80 percent of its useful life), and (c) use sum-of-years'-digits depreciation. Assume that replacement costs are increasing at 6 percent a year (at the beginning of each year, for simplicity), and that depreciation is 20 percent of the replacement cost in each year, with no investment credit. (For example, in Year 2 the replacement cost is $1,060 and the depreciation is $212.) The company has a required rate of return of 10 percent. Assume an income tax rate of 48 percent.

Required:

A. Calculate the present value of the depreciation tax shield under each set of assumptions. Should the business community advocate depreciation based on replacement costs under these circumstances?

B. If the tax law permitted a 10 percent investment credit as well as depreciation based on replacement costs, would your answer be different?

9-30. A company owned a plot of land that appeared in its fixed assets at its acquisition cost in 1910, which was $10,000. The land was not used. In 1975 the local boys club asked the company to donate the land as the site for a new recreation building. The donation would be a taxable deduction of $110,000, which was the current appraised value. The company's tax rate was 51 percent. Some argued that the company would be better off to donate the land than to keep it or to sell it for $110,000. Assume that, other than the land, the company's taxable income as well as its accounting income before taxes was $10,000,000.

Required:

How would the company's aftertax cash inflow be affected if (a) it donated the land or (b) it sold the land for $110,000? How would its net income be affected?

9-31. Seavy Manufacturing Company owns equipment which it developed and constructed, and which it rents to Timmons Company for $16,000 per year. For this fee the Seavy Company also keeps the equipment repaired and in good working condition. These services cost Seavy $6,000 per year. When built, the equipment cost $60,000. Its useful life when new was estimated at 15 years. In 1974, Seavy has received an offer of $50,000 for the equipment, which is now ten years old. Any long-term capital gains would be subject to the 30 percent rate.

Required:

A. Calculate the aftertax income over the next five years (1) if Seavy keeps the equipment and continues to rent it, and (2) if the equipment is sold.

B. What course of action do you advise the company to follow? Why?

9–32. The Standard Parts Company has received an offer to bid on some specially machined castings and is trying to decide which of two machines could do the work more profitably. The contract calls for 1,000 units per year for five years for which the company would receive $50 per unit. Below are data related to the use of Machine A and Machine B for the contract, neither of which will be of any use to the company at the end of the contract period, nor will either have a salvage value. Disregard income taxes.

	Machine A	Machine B
Cost of machine..................	$22,000.00	$40,000.00
Cost per unit per year:		
Materials and labor...........	29.60	27.65
Factory overhead (other than depreciation)	1.40	1.35
General and administrative expense.......................	8.00	8.00
Total.....................	$39.00	$37.00

Required:

Which machine should be used if the contract is won by Standard? Comment on your decision.

9–33. S. Jones is considering the purchase of 62 acres of land, presently owned by Talcott and leased from Talcott by Weeden. Weeden uses the land as a golf driving range and pays $1,000 per month rental.

The purchase price of the land is $400,000; however, Jones has knowledge of state plans to build a highway which will run adjacent to the property. Jones is convinced that once the highway is built, the land can be sold for $650,000. Jones plans to finance the purchase with $100,000 of personal funds, plus a $300,000, five-year, 7.5 percent bank note, with interest payable on a monthly basis.

The plans for the new highway call for its completion in four and a half years, and Jones has been informed by Weeden that a five-year lease on the land at the present rental rate would be agreeable. Jones is aware of some of the risks involved in the plan and as a result wishes to evaluate the proposal, using a 15 percent aftertax required rate of return.

Required:

Assuming the following tax rates

Ordinary income 51%
Capital gains 30

should Jones undertake this venture?

CASE: THURBER COMPANY

9–34. The executive committee of the Thurber Company was considering the addition of a new super-widget to its product line. It had before it an unfavorable report from the assistant and treasurer which read as follows:

1. It is recommended that the Thurber Company *not* add the super-widget to its current product line. This is largely based on a consideration of the quantity we can sell annually versus that required to break even. According to our market research department, we can anticipate sales of about 45,000 units per year. My calculations show that the break-even sales volume is 50,000 units per year as follows:

2. The marketing department has indicated that the best selling price would be $10 per super-widget. The cost department has prepared the following per unit estimate of costs:

Materials	$3.00
Direct labor: 1 hour @ $2 per hour	2.00
Variable overhead @ 25% of direct labor	0.50
General factory overhead @ 25% of direct labor	0.50
Selling and administrative expense @ 20% of selling price	2.00
Total Cost per Unit	$8.00

Apart from the overhead costs specified above, it is expected that the new super-widget department will incur fixed costs of $100,000 per year. This includes $50,000 per year for depreciation and the remainder for supervision, indirect labor, and light and power.

The sales volume at which the unit contribution of $2 ($10 selling price less $8 variable cost) will just cover the $100,000 fixed departmental expenses is 50,000 units per year.

3. The rates used for determining the unit charges for variable overhead, general factory overhead, and selling and administrative expense are standard for all of the company's product lines.

4. The estimated depreciation expense is based on $500,000 of new equipment and an economic life of ten years. Straight-line depreciation will be used on this investment.

5. A total of $300,000 was spent last year on product development and market research for the super-widget. This has already been expensed for tax purposes, but we still have this on our books as an asset. It was planned to write this off over the first five years of super-widget sales. An additional $20,000 will be required to clean up the factory area in which the new super-widget department will go. This can propably be expensed for book and tax purposes. Since the $20,000 represents a one-shot expenditure, it has been excluded from the break-even analysis.

6. Our working capital needs will be about 25 percent of the expected annual sales volume or $112,500 (25 percent of 45,000 units times $10 per unit). Since this will be recovered any time we want to drop super-widgets from our product line, this has not been included in the break-even analysis.

7. I doubt that the company will want to incure a loss on the super-widget even though the marketing people say it would be a desirable addition to the company product line and can be handled without any increase in the sales force.

8. Setting up the new department for the manufacture of super-widgets

would also provide some administrative problems for the factory management. This would be the only factory department at Thurber whose personnel cannot be used in other departments or vice versa. In effect, the "direct labor" would become a fixed cost for the company, raising the break-even point still higher than that calculated in this memorandum.

9. Certainly this project will not earn the 10 percent return after taxes that you have specified as desirable for investments in new product introduction.

Required:

A. Evaluate the assistant treasurer's report and suggest ways, if any, in which it might be improved.
B. What will the company's accounting net income after taxes be if the new super-widget is introduced? (Assume a 51 percent tax rate.)
C. What volume of new super-widgets would be required to make this a desirable investment?
D. On the basis of the information provided, what should the Thurber Company do? What additional information is required, if any?

CASE: THE WILSON COMPANY

9-35. In March 1975 the Wilson Company was considering a proposal to replace four hand-loaded transmission case milling machines with one automatic machine. The company operated a large machine shop that did machining work on a subcontract basis for local industries in the Detroit area. One of the contracts was to machine transmission cases for truck engines for the Maynard Automobile Company. The Wilson Company had negotiated such a contract with the Maynard Automobile Company for each of the previous 14 years. For the last few years, the contract had been for 60,000 transmission cases annually.

The unfinished cases were supplied by Maynard. With a hand-loaded machine, all the faces could not be machined at the same time. Each machine required the constant attention of one skilled machine operator.

The machines used by Wilson were only three years old. Each had an annual output of approximately 15,000 cases on a two-shift, five-day week basis; therefore, four machines had been purchased at a total cost of $295,000.

The useful life of a hand-loaded machine on a two-shift, five-day week basis was estimated to be 15 years. Its residual value at the end of its useful life was estimated to be $2,000. Depreciation of $59,000 had been built up for the four machines, representing three years' accumulation. The purchase of the machines had been financed by a 10 percent bank loan, and $90,000 of this loan had not yet been repaid. It was estimated that the four machines could be sold in their present condition for a total of $120,000 net, after dismantling and removal costs. The book loss resulting from the sale would be a deductible expense for income tax purposes and would therefore result in a tax saving of 52 percent of the loss.

EXHIBIT 9–9

WILSON COMPANY
Condensed Income Statement, 1974

Net sales...	$5,364,213
Less: All costs and expenses........................	4,138,647
Profit before taxes	1,225,566
Provision for income taxes..............................	622,715
Net Income..	$ 602,851

Condensed Balance Sheet
December 31, 1974

Current assets...............	$3,051,349	Current liabilities	$ 930,327
Fixed assets (net)...........	4,239,210	8% mortgage bonds.......	500,000
Other assets..................	151,491	Capital stock.................	1,000,000
		Surplus........................	5,011,723
Total Assets	$7,442,050	Total Liabilities.....	$7,442,050

The machine being considered in 1975 was a fully automatic transfer-type milling machine, equipped with four machining stations. Automatic transfer equipment on this machine moved the part progressively from one station to the next and indexed at each station, finishing a complete case with each cycle of the machine. One skilled machine operator was required to observe the functioning of the machine and make any necessary adjustments.

An automatic transfer-type machine with an annual output of 60,000 transmission cases on a two-shift basis would be specially built by a machine tool manufacturer at an estimated cost of $340,000, delivered and installed. The useful life of this machine was estimated to be 15 years. No reliable estimate of scrap value could be made; a rough estimate was that it would approximate the removal costs.

The Wilson Company's engineering department was asked to prepare a study for the executives to use in deciding what action to take. Its findings were as follows: The direct labor rate for milling machine operators was $5 an hour, including provision for social security taxes and fringe benefits, which varied with the payroll. There would be a saving in floor space amounting to $800 annually on the basis of the charge made in 1975 for each square foot of floor space used. However, the factory layout was such that it would be difficult to use this freed space for some other purpose, and no other use was planned. Out-of-pocket savings of $10,000 a year for other cost items were estimated if the automatic machine was purchased.

The Wilson Company planned to finance any new equipment purchase with a bank loan at a rate of 10 percent.

Selected financial data for the company are shown in Exhibit 9–9. The company considered the picture given by these statistics to be normal and expected the same general pattern to prevail in the foreseeable future.

Required:

What action, if any, would you recommend? Why?

part three

Responsibility accounting

Responsibility accounting is the third type of management accounting information. It is called by that name because the accounting information is structured according to organization units, which are responsibility centers. Responsibility accounting collects and reports information that is used in an important management function, management control. Part Three discusses the management control process in some detail.

Chapter 10 describes the organizational structure in which the management control process takes place. The focus is on three types of responsibility centers, called expense centers, profit centers, and investment centers. The characteristics of each of these organization units are given, and the accounting information that is appropriate for each of them is described.

In Chapter 11 we introduce the principal steps that occur in the management control process. These are programming, budgeting, operating and measurement, and the analysis of performance. We also discuss some of the behavioral matters that are important in this process, and in this connection introduce some additional ways of describing costs.

In Chapters 12 through 15 we describe in more detail each of the steps in the management control process.

The fact that responsibility accounting is the last section of the book is not happenstance. The concepts discussed in this Part Three tend to be less concrete, and hence more difficult to grasp, than those in Parts One and Two. Also, although we introduce a third type of accounting—responsibility accounting—in Part Three, the management control process also uses the management accounting information already discussed in Parts One and Two. An understanding of these other types of accounting information is therefore necessary in order to understand the subject matter of Part Three.

For the purpose of emphasis, we repeat two points that were made previously:

1. Each of the three types of management accounting information is used for a different purpose. When a problem requiring the use of accounting information arises, one must first understand the purpose for which information is to be used for the specific problem, and then select the type of information appropriate for that purpose.

2. Although the three types of management accounting information are discussed separately, collectively they comprise the overall management accounting system. There are not three separate systems. Rather, there is a single system which contains raw data that are used to construct full cost information, differential information, or responsibility information, as the case may be. Each of these types of information is used for the purpose for which it is relevant.

10

The management control structure

PURPOSE OF THE CHAPTER

A system can be described in terms of its structure — what it is — and its process — what it does. In this chapter we describe the elements of the management control structure. Essentially, these are types of units in an organization. We also introduce the main ideas of responsibility accounting which is the type of accounting information that is relevant for planning and controlling the activities of these organization units. We start with a discussion of organizations in general and then discuss three types of organizational units that are important in management control. These are expense centers, profit centers, and investment centers.

CHARACTERISTICS OF ORGANIZATIONS

As pointed out in Chapter 1, an organization — any organization — is a group of persons working together for one or more purposes. It is important to note that an organization consists of human beings. A factory with its machines is not an organization; rather, it is the persons who work in the factory that constitute the organization. It is also important to note that in an organization the human beings work together. A crowd walking down a street is not an organization, nor are the spectators at a football game when they are behaving as individual spectators. But the cheering section at a football game is an organization; its members work together under the direction of the cheerleaders.

397

Management

An organization has one or more leaders. Except in extremely rare circumstances, persons will not—indeed, they cannot—work together to accomplish the goals of the organization unless they are led. In business organizations, the leaders are called managers, or, collectively, the management. Managers decide what the goals of the organization should be; they communicate these goals to members of the organization; they decide the tasks that are to be performed in order to achieve these goals and decide on the resources that are to be used in carrying out these tasks; they see to it that the activities of the various parts of the organization are coordinated; they match individuals to tasks for which they are suited; they motivate these individuals to carry out their tasks; they observe how well these individuals are performing their tasks; and they take corrective action when the need arises. The leader of a cheering section performs these functions; so does the president of General Motors Corporation.

Organizational hierarchy

A manager can supervise only a limited number of subordinates. Old Testament writers put this number at ten. Although there can be considerable variation in this number, depending on the nature of the job to be done and on the personality and skill of the manager, clearly there is an upper limit to the number of persons that one manager can supervise directly, and it is a small number. It follows that in a company of any substantial size there must be several layers of managers in the organization structure. If ten subordinates per manager is taken as a typical number for one organization unit, an organization consisting of 1,000 people would have to have at least three layers. Units at the lowest level of the organization would each consist of 11 people (i.e., the manager and 10 subordinates). The managers of ten such units could report to a single superior, and that person therefore would directly supervise these ten lower level managers and would be responsible for the activities of the entire group.

Ten such higher level managers would be necessary for an organization of 1,000 people, and they constitute the second layer. Above these managers there would have to be a top manager to coordinate the work of the ten groups, thus making the three layers. This, of course, is a great oversimplification of the way in which organizations are actually put together and is intended only to illustrate the point that an organization necessarily consists of a number of units, each headed by a manager, and arranged in several layers. Authority runs from the top unit down through the successive layers. Such an arrangement is called an organization hierarchy.

In Chapter 1, Exhibit 1–1, we showed the organization chart for a relatively small organization. Exhibit 10–1 is a condensed organization chart for a larger organization, one that has several levels in its organization hierarchy. At the top is the board of directors which is responsible to the shareholders for the overall conduct of the company's affairs. Reporting to the board of directors is the president, who is the chief

EXHIBIT 10–1
A schematic organization chart

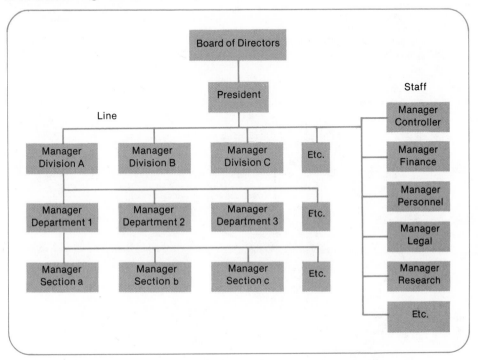

executive officer. Reporting to the president are two types of managers: line managers and staff managers. The line managers supervise the organization units that are directly responsible for achieving the goals of the organization, while the staff managers supervise the activities that provide services to the president and to other parts of the organization.

In the organization depicted in Exhibit 10–1, the top line units are called divisions. Within each division there are a number of departments, and within each department there are a number of sections. Other names are used for these organization units in different companies, but the names used in Exhibit 10–1 are common.

The term organization unit can refer to any of the boxes in Exhibit 10–1. Thus, Section *a* of Department 1 of Division A is an organization unit. Division A itself, including all of its departments and sections, also is an organization unit. Each of these organization units is headed by a manager who is responsible for the work done by the unit. As noted in Chapter 1, these organization units are called responsibility centers. A **responsibility center** is simply an organization unit headed by a responsible manager. The manager is responsible in the sense that it is the manager's job to see to it that the organization unit does its part in achieving the goals of the whole organization.

Environment

Any organization is a part of a larger society. The world outside the organization itself is called its *environment*. The organization is con-

EXHIBIT 10–2
An organization and its environment

This illustration was developed by Professor Charles Christenson.

tinually reacting with its environment. This is a two-way interaction: the organization affects the outside world, and it is affected by forces originating in the outside world. For a business organization, the nature of these interactions is suggested by Exhibit 10–2. Management is responsible for managing the organization; but since the organization is part of society, management also must see to it that the organization acts as a respectable member of that society.

Reality versus information

Accounting provides information about what is happening in an organization and about how an organization affects, and is affected by, the environment. Information about the real world is, however, only an approximation of what the real world actually is like. For example, there is a real-world territory called Rhode Island. There are also maps that give information about Rhode Island, and these maps are useful for certain purposes, such as aiding the traveler to find the best route from Providence to Newport. A map does not, however, convey a complete picture of Rhode Island, nor is it intended to do so. Rather, what the cartographer does is to select and present information that is useful for the purpose for which the map is drawn.

Accounting information is like a map. It is intended to help the user; but it is not, and does not purport to be, a complete picture of reality.

RESPONSIBILITY CENTERS

With this general description of organizations and of information about organizations, we can now discuss more specifically the nature of responsibility centers and the type of accounting that is useful in managing responsibility centers. Exhibit 10–3 provides a basis for doing this. The top section depicts a machine, which in some important respects is analogous to a responsibility center. A machine, in this case a gasoline engine, (1) uses inputs, (2) to do work, (3) which results in output. In the case of an engine, the inputs are fuel and air, the work is the production of mechanical energy, and the output is the mechanical energy.

A responsibility center has these same three essential characteristics, and they are described in Part B of Exhibit 10–3:

1. The responsibility center uses resources. These are its **inputs.**
2. It *works* with these resources. People are involved in this process. Usually, machines, inventory, and other tangible things are also involved.
3. As a result of this work, it produces **outputs.** These are classified either as goods, if they are tangible, or as services, if they are intangible. These goods or services go either to other responsibility centers within the company or to a customer in the outside world.

The foregoing is the *reality* of a responsibility center. **Information** about a responsibility center is shown in Part C of the exhibit. This information can be classified as either accounting information or nonaccounting information. Although we are here interested primarily in accounting information, we must not overlook that fact that much nonaccounting information is relevant in understanding what has happened in a responsibility center.

EXHIBIT 10–3
Nature of a responsibility center

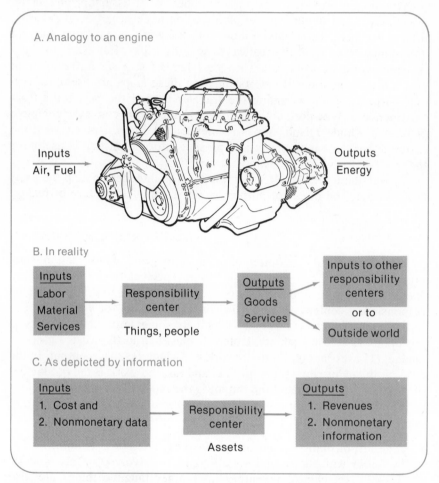

A. Analogy to an engine

Inputs
Air, Fuel

Outputs
Energy

B. In reality

Inputs		Outputs	Inputs to other responsibility centers
Labor	Responsibility center	Goods	or to
Material		Services	
Services	Things, people		Outside world

C. As depicted by information

Inputs		Outputs
1. Cost and	Responsibility center	1. Revenues
2. Nonmonetary data	Assets	2. Nonmonetary information

Accounting measures inputs in terms of cost. Although the resources themselves are physical things such as pounds of material and hours of labor, for the purposes of a management control system it is necessary to measure these physical things with some common denominator so that the physically unlike elements of resources can be combined. That common denominator is money. The monetary measure of the resources used in a responsibility centers is *cost*. In addition to cost information, nonaccounting information on such matters as the physical quantity of material used, its quality, the skill level of the work force, and so on, is also useful.

Accounting measures outputs in terms of revenues. As we shall see, accounting always measures revenues for those goods and services of the responsibility center that are sold to outside customers. In some cases, but by no means always, accounting also measures revenues for goods and services that are furnished by the responsibility center to another responsibility center within the organization. When such a monetary measure of output is not feasible, a nonmonetary measure of output, such as the number of units of product produced, may be used as a substitute. In some responsibility centers, there is no quantitative measure of output at all.

Responsibility accounting

It is apparent, from the brief description given above, that to understand what has happened in a responsibility center, managers need information about the inputs to that responsibility center, expressed as costs, and, if feasible, information about the outputs of the responsibility center, expressed as revenues. In addition to this historical information, managers also need information about estimated *future* inputs and outputs as an aid in planning the activities of the responsibility center. The type of management accounting information that is used for these purposes is called responsibility accounting. A formal definition is:

> Responsibility accounting collects and reports planned and actual accounting information about the inputs and outputs of responsibility centers.

Contrasts with other types of accounting.   Unlike the construction of differential costs and revenues, which is tailor-made for each problem, responsibility accounting involves a continuous flow of information, corresponding to the continuous flow of inputs into and outputs from responsibility centers.

An essential characteristic of responsibility accounting is that it focuses on responsibility centers. This difference in focus is what distinguishes responsibility accounting from the full cost accounting that was described in Part One. Full cost accounting focuses on products or services rather than on responsibility centers. Although full cost accounting does make use of cost centers, most of which are also responsibility centers, cost centers are used merely as a means to an end. The emphasis is always on the cost of the goods or services, and the cost center is used as a means of assembling items of cost so that they can be assigned to goods and services. (In making this distinction, we do not mean to imply that full cost accounting and responsibility accounting are two separate accounting systems. As noted in Chapter 2, they are closely related and are more accurately described as two parts of the management accounting system.)

EXAMPLE: Company X makes two products, No. 1 and No. 2. It has two production departments, A and B, each of which is a production cost

EXHIBIT 10–4

Contrast between full costs and responsibility costs

A. Full manufacturing costs

	Total	Product No. 1 Total	Product No. 1 Per unit	Product No. 2 Total	Product No. 2 Per unit
Volume (units)		2,000		1,000	
Cost item:					
Direct material	$20,000	$14,000	$ 7.00	$ 6,000	$ 6.00
Direct labor	13,000	8,000	4.00	5,000	5.00
Overhead	14,000	9,000	4.50	5,000	5.00
Total Costs	$47,000	$31,000	$15.50	$16,000	$16.00

B. Responsibility costs

	Total	Departments (responsibility centers) A	B	C	D
Cost item:					
Direct material	$20,000	$18,000	$ 2,000		
Direct labor	13,000	4,000	9,000		
Supervision	3,800	700	900	$ 800	$1,400
Indirect labor	6,600	600	800	2,100	3,100
Supplies	1,200	500	400	100	200
Other costs	2,400	300	800	500	800
Total Costs	$47,000	$24,100	$13,900	$3,500	$5,500

center. It also has two other departments, C and D, which are service cost centers. Each of the four departments is a responsibility center. The full costs of its products for a month are assembled and reported as shown in Part A of Exhibit 10–4. Responsibility costs for each of the four responsibility centers are shown in Part B. It is not possible to derive the information in Part A from that in Part B, or vice versa.

Note that from the information on full costs, it is impossible to identify what costs the manager of any department was responsible for. In particular, the costs of the two service departments are lumped together and are allocated, first to production cost centers and then to products by means of an overhead rate.

Another important characteristic of responsibility accounting is implicit in the description of organizations given earlier in this chapter. Responsibility accounting is used to measure the performance of managers, and it therefore influences the way managers behave. In discussing responsibility accounting, therefore, we must take in behavioral considerations into account. By contrast, our description of the use of differential accounting information was strictly impersonal; we made, no mention of the behavior of the human beings who used this information in analyzing alternative choice problems. There was no need to bring these behavioral characteristics into the discussion because the process was essentially an economic analysis; and economics does not deal, except peripherally, with the behavior of individuals. By contrast, in our discussion of responsibility accounting, we shall have much to say about human behavior and how managers are influenced by the nature of the accounting information they receive.

Efficiency and effectiveness

There are two key aspects to the performance of the manager of a responsibility center; they are labeled efficiency and effectiveness. Since these terms will be used frequently in the discussion that follows, it is important that their precise meaning be clearly understood. They can be defined in terms of the inputs and outputs of a responsibility center, the terms which were illustrated in Exhibit 10–3.

Efficiency. The goal of an engine is to produce energy. An efficient engine is one that uses relatively little fuel to produce a given amount of energy. Thus, efficiency expresses a relationship between inputs and outputs. The definition is:

Efficiency is the amount of output per unit of input or the amount of input per unit of output.

> *EXAMPLE:* In March, Responsibility Center E produced 1,000 units of product (its output) at a cost of $5,000 (its input). The relationship of the $5,000 to the 1,000 units measures the efficiency of the responsibility center. In this case, we can express the ratio as a cost per unit, $5 (= $5,000 ÷ 1,000). If in April, Responsibility Center E produced 1,000 units of product at a cost of $4,500, its efficiency is measured as $4.50 per unit, and the indication is that the responsibility center was more efficient in April than in March.

Note that in the above example, efficiency was expressed in relative terms; that is, it was said that the responsibility center was more efficient in April than in March. In some cases, an absolute measure of efficiency can be stated, as for example, when we say that the unit was "80 percent efficient." This is possible in the case of a physical device such as an engine, for which the theoretically perfect efficiency can be calculated by the laws of physics. An absolute measure of efficiency for a responsibility center can also be found in some circumstances; one of the functions of standard costs, which we discuss in Chapter 13, is to provide such a measure of efficiency. In a great many situations, however, the measure of efficiency is necessarily relative, rather than absolute. We say that a given responsibility center is more efficient or less efficient this month than last month, or more efficient or less efficient than some other responsibility center, rather than that it is X percent efficient.

Effectiveness. The work of a responsibility center is supposed to contribute to the overall goals of the larger organization of which it is a part. Its effectiveness is measured by how well it contributes to these goals. Since what an organization does is expressed as its outputs, a formal definition is:

> Effectiveness is the relationship between the output of a responsibility center and the goals of the organization.

> *EXAMPLE:* If Responsibility Center E is supposed to contribute to the organization's goals by producing as many units of product as it can, and if in May it produced 1,100 units of output, compared with 1,000 units in April, it was more effective in May than in April.

Relationship of efficiency and effectiveness. Effectiveness is always related to the organization's goals. Efficiency, per se, is not related to goals. An efficient responsibility center is one which does whatever it does with the lowest consumption of resources; but if what it does (i.e., its output) is an inadequate contribution to the accomplishment of the organization's goals, it is ineffective.

> *EXAMPLE:* If a department that is responsible for processing incoming sales orders does so at a low cost per order processed, it is efficient. If, however, the department is negligent in answering customer queries about the status of orders, and thus antagonizes customers to the point where they take their business elsewhere, the department is ineffective. The loss of a customer is not consistent with the company's goals.

A responsibility center should be both efficient and effective; it is not a case of one or the other.

In some situations, both efficiency and effectiveness can be encompassed within a single measure. Since an important goal of a profit-oriented organization is to earn profits, and since costs per unit of output affects profits, profit measures the combined effect of efficiency and effectiveness. When such an overall measure exists, it is unnecessary to measure effectiveness and efficiency separately. When an overall measure does not exist, however, it is feasible and useful to classify performance measures as relating either to effectiveness or to efficiency. In these situations, there is the problem of judging the relative importance of the two types of measurements. For example, how do we compare two maintenance managers, one who incurs high costs on the maintenance work that is done but has an excellent record of keeping equipment in tip-top condition, and the other who incurs lower costs but also has a poor record of equipment breakdowns? The former is less efficient but more effective than the latter. The relative weight given to these measures is a matter for management to decide.

Types of responsibility centers

A primary goal of most business organizations is to earn a satisfactory return on investment. Return on investment can be expressed as a ratio:

$$\text{Return on Investment} = \frac{\text{Revenues} - \text{Costs}}{\text{Investment}}$$

Three types of responsibility centers can be described in terms of the elements of this ratio:

1. An *expense center,* in which accounting measures costs.
2. A *profit center,* in which accounting measures revenues and costs, and the difference between them, which is profit.
3. An *investment center,* in which accounting measures profit and the investment used in earning the profit.

In the next sections we describe each of these types of responsibility centers, bringing in also the ideas of inputs and outputs, and of effectiveness and efficiency.

EXPENSE CENTERS

In most responsibility centers, the accounting system provides a monetary measure of inputs, that is, costs. For a great many of them, however, accounting does not provide a monetary measure of outputs. These responsibility centers are called expense centers.

An expense center is a responsibility center in which inputs, but not outputs, are measured in monetary terms.

Every responsibility center has outputs; that is, it does something. In many cases, however, it is neither feasible nor necessary to measure these outputs in monetary terms. For example, it would be extremely difficult to measure in monetary terms the output of the accounting department. Although generally it is relatively easy to measure the monetary value of the outputs of an individual production department, there is no reason for doing so if the responsibility of the department manager is to produce a stated *quantity* of outputs at the lowest feasible cost. For these reasons, most individual production departments, and most staff units, are expense centers. For an expense center, the accounting system records the cost incurred, but not the revenues earned.

Although the inputs to an expense center are measured in terms of cost, the term *expense center,* rather than *cost center,* is used as a name for these organizational units simply because we have already used the term *cost center* with a slightly different meaning in the description of full cost accounting in Part One. A cost center is an accounting device used to collect costs that are subsequently charged to products, whereas an expense center is a certain type of responsibility center. Most departments in a factory are both cost centers and expense centers; that is, the costs charged to the department are used both to measure the cost of products manufactured and also to measure the performance of the department manager.

There is no necessary correspondence between a cost center and an expense center, however. A cost center may or may not be an organizational unit. The machine shop in a factory may be a single department, and it is therefore an expense center; but each important machine or bank of similar machines in the shop may be treated as a cost center for the purpose of collecting costs and allocating them to products. In this case, the machines are cost centers, but not expense centers.

In an expense center, monetary information cannot be used, by itself, to measure either efficiency of effectiveness. Each of these measures requires a number for output, and in an expense center output is not expressed in monetary terms. If the expense center produces only a single product, then the number of units of product produced is a good measure of output, even though it is not a monetary measure. Efficiency can be measured as a cost per unit of product, and effectiveness measured by comparing the actual number of units produced with units produced in some previous period as was done in the example given above.

If the responsibility center produces a number of different products, however, there must be some way of aggregating the dissimilar products to arrive at an overall measure of output. Otherwise, neither the efficiency nor the effectiveness of the responsibility center can be measured. If a factory produces office furniture, consisting of a variety of chairs, desks, tables, and so on, its output cannot be measured and expressed as a single number simply by adding up units of product. One straightback chair is obviously not equivalent to one desk. In such a situation, which is common, we need some way to aggregate the dissimilar products produced in order to arrive at an overall measure of the output of the responsibility center. The profit center provides the solution to this problem.

PROFIT CENTERS

In an expense center, inputs, but not outputs, are measured in monetary terms. In a profit center both outputs and inputs are measured in monetary terms. The accounting measure of outputs is called revenue. In accounting, profit is the difference between revenues and expenses, hence the name, profit center. The definition is:

A profit center is a responsibility center in which inputs are measured in terms of expenses and outputs are measured in terms of revenues.

Although in financial accounting, revenue is recognized only when sales are made to outside customers, in management accounting it is necessary to define revenue as a monetary measure of the output of a profit center in a given accounting period, such as a month, *whether or not the company realizes the revenue in that period*. Thus, a factory is a profit center if it "sells" its output to the sales department and records the revenue from such sales. Likewise, a service department, such as the maintenance department, may "sell" its services to the responsibility centers that receive these services. These "sales" generate revenues for the service department; and in these circumstances, the service department is a profit center.

Revenues that arise when one responsibility center "sells" its outputs to other responsibility centers within the company differ from revenues that arise from sales to customers, in that outside sales increase the company's assets (either accounts receivable or cash), while internal sales do not. These internal transfers are therefore called by some people "mere bookkeeping entries." As we shall see, they nevertheless can provide extremely useful information to management.

A given responsibility center is a profit center only if management *decides* to measure its outputs in monetary terms. Revenues for the company as a whole are automatically generated when the company makes sales to the outside world. By contrast, revenues for an internal responsibility center are recognized only if management decides that it is a good idea to do so. No accounting principle *requires* that revenues be measured for individual responsibility centers within a company. With some ingenuity, practically any expense center could be turned into a profit center because some way of putting a selling price on the output of most responsibility centers can be found. The question is whether there are sufficient positive benefits in doing so.

Advantages of profit centers

The difference between revenues and expenses is in accounting called income, or profit. Profit is a combined measure of both effectiveness and efficiency. The profit of a profit center therefore provides a powerful tool for measuring how well the manager of the profit center has performed. It is not a perfect measure of performance for many reasons, as will be discussed in Chapter 15; but it is often better than any other measure.

The profit center idea was invented in the 1920s, probably by General Motors Corporation. Originally, it was regarded as a management tool that was useful in large corporations; and it is generally recognized today that most large corporations could not be managed successfully without the use of profit centers.[1]

---

[1] For an excellent description of the development of the profit center idea and its importance to management, see Alfred D. Chandler, Jr., *Strategy and Structure* (Cambridge: MIT Press, 1962).

In recent years, managers have recognized that the profit center idea is also applicable to relatively small companies, as well as to corporate giants. It is also applicable to nonprofit organizations, although because of the apparent contradiction of using the term *profit center* in a nonprofit organization, some other term such as *revenue center* is often used for the same idea.

A profit center resembles a business in miniature. Like a separate company, it has an income statement that shows revenue, expense, and the difference between them, which is profit. Most of the decisions made by the manager of a profit center affect the numbers on this income statement. Because the manager's performance is measured by profit, managers of profit centers are motivated to make decisions about inputs and outputs that will increase the profit that is reported for their profit center. Since managers of profit centers act somewhat as they would if they were running their own business, the profit center is a good training ground for general management responsibility. The profit center concept is relatively new. It is becoming increasingly popular, but its possibilities have not yet been fully exploited.

Decentralization.   The profit center is closely related to the organizational principle of decentralization; profit centers make decentralized organizations feasible. In a centralized organization, decisions tend to be made at the top level in the organization hierarchy. Since top management cannot have an intimate firsthand knowledge of what is happening at the lower levels of the organization, such decisions must be made without the benefit of knowledge of all the factors that are known to lower level managers. In a decentralized organization, decisions tend to be made on the "firing line," by managers who are best informed about conditions at these lower levels. Top management can safely delegate the authority to make such decisions because the profit center reports provide adequate information about how well the operating managers are doing their job.

The difference between a centralized and a decentralized organization is illustrated by the simplified organization charts in Exhibit 10–5. Assume, to take the simplest possible case, that the company makes two product lines, A and B, each produced in a separate plant and each marketed by a separate sales organization. In a centralized organization, all production activities would be the responsibility of a production vice president and all marketing activities the responsibility of a marketing vice president. Decisions involving both the production and marketing aspects of either product line, such as the quantity to be produced, the selling prices to be charged, and whether to accept special orders at lower than normal prices would have to be made by the president. Furthermore, there is no way of holding one individual responsible for the profitability of either product line. In a decentralized, or **divisionalized organization,** a division manager is responsible for each product line. The division manager has the information necessary to make sound decisions about

EXHIBIT 10–5
Centralized and decentralized organizations

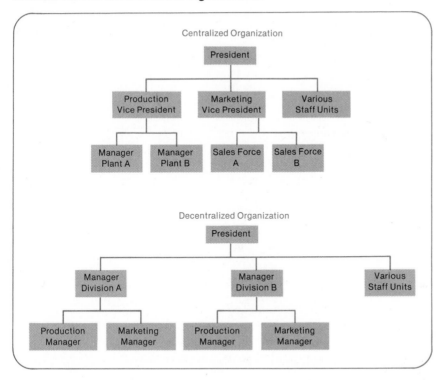

that product line, and his performance can be measured in terms of the profitability of the division since the division manager is responsible for both the revenue and expense elements of performance.

Few situations are as clear-cut as the simple illustration given above, but the general idea nevertheless holds: if the company is organized so that managers are responsible for both the revenue and expense aspects of performance, the contribution of each manager to the overall goals of the organization is easier to measure than when no single manager is responsible for both revenues and expenses. When profit centers exist, accounting provides a broader, more inclusive measurement of performance than when accounting focuses on expense centers, in which expenses, but not revenues, are measured.

Criteria for profit centers

Although the profit-center approach has become a powerful force for promoting good management control, it does not work well for all responsibility centers. In deciding on whether to set up a given responsibility center as a profit center, the following points should be kept in mind:

1. Extra recordkeeping is involved if the profit center idea is used. In the profit center itself, there is the extra work of measuring output in monetary terms; and in the responsibility centers that receive its outputs, there is the work of recording the cost of goods or services received.

2. When top management *requires* responsibility centers to use a certain service furnished by another responsibility center within the company, the service probably should be furnished at no charge, and the service unit therefore should not be a profit center. For example, if top management requires that internal audits be made, the responsibility centers probably should not be asked to pay for the cost of the internal auditing service, and the internal auditing unit should therefore not be a profit center.

3. If the manager of a responsibility center has little authority to decide on the quantity and quality of its outputs or on the relation of output to costs, then a profit center is usually of little use as a control device. This does not imply that the manager of a profit center must have *complete* control over outputs and inputs, for few, if any, managers have such complete authority.

4. If output is fairly homogeneous (e.g., cement), a nonmonetary measure of output (e.g., hundredweight of cement produced) may be adequate, and there may be no substantial advantage to be gained in converting this output to a monetary measure of revenue.

5. To the extent that a profit center puts a manager in business for himself, it promotes a spirit of competition. Up to a certain point, this is desirable. Beyond that point, however, the device may generate excessive friction between profit centers, to the detriment of the whole company's welfare. Also, it may generate too much interest in short-run profits to the detriment of long-run results. These difficulties are likely to arise when managers have an inadequate understanding of the management job. Often, the misuse of profit centers can be corrected by educating the managers. If, however, these problems cannot be overcome, the profit center technique should not be used.

Measurement of expenses

In general, the expense component of the profit center is measured in the same way as expenses in an expense center are measured, that is, according to the usual principles of accounting. A problem does arise with respect to the treatment of general and administrative expenses that relate to company as a whole. Some companies allocate these expenses to profit centers; others do not. When these expenses are allocated, the "bottom line" on the profit center income statement measures net income in approximately the same way that it would be measured if the profit center were an independent entity, and thus facilitates comparisons with other entities. These expenses are, however, not the responsibility of the profit center manager; and some people believe that the statement should show only the items for which he or she is responsible. This topic is discussed further in Chapter 11.

Transfer prices

In the simple situation illustrated in Exhibit 10–5, the manufacturing facilities of Division A were used exclusively to make the products of Division A, and the marketing organization of Division A sold only these products. Thus, both the production and marketing aspects of Division A's work would be reflected clearly on its income statement. In the more usual situation, the lines of responsibility are not so clear-cut. A manufacturing plant might, for example, make products that are sold by one division, or it might manufacture components which are shipped to another plant for incorporation into final products sold by several divisions. If the outputs of this plant are to be measured in terms of revenues, there must be a way of placing a value on the shipments that are made to other profit centers within the company. Similarly, if a maintenance department or other service unit is set up as a profit center, there must be a way of arriving at a monetary amount for the services it provides to other profit centers, for this measures the output or revenue of the service unit. The number used to arrive at a monetary amount for these transfers of goods and services is called a transfer price.

A transfer price is a price used to measure the value of goods or services furnished by a profit center to other responsibility centers within a company.

A transfer price is to be contrasted with a market price, which measures exchanges between a company and the outside world. Internal exchanges that are measured by transfer prices result in *revenue* for the responsibility center furnishing the goods or services and in *cost* for the responsibility center receiving the goods or services. Whenever profit centers are established, transfer prices must also be established. There are two general approaches to the construction of a transfer price: the market-based price and the cost-based price.

Market-based transfer prices. Since a profit center is supposed to be a miniature "company," it is reasonable to expect that its selling prices would be the same as those it would charge if it were in fact an independent entity. Thus, if a market price for its products exists, this price is normally used as the transfer price. The market price is the appropriate price because the "buying" responsibility center should ordinarily not be expected to pay more internally than it would have to pay if it purchased from the outside world, nor should the "selling" center ordinarily be entitled to more revenue than it could obtain by selling to the outside world. If the market price is abnormal, as for example when an outside vendor sets a low "distress" price in order to use temporarily idle capacity, then such temporary aberrations are ordinarily disregarded in arriving at transfer prices. The market price may be adjusted for cash discounts and for certain selling costs that are not involved in an internal exchange.

> EXAMPLE: A profit center makes a variety of products which it sells both to outside customers and to other responsibility centers within the company. Its normal prices are listed in its sales catalog. Since it knows that there will be no bad debt losses from intracompany sales, it may use a schedule of transfer prices that is 2 percent below its catalog prices, because it does not need to provide for such losses. Many companies, however, disregard such refinements and use the regular catalog price in the interest of simplicity.

If the company has more than one market price for the same product, depending, for example, on the quantity purchased, the transfer price ordinarily is the lowest price that is normally charged to outside customers.

Cost-based transfer prices. In many situations there is no reliable market price that can be used as the basis for the transfer price. In a job shop such as a printing plant, for example, each job is different, and the selling price must be set in relation to the cost of doing that job. A manufacturing plant in one division may fabricate components, or even completed products, for another division that are unlike any products that it sells to outside customers. In these circumstances, there is no market price as a guide, and the transfer price must therefore be based on cost.

The principles for constructing a cost-based transfer price are the same as those used in arriving at normal selling prices to outside customers, as described in detail in Chapter 2. Ideally, the normal price is calculated from the full cost of manufacturing the product plus a profit margin that is related to the amount of capital employed in the manufacturing process. The rate of return on capital employed would be the rate that the profit center would normally expect to earn if it made sales to outside customers. As described in Chapter 2, however, it is not always feasible to construct such a price; and various alternative approaches may be used, such as a margin over full cost, or a margin over direct costs. The mechanics of calculating a cost based transfer price are exactly the same as those used in calculating normal selling prices, as described in Chapter 2.

Marginal-cost pricing. Some authors advocate that products should be transferred at their marginal cost, which is approximately the same as their variable cost. The argument essentially is that in a purely competitive environment, a firm should be willing to sell its products at any price that exceeds marginal cost because the other component of costs do not vary with the transaction and hence are irrelevant.[2] The effect of this practice, however, would be a very low transfer price which would understate the revenue, and hence the profit, of the "selling" division, and understate the expenses, and hence overstate the profit, of the "buying" division.

The fact is that companies normally will not sell their products to outside customers at prices that are as low as marginal costs. For the same reasons that the whole company is unwilling to do this, a profit center is unwilling to sell at marginal cost to other responsibility centers within the company. Thus, the practice of transferring products at marginal cost is rarely found in the real world.

Contribution pricing. In Chapter 7 we made a distinction between the normal price at which a product is sold in the ordinary course of business and the contribution price, which is a lower price that a company is sometimes willing to accept in order to use production capacity that otherwise would be idle. The same distinction is relevant in transfer pricing. If a manufacturing division has idle capacity, it may be willing to use this capacity to make products for another division at a lower-than-normal price, rather than to have facilities remain idle. By doing so, it makes a contribution to its fixed costs and profit; hence the name, contribution pricing. In these circumstances, representatives of the buying and selling profit centers would meet to work out a mutually agreeable transfer price. Conceptually, this price would be based on the lowest price that the selling division would receive if the equivalent amount of capacity were used for products that could be sold to an outside customer, and/or the highest price that the buying division would have to pay if it purchased the product from an outside supplier.

Transfer price policies. From the above discussion, it is apparent that there is no mechanical way of calculating a transfer price that fits all cricumstances. Top management must therefore prescribe policies that govern its calculation under various circumstances. If the transfer price is to be a cost-based price, the policy must state which method, among the various acceptable methods of cost accounting, is to be used in arriving at it. If the price is a contribution price, there must be a mechanism for **negotiating** the price of actual transactions between the buying and the selling responsibility centers. For example, the selling responsibility center may be willing to sell below the normal market price rather than lose the business, which could happen if the buying responsibility center took advantage of a temporarily low outside price. In such circumstances,

---

[2] For the argument for the marginal cost approach, see Jack Hirshleifer, "On the Economics of Transfer Pricing," *Journal of Business,* July 1956, pp. 172–84; and his "Economics of the Divisionalized Firm," *Journal of Business,* April 1957, pp. 96–108.

EXHIBIT 10–6
Examples of transfer prices

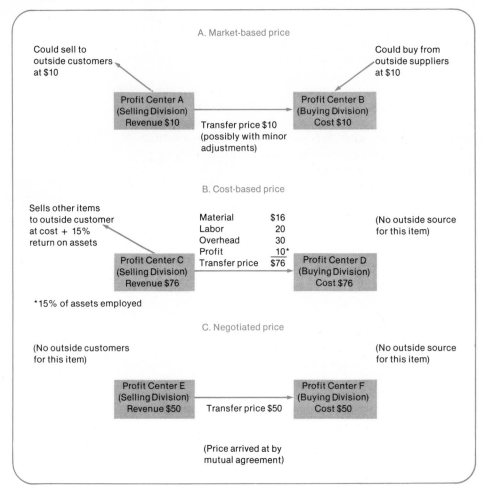

A. Market-based price

Could sell to
outside customers
at $10

Could buy from
outside suppliers
at $10

Profit Center A
(Selling Division)
Revenue $10

Transfer price $10
(possibly with minor
adjustments)

Profit Center B
(Buying Division)
Cost $10

B. Cost-based price

Sells other items
to outside customer
at cost + 15%
return on assets

Material	$16
Labor	20
Overhead	30
Profit	10*
Transfer price	$76

(No outside source
for this item)

Profit Center C
(Selling Division)
Revenue $76

Profit Center D
(Buying Division)
Cost $76

*15% of assets employed

C. Negotiated price

(No outside customers
for this item)

(No outside source
for this item)

Profit Center E
(Selling Division)
Revenue $50

Transfer price $50

Profit Center F
(Buying Division)
Cost $50

(Price arrived at by
mutual agreement)

the two parties negotiate a "deal." Unless both responsibility center managers have complete freedom to act, these negotiations will not always lead to an equitable result because the parties have unequal bargaining powers; that is, the prospective buyer may not have the power of threatening to take its business elsewhere, and the prospective seller may not have the power of refusing to do the work. Thus, there usually needs to be an **arbitration** mechanism to settle disputes concerning transfer prices.

Exhibit 10–6 diagrams the general approach to transfer pricing problems, as a way of summarizing the practices described above.

It is important to note that the transfer price used in modern management accounting systems is fundamentally different from the amount at which the transfer of products was accounted for before the profit center idea became widely adopted. In the old days, goods were transferred at cost, and services were usually provided by one organization unit to another without any charge at all.

Relation to financial accounting. The financial accounting reports do not include revenues arising from transactions between profit centers. In financial accounting, revenues are earned only from transactions with outside customers. Thus, the sum of the revenue of profit centers, as shown in the responsibility accounting system, will be greater than the revenue of the whole entity, as shown in the financial accounting system. The amounts in the two systems can be reconciled by taking account of the effect of transfer prices. The procedure is same as that used in preparing consolidated financial statements, as described in Chapter 17 of *Fundamentals of Financial Accounting.*

INVESTMENT CENTERS

In a profit center the measure of managerial performance is broader than in the expense center because in an expense center the accounting system measures only inputs, whereas in the profit center, both inputs and outputs are measured in monetary terms. The third type of responsibility center, the investment center, permits an even broader measure than the profit center. In an investment center, performance is measured not only in terms of profits but also in terms of the assets that are employed in generating those profits.

> An investment center is a responsibility center in which inputs are measured in terms of expenses and outputs are measured in terms of revenues, and in which assets employed are also measured.

An investment center is the ultimate extension of the responsibility center idea because it encompasses all the elements that are involved in the company's overall goal of earning a satisfactory return on its investment.[3] Investment centers are normally used only for relatively large units, such as a division that both manufactures and markets a line of products. It has the effect of "putting the manager into business for himself" to an even greater extent than does the profit center. Reports on performance show not only the amount of profit that the investment center manager has earned, which is the case with reports for a profit center, but also the amount of assets that was used in earning that profit.

---

[3] Many people make no distinction between investment centers and profit centers. They use the term *profit center* to apply to both. This causes no problem in practice because it is obvious from the accounting reports whether the system does, or does not, report assets employed, and this is the only difference between the two. A distinction is made here primarily because it facilitates a separate description of the characteristics of each.

This is obviously a more encompassing report on performance than a report which does not relate profits to assets employed. On the other hand, the possible disadvantages mentioned above for profit centers exist in a magnified form in investment centers. Recordkeeping costs increase, and there is the possibility that the manager will be motivated to act in ways that are not consistent with the long-run best interests of the company as a whole.

Investment base

Since the investment center is an extension of the profit center idea, no new problems arise in measuring revenues and expenses. The new problem relates to the measurement of the assets employed in an investment center. Assets employed is often called the **investment base.**

Although an investment center is in many respects similar to an independent company, it is not exactly like such a company because it can count on financial and other support from the company of which it is a part. In particular, an investment center does not need as large a cash balance as it would need if it were a separate company. The cash balance is a safety valve, or shock absorber, protecting the company against short-run fluctuations in funds requirements. Compared with an independent company, an investment center needs relatively little cash, however, because it can obtain funds from its headquarters on short notice. Because part of the headquarters cash balance exists for the financial protection of the investment centers, headquarters cash can logically be allocated to the investment centers as part of their capital employed. There are several ways of allocating this cash to investment centers just as there are several ways of allocating general overhead costs.

Problems also arise in measuring other assets that are employed in an investment center and in deciding whether some or all of the liabilities should be deducted from total assets in measuring the net assets employed. In particular, the treatment of fixed assets (i.e., plant and equipment) is a vexing problem. Cost accounting, as described in Part One, provides a way of allocating expenses to cost objectives, but cost accounting has no need to allocate assets. This need does arise in the case of investment centers that benefit from assets that are owned by the general and administrative units of the company. Furthermore, in measuring investment center performance there is a great debate as to whether depreciable assets should be recorded at their original cost, at their depreciated book value, or at some other amount. These problems are beyond the scope of this introductory treatment.[4]

---

[4] For a discussion of them, see Robert N. Anthony and John Dearden, *Management Control Systems: Text and Cases,* 3d ed. (Homewood, Ill.: Richard D. Irwin, Inc., 1976) chap. 8.

EXHIBIT 10–7

Components of an Investment Center Report
Responsibility Center A
May 1977

000 omitted

Revenues:

Outside sales		$ 800
Intracompany sales		200
Total Sales		1,000
Less: Cost of goods sold		600
Gross margin		400
Direct expenses	$250	
Allocated general and administrative expenses	50	300
Income		100
Capital charge (8 percent)		72
Residual income		$ 28
Assets employed		$ 900
Return on investment ($100 ÷ $900)		11%

Measures of performance

In the income statement of a profit center, the "bottom line" is income. Some companies use pretax income; others calculate net income after the deduction of income taxes. (For simplicity, we shall use pretax income in the examples.) In an investment center, the amount of income must be related to the amount of assets employed. There are two ways of doing this: (1) return on investment and (2) residual income.

The **return on investment** (ROI) is calculated by dividing income by the amount of assets employed. The result is a percentage. It is a measure of investment center performance corresponding to the return on total capital that is frequently calculated for the company as a whole.

Residual income is calculated by subtracting a capital charge from income. **The capital charge is found by multiplying assets employed by a percentage that represents the percentage return normally expected on the company's capital.** The amount of residual income indicates the investment center's ability to earn more than a normal profit on the amount of capital that it uses. Residual income has no counterpart in published financial statements, and it is therefore less familiar and less widely used than return on investment as an overall measure of the investment center's performance. Conceptually, however, it gives a more valid measure of performance than does return on investment.[5]

Exhibit 10–7 shows the main components of an investment center

---

[5] The reasons for the superiority of residual income as compared with return on investment are discussed in Anthony and Dearden, *Management Control Systems*, chap. 8.

report. It can be used to highlight the differences among an expense center, a profit center, and an investment center. The report is highly condensed so as to focus on these relationships; an actual report would show additional detail for the principal items of expense and would also provide a basis for comparison, as will be illustrated in Chapter 15.

If Responsibility Center A were an expense center, its performance report would show only the information about cost of goods sold ($600,000), direct expenses ($250,000), and, in some cases, allocated general and administrative expenses ($50,000). If the unit were a profit center, the report would show, in addition, the unit's revenue — consisting of both revenue from sales to outside customers ($800,000) and intra-company sales as measured by transfer prices ($200,000). Some companies allocate general and administrative expenses to profit centers; others show only the expenses for which the manager is responsible. The bottom line on the profit center report would be the income of $100,000 if these expenses were allocated.

If the unit were an investment center, its income of $100,000 would be related to its assets employed of $900,000 in either of two ways. Companies that use the return-on-investment method divide income by assets employed to arrive at an ROI of 11 percent. Companies that used the residual income method calculate a capital charge by multiplying assets employed by a normal rate of return, here assumed to be 8 percent. The capital charge of $72,000 is then subtracted from income to give a residual income of $28,000.

MANAGEMENT BY OBJECTIVES

The foregoing description of the measurement of performance in the three types of responsibility centers emphasized monetary information because such information is incorporated in an accounting system. Accounting information cannot provide an adequate record of the performance of a responsibility center, however. At best, it measures profitability; and although profitability is one important goal in a profit-oriented company, it is by no means the only goal. In a nonprofit organization, profit is not a goal at all. Furthermore, the income reported for a profit center or an investment center measures only short-run performance; it shows the results of the manager's decisions on *current* profits, but it tells nothing about actions that the manager may have taken that influence *future* profits. Top management is primarily interested in profits over the long run, not merely profits of the current period.

As a way of overcoming these inadequacies, many companies supplement the monetary accounting information with other information about the results of the manager's actions. A system that does this is called a *management by objectives* system. It gets this name because the system describes specific objectives that the responsibility center manager is expected to achieve, and then measures progress in meeting these objectives. In the terminology used above, these objectives are *outputs,* and the comparison of actual performance with the stated objectives is a measure of *effectiveness*.

For example, a sales manager may be expected to open three new sales offices next year, or a factory superintendent may be expected to have a new training program developed and installed or to take certain steps to improve safety standards. Such actions often cause the incurrence of additional expenses in the current period, which reduces current profits, but they are expected to lead to improved profitability in future periods or to the attainment of other company goals.

Since the overall performance of a nonprofit organization obviously cannot be measured by profit, or by any accounting number that corresponds to profit, a system of management by objectives is especially important in such organizations. If properly devised, the objectives that are set forth in such a system can measure the outputs of the organization in roughly the same way that revenue measures the output of a profit-oriented organization.

SUMMARY

An organization is a group of persons working together for one or more purposes. These persons require leadership, and since one leader, or manager, can supervise only a small number of persons, the employees must be organized into relatively small groups. Each such group is called a responsibility center. A responsibility center uses resources, which are its inputs, to produce goods and services, which are its outputs. Responsibility accounting measures costs and revenues in terms of the inputs and outputs of responsibility centers. The performance of a responsibility center is measured in terms of its efficiency, which is the relationship of inputs to outputs and/or in terms of its effectiveness, which is the relationship of outputs to the goals of the organization.

There are three types of responsibility centers. In the simplest type, the expense center, only inputs (i.e., costs) are measured in monetary terms. In a profit center, both inputs and outputs are measured in monetary terms; inputs as costs, and outputs as revenues. The difference between revenues and costs is profit. In an investment center profit is related to the assets employed in generating that profit.

A special problem in a profit center is accounting for goods and services that are transferred within the company. This is done by valuing these products at a transfer price, which should be a market price if one exists and is otherwise a price built up from cost or arrived at by negotiation.

Performance in responsibility centers is also measured by nonmonetary amounts. A system that incorporates such measures is called a management-by-objectives system.

IMPORTANT TERMS

Inputs	**Transfer price**
Outputs	**Market-based transfer price**
Responsibility accounting	**Cost-based transfer price**
Efficiency	**Investment center**
Effectiveness	**Investment base**
Expense center	**Return on investment**
Profit center	**Residual income**
Decentralization	**Capital charge**
Divisionalized organization	**Management by objectives**

QUESTIONS FOR DISCUSSION

1. Distinguish between "reality" and "information," using the terms "territory" and "map" in your explanation.

2. A map of Rhode Island does not convey a complete picture of Rhode Island. Suppose that it were possible to draw a map that did convey a complete picture, would it be useful?

3. What is the relevance of Question 2 to reports showing inputs and outputs of a responsibility center?

4. Give examples of the types of information that the management of a company manufacturing and selling women's apparel is likely to receive from the several parts of the environment depicted in Exhibit 10–2.

5. Why are inputs to a responsibility center reported in terms of their cost, rather than in terms of the actual resources used?

6. What are the differences between full cost accounting and responsibility accounting?

7. Refer to Exhibit 10–4. If the full jobs were obtained from a job-cost system, the job-cost records would show the direct labor costs incurred in Departments A and B, respectively, for Product No. 1. Would these records show the indirect labor incurred in each department for Product No. 1? Explain your answer.

8. In the U.S. Postal Service efficiency is measured, in part, by the cost per letter handled and effectiveness is measured by the number of days required to deliver letters, on the average. What would probably be the effect on the efficiency and on the effectiveness of the Postal Service if each of the following steps was taken, assuming no change in the total number of letters processed. Consider each action separately:
   a. The number of employees was increased.
   b. The number of overtime hours was reduced.
   c. Collection of mail on Saturdays was eliminated, and the number of employees was correspondingly reduced.
   d. Employees were granted an additional paid holiday.

9. What is the difference between an expense center and a cost center? Can one department in a company be both?

10. Explain how a responsibility center in a nonprofit organization can be a profit center?

11. What is the connection between the concept of profit center and the concept of a decentralized organization?

12. Under what circumstances should a responsibility center *not* be organized as a profit center?

13. Contrast the cost construction used to transfer products from one department to another in a product cost accounting system and the amount used to transfer products from one profit center to another.

14. Under what circumstances should a transfer price be a cost-based price?

15. Divisions A and B are profit centers. Division A manufactures stove tops which Division B uses in manufacturing complete stoves. Division B sells the stoves. In negotiating a transfer price for the stove tops, under what circumstances would the bargaining power of the two departments be unequal? Is there any way in which the two departments could be given approximately equal bargaining power?

16. Welter Company has a typing and secretarial pool which various offices may call on for assistance when their own staffs are too busy to handle the workload. What factors should be considered in deciding whether or not to make this pool a profit center? If it is made a profit center, how should the transfer price for typing services be arrived at? If the typing pool is a profit center, should other departments be permitted to hire temporary outside help to handle their overflow workload?

17. Why is the amount of cash in an investment center's bank account not a good measure of the cash that should be part of the investment base?

18. What is the difference between the way return on investment and residual income are calculated?

19. Refer to Exhibit 10–7. Give examples of information that would *not* be revealed by an accounting report if Responsibility Center A were an expense center, rather than an investment center. If it were a profit center.

20. In view of the broad scope of information contained in an investment center report, why does a company also need a management-by-objectives system?

PROBLEMS

10–1. Department 12 of the Minow Company manufactures a variety of components for products, one of which is Part No. 106. Data on this part are as follows:

Item of cost	Monthly planned cost, 1977 Per unit	Actual cost, June 1977 Per unit	Total
Direct material and direct labor ...	$ 8.00	$ 7.80	$ 7,800
Fixed costs, Department 12	2.00	2.20	2,200
Costs allocated to			
Department 12.........................	3.00	3.30	3,300
Total	$13.00	$13.30	$13,300

Required:

A. What costs are relevant for preparing financial statements for June 1977? Show the cost of goods sold if 1,000 units were sold. What amount would be shown on the balance sheet if 1,200 units remained in finished goods inventory?

B. What costs are relevant in deciding whether to make or buy Part No. 106? If an outside vendor offered to sell this part to Minow for $11 per unit, should they be bought outside? For $9? For $7?

C. If the Minow Company had idle facilities, should it accept an offer to sell Part No. 106 for $11? For $9? For $7?

D. What costs are relevant in assessing the performance of the manager of Department 12? Has the manager been effective? Efficient?

10–2. Kentow Company manufactures three products: A, B, and C. It has three marketing managers, one for each product. During the first year of operations, the company allocated its $30,000 of actual advertising expense to products on the basis of the relative net sales of each product. In the second year, the advertising budget was increased to $50,000. Half was spent on general institutional advertising in the belief the company image would be enhanced. The other half was spent $8,000 on Product A, $12,000 on Product B, and $5,000 on Product C. For purposes of income measurement, all advertising expenses continued to be allocated on the basis of sales. Certain data in the second year were as follows:

	Total	Product A	Product B	Product C
Net sales	$450,000	$193,500	$126,000	$130,500
Advertising expense	50,000	21,500	14,000	14,500
Net income	55,000	25,500	12,000	17,500

When the marketing manager of Product A received these figures, he complained that his department was charged with an unfair portion of advertising, and that he should be held responsible only for the actual amount spent to advertise Product A.

Required:

A. Comment on the sales manager's complaint.

B. How much advertising expense would have been charged to Product A under the existing cost allocation method if net sales of A and B were as given, but net sales of C were less by a total of $50,000? More by $50,000?

C. Assuming net sales of B and C were as given, but sales of A increased by $50,000, how much advertising expense would have been charged to Product A under the existing cost allocation method?

D. Assuming net sales of B and C were as given, but just before the accounting period closed, the marketing manager of Product A had an opportunity to increase its sales by $50,000 by selling goods which had a cost of $48,000. If you were the marketing manager, would you make the sale?

E. Assuming the situation as presented in D, if you were the president of Kentow Company, would you want the marketing manager to make the sale?

F. In its responsibility accounting system, how much advertising expense should be charged to the department responsible for marketing Product A under each of the conditions presented above? Explain.

10–3. Jersey Company, a distributor of hardware items offers a cash discount of 2 percent for customers paying their accounts within 10 days of sale, but charges $1\frac{1}{2}$ percent per month on all accounts not paid within 30 days of sale. Each department decides which of its customers will be allowed to buy on credit. The net sales of each department are computed by subtracting the cash discount actually taken on department sales. Revenue from finance charges is allocated to the departments on the basis of credit sales made during the current month. A summary of these monthly transactions follows:

	Total	Department 1	Department 2	Department 3
Cash sales........	$ 740,000	$180,000	$260,000	$300,000
Cash discounts.......	9,400	3,600	5,200	600
Total sales........	1,340,000	280,000	560,000	500,000
Finance charges collected	31,200	5,200	15,600	10,400

Required:

A. Comment on the method of allocating cash discounts and the revenue from finance charges for responsibility accounting purposes.

B. Compute the net revenue due to credit sales, assigning the discounts and finance revenue in a manner which you believe would produce more useful results for management use.

C. Eleven days before the month ends, the manager of Department 1 learns that a large quantity of goods remaining in his inventory could be sold for $50,000 to either Fetters Corporation or Janell, Inc. Typically, Fetters takes advantage of the discount offered by Jersey Company; and Janell, Inc., takes 90 days to pay for deliveries. To whom would the manager of Department 1 sell? Explain. Show the impact of this decision on net sales attributable to the department.

D. Refer to Requirement C. As president of Jersey Company what would your preference be?

E. If you were the manager of Department 1, what would be your attitude toward sales to poor risk customers?

F. If you were the supervisor of Departments 1, 2, and 3, how would you discourage sales to poor risk customers?

10–4. The Lane Confectionery Company is a wholesaler of candies and tobacco products. At the end of each month the controller prepares statements for each of the three branch managers and the company president. The statement for the current month is as follows:

	Branch 1	Branch 2	Branch 3
Sales.	$300,000	$200,000	$400,000
Direct costs:			
Cost of sales.	180,000	124,000	220,000
Salespersons' salaries.	34,000	26,000	38,000
Supplies.	400	300	450
Utilities.	1,100	900	1,200
Delivery expense	5,000	3,800	6,200
Depreciation—branch assets	20,000	19,200	22,500
Branch contribution	59,500	25,800	111,650
Allocated costs:			
Advertising expense	12,000	8,000	16,000
Administrative salaries and other			
administrative expense	32,000	32,000	32,000
Operating income.	$ 15,500	$(14,200)	$ 63,650

Required:

A. Comment on the strengths and weaknesses of this statement.
B. Comment on the basis of allocation of the overheads.
C. Under what circumstances would it be possible for a promotion as a reward for superior performance be given to Branch 2 manager and a criticism for poor performance be given to Branch 3 manager?
D. Should Branch 2 be discontinued? Support your answer with appropriate computations.

10-5. Happy Foods, Inc., operates several hundred fast-food drive-in restaurants. As an experiment, the top management selected three nearly identical restaurants and provided a different compensation plan to the manager of each. One manager was paid a flat salary. Another manager was paid 10 percent of net sales. The third manager was paid a salary plus 25 percent of the amount by which he reduced actual operating expenses below the planned amount. Results for the first year were as follows:

	Restaurant		
	A	B	C
Sales.	$240,000	$200,000	$160,000
Raw food costs	96,000	80,000	64,000
Gross margin	144,000	120,000	96,000
Operating expenses:			
Wages and salaries.	90,000	70,000	60,000
Advertising	30,000	20,000	10,000
Other	15,000	15,000	12,000
Total Expenses.	135,000	105,000	82,000
Operating income.	$ 9,000	$ 15,000	$ 14,000

Required:

A. Which compensation plan was probably used in restaurants A, B, and C respectively?
B. As well as you can, explain how the compensation plans affected the performance of the managers.
C. Which of the three plans, or what alternative plan, would you recommend? (Hint: Consider probable long-run as well as short-run effects.)

10–6. Exhibit 10–2 represents the flow of information between an organization and its environments. Taking General Motors Corporation (or any other industrial company if you happen to be more familiar with another one) as an illustrative situation, list a specific example of a piece of information for each of the flows depicted by an arrow on that exhibit. For the box labeled "other environmental forces," think of either the general public or the government, whichever you prefer.

10–7. Fred Louis has just been promoted to manager of the Resin Division of Mounds Corporation. When Louis took over, the division was earning a 15 percent return on gross investment annually and this was expected to continue. The new division manager was informed that corporate headquarters could borrow funds at 8 percent and make them available for investment in projects which Louis selected. Anxious to show he had good control of his managerial skills, he considered the following projects from which he could select one:

Project	Gross investment (in millions of dollars)	Annual net income (in dollars)
A	8	680,000
B	9	810,000
C	10	1,100,000
D	11	1,155,000

Required:

A. Assuming the division manager's performance evaluation is based on overall return on gross investment, which project will Louis choose, if any? Explain.
B. Is the action to be taken by Louis in the best interest of the Mounds Corporation? Explain.
C. If the cost of corporate borrowing is 12 percent, will Louis take an action which is in the Mounds Corporation's best interest?
D. Assuming the division manager's performance is based on overall return on gross *new* investment (i.e., investments which Louis decides upon, not investments which someone else has made prior to his arrival), which project will Louis choose?
E. Is the action to be taken by Louis in D in the best interest of the

Mounds Corporation if the cost of borrowing is 8 percent? 12 percent? 10 percent?

10–8. Refer to Problem 10–7.

Required:

Answer Requirements A through E assuming that Louis could select more than one project.

10–9. Fisk has just become the manager of the Mitten Division of Sacks, Inc. When Fisk took over, the division was earning a 15 percent return on gross investment annually, and this was expected to continue. Corporate headquarters was able to raise funds which it made available to managers at a capital charge of 8 percent upon written request. Fisk was considering the following projects from which one could be selected:

Project	Gross investment (in millions of dollars)	Annual net income (in dollars)
A	8	680,000
B	9	810,000
C	10	1,100,000
D	11	1,155,000

Required:

A. Assuming the division manager's performance is based on residual income, which project will Fisk choose, if any? Explain.
B. Is the action taken by Fisk in the best interest of Sacks, Inc? Explain.
C. If the capital charge is raised to 12 percent, which project will Fisk choose, if any? 10 percent? Explain.
D. Is this in the best interest of Sacks, Inc.? Explain.
E. Does the 15 percent return on gross investment have a bearing on the decision Fisk will make based on the facts presented in this problem? Explain.

10–10. Refer to Problem 10–9.

Required:

Answer Requirements A through E assuming that Fisk could select more than one project.

10–11. Gem Rice, Inc., hired a new division manager, F. Fredlin, to take over the Evans Division. Fredlin was in a quandry over the selection of the best project from the list provided her by her staff. The project selection was difficult since Gem Rice, Inc., top executives gave Fredlin the option of having her performance based on ROI or residual income where the capital charge is 4 percent. The project data are given as follows:

Project	Gross investment (in millions of dollars)	Annual net income (in dollars)
A	5	250,000
B	6	360,000
C	7	560,000
D	8	800,000
E	9	855,000
F	10	900,000

Required:

A. If only one project can be accepted, which project will Fredlin take if ROI is the basis for performance measure?

B. Compare the answer to A with the selection if performance review is based on residual income with a capital charge of 4 percent. Explain the dilemma.

C. What would happen to the dilemma if the capital charge were raised to 6 percent? 8 percent? 15 percent?

10–12. Otto Manufacturing Company has a division which produces auto batteries. It sells them to its assembly plant and also to outsiders through regular market channels. Operating details are as follows:

To assembly plant		To outsiders		Total
Sales 100,000 units @ $7*......... $700,000		50,000 @ $10	$500,000	$1,200,000
Variable costs				
100,000 units @ $5............... 500,000		100,000 @ $ 5	250,000	750,000
Fixed costs 150,000			75,000	225,000
Total Costs 650,000			325,000	975,000
Operating Income................... $ 50,000			$175,000	$ 225,000

* The $7 price is ordinarily determined by the outside sales price less selling and administrative expenses wholly applicable to outside business.

The Assembly Division manager has a chance to get a firm contract with an outside supplier at $6.50 for the ensuing period. The Battery Division manager says that he cannot sell at $6.50 because no operating income can be earned. Assume that fixed costs would be unaffected no matter what is done.

Required:

A. What would be the impact on operating income for the Battery Division if the Assembly Division manager bought outside?

B. What would be the impact on operating income for the Otto Manufacturing Company if the Assembly Division manager bought outside?

C. What do you expect the Assembly Division manager to do? Explain.

D. Does the transfer price of $7 motivate the managers to act in the corporation's best interest? Explain.

E. What would be your advice to the Battery Division manager?
F. As Battery Division manager, what is the minimum price you would set in bargaining with the Assembly Division manager?

10–13. Refer to the data in Problem 10–12. Assume that selected Assembly Division's average controllable assets are as follows:

Receivables	$300,000
Inventories.............................	200,000
Fixed assets, gross..................	500,000

Assume further that the budgeted residual income is based on the following capital charges:

Receivables...................................	5%
Inventories	10
Fixed assets, gross.........................	20

Before considering any outside acquisitions of batteries for the coming year, the Assembly Division manager anticipates that the divisional operating income will be $200,000.

Required:

A. Calculate the budgeted residual income for the Assembly Division.
B. Assume that the Assembly Division manager, if he buys from the outside supplier at $6.50, must buy 200,000 units in order to get that price. Since the division can only produce at a volume of 100,-000, the remaining 100,000 must go into inventory for one year.
   Calculate the change in the budgeted residual income for the Assembly Division taking into account the savings of $0.50 per unit and the increased investment in the inventory if the division manager buys outside.
C. What do you recommend to the Assembly Division manager? Explain.
D. Under these circumstances do you judge the transfer price of $7 as efficient? Explain.
E. Do you prefer the responsibility system as it was in Problem 10–12 or as modified with capital charges?

10–14. Division A produces a product that can be sold either to Division B or to outside customers. During 1977, the following data were collected for Division A:

Units produced	1,500
Units sold to Division B....................................	300
Units sold to outside customers.......................	1,200
Unit selling price	$30
Unit cost of production – variable.....................	$18
Unit cost of production – fixed	$ 5

The units acquired by Division B were processed further at a cost of $12 per unit, and sold to outside customers for $43. All transfers between divisions were made at the market price.

Required:

A. Prepare income statements for Divisions A and B and the company as a whole.
B. Should the manager of A be encouraged to sell more to outsiders or to B?
C. If you were the manager of B, would you buy from A and sell to outsiders after further processing?
D. As the president of the company, would you want A to sell to B or to outsiders?
E. Assume that the capacity of Division A is 1,500 units and Division B wants to buy 600 units in 1978. Should Division A sell the extra units to Division B, or continue selling the units to outside customers? Explain.

10–15. Assume the same facts as in Problem 10–14. When you return to your classroom, your instructor will assign you to act as if you were either the division manager of A or B. Role-play the following situation:

Capacity limits production to 1,500 units for Division A, and sales to outsiders directly by Division A are limited to 1,200 units. B wants to continue buying from A, but at a price of $22 per unit since an outside vendor has offered to sell B the product at that price.

Required:

A. Acting in your role as assigned, discuss the situation aloud in the classroom assuming Division B manager has approached Division A manager with his new proposal.
B. What is the minimum price for which division manager A will sell to B?
C. Review the points brought out in the classroom discussion in regard to each person's role in promoting a responsibility system.

10–16. Beyer, the purchasing agent for Pro Engineering Corporation has just received an order for a special part No. 1234 from Maker, the production supervisor who related that the part was too seldomly called for and too expensive to keep in stock. It was further stated that the part would not be needed for inclusion into the production sequence for 12 weeks. Beyer reminded Maker that this part should have been ordered as part of the six-month purchasing budget submitted by all production supervisors, but confidently accepted the order as one not too difficult to fill with a 12-week lead time.

Beyer placed the order for part No. 1234 with a reputable supplier who promised to deliver the part in time for inclusion into production sequencing. Beyer checked up several times and did everything in his power to assure delivery on time.

On the specified production date, Maker received a call from Dewey Delivery Service explaining the part will arrive a day or two late because the truck broke down somewhere between Chicago and Boston. As a result, Maker had to shift all of his production plans. Change-over costs and downtime are estimated to be about $10,000.

Numero, the controller, was mulling over who should be charged with the $10,000 idle capacity burden.

Required:

When you return to your classroom, your instructor will assign you to act as if you were either Beyer, Maker, or Numero.

1. Acting in your role assigned, discuss the situation aloud in the classroom to resolve the issue of who should bear the burden of the downtime cost of $10,000.
2. Review the points brought out in the classroom discussion in regard to each person's role in promoting a responsibility system.

10–17. Advice Incorporated, a management consulting firm, is structured into three independent groups entitled Human Resources Group, Computer Systems Group, and Engineering Systems Group. The manager of each group is told to operate his group as if it were a separate company. Revenues are generated by billing consulting hours worked to outside clients. Quite frequently, one of the groups will call upon the others to perform certain services. The usual pricing and cost schedule for each group is as follows:

Group	Per consulting hour		Total fixed cost
	Billing rate	Variable cost	
Human Resources.................	$50	$15	$240,000
Computer Systems	60	20	280,000
Engineering Systems	45	25	200,000

Required:

A. The Engineering Systems Group is working its staff to capacity with outside consulting. The Human Resources Group wants to buy consulting services from the Engineering Systems Group. At what price per hour should the Engineering Systems Group bill the Human Resources Group?
B. Under what conditions should the Engineering Systems Group bill the Human Resources Group at less than $45 per hour?
C. Under what conditions should the Engineering Systems Group bill the Human Resources Group at more than $45 per hour?
D. The Computer Systems Group has been using about 1,000 hours per quarter of Human Resources Group personnel at a rate of $50. If the Human Resources Group manager decides to raise the rate to $55, should the Computer Systems Group be forced by top management to pay the new rate in order to keep the business inside?

10–18. Supply the missing data in the tabulation below:

| | Division | | | |
	A	B	C	D
Sales..	$65,000	$45,000	$105,000	$90,000
Operating income.................................	2,800	4,500	?	?
Operating assets	?	30,000	60,000	50,000
Rate of return	4%	?	?	25%
Minimum required rate of return:				
Percentage..	?	12%	10%	?
Dollar amount....................................	4,200	?	?	?
Residual income	?	?	0	2,500

10-19. Intercontinental Manufacturing Company has three divisions whose
income statements appeared as follows:

| | Division | | |
	A	B	C
Sales..................................	$200,000	$320,000	$400,000
Cost of goods sold	120,000	198,400	220,000
Gross margin	80,000	121,600	180,000
Operating expenses................	60,000	96,000	150,000
Operating income...................	20,000	25,600	30,000
Interest expense.....................	4,000	7,000	9,500
Income before tax	16,000	18,600	20,500
Income tax (51%)...................	8,160	9,486	10,455
Net Income	$ 7,840	$ 9,114	$ 10,045

All costs and expenses were considered to be controllable at the divisional level. During 1977 the average controllable gross operating
assets traceable to the divisions were $80,000,000, $142,200, and
$125,000 for A, B, and C, respectively. Intercontinental Manufacturing
has a minimum desired rate of return of 16 percent on assets.

Required:
A. Compute the rate of return earned by each division during 1977 and
rank the division from highest to lowest in terms of rate of return.
B. The manager of Division A is considering adding a new product
line which would require an additional investment of $40,000,000.
Interest expense would increase by $2,000,000, and net income
after taxes by $2,940,000. What impact will the additional invest-
ment have on the next rate of return ranking? Is the new investment
desirable to Intercontinental Manufacturing as a whole? If you
were the manager of Division A would you add the new product
line? Explain.
C. If you were the manager of Division B and had the opportunity,
would you add the line being considered by the manager of Division A?
D. Calculate the residual income earned by each division before the

new investment and rank the divisions. How does this compare to the rankings by rate of return?

E.   Review the new investment decision discussed above and its impact on residual income. If you were the manager of Division A, would you add the new product line? Explain.

10–20.   Refer to the income statement of Division A of Intercontinental Manufacturing Company in Problem 10–19. This division is currently organized as an investment center.

Required:

A.   Suggest some inefficiencies or unwise actions that would be revealed in such a report that would not be revealed if Division A were organized as a profit center rather than as an investment center.

B.   Suggest some additional inefficiencies or unwise actions that would not be revealed in the financial report if Division A were organized as an expense center rather than as a profit center.

C.   Suggest some actions that the manager of Division A could take that would improve the reported performance of the division but that would nevertheless be contrary to the long-run best interests of the Intercontinental Manufacturing Company.

10–21.   The Box Division of Maple Company manufactures cardboard boxes which are used by other divisions of Maple Company and which are also sold to external customers. The Hardware Division of Maple Company has requested the Box Division to supply a certain box Style K, and the Box Division has computed a proposed transfer price on this box, as follows:

	Per thousand boxes
Variable cost	$180
Fixed cost	40
Total cost	$220
Profit (to provide normal return on assets employed)	30
Transfer price	$250

The Hardware Division is unwilling to accept this transfer price because Style K boxes are regularly sold to outside customers for $240 per thousand. The Box Division points out, however, that competition for this box is unusually keen, and that this is why it cannot price the box to external customers so as to earn a normal return. Both divisions are profit centers.

Required:

What should the transfer price be? (Explain your answer.)

10–22.   Six months after the Box Division of Maple Company started to supply Style K boxes to the Hardware Division (see Problem 10–21), Eastern Company offered to supply boxes to the Hardware Division for $235 per thousand. The Hardware Division thereupon informed the Box Division that the transfer price should be reduced to $235 because this was now the market price.

Required (explain your answers):

A. Should the transfer price be reduced to $235 per thousand?

B. Under what circumstances should the Box Division refuse to supply boxes to the Hardware Division?

C. If the Box Division refused to supply boxes at $235 per thousand, should the Hardware Division be permitted by top management to buy boxes from the Eastern Company?

D. If outside market prices continued to decrease, and eventually reached $210 per thousand, would this change your answer to any of the preceding questions?

10-23. The Transistor Division of Mador Company manufactures certain components that are used in radio transmitters that the Electronics Division sells to the U.S. Air Force. Data used in the negotiation of a selling price are as follows:

	Cost per transmitter	
	Transistor division components	Complete transmitter
Components from Transistor Division		$ 220
Other direct material	$ 20	480
Direct labor	80	100
Indirect costs	100	200
Total cost	$200	$1,000
Profit margin	20	100
Price	$220	$1,100

The Air Force representative argued that the $1,100 price was too high because profit was double counted.

Required:

A. If Mador Company calculated its profit margin on the basis of assets employed, is the Air Force position correct?

B. If Mador Company calculated its profit on the basis of a percentage of cost, is the Air Force position correct?

C. From the data given above, which method of calculating profit did the Mador Company probably use?

CASE: JESSUP MOTORS (A)

10-24. John Jessup, the part owner and manager of an automobile dealership, felt the problems associated with the rapid growth of his business were becoming too great for him to handle alone. Accordingly, Jessup divided the business into three departments: a new car sales department, a used car sales department, and the service department. He then appointed three of his most trusted employees as managers of the new departments: John Ward was named manager of new car sales; Marty Ziegel, manager of used car sales; and Charlie Lassen, manager of the service department.

Each of the managers was told to run his department as if it were an independent business. In order to give the new managers an incentive, their remuneration was calculated as a straight percentage of their department's profit.

Soon after taking over as the manager of the new car sales department, John Ward had to settle upon the amount to offer a particular customer who wanted to trade his old car as part of the purchase price of a new one with a list price of $5,400. Before closing the sale, Ward had to decide the amount of discount from list he would offer the customer and the trade-in value of the old car. He knew he could deduct 15 percent from the list price of the new car without seriously hurting his profit margin. However, he also wanted to make sure that he did not lose out on the trade-in.

During his conversations with the customer, it had become apparent that the customer had an inflated view of the worth of his old car, a far from uncommon event. The new car had been in stock for some time, and the model was not selling very well, so Ward was rather anxious to make the sale if this could be done profitably.

In order to establish the trade-in value of the car, the manager of the used car department, Ziegel, accompanied Ward and the customer out to the parking lot to examine the car. In the course of his appraisal, Ziegel estimated the car would require reconditioning work costing about $300, after which the car would retail for about $1,500. On a wholesale basis, he could either buy or sell such a car, after reconditioning, for about $1,350.

The new car department manager had the right to buy a trade-in at any price he thought appropriate, but then it was his responsibility to dispose of the car. He had the alternative of either trying to persuade the used car manager to take over the car, accepting the used car manager's appraisal price, or he himself could sell the car through wholesale channels. Whatever course Ward adopted, it was his primary responsibility to make a profit for the dealership on the new cars he sold, without affecting his performance through excessive allowances on trade-ins. This primary goal, Ward said, had to be "balanced against the need to satisfy customers and move the new cars out of inventory—and there is only a narrow line between not allowing enough on the used car and allowing too much."

After weighing all these factors, with particular emphasis on the personality of the customer, Ward decided he would allow $1,800 for the used car, provided the customer agreed to pay the list price for the new car. After a certain amount of haggling, the $1,800 allowance was agreed upon.

Ward returned to the office and explained the situation to Ronald Bradley, who had recently joined the dealership as an accountant. After listening with interest to Ward's explanation of the sale, Bradley set about recording the sale in the accounting records of the business. Since the new car's list price was $5,400 and it had been purchased from the manufacturer for $4,100, Bradley reasoned the gross margin on the new car sale was $1,300. Yet Ward had allowed $1,800 for the old car, which needed $300 repairs and could be sold retail for $1,500 or wholesale for $1,350. Did this mean that the new car sale involved a loss? Bradley was not at all sure he knew the answer to this question. Also, he was uncertain about the value he should place on the used car for inventory valuation purposes.

Required:

How should this transaction be recorded so as to motivate properly the managers of the departments involved?

CASE: JESSUP MOTORS (B)

10–25. Ronald Bradley, the recently appointed accountant of Jessup Motors, was unable to resolve the problem he faced as to the valuation of a trade-in car. The car had been taken in trade at an allowance of $1,800 against the list selling price of the new car of $5,400. The cost of the new car to the company had been $4,100. The old car could be sold wholesale or retail, at prices of about $1,350 and $1,500 respectively. Bradley decided that he would put down a valuation of $1,800 and then await instructions from his superiors.

When Marty Ziegel, manager of the used car department, found out what Bradley had done, he went to the office and stated forcefully that he would not accept $1,800 as the valuation of the used car. His comment was as follows:

"My used car department has to get rid of that used car, unless John [new car department manager] agrees to take it over himself. I would certainly never have allowed the customer $1,800 for that old tub. I would never have given any more than $1,050, which is the wholesale price less the cost of repairs. My department has to make a profit too, you know."

Whatever response Bradley was about to make to this comment was cut off by the arrival of John Jessup, the general manager; Charlie Lassen, the service department manager; and John Ward, the new car sales manager.

"All right, Charlie," said Jessup, "now that we are all here, would you tell them what you just told me."

Lassen, who was obviously very worried, said:

"Thanks, Bill; the trouble is with this trade-in. John and Marty were right in thinking that the repairs they thought necessary would cost about $300. Unfortunately, they failed to notice that the rear axle is cracked, which will have to be replaced before we can sell the car. This will use up materials and labor costing about $225.

"If I did work costing $525 for an outside customer, I would be able to charge him about $700 for the job. That would give a contribution to my department's gross profit of $175, and my own income is based on that gross profit. Since a high proportion of the work of my department is the reconditioning of trade-ins for resale, I figure that I should be able to make the same charge for repairing a trade-in as I would get for an outside repair job. In this case, the charge would be $700."

Ziegel and Ward both started to talk at once at this point. Ziegel, the more forceful of the two, managed to edge Ward out:

"This axle business is unfortunate, all right, but it is very hard to spot a cracked axle. Charlie is likely to be just as lucky the other way next time. He has to take the rough with the smooth. It is up to him to get the cars ready for me to sell."

Ward, after agreeing that the failure to spot the axle was unfortunate, added:

"This error is hardly my fault, however. Anyway, it is ridiculous that the service department should make a profit out of jobs it does for the rest of the dealership. The company can't make money when its left hand sells to its right."

John Jessup, the general manager, was getting a little confused about the situation. He thought there was a little truth in everything that had been said, but he was not sure how much. It was evident to him that some action was called for, both to sort out the present problem and to prevent its recurrence. He instructed Bradley, the accountant, to "work out how much we are really going to make on this whole deal," and then retired to his office to consider how best to get his managers to make a profit for the company.

Required:

How should this transaction be recorded?

CASE: JESSUP MOTORS (C)

10–26.   A week after the events described in Problem 10–25 had occurred, Charlie Lassen, the service manager, reported to John Jessup, the general manager, that the repairs to the used car had cost $580 in materials and labor of which $270 represented the cost of those repairs which had been spotted at the time of purchase, and the remaining $310 was the cost of replacing the cracked axle.

To support his case for a higher allowance on reconditioning jobs, Lassen had obtained from Bradley, the accountant, the cost analysis shown in Exhibit 10–8. Lassen told Jessup that this was a fairly typical distribution of the service department expense.

Required:

A.   In view of the new information, how should the complete transaction relating to the cars described in Problems 10–24 and 10–25 be recorded?

B.   Does the system motivate the department managers properly? If not, what changes would you recommend?

EXHIBIT 10–8

JESSUP MOTORS
Analysis of Service Department Expenses
For the Year Ended December 31, 1977

	Customer jobs	Reconditioning jobs	Total
Number of jobs	183	165	348
Direct labor........................	$ 42,772	$ 39,528	$ 82,300
Parts and supplies..............	23,699	23,885	47,584
Department overhead (fixed)	12,624	10,426	23,050
Total Cost................	79,095	73,839	152,934
Charges made for jobs to customers or other departments...................	139,004	94,632	233,636
Profit (loss).......................	$ 59,909	$ 20,793	80,702
General overhead allocation			22,832
Departmental profit for the year			$ 57,870

CASE: IVY UNIVERSITY

10–27.   In Ivy University, there are about 15 profit centers, each headed by a Dean. Each Dean is responsible for the revenue and expenses of his profit center. There are a number of service and support units, of which the largest is the buildings and grounds department (B&G).

B&G is responsible for most maintenance work throughout the university. Among other things, it does repairs of equipment, office alterations, and similar projects as requested by the profit centers. It has shops and equipment with a book value of several million dollars.

Required:
A.   On what basis should the project work be charged to profit centers?
B.   If the charge made for this project work were based on cost, should the cost include (*a*) depreciation and/or (*b*) a charge for the capital invested in fixed assets?

CASE: BIRCH PAPER COMPANY

10–28.   "If I were to price these boxes any lower than $480 a thousand," said James Brunner, manager of Birch Paper Company's Thompson division, "I'd be countermanding my order of last month for our salesmen to stop shaving their bids and to bid full-cost quotations. I've been trying for weeks to improve the quality of our business, and if I turn around now and accept this job at $430 or $450 or something less than $480, I'll be tearing down this program I've been working so hard to build up.

The division can't very well show a profit by putting in bids that don't even cover a fair share of overhead costs, let alone give us a profit."

Birch Paper Company was a medium-size, partly integrated paper company, producing white and kraft papers and paperboard. A portion of its paperboard output was converted into corrugated boxes by the Thompson division, which also printed and colored the outside surface of the boxes. Including Thompson, the company had four producing divisions and a timberland division, which supplied part of the company's pulp requirements.

For several years, each division had been judged independently on the basis of its profit and return on investment. Top management had been working to gain effective results from a policy of decentralizing responsibility and authority for all decisions except those relating to overall company policy. The company's top officials believed that in the past few years the concept of decentralization had been successfully applied and that the company's profits and competitive position had definitely improved.

Early in 1957, the Northern division designed a special display box for one of its papers in conjunction with the Thompson division, which was equipped to make the box. Thompson's staff for package design and development spent several months perfecting the design, production methods, and materials to be used. Because of the unusual color and shape, these were far from standard. According to an agreement between the two divisions, the Thompson division was reimbursed by the Northern division for the cost of its design and development work.

When all the specifications were prepared, the Northern division asked for bids on the box from the Thompson division and from two outside companies. Each division manager was normally free to buy from whatever supplier he wished; and even on sales within the company, divisions were expected to meet the going market price if they wanted the business.

In 1957, the profit margins of converters such as the Thompson division were being squeezed. Thompson, as did many other similar converters, bought its paperboard, and its function was to print, cut, and shape it into boxes. Though it bought most of its materials from other Birch divisions, most of Thompson's sales were made to outside customers. If Thompson got the order from Northern, it probably would buy its linerboard and corrugating medium from the Southern division of Birch. The walls of a corrugated box consist of outside and inside sheets of linerboard sandwiching the fluted corrugating medium. About 70 percent of Thompson's out-of-pocket cost of $400 for the order represented the cost of linerboard and corrugating medium. Though Southern had been running below capacity and had excess inventory, it quoted the market price, which had not noticeably weakened as a result of the oversupply. Its out-of-pocket costs on both liner and corrugating medium were about 60 percent of the selling price.

The Northern division received bids on the boxes of $480 a thousand from the Thompson division, $430 a thousand from West Paper Company, and $432 a thousand from Eire Papers, Ltd. Eire Papers offered to buy from Birch the outside linerboard with the special printing already on it, but would supply its own inside liner and corrugating medium. The outside liner would be supplied by the Southern division at a price equivalent of $90 a thousand boxes, and it would be printed for $30 a thousand by the Thompson division. Of the $30, about $25 would be out-of-pocket costs.

Since this situation appeared to be a little unusual, William Kenton, manager of the Northern division, discussed the wide discrepancy of bids with Birch's commercial vice president. He told the vice president: "We sell in a very competitive market, where higher costs cannot be passed on. How can we be expected to show a decent profit and return on investment if we have to buy our supplies at more than 100 percent over the going market?"

Knowing that Mr. Brunner had on occasion in the past few months been unable to operate the Thompson division at capacity, it seemed odd to the vice president that Mr. Brunner would add the full 20 percent overhead and profit charge to his out-of-pocket costs. When asked about this, Mr. Brunner's answer was the statement that appears at the beginning of the case. He went on to say that having done the developmental work on the box, and having received no profit on that, he felt entitled to a good markup on the production of the box itself.

The vice president explored further the cost structures of the various divisions. He remembered a comment that the controller had made at a meeting the week before to the effect that costs which were variable for one division could be largely fixed for the company as a whole. He knew that in the absence of specific orders from top management Kenton would accept the lowest bid, which was that of the West Paper Company for $430. However, it would be possible for top management to order the acceptance of another bid if the situation warranted such action. And though the volume represented by the transactions in question was less than 5 percent of the volume of any of the divisions involved, other transactions could conceivably raise similar problems later.

Required:

A. In the controversy described, how, if at all, is the transfer price system dysfunctional?

B. Describe other types of decisions in the Birch Paper Company in which the transfer price system would be dysfunctional.

SUGGESTIONS FOR FURTHER READING

(These books relate to the material in Chapters 10 and 11.)

Anthony, Robert N. *Planning and Control Systems: A Framework for Analysis.* Boston: Harvard Business School Division of Research, 1965.

————, and Dearden, John. *Management Control Systems; Text and Cases,* 3d ed. Homewood, Ill.: Richard D. Irwin, Inc., 1976.

————, and Herzlinger, Regina. *Management Control in Nonprofit Organizations.* Homewood, Ill.: Richard D. Irwin, Inc., 1975.

Bruns, William J., Jr., and Decoster, Don T. *Accounting and Its Behavioral Implications*. New York: McGraw-Hill, Inc., 1969.

Chandler, Alfred D., Jr. *Strategy and Structure*. Cambridge, Mass.: MIT Press, 1962.

Dalton, Gene W., and Lawrence, Paul R. *Motivation and Control in Organizations*. Homewood, Ill.: Richard D. Irwin, Inc., 1971.

Lawrence, Paul R., and Lorsch, Jay W. *Organization and Environment*. Homewood, Ill.: Richard D. Irwin, Inc., 1969.

Tannenbaum, Arnold. *Control in Organizations*. New York: McGraw-Hill, Inc., 1968.

11

The management control
process

PURPOSE OF THE CHAPTER

In this chapter we describe the nature of the management control process, the nature of the accounting information that is used in this process, and some behavioral considerations that are important in understanding how this information is used. In the first part of the chapter, management control is defined and its relation to other planning and control processes is explained. Each of the steps in the management control process is then described briefly; they are described in greater detail in Chapters 12 through 15. Types of cost constructions that are important in management control are described. Finally, there is an introductory discussion of how these cost constructions influence human behavior.

PLANNING AND CONTROL PROCESSES

Two of the important activities in which all managers engage are (1) planning and (2) control. *Planning* is deciding what should be done and how it should be done. It is an activity that goes on at all levels in an organization. When a salesperson decides what customers to call on tomorrow, he is engaged in planning. When the president decides on a five-year expansion program, he also is engaged in planning. *Control* is assuring that the desired results are attained. It is also an activity that is carried on throughout the organization. When a supervisor observes how diligently the employees are working, he is engaged in control, and so is

443

the president when discussing a current report on performance with one of the vice presidents.

It is important to understand that **control relates to desired results, which are not always the same as planned results.** The basic job of the organization is to attain the organization's goals. Plans are made with the organization's goals in mind. It may happen, however, that a change in the situation makes it desirable for a manager to depart from the plan. For example, if the sales manager sees an opportunity to exploit an unexpectedly favorable demand for a product, he should be encouraged to do so, even though this opportunity was not foreseen when the plans were being prepared. Thus, although in the normal course of events the plans indicate the results that the organization wants to attain, there are many circumstances in which rigid adherence to plans is not the best course of action. It is therefore an oversimplification to say, as some people do, that control is the process of securing adherence to plans. Such an attitude can lead to an excessive reliance on planned results as a basis for judging actual performance.

In most organizations, three different types of planning and control processes can be identified: (1) strategic planning, (2) management control, and (3) operational control. Our interest is primarily in the management control process, but the best way of explaining where this process fits in the total picture is to describe each of the processes briefly. Although either the word "planning" or "control" occurs in the name of each of these processes, it should be understood that all three processes involve *both* planning activities and control activities; the names merely suggest the relative emphasis on planning as compared with the emphasis on control.

Strategic planning

As noted in Chapter 1, an organization chooses certain strategies in order to achieve its goals, and these determine the nature of its operations. The organizers of a company do not decide simply that, for example, they are "going into the shoe business." They must be more specific than this. Should they manufacture shoes or buy them from another company? Should the shoes be men's shoes, women's, or children's? What should be the quality level and the corresponding price range? How large should the factory be? What manufacturing process should be used? Should a factory be built or should rented facilities be used? Should the shoes be sold to distributors, to retail stores, or directly to consumers? How much of the funds required to start the business should come from shareholders and how much should be borrowed? What is the best source of borrowed funds? Answers to questions like these determine the initial character of the business.

A business entity and its environment are dynamic, not static. As time goes on, the situation changes, and questions similar to those listed above need to be addressed again and again. The process of raising and answering these basic questions is what is meant by strategic planning. Specifically:

> Strategic planning is the process of deciding on the goals of the organization and the strategies that are to be used in attaining these goals.

Management control

Once the strategies of an organization have been decided upon, it is management's responsibility to see that these strategies are carried out. In a small business, this may involve primarily the development of an informal implementation plan by the manager, his explanation to other members of the organization of what he wants done, and his subsequent observations to ascertain how well the members carry out the tasks assigned to them. This face-to-face control is feasible only in the tiniest of organizations, however. In a company with many separate responsibility centers, each with its own specialized job to do, the strategies must be communicated to the managers of all these units, a formal implementation plan must be developed, and the efforts of each manager must be brought into harmony with one another. This is the management control process. Its definition is:

> Management control is the process by which management assures that the organization carries out its strategies effectively and efficiently.

Operational control

The third type of planning and control process is called operational control. It is to be distinguished from management control primarily in that it involves relatively little management judgment and relatively little interaction among managers. Inventory control is a case in point. Top management prescribes a rule which says that when the inventory of an item drops to a two months' supply, an order should be placed for x additional units. Records can then be set up which show how rapidly the item is moving out of inventory and what the quantity on hand is. When the quantity on hand reaches the prescribed minimum, a purchase order for x units can be placed. The quantity to be ordered is given by the rule; it does not require a management judgment. Since this process does not involve a management decision or judgment, except in the creation of the initial rules and in handling exceptional situations, it is quite different from the process we have labeled management control. The formal definition is:

> Operational control is the process of assuring that specific tasks are carried out effectively and efficiently.

Distinctions among the processes

The purpose of the foregoing brief description of the three planning and control processes is to provide an overview so as to place in perspective the management control process, the process in which we are primarily interested. As an additional way of explaining the distinction,

EXHIBIT 11-1

Examples of planning and control activities in a business organization

Strategic planning	Management control	Operational control
Defining goals		
Deciding strategies	Preparing budgets	
Planning the organization structure	Planning staff levels	Controlling hiring
Setting personnel policies	Formulating personnel practices	Checking attendance
Setting financial policies	Working capital planning	Controlling credit extension
Setting marketing policies	Formulating advertising programs	Controlling placement of advertisements
Setting research policies	Deciding on research projects	
Planning new product lines	Planning product improvements	Controlling work flows
Acquiring a new division	Deciding on plant rearrangement	Scheduling production
Deciding to build a new plant	Deciding to buy a new machine	Controlling construction of new assets
	Formulating decision rules for operational control	Controlling inventory
	Measuring and appraising management performance	Measuring and appraising workers' efficiency

Exhibit 11-1 shows some of the activities that are classified under each of the three processes. The relative importance of planning activities and control activities differs among the three processes as indicated in Exhibit 11-2.

The strategic planning process involves primarily planning, but a certain amount of control is necessary to insure that the information and analyses are made available to the decision maker at the proper time. Control also insures that strategic problems, once identified, are resolved rather than being allowed to fall through the cracks. At the other extreme, operational control involves primarily control activities; that is, most of

EXHIBIT 11–2
Relative importance of planning and control

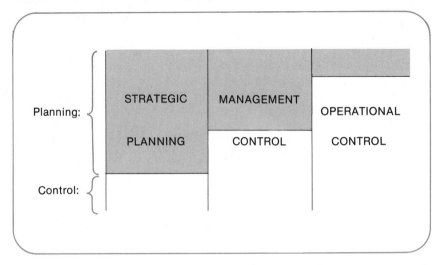

the effort is devoted to insuring that prescribed rules and procedures are being carried out. Some planning is involved in operational control, however. Preparing detailed work schedules, deciding what work stations to use, and deciding how to handle special situations that are not covered by the prescribed rules, are examples of planning activities.

The management control process, which is between these two extremes, involves approximately equal amounts of planning activities and control activities. Planning is as important as control, and managers spend roughly the same amount of time on each. Moreover, in the management control process, planning activities are closely related to control activities. We shall, for example, discuss the use of the budget as a planning tool in Chapter 12, and in Chapter 14 we shall describe how information in the same budget is used for control purposes.

STEPS IN THE MANAGEMENT CONTROL PROCESS

Much of the management control process involves informal communication and interactions. Informal communication occurs by means of memoranda, meetings, conversations, and even by such signals as facial expressions. Although these informal activities are of great importance, they are not amenable to a systematic description. In addition to these informal activities, most companies also have a *formal* management control system. It consists of the following phases, each of which is described briefly below and in more detail in succeeding chapters:

EXHIBIT 11-3
Phases of management control

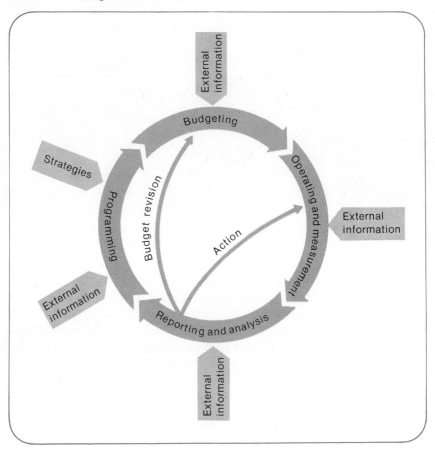

1. Programming.
2. Budgeting.
3. Operating and measurement.
4. Reporting and analysis.

As indicated in Exhibit 11-3, each of these activities leads to the next. They recur in a regular cycle, and together they constitute a "closed loop."

Programming

Programming is the process of deciding on the programs that the company will undertake and the approximate amount of resources that are to be allocated to each program. Programs are the principal activities that the organization has decided to undertake in order to implement the strategies that it has decided upon. In a profit-oriented company, each principal product or product line is a program. If several product lines are manufactured in the same plant, the plant itself and additions or modifications to it may be identified as a program. There are also various research and development programs, some aimed at improving existing products or processes, others searching for marketable new products. Program decisions are made within the context of the goals and strategies that have previously been decided upon.

Many companies do not have a formal system that is used in making program decisions; instead, they make these decisions informally, whenever the need to do so arises. Other companies do have a formal system for evaluating their total program and proposed changes in it. We discuss such systems and other aspects of the programming process in Chapter 12.

Budget preparation

Programing is a planning process. Another planning process is called budgeting. An essential difference between programming and budgeting is that programming looks forward several years into the future, whereas budgeting focuses on the next year. **A budget is a plan expressed in quantitative, usually monetary, terms that covers a specified period of time, usually one year.** Most companies have a budget.

In preparing a budget, each program is translated into terms that correspond to the responsibility of those managers who have been charged with executing the program or some part of it. Thus, although the plans are originally made in terms of individual programs, in the budgeting process the plans are translated into terms of responsibility centers. The process of developing a budget is essentially one of negotiation between the manager of a responsibility center and his superior. The end product of these negotiations is an approved statement of the revenues that are expected during the budget year, and the resources that are to be used in achieving the company's objectives for each responsibility center and for the company as a whole. The process of preparing a budget will be described in more detail in Chapter 12.

Operating and measurement

During the period of actual operations, records are kept of resources actually consumed (i.e., costs) and of revenues actually earned. These records are structured so that costs and revenue data are classified both by programs (that is, by products, research/development projects, and the like) and also by responsibility centers. Data classified according to programs are used as a basis for future programming, and data classified by responsibility centers are used to measure the performance of responsibility center managers. For the latter purpose, data on actual results are reported in such a way that they can be readily compared with the plan as set forth in the budget.

Reporting and analysis

One function of a management control system is to communicate information to managers throughout the organization. This information consists of both accounting numbers and also various types of nonaccounting information. Some of the nonaccounting information is generated within the organization, and some of it describes what is happening in the environment outside the organization. This information keeps managers informed as to what is going on and helps to insure that the work done by the separate responsibility centers is coordinated. This information is conveyed in the form of reports, as will be described in Chapter 15.

Reports are also used as a basis for control. Essentially, control reports are derived from an analysis that compares actual performance with planned performance and attempts to explain the difference. Planned performance is set forth in the budget. Techniques for making such analyses are described in Chapter 14.

Based on these formal control reports, and also on information received through informal communication channels, managers decide what, if any, action should be taken. They may, for example, decide to change the plan as set forth in the budget, and this leads to a new planning process. It is for this reason that the phases shown in Exhibit 11–3 are depicted as a closed loop, with one activity leading to the next.

ACCOUNTING INFORMATION USED IN MANAGEMENT CONTROL

The types of management accounting information discussed in Parts One and Two—full cost accounting and differential accounting—are both used in the management control process. Full cost accounting is used to make planning decisions of the type described in Chapter 2, particularly those relating to pricing products and changes in product specifications. Differential accounting data are the principal type of accounting data used in the programming phase. These data assist managers in deciding what capital investments to make, what the make-or-buy policy should be, and other matters described in Chapters 7–9.

In addition, the new type of accounting introduced in Chapter 10—responsibility accounting—is an important aid in the management control process. Responsibility accounting focuses on responsibility centers.

This is also the focus in preparing budgets and in comparing actual performance with budgeted performance. Control can be exercised only through the managers who are responsible for what the organization does. From the above brief description, it should also be apparent that responsibility accounting deals both with data relating to plans and also with data relating to actual performance, that is, with both future data and with historical data.

In explaining the nature and use of responsibility accounting information, we need to introduce two new ways of classifying costs: (1) as controllable or noncontrollable; and (2) as engineered, discretionary, or committed.

Controllable costs

An item of cost is controllable if the amount of cost incurred in (or assigned to) a responsibility center is significantly influenced by the actions of the manager of the responsibility center. Otherwise, it is noncontrollable. There are two important implications of this definition: (1) it refers to a specific responsibility center, and (2) it suggests that controllability results from a *significant* influence rather than from a *complete* influence. Each of these implications is discussed below.

The word *controllable* must be used in the context of a specific responsibility center rather than as an innate characteristic of a given cost item. **When a company is viewed as a single entity, all costs are controllable.** For any item of cost, there is someone, somewhere in the company, who can take actions that influence it. In the extreme case, costs for any segment of the business can be reduced to zero by closing down that segment; costs incurred in manufacturing a component within the company can be changed by purchasing that component from an outside vendor; and so on. Thus, the important question is not what costs are controllable in general but rather what costs are controllable in a *specific responsibility center,* for it is these costs on which the management control system must focus.

Degree of influence. The definition of *controllable* refers to a *significant* influence rather than to *complete* influence because only in rare cases does one individual have complete control over all the factors that influence an item of cost. The influence that the manager of a manufacturing department has over its direct labor costs may actually be quite limited. Wage rates may be established by the personnel department or by union negotiations. The amount of direct labor required for a unit of product may be largely determined by the engineers who designed the product and who specified how it was to be manufactured. The number of units produced, and hence total direct labor costs, may be influenced by the output of some earlier department in the production process, by the ability of the purchasing department to obtain materials, or by a variety of other factors. Nevertheless, the manager of a manufacturing department usually has a significant influence on the amount of direct labor cost incurred in the department. He has some control over the amount of idle time, the speed and efficiency with which work is done, and other factors which to some extent affect labor costs.

Direct material costs and direct labor costs in a given responsibility center are usually controllable. With respect to the items of overhead cost, some elements are controllable by the responsibility center to which the costs are assigned, but others are not controllable. Indirect labor, supplies, and electricity are usually controllable. So are those charges from service centers that are based on services actually rendered by the service center. **An allocated cost is not controllable by the responsibility center to which the allocation is made.** The amount of cost allocated to a responsibility center depends on the formula used to make the allocation rather than on the actions of the responsibility center manager. This is so unless the cost is actually a direct cost that is allocated only for convenience, as in the case of social security taxes on direct labor.

> *EXAMPLE:* In Department 6, a production department, the costs recorded for April included $12,248 of factory overhead; this was Department 6's allocated share of the $83,422 total factory overhead. The manager of Department 6 had little, if any, influence on the $83,422 of total factory overhead; that cost was the responsibility of the several factory overhead departments. Neither did the manager of Department 6 influence what fraction of the $83,422 was assigned to Department 6; that amount depended on the particular bases of allocation used (as described in Chapter 4). The $12,248 of factory overhead cost was therefore noncontrollable by the manager of the Department 6.

Contrast with direct costs.   The various items of cost in a responsibility center may be classified as either direct or indirect. Indirect costs are allocated to the responsibility center and are therefore not controllable by it, as explained above. All controllable costs are therefore direct costs. Not all direct costs are controllable, however.

> *EXAMPLE:* Depreciation on departmental equipment is a direct cost of the department, but the depreciation charge is often noncontrollable by the departmental supervisor who may have no authority to acquire or dispose of equipment. The rental charge for rented premises is another example of a direct but noncontrollable cost.

Contrast with variable costs.   Controllable costs are not necessarily the same as *variable costs,* that is, costs that vary with the volume of output. Costs such as supervision, heat, light, and magazine subscriptions may be unaffected by volume, but they are nevertheless controllable. Conversely, although most variable costs are controllable, that is not always the case. In some situations, the cost of raw material and parts, whose consumption varies directly with volume, may be entirely outside the influence of the departmental manager.

EXAMPLE: In an automobile assembly department, one automobile requires an engine, a body, five wheels, and so on, and there is nothing the supervisor can do about it. He is responsible for waste and spoilage of material, but not for the main flow of material itself.

Direct labor, which is usually thought of as the obvious example of a controllable cost item, may be noncontrollable in certain types of responsibility centers. Situations of this type must be examined very carefully, however, in order to insure that the noncontrollability is real. Supervisors tend to argue that more costs are noncontrollable than actually is the case, in order to avoid being held responsible for them.

EXAMPLE: If an assembly line has 20 work stations and cannot be operated unless it is manned by 20 persons of specified skills and hence specified wage rates, direct labor cost on that assembly line may be noncontrollable. Nevertheless, the assumption that such costs are noncontrollable may be open to challenge, for it may be possible to find ways to do the job with 19 persons, or with 20 persons who have a lower average skill classification and hence lower wage rates.

Converting noncontrollable costs to controllable costs. A noncontrollable element of cost can be converted to a controllable element of cost in either of two related ways: (1) by changing the basis of cost assignment from an allocation to a direct assignment, and/or (2) by changing the locus of responsibility for decisions.

Converting allocated costs to controllable costs. As explained above, allocated costs are noncontrollable by the responsibility center to which they are allocated. Many items of cost that are allocated to responsibility centers can be converted to controllable costs simply by assigning the cost in such a way that the amount of costs assigned is influenced by actions taken by the manager of the responsibility center.

EXAMPLE: If all electricity coming into a plant is measured by a single meter, there is no way of measuring the actual electrical consumption of each responsibility center in the plant, and the electrical cost is therefore necessarily allocated to each responsibility center and is noncontrollable. Electricity cost can be changed to a controllable cost for each responsibility center in the plant simply by installing electrical meters in each responsibility center so that each responsibility center's actual consumption is measured.

Services that a responsibility center receives from service units can be converted from allocated to controllable costs by assigning the cost of services to the benefiting responsibility centers on some basis that measures the amount of services actually rendered.

EXAMPLE: If maintenance department costs are charged to production responsibility centers as a part of an overhead rate, they are noncontrollable; but if responsibility centers are charged on the basis of an hourly rate for each hour of maintenance work done and if the head of the responsibility center can influence the requests for maintenance work, then maintenance is a controllable element of the cost of the production responsibility center.

Practically any item of indirect cost could conceivably be converted to a direct and controllable cost, but for some (such as charging the president's salary on the basis of the time he spends on the problems of various parts of the business), the paperwork involved in doing so clearly is not worthwhile. There are nevertheless a great many unexploited opportunities in many companies to convert noncontrollable costs to controllable costs.

The same principle applies to costs that, although actually incurred in a responsibility center, are not assigned to the responsibility center at all, even on an allocated basis. Under these circumstances, the material or services are "free" insofar as the head of the responsibility center is concerned, and since he does not have to "pay" for them (as part of the costs for which he is held responsible), he is unlikely to be concerned about careful use of these materials or services.

EXAMPLE: Until recently, the city of New York did not charge residents for the amount of water that they used. When water meters were installed and residents were required to pay for their own use of water, the total quantity of water used in the city decreased by a sizable amount.

Changing responsibility for cost incurrence.   The most important decisions affecting costs are made at or near the top of an organization, both because top management presumably has more ability and because it has a broader viewpoint than lower level managers. On the other hand, the farther removed these decisions are from the "firing line," the place where resources are actually used, the less responsive they can be to conditions currently existing at that place. As noted in Chapter 10, many companies recognize this fact by *decentralizing,* that is, by setting up profit centers whose managers are assigned responsibility for both revenues and costs. Thus, a decentralized organization is one in which a relatively large fraction of total costs are controllable in the lower level responsibility centers.

EXAMPLE: Perhaps the most dramatic example of a shift from centralized to decentralized management is the change that has taken place in Communist countries. Beginning with Yugoslavia in the 1950s, and later extending to the USSR, there has been a recognition by the Communist top management that the highly centralized planning and control process envisioned by Lenin simply does not work well in practice. Consequently, individual plant managers have been given much more authority to make decisions affecting the costs of their plants. This shift to decentralization made many more items of cost controllable at lower level responsibility centers. It also required the installation of a more effective management control system.

Reporting noncontrollable costs.   In the performance reports for responsibility centers, it is obviously essential that controllable costs be clearly distinguished from noncontrollable costs. Some people argue that the *separation* of controllable from noncontrollable costs is not enough; they insist that noncontrollable costs should not even be reported. Actually, there may be good reasons for reporting the noncontrollable costs assigned to a responsibility center. One reason is that top management may want the manager of the responsibility center to be concerned about such costs, the expectation being that such concern may indirectly lead to better cost control.

EXAMPLE: The control report of a production department may list an allocated portion of the cost of the personnel department, even though the supervisor of the production department has no direct responsibility for costs of the personnel department. Such a practice can be justified either on the ground that the production department supervisor will refrain from making unnecessary requests of the personnel department if he is made to feel some responsibility for personnel department costs, or on the ground that the supervisor may in various ways put pressure on the manager of the personnel department to exercise good cost control in the personnel department.

Another reason for reporting noncontrollable costs in responsibility centers is that if the manager is made aware of the total amount of costs that are incurred in operating the responsibility center, he may have a better understanding of how much other parts of the company contribute to its operation. Such a practice may boomerang, however, for the manager may conclude that the controllable costs are so small, relative to the noncontrollable costs, that they are not worth worrying about.

EXAMPLE: Exhibit 11–4 shows a control report for a production department. The controllable items of cost are clearly separated from the noncontrollable items, and no variance from budgeted costs is shown for the noncontrollable items in order to avoid any implication that the department manager is responsible for explaining the behavior of these items. The departmental manager is made aware that the total cost of the department is $15,453. Some people would argue, however, that since the manager knows that $6,248 of this amount is noncontrollable, he may not be adequately concerned about the $9,205 that is controllable and especially about his $488 unfavorable variance, which is only 3 percent of total cost.

EXHIBIT 11-4
A control report

Department   107   Month: January 1976

Item	Actual cost	Difference from budget*
Controllable:		
Material spoilage	$ 681	$(107)
Direct labor...	5,234	(228)
Indirect labor	1,678	82
Supplies	340	20
Maintenance	822	(235)
Power..	450	(20)
Subtotal, controllable.............................	9,205	$(488)
Noncontrollable:		
Rent..	763	
Depreciation	1,625	
Allocated costs..	3,860	
Subtotal, noncontrollable	6,248	
Total Cost..	$15,453	

* ( ) = unfavorable.

Engineered, discretionary, and committed costs

Still another classification of costs is that among (1) engineered, (2) discretionary, and (3) committed costs. Although both engineered and discretionary costs are controllable, the approach to the control of one is quite different from that of the other. Committed costs are not controllable in the short run, but they are controllable in the long run.

Engineered costs. **Engineered costs are items of cost for which the right or proper amount of costs that should be incurred can be estimated.** Direct labor cost is an example. Given the specifications for a product, engineers can determine the necessary production operations and they can estimate, within reasonably close limits, the time that should be spent on each operation. The total amount of direct labor costs that should be incurred can then be estimated by translation of these times into money by means of a standard wage rate, to arrive at a standard labor cost per unit. The standard unit cost multiplied by the number of units of product gives what the total amount of direct labor cost should be. Since production engineering is not an exact science, this amount is not necessarily the exact amount that should be spent, but the estimates usually can be made close enough so that there is relatively little ground for disagreement. In particular, there can be no reasonable ground for denying that there is a direct relationship between volume (i.e., output) and costs; two units require approximately double the amount of direct labor that one unit requires. Similarly, in most situations, direct material costs are engineered costs.

Discretionary costs. **Discretionary costs are items of costs whose amount can be varied at the discretion of the manager of the responsibility center.** These costs are also called **programmed** or **managed** costs. The amount of a discretionary cost can be whatever management wants it to be, within wide limits. Unlike engineered costs, there is no scientific way of deciding what the "right" amount of a discretionary cost should be, or at least there is no scientific basis that the management of the particular company is willing to rely on. How much should be spent for research and development? For advertising? For public relations? For employees' parties and outings? For donations? For the accounting department? No one knows. In most companies, the discretionary cost category includes all general and administrative activities, most marketing activities, and many items of factory indirect cost.

In the absence of an engineering standard, the amount to be spent for a given item of cost must be a matter of judgment. Usually, this judgment is arrived at by agreement between the supervisor concerned and his superior, as part of the budget preparation process.

Although there is no "right" level for the total amount of a discretionary cost item, valid standards may be developed for controlling some of the detail within it.

> *EXAMPLE:* Although no one knows the optimum amount that should be spent for the accounting function as a whole, it is nevertheless possible to measure the performance of individual clerks in the accounting department in terms of number of postings or number of invoices typed per hour. Similarly, although we cannot know the "right" amount of total travel expense, we can set standards for the amount that should be spent per day or per mile.

Furthermore, new developments in management accounting result in a gradual shift of items from the discretionary cost category to the engineered cost category. Several companies have recently started to use what they believe to be valid techniques for determining the "right" amount that they should spend on advertising in order to achieve their sales objectives, or the "right" number of sales personnel.

Spurious relationships. The decision as to how much should be spent for a discretionary cost item may take several forms, such as (1) "spend the same amount as we spent last year," (2) "spend *b* percent of sales," or (3) "spend *a* dollars plus *b* percent of sales." These three decision rules result in historical spending patterns which, when plotted against volume, have the same superficial appearance as the patterns of engineered cost. Recall that the equation for the relation of costs to volume is $y = a + bx$. Using this equation, the first type of decision listed above gives a *fixed* cost line, $y = a$; the second gives a variable cost line, $y = bx$; and the third gives a *semivariable* cost line, $y = a + bx$.

These relationships are fundamentally different from those observed for engineered costs, however. For engineered variable costs, the pattern is inevitable; as volume increases, the amount of cost *must* increase. For discretionary costs, the relationship exists only because of a management decision, and it can be changed simply by making a different management decision.

> *EXAMPLE:* A company may have decided that research and development costs should be 3 percent of sales revenue. There can be no scientific reason for such a decision, for no one knows the optimum amount that should be spent for research and development. In all probability, such a rule exists primarily because management thinks that this is what the company can afford to spend. In this company there will be a linear relationship between sales volume and research and development costs. This is not a cause-and-effect relationship, however; and there is no inherent reason why research and development costs in the future should conform to the historical pattern.

Marketing costs. Marketing costs are those incurred in order to make sales. They include the costs of the selling organization, advertising, sales promotion, and so on. These costs may vary with sales volume, but the relationship is the *reverse* of that for factory costs: marketing cost is the independent variable, and sales volume is the dependent variable. Marketing costs vary not in response to sales volume but rather *in anticipation of* sales volume, according to decisions made by management.[1] They are therefore discretionary costs.

If management has a policy of spending more for marketing activities when sales volume is high, then a scatter diagram of the relationship between marketing costs and sales volume will have the same appearance as the diagrams for the relationship between production costs and production volume (see Exhibit 11–5). The two diagrams should be interpreted quite differently, however. The production cost diagram indicates that production cost *necessarily* increases as volume increases, while the selling cost diagram shows either that selling cost has been *permitted* to increase with increases in volume, or that the higher costs have resulted in the higher volume. Further, subject to some qualifications, it may be said that for total production costs, the lower they are, the better; whereas low marketing costs may reflect inadequate selling effort. The "right" level of marketing costs is a judgment made by management.

There is not always a direct relationship between marketing costs and sales volume. Take advertising costs as an example. Management may decide (1) to *increase* advertising expenditures when sales *increase,* on

---

[1] Exceptions are salesperson's commissions and other payments related to sales revenue. These items of course vary directly with sales revenue.

EXHIBIT 11–5
Superficial similarity of production and marketing cost behavior

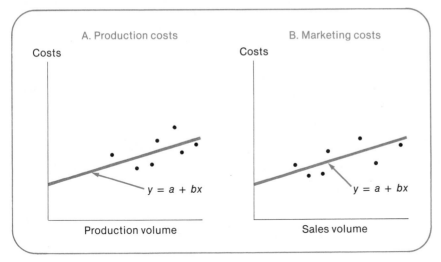

the basis that the company can afford to spend more when revenue is high; (2) to spend *the same amount* for advertising, regardless of sales volume; or (3) to *increase* advertising expenditures when sales *decrease,* in the belief that additional advertising effort is necessary to regain lost volume. Each of these policies gives a different cost-volume relationship, and the causal pattern is further obscured by the fact that sales volume is influenced not only by advertising, or indeed marketing effort in total, but also by general business conditions and other factors outside the company's control.

Committed costs. **Committed costs are those that are the inevitable consequences of commitments previously made.** Depreciation is an example; once a company has purchased a building or a piece of equipment, there is an inevitable depreciation charge so long as the building continues to be owned. When the manager of a baseball team has a five-year contract, his salary is a committed cost.

In the short run, committed costs are uncontrollable. They can be changed only by changing the commitment, for example, by disposing of the building or equipment whose depreciation is being recorded, or by buying up the baseball manager's contract. Committed costs may or may not be direct costs for a given responsibility center.

BEHAVIORAL ASPECTS OF MANAGEMENT CONTROL

The management control process involves human beings, from those in the lowest responsibility center of the organizational hierarchy up to and including each member of top management. The management control process in part consists of inducing these human beings to take those actions that will help attain the company's goals and to refrain from taking actions that are inconsistent with these goals. Although for some purposes an accumulation of the costs of manufacturing a product is useful, management cannot literally "control" a product, or the costs of making a product. What management does – or at least what it attempts to do – is **control the actions of the people who are responsible for incurring these costs.** The discipline that studies the behavior of people in organizations is called **social psychology.** It is this discipline, rather than economics, that provides the underlying principles that are relevant in the control process. We shall note briefly some aspects of behavior that are essential to an understanding of this process.

Behavior of participants

Each person in an organization is called a **participant.** A person becomes a participant – that is, he joins an organization – because he believes that by doing so he can achieve his *personal* goals. His decision to contribute to the productive work of the organization once he has become a member of it is also based on his perception that this will help achieve his personal goals.

An individual's personal goals can be expressed as **needs.** Some of these needs are **material** and can be satisfied by the money employees earn on the job; that is, they need enough money to provide for themselves and their dependents. Other needs are **psychological.** People need to have their abilities and achievements recognized; they need social acceptance as members of a group; they need to feel a sense of personal worth; they need to feel secure; they need the freedom to exercise discretion; they may need a feeling of power and achievement.

The relative importance of these needs varies with different persons, and their importance also varies with the same person at different times. For some people, earning a great deal of money is a dominant need; for others, monetary considerations are much less important. Most people do not attach much importance to the need to exercise discretion or the need for achievement,[2] but the few persons who do so tend to be the leaders of the organization. The relative importance that persons attach to their own needs is heavily influenced by the attitude of their colleagues and of their superiors.

---

[2] McClelland argues that there is a relationship between the strength of the achievement motivation of the leaders of an organization and the success of that organization and that a similar relationship helps explain why certain countries have a rapid economic growth at certain times while others do not. See David McClelland, *The Achieving Society* (1971); and David C. McClelland and David G. Winter, *Motivating Economic Achievement* (New York: The Free Press, 1969).

Motivation and incentives

- Individuals are influenced both by positive incentives and by negative incentives. *A positive incentive is the satisfaction of a need or the expectation that a need will be satisfied. A negative incentive is the deprivation of satisfaction of a need or the fear of such deprivation.* Positive incentives are also called *rewards,* and negative incentives, *punishment.* Research on incentives tends to support the following:

- Top management's attitude toward the system can be a powerful incentive. If top management signals, by its actions about the management control system, that it regards the system as important, operating managers will react positively. If top management pays little attention to the management control system, operating managers are likely to pay relatively little attention to it also. Basically, management action involves praise or other award for good performance and criticism of poor performance, and questions that seek to determine whether performance is good or poor.

- Individuals tend to be more strongly motivated by reward than by punishment.

- Monetary compensation is an important means of satisfying certain needs, but beyond the subsistence level the amount of compensation is not necessarily as important as nonmonetary rewards. Nevertheless, the amount of a person's earnings is often important indirectly as an indication of how his achievement and ability are regarded. For example, a person earning $50,000 a year may be disgruntled if a colleague of perceived equal ability receives $51,000 a year.

- The effectiveness of incentives diminishes rapidly as the time elapses between an action and the reward or punishment administered for it. This is why it is important that reports on performance be made available and acted on quickly. Management control cannot wait for the annual financial statements that appear three months or so after the year has ended.

- Needs may be unconscious, or they may be expressed as aspirations or goals. Motivation is weakest when the person perceives a goal as being either unattainable or too easily attainable. Motivation is strong when the goal can be attained with some effort and when the individual regards its attainment as important in relation to his needs.

- A person tends to accept reports of his performance more willingly and to use them more constructively when they are presented to him in a manner that he regards as objective; that is, without personal bias.

- Persons are receptive to learning better ways of doing things only when they personally recognize the inadequacies of their present behavior.

- Beyond a certain point, pressure for improved performance accomplishes nothing. This optimum point is far below the maximum amount of pressure that conceivably could be exerted. (When the coach says, "Don't press; don't try too hard," he is applying this principle.)

Rewards

Many management control systems rely for the strength of their motivation on the attitude and actions that top management takes in response to reported performance. In some situations a quite simple signal can be effective.

> EXAMPLE: In the New York City government there was a project to sort out and discard files on those Medicaid cases that had been closed. These files occupied 1,200 file cabinets. When the job started, each clerk was examining an average of 150 files a day, which was unsatisfactory. The supervisor then made the following change: instead of discarding files in a common container, each clerk was asked to pile them in front of his work station. As the piles mounted, it became apparent to everyone how much work each clerk was doing. Production immediately increased to 300 files a day.[3]

At the other extreme, the reward can be that the managers' compensation is related to their performance, that is, managers are paid a performance bonus. In view of the importance which many people attach to monetary compensation, this is a strong motivation indeed. In some cases it is too strong, for unless the standards are very carefully worked out, incessant arguments will go on about the justice and equity of the reported results. If the system is being used only for praise or blame, inequities in the figures can be allowed for when interpreting the results, but this is not possible when a bonus is computed mechanically on the basis of reported performance. Thus, a bonus plan is most successful when there is general agreement that the basis of measurement is fair.

Focus on line managers

Since subordinates are responsible to their superiors, they should receive praise, criticism, and other forms of reward and punishment from their superiors. Staff people should not be directly involved in these motivation activities (except with respect to control of the staff organizations themselves). Line managers are the focal points in management control. They are the persons whose judgments are incorporated in the approved plans, and they are the persons who must influence others and whose performance is measured. Staff people collect, summarize, and present information that is useful in the process; and they make calcula-

---

[3] From *Management Accounting*, December 1972, p. 63.

tions that translate management judgments into the format of the system. There may be many such staff people; indeed, the controller department is often the largest staff department in a company. However, the significant decisions and control actions are the responsibility of the line managers, not of the staff.

Goal congruence

Since an organization does not have a mind of its own, the organization itself literally cannot have goals. The "organizational goals" that we have referred to are actually the goals of top management. Top management wants these organizational goals to be attained, but other participants have their own personal goals that *they* want to achieve. These personal goals are the satisfaction of their needs. In other words, participants act in their own self-interest.

The difference between organizational goals and personal goals suggests the central purpose of a management control system: **the system should be designed so that actions that it leads people to take in accordance with their perceived self-interest are actions that are also in the best interests of the organization.** In the language of social psychology, the management control system should encourage **goal congruence;** that is, it should be structured so that the goals of participants, so far as feasible, are consistent with the goals of the organization as a whole.

Perfect congruence between individual goals and organizational goals does not exist, but as a minimum the system should not encourage the individual to act *against* the best interests of the company. For example, if the management control system signals that the emphasis should be only on reducing costs, and if a manager responds by reducing costs at the expense of adequate quality or if he responds by reducing costs in his own responsibility center by measures that cause a more than offsetting increase in costs in some other responsibility center, he has been motivated, but in the wrong direction. It is therefore important to ask two separate questions about any practice used in a management control system:

1. What action does it motivate people to take in their own perceived self-interest, and
2. Is this action in the best interests of the company?

An example: The computer department

As an illustration of how management control practices affect the behavior of individual managers, let us consider the problem of controlling the costs of processing information in a company that has a central computer department. The computer department processes most of the information used by the accounting department and prepares accounting reports, it develops and operates systems for controlling certain production operations, it provides information to the marketing department, it processes special studies for any manager who requests them, and it does a variety of other jobs. The costs of the computer department are determined essentially by two factors: (1) the efficiency with which the computer department manager runs the operation, and (2) the volume of requests for computer services that are made by users. Top management presumably wants the computer department to operate at an optimum level of costs, and it also wants the operating departments to use computer processing, but only up to the point where the results are worth more than the costs.

There are many ways in which the costs of the computer department can be assigned to users, each of which gives a different message, and hence a different motivation, both to the computer department manager and to the managers of responsibility centers that use its services. Some of them are described below.

Method No. 1. Do not charge any computer department costs to the using responsibility centers.

Message: Users have no responsibility for computer costs. They are encouraged to request whatever computer work they want.

Motivation: Users are encouraged to use the computer freely because its services are "free." This motivates them to seek new ways of using the computer; when a computer is newly installed in a company, such motivation is probably desirable. (In a college or university, students may be permitted to use a computer without charge for a similar reason: to encourage them to investigate its possibilities.) With such a system, however, top management has an inadequate basis for judging the performance of the computer department manager. An increase in costs may be the result of inefficiency, or it may be the result of an increase in services requested, and there is no way to separate the two causes. Furthermore, if the requests of users exceed the computer's capacity, the computer department manager must decide which requests have priority, and this lessens the control of the users over their information needs.

Method No. 2. Do not charge for routine reports but make a charge for special analyses requested by users.

Message: Routine information is furnished as a service, and users are not to worry about its cost. Users are, however, required to decide whether the value of special analyses to them is worth the charge that will be made for it.

Motivation: With respect to routine reports, the implications are the same as those in Method No. 1, but with respect to special reports, Method No. 2 introduces a different motivation. Users presumably want to keep their costs down, and they will therefore think carefully before ordering expensive work from the computer department. Furthermore, charging for these analyses tends to lessen the problem of setting priorities. The message to the user is: if you are willing to pay, you can have the job done; otherwise not.

Method No. 3. Allocate computer department costs to the operating responsibility centers as an item of general and administrative costs, the amount allocated to each responsibility center depending on its size.

Message: Users are not directly responsible for computer department costs, but they should to be aware of the magnitude of these costs.

Motivation: This method could lead responsibility center managers to raise questions about the overall size of the computer department if they thought its costs were getting out of line and having an adverse effect on the total costs charged to their responsibility centers. Fundamentally, however, it places responsibility for computer costs primarily on the computer department manager. Users are not motivated to consider whether services requested are worth their cost.

Method No. 4. Charge all users a price that is based on the cost of the services they receive, plus a profit margin.

Message: Operating departments should use the computer only for services that are believed to be worth what they cost.

Motivation: This method has the effect of putting the computer department manager in business for himself. The department is a profit center, and the prices are transfer prices (see Chapter 10). Under some circumstances, users are permitted to use services from outside companies if they can buy the services at lower cost. If the computer department manager cannot provide satisfactory service at competitive prices, the department will not earn enough revenue to cover its costs, and this is a signal that something is wrong. On the other hand, this method does not encourage the development of new services, as does Method No. 1, and the task of developing fair transfer prices may be quite complicated because many reports are used jointly by several responsibility centers.

Method No. 5. Charge for all computer services at prices that on the average equal cost plus profit margin, but charge lower prices to users who are willing to have their work done at night and higher prices for daytime work.

Message: If users are willing to be a little inconvenienced, they can have computer services at a lower price.

Motivation: This is one of several possible variations of the transfer price idea. The motivation here is to encourage the use of the computer during unattractive hours by charging a lower price for such usage. The transfer price principle can be used to motivate users in whatever direction management wishes.

Some of these methods use costs as in the cost accounting system described in Part One; some use transfer prices that may or may not be based on cost. Each of these methods of handling the cost of computer services motivates the managers involved—both the managers of operating responsibility centers and the manager of the computer department—to act differently. The best method is the one that motivates operating managers to act as top management wants them to act. Any of those described, or any of a number of others, can be "best" under a certain set of conditions.

The above example indicates the considerations that are important in structuring responsibility accounting information. These considerations are basically different from those involved in full cost accounting, where the purpose is to measure the amount of resources used for products or services, or from those involved in differential accounting, where the purpose is to estimate the amounts that are differential for a proposed course of action. Neither full cost accounting nor differential accounting is influenced by behavioral considerations; whereas in responsibility accounting, behavioral considerations are dominant.

Cooperation and conflict

In looking at an organization chart and noting the lines of authority running from one box to another, one could easily get the impression that the way in which organizational goals are achieved is that the top manager makes a decision, communicates that decision down through the organizational hierarchy, and managers at lower levels of the organization proceed to implement it. It should now be apparent that this is *not* the way in which an organization actually functions. Because individuals have their own goals, and because they react in different ways, this view of what happens in an organization is unrealistic.

What actually happens is that each subordinate reacts to the instructions of top management in accordance with how those instructions affect the subordinate's personal needs. Since usually more than one responsibility center is involved in carrying out a given plan, the interactions between their managers also affects what actually happens. For example, although the manager of the computer department is supposed to see to it that the information processing needs of the operating departments are satisfied, if there is friction between the computer department manager and an operating manager, the needs of that operating manager's department may, in fact, be slighted. For these and many other reasons, **conflict** exists within organizations.

Nevertheless, the work of the organization will not get done unless its participants work together with a certain amount of harmony. Thus, there is also **cooperation** in organizations. Participants realize that unless there is a reasonable amount of cooperation, the organization will dissolve, and the participants will then be unable to satisfy *any* of the needs which motivated them to join the organization in the first place.

An organization attempts to maintain an appropriate balance between the forces that create conflict and those that create cooperation. Some conflict is not only inevitable, it is desirable. Conflict results in part from the competition among participants for promotion or other forms of need satisfaction; and such competition is, within limits, healthy. A certain amount of cooperation is also obviously essential, but if undue emphasis is placed on engendering cooperative attitudes, the most able participants will be denied the opportunity of demonstrating their full potentialities.

SUMMARY

Planning and control activities in an organization can be classified into one of three categories: (1) strategic planning, which involves deciding on the goals of the organization, and the strategies that are to be used in attaining these goals; (2) management control, which seeks to assure that the strategies are implemented effectively and efficiently; and (3) operational control, which has to do with the performance of specific tasks. All three processes involve both planning and control.

Our interest is focused on the management control process. The main steps in this process are (1) programming, in which decisions on programs are made; (2) budget preparation, which involves the preparation of a financial plan, usually annual; (3) operating and measurement; and (4) reporting and analyzing results of operations and taking the necessary action.

All types of accounting information are used in the management control process, but the most important type is responsibility accounting, which reports both planned and actual costs in terms of responsibility centers. In understanding the use of responsibility accounting information, it is important to distinguish between controllable costs—those over which a manager can exert a significant influence—and noncontrollable costs. It is also important to distinguish among engineered, discretionary, and committed costs, and especially to realize that although engineered and discretionary costs superficially appear to behave in a similar way, they actually are fundamentally different with respect to how they are planned and controlled.

The management control process involves human beings, so behavioral considerations are important. Such psychological principles as motivation, goal congruence, and cooperation and conflict are at least as important as the principles of accounting in understanding how the process works.

IMPORTANT TERMS

Planning	Discretionary cost
Control	Committed cost
Strategic planning	Motivation
Management control	Reward
Operational control	Punishment
Controllable cost	Goal congruence
Engineered cost	Cooperation and conflict

QUESTIONS FOR DISCUSSION

1. Why is it important to define control as relating to *desired* results, rather than to *planned* results?

2. What are the differences among the planning activities that take place in the strategic planning process, the management control process, and the operational control process, respectively? Give examples.

3. What are the differences among the control activities that take place in the three processes? Give examples.

4. In Exhibit 11–3, there is an arrow going from "Reporting and analysis" to "Budgeting." What does this arrow mean?

5. What are the differences between a controllable cost and a noncontrollable cost?

6. It is said that when a company is viewed as a single entity, all costs are controllable. Does this mean that the top management conceivably could change any item of cost in the near future? Give examples of costs that top management might well change, as a practical matter, and costs that could be, but probably will not be, changed.

7. Contrast controllable costs with direct costs. With variable costs.

8. A company operates a fleet of automobiles which personnel may use for company business. If the company wanted to treat the costs of these automobiles as a controllable cost, how would it account for their use? If it wanted to treat these automobiles as a noncontrollable cost, how would it account for their use?

9. Why is an allocated item of cost not controllable in the responsibility center to which it is allocated?

10. The cost of processing sales invoices in an accounting department is an engineered cost, but the cost of operating the whole accounting department is a discretionary cost. Explain the difference.

11. Consider each item on Exhibit 11–4. Although you cannot determine the category with certainty, is it *probably* an engineered, discretionary, or committed cost item?

12. "An item of cost that is committed in the short run is likely to be discretionary in the long run." Explain why? For a given item, such as depreciation on a certain machine, what time period is "short run" and what is "long run"?

13. The "optimum" level of cost is the level that is neither too high nor too low. When is a cost "too high" and when is it "too low," selecting any item you wish as an example?

14. "The controller presumably knows more about the nature and meaning of responsibility accounting information than anyone else. He therefore, should be the principal person who discusses this information with line managers." Comment on this assertion.

15. Why do a participant's personal goals differ from those of the organization of which he or she is a part? Give some examples.

16. Can all influences on individuals be classified as either rewards or punishments?

17. A school wants its students to (a) work diligently on their studies and (b) to learn as much as they are capable of learning. What motivational devices might it use for each of these purposes? Might some of these devices conflict with one another?

18. What method of charging maintenance costs to responsibility centers is appropriate under each of the following circumstances:
    a. Top management wants line managers to have complete responsibility for the operation of their responsibility centers.
    b. The responsibility centers are research and development departments. Top management wants them to devote all their energies to research projects.
    c. Top management wants the maintenance department to be responsible for the normal painting and other upkeep work of buildings, but wants the responsibility centers to be responsible for the cost of alterations, such as new partitions.

19. Why are both cooperation and conflict desirable in an organization?

20. A university operates a bus service partly for the convenience of students who do not have automobiles, partly for student safety, and partly to discourage the use of private automobiles on campus because parking space is limited. Should the university charge a fee to users of the bus service? How does this question relate to the subject matter of this chapter?

PROBLEMS

11-1. Department managers at Modified Structures Corporation are authorized to hire labor for their departments, purchase supplies, and requisition repairs and maintenance services. The manufacturing overhead cost report for the aluminum molding department No. 4 is shown for the month as follows:

Repairs and maintenance.................................	$12,700
Factory superintendence..................................	4,800
Depreciation of equipment in department No. 4 ...	11,500
Depreciation – building	4,200
Plant personnel and medical costs....................	850
Supplies...	11,200
Indirect labor – department No. 4	31,200
Supervisor's salary	7,800
Factory heat, light, and power	1,100
Total cost	$85,350

Required:

A. Show the department managers' controllable costs.
B. Show the traceable department costs.
C. Show the costs which have been allocated to department No. 4.

11–2. Police protection and the operation of a city waterworks are two common functions of municipal governments. Middletown published a budget for 1977 operations and a report of actual results for 1977 which included the following data:

	Police department		Waterworks	
	Budgeted	*Actual*	*Budgeted*	*Actual*
Revenues	$ 0	$ 0	$62,000	$61,000
Expenses	60,000	58,000	55,000	57,000

Required:

A. Explain how the efficiency and effectiveness of these two government services could be judged.
B. Discuss the differences between these two services which accounts for the difference in methods of judging efficiency and effectiveness.

11–3. The Robinson Company has several producing departments which use the service bureau for their computer functions. The service bureau has control over all costs except depreciation. Raw materials used and other supplies vary directly with the number of computer units produced. All other costs are fixed.

In the month just completed, the actual computer units produced were less than the budgeted output. Despite the lower production, the actual cost exceeded the budget in several cost categories. The total cost budget and the actual results for the month for the service bureau are as follows:

Cost	Budget	Actual
Raw materials...............................	$ 13,000	$ 14,300
Programming labor	1,500	1,800
Supervision.................................	3,000	3,000
Depreciation...............................	16,000	16,000
Other supplies	2,500	4,900
Total cost............................	$ 36,000	$ 40,000
Computer units produced	120,000	100,000
Unit cost.....................................	$0.30	$0.40

Required:

A. For performance evaluation purposes should the charge to the using departments be based on the budgeted rate of $0.30 or the actual rate of $0.40? Explain.

B. In what way will the user charge from the service bureau influence the decision making of the using department managers?

C. What user charge system do you recommend if fixed costs are to be allocated to the producing departments?

11–4. Farragut Manufacturing Company vice president Chester Mills was reviewing the performance report for the equipment maintenance department for the month just ended. He was particularly scrutinizing this month's report because he was considering Russ Olive, the department supervisor, for promotion. He recalled having praised Olive for coming in under the budget the previous month and was looking to see whether that month was a fluke or if Olive was as industrious and as good at reducing maintenance costs as the earlier report suggested.

Olive knew he was being considered for promotion and let it be known that he was working hard at cutting costs and that he had ambitions to move up the ladder to a more responsible, higher paying job. He had been head of the equipment maintenance department for only four months, taking over from a department manager who was notorious for spending more than the budget allowed for monthly equipment maintenance. Chester Mills was quite hopeful that Olive would be the person who could take over supervision of one or two of the stamping or drilling departments which have been experiencing cost overruns lately.

Partial information taken from the current monthly performance report showed the following:

	Budget	Actual
Maintenance labor hours worked........	1,000	700
Oils and lubricants............................	$ 3,500	$ 2,200
Maintenance labor............................	5,000	4,000
Depreciation	2,000	2,000
Department head salary......................	1,800	1,800
Other materials and supplies..............	1,500	500
Total costs.............................	$13,800	$10,500

Required:

A. Discuss the pros and cons of Olive's potentiality for promotion.

B. What equipment maintenance department cost data should be examined in order to evaluate Olive?

C. What other data should be considered?

D. What are your views on the promotion policy of Farragut Manufacturing Company as far as the equipment maintenance department is concerned?

11–5. Bosworth Corporation has a power generating department that supplies power to other departments. Since this department must be prepared to operate at capacity if the other departments have a heavy need for power, the budget of the power generating department lists the costs that are planned at full capacity operations, 10,000 operating hours. In April the department operated at 90 percent of capacity. Its performance report for April was as follows:

	Budget	Actual
Building depreciation	$ 24,000	$ 24,000
Building taxes and insurance	7,000	8,000
Equipment depreciation	12,000	12,000
Fuel	90,000	80,000
Direct labor	40,000	35,000
Supplies	10,000	9,000
Miscellaneous	4,000	4,000
Total Cost	$187,000	$172,000

Required:

A. Recast this report in a form that would be more useful in assessing the performance of the power generating department. Change any numbers that you believe should be changed, using assumed amounts if you do not know exactly what the amounts should be. Explain the changes that you make.

B. The following producing departments and the actual operating hours of power each consumed is shown below. How much of the actual cost of $172,000 will be charged to each producing department if service costs are redistributed on the basis of actual operating hours?

Department	Budgeted operating hours	Actual operating hours
Cutting	2,600	2,400
Milling	2,000	1,800
Grinding	1,300	1,200
Drilling	1,000	900
Assembling	2,300	2,100
Packing	800	600
	10,000	9,000

C. Assume that the actual and budgeted operating hours were as given in B, but that the actual cost for the power generating department rose to $180,000. How much will be absorbed by each department?

D. The cutting department manager wants to buy a power generator for the cutting department which will provide adequate power but will cost only $15 per hour to operate. What are the implications of this possibility of buying from other than the service center on—
    1. The performance evaluation of the cutting department manager?

2. The power generating manager's performance evaluation?
3. The costs distributed to other departments?
E. The assembling department manager announces that the power need of the assembling department for the coming month is going to be only 500 operating hours because part-time summer help is going to be used and much of the work will be done by hand instead of machine. The manager complains that the assembling department is going to have to absorb a disproportionate share of the power generating department's overhead. What are the implications of this move?
F. Evaluate the cost distribution method used at Bosworth for planning and control purposes. What major change, if any, would you make?

11–6. A department of Tilton Instrument Corporation produces casings used in the assembly of thermo controls. Usually, 80,000 casings can be manufactured by operating at 30,000 direct labor hours a month. The direct labor is paid at the rate of $7 per hour. However, as an incentive to save time per unit produced, Tilton Instrument Corporation offers to pay a bonus equal to the regular hourly rate for each hour saved in casings production. The following other costs are anticipated at the 30,000 direct labor hour level:

Cost of direct materials used per unit.............................	$3.50
Variable manufacturing overhead per direct labor hour:	
Supplies..	0.48
Indirect materials	0.80
Repairs	0.42
Lubrication..	0.18
Power	0.12
Variable overhead per hour...	$2.00
Fixed manufacturing overhead for the month:	
Superintendence...	$ 1,875
Indirect labor...	12,025
Depreciation..	17,800
Property taxes and insurance	12,200
Repairs	1,000
Lubrication..	1,400
Power	1,500
Total Fixed Overhead	$47,800

The department manager called the casing production personnel to a meeting, explained the incentive plan, and suggested that by working faster and less wastefully the department could produce 80,000 casings in 22,500 direct labor hours. The department will operate at a normal capacity of 30,000 direct labor hours during the month, using the time saved for production of instrument panels which are used in other products.

Required:

A. Compute the expected cost to manufacture 80,000 casings in the regular time.

B. Compute the expected cost to manufacture 80,000 casings in 22,-500 hours assuming that the actual costs will conform to the budget pattern.

C. If you were an employee of the department in question, would you want to participate in this plan?

D. What incentives exist for the department manager?

E. Discuss the opportunity for employees and the corporation to share the benefits from an incentive system which pays the employees a full wage per hour for the time saved. Mention the pitfalls.

F. Do you know of similar plans? Discuss.

11-7. Department managers at Allen Toy Manufacturing Company are responsible for all indirect costs incurred and all costs related to the care and use of equipment. The productive energy power for each department is also controlled by the department managers and is separately metered to each department.

Allen Toy Manufacturing Company expected to work at its normal capacity and budgeted the following manufacturing overhead costs:

	Budgeted manufacturing overhead			
	Cutting	Painting	Assembling	Total
Plant supervision.....................	$18,000	$20,000	$21,000	$ 59,000
Indirect labor...........................	27,200	28,900	34,900	91,000
Depreciation	7,400	8,400	7,600	23,400
Equipment maintenance parts ...	5,800	6,300	7,100	19,200
Equipment repairs....................	3,700	4,600	3,300	11,600
Lubrication of equipment..........	2,600	700	2,400	5,700
Taxes and insurance on plant	3,300	3,300	3,300	9,900
Heat and light allocated	2,500	2,400	2,300	7,200
Power	3,300	3,800	2,400	9,500
Total	$73,800	$78,400	$84,300	$236,500

Overhead costs are assigned to each toy or game on the basis of machine-hours which have been estimated for a year at normal operating capacity as follows:

Cutting	20,000
Painting.........................	35,000
Assembling	40,000

At the end of the year actual overhead costs were calculated as follows:

Actual manufacturing overhead

	Cutting	Painting	Assembling	Total
Plant supervision.....................	$18,000	$20,000	$21,000	$ 59,000
Indirect labor.........................	30,900	29,400	34,400	94,700
Depreciation..........................	7,500	8,600	8,200	24,300
Equipment maintenance parts...	9,000	6,000	7,900	22,900
Equipment repairs...................	6,400	4,700	3,100	14,200
Lubrication of equipment.........	3,300	1,100	3,900	8,300
Taxes and insurance on plant...	3,300	3,300	3,300	9,900
Heat and light allocated...........	2,900	2,800	2,700	8,400
Power..................................	4,800	4,500	4,000	13,300
Total...........................	$86,100	$80,400	$88,500	$255,000

Required:

A. Prepare performance control budgets for each of the three departments and compare the actual costs against these budgets.
B. Show which of these departments had the poorest record.
C. Which particular costs in the department chosen in B were farthest from expectations?
D. Which costs were farthest from budget across all departments?
E. What possible explanations could be given to explain the deviation from budget for costs across all departments?
F. If you were supervisor of these departments, what would you do in regard to these deviations for costs across all departments?

11–8. The Leopold Company's budgeted income statement for the coming year is as follows:

	Total company	Divisions	
		Alpha Division	Bravo Division
Sales...	$385,000	$165,000	$220,000
Less variable expenses:			
Manufacturing...............................	176,000	66,000	110,000
Other..	19,000	8,000	11,000
Total.......................................	195,000	74,000	121,000
Contribution margin...........................	190,000	91,000	99,000
Less direct fixed expenses..................	57,000	17,000	40,000
Divisional margin...............................	133,000	$ 74,000	$ 59,000
Less common fixed expenses..............	65,000		
Operating Income..............................	$ 68,000		

Selected additional departmental information of Bravo Division is as follows:

	Departments		
	Clamps	Tamps	Ramps
Sales..	$80,000	$80,000	$60,000
Variable manufacturing costs as a percent of sales	40%	60%	50%
Other variable costs as a percent of sales	5%	5%	5%
Direct fixed expenses.............................	$10,000	$10,000	$10,000

Clamps are to be sold in a local market and in a regional market. Sales budgeted and other data on clamps are given below:

		Sales markets	
	Clamps	Local	Regional
Sales..	$80,000	$60,000	$20,000
Variable manufacturing costs as a percent of sales.................................	40%	40%	40%
Other variable costs as a percent of sales.................................	5%	4%	8%

Direct fixed expenses of $8,000 are expected to be divided equally between the local and regional markets. Common fixed expenses will total $2,000 for the two markets.

Required:

A. Prepare a budgeted income statement for Bravo Division in a format which would be useful for planning and control purposes.

B. Do the same for the clamps department.

C. A. Leopold, the company president, is considering an advertising program which will cost $3,500 for clamps made by Bravo Division. The advertising manager contends that if the money is spent in a local market, clamps sales in the local market will increase by $6,000. If the money is spent in a regional market, clamps sales will increase by $7,000. Should the advertising be done on a local or regional basis? Explain.

D. Assume Leopold has another advertising program which will cost $4,000 for clamps made by Bravo Division. The advertising manager contends that if the money is spent in a local market, clamps sales in the local market will increase by $10,000. If the money is spent in a regional market, clamps sales will increase by $10,500. In which market should the advertising be done?

11–9. Under normal conditions in a six-month period, Dooley Manufacturing Company produces 198,000 dials which are used in the manufacture of crock pots. Each dial contributes $1.75 to fixed overhead costs and to profits. The fixed overhead costs for six months usually amount to $180,000. Recently, a market slowdown in other companies which buy this product has reduced sales to a level of 8,800 units per month. As a result, Dooley Manufacturing Company stands to show a loss of $87,-

600 for the six-month period ahead. Therefore, Dooley Manufacturing Company is thinking about closing the plant for six months, anticipating that the market will be back to normal in another six months. The fixed overhead costs can be expected to decline to $49,500 for the entire period the operation is halted, but the additional costs required to protect the facilities and to start up again are estimated to be $67,500.

Required:

A. Show whether the plant should be closed for the six-month period ahead.

B. At what average minimum monthly volume of anticipated activity for the six-month period should Dooley Manufacturing Company temporarily close operations?

C. What other factors enter into the decision?

11–10. A. Mandel is the newly appointed production manager of the nautical rope department of Twilly Twine Corporation. Mandel is eager to do a good job because the production manager's job has usually been a stepping stone to a more responsible job at corporate headquarters. In order to become familiar with the new duties of the job, Mandel pulled from the files the following data:

	Actual data				Budgeted
	1973	1974	1975	1976	1977
Sales...........................	$12,000	$14,000	$16,000	$18,000	$20,000
Cost of goods sold..........	7,560	10,070	9,280	9,390	?
Gross margin	$ 4,440	$ 3,930	$ 6,720	$ 8,610	?
Sales in units	3,000	3,500	4,000	4,500	5,000
Production in units	4,000	3,000	5,000	6,000	?
Ending inventory in units......................	1,000	500	1,500	3,000	0

The bulk of the manufacturing costs in the nautical rope department are fixed. The plant manager told Mandel, "We had a bad year in 1974, but we got squared away in 1975, and it looks like we're shipshape from here on in. Nineteen seventy-seven should be a banner year, profitwise. If it is, corporate headquarters will really appreciate the good management effort. The only request of corporate headquarters is to get the inventories down to zero by the end of 1977."

Required:

A. What caused the drop in the gross margin in 1974 and the dramatic increase in gross margin in 1975 and 1976?

B. Calculate the total fixed costs and the variable costs per unit. Assume first-in, first-out cost flows.

C. What will be the planned gross margin for 1977?

D. What dilemma is faced by Mandel as production manager for 1977?

E. What would you advise Mandel to do?

11–11. Budgeted costs for the glass products department of Fisher Kitchen Products Corporation, headed by Kathy Kane, is given below for two different levels of production. One budget shows the costs expected at normal levels of production, the other at 80 percent of normal. The figures include Kane's salary of $34,000. The remainder of the supervisory salaries consists of allocated costs of plant supervisors. Kane hires all labor personnel and requisitions all materials used in the department. The entire amount of power and electricity costs and all repairs and maintenance costs are measured at the plant level and are distributed to the departments. Equipment acquisitions are decided at the division level.

	Budgets	
	60,000 hours	48,000 hours
Direct materials...	$210,000	$168,000
Direct labor	63,700	50,960
Indirect labor—glass products	21,000	16,800
Supplies used	28,500	22,800
Supervisory salaries.....................................	62,000	62,000
Power and light—fixed.................................	9,000	9,000
Power and light—variable	2,000	1,600
Depreciation—equipment	4,000	4,000
Depreciation—building	1,100	1,100
Repairs and maintenance—fixed....................	4,200	4,200
Repairs and maintenance—variable................	500	400
Property taxes...	4,500	4,500
Insurance	3,400	3,400
	$413,900	$348,760

Required:

A. Show the total costs controllable by Kane.
B. Show the costs traceable to the glass products department.
C. Explain why costs which are not controllable by Kane are shown as part of the glass products department costs.

11–12. The athletic facilities and the library are two elements commonly used by students in an academic environment. The Browning School has produced its annual report for the past year showing the budgeted and actual results. Part of that report is shown as follows:

	Athletic department		Library services	
	Budgeted	Actual	Budgeted	Actual
Revenues............	$3,500,000	$3,600,000	$ 1,000	$ 200
Expenses............	1,900,000	1,950,000	165,000	170,000

Required:

A. If you were the chancellor of Browning, how would you judge the effectiveness and efficiency of these two elements?
B. Discuss the differences between these two services and the methods used to judge efficiency and effectiveness to Jock O'Burly, a student

who is complaining about the high tuition cost and suggests that the library services be curtailed and athletic operations be expanded, shifting energies from a loser to a winner.

11–13. The Marcus Meat and Produce Company has four departments: meat, fruit and vegetables, groceries, and transportation. Three departments use the services of the transportation department which has control over all costs of delivery to these three departments except for depreciation. Gasoline and oils, transport wages and billing, and other maintenance supplies vary directly with the number of traffic miles logged. All other costs are fixed.

For the last month worked, the actual traffic miles logged were more than the budgeted miles. However, even though more traffic miles were logged, the actual costs were less than budget in some cost categories. The total cost budget and the actual results for the transportation department are as follows:

Cost	Budget	Actual
Gasoline and oils	$ 3,400	$ 5,010
Supervision	2,040	2,040
Transport wages and billing	9,720	8,840
Depreciation.............................	1,200	1,200
Other maintenance supplies........	1,640	390
Total Cost........................	$18,000	$17,480
Traffic miles logged...................	72,000	76,000
Cost per mile	$0.25	$0.23

Required:

A. If you were going to allocate the costs of operating the transportation department to the three user departments, would your charge be based on the budgeted rate of $0.25 or the actual rate of $0.23? Explain.

B. Explain the impact the user charge from the transportation department has on the decision making of the user department managers.

C. How do you think fixed costs should be allocated as part of a user charge?

D. What questions would you raise about the transportation manager's ability to come in under budget even though a higher volume was worked?

11–14. Bob Parsons, president of Belton Manufacturing, called for the advertising manager's performance report for the year just ended. He noticed that all of the advertising budgets for each area manager were pretty much on target except for Joe King's which was over budget. Joe was hired just about a year ago fresh out of one of the better known business schools. He impressed Parsons as an agressive and imaginative person with definite top executive potential.

Joe King took over as advertising manager in a division which in

Parson's opinion had not been capturing its share of what was an active market region for competitors.

Partial information taken from the annual divisional performance reports for the past four years showed the following:

| | Actual | | Budgeted |
	1976	1977	1977
Sales...	$810,000	$930,000	$840,000
Variable production costs......................	540,000	651,000	560,000
Fixed production costs	200,000	200,000	200,000
Gross margin	70,000	79,000	80,000
Selling and Administrative, direct............	40,000	60,000	40,000
Selling and Administrative, Operating, allocated	15,000	15,000	15,000
Income.......................................	$ 15,000	$ 4,000	$ 25,000
Sales in units	13,000	15,500	14,000

Required:

A. Evaluate the divisional performance report for 1977.

B. Discuss the pros and cons of King's potentiality for promotion. Mention any additional data you need.

C. What counsel do you think Bob Parsons gave to Joe King?

11–15. The Greenbay Corporation allocates general and administrative overhead to each of its autonomously functioning operating departments on the basis of departmental direct labor dollars incurred. The general and administrative overhead budget and the allocation rate are shown as follows:

General and Administrative
Expenses	Amount
Occupancy........................	$150,000
Accounting........................	30,000
Advertising........................	40,000
Legal	15,000
Personnel........................	15,000
Total.......................	$250,000

The total estimated direct labor dollars in operating departments is expected to be $500,000. Therefore, the allocation rate will be ($250,000 ÷ $500,000) = $0.50 per labor dollar and will remain the same for the entire year. The general and administrative costs are all fixed.

The manager of the special products department, because of increased business, needs to hire two more special products packers to bring its departmental employee level to 12. If the manager hires through the company's personnel department, two packers will be hired for $600 per month for each packer. In addition, the usual 50 cents per dollar of payroll will also be charged to the special products department for general and administrative overhead.

While driving to work, the manager heard an advertisement on the car radio suggesting the services of Pickwick Placement Bureau, an employment agency for experienced general factory help. A quick telephone call to Pickwick Placement Bureau revealed that two Pickwick packers can be made available at a cost of $650 per month per packer for a 40-hour week. The manager can hire the additional packers for as long as they are needed, and the cost will not be added to the payroll but will be paid through an account called, Other Expenses.

Required:

A. What is the special products department manager likely to do? Show calculations to support your conclusion.
B. Is this in the best interest of Greenbay Corporation? Explain.
C. How should the general and administrative overhead costs be allocated so that hiring decisions of the department manager are not affected?

11–16. Puritan Cleaners has been operating a large clothes cleaning firm for a number of years and has a citywide reputation for doing high-quality work with a fast turnaround time to the customer. "Bring it by 9, wear it by 6" was the byline which Puritan Cleaners has been known by. The outlets in each neighborhood serve as pickup and drop-off stations for the central cleaning facility. The company is always faced with an irregularity of business over the months of the year. It has been company policy to lay off shirt press operators from the shirt pressing department as soon as there was an insufficient amount of work to keep them busy, and to rehire them when demand picked up again. Because of this policy the company has developed poor labor relations and finds it very difficult to hire good shirt press operators. As a result, the quality of the work has been continually worsening.

The plant manager has proposed that shirt press operators who earn $6 per hour be retained during slow periods to do some general light-duty cleanup work which is usually performed by persons earning $3.75 per hour in the plant maintenance department.

Required:

A. Indicate which department or departments should be charged with wages paid to shirt press operators who do plant maintenance work.
B. Discuss the implications of ·your plan from the plant manager, department manager, and employee view.
C. Assume that the paid shirt presser workday is 8:00 A.M. to 3:00 P.M. and that there is plenty of shirt pressing work generally. However, the volume differences sometimes require the shirt press operators to work right up to 3:00 P.M. on busy days. On other days, the shirt press operators are finished at 1:30 P.M. and they are allowed to leave but receive pay to 3:00 P.M. Comment.

11–17. To save on outside alterations costs, Marshal Jordan Company, a large department store, has established an autonomously operated tailor shop which services the men's and women's clothing departments. The tailor shop is housed in otherwise useless space and is equipped with an insignificant amount of supplies, machinery, and other materials. The only added costs would be the tailor's wages agreed upon to be $7 per hour and estimated electricity and other expenses amounting to $3 per hour. The alterations are offered free of charge to customers who purchase garments in the store.

In order to keep track of the activity between the selling departments and the tailor shop, the tailor bills the selling department at a rate of $20 per hour for time spent on the garments. The store manager has decided that the charge should be double the hourly tailor rate because the manager feels that the men's department is presently using too much tailor time and that this department could cut down on hours used by taking more care in fitting the customers to the stocked garments.

Required:

A. Discuss the advantages and disadvantages in the store manager's action of establishing an in-house tailor shop.
B. Do you agree or disagree with the store manager's billing policy as a means of lowering tailoring time spent? Explain.
C. If you were the store manager of Marshal Jordan Company, what would be the nature of the planning and control mechanisms you would want to assure that adequate tailoring service is given?

11–18. The Valerie Company's budgeted income statement is anticipated to look as follows:

	(000's)	Percent
Sales	$1,200	100.0
Cost of goods manufactured – variable	780	65.0
Cost of goods manufactured – fixed	72	6.0
Total Manufacturing Cost	852	71.0
Gross margin	348	29.0
Selling and administrative expenses – variable	60	5.0
Selling and administrative expenses – fixed	204	17.0
Total Selling and Administrative Expenses	264	22.0
Operating Income	$ 84	7.0

Selected additional product line and market data for one of its three divisions, the Appleton Division, have been gathered as follows:

	Product			Market	
	A	B	C	East	West
Sales as a percent of company sales	15%	20%	10%		
Product A				70%	30%
Product B				50%	50%
Product C				60%	40%
Variable manufacturing costs as percent product sales	70%	65%	70%		
Fixed direct manufacturing costs	$10,000	$10,000	$5,000	$12,000	$8,000
Variable selling and administrative expenses as percent product sales	5%	5%	5%		

The total fixed costs for Appleton Division are estimated to be $30,000. Fixed direct manufacturing costs for Product A of $8,000 are divided equally between east and west markets.

Required:

A. Prepare a budgeted income statement for the Appleton Division in a format which would be useful for planning and control purposes.
B. Prepare a budgeted income statement suitable for planning and control involving a marketing manager of Product A.
C. M. Valerie, the president of the company, is thinking about spending funds for research and development on marketing methods. Valerie feels that if $3,100 are spent with experimentation on Product A of Appleton Division, sales for Product A will increase by $12,000. Valerie also feels that if the money is spent on Product B, sales will increase by $10,000. On which product should the research and development experiment be conducted?

11-19. A summary statement has been prepared by the operating divisions of Sanford Industries showing the results of the past quarter. Costs incurred at the corporate headquarters level have been distributed to each division in proportion to sales revenue. All costs incurred by each division except the allocated corporate headquarters costs are considered to be avoidable if a division is shut down. The corporate headquarters costs amount to $1,540,000.

		Divisions (000's)			
	Total	North	East	West	South
Sales......................	$6,600	$990	$2,640	$ 990	$1,980
Costs......................	6,226	572	2,090	1,276	2,288
Profits (losses)	$ 374	$418	$ 550	$ (286)	$ (308)

Required:

A. Based on the data presented, show which division or divisions should be shut down.
B. What other variables should be included in the decision to shut down?

11-20. Phil Crotty has been managing the diet soft drink division of Popsie Kola Beverage Company for the past three months, and his record has been so outstanding as compiled in the monthly divisional profit reports that he has been pirated away from Popsie Kola by the Kooky Cola Bottling Company at the end of May.

John Jordan was hired as successor to Crotty, and the two met for a brief meeting so that the experienced Crotty could pass on to the fledgling manager some of his tips to success. "The whole secret is being ready for the market, my boy," he said. "When I came here in March we didn't have a case of beverage in inventory. Our big sales exceed our capacity. So you've got to prepare for the market and build your inventory accordingly."

Jordan knew he had a big pair of shoes to fill, and he was hopeful that his performance was going to be on a par with Crotty. He figured the first two months would be made easier because the bulk of the inventory for the anticipated June and July sales are ready for shipment. The corporate managers have told Jordan that the inventories of the diet soft drink should be brought to zero by the end of July because a new lemony flavored soft drink is going to be the future big seller. The fixed costs are $21,000 per month, and the variable cost is $0.10 per case. The monthly divisional profit reports including the sales projections are shown as follows:

	Actual data			Budgeted data	
	March	April	May	June	July
Sales	$5,000	$5,000	$15,000	$50,000	$55,000
Cost of goods sold.............	4,500	4,500	13,500	?	?
Gross margin.....................	$ 500	$ 500	$ 1,500	?	?
Sales in cases....................	10,000	10,000	30,000	100,000	110,000
Production in cases	60,000	60,000	80,000	?	?
Ending inventory in cases...	50,000	100,000	150,000	?	0

Corporate headquarters has instructed Jordan that they would like to see the summer month production to be as equal as possible based on sales projections and inventory supply.

Required:

A. How reliable do you anticipate the gross margin measures will be as a measure of Jordan's performance during the months of June and July?

B. Calculate the budgeted gross margin for June and July. Assume first-in, first-out cost flows.

C. Show the total gross margin for the five-month period and make any comments you believe to be appropriate about Crotty's actions in March, April, and May.

D. What dilemma is faced by Jordan as division manager in June and July?

E. What would you advise Jordan to do?

11–21. The Box Division of Maple Company manufactures cardboard boxes which are used by other divisions of Maple Company and which are sold to external customers. The Hardware Division of Maple Company has requested the Box Division to supply a certain box Style K, and the Box Division has computed a proposed transfer price on this box, as follows:

	Per thousand boxes
Variable cost	$180
Fixed cost	40
Total Cost	$220
Profit (to provide normal return on assets employed)	30
Transfer price	$250

The Hardware Division is unwilling to accept this transfer price because Style K boxes are regularly sold to outside customers for $240 per thousand. The Box Division points out, however, that competition for this box is unusually keen, and that this is why it cannot price the box to external customers so as to earn a normal return. Both divisions are profit centers.

Required:

What should the transfer price be? (Explain your answer.)

11-22. Six months after the Box Division of Maple Company started to supply Style K boxes to the Hardware Division (see Problem 11-21). Eastern Company offered to supply boxes to the Hardware Division for $235 per thousand. The Hardware Division thereupon informed the Box Division that the transfer price should be reduced to $235 because this was now the market price.

Required (explain your answers):

A. Should the transfer price be reduced to $235 per thousand?

B. Under what circumstances should the Box Division refuse to supply boxes to the Hardware Division?

C. If the Box Division refused to supply boxes at $235 per thousand, should the Hardware Division be permitted by top management to buy boxes from the Eastern Company?

D. If outside market prices continued to decrease, and eventually reached $210 per thousand, would this change your answer to any of the preceding questions?

11-23. The Transistor Division of Mador Company manufactures certain components that are used in radio transmitters that the Electronics Division sells to the U.S. Air Force. Data used in the negotiation of a selling price are as follows:

	Cost per transmitter	
	Transistor Division components	Complete transmitter
Components from Transistor Division	—	$ 220
Other direct material	$ 20	480
Direct labor...	80	100
Indirect costs	100	200
Total Cost......................................	200	1,000
Profit margin...	20	100
Price	$220	$1,100

The Air Force representative argued that the $1,100 price was too high because profit was double counted.

Required:

A. If Mador Company calculated its profit margin on the basis of assets employed, is the Air Force position correct?

B. If Mador Company calculated its profit on the basis of a markon over cost, is the Air Force position correct?

C. From the data given above, which method of calculating profit did the Mador Company probably use?

SUGGESTIONS FOR FURTHER READING

Barnard, Chester I. *The Functions of the Executive.* Cambridge, Mass.: Harvard University Press, 1938.

Bonini, Charles P. *Simulation of Information and Decision Systems in the Firm.* Englewood Cliffs, N.J.: Prentice-Hall, Inc., 1963.

Bruns, William J., Jr., and DeCoster, Don T. *Accounting and Its Behavioral Implications.* New York: McGraw-Hill, Inc., 1969.

Caplan, Edwin H. *Management Accounting and Behavioral Science.* Reading, Mass.: Addison-Wesley Publishing Co., Inc., 1971.

Cyert, Richard M., and March, James G. *A Behavioral Theory of the Firm.* Englewood Cliffs, N.J.: Prentice-Hall, Inc., 1963.

Hofstede, G. H. *The Game of Budget Control.* Assen, The Netherlands: Van Gorcum & Co., N.V., 1967.

Lawrence, Paul R., and Lorsch, Jay W. *Organization and Environment.* Homewood, Ill.: Richard D. Irwin, Inc., 1969.

March, James G., and Simon, Herbert A. *Organizations.* New York: John Wiley & Sons, Inc., 1958.

Prince, Thomas R. *Information Systems for Management Planning and Control,* 3d ed. Homewood, Ill.: Richard D. Irwin, Inc., 1975.

Simon, Herbert A. *Administrative Behavior,* 2d ed. New York: The Macmillan Co., 1957.

Skinner, B. F. *Beyond Freedom and Dignity.* New York: Appleton-Century-Crofts, 1971.

Tannenbaum, Arnold. *Control in Organizations.* New York: McGraw-Hill, Inc., 1968.

12

Programming and budget preparation

The planning activities that are part of the management control process consist of two principal parts: programming and budgeting. They are described in this chapter. Programming deals with the formulation of long-range plans. Our description of it is brief because a thorough treatment would go far beyond the scope of this book.

Budgeting is the process of planning for next year. Most companies prepare budgets. In order to understand this activity, one needs to know not only what managers and others do in the course of preparing and using budgets, which is the *behavioral* aspect of budgeting, but also how the amounts in the budget are calculated and assembled, which is the *technical* aspect of budgeting. The chapter text focuses primarily on the behavioral aspect. An Appendix illustrates the technical aspect by showing the details of budget preparation in a simple situation. Since the interrelationships among the various parts of a budget can be understood most clearly if all these parts are grouped together, the usual practice of having exhibits appear close to the text material to which they relate has not been followed in this chapter. Instead, all exhibits appear in the Appendix, where they are arranged in an order that facilitates the tracing of information from one exhibit to another.

PROGRAMMING

Successful managers spend a considerable amount of time thinking about the future and making decisions that have an effect on future operations. Some actions, such as the construction of a new plant, take a long time to implement; and it is therefore necessary that decisions be made years in advance so that the resources will be available when they are needed. In thinking about these future needs, managers tend to focus on product lines and other programs, and the process is therefore called programming. It is also called **long-range planning.** Programming is the process of deciding on the programs that the company will undertake and the approximate amount of resources that will be allocated to each major program.

There are three main parts to the programming process: (1) reviewing ongoing programs, (2) considering proposals for new programs, and (3) coordinating separate programs by means of a formal programming system.

Ongoing programs

In the typical company, most activities in which the company will engage in the next few years are similar to those it is carrying on this year. If a company manufactures and sells 20 lines of packaged foods currently, it is likely that it will handle almost all of those 20 lines next year, and the year after. It is dangerous to be complacent about these ongoing programs, however. Consumer tastes change, competitive conditions change, manufacturing methods change. It is important that the implications of these changes be recognized and that decisions be made to adapt to the changed conditions. Thus, there needs to be a systematic, thorough way of reviewing each of the existing programs to insure that new conditions are anticipated and the appropriate action decided upon.

Zero-base review. A systematic way of making an analysis of ongoing programs goes by the name of a **zero-base review.** It gets this name because in deciding on the costs that are appropriate for a program, the cost estimates are built up "from scratch," rather than taking the current level of costs as a starting point as is customary in the annual budgeting process. Such reviews are useful for major programs in order to overcome the natural tendency toward complacency. They are also useful for individual expense centers in which the amount of discretionary costs is relatively large. These include the accounting department, the personnel department, and indeed most staff activities. Because a zero-base review is time consuming and upsetting to the normal functioning of the responsibility center, it cannot be conducted every year for every program and every discretionary expense center. About the most that can be expected is that each part of the whole company will be reviewed every five years or so.[1]

---

[1] There are references in the literature and in political speeches to "zero-base budgeting." This term implies that such reviews should be made *annually* for all programs, as a

In making a zero-base review of a discretionary expense center, basic questions are raised about the activity, such as:

1. Should this activity be performed at all?
2. Is too much being done? Too little?
3. Should it be done internally, or should it be contracted to an outside firm (the familiar make-or-buy question)?
4. Is there a more efficient way of obtaining the desired results?
5. How much should it cost?

In making a zero-base review of a product line, basic questions are asked about the demand for the product, the impact of competition, the marketing strategy, the manufacturing strategy, and so on.

Proposed new programs

Management should be on the alert for proposed new programs, either to counter a threat to existing operations or to take advantage of new opportunities. These proposals are analyzed whenever the need or the opportunity comes to management's attention. They usually involve new capital investments, and the appropriate analytical techniques are therefore those described in Chapters 8 and 9 which dealt specifically with this topic.

Formal programming systems

Every company should review its ongoing programs and make decisions on proposed new programs. Many companies do this informally, but most large companies have a formal system in which the financial and other consequences of these programs are projected for a number of years in the future. Such a projection is called a **long-range plan.** It shows revenues, costs, and other information for individual programs for a number of years ahead—usually 5 years, but possibly as few as 3, or, in the case of certain public utilities, as many as 20. Assuming that the company's fiscal year begins January 1, the programming process would begin the preceding spring. At that time top management discusses and decides on changes in its basic goals and strategies, and disseminates these to operating managers. These managers prepare tentative progams, following the guidelines set forth by top management. In the summer or early fall, these proposed programs are discussed at length with top management, and out of these discussions emerges a program for the whole company. This approved program forms the basis of the budgeting process, which begins in the fall.

---

part of the annual budget process. A good zero-base review requires far more time than is available during the preparation of the annual budget, however. There is therefore no such thing as a zero-base budget in the real world.

BUDGET PREPARATION

Although not all companies have a formal programming system, nearly all prepare an annual budget.[2] A budget is a plan that is expressed in quantitative, usually monetary, terms and that covers a specified period of time, usually one year. The budget for a business company is frequently referred to as a **profit plan** since it shows the plan that the company expects to follow in order to attain its profit goal.

Uses of the budget

The budget is useful for these purposes:

1. For making and coordinating plans.
2. For communicating these plans to those who are responsible for carrying them out.
3. In motivating managers at all levels.
4. As a standard with which actual performance subsequently can be compared.

Planning. Managers know they are supposed to think ahead. The pressures of day-to-day operating problems are often so strong, however, that there is a temptation to put this off. The budgeting process requires that such thinking be done. In preparing the budget, managers must consider how conditions in the future may change and what steps they should take to get ready for these changed conditions. Furthermore, each responsibility center affects, and is affected by, the work of other responsibility centers; the budgetary process helps to coordinate these separate activities to insure that all parts of the company are in balance with one another. Most importantly, the production plans must be coordinated with the marketing plans so as to insure that the factory is geared up to produce the planned sales volume.

Communication. Management's plans will not be carried out (except by accident) unless the organization understands what the plans are. Adequate understanding includes not only a knowledge of specific plans (e.g., how many units are to be manufactured, what methods and machines are to be used, how much material is to be purchased, what selling prices are to be), but also a knowledge about policies and constraints to which the organization is expected to adhere. Examples of these policies and constraints are: the maximum amounts that may be spent for such items as advertising, maintenance, administrative costs; wage rates and hours of work; and desired quality levels. A most useful device for communicating quantitative information concerning these plans and

---

[2] In a study of 338 member companies of the Financial Executives Institute, 99 percent of the respondents reported that they prepared budgets. (Financial Executives Research Foundation, *Public Disclosure of Business Forecasts* [New York, 1972], p. 68.)

limitations is the approved budget. Moreover, much vital information is communicated during the process of preparing the budget.

Motivation. If the atmosphere is right, the budget process can be a powerful force in motivating managers to work toward the goals of the overall organization. Such an atmosphere is created when the manager of each responsibility center understands that top management regards the process as important, and when he participates in the formulation of his own budget in the manner to be described later in this chapter. The budget tells the operating manager what performance is expected from him. A person who knows what he is expected to do is much more likely to perform properly than one who operates in an atmosphere of vagueness and uncertainty.

Standard for performance measurement. A carefully prepared budget is the best possible standard against which to compare actual performance, and it is increasingly being used for this purpose. Until fairly recently, the general practice was to compare current results with results for last month or with results for the same period a year ago; this is still the basic means of comparison in many companies. Such a historical standard has the fundamental weakness that it does not take account of either changes in the underlying forces at work or in the planned programs for the current year.

> *EXAMPLE:* In a favorable market situation, a certain company increased its volume and its selling prices and hence increased its net income in 1977 by 5 percent over the net income of 1976. If 1977's results are compared with 1976's, there is apparent cause for rejoicing. However, the company had *planned* to increase profits by 15 percent, and performance when measured against the plan was, therefore, not so good. The company took steps to find out, and if possible to correct, the factors that caused the difference between actual and budgeted results in 1977.

In general, it is more significant to answer the question, "Why didn't we do what we planned to do?" than the question, "Why are this year's results different from last year's?" Presumably, the principal factors accounting for the difference between this year and last year were taken into consideration in the preparation of the budget. Of course, the budget is a reliable standard only if it has been carefully prepared. If management doubts the realism of the budget, then there is good reason to use last year's performance as a benchmark, for this at least has the merit of being a definite, objective figure.

Types of budgets

Although we have referred to "the" budget, the complete "budget package" in a company includes several items, each of which is also referred to as a budget. We shall therefore refer to the total package as the **master budget,** and shall use appropriate names for each of its components. Exhibit 12–2 (page 510) shows the components used in a company whose budget preparation will be described in detail. The three principal parts of the master budget are:

1. An **operating budget,** showing planned operations for the forthcoming year, including revenues, expenses, and related changes in inventory.
2. A **cash budget,** showing the anticipated sources and uses of cash in that year.
3. A **capital expenditure budget,** showing planned acquisitions of fixed assets.

We shall first describe the nature of the operating budget and the steps involved in its preparation. We shall then describe the cash budget and the capital expenditure budget. Another document, the *budgeted balance sheet* is derived directly from the other budgets and is therefore not described separately.

The operating budget

The operating budget is essentially a projected income statement. It shows estimated revenues and expenses for the year ahead. Behind the overall summary shown on the income statement, there are separate, detailed budgets. These are prepared for each responsibility center and therefore are sometimes called responsibility budgets.

A responsibility budget sets forth plans in terms of the persons responsible for carrying them out. A responsibility budget is an excellent control device since it is a statement of the performance that is expected for each responsibility center manager, and therefore is a standard for evaluating his actual performance later on. As explained in the Appendix, each manager listed on the organization chart in Exhibit 12–1 (page 509) is responsible for preparing those parts of the operating budget that correspond to his sphere of responsibility. In the factory, for example, there should be a responsibility budget for each department, showing the costs that are controllable by the supervisor of the department.

Variable or flexible budgets

If the total costs in a responsibility center are expected to vary with changes in volume, as is the case with most production and sales responsibility centers, the responsibility budget may be in the form of a **variable budget** or **flexible budget.** Such a budget shows the planned behavior of costs at various volume levels. The variable budget is usually expressed in terms of the cost-volume equation described in Chapter 6, that is, a fixed amount for a specified time period plus a variable amount per unit of volume. (Recall from Chapter 6 the basic equation for determining the costs [y] at any volume [x]; it is $y = a + bx$, in which a is the fixed amount and b is the variable amount per unit of volume x.)

> *EXAMPLE:* Schedule 6 in the Appendix shows a factory overhead budget. The first group of items thereon are for budgeted costs in the machining department, as follows:

	Variable budget formula		January budget
	Fixed	Variable	(2,900 DLH)
Supervisory salaries	$3,000 + $	0 per DLH*	$ 3,000
Depreciation..........................	1,200 +	0	1,200
Factory supplies	0 +	1.00	2,900
Power...................................	2,000 +	0.10	2,290
All other overhead	400 +	0.90	3,010
Total............................	$6,600 +	$2.00	$12,400

* DLH means direct labor hours, which is the measure of volume used in the illustration.

The columns labeled "Variable budget formula" give the variable budget. The budget for any month is calculated on the basis of the volume planned for that month. The supervisory salaries, factory supplies, and power items are examples of fixed, variable, and semivariable costs, respectively. The supervisory salaries item is a fixed cost, and the budgeted amount for any month is the fixed amount, $3,000, regardless of volume. The factory supplies item is a variable cost; the budgeted amount for January is $1 times the 2,900 direct labor hours budgeted for January, or $2,900. The power item is a semivariable cost; the budgeted amount for January is the fixed component, $2,000, plus the variable component of $0.10 times the 2,900 direct labor hours ($290), a total of $2,290.

When there is a variable budget, the costs at *one* volume level are used as part of the master budget. That volume level is the volume at which the company plans to operate during the budget period.
In addition to the responsibility budgets for costs, there are also:

- A budget of sales revenue (Schedule 1, in the Appendix to this chapter).
- A budget of planned production and inventory levels of finished products and raw materials (Schedule 2).
- A budget of the planned usage of material (Schedule 3) and planned purchases of material (Schedule 4).
- A budget of planned personnel costs (Schedule 5).

There may also be a budget for planned personnel promotions, participation in training programs, and retirements — and budgets for a variety of other special purposes that are not illustrated in this description.

Relationships among the budget components

The budget should constitute a coherent whole; therefore, the pieces must be consistent with one another. The costs for the several production centers in the responsibility budget must add up to the same amount as the total factory product costs used to calculate cost of goods sold and inventory amounts. The volume level used to calculate budgeted costs from the variable budget must be the volume that is planned for the period. Changes in raw material inventory must be consistent with the planned purchases of raw material and the planned usage of raw material in production. Changes in finished goods inventory must be consistent with production volume and with sales volume. The manpower budget must be consistent with labor costs. These relationships are illustrated in the various schedules in the Appendix to this chapter.

ORGANIZATION FOR PREPARATION OF BUDGETS

A budget committee, consisting of several members of the top management group, usually guides the work of preparing the budget. This committee recommends to the chief executive officer the general guidelines that the organization is to follow, disseminates these guidelines after his approval, coordinates the separate budgets prepared by the various organizational units, resolves differences among them, and submits the final budget to the president and to the board of directors for approval. In a small company, this work is done by the president or by his immediate line subordinate. Instructions go down through the regular chain of command, and the budget comes back up for successive reviews and approvals through the same channels. Decisions about the budget are made by the line organization, and the final approval is given by the chief executive officer, subject to ratification by the board of directors.

Budget staff

The line organization usually is assisted in its preparation of the budget by a staff unit headed by the **budget director.** As a staff person, the budget director's functions are to disseminate instructions about the mechanics of budget preparation (the forms and how to fill them out), to provide data on past performance that are useful in preparation of the budget, to make computations on the basis of decisions reached by the line organization, to assemble the budget numbers, and to see to it that everyone submits his portion of the budget on time. The budget staff may do a very large fraction of the budget work. It is not the crucial part, however, for the significant decisions are always made by the line organization. Once the members of the line organization have reached an agreement on such matters as labor productivity and wage rates, for example, the budget staff can calculate the detailed amounts for labor costs by products and by responsibility centers; this is a considerable job of computation, but it is entirely based on the decisions of the line supervisors.

The budget staff is like a telephone company. It operates an important communication system; it is responsible for the speed, accuracy, and clarity with which messages flow through the system, but it does not decide on the content of the messages themselves.

PREPARING THE OPERATING BUDGET

The budget period

Most companies prepare an operating budget once a year, and the budget covers a year. Separate budget estimates are usually made for each month or each quarter within the year. In some companies, data are initially estimated by months only for the next three months or the next six months, with the balance of the year being shown by quarters. When this is done, a detailed budget by months is prepared shortly before the beginning of each new quarter.

Some companies follow the practice of preparing a new budget every quarter, but for a full year ahead. Every three months the budget amounts for the quarter just completed are dropped, the amounts for the succeeding three quarters are revised if necessary, and budget amounts for the fourth succeeding quarter are added. This is called a **rolling budget.**

Relation to accounting

The preparation of a budget can be studied both as an accounting process and as also a management process. From an accounting standpoint, the focus is on the mechanics of the system, the procedures for assembling data, and budget formats. The procedures are similar to those described in *Fundamentals of Financial Accounting* for recording actual transactions, and the end result of the calculations is a set of financial statements—a balance sheet, income statement, and statement of changes in financial position—identical in format with those resulting from the accounting process that records historical events. The principal difference is that the budget amounts reflect planned future activities rather than data on what has happened in the past.

Since the relationship to financial accounting is so close, we trust that the reader can trace the numbers through the several schedules in the Appendix to this chapter by recalling how financial accounting transactions are recorded. We therefore have not provided a detailed description of these schedules. Instead, we shall focus here on the preparation of an operating budget as a *management* process, and we shall now describe the principal steps in that process.

Relation to programming

The budget preparation process is *not* the mechanism through which most major decisions are made, but rather a means of implementing these decisions. If the company has a formal programming process, most major decisions are made as part of that process. Although some major decisions may be made during the budget preparation process, because the act of preparing the budget may uncover unforeseen problems, these are exceptions to the general rule.

When budget preparation begins, a great many decisions affecting the budget year already have been made. The maximum level of manufacturing operations has been set by the amount and character of available production facilities. (If an expansion of facilities is to take place during the budget year, the decision would ordinarily have been made a year or more previously because of the time required to build buildings and to acquire and install machinery.) If a new product is to go into volume production, considerable time would have already been spent prior to the budget year on product development, testing, design, and initial promotional work. Thus, the budget is not a brand new creation each year; rather, it is built within the context of the ongoing business and is governed by programming decisions that have been made previously.

Steps in the process

Most budget components are affected by decisions or estimates made in constructing other components. Nearly all components are affected by the planned sales volume and decisions as to inventory levels; the purchases budget is affected by planned production volume and decisions as to raw material inventory levels; and so on. Thus, there has to be a carefully worked out timetable specifying the order in which the several parts of the operating budget are developed and the time when each must be completed. In general, the steps covered by this timetable are as follows:

1. Setting planning guidelines.
2. Preparing the sales budget.
3. Initial preparation of other budget components.
4. Negotiation to evolve final plans for each component.
5. Coordination and review of the components.
6. Final approval.
7. Distribution of the approved budget.

In a company of average complexity, the elapsed time for the whole budget preparation process is approximately three months, with the most hectic part (steps 4, 5, and 6 above) requiring approximately one month. In highly complex organizations, the elapsed time may be somewhat longer. At the other extreme, a small business may go through the whole process in one afternoon.

Step 1. Setting planning guidelines. If the company has a formal program or long-range plan, this plan provides a starting point in preparing the annual budget. Alternatively, or in addition, top management establishes policies and guidelines that are to govern budget preparations. These guidelines vary greatly in content in different companies. At one extreme, there may be only a brief general statement, such as, "Assume that industry volume next year will be 5 percent higher than the current year."

More commonly, detailed information and guidance are given on such matters as projected general economic conditions, allowances to be made for price increases and wage increases, changes in the product line, changes in the scale of operations, allowable number of personnel promotions, and anticipated productivity gains. In addition, detailed instructions are issued as to what information is required from each responsibility center for the budget, and how this information is to be recorded on the budget forms. In the absence of statements to the contrary, the organization customarily assumes that the factors affecting operations in the budget year will be similar to those in the current year.

> *EXAMPLE:* The following guideline statement was developed by the budget committee of a large bank; it is relatively general and brief.
>
> It is customary for the committee to summarize for your general guidance current thinking regarding deposits, loans, and loan rates. The expectations outlined below are for the overall bank. Therefore, it is important that the head of each department analyze the impact of expected general economic trends on the conditions peculiar to his own area of activity in order to project specific goals which he may reasonably expect to attain.
>
> ### Deposits
>
> There is every indication that money market conditions will be such that demand deposit levels in our area will expand. In our judgment, we anticipate at least a 5 percent growth in demand deposits for all banks. Our overall goal, however, should be set somewhat higher to reflect an improvement in our relative position. Savings deposits will continue to climb moderately. Current rates for time and savings deposits should be used to project interest costs.
>
> ### Loans and Loan Rates
>
> In all probability, loan demand will slacken seasonally in the early months of next year; in fact, many economists believe that the decline may continue through the second quarter of the year. We firmly believe that sometime between April and July loan demand should strengthen.
>
> For the most part, the recent decline in the prime rate is reflected in the loan rate structure at this time. Accordingly, except where necessary rate adjustments are still anticipated, the existing rate structure should prevail.

Expenses

Before preparing the budget, it is imperative that each supervisor closely evaluate controllable expense in his area and consider all means of economizing and reducing costs, particularly in such areas as personnel staffing, overtime, entertainment, stationery, and so on. The salary administration policies explained in the Budget Instructions should be strictly followed.

In order to complete the budget for the entire bank by year-end, your full cooperation is necessary in meeting the deadlines which appear in the attached General Instructions.

Budget Committee

Step 2.   Preparing the sales budget.   The amount of sales and the sales mix (i.e., the proportion of total sales represented by each product or product line) govern the level and general character of the company's operations. Thus, a sales plan must be prepared early in the budget process, for it affects most of the other plans. **The sales budget is different from a sales forecast.** A forecast is merely passive, while a budget should reflect the results of positive actions that management plans to take in order to influence, or adapt to, future events. For example, this may be the sales *forecast:* "With the present amount of sales effort, we expect sales to run at about the same level as currently." By contrast, the sales *budget* may show a substantial planned increase in sales, reflecting management's intention to add sales personnel, to increase advertising and sales promotion, or to add or redesign products.

It follows that at the same time the sales budget is prepared, a selling expense budget must also be prepared because the size and nature of the marketing efforts that are intended to influence sales revenue are given in the selling expense budget. However, in this early stage, it may suffice to show the main elements of selling expense, with such details as the expenses of operating field selling offices left until the next step.

In almost all companies the sales budget is the most difficult plan to make. This is because a company's sales revenue depends on the actions of its customers, which are not subject to the direct control of management. In contrast, the amounts of cost incurred are determined primarily by actions of the company itself (except for the prices of certain cost factors), and therefore can be planned with more confidence.

Sales estimates.   Basically, there are two ways of making forecasts as a basis for the sales budget:

1.   Make a **statistical forecast** on the basis of an analysis of general business conditions, market conditions, product growth curves, and the like; or
2.   Collect the **opinions** of executives and salespersons. In some companies sales personnel are asked to estimate the sales of each product to each of their customers; in others, regional managers estimate

total sales in their regions; in still others, the field organization does not participate in the estimating process.

There are advantages and weaknesses in both the statistical and the opinion methods. Both are often used together, but neither can be guaranteed to yield an even reasonably close estimate in view of the inevitable uncertainties of the future.

Statistical techniques rest on the assumption that the future is likely to resemble the past. Such an assumption is reasonable in many situations. Thus, if sales have been increasing at the rate of 5 percent a year, and if there is no evidence that new factors will change this rate of increase, it is reasonable to predict that next year's sales will be 5 percent above this year's. This is the simplest type of forecast since it depends only on an extrapolation of past performance. A more complicated, and usually more reliable, procedure is to analyze the several factors that affect sales revenue and then predict the future behavior of each of these factors.

> EXAMPLE: Able Pharmacy is the leading drugstore in its town. Its management observes that sales revenue in the past has increased proportionately with (a) increase in the local population, and (b) increases in the general level of prices, that is, the rate of inflation. If the local population is expected to increase 5 percent next year, and if prices are expected to increase 3 percent, then one could predict a sales revenue increase of about 8 percent. (The arithmetic of combining percentages is more complicated than simple addition, so the mathematically calculated increase is not exactly 8 percent; nevertheless, 8 percent is close enough in view of the margin of error that is present in any forecast.)

The forecasting technique used in the preceding example is called **correlation;** that is, a change in one number was predicted in terms of the change in another number because there was reason to believe that there was an identifiable association between the movement of the two numbers. Companies are continually searching for factors that correlate with sales revenue as an aid to improving their prediction of this difficult number.

The foregoing description of forecasting techniques omitted the effect on sales revenue of changes in marketing policy. The estimated impact of such changes would be incorporated before the final sales budget was determined.

Schedule 1 in the Appendix to this chapter shows a completed sales budget.

Step 3. Initial preparation of other budget components.   The budget guidelines prepared by top management, together with the sales plan, are disseminated down through the successive levels in the organization. Managers at each level may add other, more detailed, information for the guidance of their subordinates. When the guidelines arrive at the lowest responsibility centers, the managers of these responsibility centers prepare the budget plans for the items within their sphere of responsibility, working within the constraints specified in the guidelines.

Planning expenses.   Based on planned output, the manager of a responsibility center makes an estimate of each significant element of expense in his responsibility center. These estimates are made by a combination of analytical techniques and judgment. Techniques for separating the variable and fixed components of cost that were discussed in Chapter 6 are widely used for this purpose. Schedules 3, 5, 6, and 7 in the Appendix to this chapter reflect such estimates.

Whenever feasible, estimates for physical quantities and for unit prices should be shown separately in order to facilitate the subsequent analysis of performance; that is, material cost is preferably shown as number of pounds times cents per pound, labor costs as number of hours times the hourly wage rate, and so on. The basic reason for such a separation is that different factors, and often different managers, are responsible for changes in the quantity component and the price component, respectively. For example, the purchasing officer is responsible for the cost per pound of raw material purchased, but the factory supervisor is responsible for the quantity of raw material used. For similar reasons, the estimates are broken down by product lines, by significant items of cost, and in other ways that will facilitate subsequent analysis of actual performance as compared with the budgeted amounts.

Usually, the most recent data on actual costs is used as a starting point in making the expense estimates. The guidelines may provide specific instructions as to the permitted changes that can be made from current expenses, such as, "Assume a 5 percent price increase for purchased materials and services." In addition to following these instructions, the manager who prepares the budget, that is, the **budgetee**, expresses his judgment as to the behavior of costs not covered by the instructions.

Step 4.   Negotiation.   Now comes the crucial stage in the process from a control standpoint, the negotiation[3] between the budgetee and his superior. The value of the budget as a plan of what is to happen, as a motivating device, and as a standard against which actual performance will be measured, depends largely on how skillfully this negotiation is conducted.

Several recent studies have shown that the budget is more effective as a motivating device when it represents a tight, but attainable, goal. If it is too tight, it leads to frustration; if it is too loose, it leads to complacency. The budgetee and his superior therefore seek to arrive at this desirable middle ground.

---

[3] In a perceptive study, G. H. Hofstede describes this process as a "game"; see *The Game of Budget Control* (Assen, The Netherlands: Van Gorcum & Co., N.V., 1967). A negotiation is a game, in the formal sense.

Slack. The superior is mindful of the phenomenon called *slack.* Although the engines on an airplane have a maximum rated horsepower, the pilot knows that they cannot be operated at this horsepower except for short intervals of time; if the pilot tried, the engines would tear themselves apart. Pilots therefore normally operate at a much lower speed, the cruising speed. Similarly, a business organization normally operates well below its theoretical potential. However, there is no way of determining the optimum "cruising speed" of a business, that is, the proper middle ground between overexertion on the one hand and laziness or inefficiency on the other. **Slack is the difference between the potential output and the actual output.** Managers know that some slack is inevitable, but they seek to avoid incorporating too much slack in the budget.

The superior's analysis. As did the budgetee, the superior usually must take the current level of expense as his starting point in the negotiations, modifying this according to his perception of how satisfactory the current level is. He simply does not have enough time during the budget review to reexamine each of the elements of expense so as to insure that the budgetee's estimates are optimum. It is a fact, however, that the operation of Parkinson's First Law ("costs tend to increase regardless of the amount of work done") strongly suggests that costs do drift out of line over a period of time, and that the current level of spending may therefore be too high. One way of addressing this problem is to make an arbitrary cut, say 5 percent, in the budget estimates, but this has the weakness of any arbitrary action; it affects the efficient and the inefficient managers alike. Furthermore, if budgetees know that an arbitrary cut is going to be made, they can counter it by padding their original estimates by a corresponding amount.

There are more reasonable tactics for keeping costs in line during the negotiating process. The superior should require a full explanation of any proposed cost increases. He attempts to find reasons why costs may be expected to decrease, such as a decrease in the work load of the responsibility center or an increase in productivity resulting from the installation of new equipment or a new method, recognizing that these prospective decreases may not be voluntarily disclosed by the budgetee.

For his part, the budgetee defends his estimates. He justifies proposed cost increases by explaining their underlying causes, such as additional work that he is expected to do, the effect of inflation, the need for better quality output, and so on.

The commitment. The end product of the negotiation process is an agreement which represents a **commitment** by each party, the budgetee and his superior. By the act of agreeing to the budget estimates, the budgetee says to his superior, in effect: "I can and will operate my responsibility center in accordance with the plan described in this budget." By approving the budget estimates, the superior says to the budgetee, in effect: "If you operate your responsibility center in accordance with this plan, you will do what we consider to be a good job." Both of these statements contain the implicit qualification of "subject to adjustment for unanticipated changes in circumstances." In other words, both parties recognize that actual events, such as changes in price levels and in general business conditions, may not correspond to those assumed when the budget was prepared and that these changes may affect the plans set forth in the budget. In judging whether the commitment is in fact being accomplished as the year progresses, management must take these changes into account.

The nature of the commitment, both as to individual elements of expense and as to the total expense of the responsibility center, may be one of three types: (1) it may represent a **ceiling** (e.g., "not more than $X should be spent for books and periodicals"); (2) it may represent a **floor** (e.g., "at least $Y should be spent for employee training"); or (3) it may represent a **guide** (e.g., "approximately $Z should be spent for overtime"). In some companies, the individual items are not explicitly identified as to which of these three categories they belong in, but it is obviously important that the two parties have a clear understanding as to which item belongs in which category.

Step 5.   Coordination and review.   The negotiation process is repeated at successively higher levels of responsibility centers in the organizational hierarchy, up to the very top. Negotiations at higher levels may, of course, result in changes in the detailed budgets that have been agreed to at lower levels. If these changes are significant, the budget is recycled back down the organizational hierarchy for revision. If, however, the guidelines are carefully described, and if the budget process is well understood and well conducted by those who participate in it, such recycling ordinarily is not necessary. In the successive stages of negotiation, the person who has the role of superior at one level becomes the budgetee at the next higher level. Since he is well aware of this fact, he is strongly motivated to negotiate budgets with his budgetees that he can then defend successfully with his superiors. If his superior demonstrates that the proposed budget is too loose, this reflects adversely on the budgetee's ability as a manager and as a negotiator.

As the individual budgets move up the organizational hierarchy in the negotiation and review process, they are also examined in relationship to one another, and this examination may reveal aspects of the plan that are out of balance. If so, certain of the underlying budgets may need to be changed. Major unresolved problems are submitted to the budget committee. Various summary documents, especially the budgeted income statement, the budgeted balance sheet, and the cash-flow budget, are also prepared during this step.

Steps 6 and 7.   Final approval and distribution.   Just prior to the beginning of the budget year, the proposed budget is submitted to top management for approval. If the guidelines have been properly set and adhered to, the proposed budget should contain no great surprises to top management. This approval is by no means perfunctory, however, for it signifies the official agreement of top management to the proposed plans for the year. The chief executive officer therefore usually spends considerable time discussing the budget with each of the managers who reports to him. After top management approves the budget, it is submitted to the board of directors for final approval.

The approved budget is then transmitted down through the organization. It constitutes authority to carry out the plans specified therein.

Revisions

The budget is formulated in accordance with certain assumptions as to conditions that will prevail during the budget year. Actual conditions during the year will never be exactly the same as those assumed, and the differences may be significant. The question then arises as to whether or not the budget should be revised so that it will reflect what is now known about current conditions. There is considerable difference of opinion on this question.

Those who favor revising the budget point out that the budget is supposed to reflect the plan in accordance with which the company is operating, and that when the plan has to be changed because of changing conditions, the budget should reflect these changes. If the budget is not revised, it is no longer a statement of plans, they maintain.

The opponents of revising the budget argue that the process of revision not only is time consuming but also may obscure the goals that the company originally intended to achieve and the reasons for departures from these goals, especially since a revision may reflect the budgetee's skill in negotiating a change, rather than one that reflects an actual change in the underlying assumed conditions. Since revisions for spurious reasons destroy the credibility of the budget, critics refer to such a revised budget as a "rubber standard." Many companies therefore do not revise their budgets during the year, and take account of changes in conditions when they analyze the difference between actual and budgeted performance.

Other companies solve this problem by having two budgets: a **baseline budget** set at the beginning of the year, and a **current budget** reflecting the best current estimate of revenue and expenses. A comparison of actual performance with the baseline budget shows the extent of deviation from the original plan, and a comparison of the current budget with the baseline budget shows how much of this deviation is attributable to changes in current conditions from those originally assumed.

Variations in practice

The preceding is a generalized description of the budget preparation process. Not all companies prepare a budget for each responsibility center, and some companies that do develop a comprehensive budget treat the process more casually than is implied in the above description. Some companies formulate their budgets in a process that is essentially the reverse of that described; that is, instead of having budget estimates originate at the lowest responsibility centers, the budget is prepared by a high-level staff, blessed by top management, and then transmitted down to the organization. This **imposed budget** is an unsatisfactory motivating device, and it is therefore not widely used.

Nonprofit organizations.   In government agencies, schools, hospitals, and other nonprofit organizations, the budgeting process is even more important than in a profit-oriented company. This is because in a profit-oriented company, the profit measure itself provides a rough guide to the actions that should be taken, whereas in a nonprofit organization, operating managers must conform closely to mandates imposed by the Congress, or by other governing bodies, and these mandates are expressed in the approved budget.

In addition to the responsibility budget described above, many nonprofit organizations also prepare a program budget. (The word *program* is used in the same sense as in the preceding section on programming.) **The program budget sets forth the programs that the organization plans to undertake during the year and the amount to be spent on each program.** The total costs in the program budget are the same as the total costs in the responsibility budget; the two budgets are two different ways of slicing the same pie. Some profit-oriented companies also prepare a program budget, in addition to a responsibility budget, as a part of the annual budget process.

Merchandising companies.   In retail stores and other merchandising companies, the budgeting process is considerably simpler than that described above for a manufacturing company. This is because the complexities of preparing a production budget and coordinating it with a sales budget are not present. Each responsibility center does, of course, prepare an expense budget, and the selling departments also prepare sales budgets. Merchandising companies ordinarily do not prepare a purchasing budget showing the amount of goods to be purchased each month. Instead, the buyers operate according to what is called an **open-to-buy** procedure. They are given a dollar maximum for the amount of goods that can be on hand and on order at any time, and they must govern their purchases so that this maximum is not exceeded. Thus, if the luggage buyer has an open-to-buy of $50,000, and has $40,000 of luggage on hand and on order, he can place additional orders for a maximum of $10,000.

THE CASH BUDGET

The operating budget is usually prepared in terms of revenues and expenses, that is, on the accrual basis. For financial planning purposes, it must be translated into terms of cash inflows and cash outflows. This translation results in the **cash budget.** The financial manager uses the cash budget to make plans to insure that the company has enough, but not too much, cash on hand during the year ahead.

There are two approaches to the preparation of a cash budget:

1. Start with the budgeted balance sheet and income statements, and adjust the amounts thereon to reflect the planned sources and uses of cash. This procedure is substantially the same as that described for the cash-basis statement of changes on financial position in Chapter 15 of *Fundamentals of Financial Accounting,* except that the data are estimates of the future rather than historical. Its preparation is therefore not described again here.

2. Analyze those plans having cash-flow implications to estimate each of the sources and uses of cash. This approach as shown in Schedule 7 of the Appendix to this chapter, and subordinate Schedules 7a and 7b. Some points about this approach are briefly described below.

Collection of accounts receivable is estimated by applying a "lag" factor to estimated sales or shipments. This factor may be based simply on the assumption that the cash from this month's sales will be collected next month; or there may be more elaborate assumptions about discounts and uncollectible accounts. Schedule 7a is constructed on the assumption that 50 percent of a month's sales are collected in the current month, and that the other 50 percent of the month's receivables are collected in the following month.

The estimated amount and timing *of raw materials purchases* is obtained from the materials purchases budget (Schedule 4). In Schedule 7b the assumption is made that all purchases will be paid for in the month in which they are received; more commonly, a lag factor, similar to that described above, would be applied to the amount of purchases in a given month. This lag factor is the time interval that ordinarily elapses between the receipt of material and the payment of the invoice. Estimated purchase discounts would also be taken into account.

Other operating expenses are often taken directly from the expense budget, since the timing of cash disbursements is likely to correspond closely to the incurrence of the expense. Depreciation and other items of expense not requiring cash disbursements in the current month are excluded. Capital expenditures are also shown as an outlay, with amounts taken from the capital budget.

Schedule 7 shows how cash plans are made. The company desires a minimum cash balance of $50,000 as a cushion against unforeseen needs. From the budgeted cash receipts and cash disbursements, a calculation is made of whether the budgeted cash balance exceeds or falls below this minimum. In January and February the budgeted cash balance exceeds the minimum. In this company no action is planned, but in other situations, the company might well decide to invest the extra cash in marketable securities. In March the budget indicates a cash deficiency of $83,-500; consequently, plans are made to borrow $84,000 to offset this deficiency. The lower portion of the cash budget therefore shows the company's financing plans.

THE CAPITAL EXPENDITURE BUDGET

The **capital expenditure budget** is essentially a list of what management believes to be worthwhile projects for the acquisition of new plant and equipment together with the estimated cost of each such capital investment project, and the timing of capital expenditures. Proposals for capital expenditure projects are analyzed as a part of the programming process described earlier. The capital expenditure budget is usually prepared separately from the operating budget, and in many companies it is cleared through a capital appropriations committee that is separate from the budget committee.

In the capital expenditure budget, individual projects are often classified by purposes such as the following:

1. Cost reduction and replacement.
2. Expansion and improvement of existing product lines.
3. New products.
4. Health and safety.
5. Other.

Proposals in the first two categories usually are suceptible to an economic analysis in which the net present value can be estimated. Some proposals for the addition of new products can also be substantiated by an economic analysis, although in a great many situations the estimate of sales of the new product is pretty much a guess. Proposals in the other categories usually cannot be sufficiently quantified so that an economic analysis is feasible.

Justification

Each proposed capital investment, except those for minor amounts, is accompanied by a justification. For some projects, the net present value or other measure of desirability can be estimated by methods described in Chapters 8 and 9. Other projects, such as the construction of a new office building or remodeling of employee recreation rooms, are justified on the basis of improved morale, safety, appearance, convenience, or other subjective grounds. A lump sum usually is included in the capital expenditure budget to provide for capital expenditure projects that are not large enough to warrant individual consideration by top management.

As proposals for capital expenditures come up through the organization, they are screened at various levels, and only the sufficiently attractive ones flow up to the top and appear in the final capital expenditure budget. On this document, they are often arranged in what is believed to be the order of desirability. Estimated expenditures are shown by years, or by quarters, so that the cash required in each time period can be determined. At the final review meeting, which is usually at the board-of-director level, not only are the individual projects discussed but also the total amount requested on the budget is compared with estimated funds available. Many apparently worthwhile projects may not be approved, simply because the funds are not available.

Authorization

Approval of the capital budget usually means approval of the projects *in principle,* but does not constitute final authority to proceed with them. For this authority, a specific authorization request is prepared for the project, spelling out the proposal in more detail, perhaps with firm bids or price quotations on the new assets. These **authorization requests** are approved at various levels in the organization, depending on their size and character. For example, each supervisor may be authorized to buy production tools or similar items costing not more than $100 each, provided his total for the year does not exceed $1,000; and at the other extreme, all projects costing more than $500,000 and all projects for new products, whatever their cost, may require approval of the board of directors. In between, there is a scale of amounts that various echelons in the organization may authorize without the approval of their superiors.

Some companies use procedures to follow up on capital expenditures. These include both checks on the spending itself and also an appraisal, perhaps a year or more after the project is completed, as to how well the estimates of cost and revenue actually turned out.

SUMMARY

In the programming process, a periodic, but not annual, review of on-going programs is made, and proposals for new programs are analyzed and decided on. Some companies also prepare a formal program, or long-range plan, in order to insure that all programs are considered and coordinated and that the projected total net income is satisfactory.

Budgets are used as a device for making and coordinating plans, for communicating these plans to those who are responsible for carrying them out, for motivating managers at all levels, and as a standard with which actual performance subsequently can be compared. In a comprehensive budget system, there is a package of interrelated budgets, including the operating budget, the variable budget, the cash budget, the capital expenditure budget, and perhaps others.

The operating budget is prepared within the context of basic policies and plans that have already been decided upon in the programming process. The principal steps are as follows: (1) dissemination of guidelines stating the overall plans and policies and other assumptions and constraints that are to be observed in the preparation of budget estimates; (2) preparation of the sales budget; (3) preparation of other estimates by the managers of responsibility centers, assisted by, but not dominated by, the budget staff; (4) negotiation of an agreed budget between the budgetee and his superior, which gives rise to a bilateral commitment by these parties; (5) coordination and review as these initial plans move up the organizational chain of command; (6) approval by top management and the board of directors; and (7) dissemination of the approved budget back down through the organization.

The *cash budget* translates revenues and expenses into cash receipts (inflows) and disbursements (outflows) and thus facilitates financial planning.

The *capital expenditure budget* is a list of presumably worthwhile projects for the acquisition of new capital assets. Often it is prepared separately from the operating budget. Approval of the capital expenditure budget constitutes only approval in principle, for a subsequent authorization is usually required before work on the project can begin.

APPENDIX: THE MECHANICS OF BUDGET PREPARATION

Following is a detailed description of the mechanics involved in preparing a budget for Lake Erie Table Company, Inc. It is presented primarily to illustrate the relationships among the various parts. It should be emphasized that this example deals only with mechanics. It does not describe the judgmental process that led to the assumptions on which the budget was based, nor the process of negotiation that led to approval of the estimates. In order to save space, only the data for three months are shown. In actuality, the budget was prepared for the first three months and for each of the other three quarters of the year.

Lake Erie Table Company employs 128 people (21 in sales, 24 in administration, and 83 in production). Exhibit 12–1 is the company's organization chart. The company manufactures and sells directly to retailers (department stores, discount houses, furniture stores) along the eastern seaboard, two types of folding card tables, the Royal and Superior models.

The Royal and Superior card tables have suggested retail prices of $24.95 and $19.95, respectively, and are sold to the retailers at $15 and $12, respectively, which is approximately 40 percent less than the retail price. Both tables have tubular steel frames with a baked enamel finish. Both tops are made of plywood covered with vinyl. Both tables come in forest

EXHIBIT 12–1
Lake Erie Table Company organization chart*

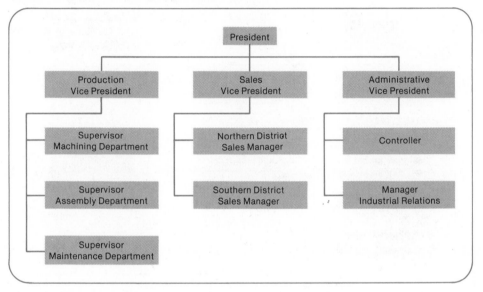

* Note: Each box represents one of the 11 responsibility centers of the company.

green, desert tan, or ivory color. Each table requires the same amount of direct labor and factory overhead to manufacture. Although the Royal model has only slightly more material in it, the company can sell the Royal model to retailers for $3 more than the Superior.

Exhibit 12–2 shows the relationships among the various schedules that constitute the budget. The responsibility for the preparation of the various schedules parallels the responsibility structure of the organization as defined in the organization chart.

Exhibit 12–3 contains basic data and calculations that are part of the budget preparation.

The master budget is made up of the following schedules:

Schedule 1: The *sales budget* is the responsibility of the sales vice president. The sales budget is the foundation of all other budgets since

EXHIBIT 12–2

Lake Erie Table Company schematic of budget relationships

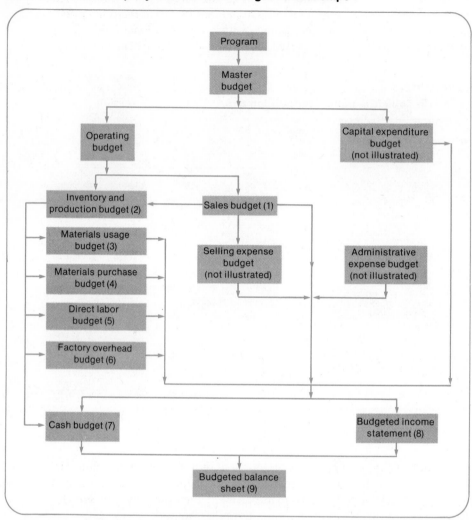

* Figures in parentheses are schedule numbers.

Note: This exhibit should be examined carefully and then Schedules 1 through 9 should be examined also and integrated into this framework.

EXHIBIT 12–3

LAKE ERIE TABLE COMPANY
Machining and Assembly Departments Cost Data
For the Quarter Ending March 31, 1977

			Estimated cost per table	
Machining department	Quantity	Price	Royal	Superior
Materials:				
A—Steel legs...............................	10 ft.	$0.20	$ 2.00	
	9 ft.	0.20		$ 1.80
B—Plywood top	12 sq. ft.	0.10	1.20	
	9 sq. ft.	0.10		0.90
Total Material Cost...............................			3.20	2.70
	DLH*	Budgeted rate		
Direct labor	0.10	$6.00/DLH	0.60	0.60
Factory overhead	0.10	6.00/DLH	0.60	0.60
Total Machining Cost per Unit..............			4.40	3.90
Units produced (from Schedule 2)			31,000	55,000
Total Machining Department Costs			136,400	214,500
Assembly department	Quantity	Price		
Materials:				
C—Vinyl top	12 sq. ft.	$0.05	0.60	
	9 sq. ft.	0.05		0.45
D—Assembly kit...	1 each	1.00	1.00	1.00
Total Material Cost...............................			1.60	1.45
	DLH	Budgeted rate†		
Direct labor:	0.20	$5.00/DLH	1.00	1.00
Factory overhead	0.20	6.00/DLH	1.20	1.20
Total Assembly Cost per Unit			3.80	3.65
Units produced (from Schedule 2)			31,000	55,000
Total Assembly Department Costs..........			117,800	200,750
Total Production Costs			$254,200	$415,250
Total Cost per Unit‡			$8.20	$7.55

* Direct labor hours.
† The factory overhead rate was calculated from data in Schedule 6.

Total budgeted factory overhead..	$154,800
Total budgeted DLH (8,600 + 17,200)	25,800
Rate per DLH ($154,800 ÷ 25,800)..	$ 6.00

‡ Check: 31,000 Royal units   × $8.20 per unit = $254,200
      55,000 Superior units × $7.55 per unit = $415,250

they are related partially or completely to the budgeted sales volume. The sales budget is influenced by the planned unit sales price and the planned advertising and selling expenses. The planned unit sales prices are decided by top management.

Each district sales manager prepares a district *selling expense budget* concurrently with the sales budget. The sales vice president prepares the general sales overhead budget and approves the district sales managers' budgets. These become part of the cash budget and the income statement.

Schedule 2: The *inventory and production budget* and all of the budgets supporting it (Schedules 3 through 6) are the responsibility of the production vice president. The inventory and production budget is prepared after the sales budget. It includes the planned inventory policy of top management. The company uses first-in, first-out cost flow for all inventories.

Schedule 3: The *materials usage budget* is prepared by the supervisors of the machining and assembly departments. The machining department supervisor prepares the estimates for materials A and B, and the assembly department supervisor prepares the estimates for materials C and D.

Schedule 4: The *materials purchases budget* is the responsibility of the purchasing manager who in this case is also the production vice president. It is his responsibility to provide the planned unit purchase price for raw materials.

Schedule 5: The *direct labor budget* is the responsibility of the managers of the machining and assembly departments. They prepare estimates of their departments' total direct labor hours. The budgeted rate per hour is prepared by the industrial relations department.

Schedule 6: The *factory overhead budget* is also the responsibility of the production department managers. The production and direct labor budgets provide the basis for projecting the planned volume of work for the machining and assembly departments, which in turn is used in planning the volume of work in the maintenance and general factory overhead departments.

Schedule 7: The chief financial officer, in this case the controller, is responsible for preparing the *cash budget.* Note that some expenses such as taxes do not require an immediate cash outlay and some expenses such as depreciation never require a cash outlay.

The controller and industrial relations manager prepare their departmental budgets and the administrative vice president prepares the general *administrative budget* and approves the accounting and industrial relations budgets.

Schedules 8 and 9: The budget director uses all of the preceding budgets to prepare the budgeted income statement and the budgeted balance sheet.

SCHEDULE 1

LAKE ERIE TABLE COMPANY
Sales Budget
For the Quarter Ending March 31, 1977

District and product	Unit selling price	January Units sold	January Sales $	February Units sold	February Sales $	March Units sold	March Sales $	Quarter total Units sold	Quarter total Sales $
Northern:									
Royal	$15.00	6,000	$ 90,000	6,000	$ 90,000	5,000	$ 75,000	17,000	$ 255,000
Superior	12.00	10,000	120,000	10,000	120,000	11,000	132,000	31,000	372,000
Total			210,000		210,000		207,000		627,000
Southern:									
Royal	15.00	4,000	60,000	5,000	75,000	5,000	75,000	14,000	210,000
Superior	12.00	8,000	96,000	8,000	96,000	8,000	96,000	24,000	288,000
Total			156,000		171,000		171,000		498,000
Totals:									
Royal	15.00	10,000	150,000	11,000	165,000	10,000	150,000	31,000	465,000
Superior	12.00	18,000	216,000	18,000	216,000	19,000	228,000	55,000	660,000
Totals to Income Statement and Cash Budget			$366,000		$381,000		$378,000		$1,125,000

Estimated sales for April, which are necessary for the production budget, are:

	April sales in units Royal	April sales in units Superior
Northern district	6,000	10,000
Southern district	4,000	8,000
	10,000	18,000

Schedule 1: The *sales budget* is the responsibility of the sales vice president. The sales budget is the foundation of all other budgets since they are related partially or completely to the budgeted sales volume. The sales budget is influenced by the planned unit sales price and the planned advertising and selling expenses. The planned unit sales prices are decided by top management.

Each district sales manager prepares a district *selling expense budget* concurrently with the sales budget. The sales vice president prepares the general sales overhead budget and approves the district sales managers' budgets. These provide inputs to the cash budget and the budgeted income statement.

SCHEDULE 2

LAKE ERIE TABLE COMPANY
Inventory and Production Budget (units)
For the Quarter Ending March 31, 1977

Product	January	February	March	Quarter total
Royal:				
Units to be sold (from Schedule 1)...........	10,000	11,000	10,000	31,000
Add: Planned ending inventory*............	11,000	10,000	10,000	10,000
Total Units Needed for Sales and Stock..	21,000	21,000	20,000	41,000
Less: Planned beginning inventory........	10,000	11,000	10,000	10,000
Units to be produced (to Schedules 3 and 5)...	11,000	10,000	10,000	31,000
Superior:				
Units to be sold (from Schedule 1)...........	18,000	18,000	19,000	55,000
Add: Planned ending inventory*............	18,000	19,000	18,000	18,000
Total Units Needed for Sales and Stock..	36,000	37,000	37,000	73,000
Less: Planned beginning inventory........	18,000	18,000	19,000	18,000
Units to be produced (to Schedules 3 and 5)...	18,000	19,000	18,000	55,000

* At the end of any month the company wishes to maintain a basic inventory equal to the next month's sales. The March figure multiplied by the unit cost gives the dollar value for the finished goods inventory on the budgeted balance sheet.

Schedule 2: The *inventory and production budget* and all of the budgets supporting it (Schedules 3 through 6) are the responsibility of the production vice president. The inventory and production budget is prepared after the sales budget. It includes the planned inventory policy of top management. The company uses first-in, first-out cost flow for all inventories.

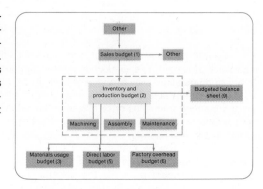

SCHEDULE 3

LAKE ERIE TABLE COMPANY
Materials Usage Budget (units)
For the Quarter Ending March 31, 1977

	Royal			Superior			Total		
Material and month	Production planned*	Quantity per unit†	Quantity needed for production	Production planned*	Quantity per unit†	Quantity needed for production	Quantity needed for production‡	Unit cost†	Total material cost
A (steel legs):									
January	11,000	10	110,000	18,000	9	162,000	272,000	$0.20	$ 54,400
February.........	10,000	10	100,000	19,000	9	171,000	271,000	0.20	54,200
March............	10,000	10	100,000	18,000	9	162,000	262,000	0.20	52,400
Total	31,000		310,000	55,000		495,000	805,000		161,000
B (plywood top):									
January	11,000	12	132,000	18,000	9	162,000	294,000	0.10	29,400
February.........	10,000	12	120,000	19,000	9	171,000	291,000	0.10	29,100
March............	10,000	12	120,000	18,000	9	162,000	282,000	0.10	28,200
Total	31,000		372,000	55,000		495,000	867,000		86,700
C (vinyl top):									
January	11,000	12	132,000	18,000	9	162,000	294,000	0.05	14,700
February.........	10,000	12	120,000	19,000	9	171,000	291,000	0.05	14,550
March............	10,000	12	120,000	18,000	9	162,000	282,000	0.05	14,100
Total	31,000		372,000	55,000		495,000	867,000		43,350
D (assembly kit):									
January	11,000	1	11,000	18,000	1	18,000	29,000	1.00	29,000
February.........	10,000	1	10,000	19,000	1	19,000	29,000	1.00	29,000
March............	10,000	1	10,000	18,000	1	18,000	28,000	1.00	28,000
Total	31,000		31,000	55,000		55,000	86,000		86,000

Total Materials Usage (to budgeted income statement) $377,050

* From Schedule 2.
† From Exhibit 12–3.
‡ To Schedule 4.

Schedule 3: The *materials usage budget* is prepared by the supervisors of the machining and assembly departments. The machining department supervisor prepares the estimates for materials A and B, and the assembly department supervisor prepares the estimates for materials C and D.

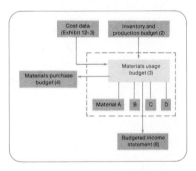

SCHEDULE 4

LAKE ERIE TABLE COMPANY
Materials Purchases Budget (units)
For the Quarter Ending March 31, 1977

Material and month	Quantity needed for production*	Add ending inventory	Total quantity required	Less beginning inventory	Purchases (in units)	Unit cost	Total cost
A (steel legs):							
January......	272,000	271,000	543,000	272,000	271,000	$0.20	$ 54,200
February.....	271,000	262,000	533,000	271,000	262,000	0.20	52,400
March........	262,000	262,000	524,000	262,000	262,000	0.20	52,400
Total..........	805,000	795,000	1,600,000	805,000	795,000		159,000
B (plywood top):							
January......	294,000	291,000	585,000	294,000	291,000	0.10	29,100
February.....	291,000	282,000	573,000	291,000	282,000	0.10	28,200
March........	282,000	282,000	564,000	282,000	282,000	0.10	28,200
Total..........	867,000	855,000	1,722,000	867,000	855,000		85,500
C (vinyl top):							
January......	294,000	291,000	585,000	294,000	291,000	0.05	14,550
February.....	291,000	282,000	573,000	291,000	282,000	0.05	14,100
March........	282,000	282,000	564,000	·282,000	282,000	0.05	14,100
Total..........	867,000	855,000	1,722,000	867,000	855,000		42,750
D (assembly kit):							
January	29,000	29,000	58,000	29,000	29,000	1.00	29,000
February......	29,000	28,000	57,000	29,000	28,000	1.00	28,000
March	28,000	28,000	56,000	28,000	28,000	1.00	28,000
Total	86,000	85,000	171,000	86,000	85,000		$ 85,000

Quarter totals	A	B	C	D	Total
January	$ 54,200	$29,100	$14,550	$29,000	$126,850†
February..........	52,400	28,200	14,100	28,000	122,700†
March	52,400	28,200	14,100	28,000	122,700†
	$159,000	$85,500	$42,750	$85,000	$372,250

*From Schedule 3. At the end of any month the company wishes to maintain a basic inventory of the next month's units needed for production. The March figure gives the dollar value for the raw materials inventory on the budgeted balance sheet ($122,700).

† To the cash budget (Schedule 7b). It is assumed that all raw materials purchases will be paid for in the month received.

Schedule 4: The *materials purchase budget* is the responsibility of the purchasing manager who in this case is also the production vice president. It is his responsibility to provide the planned unit purchase price for raw materials.

The company's inventory policy is to have on hand one month's supply of each item. Purchases are budgeted so as to attain this. For example, for Item A (Steel legs):

	Quantity feet
Needed for January production	272,000
Needed for February production, and hence inventory at end of January................. ...	271,000
Total Requirements............................ ...	543,000
Less on hand January 1	−272,000
Quantity to be purchased in January	271,000

SCHEDULE 5

LAKE ERIE TABLE COMPANY
Direct Labor Budget
For the Quarter Ending March 31, 1977

Month and dept.	Royal			Superior			Totals		
	Units to be pro- duced*	DLH per units†	Hours	Units to be pro- duced	DLH per unit†	Hours	Total hours	Rate per DLH	Labor cost
January:									
Machining	11,000	0.10	1,100	18,000	0.10	1,800	2,900	$6.00	$ 17,400
Assembly...	11,000	0.20	2,200	18,000	0.20	3,600	5,800	5.00	29,000
			3,300			5,400	8,700		46,400‡
February:									
Machining	10,000	0.10	1,000	19,000	0.10	1,900	2,900	6.00	17,400
Assembly...	10,000	0.20	2,000	19,000	0.20	3,800	5,800	5.00	29,000
			3,000			5,700	8,700		46,400‡
March:									
Machining	10,000	0.10	1,000	18,000	0.10	1,800	2,800	6.00	16,800
Assembly...	10,000	0.20	2,000	18,000	0.20	3,600	5,600	5.00	28,000
			3,000			5,400	8,400		44,800‡
Quarter totals									
Machining	31,000	0.10	3,100	55,000	0.10	5,500	8,600	6.00	51,600
Assembly...	31,000	0.20	6,200	55,000	0.20	11,000	17,200	5.00	86,000
			9,300			16,500	25,800		

Total Labor Cost to Budgeted Income Statement.......................... $137,600

* From Schedule 2.
† From Exhibit 12–3.
‡ To the cash budget (Schedule 7b).

Schedule 5: The *direct labor budget* is the responsibility of the machining and assembly department managers. They prepare estimates of their departments' total direct labor hours. The budgeted rate per hour is prepared by the industrial relations department.

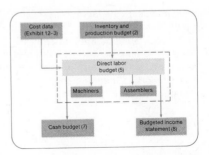

SCHEDULE 6

LAKE ERIE TABLE COMPANY
Factory Overhead Budget
For the Quarter Ending March 31, 1977

Department and account	Variable budget formula	January	February	March	Total
Machining:		(DLH, 2,900)*	(DLH, 2,900)	(DLH, 2,800)	(DLH, 8,600)
Supervisory salaries	$3,000 + $ 0/DLH	$ 3,000	$ 3,000	$ 3,000	$ 9,000
Depreciation	1,200 + 0	1,200	1,200	1,200	3,600
Factory supplies	0 + 1.00	2,900	2,900	2,800	8,600
Power	2,000 + 0.10	2,290	2,290	2,280	6,860
All other overhead	400 + 0.90	3,010	3,010	2,920	8,940
Total	$6,600 + $2.00/DLH	$12,400	$12,400	$12,200	$ 37,000
Assembly:		(DLH, 5,800)	(DLH, 5,800)	(DLH, 5,600)	(DLH,17,200)
Supervisory salaries	$4,800 + $ 0/DLH	$ 4,800	$ 4,800	$ 4,800	$ 14,400
Depreciation	1,000 + 0	1,000	1,000	1,000	3,000
Factory supplies	0 + 2.00	11,600	11,600	11,200	34,400
Power	1,000 + 0.20	2,160	2,160	2,120	6,440
All other overhead	600 + 0.80	5,240	5,240	5,080	15,560
Total	$7,400 + $3.00/DLH	$24,800	$24,800	$24,200	$ 73,800
Maintenance:		(DRH, 300)†	(DRH, 300)	(DRH, 400)	(DRH, 1,000)
Supervisory salaries	$1,100 + $ 0/DRH	$ 1,100	$ 1,100	$ 1,100	$ 3,300
Indirect labor	400 + 1.00	700	700	800	2,200
All other overhead	0 + 2.50	750	750	1,000	2,500
Total	$1,500 + $3.50/DRH	$ 2,550	$ 2,550	$ 2,900	$ 8,000
General factory overhead (all fixed):					
Salaries and wages		$ 6,000	$ 6,000	$ 6,000	$ 18,000
Depreciation		4,000	4,000	4,000	12,000
All other overhead		2,000	2,000	2,000	6,000
Total		12,000	12,000	12,000	36,000
Total Factory Overhead to the Budgeted Income Statement		$51,750‡	$51,750‡	$51,300‡	$154,800

* Direct labor hours (from Schedule 5). † Direct repair hours.
‡ To the cash budget (Schedule 7b).

Schedule 6: The *factory overhead budget* is also the responsibility of the production department managers. The production and direct labor budgets provide the basis for projecting the planned volume of work for the machining and assembly departments, which in turn is used in projecting the planned volume of work in the maintenance and general factory overhead departments.

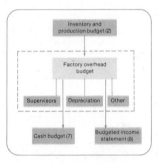

SCHEDULE 7

LAKE ERIE TABLE COMPANY
Cash Budget
For the Quarter Ending March 31, 1977

Item	January	February	March
Beginning cash balance............................	$ 50,050*	$ 90,650	$149,400
Budgeted cash receipts (see 7a below).........	358,000	373,500	379,500
Total Cash Available..........................	408,050	464,150	528,900
Budgeted cash disbursements:			
Operations (see 7b below)........................	267,400	264,750	262,400
Capital expenditures†.............................	0	0	300,000
Total Cash Disbursements..................	267,400	264,750	562,400
Minimum cash balance desired...................	50,000	50,000	50,000
Total Cash Needed	317,400	314,750	612,400
Balance (or deficiency)‡	90,650	149,400	(83,500)
Financing:			
Bank loan...	0	0	84,000
Bank repayments	0	0	0
Ending cash balance	$ 90,650	$149,400	$ 50,500

* Given.

† Estimated cost of new equipment to be purchased in March.

‡ Minimum cash balance desired plus any excess or less any deficiency and plus any loans less any repayments.

SCHEDULE 7a

Budgeted Cash Receipts

			Collected in—	
Month of sale	Sales	January	February	March
December............................	$350,000	$175,000		
January.................................	366,000	183,000	$183,000	
February	381,000		190,500	$190,500
March	378,000			189,000
Monthly collection of accounts receivable...............		$358,000	$373,500	$379,500

Fifty percent of each month's sales are collected during the month and 50 percent of each month's receivables are collected the following month. For simplicity it is assumed there will be no uncollectible accounts. The accounts receivable balance for March 31, 1977 is $189,000, and will appear on the budgeted balance sheet.

SCHEDULE 7b

Budgeted Cash Disbursements
Paid in—

Item	January		February		March	
Materials (Schedule 4)...	$126,850		$122,700		$122,700	
Direct labor (Schedule 5)...........	46,400		46,400		44,800	
Factory overhead (Schedule 6)...........	$51,750		$51,750		$51,300	
Less: Depreciation	6,200	45,550	6,200	45,550	6,200	45,100
Selling general and administrative.........	51,600		53,100		52,800	
Less: Depreciation	3,000	48,600	3,000	50,100	3,000	49,800
Total Disbursements...		$267,400		$264,750		$262,400

All material expenditures are in the same month the purchase is made. Disbursements for labor assumed to be in the same month as incurred. Overhead disbursements are in the same month the expenditure is incurred.

Depreciation expense does not require cash outlays. District selling and administrative expenses are $5,000 per month per district, plus $0.10 per dollar of sales for each district, and $5,000 per month is incurred for general selling and administrative expenses.

SCHEDULE 8

LAKE ERIE TABLE COMPANY
Budgeted Income Statement
For the Quarter Ending March 31, 1977

Schedule reference				
1	Sales...		$1,125,000	
	Cost of goods sold:			
3	Cost of raw materials used........................	$377,050		
5	Direct labor	137,600		
6	Factory overhead	154,800		
	Total Manufacturing Cost..................	669,450		
2*	Add: Beginning finished goods inventory.....	217,900		
	Total Cost of Goods Available for Sale ...	887,350		
2	Less: Ending finished goods inventory.........	217,900	669,450	
	Gross margin...		455,550	
7b	Selling and administrative expense		157,500	
	Income before taxes		298,050	
	Federal income taxes (50%)........................		149,025	
	Net Income...		$ 149,025	

* There was no change in the finished goods inventory for the quarter.

Royal............	10,000 units × $8.20 =	$ 82,000	
Superior.........	18,000 units × $7.55 =	135,900	
		$217,900	

SCHEDULE 9

LAKE ERIE TABLE COMPANY
Budgeted Balance Sheet
As of March 31, 1977

Assets

Schedule reference					
	Current Assets:				
7	Cash..		$ 50,500		
7a	Accounts receivable..		189,000		
4	Materials inventory..		122,700		
2	Finished goods inventory..		217,900	$ 580,100	
	Fixed Assets:				
Given	Land..		$ 50,000		
Given	Buildings..	$1,500,000			
Given	Less: Accumulated depreciation..	600,000	900,000		
Given	Equipment	1,000,000			
Given	Less: Accumulated depreciation	425,000	575,000	1,525,000	
	Total Assets...			$2,105,100	

Liabilities

	Current Liabilities:			
8	Income taxes payable..		$ 149,025	
7	Bank loan payable		84,000	$ 233,025
	Long-Term Liabilities:			
Given	Notes payable—$100,000 due January 1, 1980			100,000
	Total Liabilities...			333,025

Shareholders' Equity

Given	Common stock, $10 par value, 200,000 shares authorized; 100,000 shares outstanding..		1,000,000	
Given	Contributed capital in excess of par		400,000	
	Retained earnings:			
Given	Beginning balance...	$223,050		
8	Plus estimated earnings	149,025	372,075	1,772,075
	Total Liabilities and Shareholders' Equity................................			$2,105,100

Capital budget.   The capital budget is not illustrated. Note, however, that the company's planned capital expenditures have been included in the cash budget, Schedule 7. This $300,000 outlay represents that portion of the long-range capital spending budget that will be expended in March.

The completed budget is discussed with the company president. After the president approves it, he presents it to the board of directors for their approval.

IMPORTANT TERMS

Programming	**Negotiation**
Zero-base review	**Slack**
Budget	**Budget commitment**
Profit plan	**Baseline budget**
Master budget	**Imposed budget**
Operating budget	**Program budget**
Responsibility budget	**Cash budget**
Variable (or flexible) budget	**Capital expenditure budget**
Rolling budget	

QUESTIONS FOR DISCUSSION

1. Not all companies have a formal programming system, but most companies nevertheless engage in the programming process. How do they do it?

2. Give examples of the programs that a college or university might use in its programming system.

3. Why is there no such thing as a "zero-base budget?"

4. What is the relationship between the program and the budget?

5. Distinguish between the technical and the behavioral aspects of budget preparation.

6. Explain the purposes for which a budget would be used in Morgan Ford Company, the automobile dealership described in Chapter 1.

7. Why is an operating budget structured according to responsibility centers?

8. The example on page 493 shows a variable budget formula for a machining department. What would be the factory overhead budget for the department in a month when planned production volume was 3,500 direct labor hours?

9. Distinguish between the role of the line organization and the role of the staff in budget preparation. Does the budget director function in a line capacity when he prepares the budget for his own office?

10. What is the difference between a sales budget and a sales forecast?

11. The management team of a small printing shop consists of the president, the production manager, the sales manager and the controller. They meet one

afternoon, and at the end of the afternoon they have completed the budget for the coming year. Describe briefly, step by step, what probably happened that afternoon, identifying the part each person played.

12. Budget amounts may represent (a) a ceiling, (b) a floor, or (c) a guide. If you personally were the president of a company, in which category would you probably put the following items in the budget for the marketing department: advertising, secretarial assistance, entertainment of customers, market research, training of salespersons? If you are uncertain of the classification, explain why.

13. An approved budget is often called a "bilateral commitment." What is the nature of such a commitment?

14. Should managers try to eliminate budget slack?

15. Why is an imposed budget unsatisfactory as a motivating device?

16. A frequently revised budget is sometimes called a "rubber budget." What derogatory implication does this term have?

17. Suppose that a current budget is prepared as carefully as humanly possible, using all available current information. Can management use such a budget in lieu of actual reports on performance?

18. What is the difference between a program budget and a responsibility budget? Between a program budget and a long-range plan?

19. On a capital expenditure budget, individual projects often are listed in order of their desirability. Is "desirability" the same as net present value?

20. Trace through each schedule in the Appendix to this chapter so that you can describe what is being done on each and the interrelationship of the several schedules. One good way of doing this is to start with the budgeted income statement (Schedule 8) and the budgeted balance sheet (Schedule 9), and work backwards to find the source of each number on these statements.

21. Referring to the Lake Erie Table Company material in the Appendix to this chapter, give examples of cost items that probably are engineered, discretionary, and committed, respectively. Also, give examples of cost items that are controllable and others that are noncontrollable.

PROBLEMS

12–1. Gallo Kitchens, Inc., is preparing a budget for the second quarter of the current calendar year. The March ending inventory of merchandise was $106,000, which was higher than expected. The company prefers to carry ending inventory amounting to the expected sales of the next two months. Purchases of merchandise are paid for by the end of the next month, and the balance due on accounts payable at the end of March was $24,000. Budgeted sales follows:

April	$40,000	July	$72,000
May	48,000	August	56,000
June	60,000	September	60,000

Required:

A. Assuming a 25 percent gross profit margin is budgeted, prepare a budget showing the following amounts for the months of April, May, and June:
1. Cost of goods sold.
2. Purchases required.
3. Cash payments for merchandise purchases.

B. Assuming a balance due on accounts payable at the beginning of April was $53,000 and all merchandise acquisitions are paid, half in the month of purchase and half in the month following purchase, prepare a budget showing the following amounts for April, May, and June:
1. Cash payments for merchandise.
2. Ending balance due on accounts payable.

C. Assuming a balance on accounts receivable at the beginning of April was $35,000 and all customers pay three fourths in the month of sale and one fourth in the month following sales, prepare a budget showing the following amounts for April, May, and June:
1. Cash receipts from accounts receivable.
2. Ending balance on accounts receivable.

12-2. Carbo Products Company has budgeted sales for the next four months as follows:

	Sales in units
April	70,000
May	80,000
June	60,000
July	50,000

The managers are in the process of preparing the production budget for the quarter. The planned for end-of-month inventory levels are set equal to 25 percent of the anticipated month's unit sales. The inventory on hand at the beginning of April was 17,500 units. All units cost $3 each and are paid for in the month of production.

Required:

A. Prepare a budget showing the following amounts for the months of April, May, and June:
1. Number of units produced.
2. Cash payments for units produced.
3. Cost of goods sold.
4. Ending balance of inventories in dollars.

B. Assume the management decided to stabilize the production levels at 67,000 units per month, rather than fix inventory levels in relation to projected sales, and that units which cost $3 are to be paid for three fourths in the month of production and one fourth in the month following production. Assuming further a balance due on accounts payable at the beginning of April was $20,000, prepare a budget showing the following amounts for April, May, and June:

1. Ending balance of inventories in dollars.
2. Cash disbursements for units produced.
3. Ending balance due on accounts payable.

C. The management wants to determine the budgeted cash collections from sales at $4 per unit and has estimated that the historical collection pattern (given below) will continue over the budgeted period. The accounts receivable at the beginning of April amounted to $70,000. The sales collection data show:

> 60 percent in month of sale
> 38 percent in month following sale
> 2 percent uncollectible

From the above data, prepare a budget showing the following amounts for April, May, and June:
1. Cash receipts from accounts receivable.
2. Ending accounts receivable.

12–3. Shaulk Outlets, Inc., has just received a franchise to distribute humidifiers on the eastern seaboard. The company commenced business on January 1, 1977, with these assets:

Cash	$45,000	Delivery equipment...	$640,000
Inventory	95,000	Office equipment	160,000

First-quarter sales are expected to be $360,000, and should be doubled in the second quarter. One percent of sales is considered to be uncollectible. The gross profit margin should be 30 percent. Variable selling expenses except bad debts are budgeted at 12 percent of sales, and fixed selling expenses at $48,000 per quarter, exclusive of depreciation. Variable administrative expenses are expected to run 3 percent of sales, and fixed administrative expenses should total $34,200 per quarter. All equipment has an estimated useful life of 20 years and no residual value.

Required:

A. Prepare an operating budget for the first quarter of 1977 and another for the second quarter of 1977.
B. Management expects inventory levels to remain constant, and no new acquisitions of equipment are planned. Receivables are anticipated to increase to $350,000 by the end of the quarter, and payables will be $320,000. Prepare a budgeted statement of financial position for June 30, 1977.
C. Verify the anticipated cash balance for June 30, 1977, by preparing a worksheet which will show the expected cash receipts and disbursements for the first half year.

12–4. Rowes Garden Center has been organized to sell a line of lawn and garden equipment. The company began operations on January 1, 1977, with the following assets:

Cash	$11,250
Inventory	23,500
Land	25,000
Buildings and equipment	200,000

The buildings and equipment have an estimated useful life of 20 years, and have no residual value. The depreciable assets are used 80 percent for selling and 20 percent for general and administrative activities. Sales for January, February, and March are expected to be $30,000 per month and after that at $60,000 per month. Certain expenses are expected to vary with sales as follows:

	Percent of sales dollars
Cost of sales	70
Bad debts	1
Variable selling	12
Variable administrative	3

Expenses not expected to vary with sales:

Selling	$12,000 per quarter
Administrative	8,550 per quarter
Depreciation	2,500 per quarter

Required:

A. Prepare an opening budget for the first and second quarters of operations for Rowes Garden Center.

B. Survey data suggest that inventories will be double the beginning balance by the midyear and receivables will amount to one month's sales. Management would not want the cash balance to go below $5,000, and plans on using a line of credit with local suppliers. No new equipment or land will be purchased. Prepare a budgeted balance sheet as of June 30, 1977.

C. Prepare a schedule of expected cash receipts and disbursements which will allow the Rowes Garden Center management to identify the cash flows used to determine the cash balance on June 30, 1977.

12–5. Mitchell Company is compiling a cash forecast for 1977, its second year of operations. Total sales and unpaid customer balances have been estimated for the first four months of 1977 as follows:

	Sales	Beginning receivables balance
January	$67,000	$13,000
February	57,000	14,030
March	37,500	12,233
April	37,500	8,348

The sales and collection pattern, which Mitchell Company expects will not change significantly in the next four months, has been determined from historical data from the first year of business. During 1976 cash and credit sales have been approximately equal. Customers on the average pay their bills on the following schedule:

90 percent of accounts receivable at the beginning of the month are collected in that month.

60 percent of credit sales during the month are collected that month. 2 percent of credit sales become bad debts and are written off each month.

Required:

A. Prepare a budget of cash sales and collections on credit sales expected for the first four months of 1977.

B. Show the accounts receivable balance which will be shown on the budgeted balance sheet as of April 30, 1977.

C. Assume that Mitchell Company has cash requirements for operating expenses and loan payments which require the following cash payments:

January	$70,100
February	61,650
March	52,530
April	49,800

What minimum level of sales each month can support this payment schedule?

12–6. Farrar, Inc., estimates sales and collections of accounts receivable quarterly. The sales budget for the coming year is as follows:

	Total sales
First quarter	$300,000
Second quarter	400,000
Third quarter	400,000
Fourth quarter	600,000

Cash sales represent 30 percent of the total sales, the remaining are on open account. In the past, 90 percent of the amounts carried as a balance at the beginning of each quarter were collected in that quarter. Before a quarter ended, 80 percent of the credit sales for the quarter were collected. Because of the vigorous credit screening procedure, uncollectible accounts are insignificant. The sales characteristics are not expected to change in the forecasted period. Accounts receivable on January 1 were $100,000.

Required:

A. Prepare a budget of cash receipts from sales and accounts receivable for each quarter.

B. Estimate the balance for accounts receivable as it would be presented on each budgeted quarterly statement of financial position.

C. Assume Farrar, Inc., has been able to regulate its cash payments for merchandise, loans, and other expenditures as follows:

First quarter	$520,000
Second quarter	416,000
Third quarter	487,600
Fourth quarter	455,760

Calculate the sales level required which will allow these payments to be made without requiring a change in the ending cash balance, breaking sales into cash and credit categories.

12-7. Imports, Inc., is preparing a budget for the first quarter of next year. Sales are budgeted at $20,000 for January, $25,000 for February, $32,000 for March, $38,000 for April, and $30,000 for May. When merchandise is purchased it is paid for within 30 days, and the company intends to keep an inventory of at least two months' expected sales on hand. The December 31 inventory of the current year was $55,000 because of an unexpected slump in sales, and accounts payable were $10,000. The gross profit margin is budgeted at 25 percent.

Required:
A. Prepare a budget of the following amounts for the months of January, February, and March:
   1. Cost of goods sold.
   2. Purchases required.
   3. Cash payments for merchandise purchases.
B. Assuming that accounts payable could go to 60 days on any new merchandise acquisitions, and that management wants the inventory to go no lower than $30,000 at cost, what is the minimum cash payment for merchandise which can be planned for January, February, and March?

12-8. After being in business for one month, Soloman, Inc., had a cash balance of $12,600, accounts receivable of $80,000, and accounts payable of $53,400. All liabilities are paid in the month after they have been incurred. Customers are expected to pay for 80 percent of credit sales by the end of the next month, 15 percent by the end of the second month, and 3 percent by the end of the third month. Budgeted amounts for the next three months follow:

	April	May	June
Cash sales	$24,000	$18,000	$32,000
Sales on account	65,000	42,000	60,000
Purchases on account	48,000	43,000	38,000
Cash payments:			
Salaries and wages	7,000	7,000	7,800
Delivery truck		18,000	
Dividends			8,000
Interest	2,400	2,400	2,400
Miscellaneous	3,600	4,600	4,200

Required:
Prepare a cash budget which will show for each month:
A. The beginning cash balance.
B. Cash receipts.
C. Cash disbursements.
D. The cash balance at the end of the month.

12-9. Bill Davidson, president of Davidson Sales, sold strictly for cash in the old days; but Harley Davidson, his son and a college graduate, convinced Bill he could increase sales over the usually slow winter months by selling on open account. He tried it for the month of December, experiencing sales of $45,000 of which $5,000 represented cash sales.

On December 31, 1976, Davidson Sales had a cash balance of $7,000, an accounts receivable balance of $40,000, and an accounts payable balance of $27,000. Budgeted amounts for January, February, and March of 1977 follow:

	January	February	March
Cash sales	$12,000	$10,000	$15,000
Credit sales	27,000	20,000	29,000
Purchases on account	25,000	20,500	18,000
Cash payments to be made:			
Salaries and wages	3,500	3,600	4,000
Rent	1,000	1,000	1,000
Miscellaneous	1,500	2,200	2,000
Fixed asset purchases	0	8,000	0
Dividend payments	0	0	3,500

Eighty percent of credit sales are collected in the next month, 15 percent the second month, and 3 percent the third month, the remainder being uncollectible. Purchases are routinely paid for within a month.

Required:

Prepare a cash budget which will show for each month:
A. The beginning cash balance.
B. Cash receipts.
C. Cash disbursements.
D. The cash balance at the end of the month.

12-10. Refer to the data for Shaulk Outlets, Inc., Problem 12-3. In addition to the data given in Problem 12-3, the following estimates are available:

Other typical franchise holders collect 75 percent of receivables in the quarter in which a sale is made and 24 percent in the following quarter. Sixty percent of merchandise purchases and two thirds of operating expenses will be paid for in the quarter in which the purchase is made, and the balance in the following quarter. Ending inventory of each quarter should be equal to a third of the cost of sales of the coming quarter. An additional $90,000 investment will have to be made at the end of June to handle the expected increase in sales volume of $1,080,000 in the third quarter.

Required:

A. Prepare a cash budget for the first and second quarters of 1977.
B. Assuming that a minimum cash balance of $20,000 is desired at

all times, what steps would you advise Shaulk Outlets, Inc., to take
at the end of each of the first two quarters?

12-11. Refer to the data for Rowes Garden Center described in Problem 12-4.
In addition to the data given in Problem 12-4, the following estimates
are available:

Three fourths of the receivables will be paid in the quarter in which
the sale is made and 24 percent in the following quarter. Sixty percent
of merchandise purchased and two thirds of operating expenses will be
paid for in the quarter in which the purchase is made, and the balance in
the following quarter. The ending inventory of each quarter should be
equal to one third of the amount of estimated cost of sales for the coming quarter. An additional $22,500 investment will have to be made at
the end of the second quarter to handle the increased sales volume expected in the third quarter.

Required:

A. Prepare a cash budget for the first and second quarters of 1977.
B. Assuming that a minimum cash balance of $5,000 is desired at all
times, what steps would you advise Rowes Garden Center to
take at the end of each of the first two quarters?

12-12. Charles McVea, president of the McVea Company, a wholesaling establishment, asks your assistance in preparing a budget of cash receipts
and disbursements for the next two months, October and November.
The company borrowed $90,000 on August 5 to help meet the peak
seasonal cash needs, the note becoming due on November 30. There
is some question in the president's mind about whether the cash position
of the company will be strong enough to pay off the note on time.

The September 30, trial balance of the company shows, among other
things, the following account balances:

Cash	$ 14,200
Accounts receivable	227,000
Allowance for bad debts	9,100
Inventory	193,800
Accounts payable	86,000
Notes payable	124,000

The McVea Company sells one product only. Sales price of the
product is $100, and terms are uniform to all customers: 2 percent dis-
count if paid within the first ten days of the month subsequent to purchase, otherwise due by the end of the month subsequent to purchase.
Historically the company has experienced a 60 percent collection within
the discount period, an 85 percent collection within the month subsequent to purchase, and a 98 percent collection within the second month
subsequent to purchase. Uncollectibles average 2 percent of sales.

The company has projected annual sales for the current year ending December 31 of $1.5 million. Sales for recent months and estimates
of sales for the remainder of the year follows:

August	$180,000
September	200,000
October (estimate)	220,000
November (estimate)	280,000
December (estimate)	150,000

All purchases of merchandise are payable within ten days. Accordingly, month-end balances in accounts payable represent approximately 33 percent of the purchases of merchandise made in the month then ended. The unit purchase price is $68. Target ending inventory is set at 80 percent of next month's estimated sales in units.

Selling and administrative expenses for the year are estimated to total $400,000, of which 40 percent is fixed (including depreciation of $32,000). Variable selling and administrative expenses vary directly with sales, and all selling and administrative expenses are paid as incurred.

Required:

A. Prepare a cash budget for the McVea Company for the months of October and November.

B. Will the company be able to meet the $90,000 note due at the end of November?

12–13. Helen Carson, president of Patriots Products, was preparing a request to draw on a line of credit established at the Munney Bank in order to assist the company in building its inventories for peak June sales. Suppliers are seeking purchase commitments in order to preserve the current prices which have been offered. Taking advantage of the current purchase price will allow Patriots Products to maintain its gross margin of 50 percent of sales. The line of credit is provided for a three-month period at a flat fee of $250 plus 10 percent simple interest on any monies drawn on the line of credit. The line of credit requests that all borrowing be done on the first of the month and that the account be cleared by July 31.

This loan will be more significant in size than any Patriots Products has taken in prior years. Therefore Carson was required to demonstrate to the bank the company's ability to repay the loan. In support of the borrowing plan, Carson intended to provide the loan officer with a cash budget and income statement covering the loan period. She assembled the following budgeted information for the next three months.

	May	June	July
Sales	$40,000	$70,000	$30,000
Merchandise purchase commitments	40,000	20,000	20,000
Payroll	7,000	8,000	4,000
Lease payments	4,000	4,000	4,000
Other cash payments	4,000	4,000	2,000
Depreciation expense	2,000	2,000	2,000
Operating income	3,000	17,000	?
Equipment purchases	10,000	—	—

The beginning cash balance on May 1 will be $5,000, and Carson prefers that it does not go below that amount. Accounts receivable on that date are planned at $21,500, of which $18,000 will be collected during May, and $3,000 will be collected during June. The remainder probably will be uncollectible. The company's anticipated collection pattern for sales is 20 percent during the month of sale, 75 percent in the month following sale, and 4 percent in the second month following sale. On May 1 the accounts payable balance will be $25,000, representing April purchases of merchandise inventory. All purchases are paid for in the month following purchase.

Required:

A. Prepare a schedule of budgeted cash collections on sales and accounts receivable.
B. Prepare a cash budget, by month and by quarter, for the budgeted period assuming that any use of the credit line will be repaid as required. If the company needs a minimum cash balance of $5,000 at the beginning of each month, can the loan be repaid as planned? Explain.
C. Prepare the budgeted income statements for each month and the quarter.
D. Analyze the data and make any comments or suggestions to Ms. Carson which you feel are appropriate.

12–14. Below is the December 31, 1976, balance sheet of Bonus Bakers:

BONUS BAKERS
Balance Sheet
As of December 31, 1976

Assets

Current Assets:

Cash	$ 3,750
Accounts receivable	4,125
Prepaid rent	1,500
Prepaid insurance	450
Total Current Assets	9,825

Fixed Assets:

Improvements to leased building	12,775
Baking equipment	13,300
Baking utensils	1,310
	27,385
Less: Accumulated depreciation	8,308
Total Fixed Assets	19,077
Total Assets	$28,902

Liabilities

Current Liabilities:

Accounts payable	$ 4,219
Accrued expenses	182
Short-term notes payable	3,000
Total Current Liabilities	7,401
Long-term notes payable	7,000
Total Liabilities	14,401

Shareholders' Equity

Common stock (par $10)	6,000
Retained earnings	8,501
Total Shareholders' Equity	14,501
Total Liabilities and Shareholders' Equity	$28,902

Estimates and additional information are as follows:

a. Estimated 1977 sales, net of discounts and allowances: $105,000. Sales typically follow an even month-to-month pace, with no noticeable seasonal trends.

b. The company moved into its present building on July 1, 1976. Rent of $3,000 for one year in advance was paid on July 1, 1976. Beginning in July 1977, rent of $250 per month will be paid in cash for the current month.

c. Accounts receivable are expected to continue to experience a one-half month turnover cycle. All sales are on account.

d. Flour, yeast, and all other baking materials are purchased and consumed so quickly that no inventory accounts for these items is maintained. They are expensed upon purchase. The December 31, 1976, balance of accounts payable consists solely of this type of purchase and represents $12\frac{1}{2}$ percent of total 1976 purchases of baking materials.

e. It is estimated that 1977 cost of goods sold will be as follows:

Raw materials	$35,200
Direct labor	25,650
Fixed factory overhead (cash)*	4,160
Variable factory overhead	7,895
	$72,905

* Excludes depreciation and includes only $1,500 of rent payments.

f. The company holds an insurance policy for $1,000,000 of liability coverage. The policy runs from year to year from April 1 to March 30. The annual premium of $1,800 is due in April, and its cost is considered an administrative expense.

g. When the company moved to its new building, two bank notes totaling $10,000 were signed, the first being due in June 1977 for $3,000, and the second being due in January 1981 for $7,000. Both notes bear interest at 8 percent, payable on June 30 and December 31.

h. Data on fixed assets are as follows:

Asset	Purchase date	Life	Cost	Depreciation method
Improvements....................	7–1–76	10 yrs.	$12,775	SL
Baking equipment..............	1–1–72	15	12,000	SYD
Baking equipment..............	7–1–76	5	1,300	SYD
Baking utensils..................	1–1–72	10	1,310	SYD

All fixed assets are considered to have a zero salvage value.

i. Selling and administrative expenses other than the insurance and interest are estimated to total $24,600 in 1977, or $2,050 per month.

j. It is expected that accrued expenses balance, which is for raw materials, will double by the end of 1977.

k. Management does not anticipate the payment of any dividends during the coming year.

Required:

A. Prepare a budgeted income statement for Bonus Bakers for 1977 and a balance sheet as of December 31, 1977 (ignore tax considerations).

B. Prepare a cash budget on a monthly basis for Bonus Bakers for the year 1977.

12–15. Smokey Sales Company is preparing the budget for the next three months. The company is a nationwide distributor of a revolutionary attachment for citizen band car radio, called the "Seabee," which can also be used in boats. Sales have grown so rapidly in the last year or so that it has become crucial to coordinate the company's plans in the form of a master budget for the next three months starting April 1. The company desires a minimum ending cash balance at least equal to 25 percent of the accounts payable balance each month. The "Seabee" is forecasted to sell for $20 each. Recent and forecasted sales in units were gathered from various accounting and marketing reports as follows:

January (actual)....................	4,000	June............................	12,000
February (actual)	5,000	July	4,000
March (actual)......................	6,000	August.........................	4,000
April...................................	6,000	September	3,000
May....................................	9,000		

School graduation gifts and Fathers' Day gifts suggest reasons for the peak sales in May and June. Ending inventories should be kept at 80 percent of the next month's sales in units. The "Seabee" is acquired from the manufacturer at a cost per unit of $12. Purchases are paid half in the month of acquisition and the balance in the month following. All sales are on credit, with no discount and payable within 15 days. Experience has shown, however, that only 25 percent of sales are collected in the month of sale, 50 percent is collected in the month following, and the remaining 25 percent is collected in the second month following, with bad debts insignificant.

The monthly operating expenses are as follows:

Variable:	
Sales commissions...............................	10% of sales
Fixed:	
Salaries and wages	$14,400
Utilities	9,000
Expired insurance.................................	400
Depreciation...	6,000
Other...	12,000

All operating expenses are paid in cash during the month, except for depreciation and expired insurance. New fixed assets are planned for May 1 at a cash outlay of $10,000. The Smokey Sales Company board of directors intends to continue to pay cash dividends of $7,500 per quarter. The next dividend payment would be scheduled for April 1; the next declaration, June 30. The company has a line of credit with the Fiveby 5 cents Savings Bank which allows it to borrow money at 12 percent simple interest. However, all borrowing must be made at the beginning of a month, and repayments must be made at the end of a month. Interest is computed and paid only when the principal is repaid. Repayments of principal must be in round $1,000 amounts, but borrowing may be in any amount.

The balance sheet on March 31 for Smokey Sales is as follows:

Assets

Cash	$ 9,000
Accounts receivable...	115,000
Inventory	57,600
Unexpired insurance...	3,400
Fixed assets, net of depreciation.............................	132,000
Total Assets	$317,000

Liabilities

Accounts payable	$ 36,000
Dividends payable	7,500
Total Liabilities..	43,500

Stockholders' Equity

Capital stock..	$250,000	
Retained earnings	23,500	
Total Stockholders' Equity............................		273,500
Total Liabilities and Stockholders' Equity......		$317,000

Required:

A. Prepare the following detailed budgets for the three-month period ending June 30 by month and for the quarter:

    1. Sales budget.

2. Schedule of budgeted cash collections from sales and accounts receivable.
3. Purchases budget in units and dollars.
4. Schedule of cash payments for purchases of merchandise.
5. Cash budget.

B. Prepare the budgeted income statement for the quarter ending June 30.
C. Prepare the budgeted balance sheet for June 30.

12–16. Paul Barton and Robert Doyle formed a partnership to provide professional accounting services to a consortium of business executives in a medium-sized midwestern town. The partnership hired seven employees, rented an office, purchased supplies, and contracted to purchase company automobiles for the two partners. Barton & Doyle recognized that their initial investments in the business of $4,000 each would probably not be enough to get them over the initial cash squeeze which most new businesses encounter during their first months of operation and are accordingly faced with the problem of determining their exact month-to-month cash needs so that a loan agreement can be reached with a local bank.

Monthly salary expense for the seven employees amounted to $8,200, of which Barton & Doyle estimate 55 percent, 65 percent, and 70 percent will be billable to clients at the rate of 250 percent of base pay over the first three months respectively. The partners estimated that billable hours as a percentage of total hours will level off at 75 percent by the fourth month of operations. Barton and Doyle each expect to bill approximately 50 percent of their time to clients at the rate of 300 percent of their monthly draw, which they have agreed will be $2,000 each per month.

Rent on the office space amounted to $720 per month. The invoice for office supplies amounting to $1,200 will become due during the first month of operation, while the payment for the two automobiles amounting to $8,400 need not be made until the second month of operation.

Required:

Assuming that collection of monthly billings to clients takes place in the succeeding month and that Barton & Doyle wish to keep a minimum cash balance on hand of $2,000, what loan requirements will the partnership have during each of the first four months of operation? Ignore any interest charges.

12–17. Oakmont Company will begin operations on July 1 with a cash balance of $50,000 secured through the sale of capital stock. The company will manufacture a product with material and labor costs as follows:

Material.................... $2 per unit
Labor...................... 1 per unit

Indirect manufacturing costs will be $5,000 per month which includes depreciation of $1,000. Sales and production have been budgeted as follows for the first four months of business:

	Finished units sold	Finished units produced
July	6,000	10,000
August	6,000	10,000
September...................	9,000	12,000
October......................	15,000	12,000

The inventory of raw materials at the end of each month will be an amount sufficient for one half of the next month's production requirements. It is expected that three fourths of each month's purchases will be paid for in the month of purchase and that the remainder will be paid for in the month of purchase and that the remainder will be paid for in the following month. A 2 percent cash discount will be taken on all purchases of material.

Selling and administrative expenses will be 20 percent of sales. The expenses, along with direct labor and indirect manufacturing costs, will be paid for in the month incurred.

The selling price of the product has been set at $5 per unit. Collections are scheduled as follows: 80 percent in the month of sale; 10 percent in the month following sale; 9 percent in the second month following sale; 1 percent uncollectible.

Required:

A. Prepare a schedule showing materials requirements for July, August, and September.

B. Prepare a schedule showing anticipated cash disbursements on accounts payable for materials for July, August, and September.

C. Prepare a schedule of cash receipts for July, August, and September.

D. Prepare a schedule of total cash disbursements for July, August, and September.

E. Determine the cash balance budgeted for the end of July, August, and September.

12–18. In early January, McCartney Sales, a medium-sized retailing establishment, was considering a change in its credit policy, whereby customers who were previously refused charge accounts would be granted accounts with relatively low ($100–$200) credit limits. McCartney's president, Leonard P. Harrison, estimated that the present monthly sales volume of $400,000 would increase by 50 percent with the change in policy, which can be put into effect by the end of the month.

Management of McCartney Sales recognized that as the new policy takes effect, not only would sales volume and the level of accounts receivable rise but in addition, inventories and salaries would also unavoidably increase. Salaries, which currently were $60,000 per month, were expected to increase by 25 percent. Inventories, costing an average of 70 percent of selling price, were expected to increase in proportion to sales. Sales on account presently made up 75 percent of total sales and averaged a 45-day turnover rate. It was estimated that the additional sales obtained through the change in policy would be 90 percent on account and average a 60-day lag for collection.

McCARTNEY SALES
Pro forma Balance Sheet as of January 31
(in thousands of dollars)

Cash	$ 200	Liabilities...............................	$ 700
Accounts receivable......	450	Owners' equity	510
Inventory	560	Total Liabilities	
Total Assets	$1,210	and Owners' Equity......	$1,210

Required:

Assuming the following, prepare pro forma balance sheets and income statements for McCartney Sales for the months of February, March, April, and May.

A. The new credit policy is put into effect at the end of January.
B. Expenses other than cost of goods sold and salaries are fixed at $50,000 per month.
C. A minimum cash balance of $100,000 must be maintained.
D. Expansion of accounts receivable and inventory levels are to be financed with surplus cash and debt.

12–19. Lexington Products Company manufactures and distributes several products to retailers. One of these products, Fakecrete, requires 3 pounds of cement in its manufacture. The company would like to have enough raw materials in inventory at the beginning of each month equal to one half of the production needs for the month. No work in process inventories are maintained. The sales budget for Fakecrete for the coming six months is as follows:

	Budgeted unit sales
January...........................	27,000
February	30,000
March	36,000
April	39,000
May	28,000
June	24,000

Lexington Products Company plans to keep 8,000 units plus 10 percent of the next month's sales in finished goods inventory. On January 1, the finished goods inventory totaled 10,700 units.

Required:

Prepare a budget showing the quantity of cement to be purchased for January, February, and March.

12–20. Enuring Products, Inc., has made production estimates for the next six months for two of their product lines which are to be manufactured in the following quantities:

	Mixo	Fixo
January	15,700	3,200
February	16,200	4,500
March	20,400	5,200
April	22,300	5,200
May	24,500	6,400
June	26,100	6,900

Finished goods inventories are kept one month in advance of sales. The purchasing department buys material one month in advance of production needs to be certain they are on hand. Adequate inventories are on hand for January. Materials requirements per unit of product and prices are as follows:

Materials code	Product line	Requirements per unit of product	Unit materials price
XM4L	Mixo	18	$0.80
XM9B	Fixo	6	$3.00

In order to be more efficient in the use of material XM4L, the company is planning to install new equipment on March 1 which is expected to reduce the consumption of XM4L so that only 12 units will be required for each unit of Mixo.

Required:

A. Prepare a purchases budget in units of material and in dollars for each month from January to May inclusive.

B. Compute the total savings in the cost of materials purchased that can be expected from the new equipment.

12–21. Wallace Box Company manufactures cardboard cartons which are used by other manufacturers to package a wide variety of consumer products. The sales vice president has gathered various items of information as a basis for top management's decision as to the sales budget for 1977, as follows:

Sales revenue in 1976 is estimated to be $8,000,000, based on actual sales for the first ten months. This is an estimated 5 percent of all cardboard cartons sold in Wallace's marketing territory. A trade association forecasts that industry sales, in units, will increase 4 percent in 1977 as compared with 1976.

The sales staff estimates that selling prices will be at least 5 percent higher in 1977, and may well be 8 percent higher.

Sales estimates for each territory, obtained from the salespersons responsible for that territory, add up to $9,500,000 for 1977. In the past such estimates have tended to be somewhat optimistic. Included in the $9,500,000 is a sizable increase in one territory that reflects an estimated $300,000 of sales to the Marvel Company, a possible new customer. Discussions with Marvel have been underway for several months, and the salesperson is "practically certain" that Marvel will give its carton business to Wallace in 1977.

The financial vice president, who keeps well informed on general business conditions, believes that the trade association forecast is too high and estimates that industry sales in units will not increase at all in 1977.

The sales vice president, on the other hand, not only believes that the trade association forecast is reliable but also believes that Wallace's market share (i.e., percentage of industry sales) will be 5.4 percent of industry sales in units.

Required:

A. Set boundaries on the sales budget for 1977; that is, state the lowest amount and the highest amount of sales revenue that you believe top management should reasonably consider.
B. Within this range, what number would you use as the sales budget for 1977?

SUGGESTIONS FOR FURTHER READING

Hofstede, G. H. *The Game of Budget Control.* Assen, The Netherlands: Van Gorcum & Co., N. V., 1967.

Steiner, George A., ed. *Top Management Planning.* New York: The MacMillan Co., 1969.

Welsch, Glenn A. *Budgeting: Profit Planning and Control,* 4th ed. Englewood Cliffs, N.J.: Prentice-Hall, Inc., 1976.

13

Standard costs

PURPOSE OF THE CHAPTER

In Chapter 12 we described how estimates of future manufacturing costs were developed as a part of the budgeting process. The present chapter describes a cost accounting system that incorporates such estimates and discusses the usefulness of such a system. This system is called a standard cost system.

Since a standard cost system is one type of cost accounting system, it logically could have been discussed in Part One, along with the description of other cost accounting systems. Discussion has been deferred until now for three reasons. First, although the underlying concept of standard costing is not particularly complicated, there often is difficulty in grasping this concept if it is presented early in a course. A standard cost system *appears* to be a roundabout way of measuring product costs, as contrasted with the straightforward method of collecting actual costs that was described in Part One. We shall see that the opposite is the case; that is, that a standard cost system involves less work than does an actual cost system. Secondly, standard costs are used for several different purposes, and we could not discuss the usefulness of standard costs for some of these purposes early in the book because the purposes themselves had not been described. Standard costs are useful in pricing, the topic discussed in Chapter 2; they are useful in making alternative choice decisions (Chapters 7–9); and they are useful in control (Chapter 11). Third, the development of standard costs has much in common with the formulation of budgets which was discussed in the preceding chapter.

540

NATURE OF STANDARD COSTS

A standard cost is a measure of what an item of cost should be, as contrasted with a record of what it actually was. A standard cost system is a cost accounting system that records standard costs either in addition to, or instead of, actual costs. In the typical actual cost system, manufacturing overhead costs are assigned to products by means of a predetermined overhead rate, and this is also the case with a standard cost system. The difference between the two systems is in the way direct material and direct labor costs are measured. An actual cost system collects the *actual amount* of direct costs that are incurred for each product. In a standard cost system, *standard unit costs* are developed for the direct material and direct labor elements of products costs; and it is these amounts, rather than actual costs, that are carried through the system to finished goods inventory.

Because of the similar way in which overhead costs are treated in both a standard cost and an actual cost system, the term *standard cost* applies particularly to direct material cost and direct labor cost. In describing how the system works, however, we shall include overhead costs as well as direct costs, so as to show how total standard factory costs are accumulated.

Contrast with actual costs

For direct material, the standard represents the amount of material that should be needed to produce a unit of product priced at what the price of this material should be.

> *EXAMPLE:* In a shoe factory, the unit of production may be a case (24 pairs) of shoes, Style 107. In an actual cost system, upper leather, sole leather, heels, and other items of direct material would be requisitioned from raw material inventory for this lot of shoes; the actual cost of this material would be calculated; and this cost would be entered on a cost sheet for this lot of shoes. In a standard cost system, a standard material cost for Style 107 is determined, perhaps once a year, by methods to be described below. Whenever a lot of Style 107 is manufactured, it is assigned this standard material cost.

If the standard direct material cost is $50 per case, the difference between the two systems is illustrated in the following:

Direct material cost, Style 107

Job no.	Quantity (cases)	Actual cost system	Standard cost system*
1	1	$ 51,23	$ 50.00
2	1	49.57	50.00
3	5	290.41	250.00
4	2	91.87	100.00

* $50 × number of cases.

The same principle applies to direct labor. In an actual cost system, the direct labor cost of a job is found by multiplying the actual number of hours that employees worked on the job by their actual hourly labor rate. In a standard cost system, a standard direct labor cost is established for one unit of product, and the standard direct labor cost of the job is found by multiplying the number of units in the lot by this standard.

In an actual cost system, overhead is ordinarily assigned to products by means of a predetermined overhead rate. For example, if the overhead rate is $5 per direct labor hour and if a job required 100 direct labor hours, then the overhead cost would be calculated as $5 \times 100 = 500. Note that although this calculation is made in what is called an "actual" cost system, the "actual" overhead cost of this job was not necessarily $500. Indeed, there is no way of knowing for sure what the actual overhead cost was, since by definition overhead cannot be traced directly to any given product. In a standard cost system, there is also a predetermined overhead rate, but the overhead cost of a job is calculated by multiplying this rate by a *standard* quantity, such as the standard direct labor hours. With this exception, the treatment of overhead costs is the same under the two systems.

Standard costs can be used either with a job order cost system or a process cost system.

In some standard cost systems, standard costs of a job or product are recorded *instead of* actual costs. In other systems, standard costs are recorded *in addition to* actual costs. In a shoe factory, for example, no measurement is made at all of the actual direct material cost of a particular lot of shoes, such as Style 107 referred to in the preceding example. The total cost of all direct material issued to a production cost center for an accounting period, such as a month, is collected; and this total is compared with the total standard direct material cost for all shoes worked on during the period.

For large jobs, however, it is worthwhile to record *both* the standard costs and the actual costs of individual jobs.

In summary, the basic objective of an actual cost system is to charge units of products with a fair share of the *actual* costs incurred in making those products, whereas the basic idea of a standard cost system is that **the costs charged to units of products are the costs that should have been incurred on those products rather than the costs that actually were incurred.**

Standard costs and budgets

Note the similarity between standard costs and budgets. Both are estimates of what costs should be in the future. A budget is in fact a standard, against which actual costs will be compared. Customarily, however, the word *standard* is used for *unit costs,* especially direct material and direct labor costs per unit; whereas the word *budget* is used for the *total costs* in an accounting period. Thus, the budgeted direct labor cost for a month is found by multiplying the standard direct labor cost per unit by the number of units planned for production in the month. For all practical purposes, the words *standard* and *budget* can be used interchangeably.

Variances

The difference between a standard cost and an actual cost is called a variance. A standard cost system is arranged so that at appropriate points in the flow of costs, the amount of variance is recorded in one or more variance accounts. A debit balance in a variance account means that actual costs were higher than standard costs; such a variance is called an **unfavorable variance.** A credit balance means that actual costs were lower than standard costs; such a variance is called a **favorable variance.**

SETTING THE COST STANDARDS

The usefulness of a standard cost system depends in large part on how realistic the standards are. To arrive at a good standard does not necessarily require a great deal of extra effort, however. Some companies have shifted to a standard cost system simply by taking the average unit costs obtained from their former actual cost system and using these as standards. The resulting standards may be sufficiently reliable if material prices and labor rates are not expected to change significantly and if no substantial opportunities for improving efficiency are foreseen.

More commonly, the standards are built up from an analysis of direct labor, direct material, and overhead requirements.

Separation of quantity and price

Every dollar amount of direct material cost or direct labor cost in a cost accounting system results from the multiplication of a physical quantity by a price per unit of quantity. For direct material, this is the number of pounds (or other measure) of direct material multiplied by a price per pound, and for direct labor it is the number of minutes or hours of labor multiplied by a rate per hour. **In setting a cost standard, it is usually desirable to consider the quantity separately from the unit price, and to maintain their separate identity in the underlying records.**

There are two reasons for this. First, and most importantly, a separation of the quantity and price aspects facilitates analysis of the causes of the variances between the actual cost and standard cost, and for assigning responsibility for these differences. For example, the quantity of direct material used is usually the responsibility of the production department, whereas the price paid for the material is the responsibility of the purchasing department. Second, the separation facilitates revision of the standards when the need to do so arises. For example, if the standard unit price of an item of direct material increases, the standard direct material cost of each product in which this material is used can be adjusted simply by multiplying the standard quantity by the new unit price.

Types of standards

The standard cost of a product can be either an **ideal** standard or a **normal** standard. **An ideal standard represents what the costs would be if production operations were conducted at maximum efficiency;** that is, if waste or spoilage of direct material were at an absolute minimum and if direct workers produced the maximum output they are physically capable of producing and if machines never broke down. **A normal standard (or currently attainable standard) represents the degree of efficiency that reasonably can be expected under prevailing conditions;** that is, direct material costs include an allowance for the probable amount of waste and spoilage, and direct labor costs allow for the fact that workers do not actually work at peak efficiency, and that machines do break down. For a given product, a normal standard cost is of course higher than an ideal standard cost.

In most companies, the cost standards are normal standards since these represent what costs are really expected to be. An ideal standard is a goal toward which managers strive but which they probably cannot attain. Those companies that use an ideal standard argue that inefficiencies should not be built into the standard but rather should be isolated for separate examination and that managers should always strive for the best possible performance. When ideal standards are used, an allowance for inefficiency must be added to the standard cost when it is used for pricing and other decision-making purposes. In the following description, we assume the use of normal standards.

Standard direct material cost

The standard direct material cost of a product is usually derived from a **bill of materials.** This is simply a list showing the quantity of each item of material that is necessary to manufacture the article. A bill of materials is not prepared solely, or even primarily, for the purposes of the standard cost system. It must be prepared in any event in order to determine how much of what material to purchase, what storage requirements for material are, how much of each item of material should be requisitioned for a given lot, and for other production reasons. Therefore, the amount of additional effort required to develop a standard material cost is small. The bill of materials may show only the quantity of material that is re-

EXHIBIT 13-1
Calculation of standard direct material cost

A. Price per pound

	Material A	Material B
Expected invoice price per pound, delivered	$1.00	$4.00
Handling and inspection (7%)	0.07	0.28
Standard price per pound	$1.07	$4.28

B. Usage in Product 621

	Material A	Material B
Per bill of material, pounds	3.0	2.0
Allowance for waste	0.3	—
Standard usage per unit, pounds	3.3	2.0

C. Standard unit direct material cost

	Product 621
Material A, $1.07 × 3.3 pounds	$ 3.53
Material B, $4.28 × 2.0 pounds	8.56
Standard unit direct material cost	$12.09

quired to make one unit or lot of product, but if there is likelihood that material will be spoiled or wasted during the production process, an allowance for the quantity of material that will probably be lost for these reasons should be included in the calculation of standard material quantity.

The standard direct material cost is obtained by multiplying the standard quantities of material by standard unit prices. The standard unit price of each item of material is ordinarily obtained from the purchasing department.

Exhibit 13-1 illustrates the calculation of the standard direct material cost for a unit of product. In practice, the two elements of the standard cost would not be calculated on the same form. The standard unit price for each type of material would be calculated separately, and this unit price would be used in calculating the standard material cost of each product in which the material is used.

Standard direct labor costs

For direct labor costs, the estimated number of minutes required for each labor operation is often available. Production engineers have various techniques for obtaining such standard times. One is to **time study** each operation; that is, the observer uses a stopwatch to find the time that an efficient worker takes to perform the operation. However, many workers resent such direct observations; some companies are prohibited by union contracts from making them; and they are prohibited by law in many government organizations. An alternative approach is to divide each operation into the **elemental body movements** that are involved in it (e.g., "reaching," "grasping," "turning over"). Standard times for each of these body movements have been developed, and these are added up to find the standard time for the whole operation. Descriptions of these and other methods of arriving at standard time allowances will be found in books on industrial engineering. As was with the case with direct material, these standard labor times are needed not only for the standard cost system but also for other purposes: as a basis for planning labor requirements, for deciding on the best production work flow, for production scheduling, and for measuring worker efficiency.

The standard quantities of direct labor are converted to monetary amounts by multiplying each by a unit price, that is, an hourly labor rate. This rate may include not only wages earned but also an allowance for fringe benefits and other labor-related costs. In many companies one direct labor rate is established for all the direct employees in a cost center, even though the actual wages of individual employees may vary somewhat because of seniority or other reasons.

Exhibit 13–2 illustrates the calculation of the standard direct labor cost for a unit of product. The product is produced in two cost centers. An hourly rate is computed for each cost center by dividing the total estimated wages in the cost center by the number of hours of productive time that are expected to be available, and adding an allowance for fringe benefits. Note that although the normal work week is 40 hours, the productive

EXHIBIT 13–2
Calculation of standard direct labor cost

A. Rate per hour

	Cost center 1	Cost center 2
1. No. direct employees.....................................	20	50
2. Productive weekly hours per employee	35	35
3. Total hours per week, (1) × (2)	700 hrs.	1,750 hrs.
4. Estimated weekly wages, direct employees......	$4,500	$8,800
5. Wage per productive hour (4) ÷ (3).................	6.43	5.03
6. Fringe benefits (25%)	1.61	1.26
7. Standard labor rate per hour.........................	$8.04	$6.29

B. Standard direct labor cost per unit

	Product 621
Cost Center 1, 2 hours × $8.04	$16.08
Cost Center 2, 1 hour × $6.29	6.29
Standard direct labor cost..	$22.37

hours have been estimated at 35 per employee, so as to allow for personal time.

Spoilage and rework

A product may become damaged when it is part way through the production process. If it is not worth repairing, it is discarded; and the costs incurred up to that point are **spoilage costs.** If the item can be repaired, the costs incurred in doing so are **rework costs.** Some companies include an allowance for spoilage and rework costs in the standard material and labor costs of the product. Other companies treat these costs as elements of manufacturing overhead. The detailed procedures used in either case are described in texts on cost accounting.

Standard overhead costs

In Chapter 12 we described the process of preparing budgets for responsibility centers. As a part of this same process, standard overhead rates are determined. We shall therefore not repeat the description here. For the purpose of recalling what the process was and for showing the relationship between budgets and standard costs, an example is given below:

EXAMPLE: Exhibit 13-3 shows the procedure used in one company to develop both the variable budget and the standard overhead components for material handling labor costs. The top part of the exhibit is a scatter diagram in which dots show actual material handling costs plotted against direct labor hours for each of the preceding 12 months. A line fitted to these dots has the following characteristic:

Fixed cost .... $600.00 per month
Variable cost .... $ 0.40 per direct labor hour

After consultation with the departmental supervisor, it was agreed that material handling costs next year would increase 5 percent, making them

Fixed cost .... $630.00 per month
Variable cost .... $ 0.42 per direct labor hour

Normal volume for the next year was estimated at 2,000 direct labor hours per month. At this volume, costs would be:

$$\$630 + (\$0.42 \times 2,000) = \$1,470$$

The overhead rate for material handling therefore is:

$$\$1,470 \div 2,000 \text{ Hours} = \$0.735 \text{ per Direct Labor Hour}$$

(Actually, this rate would be included as part of the total overhead rate for the department, rather than being shown separately.)

EXHIBIT 13–3

Example of estimating a semivariable overhead cost

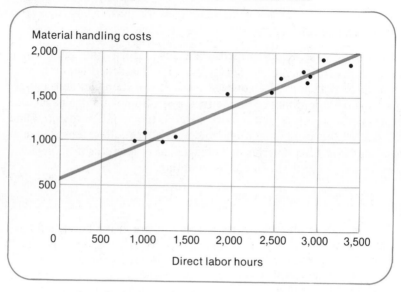

	Actual for current year	Estimated for next year
Fixed component...	$600.00	$630.00
Variable component..	0.40	0.42
Total at 2,000 direct labor hours......................................		1,470
Overhead rate per direct labor hour ($1,470 ÷ 2,000)...		0.735

The standard overhead cost of a product is found by multiplying the overhead rate by an appropriate measure of activity. This is always a standard measure, *not* an actual measure. Thus, if the overhead rate is $0.735 per labor hour, the overhead cost is found by multiplying $0.735 by the number of standard direct labor hours. (Note that if the measure of activity is standard direct labor hours, as is common, there can be a single rate, combining labor and overhead, per standard direct labor hour.)

Adjustments in standards

Standards usually change over time. Material prices and labor rates are likely to increase, and in many situations the quantity of raw material and labor per unit of product is reduced as better manufacturing methods are discovered. These changes require revisions in standard costs. As a general rule, standard costs are not adjusted more often than once a year unless some highly significant event occurs. Usually, the adjustment does not require a thorough reexamination of all elements in the standard. In some situations, the adjustment involves simply making an across-the-board increase in each standard cost element, say an increase of 6 percent to reflect overall price increases. This method, although only approximate, may be sufficiently accurate for the purposes for which the standards are used.

MECHANICS OF A STANDARD COST SYSTEM

Exhibit 13–4 is a flowchart for a standard cost system. The company depicted is the same pen company described in Chapter 3, and the flowchart is the same as that in Exhibit 3–3, with the addition of variance accounts to record the differences between actual costs and standard costs. The events in the accounting cycle are described below, numbered to correspond to numbers in Exhibit 13–4.

1. Purchase of raw materials. During the month, raw materials costing $52,000 were purchased on credit. In an actual cost system, this would be recorded as a debit to Raw Materials Inventory and a credit to Accounts Payable. In a standard cost system, the material is recorded in Raw Materials Inventory at its standard price, here assumed to be $54,000. The difference between actual price and standard price is recorded in a Material Price Variance account. The journal entry is:

Raw materials inventory	54,000	
Accounts payable		52,000
Material price variance		2,000

In this case, the material was purchased at a price that was lower than the standard price, so the price variance was favorable.

The preceding entry summarized all the purchase transactions for the month. Its nature is perhaps more easily understood in terms of a single purchase, which we shall assume to be $\frac{1}{100}$ of the total. Assume the purchase of 1,000 pounds of material at an actual price of $0.52 a pound, and a standard price of $0.54 a pound. The explanation of the entry is:

```
Purchase debited to Raw Materials Inventory:
   (Actual quantity @ standard price)
   (1,000 pounds @ $0.54 ............................................. $540
Amount owed to vendor, credit Accounts Payable:
   (Actual quantity @ actual price)
   (1,000 pounds @ $0.52) ............................................  520
Material price variance:
   (Actual quantity @ difference between
      actual and standard price)
   (1,000 pounds @ $0.02) ............................................ $ 20
```

EXHIBIT 13–4

A standard cost system

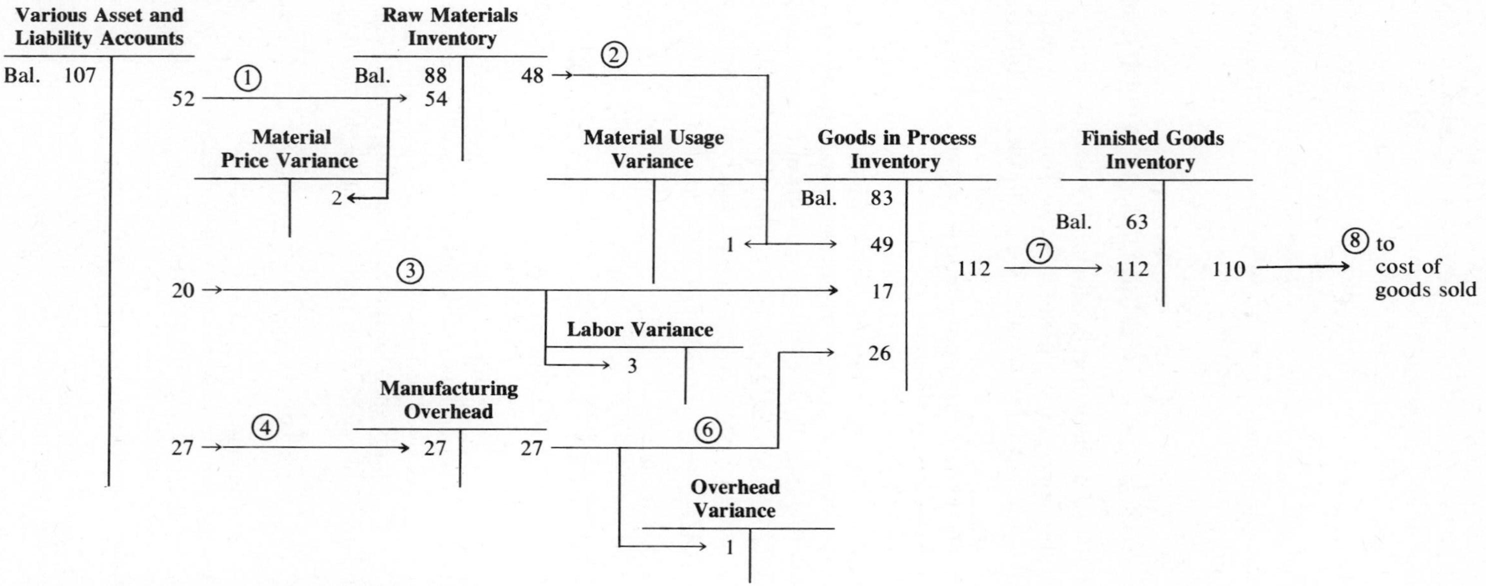

Various Asset and Liability Accounts

Bal. 107

Raw Materials Inventory

Bal. 88 | 48 →
54

Material Price Variance

52 ①
20 →
2 ↓

Material Usage Variance

②
1

Goods in Process Inventory

Bal. 83 | 112
49 →
17
26

Labor Variance

3

Manufacturing Overhead

27 → | 27
27

Overhead Variance

1

Finished Goods Inventory

Bal. 63 | 110
112 →
⑦

⑥

③

④

⑧ to cost of goods sold

Note: Circled numbers refer to events described in the text.

The variance is favorable because the price actually paid was $0.02 per pound less than the standard price.

2. Use of direct material.   During the month raw material totaling $48,000, at standard prices, was actually used in making pens. The standard raw material cost of the pens worked on was $49,000, and Goods in Process Inventory was debited for this amount. There was a difference between actual and standard raw material cost of $1,000. Since the raw material was carried in Raw Materials Inventory at standard prices, this difference represents a difference between the quantity actually used and the standard quantity included in the standard cost of the pens. It is therefore entered in a Material Usage Variance account:

Goods in process inventory	49,000	
Raw materials inventory		48,000
Material usage variance		1,000

The credit entry indicates that less material was used than the amount included in the standard material cost; it is favorable.

As was done for the preceding entry, an example of a single transaction involving the issue of one item of material to production is given. Assume that the standard cost of this item was $0.54 per pound, that the pens manufactured in the month required a standard quantity of 91 pounds of this material, but that actual usage was only 89 pounds. The explanation of the entry is:

Cost charged to Goods in Process Inventory:	
(Standard quantity @ standard price)	
(91 pounds @ $0.54)	$49.14
Amount withdrawn from Raw Materials Inventory:	
(Actual quantity @ standard price)	
(89 pounds @ $0.54)	48.06
Material usage variance:	
(Difference between actual and standard	
quantity @ standard price)	
(2 pounds @ $0.54)	$ 1.08

The variance was favorable because the quantity actually used was two pounds less than the standard quantity.

3. Use of direct labor.   During the month the actual cost of the direct labor used in the factory was $20,000, and this was a credit to Wages Payable. (Related accounts for taxes and fringe benefits are omitted in the interests of simplicity.) The standard direct labor cost of the pens worked on, however, was only $17,000; and Goods in Process Inventory was debited for this amount. The difference between actual and standard direct labor is in a Labor Variance account:

Goods in process inventory	17,000	
Labor variance	3,000	
Wages payable		20,000

The entry to Labor Variance is a debit, indicating that the variance was unfavorable; that is, actual direct labor costs were higher than standard direct labor costs.

In the case of direct material, the system showed the price variance separately from the usage variance. The entry for direct labor does not provide a corresponding separation. The labor variance could be caused by a difference between actual and standard labor rates, between actual and standard labor usage, or any combination of rates and usage. A method of separating the labor variance into its rate and usage components is described in Chapter 14.

4. Incurrence of overhead costs.   During the month, $27,000 of manufacturing overhead costs were incurred. These were debited to the Manufacturing Overhead account, with offsetting credits to Cash, Accounts Payable, Accumulated Depreciation, and various other asset and liability accounts:

Manufacturing overhead...   27,000
    (Various asset and liability accounts).......   27,000

5. Payment of employees.   Employees were paid $32,000 cash. The offsetting debit was to Wages Payable. (This transaction is not shown on Exhibit 13–4 because it involves only asset and liability accounts that are not diagrammed separately.)

6. Absorption of overhead.   Manufacturing overhead costs were applied to pens by means of standard overhead rates. The total amount of $26,000 was debited to Goods in Process Inventory. Since actual overhead costs were $27,000 (see Entry No. 4), underabsorbed overhead costs amounted to $1,000. This $1,000 is debited to the Overhead Variance account:

Goods in process inventory   26,000
Overhead variance   1,000
    Manufacturing overhead..   27,000

The variance is a debit, or unfavorable, variance. If manufacturing overhead had been overabsorbed, the entry to the variance account would have been a credit.

7. Goods completed.   During the month, pens with a standard cost of $112,000 were completed and transferred to the finished goods warehouse. Since in both the debit and credit parts of this entry the pens are valued at their standard cost, no variance account develops:

Finished goods inventory   112,000
    Goods in process inventory   112,000

8. Goods sold.   During the month, pens with a standard cost of $110,-000 were sold and shipped to customers. Again, both the debit and the credit parts of this entry are at standard cost, so no variance develops:

Cost of goods sold   110,000
    Finished goods inventory   110,000

In summary, the only mechanical difference between the accounts in a standard cost system and those in an actual cost system is that the former has variance accounts. Variance accounts are necessarily introduced whenever one part of a transaction is at standard cost and the other part is at actual cost. In the system described above, this happens when costs are debited to an inventory account; that is, debits to inventory are always at standard cost, and if the other part of the transaction involves an actual cost, there is a variance.

Disposition of variances

At the end of an accounting period, the amounts reported in the inventory accounts are at standard cost, which may be different from actual costs, and the amount shown as Cost of Goods Sold is also at standard cost. Since the inventory amounts shown on the balance sheet and the cost of goods sold item on the income statement are supposed to be at actual cost, the standard cost amounts should be adjusted to an actual cost basis.

This can be done by assigning the balances in the variance accounts to the appropriate inventory and cost of goods sold accounts. The raw material price variance can be divided among raw material inventory, goods in process inventory, finished goods inventory, and cost of goods sold in approximate proportion to the quantities of raw material in these accounts. The other variances can be divided among goods in process inventory, finished goods inventory, and cost of goods sold on a similar basis (these other variances do not affect raw materials inventory). In order to make these adjustments, only approximate proportions are used. If an attempt were made to trace each variance to the appropriate item in inventory, the work would be tremendous. This work is avoided by relying on the concept of materiality; that is, it is assumed that a good enough adjustment can be made on the basis of approximate proportions.

Some companies do not spread the variances in the manner described above. Instead, they charge or credit all variances to the income statement. They do this either in the interests of simplicity, or on the grounds that the differences between actual cost and standard cost really reflect operating conditions during the period and therefore are period costs. The Internal Revenue Service does *not* permit this practice for income tax purposes.

Variations in the standard cost idea

In the system discussed above, standard costs were introduced in the accounts when raw material entered inventory and when material, labor, and overhead were debited to Goods in Process Inventory. This is common practice, but standards can also be introduced at other points.

Instead of debiting Raw Materials Inventory at standard unit prices, some companies carry raw material at actual cost and make the conversion to standard cost when the raw material is issued for use in the production process. In such a system, there would be no material price variance, and the material variance account would incorporate both the price and the usage components of the variance. This variance can be decomposed into its price and usage components, however, by a technique to be described in Chapter 14.

Some companies do not use a *complete* standard cost system, that is, a system that treats all elements of cost on a standard basis. They may, for example, use standard direct labor costs, but actual direct material costs; or they may do the reverse. The choice depends on the advantages that are obtainable in the particular situation.

Regardless of these variations, the essential points are: **(1) in a standard cost system, some or all of the elements of cost are recorded at standard rather than at actual; and (2) at whatever point a shift from actual to standard is made, a variance account is generated.**

USES OF STANDARD COSTS

Standard costs may be used for any or all of these purposes: (1) as a basis for controlling performance, (2) to provide cost information that is useful for certain types of decisions, (3) to provide a more rational measurement of inventory amounts and of cost of goods sold, and (4) to reduce the cost of recordkeeping.

Use in control. A good starting point in the control of a manager's performance is to compare what the manager actually did with what he should have done. Standard costs provide a basis for such comparisons.

> *EXAMPLE:* The fact that the actual direct material cost of all the shoes manufactured in a month was $251,000 is not, by itself, useful. The number cannot be compared with the costs in a prior month, because the number and types of shoes manufactured were probably different. By contrast, if the manager knows that the standard direct material cost of these shoes was $230,000, there is a signal that direct material costs were $21,000 higher than they should have been.

As already indicated, differences between actual costs and standard costs are debited or credited to variance accounts. Favorable variances are an indication that performance was better than expected, and unfavorable variances are an indication that performance was worse than expected. These variance accounts are therefore an important aid in analyzing and controlling costs. Their use for this purpose will be discussed in Chapter 14.

Use in decision making. Standard costs are often used as a basis for arriving at normal selling prices, especially when each job is different from other jobs such as when jobs are done according to individual customers' specifications. This is the *time-and-material* method of pricing described in Chapter 5.

> *EXAMPLE:* A contractor who specializes in painting exteriors of houses estimates that a painter using a brush should be able to paint 60 square feet of surface per hour, and that his earnings (including fringe benefits) should be $6 per hour. He estimates that a crew (consisting of a painter and a helper) using a spray gun should be able to paint 450 square feet of surface per hour, and that the earnings of the two-person crew should be $11 per hour. He estimates his overhead costs to be $2 per direct labor hour, and decides that a satisfactory profit is 10 percent of costs. He calculates hourly rates as follows:

		Brush	Spray
1.	Standard direct labor cost per hour	$6.00	$11.00
2.	Standard overhead cost per hour ($2 per person)	2.00	4.00
3.	Total standard cost per hour	8.00	15.00
4.	Standard profit per hour (10%)	0.80	1.50
5.	Standard selling price per hour	8.80	16.50
6.	Standard square feet per hour	60	450
7.	Standard price per square foot (5 ÷ 6)	$0.147	$ 0.037

> To find the price of painting a given house, the contractor estimates the number of square feet of surface that will be painted with a brush and the number of square feet that will be painted with a spray gun, and applies the above standard unit prices, viz:

		Brush	Spray
1.	No. of square feet of surface	1,000	10,000
2.	Standard unit price (from above)	$0.147	$0.037
3.	Total price (1 × 2)	$147	$370

> The total standard price of the job (excluding paint) is therefore $147 + $370 = $517. To this he adds the price of the paint.
>
> If he gets the job at that price, he can compare actual cost with the standards used above, and this comparison provides him with a way of detecting the cause of differences between his actual profit and his expected profit.

In alternative choice decisions, of the type discussed in Chapters 7–9, standard costs are often the best available approximation of the differential costs that are relevant in making such decisions.

More rational costs. A third advantage of a standard cost system is that it eliminates what otherwise might be an undesirable quirk in the accounting system. A standard cost system records the same costs for physically identical units of products, whereas an actual cost system may record different costs for physically identical units of products. In the example of Style 107 shoes given earlier (page 541) the actual direct material cost of each lot was different. The shoes themselves, however, are physically the same. Realistically, there is no good reason for carrying one pair of Style 107 shoes in inventory at one amount and another pair of Style 107 at a different amount, or in charging cost of goods sold at different amounts. There is no physical difference in the two pairs of shoes that warrants the conclusion that one pair "cost" more than the other. In a standard cost system, all shoes of the same style would be carried in inventory and charged as cost of goods sold at the same unit cost.

Saving in recordkeeping. Because of the addition of standard costs to the system, it might appear that a standard cost accounting system requires more recordkeeping than an actual cost accounting system. In reality, when standard costs are used instead of actual costs, there may well be a *reduction* in the amount of effort required to operate the system. Consider the example of the shoe factory given above. In an actual cost system, a record must be maintained of the dollar amount of direct material used on each lot of shoes (in the example, each lot of Style 107). Requisitions of material from raw materials inventory must identify that the material is to be used for a particular lot of Style 107; the cost of each item of direct material on the requisition must be calculated, and this amount must be entered on the job cost sheet. Similarly, the direct workers must keep track of the time that they spent on each lot of shoes, each of these time records must be priced, and the total direct labor cost must be accumulated and entered on the job cost sheet for each lot.

Much of this work is eliminated in a standard cost system. All the individual material requisitions for a month can be totaled and posted as a single credit to Raw Materials Inventory. Instead of making separate entries for direct material cost on each job cost sheet, one amount, the standard unit material cost, is all that is needed. Neither is there any need for direct workers to keep track of the time they spend on individual lots. One amount, the predetermined standard direct labor cost, is all that is needed.

There is furthermore a considerable reduction in the amount of recordkeeping required for finished goods inventory and cost of goods sold. Since all pairs of Style 107 shoes have the same cost (except when the standard is changed), the complications involved in keeping track of costs according to a Lifo, Fifo, or average cost assumption disappear.

One part of a standard cost system, that of determining the individual standards, does involve additional effort. The determination of standard unit costs is done only occasionally, however. Once a standard has been determined, it is used for months, or even years, without change.

In general, there is a saving in recordkeeping costs if the occasional task of determining the standard cost is more than offset by the reduction in detailed recording that occurs each time a job is costed. If the standard cost is not used several times, there is no saving.

EXAMPLE: An automobile company may manufacture several hundred thousand units of a given model in a year. A cost must be attached to each unit, and that cost must be carried through the accounts, from Goods in Process Inventory, through Finished Goods Inventory to Cost of Goods Sold, as the automobile moves from the factory, to the storage lot, and then to the dealer. The job of accumulating the actual direct material and direct labor cost for each of these automobiles would be stupendous. It is a relatively easy matter, however, to have a standard unit cost for the basic model, and for each of the items of optional equipment that may be added to it, and to use this cost in accounting for the automobiles as they move through the inventory accounts to cost of goods sold.

A small builder of custom houses, however, would not use a standard cost system (at least not in order to save on recordkeeping). Each house is sufficiently different so that the cost of developing the standard would exceed the saving in recordkeeping. A builder of mass-produced standard houses might or might not use a standard cost system in order to save on recordkeeping costs; the choice would depend on whether a sufficient number of similar houses would be built to warrant the effort of developing standards.

DEMONSTRATION CASE

As an illustration of some of the procedural details of a standard cost system, the system of the Black Meter Company (which is the disguised name for an actual company) is described below.

Description of company

Black Meter Company manufactures water meters in one standard design but in a wide range of sizes. The water meters installed in the basements of houses are an example of its product. The meters consist basically of a hard rubber piston that is put in motion by the flow of water past it, a gear train that reduces this motion and registers it on a dial, and two heavy bronze castings which are bolted together around the measuring device.

The company has several production departments. The castings and many interior parts of meters are cast in the foundry and then are sent to one of the three machining departments, depending upon their size. Some of the mechanical parts are sent to a subassembly department where they are assembled into gear trains. Other parts go directly to the meter assembly department. There are also several departments that provide service to the production departments.

Overview of system

Since the company ships meters to customers as soon as they are completed, it does not have a Finished Goods Inventory account. It does have Raw Materials Inventory and Goods in Process Inventory accounts. It uses a standard cost system. Standard costs are established for each element of direct labor, direct material, and manufacturing overhead.

During the month, actual costs are accumulated: material is purchased, the earnings of workers are recorded, and manufacturing overhead items, such as water or electricity, are purchased and paid for at actual cost. Elements of cost are debited to inventory at predetermined *standard* costs. At the end of a month variances between actual and standard are examined. These variances assist management control of costs because they focus attention on the exceptional situations and avoid the necessity for studying the bulk of the cost data.

Establishing standard costs

A standard unit cost is established by Black Meter Company for every type of material that is purchased. This is done annually by adjusting the current market price for any changes that are expected for the following year. For example, if a certain grade of phosphor bronze currently costs $1.65 a pound, and no change is predicted, the standard unit cost for that material will be $1.65 a pound.

Standard hourly rates for direct labor and manufacturing overhead are also determined annually. These rates are used to assign costs to products according to the number of standard direct labor hours incurred in the manufacture of each product. This is done on a departmental basis. For each production department, the accountants start with data on the actual direct labor payroll, including fringe benefits, and the number of direct labor hours worked in each of the past few years. The departmental supervisor gives an opinion as to adjustments that should be made to take account of future conditions. An amount for total labor cost and an amount for hours worked under normal conditions of activity is thus derived. By dividing the payroll amount by the normal number of hours, a standard direct labor rate per standard direct labor hour for each department is found.

Overhead costs for a production department include both the overhead costs incurred in that department plus an allocated portion of the costs of service departments. Estimates are made of these amounts for each production department under normal conditions. These estimated total overhead costs are divided by the standard number of direct labor hours for each producing department, the same amount that had been used in calculating the labor rate, to arrive at a manufacturing overhead rate per standard direct labor hour. Rates used in this example are given in Exhibit 13-5.

EXHIBIT 13-5
Standard labor and overhead rates

Department number	Department name	Rate per hour		
		Labor	Overhead	Total rate
120A	Foundry--molding	$6.75	$8.67	$ 15.42
102B	Foundry--grinding and snagging	5.25	4.35	9.60
122	Small parts manufacture	5.58	5.07	10.65
123	Interior parts manufacture	5.52	5.60	11.12
130	Train, register, and interior assembly	5.55	5.96	11.51
131	Small meter assembly	5.25	6.02	11.27

STANDARD LABOR AND OVERHEAD RATES

Developing standard product costs

These standard hourly rates (which include both direct labor and overhead) are used to develop a standard cost for each type of meter. Exhibits 13-6 through 13-9 show the development of the standard cost of a $\frac{5}{8}$-inch HF meter.

Exhibit 13-6 shows the calculation for a $\frac{5}{8}$-inch chamber ring which

EXHIBIT 13-6
Foundry standard costs

FOUNDRY

		Material Cost	$150.15
Drawing No. D-2408	Part 5/8" HF Chamber Rings	Pattern Cost	14.20

Material   Phosphor Bronze #806   100 pcs.   91.0# at $1.65

Std. Man-Hrs. per 100 Pcs.	Prod. Center	Oper. No.	Operations and Tools	Machine	Std. Rate /Hr.	Total Cost	Total
1.76	120 A	1	Mold	Match Plate	15.42	27.14	
0.45	120 B	2	Grind	Wheel	9.60	4.32	
0.68	120 B	3	Snag	Bench	9.60	6.53	
							202.34

is manufactured in the foundry, and which is one component of the $5/8$-inch HF meter. As in the case with most parts, costs are calculated for a lot size of 100 units. The standard material cost is entered in the upper right-hand box. These parts are cast from bronze that has a standard cost of $1.65 a pound. Since the standard quantity of bronze required for 100 pieces is 91 pounds, the standard material cost is $1.65 × 91 = $150.15, as shown in the "Material Cost" box. The standard cost of the pattern used in the casting, $14.20, is also entered.

In order to apply the standard direct labor and manufacturing overhead rates to any part, it is necessary to have the standard direct labor hours for the operations involved in making that part. These are obtained from time studies and are entered in the first column of the foundry form. The standard time to mold 100 chamber rings is 1.76 direct labor hours; to grind them, 0.45 hours; and to snag them, 0.68 hours.

In the first column of numbers of the right-hand side of the foundry order, the combined standard direct labor and manufacturing overhead rate per standard direct labor hour for the operation is recorded. For example, Exhibit 13–6 shows the labor and overhead rate for molding in Department 120A as $15.42 per standard direct labor hour, and this

EXHIBIT 13–7
Parts department standard cost

RR–7			PARTS DEPARTMENT STANDARD COST			
Drawing No. X–2408		Part			Material Cost	
Plating H.T. & E.T.		Material 5/8″ HF Chamber Ring			$202.34	
Hours per 100 Pcs. St'd	Prod. Center	Oper. No.	Operations and Tools	Machine	Std. Rate /Hr.	Total
0.75	122	1	Broach outlet #734	P.P.	10.65	7.99
0.55	123	2	Finish tap-plate bore and face	Heald	11.12	6.12
0.93	123		Drill 6 holes	Drill	11.12	10.34
0.47	123	3	C-sink-3 holes tap-plate side	Drill	11.12	5.23
0.17	123		Tap 3 holes tap-plate side	Heskins	11.12	1.89
5.00	123	4	Rough & Finish inside & outside	Heald	11.12	55.60
0.20	123		C-sink 3 holes on bottom	Drill	11.12	2.22
0.30	123	5	Tap 3 holes on bottom	Drill	11.12	3.34
0.47	123		Spline inside	Spliner	11.12	5.23
0.50	123	6	Spline outside	Miller	11.12	5.56
5.80	123		Dress	Bench	11.12	64.50
			Total			370.36

amount appears on Exhibit 13–6 as the standard rate per hour for the molding operation. It is multiplied by the standard direct labor time of 1.76 hours to give a standard cost of labor and overhead of $27.14. The same procedure is followed for the other two foundry operations. The total standard foundry cost of 100 chamber rings is $202.34.

Exhibit 13–7 accumulates additional standard costs for these 100

EXHIBIT 13–8
Assembly department standard cost

ASSEMBLY DEPARTMENT STANDARD COST			
Drawing No. 2735		Assembly 5/8" HF ET FB	

Parts of Assembly		Cost	Parts of Assembly		Cost
X-2408	Chamber Ring	370.36	K-5030	5/8" HF Dur. Bolt (6)	125.68
K-2414	Chamber Top Plate	146.55	K-4630	5/8" HF ac Nut (6)	70.84
K-2418	Chamber Bot. Plate	140.12	K-5068	5/8" HF Washers (6)	40.23
K-2465	Disc Piston Assem.	302.70	2782	Chamber Pin	8.02
2761	Top Case	540.60	6172	Misc. Train Conn.	34.12
X-2770	Bottom Case	200.28	K-2776	Casting Gasket	26.50
3209	5/8" Closed Train	1,200.02	2779	Casting Strainer	33.04
			2412	5/8" HF Sand Plate	30.00

Rate No.	Std. Man-Hrs. per 100 Pcs.	Prod. Prod. Center	Oper. No.	Operation and Tools	Machine	Std. Rate /Hr.	Total Cost	Total
	7.5	130	1	Assem. Disc Interior	Bench	11.51	86.32	
	4.6	131	2	Assem. Train and Strainer to Case	Bench	11.27	51.84	
	5.6	131	3	Assem. Int. & Bottom to Meter	Bench	11.27	63.11	
				Total				3,470.33

chamber rings as they pass through the parts manufacture department. They enter the parts department at the standard cost of $202.34, the same cost at which they left the foundry. After the operations listed on Exhibit 13–7 have been performed on them, they become finished chamber rings. These operations have increased the standard cost to $370.36. Similar standard cost sheets are prepared for each of the other components of the $\frac{5}{8}$-inch meter.

These components and their total standard costs are listed in the upper part of Exhibit 13–8, which is the standard cost sheet for the assembly operation. Exhibit 13–8 also lists the operations involved in assembling these parts into completed meters and the standard cost of each operation. At the bottom of Exhibit 13–8 is the total standard cost of 100 completed meters, $3,470.33.

In the same manner, standard costs are calculated for all the meters that the Black Meter Company manufactures.

Accounting entries

Goods in Process Inventory is debited for the standard cost of direct material, direct labor, and manufacturing overhead. Actual costs are collected in total for the period, but no actual costs are collected for individual meters.

Material. As soon as any material is purchased, the standard cost of that material is penciled on the vendor's invoice. Each purchase is journalized in an invoice and check register. This register contains columns in which to credit the actual cost of the material to Accounts Payable, to debit an inventory account for the standard cost, and to debit or credit the difference to a purchase price variance account. When material is issued for use in production, the quantity is the standard amount (e.g., 91 pounds in the example shown in Exhibit 13–6), and the entry crediting Raw Materials Inventory and debiting Goods in Process Inventory is made at the standard cost (e.g., $150.15 in the example shown in Exhibit 13–6).

If additional material is needed, it is withdrawn from Raw Materials Inventory by means of a requisition. The total amount of such requisitions is the basis for an entry debiting Materials Usage Variance and crediting Raw Materials Inventory. An opposite entry is made for any material that is returned to inventory from the manufacturing departments, but such returns are infrequent.

A physical inventory is taken every six months and is valued at standard cost. Any difference between this amount and the balance as shown in the Inventory account is debited or credited to an Inventory Adjustment account.

Labor. The basic document for recording direct labor costs is the job timecard. Each productive employee fills out such a card for each order on which he or she works during a week. The timecard reproduced as Exhibit 13–9 shows that Harris worked all week on one order. On the timecard Harris records the quantity finished, the actual hours worked, and the standard hours. A payroll clerk enters each employee's daywork rate, the standard direct labor rate for that department, and extends the actual and standard direct labor cost of the work completed.

By totaling all the job timecards, the payroll clerk obtains the actual wages earned by each employee in each department, and also the total standard labor cost of the work done in each department. These amounts are the basis for an entry which credits accrued wages for the actual amount and debits Goods in Process Inventory account for the standard amount of direct labor. The variance is recorded in a direct labor variance account.

EXHIBIT 13–9
Sample timecard

Mach. No.	Prod. Center	Quantity Ordered	Order Number	
	130	*3,000*	*2I-86572*	**Clock No.** *337*
	Part Name			
	5/8" Cl. Trains			
Prev. Quan. Fin.	Oper. No.	Operation Name		
O	*9*	*Finish Assem.*		
Quan. Finished	Std. Hours Per 100	Std. Hours	Std. Rate	Standard Labor
2,300	*1.75*	*40.25*	*5.55*	*223.39*
Quan. Finished			TIME CARD	
2,300				**Name** *B. HARRIS*
	Stop	Actual Hours	D.W. Rate	Earnings
Sept. 20	*40.0*	*40.0*	*5.55*	*220.00*
	Start	*RHL.*		Gain or Loss
Sept. 16	*00.0*	Foreman		*3.39*

Manufacturing overhead. For each department, a cost clerk multiplies the standard direct labor hours worked by the manufacturing overhead rate for that department (as obtained from Exhibit 13–5); this gives the amount of standard manufacturing overhead cost for the department for that month. This amount is debited to Goods in Process Inventory. During the month actual manufacturing overhead expenses have been accumulated in the invoice and check register and in various adjusting entries. The difference between the sum of the actual overhead costs and the standard manufacturing overhead cost is the manufacturing overhead variance, which is debited or credited to the overhead variance accounts.

When these transactions have been recorded, all material, direct labor, and manufacturing overhead have been charged into the Goods in Process Inventory account at standard cost, and three variance accounts have been debited or credited for the difference between actual and standard.

Sales and cost of goods sold

A duplicate copy of each sales invoice is sent to the office where a clerk enters in pencil the standard cost of the items sold (see Exhibit 13–10). At the end of the month the cost clerk totals the figures on these duplicate invoices to get amounts for sales revenue and for the standard cost of those sales. The standard cost is a credit to the Inventory account and a debit to the Cost of Goods Sold account. The total sales amount is a credit to Sales and a debit to Accounts Receivable. When this work is completed, the accounting department is in a position to obtain the monthly income statement (see Exhibit 13–11). Note, incidentally, that

EXHIBIT 13–10
Carbon copy of sales invoice

```
Village of Vernon,
Attn: Village Clerk,
Vernon, N.Y.




Village of Vernon, Water Dept.,
Attn: E.J. Blackburn, Mayor
Vernon, N.Y.




              Prepaid

10    5/8" x 3/4" Model HF Meters SG SH ET FB & 3/4"        495.75


 1    Change Gear #46X -- shipped 8-10                 3.75    499.50
```

Meter Parts

347.03
2.60

```
                    Ship gear by Parcel Post
```

EXHIBIT 13–11
Monthly income statement

BLACK METER COMPANY
Income Statement for June

Net sales..		$1,198,234
Less: Cost of goods sold at standard cost................	$831,868	
Variances (detailed below)...	5,357	826,511
Gross manufacturing margin.......................................		371,723
Selling expense..	92,107	
General and administrative expense	177,362	269,469
Income before income taxes......................................		102,254
Income taxes...		49,320
Net Income		$ 52,934

Variances

	Debit	Credit
Favorable variances:		
Material price..		$ 62,608
Unfavorable variances:		
Material usage..	$ 22,457	
Direct labor..	16,234	
Overhead...	18,560	57,251
Net Variance		$ 5,357

although the net amount of the variance on this income statement is relatively small, there are sizable detailed variances that tend to offset one another. Management investigates these variances and takes action when warranted.

SUMMARY

A standard cost is a measure of what an item of cost should be, as contrasted with a record of what it actually was. Standard direct material costs per unit of product are determined by multiplying the quantity that should be used per unit by the standard price per unit of quantity. Similarly, standard direct labor costs per unit are determined by multiplying the standard number of hours (or minutes) of direct labor by a standard labor rate per hour or per minute. Standard overhead rates are determined by dividing the expected manufacturing overhead costs at normal volume by the number of units, or other measure of activity.

In a standard cost system, raw material purchased is ordinarily debited to Raw Materials Inventory at its standard unit price, and products in Goods in Process and Finished Goods Inventory are ordinarily carried at their standard costs. Variance accounts are necessary whenever one part of an accounting entry is at actual cost and the other part is at standard cost.

Standard costs may be useful for any or all of the following purposes: (1) the variance between standard cost and actual cost is an indication that actual cost performance was different than expected, and this is a starting point in the control process; (2) standard costs are used in estimating future costs, as a basis for arriving at selling prices, and are used also in certain alternative choice analyses; (3) since physically similar products have the same standard cost, standard costs provide a more rational basis for valuing inventory amounts than do actual costs; and (4) a standard cost system may involve less recordkeeping than an actual cost system.

IMPORTANT TERMS

Standard cost   **Bill of materials**
Variance   **Material price variance**
Unfavorable variance   **Material usage variance**
Favorable variance

QUESTIONS FOR DISCUSSION

1. What is the difference between an actual cost system and a standard cost system?
2. To what extent does an actual cost system not measure true actual costs?

3. A credit variance is a favorable variance. In general, do credits to accounts represent "favorable" events?

4. What is the meaning of a debit to a variance account? A credit?

5. "In setting a cost standard, it is usually desirable to maintain the separate identity of the quantity and the unit price." Why?

6. What is the difference between an ideal standard and a normal standard? Which is generally preferable, and why?

7. If raw material is credited out of Raw Materials Inventory at actual cost and debited to Goods in Process Inventory at standard cost, the difference is debited or credited to a materials variance account. What is the difference between such an account and a materials *usage* variance account?

8. Describe three ways in which the standard labor cost of an operation can be determined.

9. What are the similarities and differences between the treatment of overhead costs in a standard cost system and an actual cost system?

10. In Exhibit 13–3, the standard material handling cost per direct labor hour was stated to be $0.735. Explain, step by step, how this number was calculated. How would this number be used in the standard cost system?

11. Describe in your own words the meaning of each numbered line in Exhibit 13–4, being sure to identify whether the amounts are at actual or at standard.

12. Why should variances theoretically be disposed of by adjusting inventory and cost of goods sold? Why are such adjustments sometimes not made in practice?

13. Suppose that all costs were debited to Goods in Process Inventory at actual, and the transfer to Finished Goods Inventory were made at standard cost. How would the flowchart for such a system differ from that in Exhibit 13–4?

14. What are the advantages and disadvantages of a standard cost system as compared with an actual cost system?

15. A furniture company using an actual job cost accounting system has separate job cost records for each of two dining room tables. The recorded costs of each table are identical except in one respect: namely, the direct labor cost of assembly and finishing was $32 for one table and $36 for the other. This operation required eight hours for each table, but for one table it was performed by an employee who earned $4 per hour, while for the other it was performed by an employee who, because of seniority, earned $4.50 per hour. Did the cost of the two tables differ? Should they be sold at different prices?

16. Explain how a standard cost accounting system can reduce recordkeeping costs. Give some examples of companies in which such a system would be *more* expensive than an actual cost system.

17. Trace through the procedure described for the Black Meter Company. Can you show how the numbers on each exhibit are derived from, or help derive, the numbers on other exhibits? Can you relate each of the forms to the flowchart?

18. Imagine what an actual cost system for Black Meter Company would look like. Would it require less recordkeeping effort? Would it provide useful information to management that the standard cost accounting system does not provide?

19. In what respects, if at all, do the cost flows in the Black Meter Company differ from those depicted in Exhibit 13-4?

PROBLEMS

13-1. The production of a unit of Product 823 requires the use of direct material as follows:

	Material A	Material B
Quantity required	6 pounds	2 pounds
Allowance for waste............................	5%	10%
Delivered price per pound	$2	$3
Handling and inspection costs..............	6%	6%

Required:

Calculate the standard direct material cost per unit of Product 823.

13-2. The production of a unit of Product 823 requires one direct labor hour in Cost Center A and two direct labor hours in Cost Center B. Data on the cost centers are as follows:

	A	B
Number of direct employees.........................	30	40
Weekly productive hours per employee	35	35
Estimated weekly wages per employee...........	$220	$260
Fringe benefits...	25%	25%

Required:

Calculate the standard direct labor cost per unit of Product 823.

13-3. The Helton Company applies overhead using a rate based on standard direct labor hours. An analysis of monthly overhead costs for last year provides the following information:

	Overhead costs	Standard direct labor hours
Highest month	$9,800	2,400
Lowest month....................	8,600	1,800

For the current year, overhead costs are expected to increase 5 percent and normal volume is expected to be 2,100 standard direct labor hours per month.

Required:

A. Calculate the standard overhead application rate for the current year.

B. What would be the standard overhead cost for a product which requires three direct labor hours per unit?

C. Company engineers estimate that production at maximum efficiency would involve 2,500 standard direct labor hours per month. Assuming that the company decides to use ideal standards instead of normal, recalculate your answers to parts A and B.

D. If Helton used ideal standards while producing at normal volume, how would you expect this to affect the overhead variance? Why?

13–4. Following are standard and actual unit costs of Product Z-3 taken from the books of Alkid Company for the month of May.

	Standard unit costs	Actual unit costs
Raw materials......................	10 pounds @ $0.25	11 pounds @ $0.26
Direct labor........................	4 hours @ $5.50	4 hours @ $5.55
Factory overhead.................	4 hours @ $3.00	4 hours @ $2.95
Units produced....................		70,000
Units sold		68,000

Required:

A. Compute the total actual and standard costs and the variances for each of the three elements of production cost for the 70,000 units produced.

B. Give an analysis of the elements of cost comprising the finished goods ending inventory at standard cost. There were no beginning inventories and no ending inventory of goods in process.

C. Compute the amount of the finished goods ending inventory at actual cost.

13–5. The Crowley Company makes a single product whose standard costs per unit are as follows:

Direct materials – 10 pounds @ $0.70..........................	$ 7.00
Direct labor – 3 hours @ $6.......................................	18.00
Overhead – $2.50 per direct labor hour.......................	7.50
Total standard cost per unit.............................	$32.50

Production data for the month of May were:

Units produced	5,000
Direct materials purchased – 55,000 pounds @ $0.68.........	$37,400
Direct materials used...	52,000 pounds
Actual direct labor – 15,500 hours @ $6.10	$94,555
Actual overhead costs...	$36,250
Standard direct labor hours allowed..............................	15,000 hours

Required:

Assuming that all inventories are carried at standard cost, calculate the following variances: material price, material usage, labor, and overhead. For each variance, indicate whether it is favorable or unfavorable.

13–6. The Page Company makes Product 827 whose standard costs per unit are as follows:

Direct materials—3 pounds @ $2................................ $ 6
Direct labor—2.5 hours @ $6 15
Overhead—$4 per direct labor hour.......................... 10
Total standard cost per unit........................... $31

The following pertains to the production of Product 827 during the month of March:

Production.. 1,000 units
Raw materials purchased...................................... 3,500 pounds
Material price variance .... $350 Dr.
Material usage variance... 600 Cr.
Labor variance .... 750 Dr.
Overhead variance .... 300 Cr.

Required:

For the month of March, calculate:

A. Price per pound paid for raw materials purchased.
B. Pounds of raw materials used.
C. Actual cost of direct labor.
D. Actual cost of overhead.

13–7. The standard costs for one unit of product KLM are determined to be as follows:

Direct materials—3 units @ $5 .... $15
Direct labor—2 hours @ $7...................................... 14
Overhead—$4 per standard direct labor hour............. 8
Total standard cost per unit........................... $37

Operating results for March:

Purchases of raw materials $88,500
Actual cost of raw materials used 90,300
Standard cost of raw materials used 90,000
Actual direct labor cost...................................... 80,970
Actual overhead cost... 52,300
Standard direct labor hours 12,000
Units completed in March 6,000
Units sold in March 5,000
Inventories: Goods in process, March 1 and
  31, zero:
  Raw materials, March 1, 4,500 units @ $5
  Finished goods, March 1, 800 units @ $37

Required:

A. Prepare a flowchart for March operations assuming that all debits to inventory accounts are at standard cost.
B. Prepare journal entries for the March transactions.

13–8. The Mullis Company makes a single product whose standard costs per unit are as follows:

Direct materials—5 pounds @ $2............................. $10
Direct labor—2 hours @ $7...................................... 14
Overhead—$3 per direct labor hour......................... 6
Total standard cost per unit........................... $30

During the month of July, the following events occurred:

Production started and completed .... 6,000 units
Sales.. 5,000 units
Raw material purchases on credit—35,000 pounds
    @ $2.10.. $73,500
Raw material used in production..................................... 29,500 pounds
Actual direct labor—12,400 hours @ $7.10 .... $88,040
Standard direct labor hours allowed............................... 12,000 hours
Actual overhead costs incurred...................................... $36,850

There were no beginning inventories on July 1, and all inventories are carried at standard cost.

Required:

A.   Prepare a flowchart depicting the flow of costs through the inventory accounts during the month.

B.   Prepare journal entries for the flow of costs.

13–9. An income statement of Mono Company, which used an actual cost system, was as follows:

Sales revenue $250,000
Cost of goods sold 158,000
Gross margin 92,000
Operating expenses.. 45,000
Operating Income... $ 47,000

Suppose that instead of using an actual cost system the company had used a standard cost system and that in the same period variances were:

Raw materials usage variance........................ $3,800 Dr.
Direct labor variance .... 3,600 Dr.
Overhead variance .... 7,500 Cr.

There were no balances in either Goods in Process Inventory or Finished Goods Inventory. Variance accounts were not closed.

Required:

Calculate what the operating income would have been if a standard cost system had been used.

13–10. At the end of the first year of operations of the Standard Company, its records reflected the following cost flows:

Accounts Payable		Material Price Variance		Raw Materials Inventory	
xxx	20,000	100		19,900	12,000

Factory Payroll Payable		Direct Labor Variance		Goods in Process Inventory	
xxx	31,000		1,000	12,000	65,000
				32,000	
				32,600	

Miscellaneous Accounts				Finished Goods Inventory	
xxx	33,000			65,000	47,000

Factory Overhead		Overhead Variance		Cost of Goods Sold	
33,000	32,600	400		47,000	
	400				

Required:

A. Journalize the entries necessary to record the results of operations for the year.

B. Compute the actual cost of goods sold assuming that all variances are assigned to cost of goods sold.

13–11. The following information relates to the operations of the Forest Woodworking Corporation for the month of April.

Materials purchased	$ 9,800
Materials used	9,000
Labor	15,000
Heat, light, and power (direct costs)	1,128
Supplies used	500
General factory overhead	1,200
Machine shop (direct costs)	800
Inventories, April 1:	
Process I	0
Process II	0
Process III	0
Finished goods	1,500

All materials enter Process I at actual cost, and production flows from Process I, to II, to III. All supplies were used by the machine shop. Labor is used by all three processes equally. General factory overhead costs are allocated on the same basis as labor. Utility costs are allocated 20 percent to the machine shop, 60 percent to Process I, and 10 percent each to Processes II and III. The machine shop services only Processes I and II with 75 percent of the work being done for Process I. Six thousand units of product were started and finished during April. There were no units left unfinished at the end of the month, and 5,800 units with a standard cost of $4.50 per unit were sold.

Required:

A. Complete postings (on a separate sheet of paper) to the following T-accounts to show the accumulation of costs for the standard process cost system described above, and assuming the use of one manufacturing variance account where variances are isolated when goods are transferred to finished goods inventory.

B. Compute the actual cost per unit manufactured in April.

Selected T-accounts

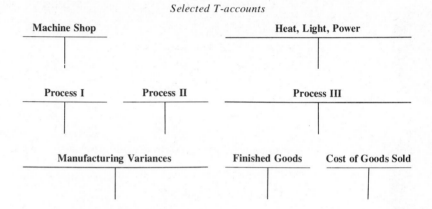

13–12. The production of a unit of Product 871 requires the use of direct materials as follows:

	Material X	Material Y
Quantity required	4 pounds	3 pounds
Allowance for waste	10%	5%
Delivered price per pound	$3.50	$4
Handling and inspection costs	6%	6%

Required:

Calculate the standard direct material cost per unit of Product 871.

13–13. The production of a unit of Product 871 requires two direct labor hours in Cost Center C and three direct labor hours in Cost Center D. Data on the cost centers are as follows:

	C	D
Number of direct employees	40	20
Weekly productive hours per employee	35	35
Estimated weekly wages per employee	$210	$230
Fringe benefits	25%	25%

Required:

Calculate the standard direct labor cost per unit of Product 871.

13–14. The Newman Company applies overhead using a rate based on standard direct labor hours. An analysis of monthly overhead costs for last year provides the following information:

	Overhead costs	Standard direct labor hours
Highest month	$16,000	4,000
Lowest month	13,000	3,000

For the current year, overhead costs are expected to increase 5 percent, and normal volume is expected to be 3,600 standard direct labor hours per month.

Required:

A. Calculate the standard overhead application rate for the current year.
B. What would be the standard overhead cost for a product which requires four direct labor hours per unit?
C. Company engineers estimate that production at maximum efficiency would involve 4,200 standard direct labor hours per month. Assuming that the company decides to use ideal standards instead of normal, recalculate your answers to parts A and B.
D. If Newman used ideal standards while producing at normal volume, how would you expect this to affect the overhead variance? Why?

13–15. Perry Gadget Company has been manufacturing a product, L400, for a number of years. Based on past experience the cost of L400 under normal operating conditions should be as follows:

Standard cost of one unit of L400

Direct materials—4 pounds @ $2	$ 8
Direct labor—1 hour @ $6	6
Overhead—@ 50% of direct labor cost	3
Total standard cost per unit	$17

The overhead rate is based on the assumption of a normal 20,000 hours of work per month.

Actual results for June production of L400 were as follows:

Units produced	10,000
Material used	40,500 pounds
Direct labor hours	10,000
Direct material cost, per pound	$2.10
Direct labor cost, per hour	$5.60
Actual overhead cost	$31,500
Sales, at $25 per unit	8,000 units

Required:

A. Compute the total actual and standard costs and the variances for each of the three elements of production cost for the 10,000 units produced.

B. Give an analysis of the elements of cost comprising the finished goods ending inventory at standard cost. There were no beginning inventories and no ending inventory of goods in process.

C. Compute the amount of the finished goods ending inventory at actual cost.

13–16. The Pack Company makes a single product whose standard costs per unit are as follows:

Direct materials – 12 pounds @ $0.65	$ 7.80
Direct labor – 2 hours @ $6.10	12.20
Overhead – $3 per direct labor hour	6.00
Total standard cost per unit	$26.00

Production data for the month of June were:

Units produced	10,000
Direct materials purchased – 130,000 @ $0.70	$ 91,000
Direct materials used	119,000 pounds
Actual direct labor – 20,500 hours @ $6	$123,000
Actual overhead costs	$ 58,750
Standard direct labor hours allowed	20,000 hours

Required:

Assuming that all inventories are carried at standard cost, calculate the following variances: material price, material usage, labor, and overhead. For each variance, indicate whether it is favorable or unfavorable.

13–17. The Edwards Company makes Product 979 whose standard costs per unit are as follows:

Direct materials – 4 pounds @ $2.50	$10
Direct labor – 3 hours @ $5	15
Overhead – $2 per direct labor hour	6
Total standard cost per unit	$31

The following pertains to the production of Product 979 during the month of October:

Production	1,000 units	
Raw materials purchased	4,500 pounds	
Material price variance	$ 900	Cr.
Material usage variance	1,500	Dr.
Labor variance	820	Dr.
Overhead variance	450	Dr.

Required:

For the month of October, calculate:

A. Price per pound for raw materials purchased.

B. Pounds of raw materials used.
C. Actual cost of direct labor.
D. Actual cost of overhead.

13–18. The standard costs for one unit of product C8J are determined to be as follows:

Direct materials—1.5 pounds @ $2 .... $ 3
Direct labor—1.0 hours @ $5 5
Manufacturing overhead $2 per direct labor hour......... 2
Total standard cost per unit $10

Results of operations for January:

Cost of raw materials purchased $9,600
Actual cost of raw materials put into production 6,200
Standard cost of raw materials used..................... 6,000
Actual direct labor cost 9,850
Actual overhead cost... 4,100
Production completed in January in units 2,000

There was no unfinished inventory at the end of
   January, and 900 units were sold.
Inventories, January 1:
   Raw materials, 1,500 pounds @ $2
   Goods in process, none
   Finished goods, 800 units @ $10

Required:

A. Prepare a flowchart for January operations assuming that all debits to inventory accounts are at standard cost.
B. Prepare journal entries for the January transactions.

13–19. The Ballard Company makes a single product whose standard costs per unit are as follows:

Direct materials—6 pounds @ $2.............................. $12
Direct labor—3 hours @ $6...................................... 18
Overhead—$4 per direct labor hour.......................... 12
Total standard cost per unit........................... $42

During the month of September, the following events occurred:

Production started and completed................................ 7,000 units
Sales... 6,000 units
Raw material purchases on credit—45,000 pounds @
   $1.90 .... $ 85,500
Raw material used in production.................................. 43,100 pounds
Actual direct labor—20,500 hours @ $5.95 .... $121,975
Standard direct labor hours allowed .... 21,000 hours
Actual overhead costs incurred .... $ 82,700

There were no beginning inventories on September 1, and all inventories are carried at standard cost.

Required:

A. Prepare a flowchart depicting the flow of costs through the inventory accounts during the month.

B. Prepare journal entries for the flow of costs.

13–20. A partial income statement for May Pex Company is as follows:

Sales revenue		$190,000
Standard cost of goods sold:		
Beginning inventory................................	$ 18,000	
Cost of goods manufactured	110,000	
Ending inventory.....................................	−16,000	112,000
Standard gross margin..............................		$ 78,000

Variances for this accounting period, which were not included in costs of goods manufactured, were:

Favorable direct labor variance of $5,000.
Favorable overhead variance of $3,900.
Unfavorable material usage variance of $3,000.

Required:

Compute the gross margin assuming actual costs were used instead of standard costs.

13–21. Data below was taken from the job cost system of Custom-Craft, Inc., as of August 31:

Job number	Actual costs		Direct labor hours
	Materials used	Direct labor	
501	$2,900	$6,000	2,000
502	3,900	4,000	1,800
503	2,200	3,000	1,300

The heating department incurred direct costs of $830, and the general maintenance department incurred $1,220 direct costs for the month. These costs of the two departments are assigned to jobs on the basis of direct labor hours per job. Actual cost for general factory overhead was $1,200, to be assigned as follows: $80 to each service department, $480 to Job No. 501, $320 to Job No. 502, and $240 to Job No. 503. During August the three jobs were started and finished, with no beginning or ending inventories of unfinished jobs. Job No. 503 was sold and shipped on August 31. The standard cost for labor is $3 per hour. Standard costs for raw materials were $3,000 for Job No. 501, $3,800 for Job No. 502, and $2,200 for Job No. 503. The standard cost for manufacturing overhead was 20 percent of standard direct labor.

Required:

A. Set up the following T-accounts and make entries to them to reflect the accumulation of costs for the standard job cost system described above, assuming all variances are isolated in one account when jobs are completed: Heating, General Maintenance, General Factory Overhead, Goods in Process, Manufacturing Variances, Finished Goods, and Cost of Goods Sold.

B. Show for each job the standard costs of material, labor, and overhead.

C. Show for each job the actual costs of material, labor, and overhead.

13–22. Prepare a flowchart for Black Meter Company, the demonstration case. Do not use dollar amounts but indicate the flows from one account to another and also indicate which amounts are at standard cost and which are at actual cost.

13–23. Suppose that the labor rate in Department 120A, Black Meter Company (Exhibit 13–5), were changed from $6.75 per hour to $7.33 per hour. (The overhead rate is not changed.) What effect would this have on the succeeding exhibits and on the total standard cost of 100 ⅝-inch HF meters?

13–24. Kodol company prepared its income statements for the current year on three alternative cost accounting systems as follows:

	A	B	C
Sales revenue	$100,000	$100,000	$100,000
Cost of goods sold	33,000	40,000	43,000
	67,000	60,000	57,000
Variances:			
Direct material	–	(2,000)	–
Direct labor	–	(1,000)	–
Factory overhead	–	(5,000)	(5,000)
Gross margin	67,000	52,000	52,000
Other operating expense	55,000	40,000	40,000
Operating Income	$ 12,000	$ 12,000	$ 12,000

Required:

Explain your answers to the following questions:

A. Match the following cost systems with alternatives A, B, and C: (1) standard cost system; (2) actual full cost system; and (3) actual direct cost system.

B. How much, if any, of the factory overhead cost was variable?

C. What was the actual factory overhead cost incurred for the year?

D. What were the nonfactory costs incurred for the year?

E. What percentage was actual factory volume for the year to normal factory volume?

F. Which of the alternative statements was *not* prepared in accordance with generally accepted accounting principles?

G. How did actual direct material cost compare with planned direct material cost?

14

Analysis of variances

In preceding chapters we discussed the preparation of plans for the conduct of future operations and the expression of these plans in the form of budgets and standard costs. In most situations, actual revenues and costs do *not* correspond to the planned revenues and costs. Management wants to know not only *what* the amount of the differences between actual and planned results were but also, and more importantly, *why* these differences occurred. Analytical techniques that are helpful in identifying the causes of the differences between actual results and planned results are discussed in this chapter. Essentially, these techniques decompose the total difference between actual and planned performance into several elements, each of which is called a variance. Having identified how much of the total difference is attributable to each type of variance, management is in a position to fix responsibility and to ask relevant questions. The answers to these questions may suggest the need for corrective action.

OVERVIEW OF THE ANALYTICAL PROCESS

We shall refer to the data with which actual performance is being compared as *budget* data because, as emphasized in Chapter 12, a care-

578

fully prepared budget is usually the best indication of what performance should be. The same techniques can be used to analyze actual performance in terms of any other basis of comparison, such as performance in some prior period, performance in some other responsibility center, or even the analyst's personal judgment as to what constitutes "good" performance. Although our principal focus is in analyzing the performance of responsibility centers in a business company, the same general approach can be used for analyzing any situation in which inputs are used to produce outputs.

In earlier chapters, we have used the term *variance* to denote the difference between actual costs and standard costs. We shall now broaden the meaning of this word to include the difference between the actual amount and the budgeted amount of *any* revenue or cost item.

An *unfavorable* variance is one whose effect is to make actual net income lower than budgeted net income. **Thus, an unfavorable revenue variance occurs when actual revenue is less than budgeted revenue, but an unfavorable cost variance occurs when actual cost is higher than budgeted cost.** Corresponding statements can of course be made about favorable variances.

In looking at the business as a whole, attention ultimately is directed to the "bottom line," that is, at the amount of the income. (We shall deal here only with *operating income,* which is the usual focus of variance analysis. We therefore exclude nonoperating items, extraordinary items, and income taxes, which are of course involved in the calculation of *net income.*) If in a certain company, budgeted operating income in April was $53,000 and actual operating income was only $49,000, the $4,000 variance indicates that something went wrong in April. It does not, however, indicate *what* went wrong. In order to take effective action, management needs to know the specific factors that caused the unfavorable variance.

Since the responsibility accounting system collects revenues and costs by responsibility centers, information from this system provides the starting point for such an analysis. Such information helps to pinpoint the responsibility centers in which the variance occurred. The system also provides data that can be used to help indicate *why* the variance occurred.

We shall divide the analysis into two parts. In the first part we shall describe the situation in which costs incurred in a month are essentially for the goods that were actually sold in that month. This happens when goods are produced to the customer's order and the production time is short, as is the case in a shop that does job printing, for example. In the second part, we shall describe the more complicated situation in which goods are produced for inventory. In this case the goods *sold* in a month are not the same physical goods as the goods that were *manufactured* in that month.

VARIANCE ANALYSIS WHEN GOODS ARE PRODUCED TO ORDER

To start with, consider the actual income statement of the Madden Company compared with the master budget amounts for April, as shown in Exhibit 14–1. This exhibit shows that the actual operating income for

EXHIBIT 14–1

MADDEN COMPANY
Master Budget and Actual Amounts
April

	Master budget	Actual	Difference*
Units produced and sold.........................	11,000	10,000	(1,000)
Sales revenue..	$440,000	$420,000	$(20,000)
Costs:			
Direct material......................................	88,000	85,000	3,000
Direct labor..	132,000	126,000	6,000
Manufacturing overhead.........................	72,000	72,000	0
Distribution and administration	95,000	88,000	7,000
Total...	387,000	371,000	16,000
Operating Income	$ 53,000	$ 49,000	$ (4,000)

*( ) = unfavorable.

April was $4,000 less than the $53,000 budgeted. The variance column indicates that revenue was $20,000 lower than expected, but that costs were $16,000 lower, so the net variance was only $4,000. How is the $4,000 to be explained?

Volume variance

We note that sales volume in April was only 10,000 units, which was 1,000 units less than the amount on the master budget. Clearly, this shortfall in sales volume had an effect on income. Can we determine what its effect was? We cannot do so from the master budget. If we recall, however, that the master budget amounts were determined from underlying relationships between revenues, costs, and volume, and that these relationships are stated in the flexible budget (as described in Chapter 12), then we can isolate the effect of the 1,000 shortfall in volume. We can do this by comparing the budgeted revenues and costs at a volume of 11,000 units, as shown in the master budget, with the revenue and costs expected at 10,000 units, as shown in the flexible budget. Recall that flexible budget amounts can be expressed as an amount per *unit* for the variable costs, and at a fixed amount per *period* for the fixed costs.

Revenues are, of course, derived from the unit selling price, a constant amount per unit.

Exhibit 14–2 gives such a comparison. It shows that at a volume of 10,000 units, revenue was expected to be $400,000, costs were expected to be $360,000, and operating income, $40,000. The $13,000 difference between this $40,000 and the $53,000 shown in the master budget arises

EXHIBIT 14–2

MADDEN COMPANY
Comparison of Master Budget and Flexible Budget
April

	Flexible budget at 10,000 units				
	Variable per unit	Fixed	Total	Master budget*	Difference†
Sales revenue............................	$40		$400,000	$440,000	$(40,000)
Costs:					
Direct material............................	8		80,000	88,000	8,000
Direct labor................................	12		120,000	132,000	12,000
Manufacturing overhead..............	2	$50,000	70,000	72,000	2,000
Distribution and administration	5	40,000	90,000	95,000	5,000
Total Costs	$27	$90,000	360,000	387,000	27,000
Operating Income......................			$ 40,000	$ 53,000	$(13,000)

* Based on budgeted volume of 11,000 units.
† ( ) = unfavorable.

because volume was 1,000 units lower than the 11,000 units given in the master budget. It is a volume variance, and it is unfavorable in that actual volume was lower than budgeted volume. Thus, **the volume variance is the difference between budgeted income at actual volume and budgeted income at planned volume.**

Exhibit 14–2 was constructed so that it matched the items in Exhibit 14–1. Actually, it is not necessary to show this amount of detail to find the volume variance. The flexible budget shows how revenues and costs vary with volume. Revenues are the selling price per unit times the number of units sold. Costs have a variable component (cost per unit times volume) and a fixed component per period. The flexible budget of the Madden Company states these relationships in the following equations:

$$\text{Revenue} = \$40 \text{ per Unit}$$

$$\text{Costs} = \$27 \text{ per Unit} + \$90,000 \text{ per Month}$$

Thus,

	Flexible budget at 10,000 units			Master budget
	Variable	Fixed	Total	
Revenue.............................	$40 × 10,000		$400,000	$440,000
Costs	27 × 10,000	$90,000	360,000	387,000
Operating income..................			$ 40,000	$ 53,000
Volume variance			$(13,000) U*	

* To emphasize the meaning, we use "U" for an unfavorable variance and "F" for a favorable variance. In practice, "favorable" or "unfavorable" is understood from the absence or presence of parentheses.

This calculation can be made even simpler if we recall the idea of the contribution margin discussed in Chapter 6. The contribution margin is the difference between unit revenue and unit variable costs, multiplied by the number of units. In the example above, the budgeted contribution margin per unit is $13 (= $40 − $27). The fact that the actual number of units sold was 1,000 units less than budgeted caused a $13,000 (= $13 × 1,000) decrease in operating income; that is,

	Per unit	Master budget	Flexible budget
Units		11,000	10,000
Revenue	$40	$440,000	$400,000
Variable costs	27	297,000	270,000
Contribution margin...	$13	$143,000	$130,000
Volume variance..		$(13,000)	

In several of the calculations to follow, we shall compute the variance by using a *difference* between an actual amount and a budgeted amount. The symbol Δ (the Greek letter *delta*) is used here to stand for a difference between two amounts.

The volume variance is Δ volume times the unit contribution margin.

Selling price variance

According to the flexible budget, at a volume of 10,000 units, sales revenue should have been $400,000. Exhibit 14–1 shows that actual sales revenue was $420,000. What explains the difference? Since sales revenue is the product of unit selling prices and the volume of units sold, and since we have already accounted for the effect of volume, the difference must arise because the actual selling price was not $40 per unit. The $20,000 is therefore a selling price variance.

The selling price variance can also be found by multiplying the difference between the actual selling price and the budgeted selling price per unit, by the actual number of units sold.[1] The actual selling price must have been $42 per unit (= $420,000 ÷ 10,000 units). The selling price variance was therefore:

Actual selling price	$42
Budgeted selling price	40
Difference	$ 2
Times actual units	10,000
Selling price variance	$20,000

The variance is favorable in that the higher selling price had a favorable effect on net income.

The selling price variance is Δ unit selling prices times actual volume; that is, it is the difference between the actual unit selling price and the budgeted unit selling price times the actual volume.

Cost variances

In computing the volume variance we took account of the effect of volume on costs. This amount was the difference between budgeted costs at the 11,000 units expected for April and the budgeted costs for the 10,000 units actually produced and sold in April. For example, referring to the data in Exhibit 14–1, for direct material costs:

Budgeted amount for April, per master budget (Exhibit 14–1)		$88,000
Actual amount for April (Exhibit 14–1)		85,000
Difference (Exhibit 14–1)		3,000
Amount due to volume:		
Master budget amount	$88,000	
Budget at actual volume ($8 × 10,000 units) (Exhibit 14–2)	−80,000	
Amount due to volume		8,000
Variance yet to be explained		$ (5,000) U

We now analyze the remaining difference between actual costs and budgeted costs. As can be seen from the material cost analysis above, the variance that remains after taking account of the volume change is the difference between actual costs and costs as shown in the flexible budget at the actual volume. In further analysis, therefore, we shall work strictly with a comparison between actual costs and budgeted costs at the actual volume, that is, amounts shown in the flexible budget for the actual volume. This comparison is shown in Exhibit 14–3.

---

[1] In this analysis, we assume that the company sells only one product. If the company sells more than one product, a mix variance also may exist. This is described in the Appendix to this chapter.

EXHIBIT 14–3

MADDEN COMPANY
Comparison of Flexible Budget and Actual Amounts
April

Flexible budget at 10,000 units

	Variable per unit	Fixed	Total	Actual	Difference*
Sales revenue	$40		$400,000	$420,000	$20,000
Costs:					
Direct material	8		80,000	85,000	(5,000)
Direct labor	12		120,000	126,000	(6,000)
Manufacturing overhead	2	$50,000	70,000	72,000	(2,000)
Distribution and administration...	5	40,000	90,000	88,000	2,000
Total Costs	$27	$90,000	360,000	371,000	
Operating Income....................			$ 40,000	$ 49,000	$ 9,000

*( ) = unfavorable.

Usage and price variances

In analyzing direct material and direct labor cost variances, we can make good use of the fact (described in Chapter 13) that the standard cost of one unit of product is composed of two components, a price component and a quantity component. For example, the standard (i.e., budgeted)[2] direct material cost of one unit of product is constructed by multiplying the standard quantity of material (e.g., pounds) required to produce that unit by a standard price per unit of quantity (e.g., price per pound). Total standard direct material cost for *an accounting period,* such as a month, is found by multiplying the standard direct material cost per unit by the actual number of units of product *produced* in that period. Actual direct material cost for the period is, of course, the product of actual quantity used times the actual price per unit of quantity. Thus,

Standard Material Cost = Standard Unit Price × Standard Quantity Used

Actual Material Cost = Actual Unit Price × Actual Quantity Used

These relationships suggest that it is possible to break the variance between actual and standard direct material costs into two components, one relating to quantity and the other relating to unit price.

Similar statements apply to direct labor costs. Standard direct labor cost for one unit of product is found by multiplying a standard price (i.e., wage rate) per hour by the quantity of labor (i.e., number of hours) re-

---

[2] In the discussion of direct labor and direct material we shall use "standard" rather than "budgeted," because the former usage is more common. In this context, these terms have the same meaning.

quired for one unit of product. Standard direct labor cost for an accounting period is the standard direct labor cost per unit times the number of units produced. Actual direct labor cost for a period is the actual wage rate per hour times the actual number of hours worked. Indeed, corresponding statements can be made for any item for which the total amount is obtained by multiplying a price per unit by a quantity. This was the reason that in Chapter 13 we emphasized the importance of identifying separately the price component and the quantity component in constructing standards.

These relationships suggest that whenever the amount of a cost element is arrived at by multiplying a unit price by a quantity, the total variance for that element can be decomposed into two elements:

• *Price variance,* which is that part of the variance caused by the difference between actual and standard unit prices, and
• *Quantity variance,* which is that part of the variance caused by the difference between actual and standard quantities. The quantity variance is more commonly called the *usage variance.*

The rules for finding these variances are:

Price Variance = Δ Unit Prices × Actual Quantity

(Δ unit price is the difference between the actual unit price and the standard unit price)

Usage Variance = Δ Quantities × Standard Price

Direct material variances

We shall first illustrate the derivation of these price and usage variances for direct material. From the underlying records, we find information about direct material unit prices and quantities. (For simplicity, it is assumed that there is only one type of material; if there were several items of material, the unit price would be an average.) The standard unit price of material is $4 per pound. The standard amount for one unit of product is 2 pounds, so the total standard quantity for 10,000 units is 20,000 pounds. The actual price in April was $5, and 17,000 pounds of material were used. These amounts are analyzed as follows:

Direct material	Unit Price	×	Quantity	=	Cost
Standard	$ 4		20,000		$80,000
Actual	5		17,000		85,000
Difference (Δ)...........	$(1)		3,000		$ (5,000)

Applying the above rules:

$$\Delta \text{ Unit Prices} \times \text{Actual Quantity} = \text{Price Variance}$$
$$\$(1) \quad \times \quad 17{,}000 \quad = \quad \$(17{,}000) \text{ U}$$

$$\Delta \text{ Quantities} \times \text{Standard Price} = \text{Usage Variance}$$
$$3{,}000 \quad \times \quad \$4 \quad = \quad \$12{,}000 \text{ F}$$

The total direct material variance, which we already know to be $5,000 unfavorable (see Exhibit 14–3) is the algebraic sum of the price and usage variances:

Material price variance................	$(17,000) U
Material usage variance...............	12,000 F
Direct material variance..............	$ (5,000) U

For direct material, the usage variance is also referred to as a *yield variance*.

Two mechanical points should be noted about the above calculations.

EXHIBIT 14–4
Direct material costs considered as rectangles

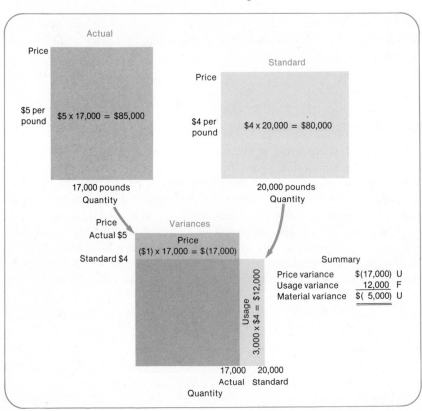

First, in calculating the differences, the actual amounts are subtracted from the standard amounts, not the other way around. This has the effect of showing a favorable variance as a positive amount and an unfavorable variance as a negative amount. Second, **the net variance cannot be obtained by multiplying the difference in unit price by the difference in quantity;** $1 × 3,000 units does *not* equal $5,000.

As described in Chapter 13, many standard cost systems identify the material price variance when the material is purchased and placed in raw materials inventory. When such a procedure is used, the calculation described above is not necessary because the material is issued to production at its standard unit cost, and there is no material price variance at that time. The difference between the cost of material used and the standard material cost of the product is entirely a usage variance.

Other ways of visualizing variances. The decomposition of a variance into its price component and its usage component is difficult to visualize. Various aids to understanding are available, two of which are shown in Exhibits 14–4 and 14–5.

In Exhibit 14–4, total direct material cost is depicted as a rectangle. Just as the area of a plot of land is the product of its length times its

EXHIBIT 14–5
Diagram of price and usage variances

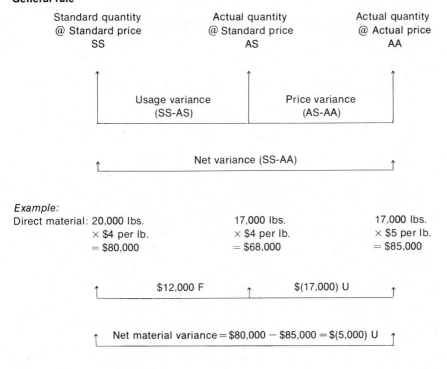

General rule

| | Standard quantity @ Standard price SS | Actual quantity @ Standard price AS | Actual quantity @ Actual price AA |

Usage variance (SS-AS)   Price variance (AS-AA)

Net variance (SS-AA)

Example:
Direct material: 20,000 lbs.
    × $4 per lb.
    = $80,000

17,000 lbs.
× $4 per lb.
= $68,000

17,000 lbs.
× $5 per lb.
= $85,000

$12,000 F $(17,000) U

Net material variance = $80,000 − $85,000 = $(5,000) U

width, so the total direct material cost is the product of a price per unit times the quantity of units. In Exhibit 14-4, one rectangle shows the standard cost, which is $4 per pound times 20,000 pounds equals $80,000. The other rectangle shows the actual cost, which is $5 per pound times 17,000 pounds equals $85,000. In the lower part of the exhibit, the actual cost rectangle is placed on top of the standard cost rectangle. The areas that do not coincide are the variances.

In Exhibit 14-5, another diagrammatic way of looking at the variances is shown. This diagram uses totals, rather than unit amounts. By placing the item "actual quantity @ standard price" (AS) between the total standard cost (SS) and the total actual cost (AA), it is possible to see how the price variance and the usage variance are derived as differences.

It should be emphasized that these diagrams tell exactly the same story as the numbers given in the text.

Significance of the variances. The separation of the direct material variance into its price and usage components facilitates analysis and control of direct material costs. The price variance is presumably the responsibility of the purchasing department while the usage variance is the responsibility of the factory supervisors who are responsible for the use of the material.

The distinction is not as clear-cut as this in all cases. For example, it may be that material of a higher than standard quality, and hence a higher unit price, was used, and that this resulted in lower spoilage. In these circumstances the two variances are *not* independent even though the decomposition of the total into two components implies that they are. Nevertheless, the use of the technique described above leads to a better understanding of what has happened than can be derived from looking only at the total direct material variance.

Although we have used direct material to illustrate how a variance can be broken into its price and usage components, it is important to note that if the company has a standard cost system of the type described in Chapter 13, the system itself will identify the direct material variances. In this case, there is no need to make the analysis described above. The material price variance is isolated when the material is debited to raw materials inventory, and the material usage variance is isolated when the raw material is debited to Goods in Process Inventory. The principles described, however, apply in all situations where the total amount is constructed by multiplying a unit price by a quantity.

Direct labor variance

The same approach can be used to decompose the direct labor variance of $6,000 (see Exhibit 14-3) into price and usage components. From detailed records, we obtain underlying data for April as follows:

Direct labor	Unit Price (rate per hour)	×	Quantity (hours)	=	Cost
Standard	$ 6		20,000		$120,000
Actual	7		18,000		126,000
Difference (Δ)............	$(1)		2,000		$ (6,000)

Applying the rules given above:

$$\Delta \text{ Unit Prices} \times \text{Actual Quantity} = \text{Price Variance}$$
$$\$(1) \qquad\qquad 18,000 \qquad\qquad \$(18,000) \text{ U}$$

$$\Delta \text{ Quantities} \times \text{Standard Price} = \text{Usage Variance}$$
$$2,000 \qquad\qquad \$6 \qquad\qquad \$12,000 \text{ F}$$

The total direct labor variance, which we already know from Exhibit 14–2 to be $6,000, is the algebraic sum of the price and usage variances:

Labor price variance	$(18,000) U
Labor usage variance.................	12,000 F
Direct labor variance..................	$ (6,000) U

Significance of the variances. For direct labor, the usage variance is also referred to as a **time variance,** or **labor efficiency variance** and the price variance as a **rate variance.** As was the case with direct material, the decomposition of the total direct labor variance into its price and usage components helps the manager to understand the cause of the variances. The price (or rate) variance may arise from a change in wage rates for which the supervisor of the responsibility center cannot be held responsible, whereas the supervisor may be entirely responsible for the usage variance because he should control the number of hours that direct workers spend in manufacturing products.

As was the case with direct materials, there may be some interdependence between the labor price and the labor usage variances. The supervisor may find it possible, for example, to complete the work in less than the standard number of hours by using workers who are more experienced and therefore earn a higher than standard wage rate.

Other variances

Two costs on Exhibit 14–3 remain to be analyzed. Manufacturing overhead consists of a long list of items: indirect labor, supplies, heat and light, depreciation, and so on. For some of these items, it would be possible to develop a price variance and a usage variance just as was done above for direct material. This is not ordinarily done, however. Instead, each significant item of manufacturing overhead is analyzed by comparing its actual cost with the amount shown in the flexible budget for the actual volume level obtaining in the month.

The same generalization applies to distribution and administration expenses, which also consist of many items. It is usually more meaningful to analyze each of these items separately than to break the total into price and usage components.

For our present purpose we shall simply develop the total variance for manufacturing overhead and for distribution and administration expense by comparing actual expenses with the budgeted expense at actual volume (10,000 units) as shown in the flexible budget (Exhibit 14–3).

| | Budgeted at 10,000 units | | | | |
	Variable per unit	Fixed	Total	Actual	Variance
Manufacturing overhead ...	$2	$50,000	$70,000	$72,000	$(2,000) U
Distribution and administration	5	40,000	90,000	88,000	2,000 F

Summary of the variances

Exhibit 14–6 is a summary of the variances developed in the preceding analysis in a form that might be used in a report to management. Note especially that although the difference between actual operating income and budgeted operating income for April was only $4,000, this $4,000 was the result of offsetting influences of major significance. This is often the case in practice, and is a principal reason why the individual vari-

EXHIBIT 14–6

MADDEN COMPANY
Summary of Variances
April

Budgeted operating income......................................	$53,000	
Actual operating income...	49,000	
Difference to be explained	$ (4,000)	

Variances	Favorable	Unfavorable
Volume..		$13,000
Selling price.......................................	$20,000	
Direct material price............................		17,000
Direct material usage	12,000	
Direct labor price................................		18,000
Direct labor usage	12,000	
Manufacturing overhead.......................		2,000
Distribution and administration	2,000	0
Total...	$46,000	$50,000
Net variance.......................................		$(4,000) U

ances are identified. If volume had been as high as budgeted, if material prices had not exceeded standard, or if labor rates had been in line with standards, the operating income would have been much greater than it was. Management will use this information to identify problem areas that need correcting.

The procedure for calculating these variances can be summarized as follows:

- **Volume variance:** Difference between budgeted operating income at actual volume and budgeted operating income at budgeted volume. (The latter amount appears in the master budget.)
- **Selling price variance:** Difference between the actual unit selling price and the budgeted unit selling price multiplied by the actual volume.

All the cost variances are found by comparing actual costs with standard or budgeted costs at the actual volume level, as shown in the flexible budget.

Direct material and direct labor costs can be decomposed into price variances and usage variances:

$$\text{Price Variance} = \Delta \text{ Unit Prices} \times \text{Actual Quantity}$$

$$\text{Usage Variance} = \Delta \text{ Quantities} \times \text{Standard Unit Price}$$

MARKETING VARIANCES SEPARATED FROM PRODUCTION VARIANCES

The preceding analysis was based on the assumption that the 10,000 units of product sold in April were also produced in April. Our reason for using this simple situation was that it permitted a description of the basic ideas of variance analysis without getting into the complications involved when goods produced in one month are sold in a later month. We now turn to the more complicated situation.

Perhaps the easiest way to visualize this situation is to regard the business as consisting of two separate entities. One entity is responsible for producing the goods, and its responsibility ends when the goods are delivered to finished goods inventory. The other entity is responsible for marketing these goods. The accounting link between these two entities is the Finished Goods Inventory account. We can visualize the goods going into Finished Goods Inventory at their standard cost, upon completion of the production process, and we can visualize the goods being sold later at a markup above their standard cost. The production entity is essentially responsible for manufacturing the goods at budgeted cost, but it is not responsible for the sales revenue nor for the volume of products sold. The marketing entity is responsible for selling the budgeted volume of goods at the budgeted markup, but it is not responsible for the cost of manufacturing the goods. We shall analyze the variances for these two parts of the business separately.

Marketing Variances

The approach to the analysis of variances in the marketing area is the same as that described in the preceding section for selling prices and volume, except that it is often more informative to work with unit *gross margins,* rather than with unit *selling prices.* The reason why this is so can be seen from the analysis given in Exhibit 14–7. In this situation, the

EXHIBIT 14–7

SEAVER COMPANY
Comparison of Budget and Actual
March

| | Unit amount | Budget | | Actual | | |
		Units	Total	Units	Total	Variance
Sales revenue	$25	1,000	$25,000	800	$20,000	$(5,000)
Cost of goods sold	15	1,000	15,000	800	12,000	3,000
Gross margin	$10	1,000	$10,000	800	$ 8,000	$(2,000)

actual unit selling price in March was exactly the same as the budgeted unit selling price, so there was no selling price variance. Actual volume was lower than budgeted volume, however; and this caused gross margin to be $2,000 lower than budgeted. If other aspects of the business were in line with the budget, this $2,000 would carry down to a $2,000 decrease in operating income. It was caused solely by the lower volume.

The lower volume caused sales revenue to be $5,000 below budget, but it also resulted in a $3,000 favorable cost of goods sold variance. The $5,000 unfavorable revenue variance overstates the real effect of the volume decrease because it was partly offset by the associated favorable variance in cost of goods sold. The real effect of the lower volume was the net of these two amounts, which is the $2,000 unfavorable variance in gross margin.

The marketing people are not responsible for the cost of goods sold; this is the responsibility of the production organization. The marketing people are responsible for maintaining an appropriate *spread* between sales revenue and cost of goods sold, whatever the cost of goods sold may be. This spread is measured by the gross margin.

The total gross margin is the product of gross margin per unit times the quantity of units sold. We can analyze the total difference between budgeted gross margin and actual gross margin by using rules similar to those used in the preceding section. The amount attributable to unit gross margin is called the margin variance, and the amount attributable to the quantity of units sold is the sales volume variance.

Margin Variance = Δ Unit Margins × Actual Volume

Sales Volume Variance = Δ Units × Budgeted Unit Margin

In setting up the calculations, actual amounts are put on the first line and budget amounts are put below them. When this is done, a positive difference will result in a favorable variance. The budget amount referred to is the amount in the master budget, that is, the budgeted amounts for the month of March, *not* the flexible budget.

EXAMPLE: In March, results were as follows:

	Gross margin per unit	Quantity of units sold	Total gross margin
Actual....................................	$11	900	$ 9,900
Budget..................................	10	1,000	10,000
Difference (Δ)........................	$ 1	(100)	$ (100)

Δ Unit Margins ×	Actual Volume	=	Margin Variance
$1	× 900	=	$900 F

Δ	Units	× Budgeted Unit Margin	= Sales Volume Variance
	(100)	× $10	= $(1,000) U

In the analysis described here, we assume that the company uses a standard cost system, and the cost of goods sold therefore is stated at the standard cost of the goods sold. Other approaches are possible. If the company used a variable cost system, cost of goods sold would include only the variable manufacturing costs, and this would lead to some differences in the analysis of variances. At the other extreme, if the company treated the factory as a profit center, goods would be transferred to the marketing department at an amount that included an element for profit, and this would affect the analysis also. These alternatives are discussed in more advanced courses.

Manufacturing variances

In analyzing manufacturing variances, direct labor and direct material variances can be calculated in exactly the same way that we have already described; that is, each can be decomposed into a price variance and a usage variance. We therefore do not discuss them further. The only point to emphasize is that the relevant volume is the *production* volume, not the sales volume, because manufacturing costs are influenced by the quantity of products manufactured, regardless of the quantity sold.

Overhead costs and overhead rates. Manufacturing overhead, however, requires a different type of analysis, the need for which arises because of the way that manufacturing overhead becomes a part of product costs. To see why this is so, we shall review briefly the effect of production volume on overhead rates; this effect was discussed in Chapters 4 and 6.

Within a relevant range, manufacturing overhead costs are expected to vary with volume, but less than proportionately. Their behavior can ordinarily be expressed as a straight line, which starts *above* zero at zero volume and rises at a constant rate per unit of volume. This is another way of saying that manufacturing overhead costs consist of a fixed component per period and a variable component, which is an amount per unit of volume times the volume. Their behavior can be described by the equation

$$y = a + bx$$

Such a line is the *budgeted* overhead cost line on Exhibit 14–8. (This line is also what we mean by a flexible budget.) In this line,

Fixed Costs (a) = \$12,000 per Month

Variable Costs (b) = \$8 per Unit

We can find the budgeted overhead cost at any volume within the relevant range by using this equation. For example, for a volume of 2,000 units,

$$y = \$12,000 + \$8(2,000) = \$28,000$$

An overhead rate is established by using the expected costs at the volume at which the company expects to operate; this is called the *standard volume.* If the standard volume is 2,000 units, and costs at this volume are expected to be \$28,000, as above, then the overhead rate is \$28,000 ÷ 2,000 = \$14 per unit.

Alternatively, the overhead rate can be calculated as follows:

	Overhead rate
Variable costs per unit (at any volume)....................................	\$ 8
Fixed costs per unit at 2,000 units (\$12,000 ÷ 2,000)	6
Total Overhead Rate...	\$14

Volume variance. Overhead costs are *absorbed* or *applied* to product costs at the rate of \$14 per unit. The line of absorbed cost on Exhibit

EXHIBIT 14–8
Budgeted, absorbed, and actual costs

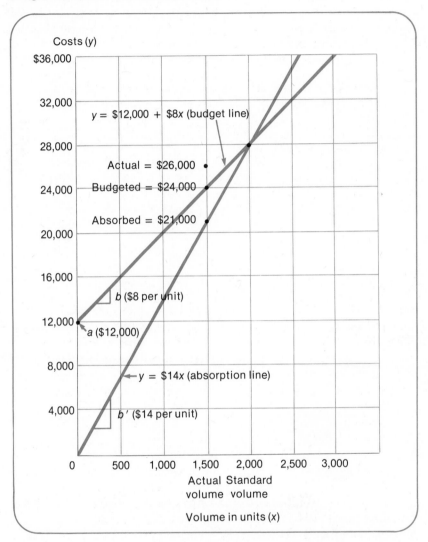

14–8 shows the total amount of overhead costs that would be absorbed at various volumes. Note that at standard volume, budgeted costs equal absorbed costs; but that at any other volume budgeted costs are different from absorbed costs, as indicated by the spread between the two lines. At lower volumes, costs are expected to be *underabsorbed;* and at higher volumes they are expected to be *overabsorbed.* They are underabsorbed or overabsorbed *because* actual volume differs from standard volume;

hence, this amount is the volume variance. **The production volume variance results solely from the fact that actual volume in a given month differed from the volume that was used in setting the overhead rate, that is, the standard volume.** Also, the production volume variance is attributable solely to the fixed component of the overhead rate; variable overhead costs per unit are, by definition, unaffected by the volume level.

EXAMPLE: The following table shows the volume variance at various volumes if the overhead rate is $14 per unit and budgeted costs are $12,000 plus $8 per unit:

(1) Volume (in units)	(2) = (1) × $14 Absorbed overhead	(3) Budgeted overhead	(4) = (2) − (3) Volume variance
1,000	$14,000	$20,000	$(6,000)
1,500	21,000	24,000	(3,000)
2,000	28,000	28,000	0
2,500	35,000	32,000	3,000
3,000	42,000	36,000	6,000

( ) = unfavorable, that is, underabsorbed.

Spending variance. If, whatever the volume level, the actual overhead costs incurred in a month were the same as the budgeted costs for that volume, as shown in the flexible budget, the net overhead variance would be entirely attributable to volume. For many reasons, however, actual costs are not likely to be the same as the amount of costs budgeted at the volume level for the period. **The difference between actual costs and budgeted costs at the actual level of volume in the period is the spending variance.**

The spending variance for overhead costs has the same significance as the *sum* of the price and usage variances (i.e., the *net variance*) for direct material cost and direct labor cost. Indeed, it would be possible to decompose the spending variance into usage and price components in the same manner as was described for these direct costs. Most companies do not do this for overhead costs, however, because they do not find this additional breakdown worthwhile.

Calculation of overhead variances. The manufacturing overhead variance, as shown in the accounting records, is the algebraic sum of the volume variance and the spending variance. In order to understand how each variance is calculated, refer again to Exhibit 14–8, which shows these variances graphically for a month in which actual volume was 1,500 units and actual overhead costs were $26,000. From the relationship indicated there, the procedure for calculating the amount of the variances can be discerned. Actual volume (1,500 units) was below standard volume (2,000 units). Actual overhead costs ($26,000) were above the amount of overhead costs absorbed into product costs ($21,000). In the accounting records, this would be shown by the entry:

Goods in process inventory 21,000
Overhead variance 5,000
    Manufacturing overhead...   26,000

The $5,000 of underabsorbed overhead is the *net overhead variance.* The net overhead variance consists of two elements:[3]

1. The production volume variance is the difference between the absorbed cost ($21,000) and the budgeted cost ($24,000). Since absorbed cost is less than budgeted cost, the volume variance of $3,000 is unfavorable. The unfavorable volume variance arises because overhead was underabsorbed, that is, because the factory did not operate at the standard volume level.
2. The spending variance is the difference between the budgeted cost ($24,000) for the actual volume of 1,500 units and the actual cost ($26,000). Since budgeted cost is less than actual cost, the spending variance of $2,000 is also unfavorable.

Thus, the volume variance is that part of the net overhead variance which results solely from the difference between actual volume and standard volume, while the spending variance shows how actual spending compared with the level of spending that was budgeted for at actual volume, as shown in the flexible budget.

Recapitulating,

- **The net overhead variance is the difference between absorbed cost and actual cost.** It is also the algebraic sum of the production volume variance and the spending variance.
- **The production volume variance is the difference between absorbed cost and budgeted cost.**
- **The spending variance is the difference between budgeted cost and actual cost.**

> *EXAMPLE:* The arithmetic calculations for deriving these variances are given below for the situation illustrated in Exhibit 14–8, in which—
>
>   **Budgeted Cost Equation = $12,000 + $8 per Unit**
>   **Absorbed Cost Equation = $14 per Unit**
>   **Actual Volume = 1,500 Units**
>   **Actual Overhead Cost = $26,000**

---

[3] If the overhead rate is applied to products by an input measure, such as actual direct labor hours, the overhead variance will include a third element, called the *efficiency variance.* The determination of this variance is discussed in advanced courses.

Calculations:

$$\text{Budgeted Cost} = \$12,000 + \$8 \ (1,500 \ \text{Units}) = \$24,000$$
$$\text{Absorbed Cost} = \$14 \qquad \times 1,500 \ \text{Units} \qquad = \$21,000$$

Absorbed Cost	−	Budgeted Cost	=	Volume Variance
$21,000	−	$24,000	=	$(3,000) U
Budgeted Cost	−	Actual Cost	=	Spending Variance
$24,000	−	$26,000	=	$(2,000) U
Absorbed Cost	−	Actual Cost	=	Net Overhead Variance
$21,000	−	$26,000	=	$(5,000) U

The reason for these calculations will be clearer if each of them is related to the "actual," "budgeted," and "absorbed" points on Exhibit 14–8.

Note that the above calculations are set up in such a way that a negative result is an unfavorable variance. Actually, it is best to check the result with a commonsense appraisal of whether the variance is favorable or unfavorable, rather than attempting to remember how the subtractions were made. In the example, the volume variance is unfavorable *because* actual volume was lower than standard volume, and the spending variance is unfavorable *because* actual costs exceeded budgeted costs.

Distribution and administration costs

As mentioned in the preceding section, many companies do not attempt to decompose the variances in distribution and administration costs into price and quantity components, preferring instead to examine the specific items of cost included in this category. It would be possible to group the selling costs in the marketing section of the analysis, and this is done in some companies, especially when the organization is a separate profit center. These are mere matters of arrangement, however. If distribution and/or administration cost variances are decomposed, the procedure would be the same as that already described for other types of cost.

Interpretation of the overhead variances

Presumably, the production manager is responsible for the overhead spending variance. Because the variable budget cannot take account of all the noncontrollable factors that affect costs, however, there may be a reasonable explanation for the spending variance. The existence of an unfavorable variance is therefore not, by itself, grounds for criticizing performance. Rather, it is a signal that investigation and explanation are required.

In some situations the production manager may also be responsible for the volume variance; that is, his failure to obtain the standard volume of output may result from his inability to keep products moving through his department at the proper speed. The volume variance is more likely to be someone else's responsibility, however. It may result because the marketing department was unable to obtain the planned volume of orders, because some earlier department in the manufacturing process failed to deliver materials as they were needed, or because vendors did not deliver raw material when it was needed.

In appraising spending performance, the analyst should look behind the total spending variance and examine the individual overhead items of which it consists. The total budgeted cost is the sum of the budgeted amounts for each of the separate items of cost. A spending variance can and should be developed for each important item; it is the difference between actual cost incurred and the budget allowance for that item. Attention should be focused on significant spending variances for individual elements.

SIGNIFICANCE OF VARIANCES

Many detailed calculations must be made in a complete analysis of the difference between budgeted operating income and actual operating income. Plowing through the detail, one easily can lose sight of the purpose of this analysis, which is to break the total difference into elements such that the *causes* of the difference are revealed. The manager wants to know what portion of the total variance is attributable to each cause so as to decide what, if any, action should be taken. He wants to be able to associate each variance with the person responsible for it. The techniques described in this chapter help the manager to do this. The manager would not personally make the computations, of course; they would be made for him as part of the control process. He needs to know how they are made, however; otherwise, he is likely not to understand their significance.

The calculation of the variances is only the first step in the control process. The existence of variances of significant size raises questions in the manager's mind, and he next takes steps to find out the answers to these questions. The president does not say to the marketing manager, "You had an unfavorable marketing volume variance; *therefore,* you performed poorly." Rather, he asks: *"Why* did you have an unfavorable marketing volume variance?" In other words, the manager does not look upon an unfavorable variance as an automatic basis for criticism, nor on a favorable variance as an automatic basis for praise. Rather, he regards the variances as pointing to situations for which an explanation of underlying causes is required. He seeks to find these causes, and only after he has found them does he act.

In this chapter we have said that the individual variances indicate the *cause* of the difference between actual and budgeted performance. In one sense, they do indicate causes; the material price variance shows how much of the total variance was caused by a difference between actual and standard material prices. The variances do not, however, indicate *why* the difference occurred. Was an unfavorable material price variance the consequence of lack of diligence on the part of the purchasing department in finding the vendor who offered the lowest price, or was it the consequence of an increase in the market price of the material? Variance analysis does not reveal these *underlying causes*. It does reveal the areas in which further investigation is needed in order to determine what the underlying causes were.

DEMONSTRATION CASE

As a way of summarizing the techniques described in this chapter, the complete analysis of a simple situation is shown in Exhibits 14–9 and 14–10. The income statement shows an unfavorable variance be-

EXHIBIT 14–9

NORRIS COMPANY
Income Statement and Summary of Variances
October
(000 omitted)

Income Statement

	Budget	Actual	Variance*
Sales	$540	$551	
Less: Standard cost of goods sold	440	418	
Gross margin at standard cost	100	133	$ 33
Less: Manufacturing variances	0	82	(82)
Gross margin	100	51	(49)
Distribution and administration expense	40	50	(10)
Operating Income	$ 60	$ 1	$(59)

Summary of Variances

Margin	$ 38
Sales volume	(5)
Marketing	$ 33
Material price	(16)
Material usage	4
Labor rate	(8)
Labor usage	(24)
Overhead volume	(15)
Overhead spending	(23)
Net manufacturing	(82)
Distribution and administration	(10)
Income variance	$(59)

* ( ) = unfavorable.

EXHIBIT 14–10

NORRIS COMPANY
Calculation of Variances

1. Marketing variances

Underlying data (given)

	Unit Margin	× Volume Sold (units)	= Total Margin
Actual	$0.70	190	$133
Budget	0.50	200	100
Difference (Δ)	$0.20	(10)	$ 33

Calculations

Δ Unit Margins ×   Actual Units = Margin Variance
$0.20   ×   190   = $38 F

Δ Volumes × Budgeted Margin = Sales Volume Variance
(10)   × $0.50   = $(5) U

2. Direct material variances

Underlying data (given)

	Unit Price	× Quantity (lbs.)	= Cost
Standard	$ 0.20	340*	$ 68
Actual	0.25	320	80
Difference (Δ)	$(0.05)	20	$(12)

* 170 units produced @ 2 pounds per unit.

Calculations

Δ Unit Prices × Actual Quantity = Material Price Variance
$(0.05)   ×   320   = $(16) U

Δ Quantities × Standard Price = Material Usage Variance
20   × $0.20   − $4 F

3. Direct labor variances

Underlying data (given)

	Unit Price	× Quantity (hours)	= Cost
Standard	$ 4.00	34*	$136
Actual	4.20	40	168
Difference (Δ)	$(0.20)	(6)	$ (32)

* 170 units produced @ 0.2 hours per unit.

Calculations

Δ Unit Prices × Actual Quantity = Labor Rate Variance
$(0.20)   ×   40   = $(8) U

Δ Quantities × Standard Price = Labor Usage Variance
(6)   × $4   = $(24) U

EXHIBIT 14–10 (continued)

4. Overhead variances

Underlying data (given)

Actual overhead costs..	$208
Budgeted overhead costs...	$100 + $0.50 per unit
Actual production volume	170 units
Standard volume..	200 units
Overhead rate [$100 + $0.50(200 units)] ÷ 200 units =...	$1 per unit

Calculations

Volume variance:

Absorbed overhead: 170 units × $1 per unit....................................	$170
Budgeted overhead: $100 + ($0.50 × 170 units)............................	185
Volume variance	$ (15) U

Spending variance:

Budgeted overhead (as above)	$185
Actual overhead...	208
Spending variance	$ (23) U

tween actual and budgeted income of $59. (For simplicity, all amounts except unit costs and selling prices are in thousands; thus $59 means $59,000.) The question is: What accounts for this $59 variance? The answer to this question is given in the summary of variances. It decomposes the total variance into elements. The remainder of the exhibit shows how each of these elements was found.

Marketing variances

The first step in the computation is to analyze the difference between budgeted and actual margins. This part of the analysis is shown in the first section of Exhibit 14–10. Gross margin is found by subtracting *standard* cost of goods sold (which is $2.20 per unit) from selling prices. Our use of the standard cost of goods sold figure means that the marketing department is not held accountable for manufacturing cost variances; rather, these are the responsibility of the manufacturing organization.

The margin variance is determined by multiplying the actual sales quantities by the difference between actual and budgeted unit margins.

The sales volume variance is the loss or gain in gross margin that results from a difference between actual and budgeted sales volume.

The algebraic sum of the unit margin variance, $38, and the sales volume variance, $(5), is the $33 shown as the gross margin variance on the income statement.

Note that margin variances are favorable when actual is greater than budget, which is of course the opposite situation from cost variances. In

Exhibit 14–9, the $33 excess of actual gross margin over standard gross margin is favorable, but the $82 excess of actual manufacturing variances over standard manufacturing variances is unfavorable.

Production variances

Next we turn to an analysis of the production variances. Note that actual production volume (170 units) is less than actual sales volume (190 units), the difference being made up out of inventory which is carried at standard cost. Carrying the inventory at standard cost means that expense variances are treated as period costs and charged directly to cost of goods sold during the period in which they occur. The labor, material, and manufacturing overhead variances described earlier in the chapter are calculated in the lower part of Exhibit 14–10. Their algebraic sum equals the $82 unfavorable cost variance noted on the income statement.

An examination of the $10 unfavorable variance in distribution and administration expenses completes the analysis of the operating income variance. This is not shown; it would consist of an analysis by class of expense of the amount of and reasons for differences between the budgeted expense and the actual expense.

SUMMARY

Our task was to analyze the difference between actual performance and the performance that was expected under the circumstances. The latter is called *budgeted* performance. The total difference between actual and budgeted net income for the company as a whole can be decomposed into a number of elements. Some or all of these elements also explain the total difference between actual and budgeted performance for a responsibility center within a company.

If goods are sold as soon as they are produced, the total difference between budgeted and actual operating income can be decomposed into the following variances: selling price, volume, direct material price, direct material usage, direct labor price, direct labor usage, and overhead.

If goods are manufactured for inventory, it is useful to divide the variances into those related to marketing and those related to production. The marketing variances are the margin variance and the sales volume variance. The production variances include the same direct labor and direct material variances as above and, in addition, a production volume variance and a spending variance.

The results of a variance analysis provide a starting point for management action. They suggest questions that need to be asked, although the analysis does not automatically give the answers to these questions.

APPENDIX: MIX VARIANCE

If the company sells only one product, then the margin variance is correctly calculated in the manner described in the text. If, however, the company sells several products, with varying unit gross margins, the margin variance as calculated is not solely the result of the difference between actual and budgeted unit gross margins. It also reflects the fact that the actual proportion of high-margin and low-margin products may differ from the proportion that was assumed in the budget. This difference is a **mix variance.** It does not show up when the variance calculations are based on the *average* unit gross margin, but it does show up when the margin variances for each product are calculated separately.

The calculation of the mix variance is illustrated in Exhibit 14–11 and described below.

The assumed situation is related to that described on page 593. In the situation described there, the budget was for sales of 1,000 units @ $10 per unit, for a total margin of $10,000. Actual sales were 900 units @ $11 per unit, a total of $9,900. We computed the margin variance as:

$$\Delta \text{ Margins} \times \text{Actual Volume} = \text{Margin Variance}$$
$$\$1 \quad\quad \times \quad\quad 900 \quad\quad = \quad\quad \$900$$

If we now assume that sales consisted of the three products listed in Exhibit 14–11, but adding up to the same totals, and computed the margin variance on each of these three products, using the same rule as above, the results are shown in Part B of Exhibit 14–11. The total of the variances on three products comes to $700. This differs from the $900 that was calculated from the total units and average margins (as in the preceding paragraph) because the earlier calculation did not take account of the shift in the proportions of the products sold. Note that actual sales of low-margin Product A were a lower proportion of total than was expected in the budget, and that actual sales of high-margin Product C were a higher proportion. It is said that the actual sales mix was *richer* than the budgeted sales mix.

We can isolate the effect of this shift in the mix by finding the difference between the budgeted unit margin of each product and the budgeted *average* unit margin for all products. The average unit margin is found by dividing the total margin by the total number of units. This difference is multiplied by the actual quantity sold for each product, and the result is the mix variance. The calculation is made in Part C. The mix variance is $200. The total of the mix variance of $200 and the margin variance of $700 is the same $900 that was computed by the use of the total units and average margins.

Computation of the mix variance and margin variance for each product, although complicated, reveals information that might not come to light if the variances were developed only from the total quantity and

EXHIBIT 14–11

Calculation of mix and margin variances

A. Assumed situation

	Budget			Actual		
Product	Unit margin	Units sold	Total margin	Unit margin	Units sold	Total margin
A..............	$ 9.00	300	$ 2,700	$10.50	200	$2,100
B..............	10.00	400	4,000	10.00	300	3,000
C..............	11.00	300	3,300	12.00	400	4,800
Total.........	$10.00*	1,000	$10,000	$11.00*	900	$9,900

* Average.

B. Calculation of margin variance

Product	Δ Margins × Actual Volume = Variance		
A........................	$1.50	200	$300
B........................	0	300	0
C........................	1.00	400	400
Margin variance....			$700

C. Calculation of mix variance

Product	Product Budgeted Margin	− Average Budgeted* Margin	= Difference	× Actual Quantity	= Variance
A........................	$ 9	$10	$(1)	200	$(200)
B........................	10	10	0	300	
C........................	11	10	1	400	400
Mix variance					$ 200

* The average margin is found by dividing the total margin ($10,000) by the number of units (1,000), not by averaging the unit margins of each product ($9, $10, $11).

average margins. It is important to know to what extent the total variance was caused by the "richness" of the product mix, that is, by the relative proportion of high-margin products.

General use of the mix concept

The mix variance for gross margin came to light when the margins for the three products were analyzed separately. A mix variance can also be developed for items of cost if the total amount of the item is broken into components and each component is analyzed separately. Some chemical companies and other companies whose manufacturing process consists primarily of combining raw materials into finished products compute a mix variance which shows the effect of variations of the proportions of the several materials.

A similar phenomenon exists with respect to direct labor costs. If instead of using the total number of direct labor hours and the *average* hourly wage rate in calculating the labor variances, we had used the number of direct labor hours in each skill category and the hourly wage rate for that skill category, a labor mix variance could be developed. This variance does not have the same meaning as a pure labor rate variance. An unfavorable pure labor rate variance means that a given employee earned more than the standard rate per hour, whereas an unfavorable labor mix variance means that a high proportion of highly paid persons were used during the period. This can happen, for example, when part of the work force is laid off, and those remaining have relatively much seniority, and hence high pay.

In general, a mix variance can be developed whenever a cost or revenue item is broken down into components, and the components have different unit prices. When a price variance is computed by use of an average price, we do not know whether the variance is caused by a true difference in prices, or whether it is caused by a change in the *proportion* of the elements that make up the total, that is, by a change in mix.

IMPORTANT TERMS

Volume variance

Selling price variance

Direct material price variance

Direct material usage (or yield) variance

Direct labor price (or rate) variance

Direct labor usage (or time) variance

Margin variance

Sales volume variance

Production volume variance

Spending variance

Net overhead variance

QUESTIONS FOR DISCUSSION

1. Suppose that in a certain month, the actual operating income of Madden Company (Exhibit 14–1) was exactly equal to its budgeted operating income. Would an analysis of variances nevertheless be desirable? Why?

2. In some contexts the word *budgeted* is used, and in other contexts the word *standard*. Is there any substantial difference between the meaning of these two words?

3. On page 582, the volume variance is calculated as $13,000, unfavorable. State in words what this $13,000 means.

4. On page 586, material price variance is given as $(17,000) and the material usage variance as $12,000. State in words what these numbers mean.

5. In Exhibit 14–5, suppose the actual quantity used had been 21,000 pounds, other numbers being as shown. What would the variances have been?

6. Recompute the direct labor variances shown on page 589, using the approach given in Exhibit 14–5.

7. Why is it useful to decompose the total direct labor variance into a rate variance and a usage variance?

8. Explain the meaning of the numbers on Exhibit 14–6, other than those already covered in Questions 3 and 4.

9. What is the reason that the analysis of variances for the Seaver Company (pages 591–98) has to be different from the analysis for the Madden Company (Exhibit 14–6)?

10. In what respects is the analysis of variances for the Seaver Company similar to that of the Madden Company?

11. Consider (a) a grocery store and (b) a company that sells used automobiles. Which would be more likely to compute a gross margin variance and which a selling price variance? Why?

12. In Exhibit 14–9 there is no volume variance for direct labor or direct material, but there is a volume variance for manufacturing overhead. Why is this so?

13. Explain the relationship among (a) fixed costs, (b) production volume, and (c) overhead costs absorbed.

14. On Exhibit 14–8, describe where the point denoting actual cost would be located under each of the following conditions:
    a. Actual volume exceeds normal volume; actual costs exceed absorbed costs.
    b. Actual volume exceeds normal volume; there is zero spending variance.
    c. There is zero net overhead variance.
    d. There is an unfavorable volume variance and an unfavorable spending variance.

15. In a certain month, actual operating income in the Seaver Company was $5,000 less than budgeted operating income, and the entire $5,000 was accounted for by the overhead spending variance. In what sense did the variance identify the *cause* of the operating income variance, and in what sense did it *not* identify the cause?

16. Under what circumstances does a mix variance arise? Why was no mix variance identified in the Madden Company example (Exhibit 14–6)?

PROBLEMS

14–1. The following data pertain to operations of the Charles Company during the month of August:

> Actual production and sales, 950 units @ $48
> Budgeted production and sales, 1,000 units @ $50
> Actual costs, $41,400
> Budgeted costs, $8,000 per month plus $35 per unit

Required:
Calculate the volume and the selling price variances.

14–2. The Watkins Company manufactures goods for inventory. Data pertaining to operations in the month of July are as follows:

Actual gross margin per unit............ $20
Budgeted gross margin per unit........ $18
Actual sales in units........................ 850
Budgeted sales in units 1,000

Required:

Calculate the margin and the sales volume variances.

14–3.   A condensed income statement for the Weems Company is as follows for the month of October:

	Master budget	Actual	Variance*
Units produced and sold	20,000	18,000	(2,000)
Sales revenue	$300,000	$288,000	$(12,000)
Costs:			
Direct materials.......................	40,000	37,000	3,000
Direct labor............................	80,000	75,000	5,000
Manufacturing overhead	95,000	89,000	6,000
Selling and administration.........	65,000	62,000	3,000
Total Costs	280,000	263,000	17,000
Operating Income....................	$ 20,000	$ 25,000	$ 5,000

*( ) = unfavorable.

Further analysis revealed the following data on costs:

	Variable rate per unit	Fixed
Direct materials.................................	$ 2	
Direct labor	4	
Manufacturing overhead	3	$35,000
Selling and administration..................	1	45,000
Totals.......................................	$10	$80,000

Required:

A.   Prepare a report comparing the master budget with a flexible budget for October.
B.   Calculate the following variances:
   1.   Volume.
   2.   Selling price.
   3.   Direct materials (net).
   4.   Direct labor (net).
   5.   Manufacturing overhead (net).
   6.   Selling and administration (net).
C.   Prepare a variance report which accounts for the difference between budgeted and actual operating income for Weems in October.
D.   Comment on the significance of the variances you calculated.

14–4.   The Powers Company uses a standard cost system in which raw materials inventories are recorded at actual cost and the material price variance is based on quantities used. The following data refer to production of Product 822 during the month of August:

Standard material cost, $2 per pound
Standard labor rate, $5 per hour
Standard quantity of material per unit of product, 4 pounds
Standard labor hours per unit of product, 6
Quantity of material actually used, 8,500 pounds
Actual material cost, $1.90 per pound
Actual labor cost, 11,500 hours, $58,075
Units of product produced, 2,000

Required:

A. Calculate the price, usage, and net variances for direct materials and direct labor.
B. Comment on the possible significance of the variances you calculated.

14-5. The Jones Company has a production overhead budget of $350,000 of fixed costs and $250,000 of variable costs for a standard monthly volume of 100,000 units of production. Actual overhead costs for July were $590,000, and the company operated at 98 percent of capacity.

Required:

A. Compute the overhead rate.
B. Compute the net overhead variance.
C. Compute the overhead spending and volume variances.
D. Comment on the significance of the variances you computed.

14-6. The graph below relates to monthly production for each of four months. The company uses standard costs and monthly budgets for production control. The items illustrated in the chart are overhead costs. Actual overhead costs are shown by the dots initialed to represent the months of September, October, November, and December.

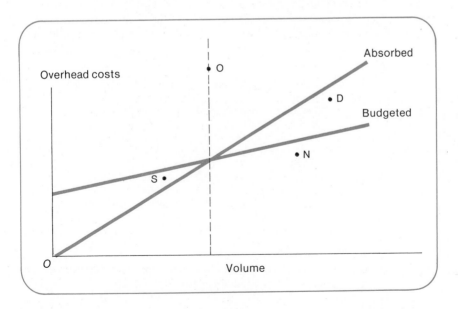

Required:

A. In what months would the net overhead variance be unfavorable?
B. In what months would a favorable volume variance appear?
C. Based only on the chart, in what two months does the control of overhead seem best?
D. In which of the months was the largest amount added to goods in process inventory?
E. In December was the amount of overhead debited to Goods in Process Inventory more than, less than, or the same as the actual overhead?
F. Which appears to be the larger for this company—the variable or the fixed overheads? How can you tell?

14-7. Bradford Products Company has the following data for production department No. 15, during the month of April:

Standard monthly volume in labor hours......................... 50,000
Standard labor hours allowed for April production.......... 51,500
Budgeted fixed overhead per month............................. $200,000
Variable overhead costs per standard labor hour............ $3
Actual overhead costs for April $358,000

Required:

A. Calculate the overhead rate.
B. Prepare the journal entry showing the application of overhead to goods in process and the net overhead variance.
C. Calculate the overhead spending and volume variances.
D. Draw a graph similar to Exhibit 14–8 showing budgeted, absorbed, and actual costs for overhead in April.
E. Comment on the significance of the overhead variances you calculated above.

14-8. The Ford Company uses a standard cost system. Raw materials inventories are recorded at actual cost, and the material price variance is based on quantities used. Overhead is applied on a units-of-production basis. The following data pertain to production of Product 879 during the month of March:

Standard material cost, $5 per pound
Standard direct labor rate, $6 per hour
Standard quantity of material per unit, 3 pounds
Standard direct labor hours per unit, 4
Quantity of material actually used, 6,100 pounds
Actual material cost, $5.25 per pound
Actual labor cost, 8,100 hours, $47,790
Budgeted fixed overhead per month, $10,000
Variable overhead costs per unit, $4
Standard monthly production volume, 2,000 units
Actual overhead costs, $17,500
Actual production, 2,050 units

Required:

A. Prepare a variance analysis to account for the difference between actual and standard production costs for March.

B. Comment on the possible significance of the variances you calculated.

14-9. The following data relate to the operations of Smith, Inc., a company using a standard cost system in which factor overhead costs are absorbed on the basis of standard direct labor hours. Smith records raw materials inventories at actual cost and calculates price variances at the time material is used.

Actual units of direct material purchased......................	600
Actual units of raw material used	300
Actual direct labor hours used in production................	170
Standard direct labor hours used in production............	150
Actual factory overhead costs.....................................	$1,500
Standard price of one unit of raw material	$3
Material price variance..	$30 Cr.
Labor time variance..	70 Dr.
Factory overhead net variance.....................................	60 Cr.
Material usage variance..	60 Dr.
Labor rate variance...	85 Dr.

Required:

Use the data available above to compute the following:

A. Standard units of raw materials put into production.
B. Standard labor rate per hour.
C. Actual labor rate per hour.
D. Standard factory overhead rate.
E. Factory overhead absorbed into product.
F. Actual raw material cost per unit.

14-10. Below are details of entries to selected T-accounts taken from the records of Midlands Corporation for the month of January. The company uses a standard cost system which removes the raw materials variance due to price upon purchase. All debits to goods in process are at standard cost.

Accounts	Debits	Credits
Accounts payable............................	xxx	50,000
Factory payroll payable....................	xxx	66,000
Various accounts	xxx	46,000
Factory overheads...........................	46,000	44,600
		1,400
Raw materials inventory....................	48,800	28,000
Goods in process inventory...............	28,800	110,400
	67,600	
	44,600	
Finished goods inventory..................	110,400	80,000
Cost of goods sold..........................	80,000	
Material price variance.....................	1,200	
Material usage variance.....................		800
Labor rate variance		2,000
Labor time variance.........................	400	
Factory overhead variance	1,400	

Required:

A. Journalize the entires which resulted in the postings to the accounts above.

B. Compute the actual Cost of Goods Sold which would appear on the January income statement after closing all variances to the Cost of Goods Sold.

14–11. Howard Machine Works employs two types of labor, skilled and unskilled, in the manufacture of Part No. 66, one of its many products. Standard cost data and actual operating results for the month of January when 100 units of Part No. 66 were manufactured, follow:

	Process	
	Assembly	Machining
Type of worker......................................	Unskilled	Skilled
Standard hours per unit........................	4	6
Standard labor rate per hour.................	$2.50	$3.50
Actual hours of operation	390	600
Actual wages......................................	$836	$2,196
Actual hours for which wages were paid:		
Unskilled...	380	
Skilled (of which ten hours were on assembly)		610

Required:

A. Calculate separately for each cost center the direct labor time and individual labor rate variances, and the mix variance attributable to the fact that skilled and unskilled labor shifted jobs for ten hours.

B. Comment on the significance of the variances you calculated.

14–12. The following data pertain to operations of the Roberts Company during the month of May:

> Actual production and sales, 1,250 units @ $57
> Budgeted production and sales, 1,200 units @ $60
> Actual costs, $63,100
> Budgeted costs, $10,000 per month plus $45 per unit

Required:

Calculate the volume and the selling price variances.

14–13. The Townsend Company manufactures goods for inventory. Data pertaining to operations in the month of June are as follows:

> Actual gross margin per unit $19
> Budgeted gross margin per unit................. $20
> Actual sales in units................................ 2,100
> Budgeted sales in units............................ 2,000

Required:

Calculate the margin and the sales volume variances.

14–14. A condensed income statement for the Davis Company is as follows for the month of March:

	Master budget	Actual	Variance*
Units produced and sold..............	15,000	16,000	1,000
Sales revenue	$315,000	$320,000	$ 5,000
Costs:			
Direct materials.......................	45,000	50,000	(5,000)
Direct labor.............................	60,000	63,000	(3,000)
Manufacturing overhead	85,000	89,000	(4,000)
Selling and administration.........	90,000	95,000	(5,000)
Total Costs	280,000	297,000	(17,000)
Operating Income.......................	$ 35,000	$ 23,000	$(12,000)

*( ) = unfavorable.

Further analysis revealed the following data on costs:

	Variable rate per unit	Fixed
Direct materials.............................	$ 3	—
Direct labor....................................	4	—
Manufacturing overhead	3	$ 40,000
Selling and administration..............	2	60,000
Totals...................................	$12	$100,000

Required:

A. Prepare a report comparing the master budget with a flexible budget for March.

B. Calculate the following variances:
1. Volume.
2. Selling price.
3. Direct materials (net).
4. Direct labor (net).
5. Manufacturing overhead (net).
6. Selling and administration (net).

C. Prepare a variance report which accounts for the difference between budgeted and actual operating income for Davis in March.

D. Comment on the significance of the variances you calculated.

14–15. The Bowers Company uses a standard cost system in which raw materials inventories are recorded at actual cost and the material price variance is based on quantities used. The following data refer to production of Product 823 during the month of September:

Standard material cost, $3 per pound
Standard labor rate, $6 per hour

Standard quantity of material per unit of product, 5 pounds
Standard labor hours per unit, 7
Quantity of material actually used, 4,800 pounds
Actual material cost, $3.05 per pound
Actual labor cost, 7,500 hours, $43,500
Units of product produced, 1,000

Required:

A. Calculate the price, usage, and net variances for direct materials and direct labor.
B. Comment on the possible significance of the variances you calculated.

14–16. Jay and Kay Enterprises have a production overhead budget of $300,-000 fixed costs and $200,000 variable costs for a standard monthly volume of 100,000 units of production. Actual overhead costs for February were $485,000, and the company operated at 90 percent of capacity.

Required:

A. Compute the overhead rate.
B. Compute the net overhead variance.
C. Compute the overhead spending and volume variances.
D. Comment on the significance of the variances you computed.

14–17. Sundry Products, Inc., has the following data for production department No. 20, during the month of May:

Standard monthly volume in labor hours 40,000
Standard labor hours allowed for May production 38,000
Budgeted fixed overhead per month......................... $200,000
Variable overhead costs per standard labor hour........ $3
Actual overhead costs for May................................ $320,000

Required:

A. Calculate the overhead rate.
B. Prepare the journal entry showing the application of overhead to goods in process and the net overhead variance.
C. Calculate the overhead spending and volume variances.
D. Draw a graph similar to Exhibit 14–8 showing budgeted, absorbed, and actual costs for overhead in May.
E. Comment on the significance of the overhead variances you calculated above.

14–18. The Posey Company uses a standard cost system. Raw materials inventories are recorded at actual cost, and the material price variance is based on quantities used. Overhead is applied on a units-of-production basis. The following data pertain to production of Product 871 during the month of January:

Standard material cost, $6 per pound
Standard direct labor rate, $5 per hour
Standard quantity of material per unit, 2 pounds
Standard direct labor hours per unit, 3
Quantity of material actually used, 2,100 pounds
Actual material cost, $5.75 per pound
Actual labor cost, 2,900 hours, $14,790
Budgeted fixed overhead per month, $8,000
Variable overhead costs per unit, $4
Standard monthly production volume, 1,000 units
Actual overhead costs, $11,300
Actual production, 950 units

Required:

A. Prepare a variance analysis to account for the difference between actual and standard production costs for January.
B. Comment on the possible significance of the variances you calculated.

14–19. Brown Company uses a standard cost system in which factory overhead is absorbed on the basis of standard direct labor hours. Brown records raw materials inventories at actual cost and calculates price variances at the time material is used. Results for the month of July appear below:

Actual units of direct material purchased	900
Actual units of raw materials put into production	750
Actual direct labor hours used in production	425
Standard direct labor hours used in production	375
Actual factory overhead costs	$3,750
Standard price of one unit of raw material	$6
Variances:	
Raw materials price	$225 Cr.
Labor time	175 Dr.
Factory overhead, total	150 Cr.
Materials usage	150 Dr.
Labor rate	170 Dr.

Required:

Use the data above to compute the following:

A. Standard units of material put into production.
B. Standard labor rate per hour.
C. Actual labor rate per hour.
D. Standard factory overhead rate.
E. Factory overhead absorbed into product.
F. Actual cost per unit of materials.

14–20. Given below are the postings to T-accounts of Northeast Company to record manufacturing costs for the month of July. The company uses a standard cost system which removes the materials price variance upon purchase. All debits to goods in process are at standard cost.

Accounts Payable		**Material Price Variance**		**Materials Inventory**	
xxx	25,000	600		24,400	14,000

Factory Payroll Payable		**Material Use Variance**		**Goods in Process Inventory**	
xxx	33,000		400	14,400	55,200
				33,800	
				22,300	

(Various accounts)		**Labor Rate Variance**		**Finished Goods Inventory**	
xxx	23,000		1,000	55,200	40,000

Factory Overheads		**Labor Time Variance**		**Cost of Goods Sold**	
23,000	22,300	200		40,000	
	700				

Factory Overhead Variance	
700	

Required:

A. Journalize the entries reflected in the postings.

B. Compute the actual Cost of Goods Sold which would appear on the July income statement after closing all variances to Cost of Goods Sold.

14–21. The Brandon Company has just completed its first year of operations. A condensed income statement follows, showing actual and standard amounts and the variances:

Income Statement

	Standard	Actual	Variance
Sales	$1,400	$1,332	
Cost of goods sold	900	800	
Manufacturing variance		(10)	
Gross margin	500	522	$22
General and administrative expense	35	30	5
Income	$ 465	$ 492	$27

Other data pertinent to first-year operations:

Raw material variances:
Price.. $15 favorable
Use.. $ 4 unfavorable

Direct labor variances:
Rate... $10 unfavorable
Time .... $12 favorable
Overhead variances:
Volume .... $29 unfavorable
Spending .... $ 6 favorable

Marketing data

	Standard selling price per unit	Expected sales in units	Actual units sold
Product A..............	$3.20	250	270
Product B	3.00	200	180

Required:

The president of Brandon Company has asked you as controller for the following data which you are to supply:

A. How much of the variance in net income was due to the fact that we sold less than expected of Product B and more of Product A?

B. What would have happened to the net income if we had produced the number of units expected?

C. What would have happened to the total net marketing variance if we had sold the number of units of both A and B that we expected to sell, but at the *actual* selling prices per unit?

D. What is the variance due to the fact that actual selling prices were less than expected? Product A sold for $3 per unit.

14-22. As part of its development activity, Vista Land Company had built a road. Its financial vice president was reviewing a report the construction superintendent had sent:

Cost Report
Wordsworth Drive

Description	Budget Price	Budget Quantity	Budget Total	Actual cost
Grading............	$20/hr.	250 hrs.	$ 5,000	$ 5,040
Paving	$6/yd.	10,000 yds.	60,000	92,400
Labor..............	$5/hr.	800 hrs.	4,000	3,840
Supervision	—	—	2,000	2,000
Overhead	—	—	4,000	4,000
			$75,000	$107,280

Notes:

1. Budget based on a 1,000-yard-long road. Actual length was 1,200 yards.

2. Grading budget based on efficiency factor of 4 yards per hour. Actual performance was 5 yards per hour.

3. Paving budget based on 10 yards of asphalt per yard of road length. Actually needed 11 yards of asphalt per yard of road length.

4. Labor based on $\frac{4}{5}$ hour per yard of road length. Actual efficiency was same as budget.

The financial vice president wanted to evaluate the performance of the work on Wordsworth Drive and specifically wanted to know the reasons why the actual cost of the road exceeded the budget by $32,280.

Required:

Prepare a variance analysis for the Wordsworth Drive project and identify the reasons why cost exceeded budget.

14-23. The diagrams shown below can represent either sales revenue, direct labor costs, or direct material costs. For each case, identify the letters.

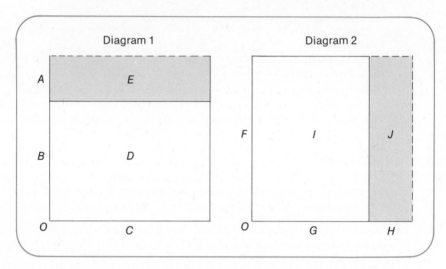

14-24. The diagram shown below reflects the amount of budgeted overhead costs and the amount of absorbed overhead cost at various volumes:

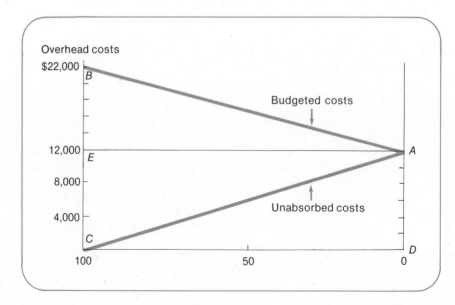

Required:

Answer the following questions based on the diagram:

A. What are the fixed and variable components of the budgeted costs at standard volume?

B. How much is budgeted for 50 percent of standard volume?

C. Compute the volume variance at 50 percent of standard volume.

D. Compute the spending variance at 50 percent of standard volume if actual overhead costs are $18,000.

E. At what percentage of standard volume will overhead costs begin to be overabsorbed?

F. At what percent of standard volume will the amount of overhead debited to Goods in Process total $8,800, of which $4,800 is fixed?

G. At what percent of standard volume will there be a favorable volume variance?

14-25. Refer to the situation depicted in Exhibits 14-9 and 14-10. In the following month the budgeted amounts were as shown in these exhibits and the actual amounts were as shown with the following exceptions:

	As shown	Following month
Sales volume, units.	190	210
Direct material quantity (pounds)	320	340
Direct labor quantity (hours)	40	36
Actual production volume (units)	170	200
Actual overhead costs	$208	$220

Required:

A. Calculate the variances.

B. Prepare an income statement and summary of variances using the format of Exhibit 14-9.

14-26. In a certain month, material costs were as follows:

	Unit price	Quantity (lbs.)	Total cost
Actual	$5	21,000	$105,000
Standard	4	20,000	80,000

Required:

A. Calculate the variances.

B. Show this situation in a diagram similar to that in Exhibit 14-4.

C. Consider the area where the price variance and the usage variance overlap. Does the procedure described in the text treat this area as part of the price variance or as part of the usage variance? Could an argument be made for treating it differently?

CASE: BROADSIDE BOAT BUILDERS, INC.

14-27. Located in Cornish, New Hampshire, Broadside Boat Builders served boaters using New England waters with a small, lightweight fiberglass sailboat capable of being carried on a car roof. While the firm could hardly be considered as one of the nation's industrial giants, its burgeoning business had required it to institute a formal system of cost control.

Pat Decatur, Broadside's president, explained, "Our seasonal demand opposed to a need for regular, level production means that we must keep a good line of credit at the bank. Modern cost control methods and consistent inventory valuation procedures enhance our credibility with the bankers and more importantly have enabled us to improve our methods and procedures. Our supervisors have realized the value of good cost accounting; and the main office has, in turn, become much more aware of problems in the barn."

Broadside's manufacturing and warehouse facilities consisted of three historic, New England barns converted to make eleven-foot "Silver Streak" sailboats. The company's plans included the addition of 15- and 18-foot sailboats to its present line. Longer term plans called for adding additional sizes and styles in the hope of becoming a major factor in the regional boat market.

The "Silver Streak" was an open cockpit, day sailer sporting a mainsail and small jib on a 17-foot, telescoping, aluminum mast. It was ideally suited to the many small lakes and ponds of the region, and after three years it had become quite popular. It was priced at $450 complete.

Manufacturing consisted basically of three processes: molding, finishing, and assembly. The molding department mixed all ingredients to make the fiberglass hull, performed the actual molding, and removed the hull from the mold. Finishing included hand additions to the hull for running and standing rigging, reinforcement of the mast and tiller steps, and general sanding of rough spots. Assembly consisted of the attachment of cleats, turnbuckles, drain plugs, tiller, and so on, and the inspection of the boat with mast, halyards, and sails in place. The assembly department also prepared the boat for storage or shipment.

Mixing and molding fiberglass hulls, while manually simple, required a great deal of expertise, or "eyeball," as it was known in the trade. Addition of too much or too little catalyst, use of too much or too little heat, or failure to allow proper time for curing could each cause a hull to be discarded. Conversely, spending too much time on adjustments to mixing or molding equipment or on "personalized" supervision of each hull could cause severe underproduction problems. Once a batch of fiberglass was mixed there was no time to waste being overcautious or it was likely to "freeze" in its kettle.

With such a situation, and the company's announced intent of expanding their product line, it became obvious that a standard cost system would be necessary to help control costs and to provide some reference for foreman performance.

Davey Jones, the molding department supervisor, and Rick Ober, Broadsides' accountant, agreed after lengthy discussion to the following standard costs:

Materials — glass cloth — 120 square feet @ $0.40 .... $48
            — glass mix — 40 pounds @ $0.75 30
Direct labor — mixing — 0.5 hours @ $4 2
             — molding — 1.0 hours @ $4 4
Indirect costs:
   *Absorb at $3 per hull 3
    Total cost to mold hull $87

* The normal volume of operations for overhead derivation purposes was assumed to be 450 hulls per month. The estimated monthly indirect cost equation was: budget = $1.44 × hulls + $702.

Analysis of operations:

After several additional months of operations, Ober expressed disappointment about the apparent lack of attention being paid to the standard costs. Molders tended to have a cautious outlook toward mixing too little or "cooking" too long. No one wanted to end up throwing away a partial hull because of too little glass mix.

In reviewing the most recent month's production results, Ober noted the following actual costs for production of 430 hulls:

Materials:
   Purchased:
     60,000 square glass cloth @ $0.39 per square foot
     20,000 pounds glass mix @ $0.76 per pound
   Used:
     54,000 square feet glass cloth
     19,000 pounds glass mix
Direct labor:
   Mixing 210 hours at $4.10 per hour
   Molding 480 hours at $4 per hour
Overhead:
   Incurred $1,400

Before proceeding with further analysis, Ober called Jones to arrange a discussion of variances. He told Ms. Decatur, "Maybe we should look into an automated molding operation. Although I haven't finished my analysis, it looks like there will be unfavorable variances again. Jones insists that the standards are reasonable, then never meets them!"

Ms. Decatur seemed disturbed and answered, "Well, some variances are inevitable. Why don't you analyze them in some meaningful manner and discuss your ideas with Jones? He is an expert in molding whose opinion I respect. Then the two of you meet with me to discuss the whole matter."

Required:

A. Determine the molding department direct cost and overhead variances. Why do you think they occurred?

B. Do you think Broadside's standards are meaningful? How would you improve them?

CASE: COTTER CO., INC.

14–28. In preparing its annual profit plan, the management of the Cotter Company, Inc., realized that its sales were subject to monthly seasonal variations but expected that for the year as a whole the profit before taxes would total $240,000, as shown below:

	Annual budget	
	Amount	Percent of sales
Sales	$2,400,000	100
Standard cost of goods sold:		
Prime costs...	960,000	40
Factory overhead	840,000	35
Total Standard Cost	1,800,000	75
Gross margin...	600,000	25
Selling and general overhead...................	360,000	15
Income before taxes..............................	$ 240,000	10

Management defined "prime costs" as those costs for labor and materials which were strictly variable with the quantity of production in the factory. The overhead in the factory included both fixed and variable costs; management's estimate was that within a sales volume range of plus or minus $1,000,000 per year, variable factory overhead would be equal to 25 percent of prime costs. Thus the total factory overhead budgeted for the year consisted of $240,000 of variable costs (25 percent of $960,000) and $600,000 of fixed costs. All of the selling and general overhead was fixed, except for commissions on sales equal to 5 percent of the selling price.

Cotter, the president of the company, approved the budget, stating that, "A profit of $20,000 a month isn't bad for a little company in this business." During January, however, sales suffered the normal seasonal dips, and production in the factory was also cut back. The result, which came as some surprise to the president, was that January showed a loss of $7,000.

Operating Statement
January

Sales		$140,000
Standard cost of goods sold......		105,000
Standard gross margin		35,000
	Favorable or	
Manufacturing variances:	(unfavorable)	
Prime cost variance..............	$ (3,500)	
Factory overhead:		
Spending variance.............	1,000	
Volume variance	(12,500)	(15,000)
Actual gross margin		20,000
Selling and general overhead ...		27,000
Loss before taxes....................		$ (7,000)

Required:

A. Explain, as best you can with the data available, why the January profit was $27,000 less than the average monthly profit expected by the president.
B. What is Cotter's monthly break-even volume?
C. What was Cotter's January production level?
D. How much did finished goods inventory change in January?
E. What were actual overhead costs in January?

15

Control reports and their use

Previous chapters in Part Three discussed the formulation of budgets and the analysis of variances between budgeted performance and actual performance. The present chapter describes how information regarding performance is communicated to managers and how managers use this information. The vehicle for communicating this information is called a control report. The chapter discusses the general nature of control reports, criteria governing their content, and their uses and limitations. Our focus is primarily on the cost and revenue aspects of performance, but other aspects of performance are discussed briefly.

TYPES OF MANAGEMENT REPORTS

We can distinguish three types of reports that are prepared for the use of managers: (1) information reports, (2) economic performance reports, and (3) personal performance, or control, reports. We shall discuss primarily the third type, but will mention briefly the nature of the other two types because they are important parts of the total communications that managers receive.

Information reports

Information reports are designed to tell management what is going on. (They are sometimes called "Howgozit" reports to highlight this purpose.) They may or may not lead to action. Each reader studies these reports to detect whether or not something has happened that requires looking into. If nothing of significance is noted, which is often the case, the report is put aside without action. If something does strike the reader's attention, an inquiry or an action is initiated.

The information on these reports may come from the accounting system, but it may also come from a wide variety of other sources. Information reports derived from accounting records include income statements, balance sheets, statements of changes in financial position, and details on such items as cash balances, the status of accounts receivable, the status of inventories, and lists of accounts payable that are coming due. A list of other possible information reports would be very long indeed. It would include reports on such *internal* information as quantities of material received, sales orders received, production that was not up to quality standards, and absenteeism; and such *external* information as general news summaries, stock market prices, information on the industry from trade associations, and economic information published by the government. An example of an information report is shown in Exhibit 15–1.

Performance reports

There are two general types of reports about the performance of a responsibility center. One type deals with its performance as an *economic entity*. A conventional income statement prepared for a division or other profit center is an **economic performance report,** and the net income shown at the bottom of such an income statement is a basic measure of economic performance. The other type focuses on the performance of the *manager* of the profit center. This latter type is usually referred to as a control report.

Economic performance reports are derived from conventional accounting information, including full cost accounting. **Control reports** are prepared from responsibility accounting information. Essentially they report how well the manager did compared with some standard of what he was expected to do.

The control report may show that a profit center manager is doing an excellent job, considering the circumstances; but if the profit center is not producing a satisfactory profit, action may be required regardless of this fact.

> *EXAMPLE:* Current control reports show that a certain downtown branch of a chain of specialty stores is operating at a loss. This loss is explainable by the fact that customers are tending to shop in suburban shopping centers rather than downtown. The store manager is not responsible for this trend. Nevertheless, an economic analysis may reveal no way to put the

EXHIBIT 15-1

Example of sales information report

SALES AND GROSS PROFIT BY CUSTOMER

BY TERRITORY THROUGH MARCH 1972

CUSTOMER NO.	NAME	TERRITORY NUMBER	SALES DOLLARS MONTH	SALES DOLLARS YEAR–TO–DATE	GROSS PROFIT DOLLARS MONTH	GROSS PROFIT DOLLARS YEAR–TO–DATE	GROSS PROFIT PERCENT OF SALES MONTH	GROSS PROFIT PERCENT OF SALES YEAR–TO–DATE
0007	ABC Company	18	1,000	5,000	200	1,250	20	25
1234	Acme Hardware	18	5,000	10,000	1,100	3,000	22	30
6600	XYZ Company	18	2,500	10,000	1,000	3,500	40	35
	TOTAL Territory 18 — Louisville		8,500*	25,000*	2,300*	7,750*	27*	31*
1300	All Purpose Supply	19	2,000	11,000	900	5,100	45	46
5000	Metro Distributor	19	6,000	42,000	1,800	15,000	30	36
6000	Union Construction	19	23,000	60,000	4,300	17,400	19	29
	TOTAL Territory 19 — Nashville		31,000*	113,000*	7,000*	37,500*	23*	33*
	TOTAL MID–SOUTH REGION		337,900**	1,200,000**	121,000**	400,000*	36**	33**

SALES STATISTICS FOR SPECIFIC CUSTOMER

Customer No. 6600 — XYZ Company

Shipping PLANT	PRODUCT CODE	PRODUCT DESCRIPTION	SALES UNITS MONTH	SALES UNITS Y–T–D	SALES DOLLARS MONTH	SALES DOLLARS Y–T–D	CLAIMS MONTH	CLAIMS Y–T–D	GROSS PROFIT MONTH DOLLARS	GROSS PROFIT MONTH %	GROSS PROFIT Y–T–D DOLLARS	GROSS PROFIT Y–T–D %
1	1111	A–1	200	700	320	1,050	–	–	200	63	630	60
1	1112	A–2	–	50	–	75	–	–	–	–	15	20
1	2222	B–1	–	100	–	125	–	–	–	–	50	40
1	2223	B–2	200	500	200	500	–	–	60	30	150	30
	Total from Plant 1		400	1,350	520	1,750	–	–	260	50	845	48
	Less Freight Absorbed		–	–	–	–	–	–	50	10	150	9
	Gross Profit		–	–	–	–	–	–	210	40	695	39
2	3333	C–1	20	50	50	75	–	–	30	60	25	33
2	3334	C–2	1,000	4,000	1,930	8,175	100	100	860	45	3,740	46
	Total from Plant 2		1,020	4,050	1,980	8,250	100	100	890	45	3,765	46
	Less Freight Absorbed		–	–	–	–	–	–	100	5	960	12
	Gross Profit		–	–	–	–	–	–	790	40	2,805	34
	GRAND TOTALS:											
	Before Freight		–	–	–	–	–	–	1,150	46	4,610	46
	Freight Absorbed		–	–	–	–	–	–	150	6	1,110	11
	After Freight		1,420	5,400	2,500	10,000	100	100	1,000	40	3,500	35

Source: H. V. Stephens, "A Profit-Oriented Marketing Information System," *Management Accounting*, September 1972, p. 40.

downtown store on a profitable basis. The decision is therefore made to close this store and open a new store in the suburbs.

There are therefore two essentially different ways in which the performance of a responsibility center is judged. First, there is the control report which focuses on the manager's responsibility for turning in an actual performance that corresponds to the commitment made during the budget preparation process. **Behavioral** considerations are important in the use of this report. Second, there is the analysis of the responsibility center as an economic entity. In such an analysis, **economic** considerations are dominant.

We mention economic performance reports primarily in order to emphasize the difference between these reports and control reports. In the balance of the chapter, we discuss control reports.

CONTENTS OF CONTROL REPORTS

Recall these basic facts about organizations: An organization has goals, and it has strategies for achieving these goals. Each responsibility center in the organization is expected to do its part in achieving the organization's goals. To the extent that these expectations can be stated in terms of revenues and costs, they are set forth in the budget for the responsibility center.

The purpose of control reports is to communicate how well managers of responsibility centers performed. If the budget was a valid statement of expected performance, the control report would simply compare actual performance with budgeted performance. It is likely, however, that during the period being reported on the circumstances were not exactly the same as those assumed when the budget was prepared. Thus, it is not necessarily correct to state that conforming to the budget represents "good" performance, and departing from the budget is "poor" performance. The interpretation of control reports is more complicated than this.

The essential purpose of a control report is to compare actual performance in a responsibility center with what performance should have been under the circumstances prevailing, in such a way that reasons for the difference between actual and standard performance are identified and, if feasible, quantified. It follows that three kinds of information are conveyed in such reports: (1) information on what performance *actually was;* (2) information on what performance *should have been;* and (3) reasons for the difference between actual and expected performance.

The foregoing suggests three essential characteristics of good control reports:

1. Reports should be related to personal responsibility.
2. Actual performance should be compared with the best available standard.
3. Significant information should be highlighted.

As a basis for discussing these points, we shall use the set of control reports shown in Exhibit 15–2.

Focus on personal responsibility

In this Part Three, we have emphasized *responsibility accounting,* that is, the type of accounting that classifies costs and revenues according to the responsibility centers that are responsible for incurring the costs and generating the revenues. Responsibility accounting therefore

EXHIBIT 15–2
Package of control reports

A. First (or, lowest) level report

Drill press department (supervisor)	Actual		(Over) or under budget	
	June	Year to date	June	Year to date
Output:				
Standard direct labor hours......	810	4,060	85	401
Direct labor cost:				
Amount..................................	$ 3,860	$ 22,140	$ 360	$ 1,140
Usage variance			622	1,807
Rate variance..........................			(262)	(667)
Controllable overhead:				
Setup costs	1,187	7,224	(265)	90
Repair and rework...................	520	2,916	180	91
Overtime premium...................	484	2,748	(75)	(530)
Supplies.................................	215	1,308	(121)	(386)
Small tools	260	1,521	160	(82)
Other	644	3,888	91	195
Total	$ 3,310	$ 19,605	$ (30)	$ (620)

B. Second level report

Production department cost summary
(general superintendent)

	Actual		Variance	
	June	Year to date	June	Year to date
Direct labor:				
Drill press................................	$ 3,860	$ 22,140	$ 360	$ 1,140
Screw machine	5,240	31,760	540	1,560
Total	$27,120	$161,970	$ 3,020	$ 5,130

	Amount		(Over) or under budget	
	June	Year to date	June	Year to date
Controllable overhead:				
Office.....................................	$ 1,960	$ 12,300	$ (115)	$ (675)
Drill press...............................	3,310	19,605	(30)	(620)
Screw machine	3,115	18,085	90	(135)
Punch press	5,740	33,635	(65)	(640)
Plating	1,865	9,795	(175)	825
Heat treating..........................	3,195	18,015	210	35
Assembly................................	5,340	35,845	(625)	(1,380)
Total	$24,525	$147,280	$ (710)	$(2,590)

C. Third level report

Factory cost summary (vice president of production)	Amount		(Over) or under budget	
	June	Year to date	June	Year to date
Controllable overhead:				
Vice president's office..............	$ 2,110	$ 12,030	$ (315)	$ 35
General superintendent............	24,525	147,280	(710)	(2,590)
Production control	1,235	7,570	(125)	(210)
Purchasing	1,180	7,045	95	75
Maintainance	3,590	18,960	(235)	245
Tool room	4,120	25,175	160	(320)
Inspection	2,245	13,680	180	(160)
Receiving, shipping, stores.......	3,630	22,965	(70)	(730)
Total	$42,635	$254,705	$(1,020)	$(3,655)

	Standard		Variance	
	June	Year to date	June	Year to date
Direct labor	$27,120	$161,970	$ 3,020	$ 5,130

provides information that meets the criterion that reports should be related to personal responsibility.

Responsibility accounting also classifies the costs assigned to each responsibility center according to whether they are controllable or noncontrollable. Many control reports show only controllable costs; nevertheless, some of them contain noncontrollable costs for information purposes. In Exhibit 15–2, only controllable costs are reported. Note that these include only direct labor cost and controllable overhead cost. Direct material cost is not included on these reports because in the departments included on these reports neither the quantity nor the price of material used is controllable by the department manager. The manager is responsible, however, for repair and rework costs of material or products that are defective, and this item of controllable cost does appear on the report.

In order to facilitate analysis and corrective action, the total amount of controllable cost is classified by item (also called *object,* or *natural element,* or *function*). Indirect labor, supplies, power, heat, overtime premiums, and spoilage are examples from the long list of cost elements that might be useful in a given situation.

In summary, **responsibility accounting requires that costs be classified: (1) by responsibility centers; (2) within each responsibility center, by whether controllable or noncontrollable; and (3) within the controllable classification by cost elements, in sufficient detail to provide a useful basis for analysis.**

Selection of a standard

A report that contains information *only* on actual performance is virtually useless for control purposes; it becomes useful only when actual performance is compared with some standard. Standards used in control reports are of three types: (1) predetermined standards or budgets, (2) historical standards, or (3) external standards.

Predetermined standards or budgets, if carefully prepared, are the best formal standard. The validity of such a standard depends largely on how much care went into its development. If the budget numbers were arrived at in a slipshod manner, they obviously will not provide a reliable basis for comparison. Methods for arriving at the best possible budgets and the related standard costs were described in Chapters 12 and 13. This is the type of standard used in Exhibit 15–2.

Historical standards are records of past actual performance. Results for the current month may be compared with results for last month, or with results for the same month a year ago. This type of standard has two serious weaknesses: (1) conditions may have changed between the two periods in a way that invalidates the comparison; and (2) when a manager is measured against his own past record, there may be no way of knowing whether the prior period's performance was acceptable to start with. A supervisor whose department's spoilage cost is $500 a month, month after month, is consistent; but we do not know, without other evidence, whether this performance is consistently good or consistently poor. Despite these inherent weaknesses, historical standards are used in many companies. There are three principal reasons for their popularity.

1. The use of budgets is a comparatively recent development. Some managers who have become accustomed to comparing current performance with past performance feel comfortable with such comparisons and are reluctant to change.

2. In some circumstances, the budget may not be reliable. Past performance is a number drawn directly from the accounting records; it cannot normally be "fudged." Although a carefully prepared budget usually is a better standard than past experience, if the future is extremely uncertain, it may not be possible to set a sound standard in advance. This can happen, for example, when budgeted sales volume is little more than a guess because of unsettled business conditions.

3. In some organizations, conditions may not in fact change significantly from one year to the next. In the dynamic society in which we live, such organizations are rare, but when this situation does prevail, the work required to prepare a budget may be viewed as being unnecessary. If past performance is judged to have been satisfactory, it can be used as a standard against which current performance is compared.

External standards are standards derived from the performance of responsibility centers other than the one for which the control report is intended. The performance of one branch sales office may be compared with the performance of other branch sales offices, for example. If conditions in these responsibility centers are similar, such a comparison may

EXHIBIT 15–3

Comparison with industry data—women's apparel department

| | Marshall Company | | Industry* |
	(000)	Ratio	
Sales	$1,647	100.0%	100.0%
Cost of goods sold	977	59.3	57.9
Gross margin	670	40.7	42.1
Sales returns	102	6.2	9.2
Selling salaries	112	6.8	7.7
Sales promotion	21	1.3	2.2
Sales per square foot ($)		$91.6	$109.2
Cash discounts (% of purchases)		6.3%	7.8%
Stock turn (times at retail)		3.4	3.9

* Source: *Department and Specialty Store Merchandising and Operating Results, 1974* (New York: Financial Executives Division, National Retail Merchants Association, 1975). Data for adult female apparel departments, department stores, sales $5–$10 million.

provide a useful basis for judging performance. The catch is that it is not easy to find two responsibility centers that are sufficiently similar, or whose performance is affected by the same factors, to permit such comparisons on a regular basis. Thus, external standards are more likely to be used in special studies, such as the zero-base review discussed in Chapter 12, than in regular control reports.

Exhibit 15–3 is an example of a report that compares performance of one department in a company with the averages of the corresponding departments of stores of similar size. Note that it does not contain a complete income statement; rather, it gives only a few key figures.

Highlighting significant information

The problem of designing a good set of control reports has changed drastically since the advent of the computer. When data had to be collected and reported manually, great care had to be taken to limit the quantity of information contained in reports because the cost of preparing them was relatively high. By contrast, a computer can print out more figures in a minute than a manager can assimilate in a day. Thus, the current problem is to decide on the *right type* of information that should be given to management. To provide managers with less information than they need is bad, but to deluge them with information that they do not need is almost as bad.

Individual cost and revenue elements therefore should be reported only when they are likely to be significant. Reporting a long list of cost items, many of which have only minor amounts, tends to obscure the few really significant ones. Related minor items should be aggregated into a single item (for example, costs for space heating, electric lighting, and air conditioning can be reported as "utilities"). Other minor items can be lumped together into a catchall classification, "other," as is done in Exhibit 15–2. Because control reports tend to have a standard format, not all the items are likely to be significant in each reporting period; the intent is that the items shown on the report are *likely to be* significant; they are items that the manager *probably* should be concerned about. If, in a given period, an item is not significant, as is the case with several of the items in Exhibit 15–2, the manager simply skips over it.

The significance of an item is not necessarily proportional to its size. Management may be interested in a cost item of relatively small amount if this item is one which is largely discretionary and therefore warrants close attention (such as travel expense, professional dues, or books and periodicals), or if costs incurred for the item may be symptomatic of a larger problem (such as spoilage and rework costs, which may indicate problems of quality control).

For repetitive manufacturing operations, **statistical quality control** techniques are available which signal when a deviation from an established standard of satisfactory quality is large enough to be significant. These techniques are usually not adaptable to control reports for an entire responsibility center, however. The factors that affect the behavior of the various cost items are so diverse and irregular that significance must be determined by judgment, rather than by statistical analysis.

The exception principle.   A management control system should operate on the **exception principle.** This principle states that a control report should focus management's attention on the relatively small number of items in which actual performance is significantly different from the standard. When this is done, little or no attention need be given to the relatively large number of situations where performance is satisfactory.

No control system makes a perfect distinction between the situations that warrant management attention and those that do not. For example, although those items for which actual spending significantly *exceeds* the budgeted amount are usually "red flagged" for further investigation, the investigation of these items may reveal that the variance was entirely justified. Conversely, even though actual spending exactly matches the budget allowance, an unsatisfactory situation may exist.

> *EXAMPLE:* When the general superintendent reads the production department cost summary report (Part B of Exhibit 15–2), his attention is not called to the performance of the drill press department in June because its actual costs were only $30 in excess of standard, an insignificant amount. We can observe from the details of drill press performance in Part A, however, that setup costs, overtime premium, and supplies are considerably in excess of standard, and these excesses may indicate that problems do exist.

The exception principle is tricky to apply in practice because it requires that the significant items be identified. As mentioned above, significance is a judgmental matter.

In order to focus attention on significant matters, control reports usually omit the arithmetic calculations used to derive the reported numbers. In Exhibit 15–2, for example, the direct labor usage and rate variances are shown, but not the calculations of these variances.

Note also that Exhibit 15–2 does not show the budgeted amounts, but only the differences between actual and budget. Some control reports have three columns: (1) actual, (2) standard (or budget), and (3) variance. The "standard" column is unnecessary. If a reader should be interested in what the standard amount is, he can find it by adding the actual and the variance. It could be argued that the significant information is the variance, and that the actual amount is also unnecessary; however, the actual does provide an indication of the magnitude of the item, and managers tend to be uncomfortable if a control report does not contain actual data.

Key variables.   In most businesses, and in most responsibility centers within a business, there are a limited number of factors which must be watched closely. These are called **key variables** or **key success factors.** They are factors that can shift quickly and in an unpredictable way, and when they do shift they have a significant effect on profits. The volume of incoming sales orders is a key variable in most businesses, for example. The number of such variables is small, six or so in a given responsibility center. The reporting system should be designed so that particular attention is paid to them.

> *EXAMPLE:* A dentist states that she needs to keep track of only three items to know how well she is doing financially: (1) billed hours (the number of hours spent daily with patients); (2) accounts receivable as a ratio of monthly billings (as an indication of whether patients are paying their bills promptly); and (3) ratio of expenses to revenues.

Management by objectives.   Our description has emphasized financial information, that is, revenues, expenses, and income. At best, such information gives an incomplete view of performance in a responsibility center. Many things happen that are not reflected in the financial amounts, or at least, are not reflected in the amounts of the current period, even though they may have an important effect on profits in future periods. Furthermore, in nonprofit organizations, profit is not a goal anyway. Thus, a control system should include information in addition to that derived from the accounting records.

Systems that do this have come to be called **management by objectives** systems. They get this name because in the course of preparing budgets, managers state specific objectives that are to be attained during the budget period. Control reports compare actual accomplishments with these planned objectives. Nonfinancial objectives are especially important in expense centers because, by definition, the financial reports do not measure the outputs (i.e., revenues) of expense centers.

> *EXAMPLE:* District sales managers may have as objectives: (1) calling on x prospective customers, (2) obtaining y new accounts, (3) training salespeople in the characteristics of specified new products, (4) increasing market share in specified geographic areas, and so on.

TECHNICAL CRITERIA FOR REPORTS

In addition to the basic characteristics described above, a well-designed system of control reports should meet certain technical criteria. Among these are:

1. Reports should be timely.
2. Information should be communicated clearly.
3. Reports should be integrated.
4. Reports must be worth more than they cost.

Timing of reports

The timing of reports has two aspects: (1) the period of time covered by one report and (2) the interval between the end of the period and the issuance of the report for that period.

The control period. **The proper control period, that is, the period of time covered by one report, is the shortest period of time in which management can usefully intervene and in which significant changes in performance are likely.** The period is different for different responsibility centers and for different items of cost and output within responsibility centers. Spoilage rates in a production operation may be reported hourly, or oftener, because if a machine starts to function improperly the situation must be corrected at once. Certain other key cost elements of a production cost center may be measured daily. Reports on sales orders received or sales revenue are often made daily or weekly or, as in the case of automobile manufacturers, every ten days, because of the variability of this item, its importance, and the necessity for taking prompt action if significant variances occur. Reports on overall performance, particularly those going to top levels of management, usually are on a monthly basis, as in Exhibit 15–2. Top management does not have either the time or the inclination to explore local, temporary problems.

Arguments for a relatively long control period are: (1) performance for a short period of time is influenced by random factors that tend to average out over longer periods; (2) reports that cover short time periods cost more per year and require more time of managers at all levels than reports that cover longer periods; and (3) frequent reports may be associated with unduly restrictive supervision. These considerations in favor of a relatively long control period may be offset, of course, by the necessity for detecting serious trouble quickly: a change in the behavior of a continuous chemical processing operation must be known as soon as it occurs, or there may be an explosion. Also if an out-of-control situation develops, the longer it continues without detection, the more unnecessary costs will be incurred.

Reporting interval. The other aspect of report timing is the interval that elapses between the end of the period covered by the report and the issuance of the report itself. Obviously, this interval should be as short as is feasible. For monthly reports, the interval desirably should be less than a week. In order to meet this deadline, it may be necessary to make approximations of certain "actual" amounts for which exact information is not available, or to take other shortcuts. Such approximations are worthwhile because an **approximately accurate report provided promptly is far preferable to a precisely accurate report that is furnished so long after the event that no effective action can be taken.** One of the benefits of a computer is that it usually speeds up significantly the process of preparing and issuing reports.

Clarity of communication

Since a control report is a communication device, it obviously is not doing its job unless it communicates the intended message clearly. This is much easier said than done. There is room for much misunderstanding in interpreting the meaning of the numbers on a report. Those who are responsible for designing control reports are therefore well advised to spend much time in choosing terms that convey the intended meaning and in arranging the numbers on the report in a way that emphasizes the intended relationships.

One small, but troublesome, matter is the way of indicating whether variances are favorable or unfavorable. The device used in Exhibit 15-2 is coming to be widely used: parentheses are used to indicate *unfavorable variances,* that is, variances that have the effect of making net income less that the budgeted amount. This means that—

- For **revenue** items, parentheses indicate that actual revenue was **less than** budgeted revenue.
- For **cost and expense** items, parentheses indicate that actual cost and expense was **greater than** budgeted amounts.

Clarity may also be enhanced if the variances are expressed as **percentages** of budget (i.e., variance ÷ budget), as well as in absolute dollars. The percentage gives a quick impression of how important the variance is relative to the budget.

Particularly in reports for profit centers, clarity may be enhanced if **ratios** are used to call attention to important relationships. Such ratios are described in Chapter 16 of *Fundamentals of Financial Accounting.*

Two devices not illustrated in Exhibit 15-2 are often useful in aiding clarity: (1) explanations and (2) graphs.

Explanatory material may do nothing more than narrate in words the highlights of what the report already says in numbers. For example, a narrative of the report in Part A of Exhibit 15-2 might begin: "Direct labor costs this June were $360 under standard, but this was the net effect of a $622 favorable usage variance and a $262 unfavorable rate variance. Controllable overhead was within $30 of budget. . . ." Such a narrative seems to help some managers comprehend the intended message of the report, but it actually does no more than restate what the report itself says.

A quite different type of explanation goes farther than this. Such an explanation of Exhibit 15-2 might say, for example: "The unfavorable rate variance was the result of the use of three machine operators in Pay Grade 6, whereas the job called for Pay Grade 5. This has been going on since April because no Pay Grade 5 employees were available. The situation should be corrected before the end of July."

The use of graphs rather than tables of numbers is primarily a matter of personal preference. A graph gives an overall impression of relationships more vividly than does a table, but not as much information can be conveyed by a graph as by a table of comparable size. Some companies use both graphs and tabular reports. Exhibit 15–4 shows a graph that could accompany the report of the drill press department (Exhibit 15–2A). It gives a clear picture of the *trend* of actual costs in relation to

EXHIBIT 15–4
Graphic report of cost performance

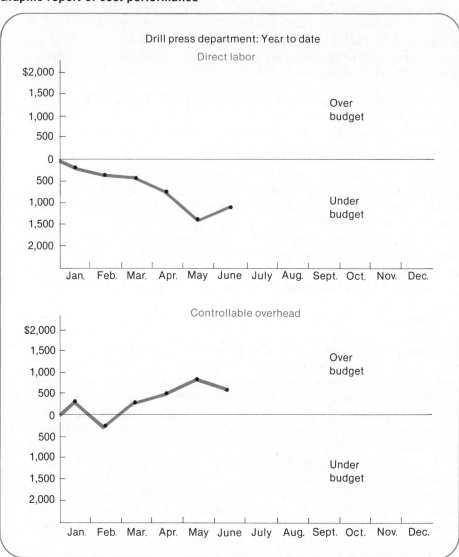

budget, but necessarily omits much of the detail that is contained in Exhibit 15–2.

Rounding. In order to focus on significant information, the numbers in control reports ordinarily are rounded. Some companies report numbers to the last penny, such as:

Direct labor............................. $127,241.83

In the underlying accounting records, such meticulousness is necessary, but it serves no useful purpose in control reports. Readers don't care about the 83 cents; they probably don't care about the 241 dollars. They can get an adequate impression about the size of direct labor costs from the $127 thousand. As a rough rule of thumb, three digits of data are usually adequate in control reports (although certain items might have more or fewer than three digits in order to make a whole column of numbers easy to understand). Thus, the direct labor item above would be reported as $127,000, or the heading of the report would say "000 omitted," or "dollar amounts in thousands," with the amount reported as $127.

The amount of rounding depends on the size of the responsibility center. Rounding to thousands of dollars will show three digits of information for items that are between $99,500 and $999,500. For smaller responsibility centers, amounts might be rounded to hundreds of dollars; this is often written as "000 omitted," but with one number to the right of the decimal point, that is, $127.2. Reports for larger responsibility centers might be rounded to millions of dollars or, as in the case of the Department of Defense, which is the largest organization in the United States, to tenths of billions.

Integrated reports

Monthly control reports should consist of an integrated package; that is, **the reports for lower level responsibility centers should be consistent with and easily relatable to summary reports that are prepared for higher level responsibility centers, and these in turn should be consistent with the summary report for the whole company.**

Parts B and C of Exhibit 15–2 illustrate this process of summarization. Part B is a control report for the general superintendent, who is on the next higher level in the organization hierarchy above the individual production departments. It is a summary report. Data for the drill press department, which is one of several departments for which the general superintendent is responsible, appear in summary form on this report. Note that the amounts reported in Part B for the drill press department are the same as the totals on the report for the drill press department, Part A. The superintendent uses this report to identify departments whose total costs appear to be out of line, and he then refers to the detailed reports for these departments. In the situation illustrated, the superintendent probably would be most interested in the plating and assembly departments because their actual controllable overhead costs were significantly in excess of budget.

Part C is a control report for an even higher level, the total production operation. It includes the general superintendent's departments, as reported in detail on Part B, plus the staff departments that report to the vice president of production, plus the expenses of the vice president's own office. Note that the totals in Part B appear as one line in Part C.

Cost of reporting

It is obvious that a reporting system, like anything else, should not cost more than it is worth. Unfortunately, there are great difficulties in applying this statement to practical situations. Although researchers are attempting in various ways to measure the value of management information, they have not had much success. Moreover, it is no simple matter to measure the cost of a given report, partly because most of the preparation costs are joint and partly because the real cost includes not only the preparation cost but also the cost of the man-hours that managers spend reading the report when they might be doing something else.

At least one practical statement can be made: If no one uses a report, it is not worthwhile. Useless reports are not uncommon. They come about because a new problem area created the need for a report at some earlier time and although the problem area disappeared, the report continues. It is therefore worthwhile to review a company's set of reports from time to time and eliminate reports that are no longer needed. A report structure, like a tree, is often better if it is pruned.

It is unfortunately true that **the more relevant a piece of information is, the more difficult it is to measure.** An estimate of future performance is more difficult to make than a record of past performance, but it is more useful. A timely report, that is, one furnished shortly after the events report on, is more difficult to compile than a report submitted long after the period has ended, but it is more useful. A measurement requiring judgment is more useful than one obtained by reading meters or other objective information, but it is more difficult. Thus, in designing a control report system, a balance must be drawn between what management would like to have and what it is feasible to furnish.

FORMAT OF CONTROL REPORTS

Exhibits 15–5 and 15–6 are additional examples of well-designed control reports.

Exhibit 15–5 is a control report for a profit center. Note that only a moderate amount of detail is shown, but that there is a breakdown be-

EXHIBIT 15–5
Control report for a profit center ($000 omitted)

Month of _____ June _____   Division _____ Seattle Stone _____

	This month			Year to date		
	Actual	Budget	Better or (worse)	Actual	Budget	Better or (worse)
Sales...	1,665	1,589	76	8,391	7,915	476
Cost of sales:						
Variable cost of sales..................	897	963	66	4,930	4,819	(111)
Fixed plant expense	232	216	(16)	1,253	1,245	(8)
Production variance	27	...	(27)	20	...	(20)
Total Cost of Sales.............	1,156	1,179	23	6,203	6,064	(139)
Gross margin............................	509	410	99	2,188	1,851	337
Expenses:						
Selling	44	40	(4)	238	234	(4)
Administration	64	62	(2)	381	365	(16)
Total Expenses	108	102	(6)	619	599	(20)
Operating income.......................	401	308	93	1,569	1,252	317
Add: Other income....................	1	10	(9)	72	18	54
Less: Other expense..................	3	2	(1)	20	11	(9)
Pretax Income...........................	399	316	83	1,621	1,259	362

EXHIBIT 15–6
Divisional performance report, May 1976 (000 omitted)

Glassware Division	Month of May	Year to date
Actual operating income.........................	$ 39	$260
Budgeted operating income	43	242
Variance...	$ (4)	$ 18

Analysis of variances*

Revenue items:		
Sales volume.....................................	$ 12	$ (24)
Margin	(3)	6
Total Revenue Variance................	9	(18)
Cost items:		
Material prices....................................	(6)	(17)
Material usage....................................	8	5
Direct labor	(7)	24
Volume	8	(13)
Overhead spending	(12)	14
Marketing..	3	5
Administration	(7)	18
Total Cost Variance......................	(13)	36
Total Variance	$ (4)	$ 18

*(   ) = unfavorable.

tween variable costs and fixed costs. The report compares budget and actual both for the current month and for the year to date, which is common practice.

Exhibit 15–6 is an even more compressed report along the same lines. It gives neither actual amounts nor budgeted amounts, but lists only the variances.

Exhibit 15–7 shows how *not* to prepare a control report. Some of its deficiencies are:

1. It covers a six months' period, with no indication of performance in the most recent month or quarter. This period is unduly long for effective control.

EXHIBIT 15–7
Expense center report

NEW JERSEY INSURANCE COMPANY
Budget Report, Corporate Loan Section
First Six Months, 1976

Costs	Budget	Actual
Employee costs:		
Salaries, full time	$109,680	$101,472
Salaries, part time		120
Salaries, overtime	1,200	280
Borrowed labor		280
Employee lunches	4,130	3,742
Insurance, retirement, etc.	13,891	11,845
Social security	3,006	2,742
Total	131,907	120,481
Direct service costs:		
Photography	655	541
Tracing	292	106
Mimeograph		27
Reproduction		14
Total	947	688
Other costs:		
Rent	16,781	16,781
Office supplies	740	1,182
Equipment, depreciation, and maintenance	3,096	3,096
Printed forms	178	366
Travel	772	752
Telephone and telegrams	910	1,134
Postage	168	156
Allocated corporate costs	7,085	6,343
Professional dues	80	80
Miscellaneous	1,073	1,165
Total	30,883	31,055
Grand Total	$163,737	$152,224
Number of full-time employees	26	24

2. It makes no distinction between controllable and noncontrollable costs. Equipment depreciation and allocated corporate costs, which are noncontrollable, are intermingled with items of controllable cost.
3. It lists items of minor importance, such as part-time salaries, borrowed labor, mimeograph costs, and reproduction costs. Conversely, the "miscellaneous" costs are greater than any single item of controllable cost, except employee cost. The miscellaneous item probably should be reclassified.
4. Readers must make their own comparison of actual and budgeted costs. The variance should have been calculated for them so that they can easily note which variances are large.

USE OF CONTROL REPORTS

The first question to be raised about a comparison between actual and expected performance is: of what use is it? A manager's performance can be measured only *after* he has performed; but at that time the work has already been done, and no subsequent action by anyone can change what has been done. Of what value, therefore, are reports on past performance? There are two valid answers to this question.

First, if a person knows in advance that his performance is going to be measured, reported, and judged, he tends to act differently from the way he would have acted had he believed that no one was going to check up on him. (Anyone who has received grades in school should appreciate the importance of this point.)

Second, even though it is literally impossible to alter an event that has already happened, an analysis of how a person has performed in the past may indicate, both to that person and to his superior, ways of obtaining better performance in the future. Corrective action taken by the person himself is important; the system should "help the person to help himself." Action by the superior is also necessary. Such action ranges in severity from giving verbal criticism or praise, to suggesting specific means of improving future performance, to the extremes of firing or promoting the person.

Feedback

In electrical engineering, there is a process called *feedback*. It refers to electrical circuits that are arranged so that information about a machine's current performance is fed back in such a way that the future performance of that machine may be changed. A thermostat is a feedback device. If the temperature of a room drops below a prescribed level, the thermostat senses that information and activates the furnace. The furnace then makes heat that increases the room temperature. In an engineering diagram, the circuitry and associated control apparatus is called a *feedback loop*.

Control reports are feedback devices, but they are only one part of the feedback loop. Unlike the thermostat, which acts automatically in response to information about temperature, **a control report does not by itself cause a change in performance. A change results only when managers take actions that lead to change.** Thus, in management control, the feedback loop requires both the control report *plus* management action. In this section, we describe how that action occurs.

There are three steps in the control process:

1. *Identity* areas that require investigation.
2. *Investigate* these areas to ascertain whether action is warranted.
3. *Act,* when investigation indicates the need for action.

Identification

The control report is useful only in the first step in the process. It suggests areas that seem to need looking into. Although significant variances between actual and budgeted performance are a signal that an investigation may be warranted, they are not an *automatic* signal. The manager interprets the numbers in the light of his own knowledge about conditions in the responsibility center. He may have already learned, from conversations or personal observation, that there is an adequate explanation for the variance, or he may have observed the need for corrective action before the report itself reaches him. Some managers say that an essential characteristic of a good management control system is that **reports should contain no surprises.** By this they mean that managers of responsibility centers should inform their superiors as soon as significant events occur and should institute the necessary action immediately. If this is done, significant information will already have been communicated informally to the superior before he receives the formal report.

The following observations by successful chief executives suggest the importance of these informal channels of communication:[1]

> The main thing is to keep your antenna sensitive, and have open management. Then the information comes in. [Walter A. Haas, Jr., Levi Strauss & Co.]

> You have to get out yourself and get around, see those flight kitchens, look at that hotel site yourself, get the smell of it and the feel of it, in order to get that extra dimension of understanding. [J. W. Marriott, Jr., Marriott Corporation]

---

[1] "It's no easy trick to be a well-informed executive," *Fortune,* January 1973.

The identification of what should be tended to by management is itself part of management. [James H. Binger, Honeywell, Inc.]

Difficulties in measuring outputs.   In examining the report, the manager attempts to judge both the efficiency and the effectiveness of the responsibility center. In order to do this, he needs information on outputs. Control reports for product departments that manufacture physical products usually contain reliable output information, such as units of products produced, but in many other responsibility centers, output cannot be expressed in quantitative terms. This is the case with most staff departments of a company, such as the research and development department, the personnel department, the controller department, the treasurer's office, and the general administrative offices. It is also generally the case with nonprofit organizations, such as government bodies of all types, schools, hospitals, foundations, churches, and social welfare organizations. If output is not stated in quantitative terms on the control report, the manager must temper his judgment of the report of cost performance accordingly. Under these circumstances, the report shows, at best, whether the manager of the responsibility center spent the amount that he was supposed to spend. It does not show what he accomplished, that is, his effectiveness; and the reader of the report must therefore form his judgment as to how effective the manager was by other means, usually by conversations with those who are familiar with the work done, or by personal observation.

Engineered and discretionary costs.   The reader must also distinguish between items of engineered cost and items of discretionary costs. **With respect to engineered costs, the general rule is "the lower they are, the better."** The objective is to spend as little as possible, consistent with quality and safety standards. The supervisor who reduces his engineered costs below the standard amounts usually should be congratulated. With respect to **discretionary costs,** however, the situation is quite different and much more complicated. **Often, optimum performance consists of spending the amount agreed on,** for spending too little may be as bad as, or worse than, spending too much. A factory manager can easily reduce his current costs by skimping on maintenance or on training; a marketing manager can reduce his advertising or sales promotion expenditures; top management may eliminate a research department. None of these actions may be in the overall, long-run best interest of the company, although all of them result in lower costs on the current (i.e., short-run) reports of performance.

Limitations of the standard.   Presumably, a particular standard is selected because it is the best available measure of the performance to be expected. Nevertheless, a standard is rarely, if ever, perfect.

Even a standard cost may not be an accurate estimate of what costs "should have been under the circumstances." This situation can arise for either or both of two reasons: (1) the standard was not set properly; or (2) although set properly in the light of conditions existing at the time, those conditions have changed so that the standard has become obsolete.

> *EXAMPLE:* The standard direct labor cost for Product 101 is $6.12 per unit. This may be an inaccurate reflection of the direct labor costs that actually should be incurred for Product 101 because it was derived from an engineering analysis that was wrong. Or, even though no such errors occurred when the rate was originally set, it may not be an accurate *current* estimate of labor costs for Product 101 because methods changes have occurred that changed the number of minutes required, or because hourly wage rates have changed.

Even though the budget is valid, a net variance may not reflect the performance of a responsible supervisor accurately since it may result from a combination of causes, some of which he can control and some of which he cannot control. The analytical techniques described in Chapter 14 makes it possible to separate, at least approximately, the controllable portion from the noncontrollable portion; however, these techniques are strictly mechanical. At best, they provide a starting point for the tasks of evaluating performance and for discovering the under-lying causes of off-budget performance.

In short, **the proper interpretation of a control report involves much more than a look at the size of the variances.** In order to determine what, if any, investigation should be made, the reader brings to bear all his experience regarding the work of the responsibility center, all the in-formation that he has obtained from informal sources, and his intuitive judgment or "feel" for what needs attention.

Investigation

Usually, an investigation of possible significant areas takes the form of a conversation between the head of a responsibility center and his superior. Such conversations are scheduled shortly after the control reports have been issued. In them, the superior probes to determine whether further action is warranted. More often than not, he learns that special circumstances have arisen that account for the variance between actual performance and the budget. A budget is always prepared under a certain set of assumptions as to the conditions that will prevail. In actual operations, some of these assumptions may not hold. If the changed circumstances are noncontrollable, this, rather than inefficiency of the responsibility center manager, may be the explanation for an un-favorable variance. If such noncontrollable changes exist, the responsi-bility center manager cannot be justifiably criticized for an unfavorable variance. Corrective action may nevertheless be required, for the un-favorable variance indicates that the company's overall profit is going to be less than planned, and steps to offset this may be feasible in other areas.

Another possible explanation of an unfavorable variance is some unexpected, random occurrence, such as a machine breakdown. The supervisor is unlikely to be as concerned about these random events as

EXHIBIT 15–8

Possible sources of trouble—high direct labor costs

Area and responsibility	Possible causes
1. *Error* (Accounting department)	• Incorrect data
2. *Supervision* (Department supervisor)	• Excessive machine downtime • Too much idle time • More moving than required • Inadequate training
3. *Production planning* (Planning supervisor)	• Work loads uneven • Runs too short • Excessive overtime • Inefficient routing
4. *Material* (Purchasing department)	• Wrong specifications
5. *Wage rate* (Personnel department)	• Jobs improperly classified • Wrong skill levels used • Poor labor relations
6. *Physical facilities* (Plant management)	• Obsolete equipment • Poor working conditions • Poor work movement

he is about tendencies that are likely to continue in the future, unless corrected. Thus, he is particularly interested in variances that persist for several months, especially if they increase in magnitude from one month to the next. He wants to find out what the underlying causes of these trends are, and how they can be corrected.

Some managers develop informal check lists of possible causes of variances that they use as a guide in making investigations of them. An example is shown in Exhibit 15–8.

Action

Based on his investigation, the manager decides whether further action is required. Usually, this action takes place at the end of the meeting described above. The superior and the manager should agree on the positive steps that will be taken to remedy unsatisfactory conditions revealed by the investigation. Equally important, if investigation reveals that performance has been good, a "pat on the back" is appropriate.

Of course, in many situations, no action at all is indicated. The superior judges that performance is satisfactory, and that is that. The superior should be particularly careful not to place too much emphasis on short-run performance. **An inherent characteristic of management control systems is that they tend to focus on short-run rather than long-run performance;** that is, they measure current profits rather than the effect of current actions on future profits. Thus, if too much emphasis is placed on results as shown in current control reports, long-run profitability may be hurt. It is easy to increase current profits by decreasing research and development maintenance or advertising expenditures, but the long-run effect of such actions may be bad.

The investigation might also reveal that conditions had changed and that the budget no longer represented a valid standard of performance. This could lead to a revision of the budget, as discussed in Chapter 12.

DEMONSTRATION CASE

For the purpose of showing how control reports are used, actions taken with respect to the reports shown in Exhibit 15–2 are described below. The reader should refer back to this exhibit in order to follow this narrative.

Drill press department

The general superintendent studied the report for the drill press department (Part A) since it was one of the departments for which he was responsible. He noted that output on the department in June, as measured by standard direct labor hours, continued to be higher than budget, and he saw no need for investigation in this area. He noted that direct labor cost continued to be below standard, because a favorable usage variance more than offset an unfavorable rate variance. He knew from his discussions of earlier reports that the usage variance resulted primarily from a methods improvement. He decided that the rate variance was of sufficient importance to investigate.

Looking down the list of controllable overhead costs, he was struck by the unfavorable variance in setup costs for June, especially since there was a favorable variance for the six months to date. He noted that repair and rework costs, which had been out of line in previous months, had a favorable variance in June. The unfavorable variance in supplies seemed to him to be significant, also.

In his regular monthly meeting with the supervisor of the drill press department, therefore, the general superintendent raised questions about the direct labor rate variance, setup costs, and supplies. The supervisor said that the direct labor rate variance arose because three machine operators were paid a higher rate than the job called for. He had been unable to obtain qualified operators at the standard rates, but he expected to be able to do so during July. The supervisor had no concrete explanation for the unfavorable variance in setup costs; it seemed to be an aggregation of unfavorable performance on a number of separate jobs. With respect to supplies, the supervisor explained that he had requisitioned a large quantity of lubricants from the central storeroom in June, and that although they were charged to his department in June, they would not be used up for another month or more.

The superintendent did not accept the explanation about setup costs or about supplies. He stressed that it was the supervisor's responsibility to keep setup costs in line, and he pointed out that the unfavorable variance on supplies was a persistent problem, not entirely explainable by the large requisition for lubricants. He balanced this criticism by making complimentary remarks about the favorable variance on repair and re-work costs.

Production departments

The vice president of production studied the factory cost summary. Since the variance for the general superintendent was sizable, the vice president looked at the production department cost summary. He did not raise a question about the drill press department because it had a favorable direct labor variance and an insignificant overhead variance for June. (As already noted, this summary report obscured some offsetting variances that were significant in the report of the drill press department.) He was particularly concerned about the unfavorable overhead variance in the assembly department. He recalled that through April the assembly department had operated close to its budget. He had raised a question about the unfavorable variance on the May report but had been assured that the situation was a temporary one. He was therefore disturbed to note that the unsatisfactory conditions apparently continued in June.

In his regular meeting with the general superintendent, the vice president therefore focused on the assembly department. He did go over the detailed reports of the other departments briefly, because this was his way of demonstrating the importance he attached to the control reports. The general superintendent had already looked into this matter, but had no convincing explanation of its cause. The vice president emphasized that he expected costs to be brought back into line promptly, and the production superintendent seemed to get the message.

The factory

The president studied the factory cost summary report, preparatory to his meeting with the vice president of production. Of the departments listed thereon, he decided that the general superintendent's departments and the vice president's own office were most in need of discussion, the former because of the relatively large size of the overhead cost variance in June, and the latter because the unfavorable variance, although small in absolute terms, might indicate the beginning of an unsatisfactory trend.

When the president discussed this report with the vice president, the vice president explained that the problem in the general superintendent's departments was primarily focused in the assembly department, and that he would keep close watch on it. The president mentioned the unfavorable variance in the vice president's office only briefly, but with enough emphasis so that the vice president understood the basis for his concern.

SUMMARY

The purpose of control reports is to communicate how well the managers of responsibility centers performed. This is done by comparing actual performance with what performance should have been under the circumstances prevailing. In most circumstances, the best standard for expressing what performance should have been is the budget, but historical standards and comparisons with other responsibility centers are sometimes used. Reports should be designed so that they highlight significant information.

The time period covered by a report should be the shortest time period in which management can usefully intervene. Reports should be issued as soon after the close of that period as is feasible. They should communicate clearly. The set of reports should be integrated with one another. The value of reports obviously should be greater than their cost.

In using reports, managers first try to identify areas that require investigation. They then investigate these areas to find out whether action is warranted, and they take action when the investigation indicates that action is needed.

IMPORTANT TERMS

Information report
Economic performance report
Control report
Historical standard
External standard

Exception principle
Key variables
Management by objectives
Feedback

QUESTIONS FOR DISCUSSION

1. Distinguish between an information report and a performance report, and also between an economic performance report and a personal performance, or control, report.

2. What use could a sales manager make of Exhibit 15–1? What changes would be necessary to convert this report to a control report? Is it of *any* use for control purposes in its present form?

3. What is meant by the statement that control reports should be related to personal responsibility? Why is this criterion important?

4. What are the strengths and weaknesses of (*a*) predetermined standards, (*b*) historical standards, and (*c*) external standards?

5. What factors can make the budget a less-than-perfect standard against which to judge actual performance?

6. If actual sales revenue is less than budgeted sales revenue, the cause could be *either* that sales effort was unsatisfactory *or* that the amount of budgeted revenue was too high. How can a manager judge which of these possibilities is the more likely?

7. What significant information about the performance of the women's apparel department is suggested by Exhibit 15–3? In what respects does the department appear to be better than the industry and in what respects worse?

8. "Numbers in reports should not be rounded. Rounded numbers indicate a lack of precision, or even sloppiness, and therefore they lessen the credibility of the report." Comment.

9. As a general rule, reports on the quality of output in a highly mechanized department should be prepared more frequently than similar reports in a department that has principally manual operations. Why?

10. A "favorable" cost variance arises when actual costs are less than budgeted costs. Explain, with examples, why a favorable variance sometimes indicates poor performance.

11. In what sense are the three reports shown in Exhibit 15–2 "integrated"?

12. Of the department's listed in Part B of Exhibit 15–2, which one do you judge has the best performance record from the information given? (Caution: You need to consider carefully which of several possible measures is the best.)

13. A thermostat and a control report are both feedback devices. What is the important difference between them?

14. It is said that "A control report should contain no surprises." If by "surprises" is meant "new information," of what use is such a report?

15. Give reasons why a report that actual cost exceeds budgeted or standard costs does not necessarily represent poor performance.

16. All the reports illustrated in this chapter omit income tax expense. Why is this omission justified? Under what circumstances would it be desirable to include income tax expenses on control reports?

PROBLEMS

15–1. Refer to the control report for the drill press department in Exhibit 15–2. Data for the department in July are as follows:

	July	
	Actual	(Over) or under budget
Standard direct labor hours...........	907	(12)
Direct labor cost:		
Amount.................................	$4,320	$ 403
Usage variance		697
Rate variance...........................		(294)
Controllable overhead:		
Setup costs	1,151	(218)
Repair and rework.....................	582	115
Overtime premium......................	542	(127)
Supplies..................................	241	(143)
Small tools	291	129
Other	720	17
Totals...............................	$7,847	$ 176

Required:

Prepare a control report for the drill press department for the month of July similar to that in Part A of Exhibit 15–2.

15–2. The Midcentral Company is a bank holding company. One method used to evaluate the performance of individual bank presidents is to compare their operating results with those of the "average" member bank of the Federal Reserve System. Data for the "average" bank and for the City National Bank, a part of Midcentral, follows:

	City National Bank (000)	FRS Average Bank
Operating revenue:		
Interest and fees on loans...........................	$1,641	76%
Interest and dividends from securities.........	454	13
Service charges on deposit accounts..........	77	2
Trust department income...........................	38	3
All others	96	6
Total Operating Revenue	2,306	100
Operating expenses:		
Salaries, wages, and benefits	429	17
Interest paid	1,072	53
Occupancy of premises	67	3
Provision for losses..................................	91	3
All other...	361	11
Total Operating Expenses....................	2,020	87
Operating Income	$ 286	13%

Required:

A. Prepare a control report for use in evaluating the performance of the president of City National Bank.

B. Comment on the president's performance when the "average" bank is used as the standard.

15–3. The Brown Company prepares monthly control reports for each sales district. The February report for the Eastern District follows:

	Budgeted	Actual
Sales	$39,000	$51,000
Cost of goods sold	23,400	31,800
Gross margin	15,600	19,200
Direct operating expenses*	15,000	18,000
Contribution to indirect expenses	$ 600	$ 1,200

* Of which $7,200 are fixed expenses.

The district manager is pleased that the budgeted contribution has been doubled.

Required:

A. Prepare a control report which will be of more value than the one above in evaluating the performance of the manager of the Eastern District.

B. Should the manager be praised or criticized for this performance? Why?

15–4. The supervisor of the maintenance department received the following monthly overhead cost report:

Item	Budget	Actual	Over (under)
Repair parts	$10,000	$11,000	$ 1,000
Lubricants and supplies	4,800	5,300	500
Depreciation of equipment	6,000	6,000	0
Training*	3,000	2,000	(1,000)
Building and grounds†	2,900	3,000	100
General plant expense*	2,100	1,800	(300)
Totals	$28,800	$29,100	$ 300

* Allocated based on numbers of employees.
† Allocated based on space occupied.

Required:

A. Discuss the appropriateness of the individual items of the report.

B. Evaluate the performance of the supervisor of the maintenance department.

15–5. The Davis Company pays a bonus to any of its four division managers who increase their percentage of operating income to sales over that of the year before. The manager of the Southern Division is unhappy because of the results of operations of this area for the current year. The Southern Division showed a decrease in operating income percentage, as can be seen below:

	Current year		Last year	
Net sales............................		$480,000		$400,000
Cost of goods sold:				
Division fixed costs..........	$ 55,000		$ 50,000	
Allocated costs................	80,000		50,000	
Variable costs..................	145,000	280,000	120,000	220,000
Gross margin......................		200,000		180,000
Selling and administrative expenses:				
Division fixed expenses.....	45,000		40,000	
Allocated expenses...........	58,000		48,000	
Variable expenses............	40,000	143,000	36,000	124,000
Operating Income		$ 57,000		$ 56,000
Operating income percentage...................		12%		14%

The items of allocated costs and expenses represent general costs and expenses of the company which were allocated to the divisions.

Required:

A. Prepare a report which shows more clearly the performance of the Southern Division.

B. Comment on the method used by the company to calculate bonuses.

15–6.   Refer to the control report for the drill press department in Exhibit 15–2. Data for department in July are as follows:

	July	
	Actual	*Over (or under) budget*
Standard direct labor hours	786	109
Direct labor cost:		
Amount......................................	$3,744	$ 371
Usage variance		641
Rate variance.............................		(270)
Controllable overhead:		
Setup costs	1,141	208
Repair and rework......................	504	203
Overtime premium.......................	469	60
Supplies.....................................	209	115
Small tools	252	152
Other...	625	83
Totals	$6,944	$1,192

Required:

Prepare a control report for the drill press department for the month of July similar to that in Part A of Exhibit 15–2.

15–7. The Northeastern Company is a bank holding company. One method used to evaluate the performance of individual bank presidents is to compare their operating results with those of the "average" member bank of the Federal Reserve System. Data for the "average" bank and for the Second National Bank, a part of Northeastern, follows:

	Second National Bank (000)	FRS Average Bank
Operating revenue:		
Interest and fees on loans	$ 933	76%
Interest and dividends from securities	148	13
Service charges on deposit accounts	32	2
Trust department income	47	3
All other	55	6
Total Operating Revenue	1,215	100
Operating expenses:		
Salaries, wages, and benefits	267	17%
Interest paid	516	53
Occupancy of premises	55	3
Provision for losses	39	3
All other	181	11
Total Operating Expenses	1,058	87
Operating Income	$ 157	13%

Required:

A. Prepare a control report for use in evaluating the performance of the president of the Second National Bank.
B. Comment on the president's performance when the "average" bank is used as the standard.

15–8. The Green Company prepared monthly control reports for each sales district. The September report for the Western District follows:

	Budget	Actual
Sales	$25,000	$20,000
Cost of goods sold	15,000	11,600
Gross margin	10,000	8,400
Direct operating expenses*	7,000	6,600
Contribution to indirect expenses	$ 3,000	$ 1,800

* Includes $2,000 of fixed expenses.

When questioned about the failure to achieve the budgeted contribution, the district manager said that sales were down because a railroad strike delayed delivery of company products to customers.

Required:

A. Prepare a control report which will be of more value than the one above in evaluating the performance of the manager of the Western District.

B. Should the manager be criticized or praised for this performance? Why?

15-9. The supervisor of the machine shop received the following monthly overhead cost report:

Item	Budget	Actual	Over (under)
Materials handling......................................	$ 6,000	$ 6,150	$ 150
Supplies..	4,200	4,000	(200)
Depreciation – equipment..........................	5,000	7,000	2,000
Training[1]...	3,500	4,300	800
Building and grounds[2].............................	2,700	2,700	0
General plant expense[1]...........................	1,500	1,600	100
Maintenance[3]	4,000	3,800	(200)
Totals	$26,900	$29,550	$2,650

Bases of allocation or assignment:
[1] Number of employees.
[2] Dollars of budgeted overhead cost.
[3] Number of hours of maintenance employees' time utilized times a standard rate.

Required:

A. Discuss the appropriateness of the individual items of the report.

B. Evaluate the performance of the machine shop supervisor.

15-10. Hogate Company pays a bonus to any of its five division managers who increase their percentage of operating income to sales over that of the year before. The manager of Division A is displeased because of the results of operations for the current year. Division A showed a decrease in operating income percentage, as can be seen below:

	Current year		Last year	
Net sales		$350,000		$300,000
Cost of goods sold:				
Division fixed costs.............	$ 40,000		$ 40,000	
Allocated costs..................	72,000		40,000	
Variable costs	100,000	212,000	100,000	180,000
Gross margin		138,000		120,000
Selling and administrative expense:				
Division fixed expenses......	35,000		30,000	
Allocated expenses............	45,000		36,000	
Variable expenses	30,000	110,000	27,000	93,000
Operating Income................		$ 28,000		$ 27,000
Operating income percentage		8%		9%

The items of allocated costs and expenses represent general costs and expenses of the company which were allocated to the divisions.

Required:

A. Prepare a report which shows more clearly the performance of Division A.

B. Comment on the method used by the company to calculate bonuses.

15–11. The following data statement of selling expenses was taken from the books of the Manten Company which sells its own line of garden tools:

(dollar amounts in thousands)

	1975		1974		1973		1972	
	$	%	$	%	$	%	$	%
Sales revenue	1,269	100.0	935	100.0	833	100.0	791	100.0
Selling expenses:								
Advertising	84	6.6	34	3.6	28	3.4	24	3.0
District branch								
expenses*............	80	6.3	41	4.4	38	4.6	32	4.1
Delivery expense								
(own trucks).........	20	1.6	15	1.6	19	2.3	22	2.8
Freight-out	21	1.7	9	1.0	11	1.3	8	1.0
Salespersons'								
salary expense......	111	8.7	76	8.1	68	8.2	61	7.7
Salespersons'								
travel expense	35	2.8	20	2.1	18	2.2	26	3.3
Miscellaneous								
selling expense.....	9	0.7	9	1.0	8	1.01	7	0.9
Totals..............	360	28.4	204	21.8	190	23.01	180	22.8

* Includes such fixed occupancy expenses as rent, advertising, and so on.

Required:

A. Calculate the average percentage amount of each expense for the four-year period.

B. Prepare a graphical report of expense performance (use percentage of sales data) for each item of expense for the four-year period similar to Exhibit 15–4. Use the average percentage amount as the standard.

C. Which items appear to need further investigation? Why?

15–12. Following are 1977 budget data for the Gateway Corporation:

	Product 1	Product 2	Product 3	Total
Sales....................................	$100,000	$60,000	$40,000	$200,000
Cost of goods sold................	60,000	42,000	32,000	134,000
Variable operating expenses...	15,000	9,000	6,000	30,000
Product contribution	25,000	9,000	2,000	36,000
Fixed costs...........................				24,000
Net Income before Tax...........				$ 12,000

Actual sales in 1977 were $220,000 as follows:

Product 1	$ 40,000
Product 2	40,000
Product 3	140,000

Cost of goods sold and variable operating expenses as percentage of sales were as expected in the budget. A loss of $1,000 resulted from operations during the year.

Required:

Prepare a report that shows 1977 results in a manner which will clearly explain the unexpected loss of $1,000 to management.

15–13. As assistant to the president, prepare a memorandum to the president, summarizing performance and pointing out matters that should be discussed with the manager of the Seattle Stone Division, based on the data in Exhibit 15–5.

15–14. As assistant to the president, prepare a memorandum to the president, summarizing performance and pointing out matters which should be discussed with the manager of the Corporate Loan Section, based on the data in Exhibit 15–7.

15–15. Department A is one of 15 production departments in the Hopewell Company. On December 15, 1976, the following variable budget and planned production schedule were approved:

1977 variable budget—Department A

Controllable costs	Fixed amount per month	Variable rate per direct machine-hour
Salaries...	$ 9,000	
Indirect labor..	18,000	$0.07
Indirect materials		0.09
Other costs...	6,000	0.03
	$33,000	$0.19

	1977				
Production plan	Total	Jan.	Feb.	Mar.	Balance
Planned output in direct machine-hours	325,000	22,000	25,000	29,000	249,000

On March 1, 1977, the manager of Department A was informed that Department A's planned output for March had been revised to 34,000 direct machine-hours. The manager expressed some doubts as to whether this volume could be attained.

At the end of March 1977 the accounting records provided the following actual data for the month for the department:

Actual output in direct machine-hours 33,000

Actual controllable costs incurred:

Salaries..	$ 9,300
Indirect labor..	20,500
Indirect materials	2,850
Other costs...	7,510
	$40,160

Required:

A. Prepare a report on performance in March.

B. Suggest what items in this report are especially significant and what possible explanations for these items may be.

CASE: DAY COMPANY

15–16. The president of the Day department store has received the facts tabulated in Exhibit 1 from one of the operating executives and has asked you to comment on the significant points revealed by these data.

EXHIBIT 1

Comparative operating statistics for Department A and similar departments of comparable stores

	1964	1965	1966	1967	1968
Department A:					
Sales	$100,000	$104,400	$109,600	$98,800	$100,600
Gross margin...........	$ 25,900	$ 28,814	$ 38,250	$35,469	$ 36,517
Direct expenses	$ 8,264	$ 8,601	$ 9,024	$ 8,861	$ 8,980
Indirect expenses.....	20,000	20,880	21,920	24,700	25,150
Total Expenses.....	$ 28,264	$ 29,481	$ 30,944	$33,561	$ 34,130
Net Profit (loss)........	$ (2,364)	$ (667)	$ 7,306	$ 1,908	$ 2,387
Percentages, Department A:					
Sales (1964 × 100).....	100%	104.4%	109.6%	98.8%	100.6%
Gross margin...........	25.9	27.6	34.9	35.9	36.3
Transactions (1966 = 100).....................	96	98	100	95	96
Percentages, other stores:					
Sales (1964 = 100).....	100%	106.1%	111.3%	112.7%	114.2%
Gross margin	25.1	27.2	29.4	30.1	34.6
Transactions (1966 = 100)			100	97	98
Published index of retail prices...........			100	102	103

The data relate to the operating results of Department A, which handles gloves and ladies' hosiery. The president is interested in the results in your analysis because the department adopted a higher markup percentage in pricing goods sold in this department beginning in 1966. The effect of this policy may be noted clearly in the percentage gross margin figures.

Required:

Respond to the president's request.

CASE: SOUTH AMERICAN COFFEE COMPANY

15–17. The South American Coffee Company sold its own brands of coffee throughout the Midwest. Sales policies and direction of the company were handled from the home office in Cincinnati, and all salespersons reported to the sales manager through two assistants. The sales manager and the president assumed responsibility for advertising and promotion work. Roasting, grinding, and packaging of coffee was under the direction of the vice president of manufacturing, whose office was in Cincinnati.

The company operated three roasting plants throughout the Midwest. Each plant had profit and loss responsibility, and the plant managers were paid a bonus on the basis of a percent of their plant's gross margin. Monthly gross margin statements were prepared for each plant by the home office (see Exhibit 1). Exhibit 2 shows gross margin for the entire company. Each month the plant manager was given a production schedule for the current month and a tentative schedule for the next succeeding month. Deliveries were made as directed by the home office.

All financial statements were prepared in the home office; and billing, credit, and collection were done there. Each plant had a small accounting office at which all manufacturing costs were recorded. Plant payrolls were prepared at the plant. Green coffee costs were supplied each plant as indicated later on a lot basis.

The procurement of green coffee for the roasting operations of the South American Coffee Company was handled by a separate purchasing unit of the company, which reported to the secretary-treasurer. Because of the specialized problems and the need for constant contact with coffee brokers, the unit was located in the section of New York City where the green coffee business was concentrated. The purchasing unit operated on an autonomous basis, keeping all records and handling all financial transactions pertaining to purchasing, sales to outsiders, and transfer to three company-operated roasting plants.

The primary function of the purchasing unit was to have available for the roasting plants the variety of green coffees necessary to produce the blends which were to be roasted, packed, and sold to customers. This necessitated dealing in 40 types and grades of coffee, which came from tropical countries all over the world.

Based on estimated sales budgets, purchase commitments were made which would provide for delivery in from 3 to 15 months from the date that contracts for purchase were made. While it was possible to purchase from local brokers for immediate delivery, such purchases usually were more costly than purchases made for delivery in the country of origin, and hence these "spot" purchases were kept to a minimum. A most important factor in the situation was the market "know-how" of the purchasing executives, who must judge whether the market trend was apt to be up or down and must make their commitments accordingly.

The result was that the green coffee purchasing unit was buying a range of coffees for advance delivery at various dates. At the time of actual delivery, the sales of the company's coffees might not be going as anticipated when the purchase commitment was made. The difference between actual deliveries and current requirements was handled through "spot" sales or purchase transactions in green coffee with outside brokers or other coffee roasters.

As an example, the commitments of the company for Santos No. 4 (a grade of Brazilian coffee) might call for deliveries in the month of May of 20,000 bags (of 132 pounds each). These deliveries would be made under 50 contracts which were executed at varying prices from 3 to 12 months before the month of delivery. An unseasonal hot spell at the end of April had brought a slump in coffee sales, and it developed that the company plants required only 16,000 bags in May. The green coffee purchasing unit therefore had to decide whether to store the surplus in outside storage facilities (which would increase the cost) or to sell it on the open market. This example was typical of the normal operation.

Generally speaking, the large volume of the company permitted it to buy favorably and to realize a normal brokerage and trading profit when selling in smaller lots to small roasting companies. Hence, the usual policy was to make purchase commitments on a basis of maximum requirements—and the usual result was that there was a surplus to be sold on a "spot" basis.

In according for coffee purchases, a separate cost record was maintained for each purchase contract. This record was charged with payments for coffee purchased, with shipping charges, import expenses, and similar items, with the result that net cost per bag was developed for each purchase. Thus, the 50 deliveries of Santos 4 coffee cited in the example would come into inventory at 50 separate costs. The established policy was to treat each contract on an individual basis. When green coffee was shipped to a plant, a charge was made for the cost represented by the contracts which covered that particular shipment of coffee, with no element of profit or loss. When green coffee was sold to outsiders, the sales were likewise costed on a specific contract basis with a resulting profit or loss on these transactions.

The operating cost of running the purchasing unit was transferred in total to the central office, where it was recorded as an element in the general cost of coffee sales.

For the past several years there had been some dissatisfaction on the part of plant managers with the method of computing gross margin subject to bonuses. This had finally led to a request from the president to the controller to study the whole method of reporting on results of plant operations and the purchasing operation.

Required:

What changes, if any, would you propose in the present reporting and control system? Explain.

EXHIBIT 1

SOUTH AMERICAN COFFEE COMPANY
Operating Statement
Plant No. 1
April

Net sales (shipments at billing prices)		$744,620
Less: Cost of sales:		
Green coffee – at contract cost		373,660
Roasting and grinding:		
Labor...	$38,220	
Fuel...	24,780	
Manufacturing expenses................	33,620	96,620
Packaging:		
Container.....................................	84,620	
Packing carton	9,140	
Labor...	12,260	
Manufacturing expenses................	25,440	131,460
Total Manufacturing Cost.........		601,740
Gross margin on sales...........................		$142,880

EXHIBIT 2

SOUTH AMERICAN COFFEE COMPANY
Income Statement
April

	Plants*			Green coffee	Total
	1	2	3		
Net sales....................	$744,620			$123,740	$2,856,400
Cost of sales:					
Green coffee	373,660			111,270	1,421,680
Roasting and grinding..............	96,620				299,440
Packaging..............	131,460				600,410
Purchasing department					78,400
	601,740				2,399,930
Gross margin	$142,880			$ 12,470	$ 456,470

*Detailed amounts for Plants 2 and 3 omitted here; total amounts include all three plants plus green coffee.

CASE: WHIZ CALCULATOR COMPANY

15-18.   In August 1973 Bernard Riesman was elected president of the Whiz
Calculator Company to fill the vacancy created by the departure of the
former chief executive. Riesman had been with the company for five
years, and for the preceding two years had been vice president in charge
of manufacturing. Shortly after taking over his new position, Riesman
held a series of conferences with the controller in which the general
subject under discussion was budgetary control. The new president
thought that the existing method of planning and checking on selling
costs was particularly unsatisfactory, and he requested the controller to
devise a system which would provide better control over these costs.

The Whiz Calculator Company manufactured a complete line of
electronic calculators, which it sold through branch offices to wholesalers and retailers, and to government and industrial users. Most of the
products carried the Whiz brand name, which was nationally advertised.
The company was one of the largest in this rapidly growing and highly
competitive industry.

Under the procedure then being used, selling expenses were budgeted
on a "fixed" or "appropriation" basis. Each October the accounting
department sent to branch managers and to other executives in charge
of selling departments a detailed record of the actual expenses of their
departments for the preceding year and for the current year to date.
Guided by this record, by estimates of the succeeding year's sales, and
by his own judgment, each department head drew up and submitted
an estimate of the expenses of his department for the succeeding year,
detailed as to main items of expense. The estimates made by the branch
managers were sent to the sales manager, who was in charge of all
branch sales. He determined whether or not they were reasonable and
cleared up any questionable items by correspondence. Upon approval
by the sales manager, the estimates of branch expenses were submitted
to the manager of distribution, Melmed, who was in charge of all selling,
promotional, and warehousing activities.

The manager of distribution discussed these figures and the expense
estimates furnished by the other department heads with the executives
concerned, and after differences were reconciled, he combined the
estimates of all the selling departments into a selling expense budget.
This budget was submitted to the budget committee for final approval.
For control purposes, the annual budget was divided into 12 equal
amounts, and actual expenses were compared each month with the
budgeted figures. Exhibit 1 shows the form in which these monthly comparisons were made.

Riesman believed that there were two important weaknesses in this
method of setting the selling expense budget. First, it was impossible
for anyone to ascertain with any feeling of certainty the reasonableness
of the estimates made by the various department heads. Clearly, the
expenses of the preceding year did not constitute adequate standards

against which these expense estimates could be judged, since selling conditions were never the same in two different years. One obvious cause of variation in selling expenses was the variation in the "job to be done," as defined in the sales budget.

Second, selling conditions often changed substantially after the budget was adopted, but there was no provision for making the proper corresponding changes in the selling expense budget. Neither was there a logical basis for relating selling expenses to the actual sales volume obtained or to any other measure of sales effort. The chief executive believed that it was reasonable to expect that sales expenses would increase, though not proportionately, if actual sales volume were greater than the forecasted volume; but that with the existing method of control it was impossible to determine how large the increase in expenses should be.

As a means of overcoming these weaknesses, the president suggested the possibility of setting selling cost budget standards on a fixed and variable basis, a method similar to the techniques used in the control of manufacturing expenses. The controller agreed that this manner of approach seemed to offer the most feasible solution to the problem, and he therefore undertook with the cooperation of the sales department a study of selling expenses for the purpose of devising a method of setting reasonable standards. Over a period of several years, the accounting department had made many analyses of selling costs.

The controller was convinced that the fixed portion of selling expenses—in other words, the portion which was independent of any fluctuation in sales volume—could be established by determining the amount of expenses which had to be incurred at the minimum sales volume at which the company was likely to operate. He therefore asked Melmed, the manager of distribution, to suggest a minimum volume figure and the amount of expenses which would have to be incurred at this volume level. A staff assistant was assigned the task of studying the past sales records of the company over several business cycles, the long-term outlook for sales, and sales trends in other companies in the industry. From the report prepared by his assistant Melmed concluded that sales volume would not drop below 45 percent of the current capacity of the factory.

Melmed then attempted to determine the selling expenses which would be incurred at the minimum volume. With the help of his staff assistant, he worked out a hypothetical selling organization which in his opinion would be required to sell merchandise equivalent to 45 percent of factory capacity, complete as to the number of persons needed to staff each branch office and the other selling departments, including the advertising, merchandise, and sales administration departments. Using current salary and commission figures, the assistant calculated the amount of money which would be required to pay salaries for such an organization. The manager of distribution also estimated the other expenses, such as advertising, branch office upkeep, supplies and travel, which he thought would be incurred by each branch and staff department at the minimum sales volume.

   The controller decided that the variable portion of the selling expense standard should be expressed as a certain amount per sales dollar.
He realized that the use of the sales dollar as a measuring stick had certain disadvantages in that it would not reflect such important influences
on costs as the size of the order, the selling difficulty of certain territories, changes in buyer psychology, and so on. The sales dollar, however, was the measuring stick most convenient to use, the only figure
readily available from the records then being kept, and also a figure
which all the individuals concerned thoroughly understood. The controller believed that a budget which varied with sales would certainly be
better than a budget which did not vary at all. He planned to devise a
more accurate measure of causes of variation in selling expenses after
he had an opportunity to study the nature of these factors over a longer
period of time.

   As a basis for setting the initial variable expense standards, using a
technique called linear regression, the controller determined a series
of equations which correlated actual annual expenditures for the
principal groups of expense items for several preceding years with sales
volume. Using these equations, which showed to what extent the principal expense items had fluctuated with sales volume in the past, and
modifying them in accordance with his own judgment as to future
conditions, the controller determined a rate of variation (i.e., slope) for
the variable portion of each item of selling expense. The controller
thought that after the new system had been tested in practice, it would
be possible to refine these rates, perhaps by the use of a technique
analogous to the time-study technique which was employed to determine
certain expense standards in the factory.

   At this point, the controller had both a rate of variation and one point
(i.e., at 45 percent capacity) on a selling expense graph for each expense
item. He was therefore able to determine a final equation for each item.
Graphically, this was equivalent to drawing a line through the known
point at the slope represented by the rate of variation. The height of this
line at zero volume represented the fixed portion of the selling expense
formula. The diagram in Exhibit 2 illustrates the procedure, although the
actual computations were mathematical rather than graphic.

   The selling expense budget for 1974 was determined by adding to the
new standards for the various fixed components the indicated flexible
allowances for the 1974 estimated sales volume. This budget was submitted to the budget committee, which studied the fixed amounts and the
variable rates underlying the final figures, making only minor changes
before passing final approval.

   The controller planned to issue each month reports showing for each
department actual expenses compared with budgeted expenses. The
variable portion of the budgeted allowances would be adjusted to correspond to the actual volume of sales obtained during the month. Exhibit
3 shows the budget report which he planned to send to branch managers.

   One sales executive privately belittled the controller's proposal.
"Anyone in the selling game," he asserted, "knows that sometimes
customers fall all over each other in their hurry to buy, and other times,

no matter what we do, they won't even nibble. It's a waste of time to make fancy formulas for selling cost budgets under conditions like that."

Required:

A. From the information given in Exhibits 1 and 3, determine insofar as you can, whether each item of expense is (1) nonvariable, (2) partly variable with sales volume, (3) variable with sales volume, or (4) variable with some other factors.
B. What bearing do your conclusions in Question 1 have on the type of budget that is most appropriate?
C. Should the proposed sales expense budget be adopted?
D. If a variable budget is used, should dollar sales be used as the measure of variation?

EXHIBIT 1

WHIZ CALCULATOR COMPANY
Budget Report—Used in 1973

		Branch Sales and Expense Performance			
DATE: October 1973		BRANCH: A		MANAGER: N. L. Darden	
	This Month				
	Budget†	Actual	Over*—Under	Percent of Sales	Over*—Under Year to Date
Net sales	$190,000	$160,000			
Executive salaries....................	2,000	2,000	—	1.25	—
Office salaries.........................	1,150	1,134	$ 16	0.71	$1,203
Salesperson's compensation.....	11,400	9,600	1,800	6.00	2,802*
Traveling expense	3,420	3,127	293	1.95	1,012*
Stationery, office supplies, and expense	1,042	890	152	0.56	360
Postage..................................	230	262	32*	0.16	21
Light and heat	134	87	47	0.05	128
Subscriptions and dues	150	112	38	0.07	26
Donations..............................	125	—	125	0.00	130
Advertising expense (local).......	1,900	1,800	100	1.12	1,200*
Social security taxes................	291	205	86	0.13	27*
Rental	975	975	—	0.61	—
Depreciation	762	762	—	0.48	—
Other branch expense	2,551	2,426	125	1.52	247*
Totals...........................	$ 26,130	$ 23,380	$2,750	14.61	$3,420*

* Over.
† 1¹¹/₁₂ of 1973 budget.

EXHIBIT 2

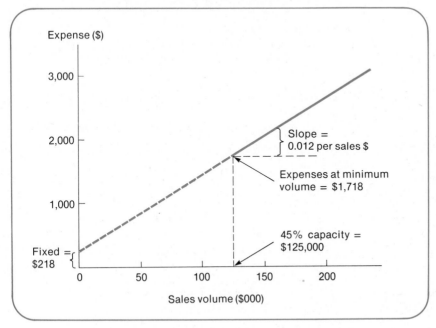

WHIZ CALCULATOR COMPANY
Budget for "Other Branch Expense," Branch A

EXHIBIT 3

WHIZ CALCULATOR COMPANY
Budget Report Proposed by Controller

Expense Budget Report						
DATE: October 1973		BRANCH: A			MANAGER: N. L. Darden	
	Budget Factors		This Month			Year to Date
	Fixed	Variable	Budget	Actual	Over* Under	Over* Under
Net sales..................................				$160,000		†
Executive salaries......................	$2,000	—	$ 2,000	$ 2,000	—	
Office salaries	110	0.0051	926	1,134	$208	
Salespersons' compensation.......	—	0.0600	9,600	9,600	—	
Traveling expense......................	568	0.0142	2,840	3,127	287*	
Stationery, office supplies, and expense	282	0.0042	954	890	64	
Postage.....................................	47	0.0010	207	262	55*	
Light and heat...........................	134	—	134	87	47	
Subscriptions and dues..............	10	0.0008	138	112	26	
Donations ....:	20	0.0005	100	—	100	
Advertising expense (local).........	150	0.0010	1,750	1,800	50*	
Social security taxes..................	42	0.0013	250	205	45	
Rental	975	—	975	975	—	
Depreciation	762	—	762	762	—	
Other branch expense................	218	0.0120	2,138	2,426	288*	
Totals.............................	$5,318	0.1091	$22,774	$ 23,380	$606*	

* Over.

† The controller had not recalculated budgets for previous months, and figures were therefore not available for this column.

16

Information processing

In this book we have focused on the *uses* of accounting information. We have given relatively little attention to the procedures and mechanics that are employed to collect and summarize this information. Since our viewpoint is that of the manager, such a focus is appropriate. Nevertheless, managers do need to have some understanding of the mechanics of processing information. They need to know enough to appreciate the quantity and quality of information that can be made available for their use, its cost, and the speed with which they can reasonably expect to get it. This chapter gives an overall view of systems for processing information that is intended to provide such an understanding.

NATURE OF INFORMATION PROCESSING

Any information processing system has these elements:

1. Recording. There must be some means of recording events at the time they happen. In accounting, events that are recorded are called *transactions*. A sales invoice is a record of an individual sales transaction; it is a piece of paper that shows the name and address of the customer, a detailed listing of the name and price of each item that was sold, and other pertinent information about the sale.

2. Classifying. The system must be designed in such a way that all the myriad bits of information that are recorded can be arranged in some orderly fashion. In *Fundamentals of Financial Accounting* we state that this is the primary function of the ledger. Data that were originally re-corded in chronological order in a journal are rearranged in the ledger in the form of accounts; each account contains all the data that relate to the subject matter that is defined by the title of the account. Such a rearrange-ment from chronological order to ledger accounts is necessary if the user is to make any sense out of the flow of data.

3. Summarizing. For some purposes, information must be available in considerable detail. If Sarah Jones, a customer, raises a question about the amount that she owes, records must be available to show exactly what items were sold to her and the detailed calculation of unit price times quantity for each item. For other purposes, however, only summaries are needed. Management has neither the time nor the need to assimilate the details of the sales transactions with Ms. Jones and every other customer. Instead, it wants summaries of sales by categories of cus-tomers, by product groupings, and so on. Thus, the detailed data on individual transactions are combined in various ways to produce the summaries that are needed for the several purposes described in this book.

4. Reporting. The information must be made available to those who need it in a form that is understandable to them, preferably one that highlights the important matters that need to be brought to their atten-tion.

Criteria for information processing

An information processing system should be designed so as to meet the following criteria:

1. Reliability. The information should state what the facts actually are. Under most circumstances, however, the information need not be abso-lutely accurate. Reasonable approximations are adequate and are much less expensive and require less time to collect than exact numbers. In order to find out exactly how many bolts are in an inventory bin, they would have to be counted, which is both time-consuming and expensive. An approximation of the number of bolts, which can be made just by looking at how full the bin is, or by weighing the bolts, is usually suffi-ciently reliable for management purposes. In arithmetic operations, how-ever, absolute accuracy is expected, and this is also the case for certain other important pieces of information, such as the amount of cash in a bank account.

2. Timeliness. Information is used as a basis for decisions. Decisions must be made promptly if they are to influence the course of events. If something is going wrong, management needs to know about it quickly. The need for speed often conflicts with the need for reliability. A reason-ably accurate report on profit for the past month that is available on the fifth working day of the following month is usually much more useful than an absolutely accurate report that is not available until several weeks later. However, a report submitted so hastily that it is little more than a guess is not useful either.

3. Clarity. The information must be presented in such a way that the person who receives it understands the message that it is supposed to communicate. If it is vague, or if the reader gets an erroneous impression from it, it cannot serve the purpose for which it is intended.

4. Economy. The information must be recorded, classified, summarized, and reported as efficiently as possible. Overall, the cost of providing the information must be less than the value that users derive from it.

Historical development of systems

The introduction of electronic computers has revolutionized business information processing systems. We shall therefore mention only briefly some important aspects of systems as they existed prior to the time when computers came into general use, and we shall discuss in more detail information processing systems as they exist currently.

Manual systems

When one thinks of systems, one thinks of *forms*. Although forms are often described as "red tape," they are essential in assuring that the correct data are recorded, and they facilitate the accuracy and clarity with which data are recorded. Once data have been recorded, the processes of classification and summarization require that data be transferred from one form to another. If this copying is done manually, it is expensive, and also copying errors creep in. Thus, the invention of **carbon paper** was a significant development in information processing. A piece of carbon paper permits the same item of information to be recorded in two or more places, without the cost and the possibility of error that is inherent in manual copying.

The process of summarizing also requires **arithmetic.** Most of this arithmetic is simple addition, so the adding machine was an important aid to information processing. More elaborate machines, collectively known as **bookkeeping machines,** essentially combine the functions of carbon paper and of adding machines; that is, they record the information in several places at once, and they simultaneously do the addition that is necessary to provide summaries. Thus, a billing machine may be used simultaneously to (1) prepare the customer's invoice, (2) adjust the ledger account, and (3) provide a summary of sales revenue credits and accounts receivable debits.

Punched card machines

From devices that copy and do arithmetic, we next proceed to punched card machines. There is a whole family of such machines. In order for them to operate, a card must be punched for each item of information. Once these cards have been punched, the machines do arithmetic and copy information from one form to another, which are the same operations done by the bookkeeping machines described above.

Punched card machines have important advantages over bookkeeping machines, however. First, they require much less human effort; once a machine has been properly set up, it will do the arithmetic and recording for an entire batch of invoices or an entire payroll, in contrast with bookkeeping machines, which require that human beings be involved in the processing of each invoice or each wage calculation. Second, they operate much more rapidly. Third, they operate virtually without error. As a consequence of these advantages, if the volume of work is large, they do this work at a much lower cost per transaction.

In addition, punched card machines perform one type of operation that could not be done by their predecessors; they can **sort** the information into categories, which greatly facilitates the classifying and summarizing operations. For example, punched card machines easily and accurately can sort a set of punched cards containing sales information for each customer into alphabetical order, or by customer size classes, or by geographical region, or in any other way that is useful.

In summary, before the advent of the computer, machines had been developed that facilitated each step of information processing. They increased reliability, speed, and clarity, and at the same time they reduced the cost of processing information as compared with manual methods. As we shall see, the computer not only represents further progress in each of these dimensions but it also introduces entirely new capabilities that none of its predecessors had.

AUTOMATED DATA PROCESSING

Automated data processing is, as the name suggests, the processing of data without human intervention. It was made possible by the development of **electronic computers.** The first computer for business purposes began operation only in 1951, and growth has been extremely rapid since then. The purpose of this section is to describe what automated data processing is — as background for the following sections in which its use in accounting is assessed. For this purpose a detailed understanding of what goes on inside the computer is not required, any more than one needs a detailed knowledge of what goes on under the hood in order to understand how to use an automobile.[1]

---

[1] This description is limited to general-purpose, digital computers, thereby omitting (a) special-purpose computers and (b) analog computers. *Special-purpose* computers are designed to perform a single task (such as calculating the course of an aircraft or missile) or a small number of related tasks. *Analog* computers use approximations rather than cardinal numbers. A slide rule is a manually operated analog computer; it is set at approximately the numbers that are to be computed, and the result of the computation is approximately correct.

EXHIBIT 16–1
Schematic of an electronic computer

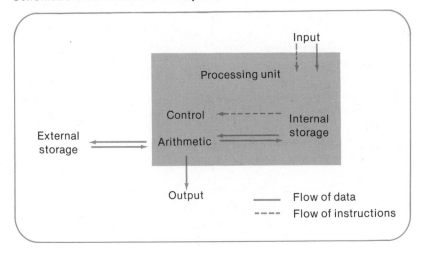

A general-purpose, digital computer (hereafter, referred to as simply "computer") performs these operations:

1. It reads and stores data.
2. It performs arithmetic operations on data.
3. It compares two pieces of data and determines whether or not they are equal.
4. It sorts; that is, rearranges, data.
5. It prepares reports, displays any desired part of the stored data, or causes some other machine to perform in a prescribed way.

The components of a computer are shown schematically in Exhibit 16–1. They are: input, storage, processing, and output. Each is described below.

Input

Computer codes.   In the computer each numerical digit, alphabetical letter, or other symbol (e.g., $, %, #, *) is represented by a combination of electrical "states." Each such combination is called a **computer character.** On the printed page, the character may be represented by a code consisting of a combination of black and white dots, as in Exhibit 16–2. Inside the computer, however, the character is not visible or tangible; it is represented by a combination of electrical states, such as the presence or absence of an electrical charge (i.e., the current is either "on" or "off"). These electrical states can be manipulated at speeds approaching the speed of electricity (which is the speed of light), and this is the basic reason that the computer operates so rapidly. (As will be explained shortly,

EXHIBIT 16–2

Visual representation of a computer character

Code	Represents
0●00●000●	1
0●00●00●0	2
0●00●00●●	3
0●00●●00●	9
●0●00000●	A
●0●0000●0	B
●0●0000●●	C

computer users do not need to know what the codes for these characters are because they will never work with the codes directly.) Since character processing is at the heart of the use of a computer system, it is common to describe a computer's capacity in terms of the number of operations on characters that it can perform in one second or other unit of time.

Input devices. In the input operations, data are fed into the computer, and each character is translated electrically into the code that the computer will use in all subsequent operations. Instructions which tell the computer what to do with these data, called the **program,** are also inputted. In the earliest computers, the input operation involved preparing punched cards containing each item of data, and these cards were then fed into the computer. This input method is still used in some companies. The preparation of punched cards is relatively expensive, however; in the typical business data processing situation, this step is many times more expensive than all the succeeding operations combined. Punched card input is also relatively slow, the maximum speed being approximately 1,300 characters per second.[2] The usual practice therefore is to convert the original data to computer code in a preliminary operation, often using an inexpensive separate machine, and to hold these data temporarily on magnetic tape or magnetic disk. The magnetic tape or disk is used subsequently as input to the main computer. A 2,400-foot reel of magnetic tape or some common magnetic disks can hold 40 million characters, and these can be inputted to the computer at a maximum rate of 300,000 characters per second.

Machine-readable input. The preparation of punched cards is expensive and slow. It also is susceptible to errors, since the punched

---

[2] All computer characteristics given in this chapter are rough approximations. There is considerable variation among computers, and speed also varies with the nature of the work being done.

cards are prepared by human beings. Much work has therefore been done to develop input mechanisms that eliminate most of this manual processing. The first such machine-readable input to come into widespread use was *magnetic ink character recognition* (MICR), which is now used on most bank checks and deposit slips. On such documents, a number identifying the depositor and his bank appears in a form that can be read by humans, viz:

⑆0511⑈00031⑆ 07⑈05141494⑊

The printing ink contains a metallic substance which permits these same characters to be read automatically by the computer. The computer does this by comparing the characteristics of each MICR character with a file of characteristics contained in its memory. When it obtains a match, it creates the corresponding computer code for the character. (This may sound like a cumbersome operation, but recall that it is done at almost the speed of light.)

Some success has also been achieved with optical devices that permit the computer to read characters that are printed with ordinary ink. Currently most of these devices work only with characters that conform to a fairly rigid format and that are positioned in a prescribed area of the document. Optical input devices that are able to read ordinary typewritten material are becoming available, and such devices will be used increasingly.

Direct input.   Another solution to the input problem is to have input information created automatically by a machine that is located at the point where the transaction originates. This information is either transmitted by wire directly to the computer, or stored on tape locally for later transmittal.

> *EXAMPLE NO. 1:* In a job shop there may be direct input devices in each department or section. When an employee begins a job, he inserts in the device one card containing his employee number, another card containing the number of the operation he is about to perform, and another with the number of the job. He inserts his employee number card again when the job is completed. The input device notes the beginning and ending time from a clock.

> *EXAMPLE NO. 2:* In a supermarket, a recording device performs all the functions previously performed by the cash register; that is, it adds up the sales price of each item and classifies the items by departments (e.g., groceries, meat, fresh vegetables). Most items now carry a machine-readable code, called the Universal Product Code (see Exhibit 16–3). With this code, the need for handkeying entries is eliminated. An optical scanner performs this operation automatically. The recording device transmits detailed sales information to a central computer. Management can obtain

EXHIBIT 16–3
Machine readable product tag showing
universal product code

> summary information on today's sales for each store in an entire chain of
> supermarkets a few minutes after the close of business.

With this mode of input, the entry of data in machine-readable form is accomplished by the primary worker as a by-product of normal operations.
Speed and accuracy are also improved. Consequently, the use of point-of-
sale and other direct input devices is growing rapidly.

Storage

The processing unit of the computer works on only one, or a few, characters at one time. A means of storing characters must therefore be provided so that they can be held until the processing unit is ready to work
on them. Since the data are represented by combinations of electrical
states, the storage medium can be anything in which there are two states
and which can be changed from one state to the other electrically. The
earliest computers used vacuum tubes which were either "on" or "off."
In more recent models the two-state characteristic is obtained by coat-
ings which can be either magnetized or not magnetized, by cores or
metallic film in which the two states are represented by the clockwise or
counterclockwise direction of a magnetic field, or by semiconductor
"flip-flop" circuits which are either "on" or "off." The newer storage
media are faster, use less power, are more compact and reliable and
easier to maintain, and, surprisingly, are also less expensive.

When a new character is entered into a particular storage cell, the
character that was previously in the cell is automatically erased. Thus,
unlike an accounting ledger page, which is also a means of storing information, computer storage can be reused indefinitely.

There are two general categories of storage, internal and external,
and several types within each category. They differ essentially because
each represents a different tradeoff between cost and access time. **Access
time** is the time required to locate a character in storage and transfer it
to the place where it will be used.

Internal storage. Internal storage or **memory** is used in the computing process, to be described next. Since hundreds of thousands of computations are to be made each second, and since for each computation data must be moved out of memory, worked on, and then returned to memory, it is essential that access time of internal storage be very short. Typically, a single group of characters can be located in one millionth of a second. Storage devices with such fast access time are much more expensive per character stored than storage devices with slow access time. Because of the high cost, internal storage is relatively small.

External storage. Until shortly before they are needed in a computation, data are stored in external storage devices. Various combinations of these devices may be used in a given computer. At one extreme are fast-access but expensive devices such as magnetic disks or drums. At the other extreme are the slow-access but inexpensive magnetic tapes already described. When magnetic tape is used, the tape must be used sequentially, which makes the process of searching for a desired piece of information very slow—as long as several minutes, if its general location on the tape is not known. In magnetic disks, there is no such sequential search process; access is direct and therefore much faster than with magnetic tape—from 50 to 500 milli-seconds (i.e., $\frac{1}{20}$ to $\frac{1}{2}$ second) to locate one character. Another large capacity but relatively fast-access storage device is the data cell. A single data cell weighs about five pounds and can store 400 million characters. About 200 of these data cells are used in one medium-sized computer system.

Processing

The processing section of the computer consists of a control unit and an arithmetic unit. Acting in accordance with the instructions of the program, the **control unit** directs the movement of characters out of and back to storage and the manipulation of these characters in the arithmetic unit. The **arithmetic unit** does only two things: (1) it **computes,** that is, performs the arithmetic operations of addition, subtraction, multiplication, and division; and (2) it **compares** two characters and determines whether or not they are equal, and if they are unequal, which one is larger. If a computer only computed, it would be nothing more than a very fast, accurate calculating machine (up to three million additions per second). It is the second operation, that of comparison, that gives the computer its extraordinary power.

> *EXAMPLE:* In February 1968, a fire demolished an Air Force warehouse and destroyed its contents which consisted of 16,000 different items of spare parts for F-4 aircraft. The fire occurred at midnight. By eight o'clock the next morning the computer had located in its records the information on the quantity of each of the 16,000 items stored in that warehouse (out of the several hundred thousand items stored on the whole base; this was a comparison operation); it had deducted these quantities from the inven-

tory record of each item and had computed the quantity to be reordered in accordance with its economic order quantity rules (these were arithmetic operations), and it had prepared 10,000 requisitions ordering replacements.

Programming. **A program is a set of instructions specifying each operation that the computer is to perform.** Data processing procedures consist of a series of operations performed one after the other. The rules for performing each of these operations must be stated precisely. For example, a program that processes incoming sales orders that are to be filled from inventory might contain the following steps:

1. For the first item on the order, compare the quantity ordered with the quantity on hand in inventory. Is the quantity ordered less than the quantity on hand? (Answer "yes" or "no.")
2a. If *yes,* deduct the quantity ordered from the amount on hand in inventory and prepare a shipping order.
2b. If *no,* prepare a backorder record (to notify the customer that the quantity ordered is not now available but that it will be shipped when inventory is replenished).

The first instruction above illustrates the comparison feature. It is this feature that permits the computer to handle any conceivable set of circumstances, *providing* that these circumstances have been foreseen and instructions for handling them have been incorporated in the program. This is a large proviso, for it requires the programmer to be aware in advance of every contingency that might arise in the procedure that he is programming, and then to provide for that contingency.

As an indication of the possibilities opened up by this comparison feature, a greatly simplified portion of an order processing program is given in Exhibit 16–4. The illustration is in the form of a **block diagram.** A block diagram shows not the detailed instructions but rather the main steps in the program for each of which there will be a detailed set of instructions. Note that at various points the program **branches** into either of two directions, depending on the results of a comparison made at that point.

The comparison, or *logic,* feature also enables the computer to sort records into numerical order, alphabetical order, or any other desired order; to merge two or more sets of records together; to update a set of records, and indeed to manipulate the data in any conceivable way that can be reduced to a set of written instructions.[3]

Computer languages. In the earliest computers the programmer had to use extremely detailed machine instructions. This is no longer neces-

---

[3] "Data" as used here means letters as well as numbers. Some computer programs operate on straight textual material; for example, the U.S. Code, the laws of many states, and abstracts of most scientific journal articles are now available in computer storage so that a computer can be used to locate references to specific topics.

EXHIBIT 16–4
Block diagram of order processing procedure

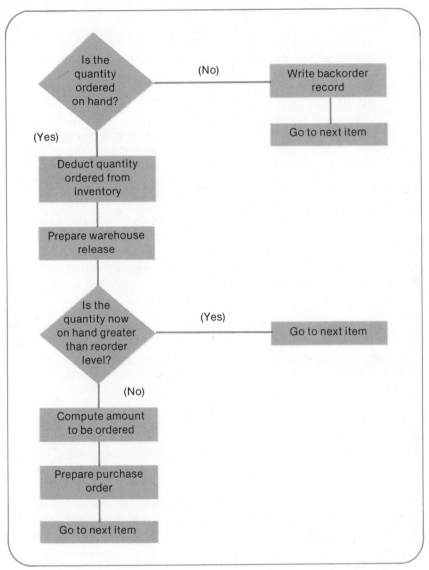

sary. Instead, the programmer uses a computer language such as BASIC, COBOL, or FORTRAN. He writes his program in the vocabulary and grammar of that language which resembles ordinary English and the symbols of algebra. The simplest of these languages, BASIC, can be learned by high school students in a few hours. The program is then inputted to the computer; and the computer, using a special *compiler program,* translates this program into the detailed instructions that it requires.

> *EXAMPLE:* In Chapter 8, the formula for finding the present value of a future payment of $1 was given as $P = 1 \div (1 + i)^n$. With CAL, which is a widely used computer language, the user would simply input the following instruction:
>
> TYPE 1/(1 + R) ↑ N FOR R = .1 FOR N = 1 TO 50.
>
> The computer would then compute the 10 percent column of the present value Table S (page 723) the whole operation requiring less than a minute. (Only a fraction of a second of this is computation time; most of the time is required for the input and output operations.)

Users of a computer language also have access to standardized instructions for many procedures such as "sort in alphabetical order," or "raise to the nth power," and also whole routines, such as those for linear programming, payroll, and order processing. Some of these routines they can use "as is," while others require modification to fit the needs of a particular company. All these developments simplify and speed up the task of preparing programs for computers.

Output

The results of the computations appear initially as characters in computer storage. They can be printed as *hard copy* on a form or a report. The program instructs the computer how to *format* these reports; that is, the program causes the computer to arrange the data in rows and columns in whatever format is desired. Some computers will print the results in the form of dots at prescribed locations on the page, thus producing graphs automatically. The output can also be displayed on a cathode-ray tube (a television screen is a cathode-ray tube). The computer can even be connected to a tape file that contains a spoken sound for each number and for certain common words, and this permits its output to be communicated audibly through an ordinary telephone.

Processing modes

Computers operate basically in one of two modes, interactive or batch.

Interactive mode.   In the interactive mode, the user is connected directly to the computer with an input-output terminal, and he inputs a specific problem or question. The computer solves this problem or answers the question and communicates the output to the user in a fraction of a second, or at most a few seconds.

> *EXAMPLE:* The first extensive application of interactive processing was for airline seat reservations. The computer storage contains the number

of seats currently available on each flight for the next month or so. At each airline reservation counter there is an input-output terminal. When ticket agents wish to inquire whether space is available on a certain flight, they query the computer via this device. The query is transmitted to the computer over ordinary telephone lines. In a second or so, the computer tells the agent whether the space is available. If the ticket agent then sells the space, the computer is notified via another input, and the computer automatically adjusts its record of space available. In some systems, the computer also calculates the price of the ticket and prints the ticket.

Many banks do deposit accounting in the interactive mode; each teller has an input-output terminal which is used both to find the current balance in a customer's account and to record deposits and withdrawals at the instant they are made. There are many other application areas in which interactive systems are in use, such as the entry and processing of sales orders, design of automobiles or electronic circuits, personnel systems, and literature search systems.

Batch mode. In the batch mode, users are not connected directly to the computer. They submit their problems to a computer center which processes each problem separately and also processes routine recurring programs. This is the older style of computer usage. Most systems are still of this type, although the proportion of interactive systems is increasing. In the batch mode, a company's payroll computation might be run weekly; order processing work, once a day; financial statements, monthly; and nonroutine jobs, whenever time is available. The batch mode is less expensive than the interactive mode, so it is used for those data processing jobs where an immediate response is unnecessary. For example, employees are willing to wait for their pay for a few days after the pay period has ended; therefore payroll programs are usually run off-line in the batch mode.

Trends in processing modes. The earlier computers used a method of operation in which the computer was loaded with a single program together with the data required for that program, and the program was run to completion. The program and data were then removed from the computer, and a new job and associated data were loaded in and executed. Under this method of operation, all pieces of the computer system not being used in executing the single program (such as the line printer or magnetic disks) were idle.

Newer computer systems, both interactive and batch, are run under the direction of an *operating system* which can manage the processing of several jobs simultaneously so that while one job uses the single computer processing unit, other jobs can share both internal and external storage and can use the line printer and magnetic disks and other devices. Some systems can handle 500 jobs in this fashion.

Even on computer systems nominally dedicated to a single function, such as airline reservations or banking transactions, other jobs for report generation or program development or other purposes are typically processed concurrently with jobs that involve the primary task. This kind of computing environment for simultaneous execution is known as **multiprogramming.** It is done under the direction of a large complex master computer program called the operating system.

More recently, computer systems have been developed in which the operating system manages the use of multiple processing units in such a way that several programs share the use of both internal and external storage and all other pieces of the computer system. With multiple processors, arithmetic operations can be performed on several jobs simultaneously. This kind of computing environment for simultaneous execution is known as **multiprocessing.** In conventional multiprocessing, all shared equipment is located at one site.

In multiple-user interactive systems, many users can input their problems to the computer, where they are held in storage until time on the processing unit becomes available, usually within a few seconds. The computer then processes the problem and transmits the output back to the user. Because in such systems the time of the central processor and other equipment is shared by the individual users, they are often called **timesharing** systems. These systems make it possible for a small business to have access to a large computer. A computer service company installs an input-output terminal in the premises of the small business, and the user pays a monthly fee plus a charge for the minutes (or seconds) of computer time. These computer service companies also have large libraries of programs which they make available to their clients.

Even more recently, a trend toward **distributed processing** or networking has developed in which computer systems at geographically dispersed locations are linked by communications lines and coding conventions so that a relatively rudimentary kind of shared processing is possible. The goal of such systems is to get the advantages of local processing where feasible, and centralized processing where necessary or desirable, all at reasonable cost. Evolution in computer equipment, operating systems, and communications equipment to support distributed processing is currently very rapid. It should be noted, however, that although these recent developments sound complicated, they are all based on the principles of automated data processing discussed earlier.

Minicomputers

A notable development in computers in recent years has been the explosive growth in the development and use of *minicomputers.* A minicomputer is usually defined as a computer which is suitable for general-purpose applications and is priced below $50,000. A minicomputer can be used alone as a special-purpose device, such as one performing numerical control of machine tools or automated testing and inspection; or it can

EXHIBIT 16–5
A minicomputer—based timesharing system

Courtesy of Digital Equipment Corporation.

be used as the processor for a computer system complete with the input, output, and external storage devices described earlier. Minicomputers are increasingly used to provide small timesharing systems for multiple-user interaction. In recent years, capabilities of minicomputers have been increasing and costs have been decreasing more rapidly than is the case with larger computers. One minicomputer has a timesharing system which serves up to four users, and currently sells for about $20,000 (see Exhibit 16–5). The continuing trend of increasing capability and decreasing cost will give minicomputers a growing share of the roughly $15 billion total U.S. market for computer-related products and services, and will make them a growing part of our everyday life as they are incorporated into automobiles, home and office environmental controls, and other products.

Hand-held calculators. A related device that in recent years has very rapidly become a part of many persons' everyday life is the hand-held calculator. These devices use much of the same integrated circuit and storage technology of advanced computers. In the terminology used earlier in this chapter, a hand-held calculator is a special-purpose com-

EXHIBIT 16-6
Hand-held calculator

Problem:
Calculate rate of return for

Investment	$1,000
Annual cash inflow	250
Economic life, years	5

Calculation:

Enter	5
Depress	n
Enter	250
Depress	PMT
Enter	1000
Depress	PV
	i

Answer: 7.93 percent

puter since it has a fixed program. The simplest calculators do the four arithmetic operations $(+, -, \times, \div)$ quietly and at electronic speed. They sell for less than $10.

A more sophisticated hand-held calculator will do automatically many of the complicated calculations that occur frequently in a business. Exhibit 16–6 shows such a machine. It is smaller than this book, sells for less than $200, and is programmed to do 50 types of calculation.

As an illustration, consider the problem of finding the rate of return on an investment such as the question: What is the rate of return on an investment of $1,000 that has a cash inflow of $250 per year for five years? By the method described in Chapter 9, this involved looking up factors in Table A and making a series of trial-and-error calculations. With the use of the calculator, one simply enters numbers and presses keys as shown in Exhibit 16–6.

IMPLICATIONS FOR ACCOUNTING

With the background of the preceding section, we shall now discuss the effect on accounting that computers are having, and are likely to have in the future. We shall first discuss this impact in general and then in relation to specific types of accounting.

General impact

It seems clear that almost all companies will make some use of computers. The individual physician's office, with perhaps one nurse and one secretary, is a very small business, but an increasing number of physicians have their billing and accounts receivable done at computer service centers.

The number of business computers in the United States rose from 1 in 1951 to 1,000 in 1956, to 31,000 in 1966, and to 87,000 in 1976. This growth will undoubtedly continue. Developments in technology are reducing both storage costs and processing costs rapidly. The cost per calculation for computers introduced in the early 1960s was roughly one tenth that of those in use in 1955, and the cost per calculation in the early 1970s was roughly one tenth of that in the early 1960s.

As new technological developments lead to still lower processing and storage costs, as programming becomes even simpler, and as more and more standardized programs become available, there will be a corresponding increase in the number of tasks that can be performed less expensively by the computer than by humans. Since the processing of data is very inexpensive once they have been converted to computer code, a business will seek additional ways to use a given item of input data. Consequently, companies will do an increasing amount of their accounting work on computers. However, although the work will be done on computers, the accounting methodology will be the same as in manual systems as described in earlier chapters.

The input problem

The least efficient part of computer-oriented information processing is input. As already noted, when input material is prepared by human beings, the process is slow, expensive, and prone to error. Although the remainder of the processing is extremely fast and virtually 100 percent accurate, the quality of the output can be no better than the quality of the input. (Computer experts refer to this truism as "GIGO" – garbage in, · garbage out.) Thus, much effort is being applied to make the initial capturing of a transaction directly usable for inputting to a computer. Devices that will convert ordinary typewritten material into computer language will probably be widely used in the near future, as will machine-readable inputs like the retail price tags described earlier. Most stores, restaurants, and service organizations already use machine-readable credit cards. As inputs become less expensive and more error free, use of computers should expand even more.

Unfortunately, the development of machine-readable input devices has created a new type of input problem, that of fraud. Criminals have found ways to use these devices to steal.

> EXAMPLE. Donn B. Parker of Stanford Research Institute described a scheme that was used in a bank in Washington, D.C. The criminal removed all the deposit slips at one writing desk and replaced them with deposits slips on which his own account number was encoded in magnetic ink. For three days every customer who used that writing desk to fill out a deposit slip was actually depositing money into the culprit's account. The thief reappeared, withdrew $100,000 from his account, and walked away. He has not yet been found.[4]

Much time is currently being devoted to plugging such loopholes in data processing systems.

Operating data

In Chapter 1, we described the main streams of operating data that provide the raw material for financial and management accounting. These streams include data for controlling the production process, for purchasing and materials inventory, for payroll and personnel, for plant and equipment, for sales and accounts receivable, and for cash and other financial transactions. The computer has brought about important changes in these data flows:

1. As noted above, with the computer data are processed more accurately, more rapidly, and at lower cost.
2. The storage capability of the computer permits large quantities of detailed data to be held in a **data bank,** where they are available for use when the need arises.
3. Many routine operations are now performed by the computer rather than by human beings. These include certain operations that require that decisions be made. For example, the computer can be programmed to decide when a purchase order should be placed to replenish a routine item carried in inventory, the quantity of that item that should be ordered, and the date when the new stock should arrive; and it can even write the purchase order without human intervention. (Humans are nevertheless necessary to supervise the operation and to make certain that the transaction is actually "routine.") The computer can do this job better than people can do it;

---

[4] *Time,* December 25, 1972.

"better" in the sense that if its program truly expresses what management intends to be done, the computer will carry out these intentions more accurately and more consistently than the humans normally employed for these routine operations.

Financial accounting

The computer speeds up the process of collecting and summarizing financial accounting information. It permits the use of accounting methods which some companies hitherto were unwilling to use because of the amount of detailed calculations involved, such as more detailed breakdowns of fixed assets in calculating depreciation; more exact methods of accruing pension benefits; and more exact methods of calculating interest, discounts, and premiums on bonds and notes. The computer permits trial runs to be made of the effect of various accounting alternatives on the financial statements.

The computer will calculate all ratios of the type we describe in Chapter 16 of *Fundamentals of Financial Accounting*. Furthermore, a service called COMPUSTAT maintains in its data bank the financial statements and ratios for over 1,700 industrial companies, going back over a period of years, and these are helpful in analyzing the financial statements of the company in question. Another service maintains a computer record of the terminology and accounting principles that companies use on their financial statements, and a company can use this service to find out how widely used various alternative practices are.

The computer has, however, created a new problem. How does one audit a set of accounts when many of the numbers and calculations are invisible, existing only in the form of electrical impulses which are often erased after subsidiary calculations have been completed? The public accounting profession has devised new tests of computer-produced data, and safeguards to prevent unauthorized manipulation of the data are also being developed.

Full cost accounting

In our discussion of full cost accounting, we pointed out that some practices that were not conceptually sound were justified on the grounds of practicality; the conceptually best method was thought to involve computations that cost more than they were worth. This was particularly the case with procedures for allocating costs. With a computer, it is feasible to use more exact methods of allocating indirect costs to cost centers. Cost pools can be narrowly defined and hence be more homogeneous, and multiple bases of allocation can be used. Shortcuts in the calculation of direct material and direct labor costs that may have been used on the ground that more exact methods were too expensive, are no longer necessary.

Differential accounting

Many of the problems for which differential costs and revenues are appropriate require extensive calculations. Some companies use approaches that they know to be conceptually unsound simply because they are unwilling to go through the arithmetic required by the better approach. This is one reason given for the use of the payback method in capital investment problems; it is not accurate, but it is simple. With a computer the drudgery of the calculation is eliminated. Computer programs are available that handle make-or-buy problems, buy-or-lease problems, product pricing problems, capital investment problems, and other problems discussed in Chapters 7, 8, and 9. They make obsolete the argument that a certain procedure should not be used because it is too complicated.

The relevant differential cost and revenue amounts depend on the nature of the particular problem being analyzed. The computer's storage capacity permits large quantities of detailed data to be held in a data bank. With proper organization of the data bank, it is practicable to use data that are "tailor-made" to the requirements of a given problem. For example, the wage rate for each job category can be held in the computer and called forth easily when the problem requires it, thus obviating the need to use average wage rates.

Mathematical models.   Perhaps most important of all, the computer permits the use of **mathematical models.** Such a model states mathematically the interrelationships among a set of variables that are believed to represent the significant factors in a given situation. The income statement is a model that shows the interrelationships of sales revenues, various elements of expense, and net income, but the relationships on the income statement are expressed in terms of a simple linear equation (Revenues − Expenses = Net Income). Much more complicated models are now being used for alternative choice problems. These models are called **simulation models** because they simulate the situation being analyzed, including what the outcome is expected to be if a proposed alternative were adopted.

Models are also available that suggest the optimum alternative out of a wide choice of possible courses of action, with many interacting variables. **Linear programming** is a widely used technique for this purpose.

> EXAMPLE NO. 1: A company that distributes its products throughout the United States wishes to locate warehouses so as to provide rapid service to its customers at the lowest combinations of transportation and warehouse costs. It has a very large number of possible choices as to the location and size of warehouses. Linear programming can be used to suggest the optimum solution.

EXAMPLE NO. 2: A petroleum refinery can make a wide variety of products, and widely varying quantities of each product, from a given quantity of crude oil of a certain chemical composition. The optimum product mix depends on the demand for various products and their relative profitability, and is affected also by limitations of the refinery process with respect to certain products. Linear programming is used by practically all petroleum refineries to find the optimum mix.

Responsibility accounting

The mechanics of programming, budgeting, measuring actual performance, and preparing control reports are facilitated by the use of computers. Computers help to insure that the calculations are accurate. More importantly they shorten the time required to compile and disseminate information, and thus they make it possible to take corrective action more quickly. Computers also make it feasible to take into account many more variables in analyzing the difference between planned and actual performance, and to use more sophisticated analytical techniques in this process.

The computer makes it feasible to use **multiple correlations** to forecast sales revenue. This is a technique that identifies the effect of each of several factors on sales, and is therefore more powerful than the simple correlation technique described in Chapter 12. It is also possible to use a similar technique in preparing variable budgets; that is, instead of adjusting costs only for changes in volume, other factors that cause costs to vary can be taken into account.

Some companies are experimenting with an **overall company model** that will predict net income on the basis of an elaborate set of assumptions as to the behavior of the various factors that affect net income. Because a company is an extremely complicated organism, construction of a realistic model of its complete operations is difficult. If it can be done, however, the company has a powerful tool that can be used to test the consequences of various proposed strategies, and also to assist in budget preparation. In the budget preparation process, for example, managers would be required to make only key decisions and assumptions, mostly those relating to marketing strategies and discretionary cost items; the model could then be used to produce all the detailed budgets, and it would do so in a way that insured that the budgets for the several parts of the organization were consistent with one another.

With a computer, standard costs can be revised more frequently. Although standard costs are supposed to be revised whenever there is a significant change in cost factors, this was not feasible in many companies. An across-the-board wage increase, for example, in a company that manufactures many different end products, components, and parts, requires recalculation of thousands of separate standard cost cards;

many companies did not judge the manual effort required to be worthwhile. When standard costs are in a computer's data bank, recalculations are a simple matter.

Fortunately for humans, the computer is limited to operations that can be precisely described. It does not eliminate the need for judgment in defining the problem and in specifying and evaluating the factors that have not been quantified, nor can a computer's calculations produce results that are more accurate than the validity of the data fed into it. Thus, the computer provides great assistance to managers and analysts, but it replaces only the computational part of their work; it does not replace the people themselves.

It is especially important to recall that the management control process is fundamentally a behavioral process. The computer does not eliminate the manager, nor does its existence alter the basic fact that managers obtain results by working with other human beings.

Integrated data processing

The dream of the system builder is to develop an information processing system in which each relevant bit of raw data is recorded once, and only once. These data are then combined, summarized, and analyzed automatically in a variety of ways so as to produce all the reports and other output documents that the business needs. Such an integrated data processing system can easily be described in general terms, but to develop it in practice is a far more complicated task than any group of mortals has so far been able to accomplish. It now appears that the computer may make feasible such a system, if not for all the data in a business, at least for substantial chunks of them. Such a system will not be developed overnight, but it is a goal that is not now completely fanciful.

Integrated data processing implies a blurring of the distinction that hitherto has existed among different categories of data. There is no longer a sharp distinction between financial accounting data and management accounting data, or between input data and output data, or between monetary data and nonmonetary data, or even between numbers and words. The computer processes them all. Thus it may soon be undesirable to discuss management accounting primarily in terms of monetary information; it may be more useful to view it as encompassing all recurring information that is of use to management.

There is a temptation to be too enthusiastic about the future of the computer. At present, computers tend to spew out too much information, and this tends to hinder rather than help managers do their job. But this is almost certainly a temporary condition caused by the haste with which computer programs have been developed and by the necessity for learning how best to use the computer's power. As time goes on, it is reasonable to expect that computer outputs will be better organized and more relevant to management's needs.

DEMONSTRATION CASE

The Marlin Company is a wholesale grocer. Retail grocery stores place orders, either by telephone or with a Marlin salesperson, and these are shipped by truck from the Marlin warehouse usually within a day or two of the receipt of the order. Terms are usually 1 percent for cash payment within 10 days, net 30 days. The company carries about 3,000 items in inventory. A few large customers get an additional 1 percent discount if their monthly purchases exceed $10,000.

Currently, when an order is received, a combination shipping document and invoice is written. The invoice is priced by multiplying the quantity of each item shipped by the unit price for that item. The cash discount is calculated, and the net dollar amount of the invoice is debited to the customer's Account Receivable and credited to Sales Revenue. The cost of each item of merchandise is entered on the company's copy of the invoice and serves as the basis for the entry debiting Cost of Goods Sold and crediting Merchandise Inventory, and for adjusting the perpetual inventory record for the item.

When the customer pays the bill, a journal entry is made, debiting Cash and crediting the customer's Account Receivable. (The account Cash Discounts Not Taken is also credited if the customer does not pay within the discount period.) These cash receipts are deposited in the bank daily.

The Marlin Company is planning to automate this system. A computer would contain a record for each customer showing the name and address, and the items ordered, with various summaries. When an order is shipped, an input to the computer would be made for the quantity of each item shipped and the name of the customer. When the payment is received, an input would be made to the computer showing the amount received, the invoice number, and the name of the customer.

Required:
1. Describe the principal steps that the computer would take (*a*) when an order is shipped and (*b*) when payment is received.
2. Suggest reports that could be developed from the information that the computer would have available.

(Exercise your imagination by trying to answer the above questions before looking at the lists below.)

Solution:
1. From the input of quantity of each item shipped, the computer can calculate the sales value by multiplying the quantity by the unit price,

which is stored within the computer. It can prepare an invoice showing amount for each item, together with the customer's name, address, and other billing information. It can calculate the cash discount. It can make the accounting entry debiting Accounts Receivable for the customer (and also to Accounts Receivable Control) and crediting Sales Revenue for the net amount. It can even prepare an envelope in which to send the invoice.

The computer can also look up the cost value of each item, and can then adjust the perpetual inventory record for the item, calculating a new balance for the quantity and value on hand. It can make a summary entry debiting Cost of Goods Sold and crediting Merchandise Inventory.

When payment is received, the computer can check the accuracy of the cash discount that the customer has taken. If the calculation is correct, it can make the entry crediting the customer's Account Receivable account and the Account Receivable control account, crediting Cash Discounts Not Taken (if appropriate), debiting Cash, and debiting Quantity Sales Discounts. It can prepare a list of the checks as a basis for the bank deposit. It can calculate the allowable quantity discount by keeping a cumulative record of quantity sold to each customer and credit the customer for this amount.

2. Among the regular and special reports that the computer can prepare from the information obtained from these transactions are the following:

   a. Sales by item, comparing current sales with averages of past periods, to indicate which items are popular and which are not. The computer could be programmed to report *only* those items for which sales are unusually high or unusually low.

   b. Sales by customer, compared with past sales, to indicate customers whose orders seem to be unusual.

   c. Inventory on hand for each item. This information, together with an economic order quantity equation, could be used to place additional orders for inventory.

   d. Overdue accounts. These could be arranged by the number of weeks the account is overdue. This information could be used to calculate an allowance for bad debts.

   e. Estimated cash receipts for each day in the future, using the due date of invoice and the customer's past record for paying, or not paying, within the discount period. This can be used as part of a cash forecast.

   f. Sales by city or other geographic region.

   g. Sales by salespersons.

   h. Sales by telephone compared with sales by salespersons for each customer. Sales by telephone may indicate that the salesperson did not anticipate the customer's needs correctly when he visited the store and took a written order.

i. Sales by item for each customer, compared with past sales, to indicate items that customers have stopped buying. This may indicate that a competitor has taken business away.

SUMMARY

A computer basically does only a few things: it stores data, it makes computations, it makes comparisons, it rearranges data, and it produces reports; however, it does these things a million times faster than a human being can do them, it can perform a long and involved sequence of such operations without human intervention, and it does its work with virtually perfect accuracy. Thus computers are rapidly taking over the routine data processing work of organizations of all types. It seems likely that they will take over such work in all businesses except the smallest, and those without a number of recurring transactions.

Computers also provide a powerful way of analyzing the data relevant to management problems to all types. They thus improve the quality of such analyses, although the results can be no better than the quality of the raw data, nor can the computer substitute for management judgment.

IMPORTANT TERMS

Automated data processing
Computer
Computer character
Computer program
Computer storage
Processing unit

Interactive mode
Batch mode
Timesharing
Data bank
Simulation model

QUESTIONS FOR DISCUSSION

1. Consider a sales invoice for a credit sale of $129 to R. Jones. Describe the several information processing steps, using what happens to the information on this sales invoice as an example.

2. Information should be "reasonably" reliable. A telephone company has considerable cash in the coin boxes of its pay phones. Should it make arrangements to count this cash on December 31 so that the cash item on its balance sheet will be accurate? If not, how should it record this uncounted cash?

3. A manual accounting system classifies a credit sale as a credit to sales and a debit to the customer's account receivable. If a computer were used, what

additional information about this transaction might well be recorded in a computer data bank?

4. Explain the advantages that a computer has over punched card machines.

5. If a computer can only determine whether one number is larger than another, how can it sort accounts numbered 14, 12, 13, and 11, so that they end up in numerical order (i.e., 11, 12, 13, 14)?

6. In what sense can a computer handle the placing of purchase orders to replenish inventory better than human beings? In what sense is the computer inferior to human beings in this function?

7. The computer can produce reports faster and more accurately than manual methods. Are such reports always better than manually prepared reports? Why?

8. Assume that a wage increase requires the revision of standard unit direct labor costs. If done manually, the revision of each direct labor unit cost (one for each operation or each product) requires 0.1 hours of clerical time at $4 cost per hour. If done on a computer, the revision effort requires that a program be prepared at a cost of $100, and then a computer operating cost of $0.01 per unit. The average product requires ten direct labor operations. How many products does the company need to have to warrant using the computer for this purpose?

9. Describe in general terms the nature of a computer program that would be used in a make-or-buy analysis (see Chapter 7).

10. A company uses the computer to estimate the net present value of new products it is considering marketing. The computer output for one such proposal reads as follows:

Rate of return	Net present value (000 omitted)
10%	$1,070
20	501
30	90
32.6	0

The above table was prepared on the assumption that sales volume would be as predicted. Additional tables were prepared on the assumption that sales volume would be 70 percent, 80 percent, 90 percent, and 110 percent, respectively, of the predicted amount. A manual computation of a single net present value required 0.5 hours, how much time, roughly, would be required to calculate this information manually? (The computer time was 11 seconds.)

11. For the information referred to in Question 10, would the computer output be more accurate than the manual calculation? Why?

12. For the information referred to in Question 10, is the computer output more useful than a manual computation showing that the proposal had a net present value of $1,070,000 at a rate of return of 10 percent?

13. If a computer is used for the problem described in Question 10, what aspects of human judgment, if any, are involved in the decision-making process?

14. "Fortunately for humans, the computer is limited to operations that can be precisely described." Why is this fortunate?

15. "If a company's accounting work is done on a computer, its employees no longer need to learn financial accounting because the computer program will incorporate the accounting principles and procedures." Do you agree? Why or why not?

PROBLEM

16–1.   The Wilson Company installed a computer in an office that was readily accessible to members of the controller organization. This terminal was rented from a "computer utility" company and connected to a large computer owned by that company. The terminal was viewed as an experiment. If profitable uses were found, and if sufficient interest developed, it was planned to install similar terminals in other offices.

Bruce Carroll, controller of the Wilson Company, discussed possible uses of the computer with the salesperson of the computer utility. One of these was the equipment replacement problem. The next day, the salesperson brought Carroll a program called PINDX, which he said would aid in solving such problems.

Exhibit 16–7 is a flowchart of this program; and Exhibit 16–8 is a sample of the actual operation of the program as it appeared on the terminal in the Wilson Company office, typed on a continuous roll of paper.

As indicated in Exhibit 16–8 the user activated the program by typing the phrase "RUN PINDX." The computer then asked whether the user wanted instructions printed out. (Presumably, this would be desirable until such time as the user was thoroughly familiar with the program.) Upon receiving a "YES," the computer printed five paragraphs of instructions, and then requested the first piece of information, the "interest rate." On the next line after this request, the computer printed a "?" and the user typed the desired information, in this case 15. The computer continued with its requests; and after "?," the user typed the requested information. The computer then typed the solution.

The problem solved in Exhibit 16–8 is as follows: a proposed machine cost $185,000 and had an economic life of five years. It was estimated to increase certain cash costs by $10,000 per year, and to reduce other costs by $70,000 in Year 1, $90,000 in Year 2, and $110,000 in each of Years 3, 4, and 5. The required rate of return was 15 percent. There was zero residual value. According to the computer, the profitability index was 1.459.

As noted on Exhibit 16–8, the total elapsed time required for running this problem (i.e., from the time Carroll typed the words PINDX to the printout of the solution) was eight minutes, of which six seconds was actually used in making the computations.

Required:

Did the PINDX program compute the profitability index accurately for the sample problem? (How many minutes did it take you to answer this question?)

EXHIBIT 16–7

Logical flowchart for profitability index program

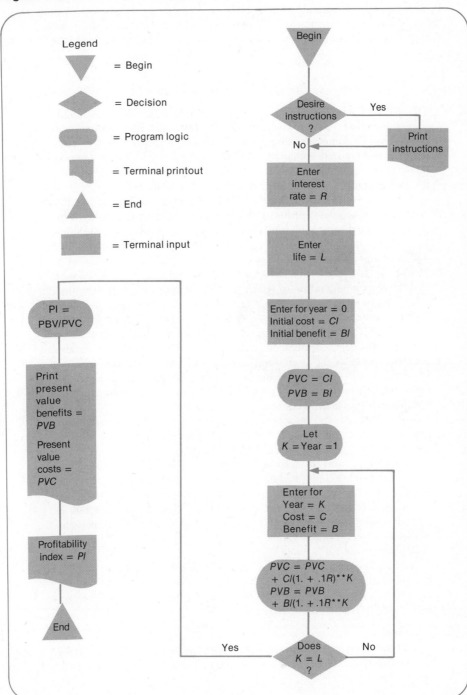

Legend

▽ = Begin

◇ = Decision

⬭ = Program logic

⬗ = Terminal printout

△ = End

▭ = Terminal input

Begin

Desire instructions ? — Yes → Print instructions

No

Enter interest rate = R

Enter life = L

Enter for year = 0
Initial cost = CI
Initial benefit = BI

PVC = CI
PVB = BI

Let K = Year = 1

Enter for
Year = K
Cost = C
Benefit = B

PVC = PVC
+ CI(1. + .1R)**K
PVB = PVB
+ BI(1. + .1R**K

Does K = L ?   Yes / No

PI = PBV/PVC

Print present value benefits = PVB

Present value costs = PVC

Profitability index = PI

End

EXHIBIT 16–8
Computer dialogue

RUN PINDX

PINDX

DO YOU DESIRE USER INSTRUCTIONS (YES OR NO)

? <u>YES</u>

PINDX CALCULATES THE PROFITABILITY INDEX (PV BENEFITS/ PV COSTS) FOR A SET OF CASH FLOWS WHICH THE USER INPUTS.

PINDX WILL FIRST ASK FOR THE INTEREST RATE. (E.G. IF YOU WISH TO USE 10% ENTER 10) NEXT PINDX REQUESTS ECONOMIC LIFE. ENTER THE LIFE OF THE SYSTEM IN YEARS TO THE NEAREST YEAR.

PINDX WILL NOW REQUEST THE COSTS AND BENEFITS FOR TIME = 0 (E.G. CASH FLOWS AT THE BEGINNING OF THE FIRST YEAR.) THE FORMAT FOR THIS INPUT IS THE COST FOLLOWED BY A COMMA FOLLOWED BY THE BENEFIT.

A LOOP IS NOW SET UP TO RUN THE NUMBER OF TIMES YOU HAVE ENTERED AS THE LIFE. IN THIS LOOP PINDX WILL PROMPT THE YEAR NUMBER AND REQUEST THE COST AND BENEFIT FOR THAT YEAR. ALL CASH FLOWS ARE ASSUMED TO OCCUR AT THE YEAR END. THE INPUT FORMAT IS THE SAME AS ABOVE— COST, BENEFIT.

ONCE THE LOOP IS FINISHED, PINDX WILL PRINTOUT THE PRESENT VALUE OF THE COSTS, THE PRESENT VALUE OF THE BENEFITS, AND THE PROFITABILITY INDEX.

NOW GIVE IT A TRY!

ENTER INTEREST RATE

? <u>15</u>

ENTER LIFE

? <u>5</u>

ENTER INITIAL COSTS AND BENEFITS FOR TIME = 0

? <u>185000,0</u>

YEAR = 1
COSTS, BENEFITS
? <u>10000, 70000</u>

YEAR 2
COSTS, BENEFITS
? <u>10000, 90000</u>

YEAR = 3
COSTS, BENEFITS
? <u>10000, 110000</u>

YEAR = 4
COSTS, BENEFITS
? <u>10000, 110000</u>

EXHIBIT 16–8 *(continued)*

YEAR = 5
COSTS, BENEFITS
? <u>10000, 110000</u>
PRESENT VALUE OF COSTS = 218522
PRESENT VALUE OF BENEFITS = 318830
PROFITABILITY INDEX = 1.459
END PINDX 8 MIN ELAPSED TIME, 6 CPU SECONDS

SUGGESTIONS FOR FURTHER READING

Davis, Gordon B. *Computer Data Processing.* New York: McGraw-Hill Book Co., 1973.

————. *Introduction to Management Information Systems: Conceptual Foundations, Structure and Development.* New York: McGraw-Hill, Inc., 1974.

Lucas, Henry C. *Computer-Based Information Systems in Organizations.* Chicago: Science Research Associates, Inc., 1973.

McFarlan, F. Warren; Nolan, Richard L.; and Norton, David P. *Information Systems Administration.* New York: Holt, Rinehart and Winston, Inc., 1973.

Meier, Robert C.; Newell, W.; and Pazer, H. *Simulation in Business and Economics.* Englewood Cliffs, N.J.: Prentice-Hall, Inc., 1969.

Murdick, Robert G., and Ross, Joel E. *Information Systems for Modern Management.* Englewood Cliffs, N.J.: Prentice-Hall, Inc., 1975.

Sanders, Donald H. *Computers in Business: An Introduction.* New York: McGraw-Hill, Inc., 1975.

Summary: The total picture

When a person studies a photograph or a painting, the eye takes in the total picture and conveys it to the brain; thus, all the parts of the picture and the relationships among the parts can be seen at one time. By contrast, when a person reads a book, instantaneous perception of the whole picture is not possible. The book must be read page by page, and it is only when one has finished the book that the total picture can be perceived. Since the study of a book is spread over a period of time, it is easy for the reader to lose sight of certain individual parts, and particularly how they relate to one another. The purpose of this chapter is to bring together the topics that have been discussed in this book, so as to convey the total picture.

In Chapter 1, a preliminary attempt was made to do the same thing, but the description in that chapter was necessarily general. Without an understanding of the terms and concepts that were discussed throughout the book, the reader could not be expected to have gained a picture of what the subject, management accounting, is.

OVERVIEW

In the course of fitting the pieces together, two key points are stressed:

1. **In a given business there is a single accounting system.** It consists of a number of related parts, and the parts are unified within the basic accounting equation: Assets = Liabilities + Owners' Equities.

2. **Different purposes require different accounting constructions.** There is no such thing as "the" cost. Information from the accounting system must be rearranged and modified to meet the needs of these several purposes.

Complexities of cost

The fundamental concept is that cost measures the use of resources. This statement is true, but it is also vague. There are few, if any, circumstances in which the word *cost,* taken by itself, has an understandable meaning. The word becomes meaningful only when a modifier is coupled with it, and even then the resulting phrase may be subject to a variety of interpretations. Listed below are general categorizations of cost that have been described in this book, and which will be referred to again in this chapter:

- Capitalized costs and operating costs.
- Product costs and period costs.
- Prime costs.
- Direct costs and indirect (or overhead or allocated) costs.
- Full costs.
- Actual costs and standard costs.
- Joint (or common) costs and by-product costs.
- Historical costs and estimated costs.
- Differential costs.
- Responsibility costs.
- Variable costs and fixed (or nonvariable) costs.
- Controllable costs and noncontrollable costs.
- Engineered costs, discretionary costs, and committed costs.

Much misunderstanding arises in business situations because the parties in a discussion do not communicate clearly what kind of cost contructions they are talking about. In particular, it is important to remember that there is no unambiguous way of stating *"the* cost" of something in any situation in which indirect, joint, or common costs are involved, and they are involved in most situations.

The appropriate meaning of *cost* depends on the purpose for which the cost information is being used. Consider a factory superintendent's salary. In costing a product for inventory purposes, some fraction of the superintendent's salary is usually included as a part of manufacturing overhead. For overall planning purposes, it is the whole amount of the salary, and not the fractions allocated to individual products, that needs to be studied. As the basis for certain specific decisions (such as whether to buy a new machine), the superintendent's salary is irrelevant and therefore is excluded from the calculations. For other types of decisions (such as whether to shut down the factory), the salary is an important consideration. In measuring the performance of a departmental supervisor, the superintendent's salary is not an element of cost, but in measuring the performance of the whole company, it is. In summary, some of these purposes require the full amount of the actual salary, some require a fraction of that amount, some require an estimate of what the amount (full or fractional) will be in the future, and some require that the amount be omitted.

The fact that different purposes require different cost constructions is obvious, but failure to appreciate this fact is perhaps the most important cause both of the misuse of cost figures and of the common but unwarranted criticism that "cost accountants can't be pinned down to a definite statement on what the cost is."

Organization of the chapter

This book has described a system. Any system can be discussed in terms of (*a*) its structure, that is, what it looks like; and (*b*) its process, that is, how it functions. In human biology, for example, anatomy is a study of a structure of the body, and physiology is a study of how the body functions. A similar approach will be used here. We shall start with a description of the accounting structure, and then describe the processes in which accounting information is used.

THE ACCOUNTING STRUCTURE

Operating information

In the typical business, vast quantities of data flow through the information system (Chapter 1).[1] When orders are received, records are kept of who has placed the order and exactly what is wanted. The production department is told exactly what to manufacture, how much, and when. The purchasing department places orders for material, and records are maintained of these orders and of the accounts payable that they generate. Inventory records show the quantity and cost of material on hand. Employees are paid the exact amount owed them. Records show the amounts billed to individual customers and payments received from customers. These and similar data collectively are called operating information.

Except for a brief description of the use of the computer in processing operating information (Chapter 16), in this book we have not focused

---

[1] These references indicate the chapter in which an expanded discussion of the topic will be found.

EXHIBIT 17–1

Types of accounting information and their *uses*

Cost, revenue, or asset construction	Uses	
	Historical data	Future estimates
1. Full	External financial reporting (especially inventory and cost of goods sold) Analyzing economic performance Cost-type contracts	Programming Normal pricing decisions
2. Differential	NONE	Alternative choice decisions (including contribution pricing)
3. Responsibility	Analyzing managers' performance Motivating managers	Budgeting

on operating information as such; rather we have focused on management accounting information. Most management accounting information is derived from appropriate *summaries* of operating information. Relatively little information is collected solely for the use of management. It follows that the cost involved in obtaining information for management is only a small fraction of the cost of processing all the information used in a business. Rearrangement and summarization of raw data for management use is a much less expensive job than recording the raw data when the transactions occur.

Management accounting information

Exhibit 17–1 gives an overview of the management accounting structure and of the management uses of accounting information.

For simplicity, the exhibit has been drawn up in terms of costs, but corresponding statements can be made about revenues and about assets. There are three types of cost constructions in management accounting:

1. Full cost accounting.
2. Differential accounting.
3. Responsibility accounting.

Full costs and responsibility costs are collected in the accounts, but differential costs are not. Some individual cost accounts are used both for full costs and for responsibility costs; other accounts are used only for one type of cost construction or the other. Differential costs are constructed in some cases by rearrangement of data obtained from full cost or responsibility cost accounts; in other cases, differential costs are constructed from information that comes from outside the accounting system.

Some companies have an additional set of accounts in order to meet the requirements of regulatory agencies. In general, these accounts are similar to its full cost accounts.

In addition to this management accounting information, the complete accounting system includes financial accounting information, that is, information used to prepare the financial statements furnished to external parties. Financial accounting is discussed in *Fundamentals of Financial Accounting* and will be referred to here only to the extent necessary to show the relationship between financial accounting and management accounting.

In the following sections, we shall describe the three types of management accounting contructions and we shall then describe the uses of this information by management.

Full cost accounting (Chapters 3, 4, and 5)

Cost measures in monetary terms the amount of resources used for (or assigned to) a cost objective. A cost objective is anything whose cost is to be measured. In the full cost structure we have used the products that a company manufactures as a case in point. In the absence of more specific information, the term "cost accounting" is usually taken to mean the measurement of costs of manufacturing goods. It could equally well refer to measuring the cost of providing services (such as the various types of telephone calls whose costs are measured by a telephone company), or to measuring the cost of performing a contract. The same principles apply whatever the cost objective may be.

Capitalized costs and operating costs.   Some costs are incurred to build or acquire capital assets. Costs of these capital assets are to be distinguished from operating costs. One of the most difficult problems of financial accounting is to decide which items of costs are to be capitalized and which are to be charged as operating expenses of the current accounting period. The following discussion relates primarily to operating costs.

Manufacturing costs and other costs.   The full cost of a product is the sum of its manufacturing cost, its distribution cost, and its general and administrative costs; however, the formal accounts usually record only the manufacturing cost of products. This is because only manufacturing costs are used in measuring finished goods inventory amounts on the balance sheet and cost of goods sold on the income statement. It would not be appropriate to include nonmanufacturing costs in finished goods inventory because these costs do not represent resources used in the manufacturing process; in general, these costs are incurred *after* the manufacturing process has been completed.

Manufacturing costs are also, and commonly, called *product costs;* and other costs are called *period costs.* Product costs enter into the inventory valuation of products, whereas period costs are expenses of the accounting period in which the costs are incurred. It must be understood that the term *product cost* in this context refers only to the manufacturing cost of the product; the full cost of manufacturing *and marketing* a product is the sum of its manufacturing cost and nonmanufacturing costs.

Direct and indirect manufacturing costs (*Chapter 4*). The manufacturing cost of a product is the sum of (1) its direct costs and (2) a fair share of the indirect manufacturing costs that are incurred for two or more cost objectives, of which the product in question is one.

Direct manufacturing costs. The direct manufacturing costs of a product (usually referred to simply as direct costs) are items of cost that are specifically traced to that product because they are caused by the manufacture of that product. They are usually classified as either (1) direct material, or (2) direct labor. They are also called *prime costs.*

Problems arise in deciding what items of cost should be classified as direct. Conceptually, direct costs should include labor-related costs such as fringe benefits, and material-related costs such as storage and handling costs, but practice varies in this regard. Except for the question of what items to include in the direct cost category, the task of collecting direct costs is straightforward. A large portion of the total paperwork in the accounting system is involved in collecting direct product costs, but only a small fraction of the conceptual problems are related to direct costs.

Indirect manufacturing costs. Indirect manufacturing costs are also referred to as *manufacturing overhead costs.* The determination of what share of the total indirect costs of the factory should be assigned to a given product involves difficult conceptual problems; it also involves more complicated procedures than those used for direct costs. Indirect costs are first collected in production cost centers and service cost centers. Total costs of service cost centers are then reassigned to production cost centers, so that all manufacturing costs eventually wind up in some production cost center. The basis of assignment reflects either the relative benefits received by the cost center or the relative amounts of costs caused by the activities of the cost center.

Indirect costs of each production cost center are allocated to products by means of an overhead rate; thus, each product passing through the production cost center is allocated a fair share of its indirect costs. The overhead rate is usually determined in advance of the accounting period. The overhead rate is arrived at by estimating the amount of factory indirect costs in the cost center, estimating the volume or activity level at which the cost center will operate, and then dividing estimated costs by estimated volume. The overhead rate is therefore a cost per unit of volume. Because some costs are fixed, the overhead rate is less for high volumes than it is for low volumes. Because actual volume and actual costs may be different than the amounts than were estimated in advance, it is likely that the amount of indirect costs allocated to products by means of the overhead rate will not exactly equal the actual amount of indirect costs accumulated in the cost center; this results in underabsorbed or overabsorbed overhead.

Job costing and process costing (Chapter 3).   Two procedures are used to accumulate the cost of products; the choice between them depends on characteristics of the production activity. In a *job cost system*, a record is kept of each product or lot of products going through the factory, and cost items are accumulated on this record. In a *process cost system*, records are maintained by cost centers only; products are assigned their proportionate share of the costs, both indirect and direct, that are accumulated in the production cost center.

As products move through production costs centers, their costs are accumulated either through job cost or process cost procedures. (It is often said that costs *attach* to products.) Simultaneously, debits to Goods in Process Inventory are made for the total amount of these costs incurred in an accounting period. When products are completed, Goods in Process Inventory is credited and Finished Goods Inventory is debited at the accumulated cost. When products are sold, a similar transfer is made from Finished Goods Inventory to Cost of Goods Sold. The costs involved in this process are manufacturing costs, excluding costs that are incurred "beyond the factory exit door."

Joint costs and by-products costs (Chapter 4).   Joint costs are costs incurred jointly for two or more products that are produced together at an early stage of the manufacturing process, but which are separated at a stage called the split-off point. They include both direct and indirect manufacturing costs incurred up to the split-off point.

When the intention is to produce as much as possible of one product and as little as possible of another product, the former is called the *main product* and the latter the *by-product*. Special accounting rules apply to the measurement of costs of by-products.

Standard costs (Chapter 13).   Instead of, or in addition to, measuring the *actual* costs of a product, a standard cost system records what its costs *should have been*. Standard direct material costs per unit and standard direct labor costs per unit are established. A standard overhead rate is also established, but it is essentially the same as the overhead rate in an actual cost system. As products move through the factory, standard costs are assigned to them; the mechanism is substantially the same as that described above for actual costs, except that at appropriate points variances between actual and standard costs are identified and recorded.

Nonmanufacturing costs (Chapter 5).   Marketing costs, logistics costs, and those general and administrative costs not attributable to the manufacturing process are not assigned to products as part of the process described above; thus such cost elements are not included in inventory or in cost of goods sold. They are period costs. Nevertheless, for certain purposes, it is necessary that full product costs, including these other costs, be measured. For these purposes, both direct and indirect non-manufacturing costs are added to manufacturing costs; this may be done on cost estimating sheets which are not part of the formal accounts. The principles governing the assignment of nonmanufacturing costs to products are the same as those for manufacturing costs. Direct costs are assigned directly, and indirect costs are allocated by means of overhead rates.

Differential accounting (Chapters 6 and 7)

Differential costs are those items of cost that are expected to be different if a proposed alternative course of action is adopted. Differential costs, as such, are not recorded in the accounts; that is, the accounting records do not label certain items as differential costs. Such items are always estimates of the future, and the relevant amounts are a function of the specific alternatives being considered. Historical costs obtained from either the full cost structure or the responsibility structure may be useful as a basis for making such estimates.

Responsibility accounting (Chapters 10 and 11)

A responsibility center is an organization unit headed by a manager. Since control can be exercised only by human beings who influence other human beings, the focus of control is on the responsibility center. In responsibility accounting, costs are assigned to the responsibility center responsible for incurring them. Many responsibility centers are also cost centers, and in these cases a single set of account serves both the needs of product costing and those of responsibility accounting. Within each responsibility center, the items of costs are classified by object or function (e.g., supervision, supplies, maintenance). Such a classification is not needed for product costing purposes. Conversely, the classification of costs by product is not needed for responsibility accounting purposes. Also, certain cost centers used in product costing are not the responsibility of a single manager (e.g., an "occupancy" cost center in which costs of using physical space are accumulated), and these cost centers are not used in responsibility accounting.

Responsibility accounting includes both *historical* costs and *estimates* of future costs. In most companies, only the historical information is recorded in the formal accounts. Estimates are shown in *programs* or *budgets* that are closely related to, but not a part of, the formal accounts.

Cost categories. Information in the responsibility accounts is classified in ways that are useful to management. The principal categories are listed below.

Variable or fixed (Chapter 6). Variable costs are those that vary with the level of activity or volume; fixed costs do not vary, within a relevant range. Some accounting systems assign only items of variable cost to products. These are called *variable cost systems* (or, but less accurately, *direct cost systems*).

Engineered, discretionary, or committed (Chapter 11). These categories refer to, respectively, costs that are *caused by* the level of activity or volume, costs that change at the *discretion of management,* and costs that are *not subject to change* in the short run. They are usually not identified as such in the accounts, but the distinctions are important in understanding the preparation of budgets and in analyzing reports on performance.

Controllable and noncontrollable (Chapter 11). These categories distinguish those items of cost over which the manager of a responsibility center, respectively, can or cannot exercise a significant amount of control. The distinction is important in analyzing reports on performance.

The account building block

Full cost accounting and responsibility accounting are part of a single system, for which detailed cost information is aggregated in two different ways for different purposes. The lowest common denominator of the system is called the *account building block.* It consists of a single item of cost (e.g., direct material, supplies, overtime) incurred in the *smaller* of either a cost center or a responsibility center. Summaries of cost information are obtained by combining these building blocks in either of two principal ways: (1) by *products* using full cost procedures or (2) by the hierarchy of *responsibility centers* in the responsibility system.

> *EXAMPLE:* Supplies consumed in the month of June in the drill press department were $215. This fact is recorded in the appropriate account. The $215 becomes part of the overhead rate and is thereby allocated to and becomes part of the cost of the products passing through the drill press department. The $215 also is part of the total cost of the drill press department and appears on the control report for that department. Total drill press department costs, in turn, are part of the total costs of the factory, which is a responsibility center aggregating all factory departments. The account building block is therefore aggregated in two ways.
>
> If the smallest account is *supplies,* the accounting system will not identify the cost of a particular type of supplies, such as lubricants. If such an identification is desired, the supplies account must be subdivided by types of supplies, and each of these becomes a building block.

When accounts are maintained in the *data base* of a computer (Chapter 16), it is easy to aggregate and combine them in whatever way is useful for various purposes.

USES OF ACCOUNTING INFORMATION

We turn now to a description of the processes in which the accounting information is used, namely:

1. Financial reporting.
2. Full cost measurement.
3. Alternative choice decision making.
4. Management control.

Financial reporting

Product manufacturing costs are used in measuring goods in process inventory, finished goods inventory, and cost of goods sold in the external financial statements. Expense accounts are also summarized to provide the amounts for expenses on the income statement. The principles and techniques governing the preparation of these financial statements are the subject matter of financial accounting.

Full cost measurement (Chapter 2)

In conducting its current operations, a business uses full cost information for many purposes.

In a business with several products, and especially in job shops, the most extensive and more frequent use of full cost information is as an aid in arriving at selling prices. In some circumstances, the company may price on the basis of differential costs in order to obtain business that it might otherwise lose. In the great majority of cases, however, companies arrive at the first approximation of the selling price, which is the *target price,* by following the principle that the price of a product should cover all its direct costs, plus a fair share of its indirect costs, plus a reasonable profit margin. This is the full cost approach to product pricing. In still other situations, the company must sell at prices that exist in the marketplace, and in these situations cost information is useful only in deciding what the company can afford to spend on producing and marketing the product.

Conceptually, selling prices should be based on an estimate of future costs rather than on historical costs as shown in the accounting records. The accounting records nevertheless provide the starting point in the calculation; that is, historical costs are adjusted for estimated changes in cost in order to arrive at the target price. If the company has a standard cost system (Chapter 13), the standard unit costs presumably incorporate these adjustments to historical cost, and they are used directly as a basis for pricing. In arriving at the actual selling price, marketing executives adjust the target price according to their judgment of what the best pricing tactic is under the market conditions currently prevailing.

Full costs are also used for many other operating purposes. They are used in situations in which a buyer agrees to pay cost plus a certain profit margin for goods produced or services rendered under a contract. This is the way automobile repair services, TV repairs, job printing, machine shop work, and a great number of other goods and services are priced. Full cost is also the method used for pricing billions of dollars worth of government contracts. Whenever a congressional investigating committee, or any other group asks the question, "What did such-and-such cost?" the answer is usually given in terms of full cost.

Alternative choice decisions (Chapters 7, 8, and 9)

Most business problems require that management make a choice between two or more alternate courses of action; for example, shall we or shall we not buy a proposed new machine? Shall we make a certain part, or shall we buy it from an outside vendor?

The best alternative is usually the one that adds the most to profits (or, if additional assets are involved, the alternative that produces the largest return on investment). This test is not always appropriate, however, because objectives other than profits usually are relevant in alternative choice problems, and in some situations such objectives are dominant. Accounting information is useful in estimating the costs that are associated with each alternative. These costs are differential costs. If an alternative involves a capital investment, it is the differential investment that is relevant.

In comparing two or more alternatives, the important question to be addressed is how the estimated costs differ, that is, how the costs for one alternative differ from those of the other; this is the concept of differential costs. Costs that are unaffected by either alternative need not be considered at all. In particular, allocated indirect costs can lead to misunderstanding in problems of this type. Since these costs are expressed as overhead rates that are often tied to direct costs, they may give the appearance of varying with whatever measure of activity causes costs to vary, whereas actually the overhead costs may not have such a casual connection with activity.

> *EXAMPLE:* If the overhead rate is $2 per direct labor dollar, and if one alternative is estimated to require $10,000 of direct labor, it may appear that the alternative will also require $20,000 of overhead. This conclusion is not warranted.

In most alternative choice problems, overhead allocations and the resulting overhead rates should be disregarded; instead, the expected behavior of the various components of overhead should be studied.

Neither full cost accounts nor responsibility accounts necessarily contain cost information that is relevant for an alternative choice problem. The task of the analyst is to put together the costs that *are* relevant for the particular problem being examined. In doing this, historical cost accounting information may be used as a starting point and adjusted so that it reflects expected future conditions. In making such adjustments, the analyst needs to understand how costs behave, and particularly how costs vary with volume (Chapter 6). Thus, unlike full cost accounting, which is associated with the financial statements, and unlike responsibility accounting, which is associated with the management control process, there is no identifiable part of the accounting structure that is associated with alternative choice decisions. Data from various parts of the structure are massaged and reassembled to fit the requirements of the specific situation being analyzed.

Management control (Chapters 11–15)

Management control is the process by which management assures that the organization carries out its strategies effectively and efficiently. The process consists of these steps, in chronological order: programming, budgeting, measuring, appraising, and acting on performance. Programming and budgeting are *planning* activities; appraising and acting are *control* activities. In the management control process, behavioral considerations are at least as important as accounting considerations.

Programming (Chapter 12). In the programming activity, management decides on the principal programs that the organization will undertake in the future and on the approximate amount of resources that are to be used for each program. Programs consist of product lines plus research/ development and other special activities. In the programming process, ongoing programs are reviewed (sometimes by a zero-base review) and proposed new programs are analyzed and acted upon. In most companies, the programming activity is relatively unstructured and informal; but some companies have a formal programming, or long-range planning, system. Differential costs are used in the analysis of proposed programs; but when the proposal covers a long period of time, differential costs are practically equivalent to full costs.

Budget preparation (Chapter 12). In the budgeting activity, an annual profit plan is prepared. The plan is prepared within the context of decisions made during the programming process. It is prepared in terms of responsibility centers, and responsibility costs are relevant.

The planned costs that are decided on in the budgeting activity are used as the basis for calculating overhead rates. If a standard cost system is used, the standard costs are also consistent with the budget.

For those responsibility centers in which overhead costs vary with the level of activity, a flexible overhead budget is prepared. The flexible budget states a fixed amount per period and a variable amount per unit of output.

Performance measurement, appraisal, and action (Chapters 14 and 15). As performance takes place, actual costs are recorded in the responsibility accounts. These are summarized in reports to management. Among other things, these reports compare actual costs with standard or budgeted costs. Techniques are available for analyzing the variances as a first step in determining their causes (Chapter 14). On the basis of such an analysis of variances, further investigation is conducted and, if warranted, appropriate action is taken.

In making these analyses of variances, distinctions between controllable and noncontrollable costs, between engineered and discretionary costs, and between variable and fixed costs must be understood. These distinctions are not ordinarily reflected in the account classifications. Rather, the identification is made in reports prepared *from* the accounts. In particular, in analyzing the performance of a responsibility center, it is essential that a distinction be made between controllable and noncontrollable costs.

Relative importance of the cost types

Debate as to the relative importance of the three types of cost constructions is pointless. Each type is important for its appropriate purpose, and a company needs all three of them. In a classroom environment, however, there may be a tendency to overemphasize the importance of differential costs and to downgrade the importance of full costs. This is because problems involving differential costs tend to be glamorous, challenging to the intellect, and having important consequences to the company. Furthermore, students who have had a course in economics know that differential costs are emphasized in such courses.

Nevertheless, in most manufacturing companies, problems involving the use of full costs arise much more frequently than problems involving differential costs. A selling price must be arrived at for every product, and, particularly in companies that manufacture a large number of products or which manufacture to each customer's specifications, the calculation of full costs is made perhaps 100 times as frequently as the calculation of differential costs. The calculations are not difficult, nor do they involve much judgment once the cost accounting system has been properly set up, but it is nevertheless of crucial importance that they be made correctly.

DEMONSTRATION CASE

As a further aid in showing how the elements of an accounting system are related to one another, this section summarizes the accounting system of the Stewart Box Company.

The company and its products

Stewart Box Company is a well-established manufacturer of paperboard cartons and boxes which are sold primarily as packages for consumer products. The cartons are manufactured in the company's carton factory. The raw material for the carton factory is paperboard which is manufactured in the company's paperboard mill, adjacent to the carton factory. The plant complex also includes a 60,000-square-foot warehouse where finished orders are stored pending delivery. The company has approximately 425 employees in 1976. Robert Stewart, the president, is also a large stockholder.

The company markets its products within a radius of about 500 miles from its factory which is located in a fairly small town. It has seven sales engineers, who are compensated on the basis of a nominal salary, plus commission. In the marketing organization are six other persons, including three who prepare price quotations for prospective customers, according to specifications obtained from the customers. The company has an excellent reputation for product quality and customer service.

The paperboard and carton industry is characterized by strong competition because of the potential overcapacity that exists in most plants. Because of this overcapacity, competition for large orders is particularly keen, and price cutting is common. Stewart meets this competition by designing special boxes to customer specifications, by actively catering to its customers' wishes, and by strict adherence to promised delivery dates.

The production process requires that the paperboard mill operates continuously on three shifts for maximum efficiency, but the carton factory operates an average of only one and one-half shifts per day.

A partial organization chart is shown as Exhibit 17–2. The paperboard mill and the carton factory are profit centers. In the carton factory are ten production departments, each consisting of a printing press or a group of similar presses and associated equipment and each headed by a foreman. There are five service departments, which perform functions such as ink manufacture, quality control, and warehouse storage; each is headed by a supervisor. Each of these 15 departments is an expense center. The ten production departments are production cost centers, and the five service departments are service cost centers.

EXHIBIT 17–2
Stewart Box Company organization chart

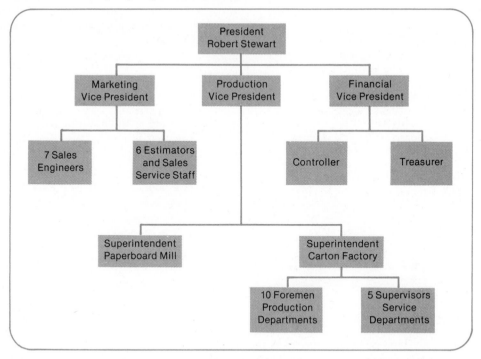

Accounting system

The company has a job cost accounting system, using standard costs. The board mill is a single cost center, operating a single paperboard manufacturing machine. A rate per machine-hour is established annually, which combines direct labor and manufacturing overhead costs. Manufactured paperboard is charged to the carton factory at a transfer price that includes standard cost plus a standard return on the assets employed in the board mill. The profit component of this charge is subtracted from the inventory amounts as shown on the financial statements (because generally accepted accounting principles do not permit a profit allowance to be included in inventory).

In the carton factory, each order is a job. The job is costed at the standard cost of the materials used on the job, a standard rate per press hour for the time that the job uses on presses, and a standard rate per direct labor hour for other operations. These rates include both labor and factory overhead costs and are estimated annually. The system also collects actual labor and overhead costs for each responsibility center.

EXHIBIT 17–3

Analysis of proposed printing press

	Tax calculation	Present value calculation
Annual cash inflows:		
Saving in maintenance costs		$ 2,000
Saving in direct labor costs		6,200
Saving in power		1,000
Saving in supplies		500
Annual pretax cash inflow	$9,700	9,700
Less: Depreciation* $20,000 ÷ 10	2,000	
Additional taxable income	$7,700	
Additional income tax 50% × 7,700.........................		3,800
Annual aftertax cash inflow		5,900
Present value of cash inflows ($A_{10|10\%} = 3.791$).........		22,400
Investment in press, installed..............................		20,000
Net present value		$ 2,400
Profitability index $22,400/$20,000		1.12

*For simplicity in this illustration, straight-line depreciation is used. The company actually used sum-of-years'-digits depreciation for income tax purposes.

Programming

The company has a five-year plan, which it revises annually. The management team (president, vice presidents, and superintendents) spend a total of about two days each summer discussing and agreeing on this revision. In 1976, for example, the sales estimates for 1977–81 indicated that the capacity of the warehouse would become inadequate by 1978. This led to an investigation of alternative warehousing arrangements, and a decision to build a larger warehouse and to tear down the existing one. The capital required for this warehouse was significant, and it was decided to borrow part of the cost and to finance the remainder from funds generated by operations.

As an aid in deciding on proposed capital acquisitions, the company calculates the net present value and a profitability index whenever the available information is sufficiently reliable to warrant a formal analysis. About 85 percent of the proposals in terms of numbers, but less than 50 percent in terms of dollar magnitude, are in this category. Exhibit 17–3 is an example of the numerical part of such an analysis. (The accompanying explanation is omitted.) It is for the replacement of a printing press which was so old and worn that maintenance and operating costs were high. The decision was made to acquire this press in 1977, and the $20,000 cost was included in the capital budget for 1977.

Over a period of about five years the company conducts a review of each facet of its operations. For production operations, it usually hires a consulting firm expert in carton manufacturing methods to conduct this review. For marketing and general administrative functions, it uses the management services division of the firm of Certified Public Accountants that audits its financial statements.

Budget preparation

The controller is responsible for the mechanics of the annual budgeting process. He sees to it that the sales staff prepares sales estimates. These are discussed at length in a meeting attended by Mr. Stewart, the marketing vice president, and the controller. After final sales estimates are agreed upon, the controller communicates these estimates to heads of responsibility centers as a basis for their budget preparation.

Some budget items are stated as a fixed amount per month, others are stated as variable amounts per unit of output, and still others are stated as a fixed amount per month plus a variable amount per unit of output. For the production departments, output is measured in terms of machine-hours or direct labor hours, and for the service departments it is measured in terms of an appropriate measure of activity, such as pounds of ink manufactured.

Each responsibility center head discusses his proposed budget first with the controller (who has had long experience in the industry and hence can point out discrepancies or soft spots), and, in the case of the carton factory, with its superintendent. Mr. Stewart then discusses the proposed budgets for the board mill and the carton factory with the superintendents of these profit centers. He discusses the marketing budget with the marketing vice president. From these discussions, an approved budget emerges. It consists of a master budget showing planned revenues and expenses at the estimated sales volume, a variable budget for each responsibility center showing the fixed amount per month and the variable rate per unit of output for each significant item of expense, a purchasing budget, and a cash budget. Standard unit costs and overhead rates are revised if necessary, so that they are consistent with the approved budget.

Product pricing

Pricing is a crucial element in the company's marketing tactics. Prices are prepared by the company's estimators for each bid or order, on the basis of sales specifications and the appropriate standard cost elements as shown in tables the company has developed for this purpose. To the calculated amount of total factory costs, there are added allowances for selling and administrative expenses, sales commissions, cash discounts, and a profit margin. These allowances are expressed as percentages, and are based on the budget. A sample price estimate is reproduced

EXHIBIT 17–4
Price estimate

Item: 500,000 boxes, 6 1/16 x 2 3/4 x 1 1/2, printed 2 colors and
varnish, on .024 caliber White Patent Coated, News Backed

PREPARATORY COST	Production per Hours	Rate	Unit	Material Cost		Mfg. Cost	
Original Plates	F. or E.						
Electros 9 3/4 x 9 1/4		18.94	.28	530	32		
Wood				15	99		
Rule				34	09		
Composing							
Die Making	③	4.85	41.8			202	73
Make Ready—Ptg.	2 x	12.80	30.0			384	00
Make Ready—C. & C.	11.55	11.25	15.8			177	75
Total Preparatory Cost				580	40	764	48
QUANTITY COST							
Board 65,005 (3 3/4)	171.00+25			5557	93		
Board (32, 5025)				25	00		
Ink		.37	300	111	00		
Ink 30"		.75 / .13	300 / 231	328	95		
Cases Corrugated	700	.30	1429	428	70		
Cellulose Material							
Board, Storage, & Handling		1.87				60	78
Cutting Stock							
Printing		⎰ 22.766					
Cut and Crease		⎱				813	09
Stripping	.933-4	.178+	120			391	60
Cellulose							
Auto Gluing		1.562 .466+11.24				477	24
Hand Gluing							
Wrapping or Packing		6.503				92	93
Inspection							
Total Quantity Cost				6451	58	1835	64
Total Preparatory Cost				580	40	764	48
Total Cost to Make				7031	98	2600	12
Selling & Commercial		45+8 (%+$)				1178	05
Material Forward						2031	98
Shipping 56+		7.25+2	60,287			220	54
Freight and Cartage		.40				241	15
Total Cost						11271	84
Profit		20%				2254	37
Total Selling Price						13526	21
Finished Stock Price							
Commission & Discount		4%				541	05
Total Selling Price						14067	26
Selling Price per M – Calculated						28	14
Selling Price per M – Quoted						30	60

as Exhibit 17–4.[2] The price calculated in the estimate is often adjusted, for quotation purposes. It may be lowered to meet competitive conditions, or it may be increased because the design job on the order is judged to be particularly good, or for other reasons. In Exhibit 17–4, the calculated selling price comes to $28.14 per thousand boxes, but the actual quotation was increased to $30.60.

Estimators of several companies meet regularly under the auspices of a trade association to price sample boxes according to their own formulas. Based on these meetings, Mr. Stewart has concluded that while most of his competitors were shaving prices below formula, Stewart's quoted prices were higher than the calculated estimate about 65 percent of the time, and lower 15 percent of the time. "It all depends on the competition, and on your assessment of the whole situation," he once said.

On some occasions, the company departs from its normal pricing practices. This usually happens when orders for cartons were not in sufficient volume to keep the board mill working at capacity. On these occasions the company took orders for paperboard at prices below full cost, in order to keep the board mill busy. Such contribution pricing is not used often, however.

Reports

Each month an income statement is prepared (Exhibit 17–5). It is constructed so as to focus on the performance of the two profit centers. Also, a spending report is prepared for each of the 15 expense centers in the carton factory. An example is given in Exhibit 17–6.

In addition, Mr. Stewart receives a variety of other reports on a regular basis. The *internally generated* reports are as follows:

1. Balance sheet, monthly.
2. Selling, general and administrative statement, monthly.
3. Overdue accounts receivable, monthly.
4. Overdue shipments, monthly.
5. Inventory size, monthly.
6. Raw materials shrinkage report, monthly.
7. Cash and securities listing, monthly.
8. Actual sales, weekly, with a monthly comparison of actual and budgeted sales.
9. Carton factory production, monthly. This included operating hours statistics and efficiency percentages.

---

[2] Many of the abbreviations and terms in this form are peculiar to the company. The purpose of Exhibit 17–4 is only to illustrate the form used in preparing a price estimate. An understanding of its details is not necessary for this purpose.

EXHIBIT 17–5

STEWART BOX COMPANY
Income Statement
($000 omitted)

December 1976			12 months 1976	
Actual	Variance*		Actual	Variance*
		Board Mill		
52	12	External sales..................................	344	38
168	16	Transfers to carton factory	1,970	130
220	28	Total revenues................................	2,314	168
169	(16)	Cost of goods sold	1,831	(154)
51	12	Gross margin	483	14
	15	Volume variance............................		34
	(13)	Other variances.............................		(14)
		Selling and administrative		
30	(4)	expenses	374	(6)
21	10	Board mill profit.............................	109	28
		Carton Factory		
666	22	Sales...	7,968	248
492	(18)	Standard cost of goods sold............	5,664	(130)
174	4	Gross margin	2,304	118
	16	Manufacturing variances		40
50	(5)	Selling expenses	552	(12)
12	1	Administrative expenses.................	143	7
112	16	Carton factory profit	1,609	153
		Company		
133	26	Total factory and mill profits............	1,718	181
52	2	Corporate expenses.......................	457	18
(4)	. . .	Nonoperating income (loss).............	(12)	2
77	28	Income before income tax	1,249	201
38	(13)	Income tax....................................	617	(96)
39	15	Net Income	632	105

*( ) = unfavorable.

10. Outstanding orders (backlog) weekly.
11. Machine production report, daily.
12. Quality control report, monthly.

Mr. Stewart examines the reports illustrated in Exhibits 17–5 and 17–6 carefully. If there are important departures from plan, he discusses them with the manager responsible. Other reports are prepared primarily for the use of some other executive, and Mr. Stewart receives only an information copy. He may or may not glance at these reports in a given

EXHIBIT 17–6

STEWART BOX COMPANY
Spending Report
Department 14 (two-color Meihle printing presses)

December 1976			12 months 1976	
Actual	Variance		Actual	Variance
5,885	(107)	Labor – pressmen.........................	81,057	(647)
2,074	(46)	Labor – helpers	28,978	(235)
373	120	Press supplies	3,279	146
1,472	(604)	Repairs	8,562	120
484	66	Power..	6,369	322
242	52	Other controllable overhead..........	3,444	461
10,530	(519)	Total controllable costs	131,689	167
2,426	. . .	Departmental fixed cost................	29,112	. . .
3,352	. . .	Allocated costs	40,224	. . .
16,308		Total costs	201,025	
	(340)	Volume variance..........................		1,012
	(859)	Total variance.............................		1,179

( ) = unfavorable.

month, but he is certain to do so if he suspects that trouble may be brew-
ing in the area covered by the report.

Mr. Stewart also pays close attention to several *external* reports he
receives regularly from the industry trade association. They show current
economic trends, the probable effects of these trends on different segments of the paperboard carton industry, and sales orders, actual sales,
production volume, and other related statistics for all members of the
association.

QUESTIONS FOR DISCUSSION

1. Exhibit 17–1 indicates that there are no historical differential costs. Historical costs nevertheless have a place in analyzing certain alternative choice
   decisions. What is their relevance in these decisions?

2. Refer to the list of modifiers of the word "cost" that is given on page 698.
   Which of the modifiers apply to the following numbers in the Stewart Box
   Company? (Each number has several modifiers.)
   a. The numbers on Exhibit 17–3, collectively.
   b. On Exhibit 17–4, the board material cost of $5,557.93 (11th line on
      exhibit).
   c. On Exhibit 17–4, selling and commercial of $1,178.05 (12th line from
      the bottom).
   d. On Exhibit 17–5, standard cost of goods sold, carton factory, of $492,000
      in December.

  e. On Exhibit 17–5, selling expenses, carton factory, of $50,000 in December.

  f. On Exhibit 17–6, labor–pressman in December of $5,885.

  g. On Exhibit 17–6, departmental fixed cost in December of $2,426.

  h. On Exhibit 17–6, allocated costs in December of $3,352.

 3. The following questions relate to Exhibit 17–5 and the December 1976 amounts.

  a. A transfer price was used in connection with *two* items. What are these two items?

  b. Assuming that inventory levels did not vary in December, what was the actual cost of goods manufactured in the carton factory?

  c. Why is the assumption in question (*b*) necessary in order to answer that question?

  d. What is the budgeted amount of corporate expenses?

  e. In December was activity in the board mill above or below the standard volume?

 4. The following questions relate to Exhibit 17–6 and the December amounts:

  a. What was the actual cost of labor–pressmen?

  b. What was the budgeted amount of total controllable cost?

  c. What amount of total controllable cost was applied to products?

  d. Why do no amounts appear in the spending variance column for departmental fixed costs and allocated costs?

PROBLEMS

17–1. As his assistant, write a memorandum calling Mr. Stewart's attention to matters you think he should note when he reads Exhibit 17–5.

17–2. Do the same with Exhibit 17–6.

CASE: MAMMOTH MANUFACTURING COMPANY

17–3. The Mammoth Manufacturing Company was a large producer of manufactured metals parts. It produced stampings, machined castings, and assemblies of stamped and machined parts for the automobile industry, the appliance industry, the tractors and implements business, and several other types of manufacturers and assemblers all over the United States. The company produced few parts for direct sale to the consumer. Instead, the parts were included in the final assembly of a consumer product such as an automobile or a home appliance sold by Mammoth's customers.

  The Mammoth Manufacturing Company had 41 manufacturing plants spread out over the country. Total sales were in excess of one-half billion dollars.

The cost control system

  For many years, Mammoth had no cost control system worthy of the name. The plants had an historical cost system, and reports were submitted monthly to the central office in Cleveland, Ohio. Nothing much was done with these reports, and as long as the plant managers met their production commitments, no one bothered much about costs. In the 1970s, however, competition became quite severe in the type of products Mammoth produced. As a consequence, profit margins were reduced drastically and the management of the company began looking around for means of improving their competitive position. Manufacturing cost control was an obvious area. The management decided that they must install a system of control over their manufacturing costs.

Several people with experience in standard costing and budgeting were hired to develop and install a cost control system in the manufacturing plants. Each manufacturing plant was considered to be a cost responsibility center, with the plant manager responsible for meeting his cost targets.

At each plant, industrial engineering departments were established and labor standards were set for each part. The accounting department at each plant was expanded to include a budgeting section. This section was responsible for developing flexible budgets to cover manufacturing overhead costs in accordance with instructions from the corporate controller's staff.[1]

The budget analysis department:

Under the corporate controller, at the central staff in Cleveland, was the budget analysis department. It was the responsibility of this department to establish timetables for budget submission; to provide forms and instructions so that the budgets would be prepared in a uniform manner; and to analyze the budget proposals and recommend whether they should be accepted or not. This was to insure a uniform "task" in each budget. The budget analysis department also had responsibility for prescribing the budget performance reports. Each month the direct labor and overhead cost performance of each plant was analyzed and the results summarized for management.

Results of the control system:

Almost from the beginning the effect of the new control system was to reduce manufacturing costs significantly. Part of these savings came from the industrial engineering studies required to set the labor standards. Part of the savings resulted from the analysis of overhead costs that was required to prepare the budgets. Often, it became evident on analysis that certain costs were seriously out of line. Much of the savings came because the system made the plant managers and the line foremen cost-conscious. The system, however, was not installed without problems; and the purpose of this case is to describe three situations that occurred during the initial period of installation.

Situation 1: Definition of fixed expense

Several of the people in the budget analysis department came from a large automobile company where the flexible budget equation was calcu-

---

[1] Material costs were controlled by a different system and will not be considered in this case.

lated by using the budgeted costs at two volumes: zero and standard volume. The budget expense at zero volume was defined as the "level of costs that would be required with a six months' shut down." This resulted in a low fixed cost and, consequently, a high variable cost. Since the variable cost per unit was relatively high using this method, the reduction in budgeted cost for each unit below standard volume was also high. This meant that when a plant was operating below standard volume, the budget allowance was squeezed. On the other hand, when volume exceeded standard, the budget authorization would be relatively high. This relationship is shown in Exhibit 1.

EXHIBIT 1

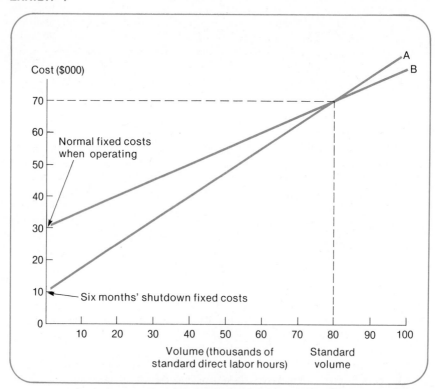

Line A shows the relation of budgeted expenses to volume assuming that there is a fixed cost at zero volume of $10,000. This is the estimated fixed cost that would be incurred after a six months' shutdown.
Line B shows the relation of budgeted expenses to volume assuming that there is a fixed cost at zero volume of $30,000. This is the estimated normal fixed cost incurred when the plant is operating.

At a standard volume of 80,000 hours, the total budgeted expense is estimated to be $70,000. Note that at less than SV, Line B gives the greater budget authorization. At more than SV, Line A provides the higher budget.

The argument for using this method was that it forced costs down when volume fell and the company really needed the cost savings, whereas when volume was above standard, the company could afford to be a little more liberal above the expenditures because they were earning increased profits from the additional volume.

Required:

A. What do you think of the method of determining the budget equation used by the automobile company.
B. How do you think the budget equation should be calculated at Mammoth?

Situation 2: Reasonable and consistent "task"

The budget analysis department was responsible for analyzing the proposed budget from each plant and recommending to top management whether it would be accepted as proposed, accepted with adjustment, or rejected. The ideal budget was one that could be attained if plant management was consistently efficient. The variance from budget, then, represented the extent of the plant's inefficiency.

It was important not only that the approved budget represent an efficient "task" but that the degree of "task" be consistent among the divisions. Although each plant's budget performance was analyzed individually, comparison among the plants was inevitable. If the budget levels did not represent a consistent task, some managers would be judged unfairly.

One of the principal problems facing the budget analysis department was how to insure that the approved budgets included a reasonable task and that the degree of task was consistent among the divisions. This problem was made particularly difficult because the plants realized that it was to their benefit to have a "loose" budget since they were being evaluated against it. Furthermore, no absolute standards existed. Overhead rates differed because of differences in automation, in facilities, in location, and so forth. Also, it was not possible to compare plants directly. No two plants produced exactly the same product line. Even where production processes were similar, there were enough differences because of geographic location, type of equipment, and mix of products that direct comparisons were not meaningful.

Required:

How would you solve the problem described above if you were the manager of the budget analysis department? The constraints within which you must work are:

A. The budget analysis department consists of 30 analysts, varying in experience from one to ten years.
B. Each plant budget department consists of a supervisor and three to five analysts. The budgeting people, however, tend to identify themselves with the plant rather than with the central controller's office.

Situation 3: The Oak Park Plant

The Oak Park Plant produced machined parts and assemblies almost exclusively for the automobile industry. At the time that the budget system was first being introduced, a new plant manager, Lou Hart, was placed in charge of the Oak Park Plant. Hart came from one of the large automotive manufacturers where he had developed a reputation as a "cost cutter."

Hart went to work on cost cutting at Oak Park with vigor. His first budget proposal was 15 percent less than the previous year's actual expense, adjusted to a comparable volume of production. Although the budget represented substantial reduction in all areas of cost, Hart's proposal represented a 25 percent reduction in indirect labor.

The Oak Park Plant's actual costs for the first year of the budget system (also Hart's first year with the company) were *10 percent less than budget.* In other words, Hart's actual overhead costs for his first year as manager of the Oak Park Plant were about 25 percent less than the preceding year's, at comparable volumes. Because of this performance, Hart was given a special award by the president of Mammoth.

Hart's proposed budget for his second year was 10 percent less than his first year's actual costs. The proposed indirect labor budget was now about one half of the amount being spent when Hart first took over the Oak Park Plant. Hart's actual costs continued to be better than budget until the autumn of his second year.

The Oak Park Plant had been producing the same parts, with only slight modifications, for the past several years. During Hart's second year at Oak Park, almost all of the automobile companies made drastic changes in the design of the parts that were being produced at the Oak Park Plant. Hart was faced with the necessity of changing over nearly every production line in the plant. This process was made particularly difficult because one of the automobile producers failed to finalize several designs until very close to the time that production on the parts was supposed to begin. Hart had reduced his staff so drastically that he did not have nearly enough manufacturing and industrial engineers to handle the changeover. Furthermore, his supervision was spread so thin that, even where the changeover was accomplished, trouble developed on several lines and production was severely curtailed. As a result, Hart failed to meet production schedules on several major parts and, consequently, the business was given to competitors. By the time the production had been straightened out, the Oak Park Plant had lost nearly half of its business. Needless to say, Hart was replaced.

Required:

How do you make sure that a budget system does not motivate a manager to take too drastic cost-cutting action?

TABLE S
Present value of $1 received n years hence

Note: Indicate by the symbol $S_{\overline{n}|i}$

Years Hence	1%	2%	4%	6%	8%	10%	12%	14%	15%	16%	18%	20%	22%	24%	25%	26%	28%	30%	35%	40%	45%	50%
1	0.990	0.980	0.962	0.943	0.926	0.909	0.893	0.877	0.870	0.862	0.847	0.833	0.820	0.806	0.800	0.794	0.781	0.769	0.741	0.714	0.690	0.667
2	0.980	0.961	0.925	0.890	0.857	0.826	0.797	0.769	0.756	0.743	0.718	0.694	0.672	0.650	0.640	0.630	0.610	0.592	0.549	0.510	0.476	0.444
3	0.971	0.942	0.889	0.840	0.794	0.751	0.712	0.675	0.658	0.641	0.609	0.579	0.551	0.524	0.512	0.500	0.477	0.455	0.406	0.364	0.328	0.296
4	0.961	0.924	0.855	0.792	0.735	0.683	0.636	0.592	0.572	0.552	0.516	0.482	0.451	0.423	0.410	0.397	0.373	0.350	0.301	0.260	0.226	0.198
5	0.951	0.906	0.822	0.747	0.681	0.621	0.567	0.519	0.497	0.476	0.437	0.402	0.370	0.341	0.328	0.315	0.291	0.269	0.223	0.186	0.156	0.132
6	0.942	0.888	0.790	0.705	0.630	0.564	0.507	0.456	0.432	0.410	0.370	0.335	0.303	0.275	0.262	0.250	0.227	0.207	0.165	0.133	0.108	0.088
7	0.933	0.871	0.760	0.665	0.583	0.513	0.452	0.400	0.376	0.354	0.314	0.279	0.249	0.222	0.210	0.198	0.178	0.159	0.122	0.095	0.074	0.059
8	0.923	0.853	0.731	0.627	0.540	0.467	0.404	0.351	0.327	0.305	0.266	0.233	0.204	0.179	0.168	0.157	0.139	0.123	0.091	0.068	0.051	0.039
9	0.914	0.837	0.703	0.592	0.500	0.424	0.361	0.308	0.284	0.263	0.225	0.194	0.167	0.144	0.134	0.125	0.108	0.094	0.067	0.048	0.035	0.026
10	0.905	0.820	0.676	0.558	0.463	0.386	0.322	0.270	0.247	0.227	0.191	0.162	0.137	0.116	0.107	0.099	0.085	0.073	0.050	0.035	0.024	0.017
11	0.896	0.804	0.650	0.527	0.429	0.350	0.287	0.237	0.215	0.195	0.162	0.135	0.112	0.094	0.086	0.079	0.066	0.056	0.037	0.025	0.017	0.012
12	0.887	0.788	0.625	0.497	0.397	0.319	0.257	0.208	0.187	0.168	0.137	0.112	0.092	0.076	0.069	0.062	0.052	0.043	0.027	0.018	0.012	0.008
13	0.879	0.773	0.601	0.469	0.368	0.290	0.229	0.182	0.163	0.145	0.116	0.093	0.075	0.061	0.055	0.050	0.040	0.033	0.020	0.013	0.008	0.005
14	0.870	0.758	0.577	0.442	0.340	0.263	0.205	0.160	0.141	0.125	0.099	0.078	0.062	0.049	0.044	0.039	0.032	0.025	0.015	0.009	0.006	0.003
15	0.861	0.743	0.555	0.417	0.315	0.239	0.183	0.140	0.123	0.108	0.084	0.065	0.051	0.040	0.035	0.031	0.025	0.020	0.011	0.006	0.004	0.002
16	0.853	0.728	0.534	0.394	0.292	0.218	0.163	0.123	0.107	0.093	0.071	0.054	0.042	0.032	0.028	0.025	0.019	0.015	0.008	0.005	0.003	0.002
17	0.844	0.714	0.513	0.371	0.270	0.198	0.146	0.108	0.093	0.080	0.060	0.045	0.034	0.026	0.023	0.020	0.015	0.012	0.006	0.003	0.002	0.001
18	0.836	0.700	0.494	0.350	0.250	0.180	0.130	0.095	0.081	0.069	0.051	0.038	0.028	0.021	0.018	0.016	0.012	0.009	0.005	0.002	0.001	0.001
19	0.828	0.686	0.475	0.331	0.232	0.164	0.116	0.083	0.070	0.060	0.043	0.031	0.023	0.017	0.014	0.012	0.009	0.007	0.003	0.002	0.001	
20	0.820	0.673	0.456	0.312	0.215	0.149	0.104	0.073	0.061	0.051	0.037	0.026	0.019	0.014	0.012	0.010	0.007	0.005	0.002	0.001	0.001	
21	0.811	0.660	0.439	0.294	0.199	0.135	0.093	0.064	0.053	0.044	0.031	0.022	0.015	0.011	0.009	0.008	0.006	0.004	0.002	0.001		
22	0.803	0.647	0.422	0.278	0.184	0.123	0.083	0.056	0.046	0.038	0.026	0.018	0.013	0.009	0.007	0.006	0.004	0.003	0.001	0.001		
23	0.795	0.634	0.406	0.262	0.170	0.112	0.074	0.049	0.040	0.033	0.022	0.015	0.010	0.007	0.006	0.005	0.003	0.002	0.001			
24	0.788	0.622	0.390	0.247	0.158	0.102	0.066	0.043	0.035	0.028	0.019	0.013	0.008	0.006	0.005	0.004	0.003	0.002	0.001			
25	0.780	0.610	0.375	0.233	0.146	0.092	0.059	0.038	0.030	0.024	0.016	0.010	0.007	0.005	0.004	0.003	0.002	0.001	0.001			
26	0.772	0.598	0.361	0.220	0.135	0.084	0.053	0.033	0.026	0.021	0.014	0.009	0.006	0.004	0.003	0.002	0.002	0.001				
27	0.764	0.586	0.347	0.207	0.125	0.076	0.047	0.029	0.023	0.018	0.011	0.007	0.005	0.003	0.002	0.002	0.001	0.001				
28	0.757	0.574	0.333	0.196	0.116	0.069	0.042	0.026	0.020	0.016	0.010	0.006	0.004	0.002	0.002	0.001	0.001	0.001				
29	0.749	0.563	0.321	0.185	0.107	0.063	0.037	0.022	0.017	0.014	0.008	0.005	0.003	0.002	0.002	0.001	0.001	0.001				
30	0.742	0.552	0.308	0.174	0.099	0.057	0.033	0.020	0.015	0.012	0.007	0.004	0.003	0.002	0.001	0.001	0.001	0.001				
40	0.672	0.453	0.208	0.097	0.046	0.022	0.011	0.005	0.004	0.003	0.001	0.001										
50	0.608	0.372	0.141	0.054	0.021	0.009	0.003	0.001	0.001	0.001												

Derivation

$$S_{\overline{n}|i} = \frac{1}{(1+i)^n}$$

TABLE A

Present value of an annuity of $1 a year for n years

Years (n)	1%	2%	4%	6%	8%	10%	12%	14%	15%	16%	18%	20%	22%	24%	25%	26%	28%	30%	35%	40%	45%	50%
1	0.990	0.980	0.962	0.943	0.926	0.909	0.893	0.877	0.870	0.862	0.847	0.833	0.820	0.806	0.800	0.794	0.781	0.769	0.741	0.714	0.690	0.667
2	1.970	1.942	1.886	1.833	1.783	1.736	1.690	1.647	1.626	1.605	1.566	1.528	1.492	1.457	1.440	1.424	1.392	1.361	1.289	1.224	1.165	1.111
3	2.941	2.884	2.775	2.673	2.577	2.487	2.402	2.322	2.283	2.246	2.174	2.106	2.042	1.981	1.952	1.923	1.868	1.816	1.696	1.589	1.493	1.407
4	3.902	3.808	3.630	3.465	3.312	3.170	3.037	2.914	2.855	2.798	2.690	2.589	2.494	2.404	2.362	2.320	2.241	2.166	1.997	1.849	1.720	1.605
5	4.853	4.713	4.452	4.212	3.993	3.791	3.605	3.433	3.352	3.274	3.127	2.991	2.864	2.745	2.689	2.635	2.532	2.436	2.220	2.035	1.876	1.737
6	5.795	5.601	5.242	4.917	4.623	4.355	4.111	3.889	3.784	3.685	3.498	3.326	3.167	3.020	2.951	2.885	2.759	2.643	2.385	2.168	1.983	1.824
7	6.728	6.472	6.002	5.582	5.206	4.868	4.564	4.288	4.160	4.039	3.812	3.605	3.416	3.242	3.161	3.083	2.937	2.802	2.508	2.263	2.057	1.883
8	7.652	7.325	6.733	6.210	5.747	5.335	4.968	4.639	4.487	4.344	4.078	3.837	3.619	3.421	3.329	3.241	3.076	2.925	2.598	2.331	2.108	1.922
9	8.566	8.162	7.435	6.802	6.247	5.759	5.328	4.946	4.772	4.607	4.303	4.031	3.786	3.566	3.463	3.366	3.184	3.019	2.665	2.379	2.144	1.948
10	9.471	8.983	8.111	7.360	6.710	6.145	5.650	5.216	5.019	4.833	4.494	4.192	3.923	3.682	3.571	3.465	3.269	3.092	2.715	2.414	2.168	1.965
11	10.368	9.787	8.760	7.887	7.139	6.495	5.937	5.453	5.234	5.029	4.656	4.327	4.035	3.776	3.656	3.544	3.335	3.147	2.757	2.438	2.185	1.977
12	11.255	10.575	9.385	8.384	7.536	6.814	6.194	5.660	5.421	5.197	4.793	4.439	4.127	3.851	3.725	3.606	3.387	3.190	2.779	2.456	2.196	1.985
13	12.134	11.343	9.986	8.853	7.904	7.103	6.424	5.842	5.583	5.342	4.910	4.533	4.203	3.912	3.780	3.656	3.427	3.223	2.799	2.468	2.204	1.990
14	13.004	12.106	10.563	9.295	8.244	7.367	6.628	6.002	5.724	5.468	5.008	4.611	4.265	3.962	3.824	3.695	3.459	3.249	2.814	2.477	2.210	1.993
15	13.865	12.849	11.118	9.712	8.559	7.606	6.811	6.142	5.847	5.575	5.092	4.675	4.315	4.001	3.859	3.726	3.483	3.268	2.825	2.484	2.214	1.995
16	14.718	13.578	11.652	10.106	8.851	7.824	6.974	6.265	5.954	5.669	5.162	4.730	4.357	4.033	3.887	3.751	3.503	3.283	2.834	2.489	2.216	1.997
17	15.562	14.292	12.166	10.477	9.122	8.022	7.120	6.373	6.047	5.749	5.222	4.775	4.391	4.059	3.910	3.771	3.518	3.295	2.840	2.492	2.218	1.998
18	16.398	14.992	12.659	10.828	9.372	8.201	7.250	6.467	6.128	5.818	5.273	4.812	4.419	4.080	3.928	3.786	3.529	3.304	2.844	2.494	2.219	1.999
19	17.226	15.678	13.134	11.158	9.604	8.365	7.366	6.550	6.198	5.877	5.316	4.844	4.442	4.097	3.942	3.799	3.539	3.311	2.848	2.496	2.220	1.999
20	18.046	16.351	13.590	11.470	9.818	8.514	7.469	6.623	6.259	5.929	5.353	4.870	4.460	4.110	3.954	3.808	3.546	3.316	2.850	2.497	2.221	1.999
21	18.857	17.011	14.029	11.764	10.017	8.649	7.562	6.687	6.312	5.973	5.384	4.891	4.476	4.121	3.963	3.816	3.551	3.320	2.852	2.498	2.221	2.000
22	19.660	17.658	14.451	12.042	10.201	8.772	7.645	6.743	6.359	6.011	5.410	4.909	4.488	4.130	3.970	3.822	3.556	3.323	2.853	2.498	2.222	2.000
23	20.456	18.292	14.857	12.303	10.371	8.883	7.718	6.792	6.399	6.044	5.432	4.925	4.499	4.137	3.976	3.827	3.559	3.325	2.854	2.499	2.222	2.000
24	21.243	18.914	15.247	12.550	10.529	8.985	7.784	6.835	6.434	6.073	5.451	4.937	4.507	4.143	3.981	3.831	3.562	3.327	2.855	2.499	2.222	2.000
25	22.023	19.523	15.622	12.783	10.675	9.077	7.843	6.873	6.464	6.097	5.467	4.948	4.514	4.147	3.985	3.834	3.564	3.329	2.856	2.499	2.222	2.000
26	22.795	20.121	15.983	13.003	10.810	9.161	7.896	6.906	6.491	6.118	5.480	4.956	4.520	4.151	3.988	3.837	3.566	3.330	2.856	2.500	2.222	2.000
27	23.560	20.707	16.330	13.211	10.935	9.237	7.943	6.935	6.514	6.136	5.492	4.964	4.524	4.154	3.990	3.839	3.567	3.331	2.856	2.500	2.222	2.000
28	24.316	21.281	16.663	13.406	11.051	9.307	7.984	6.961	6.534	6.152	5.502	4.970	4.528	4.157	3.992	3.840	3.568	3.331	2.857	2.500	2.222	2.000
29	25.066	21.844	16.984	13.591	11.158	9.370	8.022	6.983	6.551	6.166	5.510	4.975	4.531	4.159	3.994	3.841	3.569	3.332	2.857	2.500	2.222	2.000
30	25.808	22.396	17.292	13.765	11.258	9.427	8.055	7.003	6.566	6.177	5.517	4.979	4.534	4.160	3.995	3.842	3.569	3.332	2.857	2.500	2.222	2.000
40	32.835	27.355	19.793	15.046	11.925	9.779	8.244	7.105	6.642	6.234	5.548	4.997	4.544	4.166	3.999	3.846	3.571	3.333	2.857	2.500	2.222	2.000
50	39.196	31.424	21.482	15.762	12.234	9.915	8.304	7.133	6.661	6.246	5.554	4.999	4.545	4.167	4.000	3.846	3.571	3.333	2.857	2.500	2.222	2.000

Note: Indicate by the symbol $A_{\overline{n}|i}$

Index

This book has been set in 10 point and 9 point Times Roman, leaded 2 points. Part and chapter numbers are in 30 point (large) and 48 point Helvetica Medium. Part and chapter titles are in 24 point (small) and 18 point Helvetica. The size of the type page is 27 by 46½ picas.